Canadian Studies:
An Introductory Reader

Edited by

Donald Wright
Brock University

KENDALL/HUNT PUBLISHING COMPANY
4050 Westmark Drive   Dubuque, Iowa 52002

Cover: National Gallery of Canada, Ottawa, Purchased 1994. © Robert Houle.

Copyright © 2004 by Kendall/Hunt Publishing Company

ISBN 0-7575-1271-2

Printed in the United States of America
10 9 8 7 6 5 4 3 2

Contents

Introduction

IN HIS 1975 REPORT, *To Know Ourselves,* Tom Symons argued that Canadian studies must not be understood as a patriotic project, one designed to preserve and promote a particular Canadian identity. The "soundest justification for Canadian studies," he said, is the "need for self-knowledge"; it is the need to know ourselves. The quest for self-knowledge, Symons continued, is "the highest aim of culture" and "the indispensable condition for health and growth in the life of the mind."[1] He was right then and he is right now. Patriotism has no place in the university and the unexamined life isn't worth living.

Twenty years after the publication of the Symons report, the Department of Canadian Heritage commissioned a follow-up study on the state of Canadian studies. In *Taking Stock: Canadian Studies in the Nineties,* David Cameron expanded the rationale for Canadian studies offered by Symons. Related to self-knowledge, Cameron argued, is citizenship. "[S]upporting the study of Canada is the shared concern to strengthen citizenship and public values, particularly by advancing aspects of what might be called 'civic education'."[2] Like Symons, Cameron was right. Citizenship must be strengthened and universities play a part in preparing young people to become informed citizens.

This reader aims to foster self-knowledge and to strengthen citizenship where citizenship is understood as an ongoing conversation between members of a community about the kind of society they want to build together. For that conversation to be meaningful, citizens must know themselves, where they have come from and where they want to go. In short, citizenship demands self-knowledge and self-knowledge deepens citizenship.

It is on the idea of conversation that this reader is premised. Readings have been selected because they are either a conversation in and of themselves or part of a larger conversation. That conversation may be self-conscious and obvious or it may be unconscious and opaque. It can be about an event, an individual, an idea or a place. It may have taken place in the past or it may be taking place now or it may be a conversation between the present and the past. A good conversation is one that generates questions because questions lead to more conversation. A robust conversation is one that assumes nothing is fixed, that meaning is contestable, that history can be re-written and different futures imagined.

---

[1] T.H.B. Symons, *To Know Ourselves: The Report of the Commission on Canadian Studies* (Ottawa: Association of Universities and Colleges of Canada, 1975): 13

[2] David Cameron, *Taking Stock: Canadian Studies in the Nineties* (Montreal: Association for Canadian Studies, 1996): 25

The example of Robert Houle illustrates my point. Born in 1947 on Sandy Bay Indian Reserve 200 kilometers northwest of Winnipeg, Houle is from the Saulteaux Nation. An artist with an international reputation, Houle explores themes of injustice, assimilation and extinction in his art. His 1992 painting *Kanata*—which has been printed on the cover of this reader—hangs at the National Gallery of Canada in Ottawa. *Kanata* takes one of the most famous paintings in art history—Benjamin West's 1770 *Death of Wolfe*—and transforms not only its meaning but the meaning of Canada as well. Houle reproduced the *Death of Wolfe* but he drained it of its colour; at one end he added a blue band, at the other a red band. Symbolizing the French and British empires, blue and red colour the blanket and head-dress of the Native warrior seated at Wolfe's feet. The effect is enormous: General Wolfe has been decentred and the Native warrior centred; no longer about Wolfe's heroic death and the glory of the British empire, the painting is about Native peoples and their assimilation. *Kanata* reminds us that Canada is not only the story of Europeans in North America, it is also the story of Native peoples, their colonization, dislocation and assimilation. *Kanata* is part of Houle's ongoing conversation with the past and with what it means to be a First Nations person in a country where, for far too long, the first have been last. Houle knows that meaning is not cast in stone, that history can be re-written and that a more just future, one that includes all Canadians, can be imagined.

Against the backdrop of self-knowledge, citizenship and conversation, this reader moves both chronologically and thematically. It opens with a chapter on Canada's origins, on when and where Canada's beginnings can be located, and it closes with a chapter on Canada's destinies, on what the future might hold. In between are a series of chapters on events (for example, contact between Europeans and First Nations peoples, the defeat of the French by the British on the Plains of Abraham in 1759, World War I and the 1988 Free Trade Agreement), individuals (including Grey Owl, Tom Thomson and Harold Innis), ideas (French-Canadian nationalism, multiculturalism and the place of First Nations peoples in Canada today) and Canada's regions (Atlantic Canada, western Canada and the North).

Like all readers, this one does not pretend to be exhaustive. Choices about what to include and what to exclude had to be made. My intent is to offer readings that are at once representative and suggestive, readings that will excite your curiousity and incite you to read more Harold Innis, Margaret Atwood, Karen Connelly, matt robinson and George Sioui. Finally, it is my hope that, as you make your way through this reader, you will begin to make connections not just within but between the chapters, and that you will think about Canada in new and original ways. That is why I have dedicated this reader to you, my students in Canadian Studies 1F91 at Brock University, past, present and future.

CHAPTER ONE

Origins

Introduction

Where and when do we locate the origins of Canada? Because it points to issues of power, of inclusion and exclusion, the question is a political one. Arthur Lower was one of English Canada's great historians; his career spanned five decades, from the 1920s to the 1970s. In 1946 he published one of the first surveys of Canadian history. Entitled *From Colony to Nation*, it locates Canada's origins in Europe. Writing their introductory textbook some 50 years later, Margaret Conrad and Alvin Finkel locate Canada's origins in North America itself. How are we to explain this change? What is the significance of locating Canada's origins in First Nations history and not in European history?

The First Hundred Years of Europe in America

Arthur Lower

1. Expansive Forces Within Europe

THE HISTORY OF Canada must begin, as it were, pre-natally. The country of today was not born until generations of Europeans had tramped across the surface of the New World, had fought each other in its fastnesses, had given themselves in toil against the wilderness and had debated in their new homes the great questions that lie at the base of society. These men from overseas and that northern region into which they came, thrown together through four centuries of effort, brought to birth Canada, child of European civilization and the American wilderness.

All America might be said, in this sense, to have its fatherhood in that complex of European forces known as the Renaissance. A new and dynamic civilization had developed in medieval Europe. The scattered communities of feudalism had given way to great states. Some of the modern nations, such as England and France, had been built. Systems of law and administration had been formed. A money economy and intra-continental trade had taken the place of the barter and localism of manorial days. A middle class was growing up in the more advanced areas, the precursor of the capitalist class of later days. Considerable progress had been made in inventions and in the arts of life. Clothing, iron, and paper were all more abundant than a century or two earlier. Gunpowder had become an ordinary commodity; printing was common. Those who read the old Norse accounts of the Vinland voyages and compare them with the Columbian will see at a glance how much progress had been made in Europe in the five hundred years' interval: the Norse met the Skraelings on terms not far from equality, insofar as weapons went; but between the equipment of the Columbian discoverers and that of the natives, the gap was vast.

By the end of the fifteenth century, something like modern Europe had emerged. A similar way of life extended from the Mediterranean to the Baltic, from the Atlantic to the Vistula. In the north, Christianity had just pushed back the last of the heathen gods into the fastnesses of Karelia. In the east, Teutonic Knights, the outermost pillars of Christendom, were still engaged in wrestling from Slavdom souls for the Church and good lands for themselves. While the Turk remained seated firmly in the south-east, the other unbeliever, the Moor, had just been expelled from Spain. Europe, especially Latin Europe, was discovering its soul. Its energies were buoyant and youthful, fit for any task, ready for any adventure.

In the subtler aspects of civilization growth had been as marked as in the practical. The aridity of scholasticism was disappearing before the resurrection of the classical world. The intensity and passion of medievalism was mellowing and, in Italy especially, giving way to a tolerant open-mindedness that, like its counterpart, modern liberalism, passed over into elegant self-indulgence on the one hand and a scientific objectivity on the other. This objectivity permitted speculation upon the nature of man and the universe that would have been impossible earlier. Speculation led to observation, and observation led to extension of knowledge. All sciences grew rapidly, not least that group with which we are here primarily concerned, the astronomical and geographical. The conception of the earth as a sphere was becoming familiar to cultivated Mediterranean minds, and the old travel stories of the Polos about the marvels of a distant east were not forgotten. It may even be that echoes of the Norse voyages and of Greenland had been heard as far afield as Italy: there were few things that escaped the alert intelligences of Genoa, Florence, Pisa and the other northern Italian towns.

2. The Discoveries

The wider horizons of the spirit could not fail to evoke their counterparts in the physical world; consequently it may be said that the discovery of America lay in the logic of things. When the new civilization had grown to a certain point it burst its containing envelope, old Europe, and began to disperse itself throughout the world. If Columbus had not been the lucky man, there would soon have been someone else. America had to be discovered!

And it had to be discovered by an Italian, or at least a Mediterranean. Columbus brought his knowledge and his disposition towards scientific adventure from the most logical place; from a highly sophisticated Italian city state, where men had leisure for thought, uninhibited curiosity and a surplus of energy above mere subsistence. Like other great explorers, he came from a centre of civilization. He offered his knowledge and his skills in the most likely market, Spain, a rising state anxious to emulate the navigational feats of its neighbour Portugal. For the Italians, geographical science was interesting intellectual fare. For that marginal and maritime people, the Portuguese, it had been for a whole pre-Columbian century a matter of applied science in the interests of commerce. And now for the Spaniards, it was to be the occasion of dignity, power and profit. They were not long in realizing all three. Within less than a generation, the Atlantic coasts of both Americas had been laid open, and part of the Pacific coast too. The world had been circumnavigated. Gold, lands, and pomp had been obtained. Kingdoms had been conquered, cities founded. There remained only the tasks of detail such as the sketching in of local features, the penetration of the interior, the building of additional posts.

The discoveries rested on great individuals and on the organized power of states. Backward countries had little part in the process. The discovery of the New World represented no mass movement, no *Völkerwanderung*, such as had changed the face of Europe a thousand years before. It was aristocratic and classical, a new bud on the great Latin tree flung across the Atlantic.

3. The European Powers and America in the Sixteenth Century

If scientific curiosity and commendable personal ambition inspired the first great voyages, less worthy motives soon crept in. The New World became "a good thing". Greed awakened. A treasure house of riches stood revealed, and men hastened to possess themselves of them. Gold they had dreamed about, and gold, by great coincidence, they found. American gold changed the course of history. Peruvian gold destroyed the Peruvians, and by the habits it induced and the prices it set up, it almost destroyed the Spaniards for it encouraged all their worst characteristics. A people who had been fighting Moors in crusading fervour for seven centuries needed no inducements to cruelty; but when opposition was slight and greed great, cruelty mounted, and the natives were enslaved or extinguished. The backwash on Spain itself was sufficient to cripple native industry and to give the less fortunately situated northern races a chance to sell their wares in a luxury market. On rising Spanish prices, forced up by American gold, the English founded their new woollen export trade and flourished thereby, despite Spanish attempts to prevent the exportation of the imported gold. Spain moved into greatness on the wealth of her overseas possessions, but once the easy job of ruthless exploitation had been done, her progress stopped. As her empire expanded, she herself declined.

The lure of gold had led her men all over South America and over a good part of the north. Where no gold was to be found, they tried for other things. They had before them the example of the Portuguese and their spice islands; many good things, they knew, could come out of the heat of the tropics. And Europe hungered for good things. One of the best was sugar. Men everywhere have a sweet tooth, but before sugar became available, few there were who could satisfy their tastes. It was no accident that it was the queen who sat in the parlour eating bread and honey; ordinary people had to get along as best they could with beer and fat meat. Once sugar appeared, it added greatly to the joy of living and to the profit of the country that controlled the delectable lands from which the new supplies of it came—the West Indies, or "sugar islands".

With sugar, an agricultural product, came the need for labour. Lordly Spaniards did not go to the colonies to toil, so that it became necessary to find others to work for them. The native Indian seemed the natural solution, but he proved too proud or too tender and, consequently, as an alternative to slavery, died. A satisfactory substitute was eventually found in the African negro.

On gold, sugar and slaves, the Spanish and Portuguese colonies grew up. From Europe they were founded, and for Europe they existed. Those who came out to them sought fortunes, not homes; for almost all of them, the new world represented material gain. In America the exploitative attitude received from the first a strong emphasis.

One partial exception there was—the Church. In a religious age, the Church must have a large official place in the possession of a new world. To the credit of medieval Catholicism, its missionary instincts had never entirely faded, and with the prospect of new fields to conquer for the cross, they awoke to full life. In the Catholic world the evangelization of the natives, new souls for Christ, was always expressed as the foremost motive for overseas expansion. Nor did it remain merely a pious expression. Whether the discoverers and *conquistadores* wanted them or not, priests invariably accompanied the expeditions and devoted themselves to performing those rites that added souls to heaven. In the medieval Church, there was little incompatibility between the two types of men; for natives while being conquered could be conquered into the Church, and while being slaughtered could, by priestly miracle, be given entrance to the Christian heaven. But the latent humanitarianism of Christianity was bound to come to the surface, and it was not long before the Church was setting its face against the worst abuses. It became a moderating force and, true to Christianity's central concept that all men are equally the children of God, sought to shield its native converts from the white man. The result was a patriarchal attitude which, if it saved the natives from cruelty and death, tended to rob them of their own way of life and of their initiative. What neither aspect of white civilization—exploitative materialism or religion—would do was to leave the natives alone.

The division of the New World by the Pope between Spain and Portugal has often been decried in retrospect but it was quite a reasonable arrangement at the time. The Portuguese had been opening up new territories for a century and a half: they had already found the sea-route around the Cape to India. Spain had patronized the discoverer of America. They were the only two European powers that in a strict sense could be called maritime. They were the only two that had shown any interest worth mentioning in the discoveries and the problems growing out of them. The kings of France were more attracted by marauding expeditions into Italy. The English monarchy was absorbed in securing its own stability after the long anarchy of the wars of the Roses; Holland did not yet exist; and the Scandinavians, like the divided Italians, were too remote. Even the faint stir of interest shown by Henry VII of England when he made a gesture of assistance to the Cabots soon subsided. Spain and Portugal had a good case.

Since they naturally devoted their energies to the most profitable areas, they dismissed the coast of North America north of Florida with a cursory inspection. This left an opportunity for the more humble northerners, Englishmen and Frenchmen, to come in; but they were slow in availing themselves of it.

The Cabots, Italian geographers and navigators in search of patrons, had been fobbed off with a few pounds in England, most likely dismissed as innovating foreign nuisances. But the landfall they made in Newfoundland had results of its own, comparable almost to that of Columbus. For they found in those northern seas something that, to practical Bristol minds, was more valuable than gold: they found cod-fish.[1] To a continent that never had quite enough to eat, a new source of food supply was literally more valuable than gold. Consequently after John Cabot's return to

---

[1] See H. A. Innis, *The Cod Fisheries, the History of an International Economy*, rev. ed. (Toronto, 1954).

Bristol, others flocked out for the fishing, and the harbour of St. John's, Newfoundland, has never since been empty of ships. To the new southern staples on which Spain was building empires there was now added a northern, on which empires were some day to be built. Unlike the south, the north was not monopolized; nominally it was within the Spanish share of the tentative delimitation made by Pope Alexander VI, but to Spain it was of secondary interest. The delimitation, moreover, was indefinite and northerners did not regard it as law. None of them, however, had the organized power of a state behind them. They came as private parties, worked out their own arrangements on the spot as private parties and as private parties they departed. For nearly half a century no northern state took an official hand.

Among the fishermen there was no thought of settlement and permanent occupation; quite the contrary. Men who came to fish and remained to farm would be skilled hands lost to their employers. Worse, they might become business rivals, preparing and even marketing the fish without recourse to old country merchants. So whether the merchants who sent out the fishing expeditions were French or English, they were agreed in their hostility to any projects for settlement. Only gradually and reluctantly did they permit women to come out. Settlement in Newfoundland, based on codfish, came in time, but is was a long time. Meanwhile, French and English merchants from west-country ports brought home cargoes of the new food, or better still sent them down to Spain and Italy, where they sold them for Spanish gold. As their captains familiarized themselves with the opposite coasts, they went further afield, undertook more ambitious projects, and more especially, found that it paid to land their catch on a convenient shore and dry it.

The fishery in this way came to be divided into two halves: the green fishery—of cod caught off-shore, split and salted, and thence carried to Europe; and the dry fishery—of cod mainly caught inshore, cleaned, salted, and dried in the sun on the "flakes" still to be seen in any Atlantic coast village, and shipped to whatever market seemed best. Since northern Europe had its own abundant fisheries, it was the Spanish peninsula and the Mediterranean that provided the best consuming centres. Later on, after West Indian industry had become well organized and the slave population there had grown considerably, dried codfish from the north proved to be a cheap and economical food, so that another branch was added to this first northern staple trade. It was naturally the dry, or inshore, fishery that gave rise to settlement.

Within the limits of the sixteenth century, the codfisheries had not gone much beyond Newfoundland. In time all the Atlantic banks were exploited, and the exploitation was to be a factor in the occupation of the nearby coasts; but for the first hundred years, Newfoundland sufficed, and fishermen had little curiosity as to what lay round the next headland. Cabot had blazed a trail for them and that trail they were content to follow with little deviation. It is improbable that they had any contact of importance with the few natives of Newfoundland itself. On the other hand, some local products in addition to codfish may have come their way: sealskins and perhaps a few skins from inland like caribou and possibly beaver.

The next semi-public personage to come to northern waters, of whose voyage we have more than a mere mention, was Jacques Cartier. He seems to have kept his eyes open for valuables in fur, though his reason for coming was much the same as that of most other explorers: that is, sheer curiosity plus a bent towards adventure, cloaked in terms of science or of profit. Hailing from St. Malo, one of the French ports for the Newfoundland fishery, he would be familiar with its details, and in a subordinate capacity, he may have made the voyage before.[2] The hope of finding a north-west passage to the mysterious east or to those kingdoms from which the Spaniards were bringing back so much gold was a strong motive in his expedition.

Cartier's voyages have been made a great deal of in Canadian annals but the sum total of his achievements, viewed dispassionately, is not particularly great. Over parts of his route he had had two predecessors whose names are known, Jean Denys (1506) and Thomas Aubert (1508).[3] On his first voyage (1534), he followed a well-known route across to Belle Isle, ran down the Gulf past the Magdalens, and over to the Bay of Chaleur. Then he coasted the Gulf of St. Lawrence over to Anticosti Island, which may also have been known, and thence back to France. He had ascertained that the Gulf was no north-west passage, had erected a cross in a picturesque ceremony in Gaspé, had collected a short vocabulary of Iroquoian words, and had sailed a few hundred miles beyond the ordinary course of fishermen. His second voyage, the next year, was a little more ambitious: he penetrated the St. Lawrence up to the head of navigation at Hochelaga (now Montreal), wintered at Stadacona (now Quebec), and managed to keep himself and some of his crew alive during that very unusual experience. He returned to France in the spring, having in the grateful way of the times kidnapped a few of his Indian hosts as specimens to show off when he got home. His merit consists in his having been the first man to carry out a comparatively simple exploratory task and to record it in interesting detail.

His significance lies in his discovery that furs were to be had from the natives, and at the usual initial bargain prices, measured in trade goods. This discovery gave the French a second reason for their interest in what was already beginning to be called Canada, the lands about the Gulf of St. Lawrence, and although they did not follow it up vigorously, the connection Cartier had established was never entirely broken off again. We know that his heirs were granted some kind of trading rights, and they probably availed themselves of them to the extent of sending an occasional vessel to do a ship-to-shore trade. It has been conjectured that this obscure bargaining, possibly at the mouth of the Saguenay (where the Basques are supposed to have set up a whale fishery as early as 1544), may have set in motion Indian currents from

---

[2] M. Gustave Lanctot, former Public Archivist of Canada, has offered convincing proof that Cartier, sailing with Verrazano, investigated the Atlantic coast of Nova Scotia and Newfoundland in 1524, ten years before the voyage heretofore recorded as his first, that of 1534. See his "Cartier's First Visit to Canada in 1524," *CHR*, XXV (Sept. 1944), 233–245.

[3] Lanctot, *op. cit.*, 241.

the distant interior. Parties eager for French trade goods may at first have followed a difficult northern route to avoid the Iroquoian peoples on the St. Lawrence and at last have cleaned them out from their villages and rolled them back to where Champlain later found them. Whatever went on, little record remains, and official France stood aloof. It may be assumed that the long period from Cartier's last voyage or that of Roberval (1542–43) to Champlain's first (1603) saw the establishment in some form of what was to become the *raison d'etre* of New France, the fur trade.

If France displayed little interest in the New World, England until the reign of Elizabeth displayed even less. There are records of a few desultory private voyages that resulted in nothing, and that is all. The merchants of Bristol and other west country ports were doing well out of the new codfish trade, which took their vessels into the Gulf and perhaps a little distance up the river, but they were not interested in pushing on inland. When in Elizabethan times England began to get on its feet, the picture changed, at first through the efforts of buccaneers such as Drake. Voyages of exploration became numerous, especially into the North, and attempts were made at colonization. Then a group of colonial planners appeared, centring round men such as Hakluyt, Gilbert, and Raleigh, men full of big schemes for an English empire in the New World. These schemes were eventually to bear fruit, though not under the direction of their first proposers, but saving an abortive attempt at settlement in Newfoundland, none of them touched what is now Canada, and they do not concern us here. England does not come into the Canadian picture until long after Elizabeth was sleeping in the last of her famous beds.

The first hundred years of Europe in America close, insofar as what is now Canada is concerned, with relatively little done. The coastlines had become known in a general way; the St. Lawrence ascended as far as the first rapids; one staple trade and industry, the codfishery, had been strongly established; and another, the fur trade, just begun. To a great colonizing power like Spain, the northern part of the New World was an unconsidered trifle, and as such it was left to the somewhat barbaric peoples of the northern fringes of Europe.

Chronology

1492	Columbus discovers America.
1497	John Cabot's First Voyage.
1500	Newfoundland Codfisheries begin.
1524, 1534, 1535–6, 1541–2	Jacques Cartier's Voyages.
1542–3	Sieur de Roberval's attempted settlement on the St. Lawrence fails.
1544–1600	Era of fishing and trading voyages to the St. Lawrence.
1584	Marquis de la Roche fails in an attempt to take a colonizing expedition to Canada; marks renewal of colonization interest on part of France.

The First Nations of Canada

Margaret Conrad and Alvin Finkel

GRAND CHIEF JOCELYNE Gros Louis of the Huron-Wendat nation, speaking in 1992, weaved past and present together this way: "What we want Canada to do is to give us the support we need in order to regain our own strength so that we can once again walk the right path under our own steam. This means sharing with us the renewal of our self-respect and our pride in our heritage. This means paying attention to the use of language, symbols, and cultural opinions so that our peoples are not offended. This also means letting us take care of ourselves through equal access to the revenues generated on our traditional lands and working with us as partners on these vast expanses of land."[1]

Canada's First Nations have a strong sense of their own identity. This chapter outlines their rich history in the period before Europeans arrived in the Americas. By looking at Native societies in the precontact period, we can see how they have evolved over thousands of years in a North American environment and understand why history is so important in defining Native identities.

Writing Native History

Before the 1960s, Canadian history texts generally began with the "discovery" of the "New World" by European explorers. Arguing that the discipline of history was restricted to archival sources and therefore to literate peoples, historians relegated the study of pre-contact Aboriginal societies to anthropologists and archeologists. Fortunately, such rigid boundaries between disciplines have now begun to break down. "Ethnohistorians," whose background may be in one of many fields, study First Nations societies by piecing together evidence from European observations, anthropological studies, archeological evidence, and relevant data provided by meteorologists, biologists, and other scientists. In short, ethnohistorians consider all the evidence possible to recreate the lives of the earliest inhabitants of what was to become Canada.

The rich sources consulted by ethnohistorians often pose problems. The oral tradition of the Native peoples, accounts of early fur traders, priests, travellers, and other Europeans, and archeological evidence may each suggest different conclusions. Furthermore, for the hunting and gathering societies of pre-contact Canada—the groups dominating all regions except southern Ontario, the St Lawrence River valley, and the Pacific Coast at the time of European arrival—the archeological

30 000 BC	Native peoples begin to inhabit North America
10 000 BC	Natives use fluted points (sharpened points on a projectile) to kill giant mammals
9000 BC	Mastodons and mammoths become extinct
5000 BC	Natives in Labrador build ritual burial mounds; Natives in Alberta use corrals to kill large mammals
4000 BC	Southern Ontario Natives make use of fish nets, weirs, and grinding implements
1000 BC	Chiefdoms begin to be established on northwest coast; southern Ontario Natives begin making pottery
900 BC	Algonkian-speaking groups enter region north and west of Great Lakes, previously the preserve of Siouan speakers
500 BC	Trade relations established between Natives in southern Ontario and Atlantic region
AD 250	Natives begin using bow and arrow for hunting
AD 500	Horticulture established in southern Ontario
AD 1000	Viking settlements in Newfoundland
AD 1300	Iroquoian societies begin building palisaded villages
AD 1450	Formation of Iroquois Confederacy

record is weak. Time and tides have eroded much of the evidence that could have unlocked the secrets of the past.

Each Aboriginal nation has its own version of its pre-contact history. The tradition of handing down the history orally from generation to generation was firmly established long before the Europeans arrived, and it has continued to thrive. Historians disagree about how much credence to place in oral traditions. American historian James Axtell suggests that there are three basic problems with relying on oral traditions to recreate the past. First, our knowledge of the past is shaped by contemporary issues, so we have little perception of the past except in terms of the present. The danger, as Axtell says, is that "myth and history tend to merge." Views that are currently fashionable are easily projected back in time, making them appear to be eternal truths.[2] Second, while oral knowledge is slow to change, it also is subject to "structural amnesia." By this he means that those elements that no longer have relevance for contemporary society can be forgotten or transformed. Third, oral knowledge depends on human memory, which, of course, is fallible. Information can be lost by simple mistakes or by the death of a member of the community.

Oral traditions are often distorted by the scholars who record them. For example, until recently most people who studied Native societies were not only of European descent but were almost exclusively men. Women's roles in economic activities, religion, and warfare were given short shrift by male researchers who concentrated on interviews with men in the societies they studied. In recent years gender and other biases in scholarly research have been identified and more women and Native peoples are involved in exploring First Nations history. Nevertheless, researchers must always bear in mind that their own values often play a major role in how they interpret both oral and written historical evidence.

First Nations Before 1500

Estimates of the Native population of the Americas at the time of continuous European contact around 1500 have varied greatly, from 30 million to over 100 million. Since most Aboriginal peoples lived in areas of the Americas with warm climates, the territory now called Canada was sparsely settled—scholars estimate a population of between half a million and two million people. The smaller figure is based on the observations of early European writers, and the larger on estimates (difficult to confirm) of the numbers of indigenous people who might have succumbed to European diseases before direct contact with the invaders.

The impact of European diseases on Native populations was immense, quickly reducing some groups by 50 percent or more. Because the Aboriginal societies in first contact with the Europeans traded the goods they received far and wide, it is speculated that European germs spread throughout North America faster than the Europeans themselves. Scholars who estimate the pre-contact population of Canada at about 500 000 have based this calculation on regional estimates of 150 000 to 200 000 on the Pacific Coast, 50 000 to 100 000 in the Western Interior, 100 000 to 150 000 in the Great Lakes-St Lawrence Lowlands region, and no more than 100 000 in the rest of the country.

Although the origins of the First Nations of the Americas are debated, scholars generally argue that they are of Asiatic origin and arrived in the Americas in various waves of migration from 30 000 to 10 000 years ago. The route these pioneers followed was probably across the land bridges that connected Siberia to Alaska during the ice ages. Native peoples themselves often reject the notion that they are descended from people who originated on other continents. Each Native group has a creation myth that explains the origins of the world and its creatures, and these stories have in common the view that life began on the North American continent. As a Mi'kmaq legend claims, they have "lived here since the world began."[5]

At least 50 distinct cultures encompassing 12 language groupings have been identified among Canada's first peoples. The phrase "language grouping" refers to languages with a common origin, not necessarily mutually understandable languages. The Iroquoian-speaking Huron of southern Ontario and the Five Nations Iroquois of New York, for example, spoke languages as different as the Romance languages of French and Portuguese are from one another.

In the sixteenth century, the First Nations lived in societies ranging from the scrupulously egalitarian model of the Athapaskan tribes of the subarctic to the slave-owning, highly stratified societies on the West Coast. Contact with the Europeans would bring dramatic and often unwanted changes to Aboriginal lifestyles, but change and adaptation had always been a feature of their lives. For instance, when the last Ice Age receded about 10 000 years ago in southern Ontario and northern New York State, the region's only residents appear to have been a few Aboriginal groups hunting caribou. About 6000 years ago, the region's climate had grown warmer, boreal forest had replaced tundra, and deer had supplanted caribou. People began catching fish in nets and weirs and using milling stones and mortars to grind nuts, berries, and roots. As the food supply became more varied and reliable, the region's population expanded significantly, and trade with other nations brought in copper from Lake Superior and marine shells from the Atlantic coast.

Farming was introduced in the region about 1500 years ago and life became more sedentary than in earlier periods when the search for game forced frequent relocation. When the Europeans made contact with the Iroquoian-speaking peoples in the late sixteenth century, they encountered palisaded settlements of 1500 to 2000 people. By that time, confederacies of various nations had been formed in an attempt to bring peace to a region that had long been plagued with warfare. Well-crafted pottery suggests that the people had the wealth and leisure time to indulge in pursuits beyond mere survival.

DIVERGING VIEWS OF ORAL TRADITIONS

Not surprisingly, Native oral historians and most Euro-Canadian scholars have differing views of the objectivity of Native interpretations of the pre-contact past. Annie Ned, a Yukon elder in her nineties, cooperated with anthropologist Julie Cruikshank to record the history of her people. She told Cruikshank: "I'm going to put it down who we are. This is our Shagoon—our history. You don't put it down yourself, one story. You don't put it yourself and then tell a little more. You put what they tell you, older people. You've got to tell it right. Not you are telling it: it's the person who told you that's telling that story."[3]

While Annie Ned believes that oral histories conserve stories intact from generation to generation, anthropologist Bruce Trigger is virtually dismissive of their significance, at least for the study of the Iroquoians. He writes: "Oral traditions do not provide an independent means for studying the history of Iroquoian-speaking peoples. It is of interest when oral traditions confirm other sources of information about the past, but, except when they do, they should not be used even to supplement such sources."[4] Few Native people would agree with Trigger, and many would question the notion that European sources are an "independent means" for the study of Native history.

Even in areas where hunting and gathering remained the primary means of obtaining food, dramatic changes had occurred. During an estimated 12 000 years of human habitation on the Prairies, for example, the successive inventions of the spear thrower, the bow and arrow, and the buffalo pound increased the time available for spiritual and leisure activities. The spear thrower allowed the hunter to aim more accurately and throw with more force than with the unaided hand; the buffalo pound was a giant corral made of brush and hides into which a herd was driven to be systematically killed.

Improved possibilities of subsistence on the Prairies drew newcomers into the region. Three thousand years ago, only Siouan speakers lived on the plains of North America, but by the time of European contact the Blackfoot, who were Algonkian speakers, had come to dominate a portion of the region. The Sioux also disappeared from the thickly forested woodlands and the parklands north and west of the Great Lakes, replaced by Algonkian groups, including the Ojibwa and the Cree, who migrated in search of the caribou. By 1600, the Ojibwa and Cree were the chief inhabitants of northern Ontario, with the Sioux having been pushed southward and westward.

Common Cultural Characteristics

While change and diversity characterized Native life in the pre-contact period, the various Aboriginal groups shared a number of features. In all Native societies, religion, as much as nature, regulated everyday life. Native religions are characterized by a belief in a divinity residing within all living creatures as well as within all natural objects. Because Native religion was all-encompassing, attempts to analyze pre-contact societies have been limited by an inability to comprehend the intricacies of spiritual practices.

First Nations peoples did not see themselves as masters of their environment; rather, they believed that their communion with the spirits was the secret to any successes they might have in staking out a living and achieving happiness. An outside observer might credit the Beaver people of today's northern Alberta with intricate knowledge of the whereabouts of animals and edible plants. The Beaver themselves believed that vision quests and dreams showed them the paths to these animals and plants, and that breaking faith with their traditional religious views and practices would result in the disappearance from their lands of their sources of food and other necessities.

A common feature of Native societies was their knowledge of the uses of a wide range of materials found in the natural world. Millennia of experimentation had unlocked an extensive botanical knowledge that was evident in the effective use of plants for medicinal purposes. A familiarity with the properties of various types of wood and other natural materials was displayed in the successful production of means of transportation (including canoes, snowshoes, and toboggans), homes of varying types, cooking utensils, and weapons.

The Aboriginal peoples' knowledge of their environment would prove crucial to the Europeans when they turned their attention to the profits available from exploiting the resources of the Americas. Historian Olive Dickason writes:

> Basque whalers availed themselves of Inuit harpooning technology to improve greatly the efficiency of their own techniques; Mi'kmaq . . . sea hunters put their expertise at the service of Europeans to pursue walrus for Ivory, hides, and train oil [oil from the blubber of marine animals—Ed.], all much in demand by the latter; and later Amerindians did the same thing in the production of furs, so much sought after for the luxury trade, as status-conscious Europeans used furs (among other items) as symbols of rank. It has been estimated that by 1600 there may have been up to a thousand European ships a year engaged in commercial activities in Canada's northeastern coastal waters. Such activity would not have been possible without the co-operation and participation of the first nations of the land. When it came to penetrating the interior of the continent, Amerindians guided the way for the European "explorers," equipped them with the clothing and transportation facilities they needed, and provided them with food.[6]

The Native willingness to trade with the Europeans reflected the already established lines of trade among themselves. In the North, First Nations with a local resource not found elsewhere traded for other resources or for manufactured products. Copper, iron, flint, the ivory of walrus, bird feathers, and birchbark canoes all figured in the region's trade. Algonkian hunters in the woodlands traded furs for corn and tobacco grown by Iroquoian-speaking peoples in the Great Lakes region and by the Mandans of the southern plains. Natives on the Prairies journeyed to the summer trade fairs on the Missouri where they could buy handicrafts and dried corn. The first peoples of the Pacific Coast traded products of the sea with inland residents who could supply them with dried meat of caribou and mountain goats, moose hides, and goat-wool blankets.

Excavations at Coteau-du-Lac, near the southern point of the present Ontario-Quebec border, indicate that the earliest inhabitants of the upper St Lawrence engaged in extensive trade to meet their needs. Among the materials found there are projectile points originating in northern Labrador, conch shells from the Gulf of Mexico, and copper from the upper Lake Superior region that was heated and moulded to make tools. The various nations not only traded extensively with their neighbours, but also served as go-betweens for items that moved over long distances along well-established trade and communications networks. When Europeans arrived, Native people introduced them to, and often guided them along, the established water routes, forest paths, and prairie trails. The Europeans would find that many Natives involved in trade had learned the languages of their trade partners and could serve as interpreters between Europeans and a variety of Native groups.

Trade was the peaceful side of relations among Native groups, but warfare between neighbours apparently also occurred in every region. Although some battles had economic causes or were motivated by cycles of revenge, the major motives for warfare were bound up with Native rituals. Warrior males trained and prayed for opportunities to prove their battleworthiness. Others, particularly women and elders, might attempt to restrain warfare, but it was rarely eliminated for extended periods. The limited technology of warfare in the pre-contact period and the ritualistic motivations for battles reduced the chances of all-out warfare that many European areas experienced in the fifteenth and sixteenth centuries. On both continents, torture or enslavement of captives was common.

Aboriginal peoples also seemed to share a relatively relaxed attitude towards sexual and childrearing practices. According to the early European commentators, premarital sex was widely practised in Aboriginal society. Europeans were less shocked by such behaviour, which also occurred in their own societies, than by the fact that Natives expressed their feelings about sex openly and apparently experienced no guilt. By European standards, divorce in Aboriginal societies was an all-too-easy matter for couples who failed to get along with each other. Europeans also criticized the Native peoples' tolerant attitude towards children. The young were subject to little of the discipline, physical punishment, and exploitation that were typically the lot of children in Europe.

Unlike Europeans, who ruthlessly proscribed erotic encounters between members of the same gender, First Nations people tolerated homosexual relationships. The term *berdache*, the French word for male prostitute, was used by Europeans to describe Aboriginal people who cross-dressed, worked among members of the other gender, and sought same-sex partners in their sexual relationships. Some Native cultures believed that cross-working and cross-dressing women and men actually belonged to a third gender that combined male and female characteristics; but in most cases gays and lesbians simply seem to have assumed the work roles and dress code of the other gender rather than incorporating the behavioural patterns of both men and women.

While the relative influence of men and women in social arrangements varied among Native societies, women generally held far more social power than European women could claim. Although each of the sexes had different economic roles, women generally produced and controlled the food resources of the tribe. Men gained status through their prowess as hunters and protectors of their tribe.

Some First Nations restricted women's role in religious activities. In particular, menstruating women were often forced to absent themselves from ceremonial events. Women may have welcomed this enforced seclusion. As explorer Samuel Hearne observed, among the Athapascans, menstruation was used by women as justification for taking a holiday from their husbands. Established customs prevented husbands from protesting a woman leaving the tent for four or five days when she claimed to be menstruating, even if she made the argument several times a month.

Women had an important voice among the Athapaskans and other Native groups, but the more valued position of males was reflected in the fact that during times of famine, female infanticide was practised while male infanticide remained rare. Moreover, Athapascan men could exchange or share wives without the women's consent. When European men arrived in North America, they tended to establish trading relations with First Nations men, thus often enhancing their status.

For all their similarity, First Nations peoples, like Europeans, developed different cultural practices. What follows is a brief overview of the First Nations of Canada at the time of European contact.

The First Nations of the Atlantic and Gulf Region

In the fifteenth century, Algonkian-speaking cultures inhabited much of the northern half of the North American continent, including the Atlantic and Gulf region. The Mi'kmaq were the largest group in what is today Atlantic Canada. The region's Algonkian peoples also included the Beothuk in Newfoundland and the Maliseet of what is now southern New Brunswick.

In Newfoundland the harsh climate and rugged terrain limited the potential for population growth. The Beothuk, estimated to number only 1000 in the year 1500, depended heavily on the caribou for food and clothing, which they hunted during the herds' fall migrations. As for other Aboriginal peoples in the Atlantic region, marine resources, such as seals, seabirds, fish, and shellfish, were critical for survival. The Beothuk could travel long distances in distinctive, light-weight birchbark canoes and lived in easily assembled wigwams covered with hides or birchbark. Because they painted themselves with red ochre and were among the first Aboriginal peoples encountered by Europeans, the Beothuk may have inspired the misnomer "Red Indian."

The Mi'kmaq were relatively affluent, living in one of Canada's more favoured geographical areas. Population estimates vary widely, from 3500 to 35 000 before 1500. Whatever archeologists may conclude about their origins, the Mi'kmaq believed themselves to have been placed on the earth by the supreme deity, the Great Spirit. A lesser deity, Glooscap, created the natural features of the land during his stay on earth, and before he departed for the heavens he instructed the Mi'kmaq on how to make tools and weapons. He also foretold the coming of the Europeans.

The Mi'kmaq occupied a territory stretching from the Gaspé Peninsula to Cape Breton Island, taking in present-day Nova Scotia, Prince Edward Island, and northern New Brunswick. Unlike their southern neighbours, they did not establish permanent coastal settlements but migrated to accommodate their seasonal round. Their conical wigwams, dress, and diet were much the same at the time of European contact as archeology suggests they had been 1500 years earlier. Such continuity testifies to a culture extraordinarily well adjusted to its natural surroundings, as well as a relatively stable environment capable of regenerating its resources.

The lives of the Mi'kmaq were governed by the seasons. Each year, when spring approached they set up camp near bays and river mouths and began setting up or repairing their fish weirs in anticipation of the runs of smelt, herring, salmon, and sturgeon. Spring also meant the return of migratory birds in great numbers. Along with the year-round resident ducks and gulls, migratory birds, and their eggs and nestlings, provided an additional source of food. Shellfish, including scallops, clams, mussels, and oysters, added variety to the Mi'kmaq diet. In summer, they hunted seals and walrus that basked on the sandy beaches. The Mi'kmaq also caught dolphins and small whales and fished with baited bonehooks for cod, sea trout, and halibut. As autumn approached they hunted large flocks of migratory birds, and in September they caught eels and dried them for winter use. When the first snow arrived it was time to move inland in search of moose and caribou as well as otter, muskrat, and bear. A severe winter was often the greatest threat to supplies of food resources.

The Mi'kmaq greatly impressed the first European observers, who described them as intelligent, self-reliant, and self-confident. Even missionaries, whose professional mandate was to reconstruct Aboriginal cultures in the image of their own, admitted that these people were peaceable, hospitable, and charitable, displaying little of the greed of European societies. The Mi'kmaq were relatively egalitarian and they exalted individual liberty. Affluent by the standards of the time, their wealth was evident in the intricate quillwork that adorned their clothing and utensils.

Perhaps because of their relative well-being, the Mi'kmaq may have produced formal governmental structures that went beyond the level of the band—that is, the face-to-face group of people who worked together to guarantee subsistence. Their structures may even have extended beyond the level of the tribe—the collection of bands in a given area—to include the entire Mi'kmaq people. Although the Mi'kmaq practice of choosing a grand chief to preside over all the tribes and seven district chiefs may have developed after European contact, it probably reflected pre-contact relations. The local chiefs were assisted by councils of male elders. Consent rather than coercion kept Mi'kmaq government in place without a state apparatus of courts or police.

The Maliseet, who lived in the southern region of modern-day New Brunswick, had a somewhat different subsistence cycle from that of the Mi'kmaq. At the time of European contact, they had just begun to cultivate corn and pumpkins. Evidence is mounting that they built substantial houses near the seacoast and lived there the year round. Their oval, semisubterranean "pit houses" were conical structures framed with poles, covered with bark and hides, and held in place by stones at the base. In these small buildings, families worked, ate, and slept.

The Canadian Shield First Nations

Algonkian peoples also inhabited much of the Canadian Shield, which was, on the whole, less accommodating than the Maritime region to human habitation. In 1500 the nations of the Shield included the Innu (known as Montagnais to the Europeans), the Ojibwa, the Cree, the Nipissing and the Algonquin. Most Algonkian peoples lived in dispersed groups of fewer than 400 people who survived by cooperative endeavour. While bands in the region were generally self-governing, most had organized contact with other groups whose culture they shared and with whom they intermarried. Informal alliance systems existed for purposes of warfare. Although these groupings could not create a formal nation in the European or even Mi'kmaq sense, in modern times many of them have used the term "nation" to describe the bonds that link their members.

The Innu, whose home is in northern Quebec and southern Labrador, lived a life of rough equality. According to anthropologist Eleanor Leacock, the Innu of southern Labrador made decisions by the consensus of those affected by the decision, and men and women worked closely together to ensure survival. Leacock writes:

> All adults participated in the procuring of food and manufacture of equipment necessary for life in the north. In general, women worked leather and bark, while men worked wood, with each making the tools they needed. For instance, women cut strips of leather and wove them into the snowshoe frames that were made by men, and women covered with birch bark the canoe frames the men made. Women skinned game animals and cured the hides for clothing, moccasins and lodge coverings. Everyone joined in putting up lodges; the women went into the forest to chop down lodge poles, while men cleared the snow from the ground where a lodge was to be erected.[7]

While small groups of Innu men hunted big game away from the local camp, women, responsible for childrearing, hunted small game closer to home. They prepared dried sturgeon mixed with fish oil to provide a high-protein winter food that could be stored for several months. Everyone worked together to drive migratory caribou into compounds where they could be speared. Women as well as men became shamans, intermediaries between the people and the spirit world.

In a society without formal laws and systems of punishment, consensus was essential to prevent disunity. Ridicule, rather than corporal punishment, served to sway wayward souls from acting against collective decisions. Although each Innu band of several hundred people had ties with other Innu bands, decisions were usually made at the local rather than the tribal level. Cooperation between bands was also common. A band whose territory became temporarily short of game could hunt within the territory of another Innu band or receive food from that band.

The Ojibwa controlled the northern shores of Lake Huron and Lake Superior from Georgian Bay to the edge of the prairies. Each Ojibwa band lived in a village of dome-shaped, birchbark wigwams that served as their permanent homes. In times of warfare and during the winter hunt, Ojibwa men left their village; the women remained in the village except when they attended clan feasts or were married to a resident of another village.

Goods and work were shared within bands. Tasks were sex-segregated, and all chiefs and most shamans were male. Men were warriors and hunters of big game such as caribou, elk, and deer, as well as fishers and makers of snares, bows, and arrows. They also built the wigwams. Women hunted small game, gathered wild rice and berries, skinned the animals, prepared all the food, made the clothing, blankets, and cooking vessels, kept the wigwams in good repair, and took all responsibility for children. Before European firearms were available, the Ojibwa hunted animals with snares made of wild hemp, by placing sharp spikes on their path, by using dogs to drive them into water, or by bow and arrow. The bows were made from ironwood or red cedar, the arrows from bone and shell.

Religious beliefs were central to Ojibwa culture. Like many First Nations, the Ojibwa believed that spirits were reflected in all natural phenomena and that each person could enlist the aid of guardian spirits to deal with the natural world and other humans. Among the most feared in the human world were sorcerers who might avenge wrongs by driving the soul from the body or enticing game away from a favourite hunting area. Shamans acted as intermediaries between individuals and the spirits, prescribing herbs that could heal injuries or cure illnesses and indicating the items a hunter should carry in a medicine bag to enjoy success during the hunt.

In their relations with the spirit world, most men did not depend solely on the shamans. They also undertook fasts, which were intended to induce visions, and they served as the audience outside "shaking lodges," small barrel-shaped structures where a diviner would sing and drum to attract spirits. Once these spirits arrived, their presence would cause the lodge to shake and the audience would ask them about the location of game or the fate of relatives. Participants might also entreat the spirits for cures to illnesses.

The Midewiwin, or Grand Medicine Society, played a key role in maintaining and developing the Ojibwa traditional medical-spiritual practices (the two were usually believed to be related). Years of instruction were required before its members reached the highest of its four grades of membership. The annual feast of this society brought together various bands and served as both a social and religious event.

The bands also joined forces on a temporary basis for purposes of warfare. When a band chief wanted to make war against the Sioux, he would send an envoy with pipe and tobacco to invite other bands to participate. Warfare was never within the tribe; it occurred only between the Ojibwa and other nations and was designed to establish control over a particular hunting territory. It also provided the warriors with the opportunity to demonstrate their prowess and was accompanied by a great deal of ritual. Because of the limits imposed by the bow and arrow, the major weapon of the pre-contact period, and the relative equality of the contending groups in battle, few casualties resulted from any encounter.

While the Ojibwa bands hunted separately from one another, intermarriage between them was common, and clans held annual feasts that linked the bands. The feasts were an integral part of the entertainment of the Ojibwa, who also played a variety of ball games, including the forerunner of today's lacrosse and a game called "maiden's ball play," a rough game that was played only by women. Jumping, foot racing, tossing, and gambling were other diversions for a people whose spirituality

AN OJIBWA BALL GAME

In 1850, Kah-Ge-Gah-Bowh, an Ojibwa who deceptively styled himself as a chief, provided a graphic description of an Ojibwa ball game. His account is reproduced here with the typographical errors that are found in the original printed edition.

Each man and each woman (women sometimes engage in the sport) is armed with a stick, one end of which bends somewhat like a small hoop, about four inches in circumference, to which is attached a net work of raw-hide, two inches deep, just large enough to admit the ball which is to be used on the occasion. Two poles are driven in the ground at a distance of four hundred paces from each other, which serves as goals for the two parties. It is the endeavour of each to take the ball to his hole. The party which carries the ball and strikes its pole wins the game.

The warriors, very scantily attired, young and brave fantastically painted—and women, decorated with feathers, assemble around their commanders, who are generally men swift on the race. They are to take the ball either by running with it or throwing it in the air. As the ball falls in the crowd the excitement begins.—The clubs swing and roll from side to side, the players run and shout, fall upon and tread upon each other, and in the struggle some get rather rough treatment.

When the ball is thrown some distance on each side, the party standing near instantly pick it up, and run at full speed with three or four after him.—The others send their shouts of encouragement to their own party. "Ha! ha! yah" "A-ne-gook!" and these shouts are heard even from the distant lodges, for children and all are deeply interested in the exciting scene. The spoils are not all on which their interest is fixed, but is directed to the falling and rolling of the crowds over and under each other. The loud and merry shouts of the spectators, who crowd the doors of the wigwams, go forth in one continued peal, and testify to their happy state.

The players are clothed in fur. They receive blows whose marks are plainly visible after the scuffle. The hands and feet are unincumbered, and they exercise them to the extent of their power; and with such dexterity do they strike the ball, that it is sent out of sight. Another strikes it on its descent, and for ten minutes at a time the play is so adroitly managed that the ball does not touch the ground.

No one is heard to complain, though he be bruised severely, or his nose come in close communion with a club. If the last-mentioned catastrophe befall him, he is up in a trice, and sends his laugh forth as loud as the rest, though it be floated at first on a tide of blood.[8]

was never puritanical. Young women were free to engage in premarital sex, but women had no sexual freedom after they married and had little say in the selection of a marriage partner. Rules about marriage, like rules generally, were imposed informally.

North and west of the woodlands Ojibwa lived another Algonkian-speaking nation, the Cree. Almost as populous as the Ojibwa, the Cree had gradually migrated westward, and some of their bands lived west of Lake Winnipeg by the early sixteenth century. Pre-contact populations have been confirmed in the parklands of the Saskatchewan River and the woodlands of Alberta. Because their territory was not as abundant in game as the Ojibwa's, the Cree were more nomadic than their Algonkian neighbours and their bands were smaller. Tipis made of caribou or moose hides, assembled and disassembled by the Cree women, provided them with shelter as they followed the caribou, moose, beaver, and bear. Their sturdy birchbark canoes provided transportation for whole families and their belongings.

The Cree and Ojibwa had no concept of land ownership. Rather, they believed that a particular group had the right to establish primacy in a particular area, giving it the first right to hunt and gather food there each season. It was also understood that if the area hunted by a band did not provide enough food in a given year, that band would have a right to hunt in the territory of a band that had enjoyed a surplus. Among the Cree, a band that was starving received assistance from a band that was prospering. Large annual Cree tribal gatherings in the summer cemented the bonds that made sharing in times of famine possible. Again, it was the seasons that dictated social arrangements. In the winter, when travel was difficult, it made sense for groups to disperse over the territory of the nation, placing no more people in an area than the wildlife could support. In summer, when travel was easier, gatherings in central locations were feasible.

Like Cree social organization, Cree religious beliefs and rituals diverged from those of their Ojibwa counterparts in many ways. Nonetheless, the two groups shared a belief in the importance of dreams and vision fasts as means of communicating with the spirit world. Both also venerated the dead. The Cree buried their dead in the ground with great lamentation and held annual feasts in honour of the departed.

The Interior Plains First Nations

In the pre-contact period, a variety of Aboriginal groups occupied the territories of the Interior Plains region of North America. Only Siouan-speaking groups lived in the area of present-day Prairie Canada 1000 years ago, but by the time of European contact in the eighteenth century, the Blackfoot, an Algonkian people, had achieved dominance on the northern plains of today's Saskatchewan and Alberta. Siouan groups remained in control of the plains of what is now Manitoba, with the Assiniboine constituting the largest Native grouping in that area. The cultures of the Plains peoples of North America were varied, but they also had similarities because of a common dependence on the buffalo.

The Blackfoot were an Algonkian nation whose long separation from their eastern counterparts had produced a variant of Algonkian language that could not be understood by other Algonkian speakers. Estimated at about 9000 in the early eigh-

DREAMS AND CREE CULTURE

A Plains Cree elder presented a testimony in the 1930s regarding the power of dreams for his people. His emphasis is on the experience of men, but women were equally guided in their lives by the interpretation of dreams.

The spirit powers may come to you when you are sleeping in your own tipi when you are young. If you want to be still more powerful then you go and fast. The ordinary dreams you have while sleeping are called pawamuwin. They are not worth anything although sometimes you dream of things that are going to happen.

You can tell a power dream in this way. You are invited into a painted tipi where there is only one man. The crier, who is the Raven Spirit, calls, and many come. I myself knew right away that they were spirit powers. I sat and thought to myself, "That is Horse, that is Buffalo spirit." The one that invited me said, "That's right."

I was called many times and they always told me the same thing—that I must do more fasting. Each time they invite me to a different painted tipi. Often after I wake up I wonder why they didn't tell me anything. I had nothing to do with girls when I tried to dream.

Finally, they told me that this would be the last time. They want me to go and fast for eight days. One of them said, "Try hard to finish these eight days, for that will be all." I gathered as many offerings as I could. It was during the moon just past [July] and there was plenty of food in camp so I knew the people wouldn't move for a while.

I promised to stand and face the sun all day and to turn with the sun. Only after sunset would I sit down. I had heard that this was the hardest thing to do and that is why I resolved to do it out of my own mind. I thought that I could help myself a little that way. [By making himself suffer more, he would secure greater blessings.] The sun wasn't very high when I got tired. I suffered all day. I tried all kinds of ways to stand, but I was played out. I raised my hands and cried; I could hardly finish. The sun went down and I just fell over. That was the first day.

The next morning I got very thirsty. I was not hungry but was thirsty all the time. On the fourth night my brother came with horses to get me. I told him I would stay. He came again on the sixth night but I said I would remain for two more nights. He said, "From the way you look, I may not find you alive."

All kinds of different spirit powers came to see me every night. Each one who invited me gave me power and songs. Then one gave me the power to make the Sun dance. That is how I got power and how I know many songs. Pretty nearly every night now I sing some of those songs.[9]

teenth century, the Blackfoot peoples included three tribal groups: Blackfoot, Peigan, and Blood. Before the Europeans arrived, they had begun migrating southward into former Siouan territory, and even before they met Europeans they had used guns and horses acquired by trade with the Cree to gain more Sioux territory by force. The Blackfoot tribes first encountered by the Europeans hunted the plentiful buffalo of the plains and maintained control over their territory by creating a relatively unified armed force under centralized control. They used warfare to expand their tribal hunting grounds and to capture women who could then be adopted by the tribe to ensure its further population expansion.

Most Blackfoot men belonged to military societies involving several grades of membership according to experience and achievement. The Blackfoot tribes conferred authority upon male chiefs for purposes both of warfare and the hunt. As buffalo hunters, the Blackfoot lived a nomadic existence, following the herds and pitching tipis made of buffalo skin. A late-nineteenth-century missionary, John McDougall, aptly summed up the role of the buffalo in Blackfoot life:

> Without buffalo they would be helpless, and yet the whole nation did not own one. To look at them and to hear them, one would feel as if they were the most independent of all men; yet the fact was they were the most dependent among men. Moccasins, mittens, leggings, shirts and robes—all buffalo. With the sinews of the buffalo they stitched and sewed these. Their lariats, bridles, lines, stirrup-straps and saddles were manufactured out of buffalo hide. . . . Women made scrapers out of the legbone for fleshing hides. The men fashioned knife handles out of the bones, and the children made toboggans out of the same. The horns served for spoons and powder flasks. In short, they lived and had their physical being in the buffalo.[10]

Worshippers of sun and thunder, the Blackfoot attached special importance to Sun Dance bundles, which, along with medicine bundles, were kept in rawhide bags. They believed that each object in the bag played a role in ensuring good fortune. The transfer of a bundle from one person to another involved an elaborate ceremony lasting several weeks as the new owner was exposed slowly to the significance of each item in the bundle and to the visions and songs that justified the object's inclusion.

The deceptively named Sun Dance was an elaborate set of religious ceremonies lasting several days and involving an entire nation. Presided over by a holy woman at a site chosen by a warrior society, it was organized by the extended family of a woman who had publicly promised the Sun Spirit to sponsor the event should the Spirit spare a male relative whose life was in danger. The tribe built a lodge where its various military and secret societies performed dances and rituals in exact sequence. While the Sun Dance was practised before the Blackfoot had direct contact with Europeans, it appears that it did not predate the arrival of the horse, which made hunting easier and left more time for leisure. It is perhaps best viewed as an elaboration of older Blackfoot traditions rather than as a tradition fully in place before the European arrival.

Blackfoot society was less egalitarian than that of the Ojibwa or Cree. Chiefs and male shamans had several spouses and larger tipis than other tribal members since the ceremonial functions performed by these men were thought to require more space and people in the household. Because of male casualties in warfare and the adoption of female captives into the Blackfoot culture, women always outnumbered men. While there were some female shamans, they had no privileges. First or second wives had higher status than later wives. In the post-contact period, as some leaders acquired many wives, the number of low-status women increased dramatically.

The Great Lakes—St Lawrence Lowlands First Nations

Although most Aboriginal societies were organized around hunting, gathering, and fishing, the mainly Iroquoian-speaking tribes concentrated in southern Ontario and the St Lawrence River valley grew corn, beans, and squash. Taking advantage of moderate climate and good soils, these nations were less dependent than other groups on an abundance of game or fish to guard against famine. The sedentary lifestyle encouraged population growth, with the result that the Iroquoian nations—including the St Lawrence Iroquoians, the Huron (in the Lake Simcoe-Georgian Bay area), and the Huron's neighbours, the Petun and the Neutral—together accounted for perhaps 50 000 people in 1500.

Here, too, the seasons governed people's lives. Among the Stadaconans, for example, whose summer home was on the island of Montreal, the women planted crops in the spring and then set off by canoe with their families for the Gulf of St Lawrence where the men fished and hunted. Families returned home in time for the women to harvest the annual crop.

The large palisaded villages and the loose political confederacies of some of the Iroquoian groups marked them off culturally from most hunter-gatherer societies. Another distinctive characteristic was the longhouse. Built of elm bark and attached to wooden frames, the longhouse was six metres wide and sometimes over thirty metres long, and within it about forty members of an extended family lived and shared responsibilities. A village might contain 30 to 50 of these longhouses, each with a row of fires down the middle and bedrooms on both sides. Underground storage pits, usually about 1.25 metres deep and slightly less than 1 metre in diameter, held part of the harvest to protect it from fire and mice. In some villages, chiefs had larger longhouses to accommodate village and war council meetings.

Iroquoian societies were matrilineal (descent was traced through the mother's line) and matrilocal (a man lived with the family of his wife). While women dominated agricultural activities, the men were responsible for providing the smaller portion of the food supply that came from hunting. A minority of men were also involved in intertribal trade. By the sixteenth century, the Huron were extensively involved in barter with a variety of Algonkian groups. Corn, corn meal, and fish-nets were traded for animal skins and fish. Only a small number of families con-trolled the trade, but the wealth they earned from it was redistributed within the Huron confederacy.

While village or tribal councils involved all men over a certain age, important decisions required the approval of the women. For example, the men might decide to go to war with another tribe, but if the women, who controlled agriculture, refused to supply food for the warriors, there could be no war. Chiefs were men from cer-tain family lines, but the women of the line chose the chief and could replace him if he failed to meet their expectations. Every Huron belonged to a clan, which offered special privileges. Any member of the clan could stay with fellow clan members when passing through a village and could depend upon them for help in a lean crop year.

Burial practices among the Huron were elaborate. About once a decade the remains of the dead were disinterred in the villages and placed in a common burial ground in a ceremony called the Feast of the Dead. This ceremony was believed to make it possible for the souls of the dead, until then interred with their remains, to travel westward to the land of souls. The Huron's land of souls was thought to be much the same as their earthly home—an indication, perhaps, of their positive view of life in their own lands.

Iroquoian creation myths offered dramatic explanations of the origins of the earth and its inhabitants. For the Five Nations Iroquois, the vast land area they lived on was an island on the back of a turtle. Long ago, according to one account, be-ings similar to humans lived in longhouses in the sky. In the centre of their princi-pal village stood the celestial tree blossoming with lights, the symbols of peace and knowledge. One day a curious woman asked her husband to uproot this tree so she could discover the source of its power. As she bent forward to look into the hole where the tree had once been, she tumbled to a lower world. From the light that now shone through the hole into this lower world, the animals saw her plight. The Canada goose flew down to rescue her and then placed her on the back of the turtle. In this way Great Turtle Island, or North America, came into existence.

The confederacies of Great Turtle Island appear to have been a response to a growing cycle of violence in Iroquoian societies, resulting from blood feuds. The Five Nations Confederacy was the earliest. According to Iroquois legend, it owed its origins to the efforts of Dekanawidah—the "Heavenly Messenger," a Five Nations chief—and his disciple, Hiawatha. It proved to be the most effective and enduring of the Iroquoian confederacies, if only because the Five Nations were surrounded by enemies and their members therefore had more incentive to make it work. The Huron and Neutral con-federacies, recent phenomena in the period of first contact with the Europeans, did not develop the cohesion evident in the Five Nations Confederacy.

In the confederacies, men chosen by the women of the villages made decisions on war and peace and tried to settle disputes between villages or clans. They were

DEKANAWIDAH AND HIAWATHA

The lives of Dekanawidah and his associate Hiawatha illustrate the dynamism of pre-contact First Nations life. But efforts to piece together their life stories also illustrate the difficulties in writing biographies of individuals in pre-literate societies. What we know of Dekanawidah and Hiawatha comes from the stories passed on from storytellers of their own time to later generations of Iroquois. The legends suggest they may have lived as early as the late fifteenth century or as late as a century afterwards.

Although Dekanawidah (which means the Peacemaker) was born a Huron in today's southeastern Ontario, he lived his adult life among the Seneca in today's New York. Hiawatha, meanwhile, was born an Onondaga but lived with the Mohawk. We do not know the story of how either man ended up among a different Native group than the one of his birth. But we know they became leaders in their new homelands. These facts alone suggest societies that were, in no way, static.

Dekanawidah was disturbed by the extent of infighting that had developed among iroquoian-speaking peoples, and concerned that their disunity might entice other First Nations to invade their territories. In his travels, he met Hiawatha, who shared his concerns. The two visited all the Iroquoian groups on the south shore of Lake Erie and Lake Ontario, and possibly along the St Lawrence. They organized a congress of all of these groups. Then, according to tradition, Dekanawidah proposed an elaborate constitution with 117 sometimes quite lengthy clauses dealing with questions of relations among Iroquois peoples and between these peoples and other First Nations. Five groups—the Mohawk, Onondaga, Oneida, Seneca, and Cayuga—smoked the peace pipe to symbolize their acceptance of this constitution.

The constitution, like the legend of Dekanawidah, was preserved orally. It began: "I am Dekanawidah [the Peacemaker] and with the Five Nations' Confederate Lords I plant the tree of the Great Peace."[11] Its many clauses demonstrated an effort to create unity among the Five Nations but at the same time to assure that representatives of the five nations in the Confederacy Council truly spoke for the women and men of these nations. The constitution not only codified elaborate rituals for decision making but also guaranteed each of the nations its religious rights, confirmed women's ownership of the land and soil, and ensured that traditional rights of clans would not be violated. Rules for adoption of individuals and nations into the Five Nations demonstrated that this was not a closed society.

The Iroquois constitution was detailed and sophisticated. It had an influence on the men who drafted the American constitution, particularly Benjamin Franklin.

not always effective. Unanimity was required before a decision could be approved, and even then a tribal council that disagreed with a confederacy-level decision could disavow it. The confederacy had no permanent officials, and its decisions required the consent of tribes to be put into effect. It was a loose system of government that made little sense to the recently arrived Europeans.

While individual freedom and collective sharing of tasks and goods characterized Iroquoian society, the increased warfare of the immediate pre-contact period revealed a different side of the society. Warfare appears to have been on the rise because the young warriors had become more militant in their demands to be allowed to demonstrate their prowess in battle. Prisoners were often tortured, and sometimes captured warriors were cooked and eaten in ceremonies suggesting that cannibalism, where it involved a captured warrior, had been given religious approval within the culture. Still, casualties in battles between Iroquoian groups were relatively light, and women and children taken as prisoners were generally adopted as equals rather than enslaved by the tribe that captured them.

The Western Cordillera First Nations

The coastal societies of British Columbia stand apart from all other First Nations. Of the twelve language families that have been identified for pre-contact Canada, six are exclusive to British Columbia. With a combined population of perhaps 200 000 people in the eighteenth century, the coastal societies included the Tsimshian on the northern mainland, the Coast Salish on the southern mainland and Vancouver Island, the Southern Kwakiutl (or Kwakwaka'wakw) on the east coast of Vancouver Island, the Haida of the Queen Charlotte Islands, and the Nootka (or Nuu'chah'nulth) on Vancouver Island's west coast. These groups constituted the most affluent Native societies of pre-contact Canada, and their social structure is often attributed to this affluence.

Although different in many ways, all West Coast nations were chiefdoms characterized by social hierarchies that resembled the ordered patriarchal societies of Europe more than the relatively egalitarian Aboriginal societies of the rest of Canada. The chief, always a man, was regarded as a priest who owed his position of power and wealth to the gods. Generally holding his position by virtue of family descent and ruling between 100 and 500 people, the chief controlled the distribution of the resources of the community and took a larger proportion of the community's goods for his own use. Below the chief in the hierarchy were certain members of his family, members of several other wealthy leading families, free men (that is, non-slaves) and their families, and finally slaves.

The potlatch, a feast during which individuals distributed portions of their property in the form of gifts, reduced disparities somewhat and emphasized the connection between all free men and women of the tribe. It demonstrated that property belonged to the community even if custom dictated that its use was not equally shared. Status was indicated by a family's generosity at potlatch time. Ironically, the accumulation of goods for this ceremony encouraged aggressive competition between potlatches, and the elaborate rituals governing gift giving ensured that the social system reproduced itself.

By redistributing wealth, potlatches legitimized the social structure and served diplomatic roles as well. Within a tribe, the potlatch ensured that no free person was reduced to poverty and obviated the need for formal policing mechanisms that might have been required if some members were forced to resort to thievery to survive. Among tribes, potlatches between chiefs allowed one chief to demonstrate his control over an area by granting lavish wealth derived from it. Thus, potlatches served as a diplomatic way to stake out territory and fend off potential rivals.

Slaves, usually women and children captured in wartime (adult male captives were killed), were almost universally excluded from the potlatches. Although slaves worked alongside free people, their slave status was a badge of shame. Generally, a tribe would pay a ransom to free tribal members enslaved by an enemy nation, but slaves captured in forays far from the tribal home of their captors might never be freed; their slave status passed to their children. The treatment of slaves varied. In some villages there was little distinction between the slaves and free people except at potlatch and marriage time. In other villages there was mistreatment of slaves, but the tendency was exaggerated by European observers, particularly missionaries, who were convinced that slaves were both eaten and used in ceremonial sacrifices. Native oral tradition rejects these claims and insists that cannibalism was taboo and only animal flesh was used in ceremonies.

A favourable geographical location and ingenious use of local resources created wealthy societies on the northwest coast of North America. Plants, almost exclusively gathered by women, and plentiful stocks of fish, particularly salmon and halibut, and shellfish provided the staples of the coastal diet. The coastal peoples built weirs, or open-work fences, to divert fish so they could be easily harpooned or netted. The men made harpoons of wood with barbs of bone or horn from local animals. While the men fished, the women prepared the catch, preserving large quantities by smoke-drying. The women cooked food in pit ovens that they dug in the ground.

Abundant timber allowed the Native peoples of the coast to build large homes for extended families. Among the Tsimshian, for example, homes made of massive timbers from red cedar measured 15 by 16.5 metres. A central pit, 9 by 1.5 metres, served as the main living space, where women cooked and everyone ate and relaxed. Recreation for coastal nations included wrestling, weightlifting, tug-of-war, foot races, and gambling.

The free women wove intricate baskets from red and yellow cedar and the flexible roots of the spruce. They also made textiles from mountain-goat wool, dog wool, and the down of ducks and other birds. Men and women learned different skills. While the women wove, the men worked in stone and wood. The woodwork was particularly impressive, consisting of elaborately decorated totem poles and masks, house façades, feast dishes, canoes, storage boxes, helmets, and even cradles and chamber pots.

Aboriginal societies of the West Coast had varying resources, religious beliefs, and marriage practices. While the Nuu'chah'nulth were whalers, the Haida lived off sea otters, sea lions, fur seals, and fish. The Haida and Tsimshian were matrilineal societies: the children inherited their line of descent, and thus their position in society, from their mothers. Women in these two societies generally enjoyed a higher status than women in the other coastal groups, which traced descent through the father's line. In all coastal societies, pubescent girls were secluded for lengthy periods, restricting their freedom during a stage of life when few restraints existed for males.

Coastal peoples worshipped gods of the forests, mountains, and beaches, but they also believed that sinister forces resided in nature—sea monsters, ferocious birds in caves, ogres in the forest, and thunderbirds on mountains that could swoop down on any prey. To fend off such monsters, a person had, among other things, to carry out periodic fasts, to avoid sexual relations, and to scrub the body with branches. Shamans, both men and women, were the intermediaries between the Natives and the spirit world. Long years of training taught them how to perform rituals that would cure diseases, which were believed to be the result of souls wandering or the intrusion of foreign objects into the body at the whim of malevolent spirits.

While the coastal societies had developed cultures vastly different from those east of the Rockies, the village-based societies of the plateau (that is, the southern interior of British Columbia and the mountain regions of southwestern Alberta) were generally characterized by looser, more democratic structures similar to the ones further east. Band-level chiefs in these societies rarely appropriated more of the product from the hunt or salmon fishing than other members of the tribe. Distinctions among families were uncommon, and slavery was not practised. Among both the Carrier and Sekani of east-central British Columbia, hunting grounds and fishing spots were commonly owned by the band.

The Carrier women enjoyed a status equal to that of men. Indeed, if recent field research can be accurately projected backwards into the pre-contact period, elder women were regarded as greater repositories of wisdom than elder men. Women participated in key subsistence activities, including salmon fishing, snaring, trapping, and hunting. While most of the salmon fishing was done by men, it was the women who filleted, smoked, and stored the fish and made fish eggs into dried cakes that often were used as trade items.

The North's First Nations

A variety of Aboriginal societies whose people spoke Athapaskan languages lived in the northern regions of today's four western provinces and in the Northwest Territories and Nunavut. Harvesting local resources of the subarctic, such as fish, small game, caribou, trees, and berries, the Athapaskans lived in self-sufficient groups of about 20 or 30 related people. Tribal organization did not exist, and even band-level organization was only temporary: a coming together of people to carry out a specific task.

The lives of members of the Athapaskan groups of the western subarctic were marked by cooperation in the tasks required for eking out a subsistence in a harsh terrain. A group that had experienced a bad year could count on aid if it moved to an area where a local surplus existed. Work was sex-segregated, as it was among the Algonkian groups, but again there is little to suggest that women's work was less valued than men's. While the men hunted big game, women trapped smaller animals and prepared clothing from moose hides and rabbit skins. Women also carted the band's goods as groups moved from place to place in winter. Both women and men could become shamans.

The Athapaskans believed that, at one time, animals such as the crow and the wolf spoke and behaved like humans. They therefore felt it necessary to know details of the past of these animals as well as of plants so they could understand their nature and how they must be treated. An elaborate mythology detailing this past was passed from generation to generation.

By the sixteenth century, the Thule people, ancestors of today's Inuit, enjoyed undisputed control of the tundra region beyond the tree line from Labrador to the Yukon. The Thule, nomadic but originally concentrated in the western Arctic, had gradually followed the caribou to spread their domain as far as the Atlantic. Speaking their own language, Inuktitut, they were alone among the First Nations of Canada to have claimed a home on two continents when the Europeans first arrived. Until political pressures in the nineteenth century forced them to choose to live either in Greenland or Canada, the Inuit moved freely between the Canadian Arctic and Greenland in search of whale, caribou, and seal.

The sealskin-covered kayaks and umiaks of the Inuit were their main sea transportation; dog sleds provided land transport. With the bow and arrow and the spear thrower they caught their prey and fended off the rare intruder who might dispute their control of the far North. Although they maintained their physical distance from the other Native groups in North America, the Inuit had religious beliefs and followed cultural practices that had much in common with those of other hunter-gatherer cultures such as the Athapaskans. Like these groups, the Inuit carved out their subsistence in a harsh environment. Their famous igloos, winter homes made of ice and snow, alternated as residences with summer houses that had frames made of whalebone and driftwood and roofs covered with baleen from whales and then sod.

Although the northern peoples lived in a less favourable environment than other Aboriginal peoples, they possessed rich cultures. They developed songs and dances to celebrate their subsistence activities, beating drums made of caribou skins with sticks to accompany the dancers. Gambling, football, archery, and club-throwing were among their leisure activities. They also made every effort to bring beauty into their lives. Author Keith J. Crowe notes:

> They tattooed their bodies and embroidered their clothing with beads of horn or soapstone, with the quills of goose and porcupine, with moosehair or strips of weasel skin. Some made toothmark patterns on birchbark containers. Some people painted their skin tents and shirts with paint made from red ochre or black graphite. Any possession, a wooden bowl, a horn dipper, or a knife, might be decorated in some way. Painting, carving, embroidery, tassels, fringes and beads, dyeing, and bleaching were all used.[12]

Throughout thousands of years, Aboriginal peoples not only adapted to various geographical environments but also carved out rich, dynamic lives and relationships. As part of this process, they defined their earthly existence by developing vibrant spiritual beliefs, which also changed over time. In the fifteenth century, when Europeans began to come regularly to the shores of the Americas, the resident nations entered relationships with people whose social values, religious beliefs, and cultural practices were at sharp variance with their own.

Notes

1. Canada, Royal Commission on Aboriginal Peoples, *Report,* vol. 1 (Ottawa: Government of Canada, 1996) 687.
2. James Axtell, *The Invasion Within: The Contest of Cultures in Colonial North America* (New York: Oxford University Press, 1985) 14–15.
3. Julie Cruikshank, *Life Lived Like a Story* (Vancouver: UBC Press, 1992) 278.
4. Bruce G. Trigger, *The Children of Antaentsic: A History of the Huron People to 1660* (Montreal: McGill-Queen's University Press, 1976) 19–20.
5. Arthur J. Ray, *I Have Lived Here Since the World Began: An Illustrated History of Canada's Native People* (Toronto: Lester/Key Porter, 1996).
6. Olive P. Dickason, *Canada's First Nations: A History of Founding Peoples from Earliest Times* (Toronto: Oxford University Press, 1997) xii.
7. Eleanor Leacock, "Women in Egalitarian Societies," in *Becoming Visible: Women in European History,* ed. Renate Bridenthal, Claudia Koonz, and Susan Stuard, 2nd ed. (Boston: Houghton Mifflin, 1987) 22–23.
8. G. Copway or Kah-Ge-Gah-Bowh, Chief of the Ojibway Nation, *The Traditional History and Characteristic Sketches of the Ojibway Nation* (London, 1850; reprinted Toronto: Coles, 1972) 43–45.
9. David G. Mandelbaum, *The Plains Cree: An Ethnographic, Historical and Comparative Study* (Regina: Canadian Plains Research Centre, 1979) 160–61.
10. John McDougall, *Saddle, Sled, and Snowshoe* (Toronto: William Biggs, 1896) 261–62.
11. Ronald Wright, *Stolen Continents: The "New World" Through Indian Eyes* (Toronto: Penguin, 1993) 120.
12. Keith J. Crowe, *A History of the Original Peoples of Northern Canada* (Montreal: McGill-Queen's University Press, 1991) 22.

"Discovery"

Introduction

Who discovered who? That question lies at the heart of these two readings. The seventeenth-century French explorer Samuel de Champlain recorded his explorations for the King of France. In this excerpt, from 1615 to 1616, Champlain is an ethnographer of sorts; he records the habits and customs of the Huron people *and* his impressions of the Huron people. To what extent can we trust the "facts" of Champlain's writing and to what extent do the Huron appear as the object of a European and defining gaze? Peter MacLeod is a historian. His article turns on its head our understanding of discovery. Using Anishinabeg oral traditions, he tells a very different story of discovery. Who are the explorers and who are the discoverers? What does reading Champlain and the Anishinabeg oral accounts together tell us about agency and passivity in history?

To the King

Samuel de Champlain

TO THE KING: Sir, here is the third volume of my account of the most interesting and important things that happened on my voyages to New France. I think you will find this volume even more enjoyable to read than the first two, for there I was chiefly concerned with ports, harbours, latitudes, magnetic variations and other matters of greater interest to seamen and navigators than to laymen. In this book you will learn something of the manners and customs of the savages—their weapons, their strategy in the field, their methods of travel—all set down with enough detail to satisfy the most curious reader.

You will soon see that these people are by no means so ignorant that in course of time they cannot be taught the arts of civilization. You will see how for fifteen long and arduous years we have nourished the hope of planting the cross in the New World, knowing that our first duty was to treat the savages with patience and charity and seeking above all to bring the miserable creatures to a knowledge of God and their Saviour. It is true that some of our people think only of profit, but I am convinced that their greed is nothing more than a means to an end and part of God's holy plan.

When a tree brings forth fruit, the fruit belongs to the owner of the land, who has watered the tree and cared for it. The fruit of our labours belongs by right to your Majesty, not only because New France is part of your dominions but also because you have given us the benefit of your protection. Certain persons were unfriendly to our aims and ambitions and they used every means at their disposal to hinder the success of our expedition. Whatever we have achieved we owe to the support of your Majesty and the wisdom of the Council, which gave us the authority to act in your name.

This only makes us the more eager to establish new colonies overseas, so the savages may learn not only of the glory of God but also of the power and greatness of your Majesty. Once the savages have been taught to speak French they will soon learn to think and feel like Frenchmen, and then they will want nothing so much, after the love of God, as to serve France. If we succeed, your Majesty will share the honour and glory with God alone. Your name will always be blessed as that of the man who brought so many wretched creatures to a knowledge of their Saviour. You will always be famous for having carried the sceptre of France farther west than all your ancestors carried it to the east, so that now we hold sway over the whole known world. You alone of all kings are entitled to call yourself Most Christian. This great

The excerpts from *Voyages to New France* by Samuel de Champlain are reprinted by permission of Oberon Press.

enterprise shows that you deserve the title not only by right of inheritance but also by right of achievement. For despite all your other cares you have taken pains to see to the preaching of the gospel in many a land where the name of God had never been heard before. In course of time these people will join us in praying for the Kingdom of God and like us will bless the name of France.

I am, Sir, your most humble, faithful and obedient servant and subject,

CHAMPLAIN

To the east the country is already well-known, extending as it does to the shores of Labrador, Newfoundland, Cape Breton, Acadia and New England. I have already described this part of the country in the journals of my previous voyages and I won't say anything more about it now, since I want to tell you as much as I can of what I saw in the interior.

The Huron country lies in latitude 44° 30' and is seven hundred miles from east to west and thirty from north to south.[1] Like Brittany, it is almost completely surrounded by water. The land is fertile and most of it is cleared. There are about eighteen villages, of which six are really fortified towns, with stockades surrounding the living quarters. The stockades are made of wooden stakes set in three rows and lashed together, with galleries behind from which the defenders can throw boulders down on the enemy or pour water on him if he tries to set fire to the defences.

The population of the country is about thirty thousand, of which two thousand are warriors. They live in lodges made of bark. These lodges are about twelve yards wide and up to fifty or sixty yards long, with a gangway a foot or two across running down the middle from one end to the other. On each side there is a sort of bench about four feet high, where they sleep in summer to get away from the fleas. In winter they sleep on mats on the floor near the fire, where it is warmer. They gather dry wood all summer and pile enough in the lodges to last the winter. At one end of each lodge there is an open space where they store their Indian corn in large casks made of bark. Mice are everywhere and everything they want to keep safe, such as food or clothing, has to be hung up on wooden pegs. The average lodge will have a dozen fires and two dozen families. The smoke inside is thick and blinding and diseases of the eyes are common, in fact many of the older people have lost their sight altogether. The trouble is that there are no windows and so there is no way for the smoke to escape except through a single hole in the roof. Each lodge is built three or four yards from the next, in case one should catch fire from another. Often they will live in one place for ten, twenty or even thirty years and then move to a new site six or

Explaing the characteristics of the new land.

---

[1]By Huron country Champlain here means the whole of what is now Ontario, south of the Ottawa River. From east to west this area measures about 500 miles; from north to south it varies from a few miles to 175 miles or more. In the next sentence Champlain seems to be referring to only a part of the region, namely the Bruce Peninsula.

eight miles away. If they are driven out by their enemies they may move to a distance of a hundred and twenty miles or more, as the Onondagas once did.

They are a happy people, even though their life is wretched by comparison with ours. They have never known anything better, so they are content with what they have. The staple of their diet is Indian corn mixed with red beans and cooked in a variety of different ways. First they pound the corn and beans with a wooden mortar to make flour, then they winnow the flour with pieces of bark. To make bread they boil the dough, as if they were making corn soup. This makes it easier to whip. After it is thoroughly boiled they sometimes add blueberries or dried raspberries or occasionally (for it is very scarce) pieces of suet. After moistening the batter with warm water they make it up into loaves or biscuits which they bake under hot coals. Then when the loaves are ready they take them out and wash them.

Sometimes they take the meal and wrap it in corn leaves, fasten it together and put it into boiling water. More often they make it into a dish they call Migan. To make Migan they take two or three handfuls of corn, pound it and put it into an earthenware pot. Then they add water without removing the husks and bringing it to the boil, stirring the meal from time to time to make sure it doesn't stick to the pot and burn. Finally, they add a little fresh or dried fish, depending on the season, to give it flavour. They eat a lot of Migan, especially in winter. It usually smells foul and tastes worse, either because they don't know how to make it or because they don't bother to make it properly. They can prepare it well enough when they want to take the trouble, and when they cook it with venison it tastes all right. Usually they simply put the fish into the pot in small pieces, without bothering to remove the bones, scales or insides, and this is what gives it a bad taste. Then when it is ready they all simply help themselves from the common pot. Migan is thin enough to drink but there isn't much to it. Sometimes they make the same dish by roasting unripe corn. This they preserve and later cook whole with fish or, when they have it, with meat. Or they take dried corn and roast it over hot coals, then pound it and make it into flour. This is the way they make it when they are on the move and it's the way I like it best.

For banquets and other special occasions they take a quantity of fish and meat, cut it up into pieces and boil it in big kettles. After it has been boiled for some time they skim off the fat with a spoon. Then they add the roasted meal and stir it in until the mixture is like a thick soup. Each person gets a helping from the pot, along with a spoonful of fat, which is their idea of a delicacy. Sometimes they add beans and boil them up with the roasted meal, with a little fat and some fish stirred in. They often give banquets in winter, when they have time on their hands, and dogs are kept busy eating up the scraps. They save up their fish and game for these occasions and the rest of the time they live on thin Migan, which is no better than pig swill.

There is another dish they make with Indian corn. They take the ears and bury them in the mud and leave them to soak for two or three months. When they are good and rotten they dig them up and boil them with meat or fish and then eat them just as they are. Sometimes they roast the corn instead of boiling it and that tastes better, but I can assure you that nothing could smell worse than the ears of corn when they come up all covered with mud. However, there's nothing they like better. The women and children suck the rotten ears as if they were sugar-cane. They also eat a lot of squash, which they boil or roast over hot coals. Usually they have only two meals a day. We ourselves fasted during Lent, partly to give them an example, but it was a waste of time.

We noticed that they kept bears in captivity for two or three years at a time, to fatten them for the slaughter. I have no doubt that if they had livestock they would have no difficulty in caring for it, once they had learned how. There is plenty of good land for pasture and all they need is suitable stock—horses, cows or pigs. Without stock they will always be poor. However, they seemed to me happy enough. They live from hand to mouth but they are better off than the savages who have no permanent settlements and roam the countryside like wild animals.

Their clothing is made from skins of all sorts. Some of these they get by skinning their own game; others they get in exchange for corn, meal, beads and fish-nets from the Algonkins and Nipissings, who are great hunters. Everything they wear is cut to the same design, so there isn't any variety of style or colour, but they take great pains with the skins when they cure them. Their loincloth is usually made out of a piece of deerskin. So are their leggings, which hang in folds and come up to the waist. Moccasins they commonly make out of deerskin, bearskin or beaver. Beaver is in great demand, for they use it to make robes, which they wear like a cloak in the Irish or Egyptian fashion, with sleeves tied behind with a cord. When they go out into the bush they wrap themselves up in their furs, but when they are at home they loosen the sleeves and wear their cloak open.

They decorate their clothes with coloured bands made out of glue and strips of skin. Sometimes you will see bands painted red or brown alternating with bands of glue, which always keep their shape and colour no matter how dirty and worn they get. Some of the tribes are more skilful in dressing skins than others, and more ingenious in decorating them. The Montagnais and the Algonkins take more pains with it than any of the others. They decorate their skins with bands of porcupine quills, which they dye a bright scarlet. They prize these trimmings and when they discard a skin they take the trimmings off and use them over again. They even use them to adorn their faces when they want to look their best. Usually they paint their faces black and red, mixing the pigment with vegetable oil (sometimes made from sunflower seeds) or animal fat. They also dye their hair, which some of the men grow long; others grow it short, while still others grow it on one side of the head only. The women and girls all do their hair the same way, keeping it well combed, oiled and dyed. When they go to a dance they put it up in a tuft at the back, bound with an eelskin thong, or else in heavy plaits hung with beads. They dress just like the men except that they always keep their robe, which comes down to the knee, fastened around them. For though they aren't ashamed to show their bodies above the waist

Clothing

and below the knee, they always keep the rest covered. They like to wear bracelets and ear-rings and often have beads hanging from their belt. I have often seen girls at dances, where the elders take pride in showing off their daughters at their best, wearing more than twelve pounds of beads, to say nothing of the rest of the finery they had on.

For the most part the people are cheerful and good-natured, though some are surly enough. Both men and women are strong and well-built. Many of the women and girls are attractive and have good figures, clear skin and regular features. Most of the young girls have good breasts. The women do much of the work around the house and in the fields, sowing the corn, gathering the wood, stripping and spinning the hemp, making fishnets. They are expected to harvest the corn and store it, cook the meals and take care of the house. They are in fact no better than beasts of burden. As for the men, they do nothing but go hunting and fishing, build the lodges and fight the wars. When they have nothing else to do, they go trading in other parts of the country. On their return they eat and drink and dance until they can stay awake no longer. This is all they know of work.

They have a kind of marriage ceremony, which works like this. When a girl turns thirteen or fourteen, boys will begin to notice her, if she is attractive. Eventually one of them will ask the girl's parents for her hand. (Sometimes the girl doesn't wait for her parents' consent, but the wisest and best of them do.) Next the suitor will give the girl a present of beads, perhaps a necklace or a bracelet. If she likes him she will accept the present. He will then come and sleep with her for three or four nights and they will enjoy each other as if they were man and wife. If they don't get on well with each other, the girl will leave her lover, but she will keep his presents in return for the pleasure she has given him. The disappointed suitor is then free to look for another girl and the girl is free, if she likes, to look for another suitor. This goes on till they find what they are looking for. Some girls spend their whole youth like this, so that by the time they are married they have had twenty or more suitors. Not that these will be their only lovers. For no matter how many suitors they have, the girls go about from one lodge to another after nightfall and so do the boys, making love whenever they feel like it to any girl who will have them. The married men do the same and nobody thinks the worse of them for it, for that is the custom and everybody expects it.

The only time a woman will stay with her suitor is when she is with child. Then her most recent suitor will return and treat her with all the tenderness and affection he used to feel for her. Usually he will claim the unborn child as his and often another man will say the same. In the end it is up to the woman to decide which of them she will marry and she will choose the one that pleases her most. By that time she will have amassed a great quantity of necklaces and beads of all sorts. She will also have had the privilege of marrying the husband of her choice. Once married, the women stay with their husbands and never leave them without some very good reason. There is, of course, never any question of impotence, for each suitor must prove himself before he is married. Nevertheless, the women aren't any more particular where they find their pleasure after they are married than they were before, so long as they keep up appearances. This means that there is no way of knowing whether or not the children are the lawful issue of a man and his wife. For the same reason children never inherit property or titles from their fathers. Since there is no way for a man to know who his children are, he will choose his heirs from among his nephews and nieces, for he can be sure they are his sisters' children if not his own.

The children are fed and cared for by the women. During the day they bind the child to a piece of wood and wrap him in furs or skins, leaving an opening through which he can urinate. With girls they twist a leaf of corn and put it between their thighs in such a way that one end presses against their crotch while the other remains outside their clothing. The leaf carries off the urine and keeps the child dry. Under the child they spread the silk of a special kind of reed—the one we call hare's foot—which is soft for it to lie on and helps to keep it clean. They decorate the backboard with beads and the smallest of children wear necklaces. At night they put the child to bed with nothing on, between its father and mother. It's a wonder they don't get hurt or smothered while their parents are sleeping, but this seldom seems to happen. When they get old enough the children run free. They are never punished and for this reason are often naughty. You often see them strike their mother and sometimes, when they get big enough, they will even strike their father if he does anything they don't like. It's almost as if they were a curse from on high.

They have no laws, so far as I could see. They have no idea of justice, except to take an eye for an eye and a tooth for a tooth, so naturally they are always having quarrels and blood feuds.

They have no gods and no forms of worship and live like animals. They do have some respect for the devil, or for something of the same name, but it's hard to say what it is. The word they use means several different things, so one can't make out whether they are talking about the devil or about something else. I think it's the devil they mean, because I've noticed that when they see a man do something extra-ordinary, something more courageous or cunning than usual, or when they see a man in a frenzy or out of his mind, they address him as Oqui, that is, great all-knowing spirit or devil.

Some of them deliberately play the part of an Oqui, or Manitou as the Algonkins and Montagnais call them. They serve as medicine-men, healing the sick, caring for the wounded and foretelling the future. In other words, they practise all the tricks and deceptions of the devil in order to confuse and mislead the people. For instance, they persuade the sick that they won't recover unless they go through certain ceremonies and invite everybody to great banquets. Then, of course, the Oquis come to the banquets and make sure they get the best of it. Not satisfied with that, they will convince their patients that they have to go through further ceremonies, which I will describe more fully later on, if they hope to make a quick recovery. But though the people trust their medicine-men, you seldom see any of them actually possessed by the devil, as you do farther inland. This is why I have always felt it wouldn't be too hard to teach them the essential truths of the Christian religion, if only one was willing to take the trouble. But there's no point in sending out a few priests without adequate backing, for though the savages are eager enough to learn about God today, tomorrow, when they find out they have to give up some of their filthy habits, their bad manners and their dissolute conduct, they will change their minds. What we need are people who can keep them up to the mark, people who can set an example and encourage them to mend their ways.

Father Joseph and I often went to their councils and talked to them about their customs and their beliefs, and they always listened carefully. They couldn't always understand what it was we were trying to tell them. It wasn't always something you could put in words. More than once they suggested that if we really wanted to help them we should bring our women and children and settle down among them. Then they could see for themselves how to serve God and obey His laws. They could see how we lived out our daily lives, how we sowed the seed and tilled the soil, how we fed and cared for our stock, how we made all the many things they had seen and envied. They felt sure, they said, that they would learn more this way in one year than they would learn in twenty years of listening to us talk. If necessary, we could take their children and bring them up as our own. Seeing their life was so wretched in comparison with ours, the children would certainly make no bones about adopting our customs in preference to their own. This seemed sensible to me and showed, I felt, that they were genuinely anxious to know and understand the truth. It's a shame to let so many of our fellow-men be lost, to let them perish as it were on our doorstep, without doing what we can to save them. Surely this of all things is a work fit for kings, princes and prelates, and they alone are equal to the task, the task of establishing the Christian faith in a wild, unknown country. After all, these poor people ask for nothing but to be told what to do and what not to do. It is up to those who have the wealth and power for such a work to take it upon themselves, for one day they will have to answer to God for all the souls they, in their negligence and greed, have allowed to perish. This great work will be accomplished in due course, God willing, and the sooner the better, for it will bring glory to God, honour to the King and lustre to the good name of France.

I promised to say more about the ceremonies they use to heal the sick. The sick person sends for an Oqui. The Oqui comes and asks him to describe his symptoms. Then he sends for a number of men, women and girls, along with three or four old women, sometimes more. They all come dancing into the sick man's lodge, each wearing the head of some wild beast—usually that of a bear, since it is the most terrifying to look at. Two or three of the old women go to the sick man, who usually isn't sick at all but only thinks he is or pretends to be. In any case he is soon cured and then he usually arranges a feast at the expense of his friends and relatives. Each of them has to give something to put in the pot. The dancers also bring presents—a string of beads perhaps or some other such trinket. These they give to the old women, who take turns singing until all the presents have been handed over. Then they all join in, beating time with sticks on pieces of dry wood. At this point all the women and girls go to one end of the lodge, as if they were about to act out a ballet or a masquerade. The old women walk out in front with their bearskins on their heads and the rest bring up the rear. They have only two ceremonial dances, one of four steps, the other of twelve like the Breton *trioly*. Sometimes the young men join in and many of them dance quite gracefully. When the sick man sees that he has made all he can out of his sickness he gets up. The old women lead him out. At first he pretends to be unwilling, but once he starts to dance he soon gets into the swing of it and has as much fun as any of the others. It goes without saying that most of the sufferers aren't really sick at all. Those who are sick don't get much good out of such foolishness.

However that may be, the Oquis are often renowned for their cures. This in spite of the fact that their treatment usually does more harm than good, for sometimes they keep up their racket from dawn until two o'clock the next morning, by which time the sick man is almost out of his mind. Sometimes they get the women and girls to dance together, but only if the Oqui gives the word. Sometimes the Oqui or Manitou will get together with several of the others and start making faces and casting spells. Soon they are writhing and twisting and before long they are beside themselves. Then they will start scattering brands all over the place like madmen, swallowing hot coals or holding them in their hands and throwing red-hot cinders into the eyes of the onlookers. Anyone who saw them in such a state would think they were possessed by the devil, that is, by the great Oqui or Manitou.

When the dancing is over and the noise has died down they each go back to their own quarters. The wives of the Oquis have the worst of it, for the Oquis are quite mad by that time and will set fire to anything they can lay their hands on. Usually the women hide everything they can. The Oqui will come in with eyes flashing and stand there until the fancy strikes him, when he will start throwing things all over the place. Then just as suddenly he will lie down and sleep for a while. Before long he will wake up with a start and seize some hot coals or stones and start throwing them about. When he gets tired of that he will go off to sleep again. In time the madness passes off. To bring on a cure, the Oqui will go and sweat himself with several of his friends. For two or three hours they will steam themselves under long strips of bark, wrapped up in skins with stones heated in the fire. They sing the whole time, stopping only to catch their breath or to take a drink of water, for of course they get extremely thirsty. Eventually they become themselves again.

Usually two or three of the sick recover, more by luck than good management, and this encourages the people to believe in the Oquis. They forget that for every two that get better ten die of the noise, which is more likely to kill a sick man than to cure him. We know that a sick man needs rest and quiet, but they think they can cure him by making a racket. This just shows how the devil turns everything upside down.

Sometimes the women will go into a frenzy like the men, but they do less harm. They get down on all fours like animals. At this point the Oqui starts to sing. Then he makes a face and breathes on the woman, telling her to drink certain waters and to feast on fish or meat, no matter how scarce it is. When the feast is finished they all go back to their lodges until the Oqui comes again. This time he brings a number of other people with him. They all sing and breathe on the woman. Each of them has a dried tortoise-shell filled with pebbles, which they shake in her ear. They tell her to hold a dance and three or four feasts. The Oqui will then order costumes and masquerades, like those you see during the Mardi Gras in France, and the girls will come elaborately painted and dressed. While they are making ready for the masquerade, the Oqui will go and sing by the litter of the sick woman and then will go up and down the length of the village, singing and chanting the whole way. When it's all over everyone is hungry and they sit down and eat up all the Migan in the pot.

According to custom, each family must live on what it can get by farming and fishing. They have all the land they can use, but they find it hard to clear without proper tools. This is how they go about it. First they strip the trees of their branches. Next they burn all the cuttings at the foot of each tree, so as to kill it. Then they clean up the ground between the trees and sow their corn. They set out about ten grains to a clump, leaving a yard between clumps, and sow enough to last for three or four years, in case they have a bad season. The women sow the seed and harvest the grain, as I've already explained. They also collect wood for the winter. This they do in March or April, and by all working together they finish the job in two or three days. Each family gathers enough for its own needs. If a girl gets married, every woman in the village has to give her a load of firewood to get her started, since she wouldn't be able to get enough for herself out of season.

This is how their government works. The elders and chiefs meet in council and make all decisions necessary for the welfare of the village. Normally they act by majority vote, but sometimes they defer to someone they have special reason to respect. Such a man may be asked by the others to give his opinion on the point at issue and in that case his advice, once given, is followed to the letter. None of the chiefs has any authority over the rest, though as a mark of respect the oldest and bravest among them are known as captains. There are usually several such men in each village. They are treated with deference and respect, but they aren't allowed to put on airs.

They have no laws and no punishments. The elders make long speeches and give their opinion when asked for it, but they have no authority to enforce their decisions. Everyone has a right to speak in council and if anyone makes a proposal that pleases the others he is expected to come forward and offer to carry it out. They tell him that he is a brave man and worthy of the enterprise in hand, and say that such a work will bring him new honour and add new lustre to his name. He can excuse himself if he likes, but few do, for they are anxious to make a name for themselves.

When they decide to make war, two or three of the oldest and bravest captains will volunteer to lead the expedition. Before they start they send messengers to all the neighbouring villages with presents, to let them know their plans and to ask for help. The captains choose the time and place where they will meet the enemy, as our generals do. They also dispose of prisoners and attend to all other matters of importance, for the captains are the only superiors these people are willing to recognize and obey. If things turn out well they get all the praise; if they turn out badly they take all the blame.

So much for their councils. They also have general assemblies to which delegates come each year from distant parts of the country, one from each district. They meet in a village chosen for the purpose. This is an opportunity to renew old friendships and take whatever steps may be necessary for the defence of the country against the common enemy. The meetings last three weeks or a month and there is constant feasting and dancing. When the meetings are over they exchange presents and then each man sets out for his own district.

When a man dies and is to be buried, they take the body, wrap it in skins, cover it carefully with bark and then raise it up on four posts, over which they build a shelter roofed in with strips of bark. Sometimes they bury the body in the ground, in which case they first dig the grave and then shore up the sides to prevent it from falling in. Then they lower the body and cover it with bark before filling the grave with earth. Finally they build a small shelter over the top.

The bodies are left like this for eight or ten years, until the next festival of the dead. What happens then is that they summon a general assembly at which, among other things, the delegates decide when and where the next festival of the dead will be held. Then they each return to their own district and uncover the bones of those who have died since the last festival. These are carefully cleaned and preserved, though they smell like newly-buried bodies. At the appointed time the relatives and friends of the dead bring the bones, together with necklaces, skins, tomahawks, pots and other valuables, and a quantity of food, to the chosen place. There they lay down their burdens and give themselves up to dancing and feasting for the ten days of the festival. Tribes come from all over the country to take part in the ceremonies. The dancing, the feasting, the general councils all serve to renew and strengthen old friendships. As a symbol of goodwill they mingle the bones of their relatives and friends one with another, saying that just as the bones of the dead are gathered in one place, so also the living will be united in friendship, as one people, as long as they live. They make a number of speeches over the bones and then after making certain faces and signs they dig a big trench sixty feet square and bury all the bones in it, together with the necklaces, beads, tomahawks, pots, knives and other trinkets they have brought with them. This they cover with earth and on top of that they build a wooden canopy supported on four posts. The burial of the dead is the most solemn of all their festivals. Some of them believe in the immortality of souls; some doubt it and say that after their death they are more likely to turn into crows than angels.

So far I have said nothing about how these people spend their time in winter, that is, from the beginning of December to the end of March, when the snow melts and spring begins. Ordinary life continues in winter as in summer, with its feasts and dances for the sick. They also have festivals of song and dance called *tabagies,* to which they invite people from other villages. Sometimes there are five hundred men, women and girls at these festivals, all dressed in their best clothes. On special days they hold masquerades and go about from lodge to lodge, asking for anything that takes their fancy. So-and-so gave me this, they sing, and so-and-so gave me that—or something to that effect. Everybody gives what they have to give. If anyone refuses, the masquers get angry and make a sign: they go and find a stone and leave it, as an insult and mark of contempt, beside the man or woman who refused them. This goes on until some of them—women as well as men—have asked for and been given skins of all sorts, along with fish, Indian corn, tobacco and even such things as cauldrons, kettles, pots, tomahawks, sickles and knives. Some of the villages have clowns like the ones we have for the Mardi Gras in France, and from time to time they challenge the clowns of other villages to a contest. And so they spend the winter.

There's also work to do: the women spin and grind meal and the men go off to trade in other parts of the country. We noticed that they were always careful to leave enough men to defend each village in case of attack. By custom—for they have no laws—no-one is supposed to leave his village without the consent of the council of chiefs. The men also make their own nets and fish right through the winter. This is how they go about it. First they make a number of holes in the ice, one about five feet long and three feet wide. They fasten the net to a wooden pole six or seven feet long and lower it through the ice. Then they pass the pole under the ice from one hole to the next, until they come to the large opening. Here they let the net, which is weighted down with small stones, sink to the bottom. After leaving it for some time they will suddenly pull up both ends and bring the fish that are caught in the net to the surface.

Winter closes in during November and lasts until the beginning of April,[2] when the sap starts to rise and the buds begin to show. On the twenty-second we received our first news of Brûlé, who, you may remember, had set out for Carantouan. A party of savages had met him and brought word that he had turned back, why they didn't know. On the twentieth of May we ourselves set out for the habitation with several savages who had promised to show us the way. The journey took forty days. We caught fish of all sorts on the way and killed a lot of game. This gave us fresh food to eat and besides we enjoyed the hunting and fishing. We reached St. Louis toward the end of June and there I found the Sieur du Pont waiting for me with two ships. The savages had told him I had been killed and he had just about given me up for

---

[2]Champlain says that winter lasts *until April,* but since in a previous paragraph he spoke of winters as lasting *until the end of March,* he must mean *the beginning of April.*

lost. Some of the priests were at St. Louis and we were very happy to see each other again. As soon as we had greeted each other, however, I made arrangements to leave for the habitation with Darontal, my host. Before saying goodbye to the savages I promised to visit them again as soon as I could and to bring them presents. I begged them to forget their quarrels and they promised they would.

We set out on the eighth of July and reached the habitation on the eleventh. There the priests led us in giving thanks to Almighty God for having preserved us from all the dangers we had passed through.

When the first excitement was over I introduced Darontal to the others. He admired the buildings and our way of life, and when we had seen everything there was to see he told me privately that he wouldn't rest until as many of his people as possible had come to live with us, so they could learn to worship our God and live as we lived. He much preferred our way of life to his own and realized that his people could learn our ways more easily by living with us than by waiting for us to come and teach them. He had already pointed out to Father Joseph that if they were slow to learn, their children would be quicker. He now suggested that we build another habitation at St. Louis to secure the river from enemy attack. He assured me they would join us there as soon as there were quarters for them to live in and promised that from then on we would live together like brothers. I thought this was a good idea and told him we would build a habitation for them as soon as we could.

I entertained Darontal for four or five days and before he left I gave him a number of presents to mark the occasion. He was very pleased. I urged him not to forget what had passed between us and suggested that before long he come to see us again with some of his people. With that he rejoined his companions, who were waiting for him at St. Louis.

After his departure we enlarged the habitation by at least a third and strengthened the fortifications, for as it was it wasn't fit to live in. For the buildings we used limestone, which is an excellent material and plentiful in those parts.

Father Denis and Father Joseph had both made up their mind to return to France. They planned to take with them the story of what they had seen in the New World, in the hope of persuading more of their brethren to devote their lives to service among the savages.

Before leaving, we harvested some corn we had brought out from France. The seeds had come up well and I wanted to take some of the grain back with me to show how fertile the country is. By now our gardens were lovely. We had some fine Indian corn and some young trees and grafts that de Monts had given me in Normandy. We also had peas, beans, squash, cabbages, white beets and a number of other vegetables and herbs.

We left in the long-boats on the twentieth of July. Two of the priests, Father Jean Delbeau and Father Pacifique, stayed on at the habitation. They seemed pleased with what they had accomplished so far and now planned to wait at the habitation for Father Joseph, who was expected back the following year.

We reached Tadoussac on the twenty-third. There we found du Pont, ready and waiting for us. On the third of August we set sail. The winds were favourable and we reached Honfleur on the tenth of September, 1616. As soon as we landed we gave thanks to God for having brought us safely back to our native land. We prayed also that He would move the hearts of the King and Council to do what was necessary to nourish and succour the savages and bring them to a knowledge of the holy catholic faith, for the greater glory of God and the honour of the crown of France.

The Amerindian Discovery of Europe: Accounts of First Contact in Anishinabeg Oral Tradition

D. Peter MacLeod

THIS PAPER DEALS with one account of first contact between Amerindians and French during the seventeenth century, when a small group of people made a voyage of exploration and discovery, then returned home bearing new and exotic goods and strange tales of their encounter with a new and profoundly alien civilization. It examines how this first contact expanded into a permanent relationship between two peoples.

Narratives of first contact in the seventeenth century are of course very common. Yet, most, in fact almost all, of our narrative sources from this time are found in European documents. They naturally express the perceptions and prejudices of their writers, and thus portray the contact period as a time when Europeans discovered America. In these narratives, Europeans are the actors, and Amerindians the passive objects of discovery.

In this paper, on the other hand, we will be examining an account of the contact period which is based entirely upon Amerindian sources. This version of the history of first contact is of particular interest because the "explorers" and "discoverers" are Amerindians.

More specifically, they were Anishinabeg. The Anishinabeg, or Ojibwa, belong to the Algonquian family nations and although this is something of a simplification, during the contact period they lived in the upper Great Lakes region, roughly the area east and west of what is now Sault Ste Marie.

We know of their impressions of the contact period through their oral traditions. Those Anishinabeg who first encountered Europeans in the seventeenth century passed on their memories of events to their children. These recollections were subsequently transmitted by tribal elders, from generation to generation, until the mid-nineteenth century. Then, they were preserved in print by a group of Anishinabeg authors. These writers, who had received European-style educations, used the oral tradition as the basis for a series of histories of the Great Lakes region from the perspective of the Anishinabeg.[1] One version of the Anishinabeg traditions of the contact period was obtained by a missionary in the Lake Superior region who interviewed Peter Jones, an Anishinabeg who had become a Methodist minister.[2]

We examine here an account of first contact that tells how one group of Amerindians remembered their nation's first contact with Europeans.

In the oral traditions of the Anishinabeg first contact with Europeans occurred soon after the arrival of the French in the St Lawrence valley. At this time word reached the Anishinabeg of the existence of "some strange persons living on this continent."[3] In some versions these were supernatural "spirits in the form of men,"[4] in others they were just "extraordinary people."[5] The Anishinabeg met in council to decide how to respond to this information and eventually decided to prepare an expedition to travel eastward to seek out the strangers.[6]

This expedition, organized and led by a shaman, departed early in the spring soon after the breakup. The Anishinabeg explorers travelled down the Great Lakes, along the French River, then down the Ottawa. Towards the mouth of the Ottawa River they discovered the first physical evidence of the existence of the newcomers—a hut standing in a clearing, surrounded by the stumps of large trees that had not been cut with stone axes.[7] The trees appeared, in fact, "to have been cut through by the teeth of a colossal beaver."[8] The shaman and his party deduced that this was a campsite of the strange people and were pleased to have found this tangible indication of their reality.

Further down the river the intrepid explorers were further encouraged when they found another clearing and a cabin that had apparently been occupied by the strangers during the previous winter.[9]

Finally, the party reached the St Lawrence River. There they found a settlement occupied by the strangers who greeted them cordially. These people were indeed very odd and, in fact, rather resembled squirrels. This was because, according to the oral tradition, they kept: "their goods and provisions in hollow places, but instead of digging holes in the ground like squirrels, they took the trouble to put several pieces of wood together, in the shape of a hollow tree sometimes, fastened with hoops, where they kept their provisions."[10]

From these strangers the Anishinabeg travellers acquired, either as gifts or through trade, a variety of items, including cloth, metal axes and knives, flint and steel, beads, blankets, and firearms.[11] Then they set out for home.

Immediately following their return a second council was called. The travellers provided a complete account of their successful voyage and displayed the interesting items that they had obtained. These goods aroused considerable interest among the Anishinabeg. Hunters came in from the forest to obtain shavings or chunks of wood that had been cut with an ax. Bolts of cloth were cut into small pieces so that everyone could have one. Splinters of wood and shreds of cloth were attached to poles and sent from village to village spreading the word of the arrival of the strangers.[12]

Now this account of first contact between the Anishinabeg and the French is most notable for the fact that rather than waiting passively to be "discovered" by European "explorers," it is the Anishinabeg who discovered the French and took the initiative in opening commercial relations. Although they were impressed by some aspects of European technology and intrigued by unusual French customs it was the Anishinabeg who remained firmly in control of the situation and the Europeans who responded graciously to Anishinabeg overtures. According to these oral traditions the Anishinabeg remained in control when the first French traders travelled to the Anishinabeg country.

Some of these traders produced accounts which suggest that the Amerindians were most impressed with these heroes. Pierre Radisson, in particular, appears to have believed himself to be rather charismatic and left his readers with little doubt that the mere presence of a pair of Europeans and their goods was enough to dominate the nations of Lake Superior. In his own words:

> We weare Caesars, being nobody to contradict us. We went away free from any burden, whilst those poore miserable [Amerindians] thought themselves happy to carry our Equipage, for the hope that they had that we should give them a brasse ring, or an awle, or a needle. . . . Wee . . . weare lodged in ye cabban of the chiefest captayne. . . . We like not the company of that blind, therefore left him. He wondered at this, but durst not speake, because we were demi-gods.[13]

The Amerindians who compiled the oral traditions were apparently less impressed. Their account of this visit is rather different. According to the oral tradition:

> Early the next morning . . . the young men once more noticed the smoke arising from the eastern end of the unfrequented island, and led on by curiosity, they ran thither and found a small log cabin in which they discovered two white men in the last stages of starvation. The young Ojibways filled with compassion, carefully conveyed them to their village, where, being nourished with great kindness, their lives were preserved.[14]

So in this phase of the contact period the oral traditions contrast the resourceful, confident, and compassionate Native community with rather pathetic commercial travellers who need indigenous help to keep from starving to death in the midst of one of the richest fishing grounds in the Great Lakes region. Inspiring neither respect nor fear the two Europeans were wholly dependent upon the tolerance and charity of the peoples through whose homelands they travel. They were welcomed but valued only for the products that they sold. For they could contribute nothing else to the lives of their Anishinabeg rescuers and hosts except perhaps the entertainment afforded by the presence of such unusual individuals.

Yet these goods were valued and trade between the Anishinabeg and the French flourished. As the trade continued the two groups decided to formalize their relationship with an alliance. The terms of the alliance were amicably negotiated at a meeting near the site of Sault Ste Marie in 1671.

The reports that delegates brought home from this conference reflected widely varying interpretations of the nature of the relationship. Simon Francois Daumont de St. Lusson, representing the French crown, produced an account for his superiors that depicted the Anishinabeg as completely subordinate to the French:

> In the name of the most high, most mighty and most redoubtable Monarch Louis, the XIVth of the Christian name, king of France and Navarre, we take possession of the said place of St. Mary of the Falls as well as of Lakes Huron and Superior, the Island of Caientolon [Manitoulin] and of all other Countries, rivers, lakes and tributaries, contiguous and adjacent thereunto. . . . declaring to the aforesaid Nations that henceforward as from this moment they were dependent on his Majesty, subject to be controlled by his laws and to follow his customs.[15]

Yet St. Lusson was evidently a good deal more circumspect when negotiating with the Anishinabeg for a less baroque but more convincing account of the same meeting was preserved by the descendants of the member of the Crane Clan that represented the Anishinabeg: "Sieur de Lusson . . . the envoy of the French king, asked, in the name of his nation, for permission to trade in the country, and for free passage to and from their villages all times thereafter. He asked that the fires of the French and Ojibway nations might be made one, and everlasting."[16]

The alliance thus established was remembered by the Anishinabeg as characterized by the close adherence of the French to Anishinabeg customs and forms.[17] This alliance entailed only the granting of access to Anishinabeg villages to French traders and certainly no surrender of Anishinabeg sovereignty or freedom of action.

Yet if the impact of the Europeans themselves was something less than overwhelming their technology was nonetheless very much appreciated for both its novelty and its utility. Of all European products it was firearms that received the most attention in the oral traditions of the contact period. In these traditions, the Anishinabeg portrayed themselves as quickly mastering a new technology and using it to further their goals.

In one narrative the acquisition of firearms by the party that first set forth in search of Europeans makes their return rather more dramatic than they might have intended. For as the returning adventurers came in sight of their homes they used one of their new muskets to fire a shot into the air. According to the oral tradition:

> they arrived at their village on an exceedingly calm day, and the water was in perfect stillness. . . . The Indians saw the canoe coming towards the shore of the village, when suddenly a puff of smoke was seen and a terrific clash of sound followed immediately. All the inhabitants were panic stricken, and thought it was something supernatural approaching the shore.[18]

This confusion was resolved when the explorers landed and the Anishinabeg began to consider the strategic implications of this new military technology. One account of this process is rather charming:

> Intercourse had been opened between the French and the Ottawas and Chippewas on the straits of Mackinac and being supplied with fire arme [sic] and axes by the French people, it occurred to the Ottawas that these implements would be effective in battle.[19]

According to Anishinabeg sources some unsuspecting enemies "thought that they [firearms] were nought but clubs" but were then taken by surprise and suffered a "crushing defeat."[20] In fact, the oral traditions relate a series of victories by the Anishinabeg over enemies who were not equipped with firearms. This continues until these enemies themselves gain access to European weapons.[21] So European weapons, if not Europeans themselves, are portrayed in the oral traditions as quickly becoming a key element in the military balance in the Great Lakes region. A nation possessed of firearms was in a position to dominate its neighbours. Enemies with equal access to European military technology on the other hand met on equal terms.

Yet apart from supplying military technology the French are not portrayed as exercising any great influence on the course of events in the Great Lakes region during the contact period. At the end of the contact period the Anishinabeg remain as firmly in control of their lives as they had been when they first became aware of the existence of Europeans.

This is, on the face of it, a rather ordinary story of how the Anishinabeg hear of a new and mysterious people of unknown potential, and then follow up and investigate, establish commercial relations and an alliance, and acquire new technology. It is most important for what it reveals of Anishinabeg attitudes regarding first contact. Some historians have successfully used Anishinabeg oral traditions as a guide to actual events.[22] Here we are concerned less with what happened than with how it was perceived and remembered by Amerindians.

The Anishinabeg remembered the contact period as a time when their lives were enhanced and their power increased through contact with Europeans and access to European technology. The French appear in Anishinabeg histories of the contact period, not so much as intrusive aliens, but as a new people who are at first discovered then accepted and incorporated into the world of the Anishinabeg. They are remarkable only for a number of rather peculiar but harmless habits and for their technology. In the beginning this technology had been impressive, even frightening, but it was quickly mastered and exploited by the Anishinabeg. According to Anishinabeg oral traditions Europeans, in the contact period, posed no threat to the Anishinabeg who remained very much in control of their lives and destinies.

First contact had occurred as the result of the actions of the Anishinabeg. Their oral traditions demonstrate very clearly that the Anishinabeg did not remember their ancestors as the passive objects of discovery by Europeans. Instead, they remembered these ancestors as actors who had themselves taken the decision to seek out and contact the Europeans. So for the Anishinabeg the history of the contact period is not the story of the European discovery of America, but of the Amerindian discovery of Europe.

Notes

1. D. Peter MacLeod, "The Anishinabeg Point of View: The History of North America to 1800 in Nineteenth-Century Mississauga. Odawa and Ojibwa Historiography," *Canadian Historical Review* 72, 2 (June 1992): 70–75.
2. J. G. Kohl, *Kitchi-Gami: Wanderings Round Lake Superior* (London: Chapman and Hall, 1860), 244.
3. Andrew J. Blackbird. *History of the Ottawa and Chippewa Indians of Michigan: A Grammar of their Language, and Personal and Family History of the Author* (Ypsilanti, MI: The Ypsilantian Job Printing House, 1887), 92.
4. William Whipple Warren, *History of the Ojibways, Based Upon Traditions and Oral Statements* (St Paul, MN: Minnesota Historical Society, 1885). 118; rprt. *History of the Ojibway People* (St Paul, MN: Minnesota Historical Society Press, 1984).
5. Francis Assikinack, "Social and Warlike Customs of the Odahwah Indians." *The Canadian Journal of Industry, Science, and Art* 3, 16(July 1858): 307.
6. Kohl, *Kitchi-Gami*, 245.
7. Warren, *History of the Ojibways*, 119.
8. Kohl, *Kitchi-Gami*, 246.
9. Warren, *History of the Ojibways*, 119.
10. Assikinack, "Social and Warlike Customs," 307.
11. Ibid.: Blackbird. *History of the Ojibways and Chippewa Indians*. 93: Warren, *History of the Ojibways*, 119.
12. Blackbird. *History of the Ottawa and Chippewa Indians*, 93: Kohl, *Kitchi-Gami*, 247: Warren, *History of the Ojibways*, 119–20.
13. Pierre Esprit Radisson, *Voyages of Peter Esprit Radisson. Being an Account of his Travels and Experiences Among the North American Indians from 1652 in 1684*, ed. Gideon D. Scull (Boston: Prince Society Publications, 1885), 200–201: rprt. (New York: Peter Smith, 1943).
14. Warren, *History of the Ojibways*. 122; Grace Lee Nute, *Caesars of the Wilderness: Medard Chonart, Sieur des Groseilliers and Pierre Esprit Radisson, 1618–1710* (New York: D. Appleton-Century, 1943), 62n: rprt. (St Paul, MN: Minnesota Historical Society Press, 1978).
15. E.B. O'Callaghan. *Documents Relative to the Colonial History of the State of New York: Procured in Holland, England, and France, by John Romeym Brodhead, esq., Agent Under and by Virtue of an Act of the Legislature Entitled "An Act to Appoint an Agent to Procure and Transcribe Documents in Europe Relative to the Colonial History of the State,"* vol. 9 (Albany, NY: Weed, Parson, and Company, 1855), 803–4.
16. Warren, *History of the Ojibways*, 131.
17. Ibid., 132, 135.
18. Blackbird, *History of the Ottawa and Chippewa Indians*, 93.
19. Ibid.
20. Ibid.
21. Warren, *History of the Ojibways*, 120, 124, 126, 148, 223.
22. W.J. Eccles, "Sovereignty Association, 1500–1783," *Canadian Historical Review* 65, 4 (Dec. 1984): 475–510: Leroy V. Eid, "The Ojibwa-Iroquois War: The War the Five Nations Did Not Win," *Ethnohistory* 26, 4 (Fall 1979): 297–324; Peter S. Schmalz, "The Role of the Ojibwa in the Conquest of Southern Ontario, 1650–1701," *Ontario History* 76. 4 (Dec. 1984): 327–28.

CHAPTER THREE

Natives in the Canadian Imagination, or The Grey Owl Syndrome

Introduction

Native peoples entered the European imagination at the moment of Contact. They existed—and continue to exist—as either the "dangerous savage" or the "noble savage." Writing about Native peoples in the Canadian imagination, Daniel Francis uses the term "the Imaginary Indian." By that he means that Native peoples in Canadian art and literature exist not on their own terms but as constructions of the Canadian imagination, as symbols of something else: for example, of the environment, of simplicity, of harmony and of loss. This collection of readings focuses on Grey Owl, one of Canada's most fascinating figures. He was born Archie Belaney in Hastings, England in 1888. At 18 he immigrated to Canada where he worked as a trapper and guide near Lake Timiskaming, Ontario. In the 1920s he re-invented himself as Grey Owl, a Native man and ardent conservationist. Through his writings and public lectures he earned a national and international reputation; he even received a meeting with the King of England. In this excerpt from *Tales of an Empty Cabin,* how does Grey Owl confirm the Native in the Canadian imagination? Put another way, would anyone have read *Tales of an Empty Cabin* by Archie Belaney? Only after his death in 1938 was it revealed that Grey Owl was once Archie Belaney. Does the fact that he lied negate the truth of his insights? Grey Owl continues to figure in Canadian culture. Milton Kelly is a novelist, short story writer and playwright. His 1987 novel *A Dream Like Mine* received the Governor General's Award for Fiction. "Case History" comes from his 1991 collection of short stories, *Breath Dances Between Them.* A writer and an academic, Armand Garnet Ruffo is Ojibwa. At one point, Grey Owl lived with his great, great grandparents in northern Ontario. This selection of poems comes from *Grey Owl: The Mystery of Archie Belaney,* Ruffo's 1996 exploration in poetry of Canada's most famous Native person who wasn't Native. Or was he?

Tales of an Empty Cabin

Wa-Sha-Quon-Asin (GREY OWL)

The Keepers of the Lodge

FOR THE PAST two months I have been trying to write a book. Whether it is a good book or not I leave you to judge. But if it isn't, I can give you a number of very good reasons why.

About the best of these is a bumping, banging, thudding noise, accompanied by wailing, screeching and chattering in what sounds like a foreign tongue from some obscure corner of the earth's surface. This is caused by a number of beaver of assorted ages from one to seven years, expostulating with each other over the ownership of a pile of stove-wood that I have, in a weak moment, left before the door of Beaver Lodge. The wood is mine of course, but this is no way lessens its suitability for material to be added to the already impregnable defences of the beaver house that has lately been built a short distance down the shore. The only real difficulty seems to be that of deciding who is to have the honour of removing it. There are sounds of strife, sounds of anguish, sounds of outraged sensibilities, and sounds of supplication. When a beaver wishes to be heard, he is not without the means. Up to three years, the age of maturity, each generation has an intonation all its own, and every individual has a different voice. As a tribe, or race (or whatever division they come under), they step heavily, pound violently, haul, push and heave vigorously, and are fanatically determined in the carrying out of any project they have decided, at all costs, to complete. Hence the noise, which is unspeakable, unthinkable, indescribable and unsupportable. These are good words; I got them out of a book. But there were not enough of them; they do not begin to tell it.

I try to concentrate, to marshal my ideas for your approval. There is a fresh sound, a loud clattering as of a tin dish being thrown with monotonous and devilish persistence against a stone. I am trying to write about beaver, but begin to feel a good deal more like writing something vivid about a bullfight. So, I put down my pen and go outside. I see at a glance that I am a little late; the wood is nearly gone. It appears that while the second and third generations have been squabbling over who is going to have all the wood (the fourth is too young to do much but squall), the first, or largest generation has been quietly getting away with most of it. They are moving up and down, one coming and one going, with that clockwork regularity that makes two beaver engaged in transportation work look like an endless chain. I like my food cooked, but not at this price; it will be cheaper to eat it raw. So I push the remainder of the stove-wood into the lake, so that there will be no further discussion. This makes a difference, the difference being that the fun will now take place inside the cabin. Three of the yearlings, finding themselves temporarily unoccupied now that the wood is satisfactorily disposed of, come bustling in through the door, bringing their potentialities for mischief along with them. They wander around for a while, peering into everything, fairly dripping with curiosity and exuding wilfulness from every pore, eventually entering into a spirited contest over the remains of a box of apples, with the usual sound-effects. Having pacified these highbinders and bribed them, with an apple apiece, to go away, I pick up my pen and resume my work, although I have not yet been able to determine the cause of that exasperating tinny clattering; the only tin dish outside is the one used to hold the beavers' rice, and it is still in its place, full and intact.

I have just got nicely started when, in the middle of a word, there comes another sound, a kind of a rich, satisfying sound, as of some keen-edged tool of tempered steel cutting into very good timber; it also sounds not unlike a beaver's teeth going into a canoe. I put down my pen, go out and investigate. It is, indeed, a beaver's teeth going into a canoe. You see, an overturned canoe looks a little like part of a tree, and offers the same excellent opportunities for idle teeth; the canvas looks something like bark, is the same colour and comes off as easily, with the nice, interesting sound mentioned above. Of course, even if you are a beaver, you can't eat green paint and canvas, but it's great fun and you can always spit out the paint. After a short altercation I put the canoe on the rack out of reach, soothe injured feelings with an apple, and go in again. I pick up my pen and complete the unfinished word.

I write uninterruptedly for perhaps fifteen minutes. Then commences that infernal clattering again, as though someone were dropping a tin plate repeatedly on the hard ground. It is now broad daylight, so I take my observations through the window, and am enlightened. A beaver of the third generation, old enough to be effectively mischievous, is alternately lifting and dropping on the ground the tin dish of rice. Those of the younger beaver who haven't yet learned to eat out of a receptacle, are content to dump the rice out on the ground; they can get at the rice easier that way. They then throw the dish in the lake, to join a number of other articles, besides dishes, that they have consigned to a watery grave. But this fellow has another notion, apparently. I watch the process interestedly. He picks up the dish with his teeth, keeping it right side up, and tries to walk away with it; he wants, for some reason best known to himself, to take the whole works home with him. The container is large, and he is not a very big beaver, and as soon as he stands upright it overbalances and falls. He picks it up and tries again, and it falls again, and so on, so many times to the minute. I begin to count them. The clang of the now empty pan seems to amuse him, and he keeps experimenting, until at last he discovers the way. He finds the point of balance, stands erect with the dish in his mouth, and placing both his hands under it to support it, starts to march down the incline to the lake. Seeing my dish about to be sacrificed I rush out, whereupon the young scallawag slides down the slippery approach and throws himself, dish and all, into the water. The pan rocks for a moment or two and sinks. The beaver birls round and round in the water, in celebration of his success, and also disappears, and I am left in complete possession of the empty landing.

This is a pretty fair example of the perseverance of these animals, who will try every possible means to accomplish their ends, until they have either succeeded, or proven the project to be impossible.

And I think you will agree that any man who will attempt to write a book whilst surrounded by a number of these exceedingly active and industrious creatures, can claim to have learned from them at least the virtue of patience. And this is no idle alibi, for at the moment, even as I write, a full-grown beaver has just burst open the door and entered, bringing in, as an addition to the beaver house that stands here beside the table, a stick six or seven feet in length. And it is no unusual thing for beavers, walking erect with loads of mud supported in their arms, to pass around my chair on their way to further plaster this house within a house, and not infrequently I am obliged to cease my work, lift the chair out of their way, and stand aside until their job is done.

*

Of all the natural laws that govern this Universe, or that part of it with which we are acquainted, there is one that, although it may not at times seem to be very rigidly enforced, is in the long run inescapable—the Law of Compensation. It has caught up with me here, and is exacting the usual penalties. Having, against Nature's express decree, succeeded in partly eliminating from the mentality of a number of wild animals the natural fear that is their only safeguard, I must now afford them that protection myself. So that I no longer spend my nights in sleeping, but unceasingly patrol the scene of their activities all the hours of darkness, resting only in the forenoon. And as it is not unlikely that the beaver will live as long as I do, it seems highly probable that I will spend the term of my natural life doing penance for my meddling, in this topsy-turvy fashion.

The beaver, in their immunity, have become over bold, and instead of disappearing from view at the first unusual sound, and abolishing themselves from the landscape as though they had never even existed, they now stand waiting curiously to see what they are to run away from, long after their less cultured brethren would have been in the lake, sunk and out of danger. The cuttings are often far from water, and ever I must haunt the beaver works, armed against possible and very probable marauders such as bears, wolves, coyotes, and even great horned owls that might try for a straggling kitten. And as the mediaeval watchman passed along the streets of cities calling, "All's well,—All's well," so, as I go, I take up my own monotonous cry, "A-a-a-all r-i-i-ight,—A-a-a-all r-i-i-ight." This is my signal and identification, and well known to them, and without such utterance I never venture forth, so they may know that any unannounced approach is not I, and therefore dangerous.

One night, on checking up, as I do almost hourly, after an intensive and widespread search I could find neither hide nor hair of Jelly Roll. Bears are numerous here, and tragedy lurks always threatening in the shadows. Unable by any means to find her, I decided to remain at my original stand, and commenced to send out certain searching calls such as she only would respond to. Patiently, but with growing uneasiness, I sent out my S.O.S. at intervals, casting the beams of a powerful electric torch in all directions. I kept this up for some considerable time and was beginning to feel the least bit anxious, when all at once I felt a tug at my leg, and turned the light downward to see standing at my feet, erect and looking up at me, the missing Jelly Roll. She was bone dry, and beginning to be impatient, and must have been there all the time. I didn't blame her for being out of patience, in a way. No doubt she and Rawhide, figuring that they own me, talk me over between themselves, and I had a feeling that this fresh stupidity of mine was, to her way of thinking, only one more example of my lack of culture and training; and I sometimes imagine that they both must be at times a little disappointed in me, after all the trouble they have been to, getting me into shape.

I have sat beside her on guard whilst she, confident in my protection, tired and weary with her working, slept in the moonlight that flooded the mouth of a runway. This often happens, and as she lies there with her head on my knee as in the old days, making soft murmuring noises in her dozing, she is no more Queen of the Beaver People, but is just Jelly the old-timer—the Tub. If I move she will clutch at my clothing to keep me there, and make sounds I hear from her at no other time. And then her voice is like a muted keyboard that runs the gamut of her emotions, recording every slightest variation; or like some delicately balanced instrument on which impressions come and go, swiftly wavering back and forth, even as her rich, dark fur mirrors the gossamer touch of every imperceptible, tiny breeze that stirs it ever and anon. And when I look down at the ugly body, unlovely till you see the eyes, I cannot but think that beauty may not be all in form, but may rest in strength, in grace of motion, in symmetry and rhythm, and in fidelity, and in a harmonious conformation to an environment.

Despite her affection and the disarming innocence of her softer moments, Jelly Roll is the most self-willed creature in all the world. She knows what is forbidden, and constantly attempts to outwit me; but on being caught red-handed, as she nearly always is (she is the most guileless, transparent old bungler imaginable when it comes to artifice), she flops down and flounders around in an apparent agony of fear, though she must know that she has nothing to fear but my disapproval and reproach, to which she is very sensitive indeed. On being comforted (a little later, of course), she will jump up at once and start to frolic; yet the lesson is not forgotten—not that day, anyway. This edifying performance has by now become perfunctory, and through long practice is now more or less automatic, and she assumes her abject pose immediately I appear on the scene of her misdoings, as though to have the unpleasantness over with as soon as possible. A scolding from me puts her in the greatest misery, but a peremptory word or two, or an overt act, from another, causes instant and sometimes very active hostility. She has a strong instinct for protection towards her young, as has her partner. This is a trait possessed by most animals but, like some dogs, she goes further and without training of any kind, stands with threatening attitude and voice between a stranger and myself, should I happen to be lying down. However, if I am standing up, I can darned well take care of myself. She herself has no fear whatsoever of strangers, and will face any crowd, and go among them, inspecting them and taking charge with the most unshakeable aplomb.

She still polices the estate, as before, and should someone unknown to her be in the canoe she quickly gets to know about it, and knowing that I will not allow her to approach the canoe too closely when someone else is with me, she will play sly and swim beneath the surface, bobbing up suddenly alongside from nowhere at all with a deep, explosive grunt, not always of welcome. She cannot climb into this high-sided canoe unless her diving board is attached, but she will stick pertinaciously to the canoe, swimming underneath it, getting in the way of the paddle and doing everything possible to retard our progress; failing this she will escort the canoe ashore in the hopes of getting a chance to investigate the newcomer. This intention I must of course frustrate, as my guest will have only my word for it that she does not mean business, or that taking a leg off him is not her idea of good clean fun. Her perception of what is going on about her is very keen; she undoubtedly knows what it is all about, and takes a lively interest in many things not supposed to be of interest to animals. So also does Rawhide, though in a less obvious manner; yet on occasion arising he shows a matter-of-fact familiarity with many things about him, that his indifferent and sphinx-like demeanour would seemingly have left him unconscious of; evidently a keen observer in a quiet way. His self-possession, steadiness of mien, and unchanging equanimity of bearing are in direct contrast to the varying moods of his temperamental consort. At times genial, almost affable, withal somewhat of a busy-body and stuck into everything, there are occasions when Jelly Roll carries about her something the same air of disapproval one detects in the presence of a landlady with whom one is a little behind with the rent.

On his visits to the cabin Rawhide acts exactly as if he could not hear the radio, even closing his purse-like ears, as beaver are able to do in order to exclude water, shutting them tight against any programme of which he does not approve. But Jelly takes in this machine the almost feverish interest she has in anything new, standing sometimes stockstill, listening, with hands and fingers making queer aimless little movements, a stiff, brown column of intense attention. During one broadcast she was present at, the characters in a play became engaged in a fight and one of them was killed. The sounds of battle had a strong effect upon her. Her eyes began to stare, her hair became erect and she commenced to blow loudly. On the woman of the cast falling unconscious, the resulting uproar had such a strange effect on her, and she stood so stiffly and unnaturally, and showed, in the unmistakable way she has, such a strong disapproval of the whole business, as to be rather alarming. She began to weave and totter back and forth, and I wondered if she too were not about to faint—though actually she had more than half a mind to join in the conflict. So to save the radio from being wrecked I gave her an apple and broke the spell. She is still a paper addict, and I keep in the cabin for her special convenience a bag full of nice crackling papers, the very sound of which drives her frantic with joy, and this she always looks for in its accustomed place on her visits. These occur, in fine weather, almost hourly, and whilst on deck she likes to stir things up; she weighs all of sixty pounds, and can stir up very effectively when so minded, and her entry into any gathering that may be assembled here, injects into the proceedings all that feeling of delightful uncertainty that one has in the presence of a large fire-cracker that is liable to explode at any moment.

She has often stolen papers of some value to me, and gets all the envelopes from my correspondence, which is considerable. She has a preference for periodicals, as the advertising pages are on stiffer paper than is the reading matter, and they can be induced to make a more deliciously exciting noise, and when she gets hold of one of these she is beside herself with happiness, shaking her head back and forth as she walks out of the door with it, her whole person emanating triumphant satisfaction. Once, at the request of an onlooker who thought that her patriotism should be tested, I placed before her three separate magazines, Canadian, English, and American. After giving each one a searching examination, she chose the Canadian periodical and walked out with it. The visitor was rather taken aback, and still believes that I made some secret sign to her that she acted on. Pure accident, naturally, but the effect was quite good. Sometimes the sober Rawhide joined in these escapades, a few of which were positively uncanny, had they not been so utterly ridiculous. Here's one that would have knocked Baron Munchausen for a loop. (A loop, reader-across-the-sea, is a circle, a cipher or a nought). Beaver like to have dry cedar on which to exercise their teeth, it being nice and crunchy. As there were no cedars in that particular area, I took a bundle of shingles that had been left over from the roofing of my new cabin, and left them down on the shore for the beavers' use. Next morning I found that the fastenings had been cut off and neatly laid to one side, and the whole of the shingles removed. I wondered what was the purpose of this wholesale delivery, until, the next afternoon a man came to see me, who wanted very much to see the beaver at work. It was a few minutes' walk to the beaver house, and as we drew near to it I noticed that it had a strange appearance, and arriving there we, this man and I, stood perfectly still and stared, and stared, and *stared—one side of the beaver house was partly roofed with shingles!*

At length my visitor asked in a hushed voice, "Do you see what I see?" I replied that I did. "Exactly!" he agreed. "We're both crazy. Let's get out of here." We retired, I remember, in awe-struck silence, went to the cabin and drank quantities of very strong tea. I asked him if he didn't care to wait and see the beaver themselves, and he shook his head. "No," he answered, "I don't believe I do. I'm not long out of the hospital and just couldn't stand it, not today. Some other time—" and went out of there muttering to himself. The explanation is of course quite simple. Beaver will seize on any easily handled material they find, and make use of it for building purposes (this includes fire-wood, paddles, dish-pans, clothing, &c.), and seized on the shingles at once, and being unable to push the shingles, owing to their oblong shape, into the mesh of the structure, had just left them lay there on the sides of the house.

But the star performance, in its implication of the burlesque, was one of Jelly's very own. One afternoon, shortly after the affair of the shingles, I heard a woman's scream, long and piercing, from the direction of the beaver dam. Beside the dam ran the trail that led to my cabin. Now Jelly is a real watch-dog when I am not around, and at that time, in her younger and less judgematical days would lay in ambush, waiting for people so she could chase them (a practice since abandoned), and thinking she had caught somebody in her ambuscade and was scaring them to death, I hustled down to the dam to see about it. I found there a woman, evidently badly frightened, who exclaimed: "Do you know what I have just seen?—a beaver going by with a paint brush!" "A who going by with a what?" I demanded. "A *beaver* going by with a *paint brush*!" she affirmed. "Oh, I know you won't believe me, but that's what I saw." Accustomed though I was to the hair-brained exploits of these versatile playmates of mine, this rather floored me, so I simply said, "Oh!", and led the woman to the cabin. I left her there and went to the stump on which the man who had been painting the new roof had left his paint brush. Sure enough, it was gone, removed by busy fingers whose owner was always on the watch for something new. So I told this to the lady, and the matter was explained. But it never was explained to me why, later in the evening, I should find laying at the foot of the stump, with the fresh imprint of four very sharp incisor teeth upon it, the missing paint brush. Why was it returned? Your guess is as good as mine.

And reader, believe it or not, all during the latter part of this last paragraph, a beaver of the third, or inexperienced generation, finding that his efforts to open the door have been persistently disregarded, has been trying to get in through the window. It will I think, be cheaper, in the long run, to open the door. I have opened the door, and there are three beaver; I'll be seeing you later, reader.

To resume. Today there were a large number of visitors here. The moose, a great bull with his antlers half developed, but for all that wide and formidable-looking enough, obligingly stalked down within a distance of a few yards and had a look at the crowd. They also, with mingled feelings, had a look at him. But Jelly Roll, after all the complimentary things I have written about her, let me down rather badly. Having demolished a chocolate bar offered her by a lady, she turned her back on the entire assemblage, took a branch I proffered, smelled it, threw it to one side, launched herself into the lake, and was no more seen. This behaviour is not usual with her. In fact, at times she is rather difficult to get away from, and is one of those ladies who do *not* take "No" for an answer. She is very self-assertive, and has no intention of being overlooked when there is any company around or anything especially good to eat to be had. At these times she is very much to the fore, assuming a bustling and extremely proprietory manner, and whether excited by the presence of strangers or on account of the reward she has come to know that she will get, or from sheer devilment, I cannot pretend to say, but she will very often stage a little act. She first inspects, one by one, the visitors who, by the way, are seated well out of the way in the bunk—she thoroughly enjoys a taste of good shoe leather—and if pleased, which she generally is, she commences her show. This consists in trundling back and forth the bag of papers, the removal perhaps of the contents of the bag, with result-ant rumpus and mess, the replacing of sticks removed by me from the beaver house for that purpose, and various other absolutely unnecessary evolutions. And all this with such an air of earnestness and in such breathless excitement, and with such manifest interest in the audience and such running to and fro to them between the scenes, that those present could be excused for supposing it to be all for their espe-cial benefit. We have, of course, a slight suspicion that the anticipated reward may have some bearing on this excessive display of histrionic ability. But a good time is had by every one present, and that is all that really matters. Speaking to her conver-sationally attracts her instant, if casual attention, and often elicits a response. She has come to understand the meaning of a good deal of what I say to her; but this faculty is not confined by any means to her alone. The beaver is an animal that holds com-munication by means of the voice, using a great variety of inflections, very human in character, and the expression and tone indicate quite clearly to human ears what emotions they are undergoing; and this resemblance makes it fairly easy for them to understand a few simple words and expressions. I have made no attempt to train them in this, or in anything else; everything they do is done of their own free will, and it has all been very free and easy and casual. I do not expect them to knuckle down to me, and I would think very little of them if they did; nor do I let them domi-nate me. We are all free together, do as we like, and get along exceedingly well to-gether. Rawhide I know, for one, would not tolerate for a moment any attempt to curtail his freedom or to curb his independent spirit. He is rather a solemn indi-vidual, and he ignores nearly everything that is not directly connected with his work and family. Yet even he has his times to play, and carries always about him an unde-finable air of "howdy folks and hope everything's all right and it's a great world." The obstinacy of a beaver when opposed by any difficulty also applies if you try to get him to do anything against his will, but personal affection has a great influence on their actions, and given sufficient encouragement and a free hand they will learn, of them-selves, to do a number of very remarkable things quite foreign to their ordinary hab-its. Rawhide, for instance, has learned to kick open the door when walking erect with a load in his arms. He built his house inside mine, and will climb into a canoe and enjoy a ride, as does his life partner. Jelly Roll is able to open the camp door with ease from either side, pushing it open widely to come in, and making use of a handle I have affixed to the bottom of the door to get out again. And as the door swings shut of itself, she has succeeded in creating the impression that she always closes the door behind her, which is all to the good. Though he rarely answers me as Jelly does, Raw-hide listens closely, with apparent understanding, when I talk to him, and dearly loves to be noticed, often rushing up to me when I meet him by chance on a runway, and clasping my fingers very firmly in his little hands. But his old, wild instincts are very strong in him, nor do I try to break them; and he has not bothered to learn very many of Jelly's tricks, being, it would seem, quite above such monkey work. But he will come at my call, when disposed to do so, and can be summoned from his house upon occasion, he selecting the occasion.

In the more serious matters, however, Rawhide plays a more notable part, being direct in all his actions, and rather forceful in his quiet way, and in family matters is something of a martinet. For instance, he took a strong objection to Jelly Roll sleeping in my bed, at a time when they lived together with me in the cabin. She had been always used to sharing my bed and no doubt expected to keep it up all her life. But when he would awaken and find her absent from his couch, he would emit loud wailing noises, and come over and drive her away into their cubby-hole. To see him pushing her ahead of him, she expostulating in a shrill treble of outraged sensibilities, was about as ludicrous an exhibition as I have ever seen, and when with childish squeals she would break away and rush to me for protection from this unwelcome discipline, her wonted dignity all gone, she would stick her head in under my arm and lie there like the big tub she is, imagining herself safe but leaving her broad rear end exposed to his buffeting. And this ostrich-like expedient availed her very little, for Rawhide is about the most determined creature I ever knew, and always gained his point. And from then on, not wishing to be the cause of further family discord I discontinued my habit of sleeping on the floor.

But don't get the impression that Jelly only plays and never works. She does both with equal enthusiasm, and can be a play-girl and a builder-upper at the same time—one of those dual personalities we hear about. Jelly, when on labour bent, fairly exudes determination. She will arrive at a runway under a great head of steam, and on striking shore there is no perceptible pause for changing gears; she just keeps on, out, and up, changing from swimming to walking without losing way. Her progress on land is not so much a walk as it is the resolute and purposeful forward march of a militant crusader, bent on the achievement of some important enterprise. Her mind made up, without further ado she proceeds immediately to the point of attack, and by an obstinate and vigorous onslaught will complete in a remarkably short space of time, an undertaking out of all proportion to her size. She accepts my occasional co-operation right cheerfully, but being, as she is, an opportunist of the first water, instead of making a fair division of labour she sees her chance to get that much more work done, and attempts to haul sticks of timber or move loads that are more than enough for the two of us, attacking the project with an impetuous violence that I am supposed, apparently, to emulate. Her independence of spirit is superb, and her bland disregard of my attempts to set right any small mistakes I think she has made (a practice I have long ago desisted from) show her to be the possessor of no mean superiority-complex. She is pretty shrewd and misses no beats, and belongs to that rare type of worker who finds the day all too short for his purpose.

For a resting-place she has a little, low pavilion backed by a large fallen tree and roofed with spreading spruce limbs. This bower looks out upon the lake, and in her spare time here she lies and gazes out across the water, and heaves long sighs of pure contentment. I have often caught her talking to herself in a low, throaty little voice, which on my approach would drop to the deep-toned sound of welcome. Beaver are the most articulate of any beasts I know of and perhaps I can best describe the sounds they make as being very nearly those I imagine a child of three would utter, if he had never learned to talk in any language; and Jelly Roll's attempts to make herself intelligible to me are often quaint and childlike, and not a little pathetic. Rawhide is not nearly so talkative as some, and is much given to working apart from the others, and this self-abnegation is characteristic of most heads of beaver families. Although he takes kindly to the circumstances of his new surroundings and has, in his own quiet and unassuming way, adapted himself very thoroughly to camp life, he retains nearly all the characteristics of a wild beaver in so far as his work is concerned. He looks with a jaundiced eye on my attempts at assistance, and is expert beyond the power of even Jelly to attain to; whether as a result of his early training, or because the female is naturally more care-free, does not appear. On the rare occasions when he rests, he will sometimes share with Jelly her piazza, and with both of them my approach to this retreat is always acknowledged by some small sound of greeting, and is often the excuse for a frolic or even one of those rare sentimental spells, absurd but touching evidence of an affection that seems so firmly rooted yet is so deeply submerged, save at infrequent intervals, by the demands of a vigorous life. Though not very demonstrative, Rawhide has his softer moments too, and in a way that seems so very humble, as though he knew that Jelly had some method of expression that he can never have but does the best he can. But this is only when everything is properly squared away and he has time on his hands. For he is methodical in this as in all his ways. And if he does permit himself a little space for play, it is not for long, and becoming suddenly serious, as though he felt that he had committed himself in a moment of weakness he walks or swims very soberly away. He has a fine regard for the niceties too, and never interferes in conversation or speaks out of his turn, as Jelly often does. A visitor once said that Rawhide reminded him of some old man who had worked too hard when very young, and never had his childhood.

This methodical beast is something of an unsung hero; not that he does actually a great deal more than Jelly, but he is less spectacular and attracts less notice. Yet most of the undertakings that have been completed here bear the stamp of his peculiar methods and devising. His studious attention to what he deems to be his duty, his quiet competence, and his unruffled and unconquerable poise, are on a different plane to Jelly's violently aggressive, but none the less effective programme. So repressed are his emotions and so hidden his reactions, and he carries on so unobtrusively, that he is something of an enigma, and I have not been able to, and perhaps never will, quite gauge the full measure of his sagacity. And as he sits sometimes so motionless, regarding me so steadily with his cool and watchful eye, I often wonder what he thinks of me.

> Jelly Roll, jovial, wayward and full of whims.
> Rawhide, calm, silent and inscrutable.
> These two; King and Queen of All the Beaver People,
> These are the Keepers of the Lodge.

Tolerance

> "The brute tamer stands by the brutes, by a head's breadth only above them!
> A head's breadth, ay, but therein is hell's depth and the height up to
> Heaven."
>
> Padriac Colum

Thus says the poet. But with all due regard for his meaning, if I understand him aright, I am inclined to disagree with him. There is not so wide a difference between man and beast as all that. Often I think that the term "brute" as applied to a dissolute fellow is somewhat of a misnomer. Brutes are rarely depraved, and at least with animals you do not have to watch for symptoms of an overdeveloped business instinct, nor is it necessary to guard against the double dealings of self-interest. There is nothing much to fear save a little wilful mischief and the odd misunderstanding. These cerebral shortcomings may perhaps be the result of a lack of imagination, but it is very refreshing to be confronted by constant evidences of sincerity, even if they are at times a little vigorous. Few forms of affection are more genuine than the guileless and intense devotion that is given only by children and some animals.

As a man lives longer and longer in the woods, so he entertains, if he be of an entertaining nature, an ever-increasing respect and love for Wild Life in all its varied forms. He hesitates at last to kill, and even when necessity demands that he take life he does so with feelings of apology, even of regret for the act. So natural and compelling is this instinct for reparation that old Indians, not yet made self conscious of their pagan customs (many of which, by the way, are rather beautiful and worth perpetuating), have a ritual fitting for such occasions in respect of the more highly esteemed creatures. Years ago I came to this attitude, and it enveloped me so slowly, and yet so surely, that it seemed at last to be the natural outcome of a life spent overmuch in destroying rather than in building. I cannot believe that I am alone in this, but have pretty good evidence that of those whose experience has been such as to cause them to consider the matter at all, only the ignorant or unthinking or the arrogant, or those governed by selfishness are not so affected, at least to some degree.

A man will always lack something of being a really good woodsman, in the finer sense, until he is so steeped in the atmosphere of the Wild and has become so possessed, by long association with it, of a feeling of close kinship and responsibility to it, that he may even unconsciously avoid tramping on too many flowers on his passage through the forest. Then, and then only, can he become truly receptive to the delicate nuances of a culture that may elude those who are not so tuned in on their surroundings. Many instances have I seen of men who, half-ashamed by the presence of spectators, yet had the courage to save the lives of ants, toads, snakes and other lowly creatures in the face of ridicule. And these were virile, hard-looking "he-men," to whom such abject forms of life should supposedly have been of small consideration. And speaking of toads and harmless types of snakes, and other ill-appearing but inoffensive and often beneficial beasts, their persecution is generally the outcome of fanatical hatred, springing from an unreasoning fear of them on the part of those who know nothing whatever about them.

There are many who walk through the woods like blind men. They see nothing but so many feet of board measure in the most magnificent tree that ever stood, and calculate only so many dollars to each beaver house. (With all due respect for economic necessities, there is, I believe, even a certain amount of sentiment present in some slaughterhouses.) For such the beauties of Nature do not exist, and their reactions to the scenic splendours that surround them are similar to that of a man I once accompanied to the top of an eminence, to view a wide-spread panorama of virgin pine forest that stretched from our feet into the blue distance. He looked at the scene before him—such a one as few men are privileged to see—and I thought him rapt with appreciation, when he presently remarked, "Gosh, wouldn't that look good all piled on skidways!"

The function of the forest is *not* exclusively that of providing lumber, though judicious and *properly controlled* garnering of a reasonable forest crop is essential to industry. There are many reasons, æsthetic, economic and patriotic, for the perpetuation of large tracts of unspoiled, *original* timber—exclusive of re-forestation. This last scheme should be carried on intensively, and commercial concerns should be obliged (and many of them do, to their credit) to plant six or a dozen trees for every one they cut, thus putting in their own crop, and so be made to keep their acquisitive eyes off some of Canada's remaining beauty spots, which will be irretrievably ruined if commerce has its way with them. There is plenty for all purposes, if patronage does not outdo honesty.

It is said that all creatures are put here for our exclusive use, to be our servants. Perhaps they are. Yet the abuse of servants is no longer popular; and no one will say that the deer are put in the woods expressly for the wolves to eat, or the spruce cones especially for the squirrels. And once in the woods we are apt to be not much greater than the wolves and squirrels, and are often less. Human beings, as a whole, deny to animals any credit for the power of thought, preferring not to hear about it and ascribing everything they do to instinct. Yet most species of animals can reason, and all men have instinct. Man is the highest of living creatures, but it does not follow as a corollary that Nature belongs to him, as he so fondly imagines. He belongs to it. That he should take his share of the gifts she has so bountifully provided for her children, is only right and proper; but he cannot reasonably deny the other creatures a certain portion. They have to live too. And he should at least use some discretion about it and not take the whole works. Proper use should without doubt be made of our natural resources, whether animal or of any other kind, but it could be done more in the spirit of one who, let us say, is walking in a lovely garden where he may gather, by invitation, choice blossoms sufficient for his needs. But only too often we (I say "we" because I too have not been altogether guiltless in the past) have acted like irresponsible children who, not satisfied with the bounty that should suffice them, must needs tramp down what they cannot carry away.

Man's unfair treatment of the brute creation is too well realized to need a great deal of comment. It varies all the way from neglect, and a callous disregard of any claims the animal may have on his (the man's) sense of fair play, to active cruelty. There are those who are able to indulge a craving for a sense of power, only by exercising it over others who cannot retaliate. This is weakness, not strength such as real power bestows, and from it springs the proverbial cruelty of the coward. The bravest men are generally the kindest, as I saw very often proven during the war; and when, on returning from active service, I heard and saw demonstrations of bitter and implacable animosity, I learned that only the weakling or the non-combatant can hate with such terrible intensity. You have to meet the enemy to appreciate him; and the frank hostility that is sometimes seen to exist between some of those belonging to different social strata could be much ameliorated did each have a chance to cultivate the other. I have met the great, the near great, and the not great. Some say that the higher you go, the simpler and more unassuming they are. I will go further and say that wherever you go, be it up or down, they are quite usually just people, real folks. Kindness, hospitality and consideration are not the prerogative of any class, and a difference in accent is no indication of any great difference in heart. I have met traffic policemen who were natural born gentlemen, and one of the kindest and most courteous hosts I ever had was an ex-bartender who was also an ex-pugilist; and I have dined with a patrician whose conversation missed on every cylinder. But he was an individual.

Titles can be convenient appendages whereby those who have them may be sufficiently bedeviled by those who have not; though I observe that few refuse them. Certainly, the great ones among us, title or no, once they know that you wish only to talk with them as one human to another, with mutual respect, as we should meet all men—when they find, to their relief, that you do not propose to cross swords with them in a crackling duel of splintery, two-edged trivialities, they can be as simple, kindly and unaffected as any son of the soil. And they have so genuine an interest in what you have to tell them and have, moreover, such very well-considered things to say, and they have, altogether, brought to so fine an art that priceless ability to put at his ease the stranger within their gate, that it is at once ascertained that therein lies the real secret of their greatness. And in this they seem to me to be very close in spirit to those great trees that stand so nobly, and yet so proudly tranquil, who never will offend, and who bring grace and elegance to the landscape that they dominate.

If this tolerant attitude is so desirable, nay essential, in our dealings with our fellow humans of whatever class, race or creed, all of whom can, when put to it, ask our aid if need be, would it not seem to be at least fair, a little like good sportsmanship, to permit ourselves just a little sympathy, to exercise some small amount of thought, in our dealings with those creatures who sometimes stand so badly in need of the consideration for which they cannot ask?

That chivalry towards the weaker in which man so prides himself, does not appear to any large extent, if at all, in his attitude towards dumb animals that are unable to upbraid him, or to contribute verbally to public opinion and so damn him. Man's general reactions to his contacts with the animal world (here I speak only of that unfortunately rather large class to whom these remarks apply) are contempt or condescension towards the smaller and more harmless species, and a rather unreasonable fear of those more able to protect themselves. There are many men who inspire our respect by their love for their horses, dogs and other animal companions; yet we still have the bull fight, which I once saw described as a game in which the whole effort of the human players, they having the odds all on their side, was to commit a series of fouls and expect applause for them. I am given to understand that in at least one country whose people regard with disgust this brutal "sport," certain dealers carry on a trade in old, worn-out horses who, as a reward for their long years of service, are shipped away to be tortured in the bull ring for the satisfaction of audiences whose ancestors for hundreds of years blackened the pages of history with the most fiendish cruelties, and annihilated a whole race of Indian people in the name of God. Dogs are still beaten to death in the harness by their owners, and so-called sportsmen, willing to take a chance which only the animal will have to pay for, take flying shots at distant or moving game, and frequently their only reaction to the knowledge that the beast has escaped to die a lingering death, is one of irritation at losing a trophy or some meat.

I had a hunting partner who in attempting such snap shooting, smashed the bottom jaw of a deer. Some days later we found it dead, on which he looked at the carcase and said "Well, you . . ., I got you anyway." Nor is this an extreme case. All through the woods, in hunting season, careless hunters allow maimed animals to escape them to either die in the throes of suffering, or to slowly starve to death owing to their inability to take care of themselves in a crippled condition. Whole species of valuable and intelligent animals have been exterminated for temporary gain, and useful varieties of birds have been destroyed to the point of annihilation (and in one case completely) to tickle the palates of gourmets.

Kindness to animals is the hall-mark of human advancement; when it appears, nearly everything else can be taken for granted. It comes about last on the list of improvements as a rule, so that by the time animal care has been allowed to assume a place of real importance in the curriculum of human activities, it will generally be found that most other social advancements have already been brought to a high degree of refinement, and it is perhaps not too much to say that, using animal welfare among a people as the lowest level in the gauge of their accomplishments, the degree of culture that they have attained to may be indicated by it.

Much of the cruelty perpetrated to provide fashionable adornment is not realized, or even suspected, by the wearers who, somewhat unjustly, get most of the blame. Few perhaps, if any, of those who wear one type of lamb's wool coat, know that the excellence of texture they demand, and which is merely ornamental, is obtained by beating the pregnant mother with sticks until she, in her terror and pain, gives premature birth to her young, who provide the skins, and I have heard that ranches or sheep farms are maintained to cater to this horrible industry. Not much comment is needed on this except, on my part, that the much played-up ferocity of the North American Indian supplies nothing quite like it, and that I would like very much to believe that the general public, including those who wear the coats, did they know of this most inhuman practice, would no longer countenance it.

It would seem as though the making of money would excuse almost anything, and that nearly any undertaking, however unethical, can be termed "business" and so get itself excused, provided it is successful and does not muscle in on some big-shot monopoly. Sheep, I know, are often skinned alive, and I hear that certain kinds of fish are cut in pieces from the tail to the head, so they will remain alive to the last, in order that jaded appetites may be stimulated by the crimped appearance of the flesh that is thus obtained. Is the mere shape of the food, then, of such consequence? Can anyone really be so childish? And perhaps fish do not feel; I cannot know, but I am pretty sure, from what I have seen, that those to whom these puerilities are of such consuming importance, number such unprofitable speculations among the least of their worries. However, I think we can agree that birds are capable of feeling, and I am given to understand that live ducks are crushed in a press for some outlandish dish designed for connoisseurs of food, and that larks and other songbirds are killed by thousands in some countries, and cooked to feed the delicate sensualism of epicures. I cannot believe that these little songsters were put on earth to feed gross appetites, but to give joy to mankind in another way, and even this gift of song is perverted by the bird-catchers, who have been known to blind the tiny eyes with needles, so the helpless little creatures should sing unceasingly, and then to put them in the nets as bait.

Vivisection may be necessary, lamentably, and medical men of the utmost honesty and sincerity may be working by this means for the good of humanity, and are perhaps as merciful as circumstances allow. We understand that important results are sometimes obtained. Yet the importance of the findings provides little surcease from suffering for the poor dumb brutes that are subjected for hours, even days, to excruciating agonies on our behalf. And many a cold-blooded torturer of sadistic inclinations performs, in the name of research, as has been proved, terrible experiments that are of little or no benefit to the human race. And benefit or no, I think the price is too great for any living creature to be called upon to pay, far greater than we have any right to ask.

Personally, I could not ever feel at ease if I knew that I had prolonged my not so important life by the infliction of long-drawn-out and agonizing pain on perhaps hundreds of helpless and inoffensive creatures, tortured until they died in misery that I might live, who some day must die in any case.

Every living creature is parasitical to some degree, in one way or another, on some other form of life, in order to live; but man extracts tribute from everything, even including the less fortunate of his own kind. Almost always he extorts far beyond his needs, destroying without thought for the future—the parasite supreme of all the earth. And in spite of the high position he has gained, he has still much to learn of tolerance, moderation and forbearance towards not only the lesser of created things, but towards his fellow-man.

And now I have discovered, in my slow way, that it is actually necessary in this day and age of our civilization, to enact legislation forbidding the exploitation of children in industry, and that in one year thousands of young people were injured, and not a few killed at their work, whilst profiteers waxed rich on the proceeds of their cheap labour. It is more than a little saddening to find that even children fall a prey to the predatory instincts of a mercenary ogre, and when I first heard of it, I found some difficulty in believing that it could be true and still cannot quite grasp why a *law* should be necessary to put a stop to it.

And now, have I offended you, my readers? It has not been my intention. But if in my ignorance and little knowledge I have erred, it is because in my late travels in the centres of civilization I have seen and heard much that was unexpected, some of it not easy to grasp and leaving me at times a little bewildered. We who live in the woods have different standards—not all of them good.

*

I am still a hunter, in a little different way. The camera is my weapon today. It is, after all, more fun, and if sport is the object, a lot harder. Yet hunting calls into play many manly attributes and I would not, if I could, lay a hand to the suppression of this most noble sport (I do not refer here to either fox, stag, or otter hunting with hounds, all of which are, to my way of thinking, grossly unfair and exceedingly unsportsmanlike)—noble, that is, if carried on with at least a reasonable consideration for those creatures that are giving, not for your necessity, Mr. Sportsman, but for your amusement, all they have to give—their lives. I go so far as to say that in most cases, the circumstances of the hunt mean more to the average hunter—if he is a sportsman—than the actual kill itself. The healthful, invigorating exercise, the beauties of the scenic Wilderness, the zest of such achievements as are necessary in order to get around in a rough country, the tonic properties of the pure, fresh air, the association with his guides, the hearty meals over crackling camp fires, the romance and the adventure—all these things go to make a hunt worth while. And if you are lucky, a good, clean, merciful kill is excusable, provided the animal is put to proper use and not killed for the sake of its eye-teeth or a pair of horns, while several hundred pounds of the very best of meat are allowed to lie in the woods to rot. And hunting has this to recommend it, that everything you get you work for.

Me, I kill no more, unless in case of absolute necessity, having had perhaps my share and over. Some prefer to have a den full of trophies; others a hunting-lodge decorated with skins, maybe. Each to his own taste; I like mine alive.

I make no false claims that I am out especially to try and do the public good, or that I have some "message" for the world. I am only trying to do what little is within my power for those creatures amongst whom my life has been passed. And if by so doing I can also be of some little service to my fellow-man, the opportunity becomes a twofold privilege. I do not expect to accomplish much in the short span that is left to me, but hope to assist, even if only in a minor rôle, in laying a foundation on which abler hands and better heads may later build. In this way I may perhaps be instrumental, at least to some extent, in the work of saving from entire destruction some of those interesting and useful dwellers in our waste places, in whom lie unexpected possibilities that await but a little kindness and understanding to develop—the rank and file of that vast, inarticulate army of living creatures from whom we can never hear.

Quite the most interesting of the developments that have arisen from this self-imposed task of mine has been the opportunity given me of coming into contact with people from every walk of life. I have been privileged to make many friends, and expect to make some more. These experiences are valuable to me, and apart from their educational angle and the broadening effect they have on my views in general, I enjoy them.

One of my most absorbing tasks is that of answering the letters I receive from schools. Some are written in a childish scrawl, some are smudged, others extremely neat with the lettering all erect and very soldierly; but every one is so carefully inscribed, and all bear the signs of the labour that has been put into them by their intensely sincere and hopeful writers—labours of love if ever there were any. And in this, above all things, am I greatly honoured. I try to answer them all, either collectively or through their teachers, or, if the case should call for it, individually; for this is a responsibility I may not shirk.

This is to me my most important correspondence, for I feel that by this means it is given to me to build, even if only a very little, and to implant in fertile minds, anxious for knowledge, seeds that perhaps will blossom into deeds after the planter has been long forgotten.

Epilogue

And now the moon has risen here, on Ajawaan. It shines through a window and touches the peak of the beaver house that stands within.

I sit alone. And all the Voices of the Night are all around me, and swift rustlings, soft whisperings and almost noiseless noises encompass me about.

And the moon throws eerie shadows down along the aisles between the trees, where strange shapes and formless objects stand like waiting apparitions, where moonbeams lie in glimmering pools, and spots of light like eyes peer out from darksome ambuscade.

On the shore, in a little group, some tiny beavers sit, and sniff, and look, and whisper low, like children seeing goblins in a graveyard.

*

And now my Tales are done.

And as I wrote, I wonder if the actors in them did not come back from out the Past, and live again, and play their parts once more. And as I told of them and what they thought, and what they said or did, who can say but that they gathered there, around the Empty Cabin and listened, in that silent and enchanted grove of pine trees?

Perhaps the grove was no more silent, but was filled with all the voices of those whose tales were told here, long ago. And maybe the Cabin was not empty, but was filled again with movement, while its door stood wide in welcome and its window glowed with light, and its fire was burning brightly and it woke from all its dreaming, when those who once had lived here, lived again.

And the Cabin won't be empty any more, nor the grove again so silent and deserted, while yet remains a solitary reader whose sympathy and kindly understanding brings Life to that memory-haunted valley in the hills, and awakens those others, who have dreamed and waited there so long.

THE END

Case History

M. T. Kelly

Case History

"DEEPLY MISOGYNIST." GALLEGAR'S eyes were brilliant in his flat red face. Skin flaked off his cheeks, his nose was shiny; even the white part of his forehead, the part that had been protected by his hatband, was peeling.

"You got a lot of sun," I said, feeling I should shout, though he was standing right in front of me. Below us Hell's Gate Rapid roared. Heat reflected off the rock and the air itself seemed loud. Small blueberry bushes were growing on our sloping campsite; edges of the portage trail crumbled. The very bones of the earth seemed to be coming through the thin skin of the country. My head ached.

Unflinching, Gallegar stared at me. "She asked if you had a problem with women, and I answered, 'Oh, yes.'" When he'd finished, Gallegar's mouth set determinedly, and his eyes brightened.

"So do you," I said, "but this isn't a competition. The last thing I want to do is move around more in this heat."

What Gallegar had agreed to do was go on a "nature walk" after supper with the leader of our canoe trip. None of us had imagined she'd turn out to be the kind of leader she was, but from the moment I had first spoken to Allison there had been a problem.

For years Gallegar, Jones and I had gone on canoe trips together. We came to it late, in our early thirties; none of us were childhood friends, or had ever gone canoeing at a camp, and I usually did most of the organizing for our trips. A two-year contract job in Northern Ontario turned me into an addict, and I conveyed my enthusiasm to these two men I'd known since university.

We had been down the Spanish River, we had canoed the North Shore of Lake Superior, and we wanted to go to Labrador. There had been a strange, unifying power in all our trips, one we usually felt in retrospect, and we kept returning to them. This year, however, would be a little different. It was Allison's expedition, though it had been my idea to go with her. In an issue of *Wildculture,* a magazine in which she had written an article, she had also advertised for companions to go on a canoe journey "down the historic Mississagi, a naturalists' trip, following Grey Owl's route."

The idea was a good one, and would also save Gallegar, Jones and me a lot of preparation. This time someone else could arrange things. I knew about the river, and kept saying the name, Mississagi. Though the whole thing wouldn't cost much, Jones insisted on referring to it as a "catered trip." Gallegar was neutral, but Jones made comments about us needing help because we were getting older. We were hardly old, but middle-aged talk about getting older was familiar, or predictable, enough to be irritating; and the way he said "catered" made me uneasy. He didn't say it with conscious contempt, in fact Jones included himself as much as anyone in his good-humoured mockery, but he said it so much it began to sound like a mantra to enhance his masculinity—Jones doesn't need a catered trip, but he's taking one anyway. The warm—for there was warmth in the way he included us all and we played along—private joke became relentless. Don't blame me if you're worried about getting older, I wanted to say; you do it then. But I kept quiet and we wound up with Allison.

"'Pale emasculates'!" Jones pushed his back hard against the pack where he was resting. He drew on a cigarette, squinted, held the book out in front of him and continued. "'The rollicking chorus of the canoe brigades is replaced by the pulings . . . of pale emasculates.'"

I wasn't sure if he was reading or quoting, but it was a performance. Jones looked up at Gallegar and me as we stood above him. "That you, old buddy, a pale emasculate?" Without giving Gallegar a chance to respond, Jones went on. "'These effeminates—'"

"I'm goin'." Gallegar grabbed the peak of his baseball cap and tugged down, hard. He walked away.

"Well, I'm going to tie a rope around me and hang in that pool down there. Then I'm having a drink. You coming, Mick?" Jones exhaled. The smoke lingered by his beard. He smiled and cocked his head.

"In a minute."

"What are you, a pale emasculate?" He didn't let up.

"I didn't know that was in there. I mean, he was of his time, but . . . I'm surprised," I explained. Instantly I was angry at myself for being serious; it was a mistake. Earlier in the trip, in turning aside a jibe, I had said: "I don't find that humorous." I had meant to be gently satirical. Now, after two days, nearly everything I said was met with, "Oh, don't you find that humorous?" The kidding didn't stop. A flare of irritation seemed to leap from my chest right at Jones, as if I had a spirit self that flew at him.

Perhaps he felt it, perhaps he was just weary, but he stretched and said accommodatingly, "The guy can't write. It's shit."

Jones referred to Grey Owl, born Archie Belaney in England, who pretended he was a half-breed or Indian, and who had canoed this same stretch of the Mississagi in the early part of the century.

"I come in peace, brother," I mocked, then, mouthing some Ojibway syllables, emphasized, "*the* Grey Owl." Instead of coming to terms with Jones, or at least sitting down beside him to talk, I parodied with revulsion Grey Owl's greeting to the King of England. I tried to keep in mind that Grey Owl was an early conservationist, but then I let myself go: another tall, twisted, imperial phoney, a Brit who "seeded" native women, then abandoned the children, a violent sociopath only concerned with himself, *his* reactions to the country, *his* feelings. I saw a six-foot child in a canoe acting wilfully, turning aside from the things he'd done to other people, turning away.

He lied. He lied about the river, he lied about the rapids, at least he exaggerated; he couldn't be trusted. I thought of his books, his picture of an Indian camp: all pastels, twilight behind the white pines, a movie set with obvious, false, backlighting. And now this disappointing attitudinal crap Jones had dug up. I knew there was something wrong as I stood there hating a man dead fifty years. If I'd been persuaded to give Grey Owl a chance, to consider him, to read him, now it seemed a waste of time. Unable to finish anything he'd written, instead of indifference I felt rage. Boy, am I angry, I said to myself, easing down beside Jones.

"You got any Aspirin?" As Jones spoke he grimaced from the pain of a headache and closed his eyes against the sun. At the same time the crow's-feet that radiated out below his temples managed to let me know he was pleased with himself.

"What's the matter? A little hung?"

"Yep," he said. "But I'm going to have another drink."

"It's the heat." I relaxed. "I've never seen it so hot in the bush. You know, by the way, that he's convinced himself that she's okay just to spite us. That's why he's going."

When Jones didn't respond my anger surged again. But then maybe I was a little obsessive about Allison. I was obsessive about Grey Owl, and he wasn't even around. Some of this was my fault.

The four of us had first met at the front of a nearly empty Ontario Northland bus on the way to Biscotasing. It was the rendezvous Allison had chosen; before that we only corresponded. I suspected she was among the few people at the back laughing—there weren't that many buses to Bisco—but hadn't introduced myself. As we passed the height of land, where the rivers begin to flow north, I looked outside and saw black spruce against peach twilight. A shadow of dread passed over me as I looked out at the dark trees. Allison may have felt it too, for at that moment she came forward, put her hand on my armrest to bend down and peer out, and she said, "Heh, I didn't realize we were in the north."

Then she sat down in the aisle, hugging her knees, facing us and smiling. What a smile it was: big, open, social. There was nothing false or strained in that smile, but still the whole set of her look, her openness, had something in it of an agenda: now I'm ready to meet. It looked as if it was something she'd learned.

"I know who you are," she spoke to Jones and Gallegar.

"You're Allison," Jones said.

From the seat behind them I smiled, eager, responding the way she invited, fond, waiting my turn.

I was not addressed.

Later Jones and Gallegar pointed out that, within minutes of meeting Allison, I had criticized her.

"It wasn't her, it was something she'd written," I said.

"Same thing," Gallegar answered. "She's a first-time author."

I had done it innocently enough, using my comments to draw attention to myself when she didn't speak to me. I was also in a rush to let her know that, unlike the other guys, I had paid attention to her, close attention, before our meeting. But I did show off—the way I jumped in may have seemed aggressive, may have been aggressive—and however mild, it was a criticism. I would pay and pay for it.

What I said was: "That piece you did in *Wildculture* about the pickerel plant and the arrowhead; weren't the drawings mixed up? The arrowhead leaf is much more pronounced."

"Oh." She cocked her head, a kind of heaviness settling into her large face. "Our research is very careful."

"I really liked your piece," I said, "but isn't . . ."

Allison didn't let me finish, but got up to walk back to her seat. As she went by she didn't talk to herself or mutter, nothing like that, but she was definitely not talking to me as she said, "We're quite careful."

Turning my head, I followed Allison, not panicking but with a kind of rushing frustration that was a little like panic. A mistake had been made and I was not allowed to make up for it. With a little muscular jolt of dissatisfaction I faced forward again. Now I would have to explain myself; now I would have to wait.

Everything got much worse that night in Biscotasing.

Allison was a short woman, a little stocky, with strong features—large oval cheeks in a big face, a prominent nose—and no calves. I focused on how she had no calves as I followed along in the group she led from the bus-stop to the hotel in Bisco where we were to stay the night. At least she isn't sexually attractive, I said to myself: not with that moon face, not with that hook nose, not with those calves. Allison *was* sexual, her shorts were tight, very tight at the crotch; she kept pushing her hair away from her face in a languorous way. But she wasn't attractive to me. It was a profound relief.

The road on which we walked was red earth, surrounded by wet, marshy fields. It was heavy dusk, with a hint of rain in the air, and I was anxious, worrying if it would rain all week on the river. Just a line of pink showed in the west, under dark clouds, and swallows were active over the fields. Far off a pair of crows squawked from a dead tree. There were flickers of movement, bats or shadows, drops of rain, over the northern meadow. I tried to point out the birds.

"Could that be a nighthawk?"

"Until I was married I was liberal. Then I had kids, and I said to myself, heh, they don't have any rights. They're barbarians! Monsters." Allison repeated "monsters" and laughed, a little nervously, as if partially aware of the monster she must have appeared to her children. Her giggle was that of a nine-year-old who's done something but with darting eyes, a sly smile, evades it. Allison flushed; she was so unconscious of the strength of her emotion that she moved like a puppet, jerking away so she didn't have to look at me.

"Do bats occur this far north?" I said. "I mean, we're on the edge of the boreal forest. They must."

"Teaching," she said. "Forget it. I only lasted one year as a teacher. My husband can put up with that sort of thing but I can't. He's with the kids this week. We take turns. He can have my turn!"

"It's good to get away," I offered from the back of the pack.

"Oh look! Tree swallows."

Never have I been so actively ignored. It was like a blow.

I acted back. That's it, I said to myself, and shut up. And I shut up aggressively around her the whole week. Ignoring and avoiding Allison took an effort, took a toll, but I conceded nothing. Now, five days later, I knew she'd been complaining to Gallegar. Somehow he and Jones never became lightning rods for her dislike the way I had. But she was wearing on them, I knew that.

"So what's the word?" I asked Jones. "What will he be like after his nature walk?"

"I don't want to talk about it." He fumbled in his shirt pocket for another cigarette.

"You don't want to talk about it. Well, she's sure getting to you."

"I know. That's why I don't want to talk about it."

"The nicknames! If I hear 'The Smoker' one more time . . . I mean, okay, people often use stupid nicknames in groups. It's an easy way to relate. Easy. Stupid. But Jesus, she's in the stratosphere! Each time she sees you she says it as if she's just made it up. And she repeats it . . ." As an afterthought I added, "Gallegar says she's the unhappiest human being he's ever met."

"She is."

"I know, but . . ."

"Insecure."

"Insecure. Stalin was insecure. Insecure does more goddam damage—"

"She knows a lot."

"Oh yes. And she lets you know it."

"She spreads the shit around," he said.

That evening Gallegar and Jones stayed out on the rock, drinking and looking at the rapids. I was with them for a while, but all we talked about was the bugs and the sunset. Gallegar seemed nonchalant, immune, as if nothing had happened; as if he hadn't gone on the walk. He wore mosquito netting over his baseball cap. Maybe he liked her. I felt isolated, and went to bed.

The next day Gallegar didn't look as though he liked anyone. It wasn't simply that he was hung-over, though he was, or that he knew Jones and I were laughing at his misery, which we were. It was simply that Allison wouldn't stop talking to him. All day their canoe—Allison wanted to canoe with Gallegar—lagged behind as she steered them over to examine riverine plants. This leisurely way of canoeing was an exercise of power; continually we had to wait. The voice Allison used as she lectured was soft and rich, full of vowels that celebrated the wonder she thought she was imparting. Gallegar's furrowed face, made even fiercer by the warpaint of zinc oxide on his red nose, had no impression on her. I don't think she even looked at his face. And his hunched, enduring back had no effect either. But Gallegar was tough; no matter how irritated, no matter how he suffered, his glance over at Jones and me was baleful and challenging. He understood full well what was going on, but dared us to take it too far. He wasn't so much defending her as warning us.

That evening was even stranger. The weather changed, threatening rain. It was grey and close and still. We set up camp on a high rock, which acted as a wall and overlooked a nearly still pool of the river. There was current, but the pollen-streaked surface hardly seemed to move.

Jones and I went down to swim; the humidity was intense. Then Allison and Gallegar showed up, carrying towels and shampoo, laughing. They were a couple, as fresh as morning. Gallegar had his cap off. We all washed and swam, then, equidistant from each other, only our heads showing sleek and white against the black water, we held still and talked.

"This is the life," Allison said. "It makes you wonder why we live in cities when we could have this."

"Only in summertime," Jones said.

"It's fabulous." Half treading water, half floating, Allison moved to just in front of Gallegar. "Isn't it great?" she said, bringing her face close to his. Her smile was so big and wet and bright it seemed she was wearing lipstick, though she wasn't.

Smiling back, Gallegar nodded, his skull showing through his thin skin and making him look like a gnome under the massive rock wall.

Allison moved even closer; there were no boundaries between them. I was reminded of a mother trying to teach her child to swim, but coming too close, hysterically reassuring.

Gallegar didn't look startled, didn't pull back or dodge or try to escape; there was only a hardening in his grin, a rictus. He smiled right back at her; he looked happy.

"Feeling better?" I asked.

"It's great," he said.

We all talked about how wonderful it was for a while, then swam over and sat together on a ledge, our legs dangling in the water. In spite of the humid warmth the air on our skin was chilly—the cloud cover made it seem cooler than it was—and Allison slid back in. She asked for my soap and I handed it to her.

"Thanks."

Gallegar followed her, but came right back out, pushing himself up on his arms and slipping on the algae that covered the shelving greenstone. Jones pulled him up, then helped Allison, and we all towelled off and started back to the fire.

Allison took Jones's arm as casually as if they were a strolling couple out window shopping.

Stiffening, Jones stopped, but he didn't politely disengage. In fact, he made room so he and Allison could go up the narrow path abreast.

"Hey, you forgot your soap," Gallegar called to me as Allison and Jones went ahead.

"Thanks." I waited for him.

Single file, Gallegar and I followed. The hemlock pressing in, and green with hard little berries in it, or tiny blossoms like points of light, the dense grey air, made me dizzy; my head spun.

"Man, this is steep." I turned to Gallegar. "What do you think the elevation is?"

"My map's in the tent," he said laconically.

"Can I have a look?"

"Yep."

That evening Allison didn't talk to Gallegar. She even made arrangements to switch partners so she wouldn't have to clean up with him. Not that he had to face any overt hostility; Allison was as happy as I'd seen her. She just left him out.

She was even pleasant to me. When I was in my tent looking at the map and reading, she came by and told me she'd found some jewelweed.

"Oh," I said, looking up from my piled clothes and sleeping bag and wishing I had a shirt on. "Great."

She knelt down in front of the mosquito netting. "Touch-me-not. They're down where we pulled the canoes up."

"I think Jones went to the end of the island," I said. "In the bush."

"Okay, I'll find him." Her neutral warmth surprised me. "Did he have the bird book with him?"

"I dunno. Gallegar's still down by the fire. Did you check with him? He'd know where the bird book is."

Allison held onto, and examined, my tent flap. She made no mention of Gallegar, and no mention that I had a tent bigger than everyone else's, as she had before.

"I saw a black-backed, three-toed woodpecker!" she said. "I wanted to show him. The bird's still around. He had his binoculars."

She was talking about Jones, not Gallegar. "Looks like it's going to rain," I said, and it started to rain.

"Gotta go." Pulling her hood up, Allison scurried away, looking both ways as she left and running awkwardly, as if she was wearing a skirt and crossing a city intersection. "See you," she called.

The rain came down hard. I don't think Allison found Jones; no one sat around talking after dinner. I went to sleep early.

My tent was white. The light seemed to come right at me, like a huge face coming through the walls, coming too close. There was no sound, at least I didn't notice any wind or rain, just darkness and another startling flash.

Then came a crack of thunder, a crack from hell louder than any I had experienced.

It was the middle of the night. My tent was on the highest point of rock.

The terror was profound, intense, sickening; but it was so strong it was over quickly, or at least partially over. My nervous system seemed to shut down from being overloaded. I had seen the phenomenon in a beaten dog who snapped, fought, protested, but when the blows didn't stop just lay down under them, his face changing, drawn still; it was too much, no more could be done, like death. I was not a dog, but lightning wouldn't stop. For a moment in the blinding flash I felt I had no skin, imagining myself a skinned carcass, a muscular man become a flayed bear, with paws and yellow nerves and muscle. Or an animal seen with x-ray vision, a heart tied by a string to a gaping mouth, all in black outline.

The storm went on and on. There was too much fear, and I just let it come.

Some of it went away. I even slept a little as the glare turned blue.

My reaction was extreme, but the next day everyone was changed. The weather had made us mute, and as we canoed through a marsh, great, still, and heavy after the storm, no one spoke. The silence, a fatalistic patience, lasted for the rest of the trip; a kind of life had been bled away.

The marsh, with the forest appearing rounded at its edge, looked like a European painting of woods in fog. The bright light of the north was gone. Those days— not with fall in them, but the cool bright days unique to Canada, and the open windy days of high summer—were gone. The part of the year that was promise, and fulfilment, was over.

The river seemed obliterated; even now I can't remember too much of the trip, places where we camped. It wasn't so much obliterated as taken away, like a childhood.

She was always there, but Allison, locked in her anger and unhappiness, or associations with Grey Owl, had not transformed the place and made it other than what it was. Symbols matter, but what left me distraught was that Jones, Gallegar and I failed each other. In Sudbury, on the way home, we went drinking and made fun of Allison and needled each other as we had on the trip. Below the gossip and jabbing there was frustration and exasperation that became so intense that finally Jones said, "Just leave it!" Not once had we been serious about how she affected us. And we never admitted how moving, primordial and terrifying the river was. There'd been no support. At night, under the stars, with Allison sleeping but present like a spirit, we said nothing.

It affected the others as deeply. A year later Jones revealed that the trip had disturbed him so much he wanted to put off the next one. There would be other rivers, but the Mississagi, something, had been destroyed.

Part of it is coming back. I am beginning to see again, as if for the first time, without us, Bark Lake narrowing, grassy reeds; and far away there are other voices, ghostly on the deep blue air. I can see the same spot in spring with candling ice, the expanse of ice all distance, and above it the white, empty, loving sky.

Grey Owl
The Mystery of Archie Belaney

Armand Garnet Ruffo

Archie Belaney, 1930–31

The current is faster than I expect.
Suddenly my articles break into demand.
Letters of congratulations come flying
in from across Britain and the United States
(few from Canada which I find disconcerting).
Strangers want to visit me.
Reporters want to interview me.
They announce that I'm the first
to promote conservation:
the beaver,
the forests, the
Indian
way of life.

I begin by signing my name Grey Owl,
and saying I was adopted by the Ojibway,
and that for 15 years I spoke nothing but Indian;
then, before I know it, I have Apache blood.
Finally I'm calling myself an Indian writer.
Fast, it all happens so fast.
At first I'm hesitant.
I'm unsure of the name, the sound of it.
(Although, do I not prefer traveling at night?
Did I not hoot like an owl in Bisco?)
I think of the risk, those who know me.
There are Belaneys in Brandon.
My wife Angele in Temagami—
who knew me when I still carried an accent—

not to mention all those folks in northern Ontario.

But the thrust of self-promotion is upon me,
and head first into it, I hear myself
convincing myself that nobody's going to listen
to an immigrant ex-trapper from England,
promote an indigenous philosophy for Canada.
And if this is the only way
to get Canadians to listen,
then I'll do it, and more
if I have to. I'll be
what I have to be.
Without hesitation.

To Be A Red Indian

Red skin. Black hair. Piercing eyes.
Feathers. Beads. Moccasins. Braids.
Always slouch. Never smile.
Say How-Kola

When It Comes

There are rumours, bits and pieces,
dry as tinder, ready to catch fire
and burn me at the stake.
     (Confess! Confess!)
So when they hint to ask:
pardon me, but is it true?
I look them in the eye,
straight as a good paddle,
as though they could trust me
with their life.
And I say: I feel as an Indian, think
     as an Indian, all my ways
     are Indian, my heart is Indian.
What more can be said? What more
is there? When it comes.

Archie Belaney, 1931

The review accuses me of having a ghost writer
and, even though I take offence,
I do,
the other side of myself.
The half I don't consider Indian, although
by now I feel that side also slowly darkening.

To explain—why I can write—
I simply announce to the press
although my mother was a Jicarilla Apache,
my father was an American scout named McNeil
with a sister in England, who is to be credited
for providing me with a sound education, and to whom
as a gesture of gratitude, I have dedicated my book.
A half-breed who leans towards his Indian side, I explain,
and they're satisfied just looking at me and my scowl.

As far as I'm concerned, it's not a question of Who,
that's not the issue, but rather How.
How do I get away with it? Again, a simple answer:
you see, it's not me they see at all;
it's the face in their mind,
the one they expect (of me),
born out of themselves,
in their own image.

John Tootoosis, 1936

An Indian can tell who's Indian.
Grey Owl can't sing or dance.
But he's doing good
and when we meet
I call him Brother.

Ottawa Citizen, April 20, 1938

The chances are that Archie Belaney could not
have done nearly such effective work for conservation
of wildlife under his own name. It is an odd commentary,
but true enough.

London Times, April 21, 1938

Since the death of Grey Owl
a remarkable conflict of opinion
has arisen over his parentage,
particularly regarding his Indian blood.

Liverpool Daily Post, April 21, 1938

What, after all, does his ancestry matter?
The essential facts about his life are not in dispute,
for as a conservation officer under the Canadian
Government, and as lecturer and broadcaster
in Great Britain, he worked unceasingly for
the protection of wild life.

Manchester Guardian, April 21, 1938

Whatever his origins, he devoted his life
to the understanding of nature and the considerable
fortune his writing and lecturing brought him
to the relief of the suffering animals.

Winnipeg Tribune, April 23, 1938

His attainments as a writer and naturalist will survive
and when in later years our children's children
are told of the strange masquerade—if it was
a masquerade—their wonder and their appreciation
will grow.

Between Birth and Death Waussayuah—Bindumiwin*

Born: Archibald Stansfeld Belaney
September 18, 1888, Hastings, England.

Down the avenue of trees, I see
a spot of sunlight.
And I am trying so hard to get there.†

Dies: Grey Owl, Wa-sha-quon-asin
April 13, 1938, Prince Albert, Saskatchewan.

---

*A vision whose meaning is complete. See Basil Johnston, *Ojibway Heritage,* Toronto: McClelland & Stewart Ltd., 1976.

†Grey Owl's words recorded by Betty Somervell during her ocean voyage with him from England to the United States, 1937. Quoted in *The Green Leaf,* ed. Lovat Dickson, London: Lovat Dickson Ltd. Publishers, 1938.

CHAPTER FOUR

Conquest

Introduction

The Conquest, the defeat of the French by the British on the Plains of Abraham in 1759, presents an enormous problem in Canadian history. After all, one side won and one side lost. What is the meaning or significance of 1759? The answer depends on who asks the question. Think of the artist Robert Houle and his 1992 painting "Kanata." Think also of Donald Creighton. As English Canada's pre-eminent historian from the 1930s through to the 1960s, Creighton saw the Conquest as epiphenomenal. A contemporary of Creighton's, the great French-Canadian historian Michel Brunet could not have disagreed more profoundly. Far from being "an event of apparently unique importance" it was an event of singular importance. How are we to explain these different versions of the same event? Mark Starowicz, the force behind and the creator of the multi-volume television documentary *Canada: A People's History*, sought to create a single history of Canada, not a French-Canadian history and not an English-Canadian history. The Conquest presented a particular challenge. He could not ignore it; nor could he celebrate it. He could not turn the victorious James Wolfe into a George Washington. In this concluding excerpt to the episode on the Seven Years War in general and the Plains of Abraham in particular, how does Starowicz find symbolic unity?

The Economy of the North

Donald Creighton

I

WHEN, IN THE COURSE of a September day in 1759, the British made themselves the real masters of the rock of Quebec, an event of apparently unique importance occurred in the history of Canada. There followed rapidly the collapse of French power in North America and the transference of the sovereignty of Canada to Great Britain; and these acts in the history of the northern half of the continent may well appear decisive and definitive above all others. In fact, for France and England, the crisis of 1759 and 1760 was a climax of conclusive finality. But colonial America, as well as imperial Europe, had been deeply concerned in the long struggle in the new continent; and for colonial America the conquest of New France had another and a more uncertain meaning. For Europe the conquest was the conclusion of a drama; for America it was merely the curtain of an act. On the one hand, it meant the final retirement of France from the politics of northern North America; on the other, it meant the regrouping of Americans and the reorganization of American economies.

The conquest had a double significance, American and European, because the struggle in North America had not been one war, but two. It was a part of the history of both the old world and the new. In its more obvious and more imposing aspect, it was an extension of that war between France and England which filled the century from the Revolution of 1688 to the Peace of Paris in 1763. North America was merely one theatre in a world conflict, a struggle between imperial giants, which invaded the extremes of east and west; and this conflict appeared, in America, as in every other continent which it visited, to dominate the lives and to decide the destinies of lesser men. Its shocks and pauses both stimulated effort and imposed quiet on the seigniories of the St. Lawrence and the towns of New England. And when the war was won by the capture of Montreal and concluded by the Peace of Paris, it might well have seemed that the struggle in North America was over for ever.

Yet concealed within this majestic imperial drama was a subplot, a conflict between the first Americans in America. And for them this secondary drama was the more prolonged and therefore the more important of the two. Two colonial societies, rooted in two different American landscapes, had come into existence on the continent; and while one was scattered sparingly along the giant system of the St.

From *The Empire of The Saint Lawrence: A Study in Commerce and Politics* by Donald Creighton. Copyright © 2002 by Donald Creighton. Reprinted with permission of the publisher, University of Toronto Press.

Lawrence and the lakes, the other, more compact and populous, had grown up on the Atlantic seaboard. These two societies differed from each other, and among the differences which distinguished them were some which had been imported from Europe. Fundamentally, the civilization of each society in North America is the civilization of Europe. An inward necessity, instinctive and compelling, had driven the immigrants to preserve the mysterious accumulations of their cultural heritage; and the price they were forced to pay for its preservation should not entirely obscure the extent of their success. Undoubtedly, these two societies, one almost exclusively French and the other predominantly English, were differentiated by race, language, laws and religion. The distinctions which had been inherited from the old world lived on in the new with an almost inextinguishable vitality; and undoubtedly they helped to foster and to prolong the rivalries between the first Americans.

But the society of the St. Lawrence and the society of the Atlantic seaboard were divided by something else, which was perhaps more fundamental and which was purely American. It was, in fact, the continent of North America itself. Immediately these migrants had to come to terms with the new continent. From it they had to wrest a living; and since they were Europeans and not Indians, a living meant not merely the food to sustain life but the amenities of West-European civilization which alone could make it tolerable. They had to find means to produce their own necessities and to pay for their imports from Europe. They had to live in and by the new world; and they were driven, by this double compulsion, to understand the possibilities of the new continent and to exploit its resources. They could escape neither the brutal dictates nor the irresistible seductions of North American geography; and in an undeveloped world the pressure of these prime phenomena was enormous and insistent. Each society, after long trial and recurrent error, had read the meaning of its own environment, accepted its ineluctable compulsions and prepared to monopolize its promises. And each, in the process of this prolonged and painful adjustment, had acquired an American character, a purpose and a destiny in America.

II

Chance flung the first English colonists on the edges of the Atlantic seaboard and opened the single great eastern waterway of the interior to the French. In the history of the different economies, of the cultural patterns which were to dominate North American life, these were acts of first importance. For each cultural group, the English and the French, fell heir to one of America's geographic provinces, and both these regions had their laws, their promises and their portentous meanings. Of the two, the Atlantic seaboard conformed more nearly to the geographic conditions of western Europe, which had been for centuries a forcing-house of nations. It was, for North America, a fairly small and compact area, sharply defined by obvious natural frontiers. From the coastline the land stretched westward to rise at last in the ridges of the Appalachians, which were unbroken from the St. Lawrence valley to the

Floridas, save where the Hudson-Mohawk system gave access to the west. It was a boundary; but during colonial times it was not a barrier in the sense that it confined a restless and ambitious people determined upon its assault. Because they shaped the courses of the rivers, the mountains helped to focus the attention of the English-Americans upon that other boundary of the Atlantic seaboard, the ocean. Their faces were turned east rather than west; and during the greater part of the colonial period, the commercial energies of the population were concentrated in the numerous short rivers, in the bays and sounds and harbours which fretted the coastline, and sought their objectives eastward on the sea. For New England especially, whose economy was based upon its fisheries, the pull of the coastline and the submerged continental shelf beyond it, was enormous. The prohibitions, the invitations and the varieties of this seaboard empire directed, in a kindly fashion, the energies of an adaptive people. While the land configuration concentrated their pursuits, the climate and soil gave them variety. The area meant stolidity, gradual settlement, the inescapable necessity to produce and the possibility of diversified production. Seaward, it meant a commercial empire which would cease to be imperial because it would inevitably become oceanic.

The river up which Cartier ventured gave entrance to the totally different dominion of the north. It was a landscape marked off from the other geographic provinces of the new continent by the almost monotonously massive character of its design. A huge triangle of rocky upland lay bounded by a river and a string of giant lakes. It was a solemn country, with that ungainly splendour evoked by great, crude, sweeping lines and immense and clumsy masses. The marks of age and of terrific experience lay heavy upon it. It was an elemental portion of the earth, harshly shaped by the brutal catastrophes of geological history. The enormous flat bulk of the Precambrian formation was not only the core of the whole Canadian system, but it was also the ancient nucleus of the entire continent. It lay, old and sombre and ravaged, nearly two million square miles in extent. The ice masses, during the glacial period, had passed over and beyond it, and they had scarred and wrenched and altered the entire landscape in their advance and their retreat. Scouring the surface of the Shield itself, pouring boulder clay into the valleys to the south, the ice sheets had hollowed the beds of new lakes and had diverted the courses of ancient rivers. There was left a drainage system, grand in its extent and in the volume of its waters, but youthful, wilful and turbulent. The wrinkled senility of the Precambrian formation was touched by a curious appearance of youth. The countless meaningless lakes and lakelets, the intricately meandering rivers and spillways, the abrupt falls and treacherous rapids, which covered the face of the Shield, seemed to express the renewal of its primitive strength. To the south, below the Shield, the ice masses had throttled the waters into new lakes and had dammed the St. Lawrence into a long southern loop, leaving Niagara, the Long Sault and Lachine as evidence of the novelty of its course.

The Canadian Shield and the river system which seamed and which encircled it, were overwhelmingly the most important physical features of the area. They were the bone and the bloodtide of the northern economy. Rock and water complemented each other, fought each other's battles and forced each other's victories. The Shield itself, a huge lop-sided triangle, whose northern points were Labrador and the Arctic east of the Mackenzie, occupied over one-half of the land area which was to become the Dominion of Canada. For the French and for their successors it was unescapable and domineering. It hugged the north shore of the St. Lawrence as the river issued from the continent. Westward, in the centre of the lowlands of the St. Lawrence, the good lands began to peter out a hundred miles north of Lake Ontario in the scarred, blank rock, thin soil sheet and towering evergreens peculiar to the Shield. Relentlessly it followed the north shore of Lakes Huron and Superior and at last struck north and west for the Arctic Ocean. Its long, flat, undeviating plateau effected the complete severance of the St. Lawrence lowlands from the western plains. In the east it helped, with the northern spurs of the Appalachians, to cut off Acadia from Quebec. Settlement starved and shrivelled on the Shield; it offered a sullen inhospitality to those occupations which were traditional in western Europe and which had been transferred by the first immigrants to the Atlantic seaboard of North America. But from the beginning it exercised an imperious domination over the northerners, for though it was a harsh and an exacting country, it offered lavish prizes to the restless, the ambitious and the daring. It was an area of staples, creating simple trades and undiversified extractive industries; and its furs, its forests and its minerals were to attract three great assaulting waves of northerners. Fur was the first great staple of the north. And with the fur trade, the Precambrian formation began its long career in the Canadian economy as a primary, instead of as a subsidiary, economic region. It was upon these ancient rocks that the central emphasis of the Canadian system was placed at first, and the initial importance of the Shield is of deep significance in the history of the economy of the north.

To the south lay the lowlands of the St. Lawrence. Here the intense winters of the Precambrian formation were softened and the hot, bright summers flamed more slowly out of long springtimes and faded gradually into reluctant autumns. North of the lakes, the lowlands stretched from Quebec city to Georgian Bay—a narrow but slowly broadening band of fertility, crowded a little oppressively by the sombre masses of the Shield. South and west, beyond the river and the lakes, they lapsed easily into the central lowlands of the continent and the basin of the Mississippi. In the centre of this rich region lay that immense organization of waters which issued from the continent by the river of Canada; and this drainage system, driving seaward in a great, proud arc from Lake Superior to the city of Quebec, was the fact of all facts in the history of the northern half of the continent. It commanded an imperial domain. Westward, its acquisitive fingers groped into the territory of the plains. Aggressively it entrenched upon the dominion of the Mississippi. It grasped the Shield, reached southward into the valley of the Hudson and at last rolled massively seaward between sombre approaches which curved away southward into the Maritimes and rose north-eastward past Quebec and Labrador to Newfoundland.

It was the one great river which led from the eastern shore into the heart of the continent. It possessed a geographical monopoly; and it shouted its uniqueness to adventurers. The river meant mobility and distance; it invited journeyings; it promised immense expanses, unfolding, flowing away into remote and changing horizons. The whole west, with all its riches, was the dominion of the river. To the unfettered and ambitious, it offered a pathway to the central mysteries of the continent. The river meant movement, transport, a ceaseless passage west and east, the long procession of river-craft—canoes, *bateaux*, timber rafts and steamboats—which followed each other into history. It seemed the destined pathway of North American trade; and from the river there rose, like an exhalation, the dream of western commercial empire. The river was to be the basis of a great transportation system by which the manufactures of the old world could be exchanged for the staple products of the new. This was the faith of successive generations of northerners. The dream of the commercial empire of the St. Lawrence runs like an obsession through the whole of Canadian history; and men followed each other through life, planning and toiling to achieve it. The river was not only a great actuality: it was the central truth of a religion. Men lived by it, at once consoled and inspired by its promises, its whispered suggestions, and its shouted commands; and it was a force in history, not merely because of its accomplishments, but because of its shining, ever-receding possibilities.

For something stood between the design and its fulfilment. There was, in the very geography of the region itself, a root defect, a fundamental weakness, which foreshadowed enormous difficulties, even though it did not pre-determine defeat. In the centre, by Lake Ontario and the lower reaches of the river, the drive of the great waterway was unquestioned and peremptory. But this power was not indefinitely transmissible, and the pull of a system stretching over two thousand miles was at long last relaxed and weakened. The outer defences of the St. Lawrence contradicted its inward solidity; its boundaries were not bold and definite, but a smudged faint tracery. Between the valley of the St. Lawrence on the one hand and the valleys of Hudson Bay, the Mississippi and the Hudson river on the other, the separating heights of land were low and facile; and over these perfunctory defences invasions might pass as easily as sorties. The river's continuity was broken at Niagara: it stumbled and faltered at the Cascades, the Cedars and Lachine. As it drove east and north past Quebec and into its immense estuary, the river was caught, its influence narrowed and and focused by the uplands of the Shield to the north and the rolling highlands of the Appalachians below. There were breaks and obstacles; and over both its seaward approaches and its continental extremities the hold of the river closed and again relaxed, uncertainly and unconvincingly. Yet for all its inward contradictions and its outward weakness, the river was a unit, and its central entrance was dominated by the rock of Quebec and the island of Montreal.

III

Each of these two geographic provinces was a matrix in which a distinct American economy was crudely fashioned. The boundaries of these rival economies were co-extensive with the limits of two conflicting political dominions and two antipathetic social groups. It was certain that man, with his political capacities and economic resources, would modify the crude stamp of the geographical matrix; and it was equally certain that the geographical matrix itself would alter slightly under the force of human ingenuity and effort. Yet, in the first simplicity of early settlement, the pressure of geography bore with continuous persistence upon an unprotected people; and a brutal necessity drove the first Americans to come to terms with the landscape they had inherited. To exist as men, to live as West Europeans, they must immediately read the meanings of their respective empires, capitalize their obvious resources, fulfil their manifest destinies. The riddle of all migratory peoples confronted them; they must tie together the cut threads of their material and spiritual history, they must weave a new pattern of existence out of the stuffs of their new homeland and of the old world of Europe. It was a gigantic task; and in their deep need and desperate hurry, they turned naturally to the most immediate and the most easily obtainable of their resources. What the continent flaunted, they took; they could not be made to seek what it seemingly withheld. Their economies grew naturally, organically out of the very earth of the new world. It was not the sage wisdom of European statesmen which determined their development, but the brute facts of North American life. And the character and development of these two economies were to affect decisively not only their separate relations with the old world, but their mutual relations in the new.

In the region of the Atlantic seaboard, which by the end of the first half-century of settlement the English had acquired for their own, there developed a richly diversified way of life. The area invited a varied agricultural production; it encouraged, on the sea, a complex, cunningly adjusted and truly oceanic trade. From the stubborn soil and stern north temperate climate of New England, the coastal plain broadened out into the more fertile amplitudes of the middle colonies and passed southward into the lush richness of a region warmed by hot skies and watered by innumerable rivers and creeks. The sub-tropical products, tobacco, rice and cotton, were added to the homely, traditional roots and fruits and cereals of western Europe. But everywhere production called for husbandry, settlement, the consistent effort of a population established on the land; and, as the hewn forests receded westward, the life of the ploughed countryside collected in little villages and became concentrated in towns. There was great vitality in this economy, but its development was conditioned by certain definite limitations. For the great majority of these migrants trade was inevitably oceanic and not continental. They were granted a hundred outlets to the sea; but they were denied the single great eastern entrance to the continent. What they wanted from the Indians, the inhabitants of the interior, was chiefly land, not goods; and beyond the established settlements there extended, not a vast spectacular commercial empire, but a narrow, laborious land frontier. The rivers broke and dwindled, the forests and the hills closed in upon this agricultural community; but eastward, in generous compensation, were the inviting expanses of the sea. It was a wide horizon, bounded by the old world of England, France, Spain and Portugal, and by the new world of Newfoundland, Africa and the Indies; and across these expanses the colonial merchants drew, not a few direct and simple trade lines, but an increasingly intricate network of commercial communications. Neither they nor the English could prevent it. The abstractions of the mercantile system could not link the colonies and the motherland commercially when the practical needs of Englishmen and Americans did not necessitate a close commercial relationship. The trade of the Atlantic seaboard was not to be carried on over commercial trunk-lines which crossed the ocean undeviatingly to converge upon England. The paths of American commerce radiated over the Atlantic and no mercantilist wisdom could focus them in London.

This commerce, which in part competed with the interests of Great Britain, expanded continuously during the colonial period. Newfoundland, England, southern Europe, Africa and the West Indies were all drawn into the widening circle of American trade. Back of this expansion was the commercial energy of Philadelphia and New England; and back of New England were the resources of the forest and the cod from the "silver mines of the Atlantic". In the north, that eastern pull to which the whole of the seaboard was subject, the pull of the coast and the submerged continental shelf, was irresistible; and the hoard which the fishermen of Marblehead, Gloucester, Plymouth, Salem and Ipswich drew yearly from the banks and shoals and ledges stretching northward from Cape Cod, paid the way of the Americans around the ports of the Atlantic. The fishing industry enhanced the value and quickened the development of the subsidiary industries of the North Atlantic coast—lumbering, ship-building, distilling and the provision business. Under the rapid and magically repeated transmutations of commerce, cod became molasses, molasses rum, and rum turned into furs and manufactures and gold and slaves. The strangely varied component parts of this system were deftly combined into a great integration. It had toughness, elasticity and expansive powers. American trade burst through the imperial system to become international. The slaves which the New Englanders bought on the Guinea coast and sold to the planter plutocrats of Jamaica and Barbadoes, fulfilled the beneficent dual function of consuming inferior New England fish and of producing molasses for active New England distilleries. At last this southern trade, geared to increasing speed and capable of greater volume, broke into the French West India islands of Martinique and Guadeloupe.

On the continent, expansion paralleled and complemented expansion by the sea. Settlement, in search of closer bases for the ever-expanding fishery, felt its way instinctively and surely from New England up the coast to Acadia, which thus began to play its complicated role as an outpost of both the St. Lawrence and the north Atlantic seaboard. Trade worked more deeply inland, for though Anglo-American commerce was chiefly eastern and oceanic, there had always been an outlet to the west. This was the Hudson river, a stream of deep significance in North American history, which alone of all the rivers of the coastal plain threw off the hold of the Appalachians and alone pierced the inner defences of the St. Lawrence. It became the pathway of both military and commercial aggression. The easy route by Lake Champlain and the Richelieu led into the political centre of the St. Lawrence system; the Hudson, the Mohawk and Lake Ontario gave entrance to the western commercial empire of the French. Rum, made by New England distilleries out of molasses paid for by New England fish, English manufactures, guns, powder, kettles and cheap cloth, enabled both Dutch and English merchants to compete effectively in an area which the French regarded as their own preserve. In Albany, Schenectady, Oswego and the distant interior, was felt the final pressure of the first great synthesis of industry and commerce created on the Atlantic seaboard.

The economy of the north was in utter contrast with the industrial and commercial organization of the Atlantic seaboard. In the north, geography directed the activities of men with a blunt sternness; and it had largely helped to create a distinct and special American system. The lower St. Lawrence was for the French, as it is for the Canadians of today, the destined focus of any conceivable northern economy; and in response to an invitation which was at least half a command, settlement became inevitably concentrated on the strip of territory between Quebec and Montreal. Here were the lowlands of the St. Lawrence; but the restricted area drew men for other reasons than for its fertile land, and northern commerce was not to be built up upon a solid foundation of agricultural production. The river and the Shield, which seemed physically to overawe the valley with their force and mass, reduced the lowlands to a position of secondary economic importance. It was the final trunk-line of the western commercial system driving past Quebec and Montreal, which gave the rock and the river city their initial economic importance.

Agriculture struggled with an ineffectual persistence against the lures of the fur trade; and French officialdom, from Colbert on, tried to preserve settlement and farming from the too damaging encroachments of expansion and commerce. But the first important Canadian market and the first source of Canadian staples for export lay, not in the lowlands, but in the west. Settlement, encouraged rather by the fitful favour of French policy than by the inner necessities of commercial Canada, huddled close to the lower reaches of the St. Lawrence or ventured timidly down the Richelieu. There it stuck. The seigniory of Beaupré became the eastern limit of continuous settlement and the manor of New Longueuil was to be its outpost on the west: beyond this, east and west, there were only tiny communities and around them the forest and scarred upland closed with appalling abruptness. Population, in a country where mere numbers were unneeded and unwanted, increased slowly; and at the conquest there were but a scant sixty-five thousand French Canadians while the English in the Thirteen Colonies numbered perhaps a million and a half. Unlike the Anglo-American farmers, the peasants of the St. Lawrence valley produced food-stuffs not for export but for subsistence; and right up to the conquest there were years when they could not subsist upon what they had produced. The efforts of Talon and his successors to build up a diversified industrial system and to develop a trade in wheat and provisions were fated to be fruitless.

The trend of expansion from the St. Lawrence valley was towards the west; and the commercial empire of the north, in sharp contrast with that of the Atlantic seaboard, was inland and not oceanic. The St. Lawrence was incapable of playing an effective role in the task of building a vigorous union out of the maritime and continental colonies which had been established by the French. On the map, the number and the variety of these possessions were impressive. In the West Indies, the French held Guadeloupe, Martinique, St. Christopher and Tortuga—tropical islands which produced sugar and molasses. In the north, in that region bounded by Newfoundland, the Gulf of St. Lawrence and Acadia, where political dominion would be determined largely by mastery in the catch of fish, the French established little settlements in Gaspé and Acadia, at Isle St. Jean, Cape Breton and Placentia. These two groups of colonies—the sugar-producing and fish-producing settlements—together with the fur-producing colony of the St. Lawrence, made up the western dominion of the French. Puny and disconnected, they lay raggedly across the face of the new world; and the problem of uniting them in a robust integration despite the opposition of England and New England—of linking the St. Lawrence, the Maritimes and the West Indies together and with continental France—exhausted the strength and ingenuity of Frenchmen.

The New Englanders shouldered their way into the markets of the French West Indies. To the north, the French fishing settlements were overshadowed by Newfoundland which was growing with painful slowness as an outpost of the English fishery; and to the south, England's temporary ally, New England, flung the accumulating strength of its variously nourished economy into the fight for fishing grounds and markets. For over half the year, the connection between Canada and the French Atlantic colonies was broken by the ice barrier in the St. Lawrence; and the proximity of Acadia enabled New England to usurp the economic control of the maritime region. The French lost Acadia by the Treaty of Utrecht: and although within the restricted area of Gaspé, Isle St. Jean and Cape Breton they prolonged their resistance sufficiently to prove that the final fate of the fisheries region was uncertain, they failed either to make their maritime colonies self-sufficient or to link them effectively with the St. Lawrence and the islands to the south. France itself was incapable of exerting the inward pull which would draw these feeble and scattered American communities together. She could not compete effectively with England in the production of rough staple manufactures for colonial consumption; and, while she could take the furs and fish of America, she could not assist her north temperate colonies in supplying an adequate market for the produce of the French sugar islands. The lower St. Lawrence valley was the best possible centre of an integrated American economy of the French; but the St. Lawrence failed almost completely to emulate the example of New England and to offer independent co-operation to the motherland. The frozen river enforced the periodic isolation of Canada; and the colony was beset by the limitations and weaknesses of population, industry and commerce, which were inevitably inherent in a society based upon the river, the Shield and its furs. All this stunted the seaward expansion of the St. Lawrence; and Cape Breton depended for its existence and the French West Indies for their prosperity upon the commercial strength of New England and not of New France.

The St. Lawrence lacked energy in those very spheres where the vitality of the seaboard was abundant and insistent. The lower valley of the river was not the source of the chief Canadian export; nor was it the base of a complex oceanic trade. Canadian expansion drove impulsively westward, along the rivers and into the interior. The energy and initiative which lay dormant in the lowlands grew exuberantly in the western wilderness of rock and water and forest. Radisson, La Salle, La Vérendrye and the other heroes of exploration stand out from the ruck of men who passed westward along the waterways and unremembered out of life because in them the common compulsion troubling a whole society became the intense, solitary excitement of genius. It was trade which drew them all; for the Shield and its outlying fringes gave up the first and simplest of the Canadian staple products, beaver fur. Furs, a product of the Shield, obtainable by the river system of transportation, weighted the already heavy emphasis of the Precambrian formation and the St. Lawrence. Furs impelled the northerners to win that western commercial empire which the river seemed to offer to the daring. The expansion of the French was the penetration, not the occupation, of the west; it meant travel not home-building, and commerce not agriculture. And the future Upper Canada, the first great granary of the north, which was scarcely touched by French settlement, was passed and distanced by French trade.

Thus the society which grew up in the northern geographic province instinctively created that form of endeavour which was to dominate Canadian life until the conquest and for nearly a century thereafter. This was the northern commercial system, of which furs were the first staple; and the fur-trading organization of the French was the elementary expression of the major architectural style of Canadian business life. It was a distinct North American system, peculiar to Canada, with the immensity and simplicity which were characteristic of the landscape itself. From the ports of France, the northern commercial organization plunged in a single trunk-line across the Atlantic and up the river to Quebec and Montreal; but beyond the river city it spread out in increasing amplitude and with infinite ramifications over the enormous bulk of the Precambrian formation and over the central lowlands of the continent. This western territory, where the goods of Europe were exchanged for the goods of America, was the inland commercial empire of the St. Lawrence. The colony, weak in agriculture, weak in industry and seaward commerce, was tied in utter bondage to France; but it revenged this subordination in the east by its extravagantly ambitious pretensions in the hinterland of North America. The whole landscape annexed to the river of Canada, the lands which spread out north and south and westward of the Great Lakes were claimed and largely exploited by the commercial state which was centralized at Quebec and Montreal.

It seemed, in the first assertive youth of the northern society, as if the St. Lawrence might take possession of inland North America, as if the western edges of the continent would be the only limits of this vast, facile, unsubstantial commercial empire. The young fur-trading colony concentrated with passionate intentness upon the fulfilment of its own peculiar destiny. La Salle and La Vérendrye pressed south and westward to assert the ultimate claims of the northern system; and a long struggle began with those competitors who controlled the Hudson river and Hudson Bay, the two routes which rivalled the St. Lawrence as highways to the interior. It became at once the greatest ambition and the chief task of Canadians to enlarge the extent of their commercial dominion, to centralize it upon the lower reaches of the St. Lawrence and to protect it from the encroachments of rivals from the south and from the north.

The pressure of this system was enormous. The colony grew curiously—ungainly, misshapen, almost distorted—stamped by tasks and ambitions which were, on the whole, too great for it. The western commercial organization, which lasted as the dominant economic form for two centuries of Canadian history, rooted certain tendencies deeply in the society of the St. Lawrence: there were virtues and weaknesses, loyalties and antipathies which became fixed and almost ineradicable. It was western commerce which helped largely to determine the part which Canada would act in the affairs of European empires and the role which it would play in the politics of North America. A colony which scarcely rose above the level of feudal industry and which failed completely to develop a diversified trade, required a mature European metropolis both as a market and as a source of manufactures and supplies. Canada continued acquiescent and loyal within the French empire, for it was tied by every basic interest to the motherland. But while the northern commercial system inclined Canadian statesmen and merchants to passivity within the empire, it drove them to competition and conflict upon the North American continent. Their subserviency in the east was complemented by their aggressiveness in the west. Because they desired it as a commercial monopoly, the Canadians struggled to make the entire empire of the St. Lawrence a political unit. They sought to break the commercial competition of Hudson Bay and the Hudson river and to restrict the expansion of the Atlantic seaboard; for the bay and the river threatened to partition the western monopoly, and the march of settlement from the Atlantic seaboard involved the annihilation of the fur trade through the destruction of the hunting races. North and south of the St. Lawrence, Canada discovered its inevitable enemies; but in the centre of the continent, among the Indians, it found its natural allies. The primitive culture of the hunting Indians was essential to the fur-trading state; and the fur-trading state would alone preserve the Indians from extinction. It was more than an alliance: it was a political union. It was even a strange amalgam of two widely different cultures. The commercial system threaded through the native culture of the continent in tiny, intricate ramifications, changing it, debasing it, but effectively prolonging its existence. The Indians, giving up to the new westerners the fruits of their experience, the cunning adjustments of their heritage, and something of their proud, passionate independence, helped, in their turn, to create that curious western world of half-tones, that blent society where Europe and America met and mingled.

It was western trade, moreover, which largely determined the style of Canadian politics. Transcontinentalism, the westward drive of corporations encouraged and followed by the supercorporation of the state, is the major theme in Canadian political life; and it was stated, in its first simplicity, by the fur trade. The trade enforced commitments and determined policies. The state was based upon it: it was anterior to the state. Until 1663 Canada was governed by a series of trading corporations; then it became a commercial and military state. Colonial government derived its strength from taxes paid directly or indirectly by the western trade; and that strength was expended in an effort to extend the dominion of the fur trade and to protect it from competition. From the first, the government was committed to the programme of western exploitation by the river system. The St. Lawrence was an expensive monopoly; and its imperious demands could be met—and even then inadequately—only by the corporate effort of the northern society. The immense capital expenditures of the nineteenth and twentieth centuries were anticipated with startling clarity in the expensive military policy, the fortified posts, the presents to the Indians, by which Frontenac and his successors endeavoured to realize the destiny of the north. Inevitably, the instinct of both politicians and business men was towards unity and centralization, both for the management and the support of this monstrous western machine. Strong, centralized government was, of course, imported from old France; but its continuance in the new world was encouraged, rather than opposed, by the northern commercial system. It is true that the distant western trader, whether he was the employee or the debtor of a Montreal merchant, shouldered his aggressive individuality through an inevitably relaxed restraint. But the laxity which obtained on the frontiers of the system was abandoned as the river in its last concentration drove north-eastward towards the sea. Here trade, its management and its final defences, were concentrated; and the twin cities, Quebec and Montreal, were the two symbols, military and commercial, of a single unified system.

IV

Two worlds lay over against each other in North America and their conflict was not only probable but certain. Between those who possessed and those who were denied the single great eastern entrance to the continent, the hostility of war could subside only into the competition of peace. With the whole pressure of its material and spiritual being, each society was impelled to maintain its separateness and to achieve its dominion. They contradicted each other, they crowded each other; and the wars and raids and surprises which fill the seventeenth and eighteenth centuries are but outward manifestations of a great, essential and slowly maturing conflict. When Dongan laboured to defy Montreal from Albany, when the British built Halifax to overawe Louisbourg, when Washington toiled westward against Fort Duquesne, they did not so much initiate clashes as reveal the points at which two ponderously moving systems would be forced into reverberating collision. Here were two geographic provinces occupied by culturally distinct peoples; here were two economies controlled by antagonistic national states. Of their essence, the St. Lawrence and the seaboard denied each other. Riverways against seaways, rock against farmland, trading posts against ports and towns and cities, *habitants* against farmers and fur traders against frontiersmen—they combined, geography and humanity, in one prime contradiction.

With the excuse and with the stimulation of the imperial wars, the conflict in North America developed on its own lines, created its own strategy and tactics and discovered its own battlefields. Along the arc which stretched from the Gulf of St. Lawrence to the Mississippi and wherever these two systems touched or threatened each other, the conflict flared or smouldered. The seaward extension of the St. Lawrence cut like a boulevard through the finest fishing grounds in the West European-American world; and the French, weak as they were in the region, were determined to keep the gulf, the islands and Acadia as the outposts of their inland, and as the citadels of their maritime, empire. From Newfoundland, which lay like "a great English ship moored near the Banks", the English fishery expanded competitively into the area. From the south, New England, with the strength of its fused industrial and commercial organization, developed its fishing interests and pushed its settlements into Acadia. A little westward of this, where the river flowed between the Appalachians and the Canadian Shield the St. Lawrence temporarily threw off the clutch of its competitors; and its inner strength was fittingly expressed in the lofty symbol of the fortress of Quebec. But almost immediately beyond this, the inroads of geography and humanity began again. The Hudson river, by its two extensions, Lake Champlain and the Richelieu on the one hand and the Mohawk on the other, pierced through the easy outward defences of the St. Lawrence into the quick of the whole system. New York, backed by the industrial and commercial power of the North Atlantic seaboard, developed this natural highway with a chain of outposts from Albany past Schenectady to Oswego; and as middlemen the Iroquois extended competition throughout the west.

In the central lowlands of the continent, La Salle and those who followed him had established a counterfeit dominion. There was deception in the very grandeur of the Great Lakes. The country which spread out around them in such easy undulations was not a single geographic province: and the lakes crowded a territory which was unexpectedly narrow for them. A short way below the northern system, a low and almost indistinguishable height of land separated the waters of the Mississippi from those of the St. Lawrence. On the north, the rivers of James and Hudson Bay—the Rupert, the Moose, the Albany and the Nelson—pressed dangerously close. Radisson and La Salle passed with easy confidence into territory which, even from a geographical point of view, was competitive; and time could only reveal more fully the enormous northern and southern pull of Hudson Bay and the Mississippi. The Hudson's Bay Company, backed by the great strength of commercial England, began to invade the northwestern, fur-trading country of the French which centered at Lake Winnipeg. By the middle of the eighteenth century, land companies began the scramble for grants by the "western waters" of the Mississippi; and the first discontented pioneers from Virginia and Philadelphia began to mark out the trail that led by Cumberland Gap and the Wilderness Road to the Ohio.

At all these points, where the economy of the St. Lawrence clashed with the rival economies of North America, struggles necessarily arose. They were neither haphazard nor transitory, they were rooted in the continent; and they were to reveal an almost indestructible permanence in the future. The first inhabitants of North America did not create these prime contradictions: they discovered them. The vital quarrel in the new continent was not a mere extension of the political rivalries of Europe; it was not wholly a result of those cultural differences which had been imported from Europe by the first migrants. It was, in part, American, it was a product of North America. It was fought, not only by British and French regulars, but also by Americans—by explorers, seigneurs, fur traders and Indians, by fishermen, Boston apprentices, frontiersmen and Virginia planters. Never was this American conflict completely fused in the imperial war which overshadowed it: its beats and pulses could not be perfectly regulated by the timing of European wars and European diplomacy. To be sure, the naval and military strength of Europe helped to magnify these American disputes and European diplomacy marked the main stages in their evolution. But the tumult in the maritime region did not cease with the Peace of Utrecht and the conflict impending in the Ohio country was not prevented by the solemn affirmations of Aix-la-Chapelle. Irrepressibly, the struggle in North America developed in its own way, in response to its own inner urgencies; and, though Europe might enhance or weaken American forces, it could neither create nor destroy them.

The British conquest, therefore, while it made changes and portended others, did not alter certain fundamentals of Canadian life. The conquest did not end the rivalry between the economies of North America, for it could not. The French could be beaten in America; but the St. Lawrence could not surrender in Europe. The northern commercial system remained what it had been—a distinct and competitive American economy, strong enough, despite its undeniable weakness, to arouse jealousy and fear and to enforce a certain respect. The departure of one set of officials and the arrival of another could not change the main trend of its development. In a certain sense, the French were not really the builders of the northern commercial empire: they were its first owners, its first occupants. They read the meaning of the region, they evoked its spirit, and they first dreamed the dream which the river inspired in the minds of all who came to live upon its banks. What the French saw, what they did and what they failed to do formed an experience which had not merely a limited national significance: it was an astonishingly correct anticipation of the experience of successive generations of northerners. With the surrender of the transportation system of the St. Lawrence, there was passed on also to the victors the commercial philosophy based upon it. It was accepted without pause or question. The new northerners, who succeeded to the direction of the St. Lawrence after the conquest, diverged from the lines laid down by the French only in the attempt to repair their failures. They clung to the conquests of the French and they tried to recapture their concessions.

These facts were at first imperfectly understood. After the conquest of Canada, Great Britain held the whole of North America except the south-west sector—an empire which stretched unbrokenly from Labrador to Florida. The British imagined they could unify this empire and standardize its various parts. They tried, in 1763, to make Quebec a typical American colony in a unified continental dominion. But they were wrong: for Quebec was an unusual colony and it had no part or lot in the affairs of the Atlantic seaboard. It had its own organization and its own internal problems. It nursed a special ambition for the west of North America and it was bound by unusually strong ties to the metropolis in Europe. Thus the Peace of Paris and the subsequent efforts of the British to unify and standardize their American empire violated the logic of facts on the St. Lawrence as well as in other parts of the new continent. It is significant that the peace and the imperial reorganization were followed by twenty years of increasing tumult which culminated in the political division of the continent roughly upon the lines which the French had already established. The French and the British were both humbled in America; but through all the curious chances and reverses of the eighteenth century, the St. Lawrence managed to preserve its individuality and its separateness.

The conquest could not change Canada. In fact, in some ways, it strengthened the dominant impulse of Canadian life. It tied Canada to Great Britain, a commercial and maritime power far stronger than France; and it opened the St. Lawrence to the capital and enterprise of Britain and British America. To the defeated society of the north it brought fresh enthusiasm, a new strength and a different leadership. But this injection of new vigour, while it strengthened commercial Canada, necessarily raised the problem of assimilation. The conquest brought two groups of Americans, different even in terms of their Americanism, within the limits of a single colony; and it remained for the future to determine how long and how effectively they could co-operate in the struggle for the western trade. It was certain that the British Canadians would fight to realize the commercial empire of the St. Lawrence; but it was equally certain that they would be forced to fight in company with the Canadians of French descent.

The British Conquest:
Canadian Social Scientists and the Fate of the *Canadiens*

Michel Brunet

SOCIAL SCIENTISTS HAVE the task of describing how human societies are built, how they develop, how they are arrested in their development, how they disintegrate, how they vanish. Such an undertaking is not an easy one. It requires long research, and much hard and fresh thinking about man's behaviour. Unfortunately, social sciences are still in their infancy. This field of knowledge has always been and is still neglected. For centuries, most social scientists were mere defenders of the *status quo*. They were entrusted with the job of vindicating the ruling classes to which they belonged or whose servants they were. Only a few thinkers did sincerely try to meditate upon the motives and interests which influence human history. Some reformers did unmask the false dogmas upon which the social order of their time rested. They were looked at with scorn, fear, or hostility in official and academic circles. One always takes the risk of being persecuted or ignored when one dares to question the social and political conceptions of the dominant minority.

We are now in the second half of the twentieth century. In the natural sciences, man has freed himself of all the fallacies which formerly impeded the extension of his knowledge of material things. Every day new frontiers of learning are opened to man's inquiry. But in the social sciences there has been little progress because too many social scientists have satisfied themselves with repeating the commonplaces, platitudes, and watchwords of past generations. They have not gone beyond the romantic period of the nineteenth century. Their vocabulary is a Victorian one. Others have spent their time writing long and dull monographic studies on minor topics and have missed the fundamental questions of their craft. Were they afraid to challenge the social creeds of their time and to contest the validity of their forefathers' ideology? Was the power of the ruling class so overwhelming that they have felt compelled to keep silent? Perhaps the majority have been the unconscious victims of social conformity.

In any case, the result is that we live in a world we do not understand. We are almost powerless to meet the problems of our industrialized and urbanized society. Social scientists must reconsider their frame of reference if they want to make a real,

---

"The British Conquest: Canadian Social Scientists and the Fate of the Canadiens" from *Canadian Historical Review*, 40:1 (1959), pp. 93–107 by Michel Brunet. Reprinted by permission of University of Toronto Press Incorporated, www.utpjournals.com.

*The Gray Lecture delivered at the University of Toronto, October 31, 1958. Reprinted from *Canadian Historical Review*, XL (2), June, 1959.

scientific, attempt to explain the political, economic, and social evolution of the Atlantic world from the Renaissance to our confused contemporary age. A new approach is needed, and the need is urgent.

There are many proofs of the social scientists' failures and shortcomings. It is not my intention to draw up an inventory. I shall confine myself to an historical and sociological problem which I have long studied: what has actually been the historical evolution of the French-Canadian collectivity since the British Conquest and occupation of the St. Lawrence valley, and how have four generations of social scientists interpreted this historical fact?

With the help of France, and under the direction of their natural leaders, the *Canadiens* had organized a colonial society in North America. They had the legitimate ambition of developing alone and for their own profit the St. Lawrence valley. For a century and a half, they succeeded in maintaining their separateness and their collective freedom.

Being too weak to keep for themselves the northern half of the continent, the *Canadiens* were defeated, conquered, and occupied. Many of their leaders, having realized that their interests as a ruling class were in jeopardy under a foreign domination, decided to emigrate. The mass of the people could not follow them and had no choice but to submit to the British invaders who now ruled the colony. French Canada could no longer rely on its mother country whose support it vitally needed to grow normally. A colonial nation is always the offspring of a metropolis devoted to its progress. Deprived of this help, the *Canadiens* were left to their own resources which were very limited. Their new lay leaders had no influence in politics and business. Their priests became their principal spokesmen, yet the collaboration of the clergy was necessary to the British authorities and they skillfully managed to keep it. As a collectivity, the *Canadiens* were doomed to an anaemic survival. One must never forget that to survive is not to live.

Canada now belonged to a new collectivity. Having taken into their hands political and economic control of the St. Lawrence valley, the British administrators and merchants—the cleverer among them—wanted to establish a prosperous colonial nation of their own stock. With the generous protection of Great Britain they succeeded. Their metropolis sent them settlers, technicians, educators, capital investments, and military support. A second Kingdom of Canada was born and it was British.

The new inhabitants of Canada, who first called themselves the British Americans, had hoped that they would completely assimilate the *Canadiens*. After the 1820's, some shrewd leaders of British Canada realized that it was impossible to achieve this aim. But they knew that the *Canadiens* had no chance of remaining a majority in the St. Lawrence valley. In fact, they were finally outnumbered by the British during the fourth decade of the nineteenth century. There was then no racial reason for delaying the granting of responsible government to the colony. The French-Canadian voters no longer threatened British-Canadian domination. The

British political leaders and businessmen had the assurance that they would forever run the country they had built. The *Canadiens* had become a minority group whose survival the British majority had come to tolerate, with more or less good grace. Actually, they had no choice.

These are the bare facts. Now let us see what the social scientists have said. William Smith, who wrote his *History of Canada* at the beginning of the nineteenth century, gives an appalling description of all the wrongs the *Canadiens* were supposed to have suffered during the French régime and summons them to kneel before their British benefactors who had conquered them only to liberate them: "How happy, then, ought the Canadians to be, that God in his Providence, has severed them from the ancient stock to which they belonged, and committed them to the care of a Monarch, who, by making the success of his arms the means of extending his beneficence, has an incontestible right to their affectionate fidelity."[1] In 1828, John Fleming, a Montreal businessman and amateur historian, seriously maintained that Great Britain had waged war against the *Canadiens* and taken possession of their country "less from views of ambition and the security of the other Colonies, than from the hope of improving their situation, and endowing them with the privileges of freemen."[2] Fleming's testimony was approvingly invoked by R. Montgomery Martin in his history, *The British Colonies*, first published in the 1830's.[3]

Francis Parkman, one of the greatest romantic historians, did not think differently. He believed that France could not give to the *Canadiens* the benefits of self-government because only the "German race, and especially the Anglo-Saxon branch of it, is particularly masculine, and, therefore, peculiarly fitted for self-government." As members of the French Empire, the "people of New France remained in a state of political segregation" and were kept in order by the armed forces of the king of France, according to Parkman. But, at last, the English Conquest

> was the beginning of a new life. With England came Protestantism, and the Canadian church grew purer and better in the presence of an adverse faith. Material growth, an increased mental activity, an education real though fenced and guarded, a warm and genuine patriotism, all date from the peace of 1763. England imposed by the sword an reluctant Canada the boon of rational and ordered liberty. Through centuries of striving she had advanced from stage to stage of progress, deliberate and calm, never breaking with the past, but making each fresh gain the base of a new success, enlarging popular liberties while abating nothing of that height and force of individual development which is the

---

[1] William Smith, *History of Canada* (Québec, 1815), 1, 383.

[2] [John Fleming], *Political Annals of Lower Canada* (Montréal, 1828), lxxiii.

[3] R. Montgomery Martin, *The British Colonies* (London, n.d.), 1,15.

brain and heart of civilization; and now, through a hard-earned victory, she taught the conquered colony to share the blessings she had won. A happier calamity never befell a people than the conquest of Canada by the British arms.[4]

Parkman sang this hymn to British liberty in 1874. Ten years later, he repeated that "civil liberty was given them [the *Canadiens*] by the British sword." However, his opinion of the Catholic Church had changed. He then regretted that the British conquerors had left the *Canadiens* free to exercise a religion that had transformed them into one of the "most priest-ridden communities of the modern world."[5] As a social scientist, Parkman should have known that the ecclesiastical pre-eminence he noted in French Canada, at the end of the nineteenth century, was one of the consequences of the British conquest and occupation. But how many social scientists have realized that?

William Kingsford, who published a ten volume *History of Canada* between 1887 and 1898, had nothing new to say. He had learned well the lesson taught by all his predecessors. According to his preconceptions and the accepted historical interpretation of his time, the *Canadiens* had been exploited and mistreated when Canada was a French colony. But the situation had rapidly changed under the "British rule which first awoke the French Canadian rural population to the duties, the obligations and independence of manhood."[6] Did Kingsford believe that the *Canadiens* had all been infants when they had lived alone in the St. Lawrence valley and fully enjoyed their freedom as a collectivity? In 1894, giving a survey of the colony around 1784, the same historian declared that the "rural population had remained unchanged in their social and political views, and shewed no inclination to accept the impulse of any modern movement."[7] Should we conclude that the awakening of the *Canadiens* to "the duties, the obligations and independence of manhood" under the benevolent guidance of their fatherly conquerors had not been completed after twenty-four years of British occupation? Were they so ungrateful and unintelligent that they refused to co-operate in their own liberation? Kingsford did not concern himself with these questions. With the over-confidence and naïveté of a Victorian imperialist convinced that the British Empire, in taking its share of the white man's burden, had a mission to civilize the backward *Canadiens*, he stated: "It is plain that

---

[4] Francis Parkman, *The Old Regime in Canada* (Boston, 1889), 397–8, 398, 395, 400–1. This book was first published in 1874. One must note that Parkman uses the challenge and response hypothesis. The latter has always been popular because it pleases the imagination, but scientifically speaking its value is very limited.

[5] Francis Parkman, *Montcalm and Wolfe: France and England in North America* (Centenary Edition, Boston, 1922), II, 427. This book was first published in 1884.

[6] William Kingsford, *The History of Canada*, IV (Toronto, 1890), 451.

[7] *Ibid.*, VII, (1894), 195.

whatever be the ethnological character of the French Canadians, that it has been under the British government that they have attained to the force and power they possess, and have moulded themselves to the type they present. The political liberty they have enjoyed has enabled them thus to increase in number and prosperity." To back up his assertions, he recalled that from 1632 to 1760 the *Canadiens* had increased to a total population of only 60,000 while from 1760 to 1838 (a period of 128 years like the preceding one), they had become a people of 1,250,000.[8] A high birth rate does not necessarily prove that a people is prosperous and free. Nor did the author take into account that the *Canadiens* had lived, since the Conquest, under the political and economic domination of the British *bourgeoisie*. Even if they were 1,250,000 strong in 1888, they were a minority group whose influence and resources were very limited when compared to those of the English population of Canada. A social scientist, who has an obligation to describe the actual situation of the collectivity he studies, is bound not to overlook, or hide, these fundamental facts.

Are the twentieth century historians and sociologists more realistic? Have they been able to renounce the political and social preconceptions of the romantic and Victorian eras? Old creeds endure, even among people who are responsible for the advancement of human knowledge. Man is so lazy that he does not easily change his mind. He feels so secure when he repeats the commonplaces and slogans of past generations. Smith, Fleming, Parkman, and Kingsford still continue to influence all the social scientists who write about French Canada, even those who have never read these old authors. The ideas of these earlier writers are part of an oral tradition which is carried uncritically from one generation to the next. Nor does such a process only occur, as we are inclined to believe, among the lower and more ignorant classes. It happens frequently, too frequently indeed, in academic circles, where young scholars let themselves be directed into the well-worn tracks of their teachers.

Among the modern historians Professor A. L. Burt has devoted many years of his scholarly life to the study of Canada after the British Conquest. His book, *The Old Province of Quebec*, is still one of the major works in Canadian history. The author has enlarged our knowledge of this period. Unfortunately, he has contributed nothing new on the French-Canadian problem. Like all his predecessors, he has failed to see what was the actual position of the *Canadiens*, as a collectivity, before and after the British Conquest. He goes so far as to maintain that they "had been forced to live an unnatural life under governors of their own blood, but under rulers of an alien race they were to find themselves."[9] He is sincerely convinced that the British occupation benefited the "French in Canada [who] were the first considerable body of an alien race to taste that liberty which is larger than English liberty and is the secret of the modern British commonwealth of nations."[10] For him, the *Canadiens* obtained from

---

[8] *Ibid.*, IV, 502–3

[9] A. L. Burt, *The Old Province of Quebec* (Toronto, 1933), 12.

[10] *Ibid.*, 56.

their conquerors the "liberty to be themselves."[11] How can a people living under the domination of a conqueror be free? Has not Professor Burt himself noted that the *Canadiens* on the eve of the War of 1812, after more than sixty years of British liberty, "were now openly resenting the rule of their British masters."[12] One can then suppose that they did not feel that they had the "liberty to be themselves." In fact, they began to resent the British rule immediately after the Conquest.[13] Their reaction was that of any collectivity living under the yoke of its former enemies. It cannot be otherwise. How can a social scientist overlook this fact?

Professor Edgar McInnis, whose textbook on Canadian history is perhaps the best yet published, realizes that the British businessmen, enjoying a privileged situation, "stepped right into the key positions in the economic life of the province of Quebec, and that fact made them of salient importance in political affairs as well."[14] If the words he uses have any meaning, one must infer that the *Canadiens* were compelled to bow down before the economic and political domination of the British invaders. This is actually what happened. But the author does not seem to take into account what he himself has written for he asserts a few lines below: "The French had much cause to feel that their fortunes had been improved by the change of masters."[15] Like all his predecessors, Professor McInnis does not realize that the *Canadiens,* when they lived alone in the St. Lawrence valley, were their own masters. Their relationship with France was that of a colonial nation with her metropolis which worked, in collaboration with the colonial leaders, for their collective benefit. Associated by force with the British Empire, they were reduced to the status of a subjected people. Great Britain had not conquered Canada for the good of the *Canadiens* but for the development of British colonization in North America.

Every book published by Professor D. G. Creighton is a landmark in Canadian historiography. In reaction to the nationalist school of historians who had over-emphasized the English Canadians' struggle to achieve self-government and depicted Great Britain as the villain of the story, he has shown what is the actual basis of Canadian separateness in North America and how great is English Canada's debt to its mother country. On many topics of Canadian history, his authority is, and shall remain, unchallenged. However, his approach to French Canada is still that of

---

[11] The title of the fifth chapter of A. L. Burt's textbook, *A Short History of Canada for Americans* (Minneapolis, 1942 and 1944), 57.

[12] A. L. Burt, *The United States, Great Britain and British North America from the Revolution to the Establishment of the Peace after the War of 1812* (Toronto, 1940), 319.

[13] See Michel Brunet, "Les Canadiens après la Conquête: Les débuts de la résistance passive," *Revue d'histoire de l' Amérique française,* XII (Sept. 1958), 170–207.

[14] Edgar McInnis, *Canada: A Political and Social History* (Toronto, 1947), 131.

[15] *Ibid.,* 132.

Parkman's. He declares: "To the defeated society of the north it [the British Conquest] brought fresh enthusiasm, a new strength and a different leadership. But this injection of new vigour, while it strengthened commercial Canada, necessarily raised the problem of assimilation."[16] How can a "defeated society," placed under the domination of an alien *bourgeoisie* and engaged in a process of assimilation by its conquerors, become stronger? For Professor Creighton, the *Canadiens'* opposition to their conquerors' rule was merely a "struggle between commercialism represented aggressively by the merchants and a decadent semi-feudal society defended by peasants and professional men."[17] The *Canadiens,* for various reasons, having not been completely assimilated by the British inhabitants of the St. Lawrence valley, Professor Creighton asks himself if the Conquest has not given a "chance that an older, simpler, more devout France, the France of the seventeenth, not of the eighteenth, century, would maintain its footing and even increase its influence in North America?"[18] A society is a living organism, not a museum. Is it possible to compare the influence which the *Canadiens* have had since 1760, in the St. Lawrence valley and in North America, to that they exerted at the time of the French North American Empire?

Among contemporary Canadian historians, Professor A. R. M. Lower has made a commendable effort to understand French-Canadian collective behaviour. But his interpretation of French Canada's history follows the traditional path. He has come to the startling conclusion that: "What saved French liberty was its loss—its loss in the English conquest, for out of conquest came eventually the English institutional apparatus of freedom—popular government and all the guarantees of the common law. . . . If the rule of France had not been terminated, New France in the course of time might or might not have drifted off to some kind of independence: what it would not have done would have been to secure the institutions of freedom with which it is now familiar."[19] Does Professor Lower prefer the "English institutional apparatus of freedom" to freedom itself? As a political scientist who has studied with enthusiasm the liberal democratic way of life, he knows that a people cannot leave to another people the care of its liberty because, as he himself explains, "liberty left to others to look after turns out to be slavery."[20] A conquered nation that is unable to drive out the invaders and finally becomes a minority group in its native land loses its right to self-determination. For it, there is no independence. Professor Lower should have realized this when he once wrote: "Conquest is a type of slavery. . . . The entire life-structure of the conquered is laid open to their masters. They become

---

[16] Donald G. Creighton, *The Empire of the St. Lawrence* (Toronto, 1956), 21. This book was first published in 1937.

[17] *Ibid.,* 126.

[18] Donald G. Creighton, *Dominion of the North: A History of Canada* (Boston, 1944), 144.

[19] Arthur R. M. Lower, *Canada: Nation and Neighbour* (Toronto, 1952), 49.

[20] A. R. M. Lower, *This Most Famous Stream: The Liberal Democratic Way of Life* (Toronto, 1954), 9.

second-rate people."[21] It is evident that this author has not meditated long enough upon the historical facts submitted to his observation or the political principles he has himself enunciated. No other Anglo-Canadian historian was in a better position to describe accurately the fate of the *Canadiens*.

Sociologists who have studied the French-Canadian collectivity have simply repeated the historians.[22] One must not criticize them too severely because, after all, what can sociologists do when historians give them false references about the past history of the society they observe?[23] Without the background knowledge that historians alone can furnish, sociologists are powerless. Professor Everett C. Hughes and all his disciples (and they are numerous) have much difficulty in trying to prove that the *Canadiens* have formed a folk society since the seventeenth century. In accordance with the old historical interpretation, these writers have convinced themselves that the British Conquest and occupation did not modify the social structure of French Canada. On the other hand, they realize that French Canadians, as a group, are in a position of subordination. They have discovered the explanation for this situation. For them, the *Canadiens* are struggling under the impact of twentieth-century industrialization. The former folk society of French Canada is crumbling and its members are painfully adapting themselves to the industrial and urban age. So speak the sociologists and anthropologists. They all agree that it is a toilsome and slow social process. A few among them think that French-Canadian society will melt away by integration and acculturation. These new pedantic and mysterious words are now used to name a social phenomenon which was formerly called, more accurately, assimilation. Others are more optimistic and seem sure that the *Canadiens* will overcome this ordeal. The political, economic, social, and cultural problems to which industrialization and urbanization give rise present a challenge to any society. There is no exception for French Canada. But one must never lose sight of the fact that a foreign conquest and occupation is the greatest impact a society can ever meet. How can social scientists ignore this fact when they study French Canada? Moreover, the Redfield school of sociologists should know that the *Canadiens* have never formed a folk society!

---

[21] A. R. M. Lower, *Colony to Nation: A History of Canada* (Toronto, 1946), 63.

[22] See Everett C. Hughes, *Rencontre de deux mondes: La crise d'industrialisation du Canada français* (Montréal, 1944), 13. (This book was published in 1943 under the English title, *French Canada in Transition*, and translated into French by Professor Jean-Charles Palardeau, Director of the Department of Sociology at Laval University); Everett C. and Helen M. Hughes, *Where Peoples Meet: Racial and Ethnic Frontiers* (Glencoe, Ill., 1952), 114; Horace Miner, *St. Denis, a French-Canadian Parish* (Chicago, 1939).

[23] See also the statements of the following historians: Frank Basil Tracy, *The Tercentenary History of Canada* (Toronto, 1908), 11, 557, 562; Mary Quayle Innis, *An Economic History of Canada* (Toronto, 1935), 63, John Bartlet Brehner, *The North Atlantic Triangle* (Toronto, 1945), 32–5, 48–9; G. P. de T. Glazebrook, *A Short History of Canada* (Oxford, 1950), 82, 90, Gerald S. Graham, *Canada: A Short History* (London, 1950), 63, 74: J. M. S. Careless, *Canada: A Story of Challenge* (Cambridge, 1953), 93, 100; Mason Wade, *The French Canadians, 1760–1945* (Toronto, 1955), 44, 47–8, 88.

French Canadians themselves have been unable, for two centuries, to understand the actual causes of their ordeal as a collectivity. The first spokesmen of French Canada, after the Conquest, were obliged to collaborate with the British authorities under whose thumb they now had to live. They developed the habit of flattering their conquerors with the hope of gaining their protection. They gradually adopted all the commonplaces, watchwords, and slogans of their British masters about the rights of Englishmen and the exceptional merits of the British constitution. They spoke with scorn of the French régime knowing very well that such a language pleased the government and the British merchants. Indeed, the *Canadiens* who were responsible for dealing with the British administration and *bourgeoisie* were not free to act or think differently. They had to conciliate the invaders who occupied their country. The result was that after one generation, the leaders of French Canada had almost assimilated all the official thinking of their British rulers.

The Church did much to contribute to the dissemination of this British propaganda. One must always remember that the ecclesiastical administrators, whose influence was now very great in a society deprived of its natural lay leaders, became the most faithful supporters of the British domination immediately after the Conquest. By granting the Church a few privileges, the conquerors skilfully secured their devotion. The French Revolution strengthened this bond. The priesthood and all church-going *Canadiens* came to the conclusion that God himself had favoured the British Conquest of Canada in order to protect the Catholic Church of this country and the *nation canadienne* from the abuses and horrors of this wicked revolution. The British did their best to propagate this providential interpretation of their coming to the St. Lawrence valley. The French royalist priests whom the London government encouraged to immigrate to Canada from 1792 to 1802 were very useful to this end. Many generations of *Canadiens* have asked themselves with alarm what would have been their fate if they had been members of the French Empire during the revolutionary era. Even today, this question still troubles some conservative minded French-Canadian leaders who have not yet rejected the legends their forefathers believed in.

A speech delivered by Louis-Joseph Papineau, then Speaker of the House of Lower Canada, on the occasion of the death of George III, reveals to what extent the leaders of the conquered *Canadiens* had embraced the political thinking of their masters:

> George III, a sovereign respected for his moral qualities and his devotion to his duties, succeeded Louis XV, a prince justly despised for his debauches, for his lack of attention to the needs of the people, and for his senseless prodigality to his favorites and mistresses. Since that epoch the reign of law has succeeded to that of violence; since that day the treasure, the fleet, and the armies of Great Britain have been employed to provide us with an effective protection against all foreign danger; since that day her best laws have become ours, while our faith, our property, and the laws by which they were governed have been conserved; soon afterwards the privi-

leges of her free constitution were granted us, infallible guarantees of our domestic prosperity if it is observed. Now religious tolerance; trial by jury, the wisest guarantee which has ever been established for the protection of innocence; security against arbitrary imprisonment, thanks to the privilege of the *habeas corpus;* equal protection guaranteed by law to the person, honor, and property of citizens; the right to obey only laws made by us and adopted by our representatives—all these advantages have become our birthright, and will be, I hope, the lasting heritage of our posterity. In order to conserve them, we should act like British subjects and free men.[24]

Papineau made no distinction between individual rights and collective freedom. Under the British domination, the *Canadiens* enjoyed the right of property, although in this respect, one must not forget the confiscation of the Jesuits' estates and all the wrongs the other religous communities suffered; they could exercise their religion, but the bishop and all ecclesiastical administrators were subjected to close and suspicious supervision by the colonial and imperial authorities.[25] They were entitled to a fair trial when arrested, and they elected representatives to a House of Assembly with very limited powers. Indeed, there is no reason to cry out in admiration of the British administration. But the "English institutional apparatus of freedom" did impress Papineau for a while. When he tried to give some meaning to British liberty and claimed for the *Canadiens,* who constituted the majority of the population in Lower Canada, the right to govern themselves, he and his followers were crushed by British military forces. If the *Canadiens* had been entrusted with the government of the St. Lawrence valley, it would have seriously jeopardized the future of British colonization in North America. Lower and Upper Canada were united. The *Canadiens,* now reduced to the status of a minority group, had to accept the leadership of the British Americans who took control of the government of a united Canada. Papineau, LaFontaine, Morin, and all the other French-Canadian leaders of the 1840's did not understand what had actually happened. Some of them were naïve enough to believe that they had obtained for their people the right to self-government. The French-Canadian leaders who have since succeeded them have laboured under the same delusion. They boast that they have achieved Canada's independence for the *Canadiens!*

Social scientists of French Canada have not been more clear-sighted than its politicians. Men of action are not bound to analyse the social and political evolution of the collectivity. They have other problems to face and to solve. However, historians, political scientists, and sociologists have the task of giving a true picture of the society they study. With the exception of François Xavier-Garneau who partly realized what had been the consequences of the British Conquest for the *Canadiens* as a people,[26] French-Canadian historians have, in general, adopted with only a few slight

[24] The speech was delivered in July 1820; quoted in Wade, *French Canadians,* 127–8.
[25] For example, the bishop was forbidden to convene a synod, and be could not travel abroad.
[26] See François-Xavier Garneau, *Histoire du Canada* (4 vols., Québec, 1845–52), III, 296, 303–4; IV, 313.

differences the historical interpretation of the American and English-Canadian scholars.[27] This fact is a striking one and it has never been adequately pointed out. It indicates that the French-Canadian upper classes have been engaged, since the Conquest, in a process of assimilation to English Canada. The assimilation of one people by another always begins with its leaders. But one has also to take into consideration that the teaching of social sciences has long been and is still neglected in French-Canadian universities. Laval University, founded in 1852, and the University of Montreal, a mere branch of Laval from 1876 to 1920, have never had the intellectual traditions and the financial resources required to become genuine institutions of higher learning. The situation has somewhat improved during the last ten years but there are still too few French-Canadian scholars carrying on fresh investigations in the social sciences. The low standard of education in French Canada has been one of the numerous misfortunes which befell the *Canadiens* since the Conquest of their homeland.[28] Too many people—not always ill-intentioned—who have deplored or denounced the ignorance of the *Canadiens* have overlooked the fact that, from 1760 to the second half of the nineteenth century, they were unable to organize a decent school system. France could no longer send them the teachers they needed and the French government had discontinued its financial grants to education. On the other hand, the *Canadiens* could not count on the help of the British authorities. Is it necessary to recall the fate of the College of Quebec?

Social scientists from both French and English Canada, and foreign students of French-Canadian history, have all failed to describe the actual situation of the *Canadiens* as a people because their frame of reference was inadequate. They have never seriously asked themselves how a society forms itself—especially a colonial society—and under what conditions it comes to maturity. How can it be arrested in its development and reduced to a status of mere survival? Why does a society disappear? These are the essential questions a social scientist must bring forward and answer to fulfil his responsibility as a scholar. Unfortunately, the social sciences have not yet shaken off the limitations of amateurism and romanticism. Social scientists are too often literary men who become students of society by accident, and their approach is often that of the novelist.

---

[27] See Michel Bibaud, *Histoire du Canada sous la domination française* (Montréal, 1843), 414; and *Histoire du Canada et des Canadiens sous la domination anglaise* (Montréal, 1844), 5; G.-H. Macaulay, *Passé, présent et avenir du Canada* (Montréal, 1859), 6; Philippe Aubert de Gaspé, *Les Anciens Canadiens* (Québec, 1863), 202; *Les Ursulines de Québec depuis leur établissement jusqu'a nos jours* (Québec, 1863–6), III, 349; J.-S. Raymond, "Enseignements des évenements contemporains, *Revue canadiense,* VIII (1871), 55; Benjamin Sulte, *Histoire des Canadiens-Français* (Montréal, 1882–4), VII, 134; L.-F.-G. Baby, "L'exode des classes dirigeantes à la cession du Canada," *The Canadien Antiqustrian and Numismatic Journal,* 3rd series, II (1899), 127; Desrosiers et Fournet, *La Race française en Amérique* (Montréal, 1910), 292; Thomas Chapais, *Cours d'histoire des Canada* (Québec, 1919–40), 1, 3–5; Lionel Groulx, *Lendemains de conquête* (Montrél, 1920), 182, 183, 216, 232–3, 235; Gustave Lanctót, "Situation politique de l'Eglise canadienne sous le régime français," *Rapports de la Société canadienne d'histoire de l'Eglise catholique,* VIII (1910–1), 56.

[28] See Lionel Groulx, *L'Enseignement français au Canada* (Montréal, 1933), 1, 37–58.

Factors of an emotional nature have also exerted a very bad influence on the thinking of French- and English-Canadian historians. The latter were in a very ticklish position. Could they admit that the British Conquest and occupation of the St. Lawrence valley had wronged the *Canadiens* as a people? Being rightly proud of the British businessmen and settlers who have built, with the help of Great Britain, the second Kingdom of Canada, their first objective was to relate their achievements with a patriotic bent. The history of French Canada did not interest them very much and they did not care to study it seriously. But they could not completely ignore the fact of the Conquest. Having a feeling of solidarity with the conquerors, they were inclined to vindicate their actions. Finally, they easily convinced themselves that the fate of the *Canadiens* had been better under the British rule than it would have been if they had remained in the French Empire. This hypothesis was a mere subterfuge but it had the advantage of giving good conscience to the English-Canadian majority. All conquerors use arguments of this kind to legitimize their domination over a subjected people. One must never forget that France had not conquered French Canada but had founded it and that the *Canadiens* could not develop normally as a people without the help of their metropolis. However, English-Canadian social scientists can be excused. Were not the principal spokesmen of French Canada—the bishops, political leaders, businessmen, and historians—all eager to proclaim that, after all, the coming of the British had benefited Canada and the *Canadiens*?

Indeed, the churchmen and lawyer-politicians who, for six generations, have led the French Canadians, like to believe that the Conquest did not impair the growth of their compatriots as a people. They stubbornly refuse to recognize that the *Canadiens* are conquered people whose survival as a collectivity has been possible because the conquerors were unable to assimilate them completely. On the contrary, they have endeavoured to persuade themselves that the challenge of the British occupation has even contributed to the strength of French Canada. It is said that the *Canadiens* have learned how to avail themselves of the prosperity and liberty the British are supposed to have brought to Canada. All agree that there were some difficulties in the beginning, and that a few wicked British wanted to persecute the *Canadiens* and to assimilate them. But the *Canadiens* are told that, thanks to the cleverness of their religious and political leaders and their own courage, they have finally successfully overcome all the bad consequences of a foreign domination. The French-Canadian ruling classes, whose accession to their position of pre-eminence has always been dependent on the willingness of either the British authorities or the English-Canadian leaders, are interested in upholding this historical interpretation. Nor does this viewpoint displease too much the English-Canadian majority whose good conscience is not upset. It gives to the priesthood and politicians of French Canada the rôle of Saviours in the service of their people. It also magnifies the *Canadiens'* national pride. In any society vested interests and patriotic emotions tend to influence the writings and teaching of the social scientists. Too often they themselves are unaware of this social pressure.

The era of amateurism and romanticism is over. It is time to put Parkman aside. Social scientists should leave to the politicians and preachers the job of making pep-talks about the grandeur and virtues of British liberty, free enterprise, rugged individualism, and similar topics. They must approach the study of society with more scientific methods. They must state with candour and lucidity all the problems and challenges of our times.

In Canada, French- and English-Canadian social scientists bear heavy responsibilities. They must be conversant with all the political, economic, and social problems facing the Atlantic world in the second half of the twentieth century. Men of action who are entrusted with the orientation of Canada need their help to perform their duty. And there is in this country a peculiar problem that challenges every generation of Canadian citizens: the peaceful coexistence of the *Canadiens* and Canadians. This coexistence has begun almost two centuries ago. It seems that it will endure for many more generations.

Can we say that social scientists have up to now been equal to their task in dealing with this sociological problem? Was not their approach to it quite unsatisfactory? Their wishful thinking and their romanticism have impeded their examination of the fundamental facts that have determined the historical and sociological evolution of Canada. They have never perceived the true nature of the relations which have existed, since the Conquest, between *Canadiens* and Canadians. They do not even have the excuse of having promoted "national unity." A true and fruitful partnership between French and English Canadians cannot be based upon a common misunderstanding of Canadian history and Canadian society. Empty words about democracy, self-government, *bonne entente,* and the riches which a bilingual and bicultural state is supposed to enjoy have too often deceived the social scientists of Canada. They have first the obligation to analyse the facts without troubling themselves with the vested interests they will hurt or the unfavourable reactions of the influential people they will scandalize. For the good of Canada, and Atlantic civilization itself, they have the opportunity, by studying with a fresh approach our own historical and social problems, to make a worthy contribution to the progress of the social sciences.

The Plains of Abraham: The Abandoned Battlefield

Mark Starowicz

SHORTLY AFTER ELEVEN A.M. on September 13, 1759, Louis-Antoine de Bougainville arrived on the Plains with 1,200 French troops but by that time the battle was over and the field had been left to the dead and dying. Colonel Étienne-Guillaume de Senezergues, mortally wounded, would die the next day. François Clement Boucher de la Perrière, who had fought though his eyes were failing him, would be dead by evening.

James Wolfe, the British General who had been sick and frail before the battle, lived only a few minutes after receiving a fatal shot to the chest. His body was sent back to England where he became the Empire's newest hero. His coffin was carried through streets filled with silent mourners and he was buried beside his father at St. Alfege's, Greenwich. He was 32 years old.

Louis-Joseph, the Marquis de Montcalm, would survive for one more day. He died of his wounds at the General Hospital, glad, he said, not to have seen the fall of Quebec. There were no coffins left and his body was put into a makeshift box and buried in a crater made by a British cannonball that had landed in the Ursuline nuns' chapel. He was 47 years old.

One thousand, three hundred men were killed or wounded on the Plains of Abraham. The Canadians from the parishes and cities of New France, the youths of the English Midlands, the dispossessed of the Scottish Highlands, the unemployed from Normandy and Provence—all were buried, French and English together, in common pits on the Plains. The location of their graves would never be marked.

Ten days after the Battle, the French artillery commander Fiacre-François de Montbeillard wrote in his journal: "I have nothing but misfortune to write about. Twenty times I have picked up my pen and twenty times sorrow has made it fall from my hands. How can I bring to mind such overwhelming events? . . . We were saved and now we are lost."

CHAPTER FIVE

The Making of Laura Secord

Introduction

The War of 1812 entered English-Canadian mythology in the late-nineteenth century. Writers, poets and historians used the War to create heroes for a young nation. These included: General Brock, the British General who died at the Battle of Queenston Heights; Laura Secord, who upon learning of American plans to launch a surprise attack against the British at Beaver Dams made a difficult journey on foot to warn Lieutenant Fitzgibbon; and Tecumseh, the Shawnee Chief who fought as an ally of the British. The historian Cecilia Morgan has studied the ways in which Laura Secord has been remembered and the uses to which her image has been put. How and why has Laura Secord changed over time? Agnes Maule Machar and Katharine Livingstone Macpherson were two late nineteenth-century writers. How do they "invent" or "construct" Secord?

Creating a Heroine for English Canada: The Commemoration of Laura Secord

Cecilia Morgan

TO SAY THAT the study of 'heroines' and their place in historical narratives is a complicated endeavour, one fraught with many challenges, would be an understatement. For a feminist historian such as myself, one very basic task was that of 'uncovering' and 'restoring' women's activities, experiences, and identities to the historical record, while simultaneously engaging with the ongoing creation of the category 'woman' and its relationship to other categories and identities: class, race and ethnicity, religion, and so on. Moreover, in the case of a woman such as Secord, matters are no less challenging because her image and narrative have been deployed in the creation of 'national' and imperial narratives and representations and her justification as a person of historical significance has been intimately linked to her service to the nation. While some might see this as a cause for celebration—at the very least legitimization of their subject—I viewed it as a test of my skills as a historian and scholar of gender and culture. I leave it to my peers and colleagues to determine how well I have succeeded in providing some kind of 'unified' exploration of these identities, relationships, and locations. What concerns me more here are some of the theoretical and methodological challenges involved in the study of 'heroines,' not to mention the political nuances that overlay all of the above.

First, 'finding' Secord was the most basic and, yet, the most unsolvable task of this research. To be sure, certain biographical details exist that allowed me to sketch out the contours of her life. I can tell you her (approximate) date of birth, her family background, the date of her arrival in Upper Canada, the date and fact of her marriage to James Secord, and the number of children she bore. I can tell you about her walk to warn James Fitzgibbon, although as I have argued elsewhere that narrative is not without its own vagaries, inconsistencies, and blurred edges. And I can tell you something about her life 'post-walk': her struggle to gain state recognition, her attempts to help support her family given her husband's disability, not to mention her widowed daughters' and their children's move back to the family home, along with their children. And I would argue that it is not inconsequential to be able to narrate that much of an Upper Canadian woman's life, even when the woman was white and of 'middling' status.

Yet there are many other dimensions of Secord's life, particularly questions surrounding her own subjectivity, which remain hidden and at present are lost to the curious historian. In all likelihood, they will remain obscured. I cannot tell you, for example, how she experienced and remembered her 'walk' in any way outside of the public domain of service to the colonial state and British Empire: all I have are her petitions to the Crown which, not surprisingly, stress duty, loyal service, and her family's needs. In themselves these petitions may somehow seem to 'complete' the story—in that, as I have argued, they let us see how she framed her narrative—but I would suggest that they represent only fragments of the historical record, testimony to the power of the colonial state and to the specific kinds of linkages of public and private in this period. I cannot tell you, for example, precisely what Secord herself made of the occupation of American troops—her former countrymen—of her village and, it seems, home, nor can I do more than speculate as to how she might have weighed and assessed her responsibilities as a wife and, in particular, mother (although I do know that some of her commemorators were keen to reconcile these aspects of her life with her loyal service).

Secord's body is yet another dimension of this narrative that alerts us to absences and silences. Her commemorators, particularly women such as Curzon and Currie, were eager to write about the marks of such service on Secord's body: her innate frailty and slightness of stature, her bleeding feet, the exhaustion she suffered, the heat and insects of late June, and the trepidation and fear she experienced. In doing so it might be said that they turned her body into an archive of knowledge of the sacrifices heroines endured; certainly in their accounts her body became a historical artefact, as much a 'source' that testified to her walk as any political or military document. But we have no idea how she experienced any of this. Was the walk a daunting physical struggle for her? Did her feet in fact bleed? The answer may well be yes to both questions, yet she had also borne and raised a number of children and perhaps had endured miscarriages and/or stillbirths; early nineteenth-century childbirth was itself a test of physical endurance for women such as Secord. It is impossible to know how she incorporated and ranked the trek to Beaverdams in what might have been a lexicon of gynecological and other kinds of physical sufferings endured by women in this period.

Moreover, her fear was said to have encompassed wild animals, American soldiers, and Aboriginal warriors; as I have argued elsewhere, it was the latter who, her commemorators argued, both concerned her the most and allowed Secord to demonstrate her 'heroic' qualities. Yet, apart from a few references in some of her petitions to her trepidation and alarm upon discovering the Mohawk camp, I can do no more than speculate about her conceptions of Native peoples and her understanding of the role played by the Iroquois in the War of 1812. For example, it is possible that, as a child in Barrington, Massachusetts, Secord had been exposed to New England's narratives of white captivity at the hands of Natives and had come to see them as a group to be feared and mistrusted. Yet it is also possible that she had some contact with those Native peoples who might have been hunting and trading in the Niagara Peninsula. Moreover, given her husband's military service, particularly his involvement at Queenston Heights, she may have been aware that certain Native men, at least, were allies and not enemies of the British.

The determination of her story by the state and empire, the place of domesticity and maternity, the embodiment and corporeality of this narrative, and the place of racial fears, fantasies, and relationships are only a few of the questions and themes that impinge upon any attempt to find the 'real' Laura Secord and the 'true' narrative. Less discussed, but still important, is the question of labour. Secord's walk could well have been perceived as 'work' for Crown and colony and acknowledged as a spectrum of physical toil that also incorporated her labour for her family, particularly the nursing care—itself a very common form of women's work—expended in looking after her semi-invalid husband. To be sure, her commemorators often linked her physical sacrifice in getting to Beaverdams to her (quite likely imagined) defense of the wounded James on the Queenston Heights battlefield and argued that she had shielded him to prevent his being fatally stabbed. Some were not afraid to depict Secord as a 'hard-working' wife and mother, part of Niagara pioneer life: witness the ubiquitous and fictive cow. Yet it was equally and, for some, even more important that Secord's femininity, class, and racial identity be aligned in ways that would depict her as a 'lady.' Thus some commemorators added black servants, or her love of Lieutenant Governor's balls at Newark, and substituted silk gowns and thin slippers for plain cotton dresses and sensible shoes. Feminine consumption and love of 'finery' could be managed and controlled and could be an acceptable companion to nation and empire. Once more, Secord's own fantasies and desires lie buried.

Thus, while I am unable to do anything more than simply point to absences, Secord's commemorators were far more optimistic. Using genres and methodologies other than the kind of 'scientific' history I have been trained to practice and produce, writers such as Sarah Curzon, Emma Currie, John Price-Brown, and Merrill Denison, blended prose and poetry, history and literature, to produce a Secord who was much more than the sum of a historian's sources. And while we have argued in *Heroines and History* that their imaginings were criss-crossed by conceptions of gender, race, empire, and nation, we also have tried to point out that the issue is simply not just that of writing 'bad' history. Instead, we must recognize that Secord's commemorators conceptualized their tasks in ways both similar to and different from our notions of creating historical narratives. And yet I return once again to the problem of studying Secord and her commemoration: was there any other way of examining her life and its significance without the framework of 'the nation?' Could they have told her story with another theoretical structure that would not have relegated her experiences to the realm of not just 'the private' domain but that of the domestic, which in that context might well have been viewed as the realm of trivia?

Yet trying to construct a 'Laura Secord' whose narrative was not built on the scaffold of English-Canadian nationalism is not the only challenge or question. We have argued in *Heroines and History* that both Madeleine de Verchères and Secord's story are dependent on the presence and, at times, absence of the Iroquois; hence our narratives about these 'heroines' creation had to tackle the intermingling of nationalism with imperialism. And, as I searched for and found Secord's commemorators, I became increasingly aware that not all those active in the creation of 'Canadian' historical memory were white and middle class. While not engaged in Secord's commemoration, Iroquois historians such as John Brant-Sero, Ethel Brant Monture, Bernice Loft, and Elliott Moses, crafted narratives of both Native societies and 'Canada' that at times engaged with those of the historical societies, the builders of monuments, and the writers of textbooks.

At other times, the histories told by Native historians followed different trajectories and sought to tell a different story. Their work can be and, I would argue, should be seen as not merely a triumphant narrative of subaltern peoples' agency, although their agency and resistance should not be overlooked. But equally important is their complex, if fraught, relationship with both the Canadian nation-state and the modernity that these historical narratives engaged in and helped create. I would argue that this point is relevant even when we are faced with the issue of these narrators and their narratives' partial absences from the dominant theatres in which much of English Canada's narratives were dreamed of, rehearsed, and enacted. To be sure, the historical memories created and told by historians such as Brant-Sero and Monture are not so much historical memories that 'failed' (as one might argue de Verchères' narrative does today) but, instead, they took shape in forms and locations both similar to and different from those chosen by Secord's commemorators. For example, at times their archive was the public imperial and national one favoured by English-Canadian historians. However, their archive also could take an embodied form, as historians such as Brant-Sero, Monture, and Loft performed history, using narrative in conjunction with Iroquois poetry, music, and dance. It may well be that their labour as historians—or some facets of it—succeeded in either uniting the seemingly disparate elements of 'private' and 'public,' 'home' and 'nation,' better than their non-Native contemporaries. And it is worth considering that such designations and categories might have had very little or possibly even no meaning for them in the first place.

But to return to Laura Secord and the question of 'heroines.' We argue in the conclusion of *Heroines and History* that the latter and its creators treat the former more harshly and subject them to a greater degree of scrutiny that that meted out to 'heroes.' And while I do not of course disagree with this observation, since the book's publication I have been forced to think about contemporary meanings of Secord's story, in ways that other work I have published has not forced me to return and reflect on my own scholarship. To no small extent my repetition and reiteration of these issues has been because of issues of reception, that great question for cultural historians: both of *Heroines and History* and my own writing of history as public discourse and knowledge. Rather than being something 'over and done with,' Secord's memory and life continue to be narrated and recreated: in schools, in books for girls, and in her descendants, a number of whom have attended the public talks I have given in the Niagara area and who are themselves bridges between the domains of history and memory. The reception of the book has made me wonder if Secord's narrative and the story of her commemoration is more relevant, more 'alive,' and more central to these audiences than individuals such as Isaac Brock or those others who figured so prominently in 'traditional' political and military history. For these audiences, it seems, the image and narrative of Laura Secord bridges the public and private, the nation and the home, and provides them with a 'better story' with which to construct past and present (and possibly even future). But that would be a subject of a future, and another, study.

Laura Secord

Agnes Maule Machar

During the so-called war of 1812–14 between England and the United States, Laura Secord, the wife of a crippled British veteran, saved the British forces from surprise and possible destruction by the heroic action narrated in the ballad. Her home lay near the celebrated Queenston Heights, a few miles from the Falls of Niagara.

SOFTLY the spell of moonlight fell On the swift river's flow,
On the gray crags of Queenston Heights, And the green waves below.

Alone the whip-poor-will's sad cry Blent with the murmuring pines,
Save where the sentry paced his rounds Along th' invading lines.

But in one lowly cottage home Were trouble and dismay;
Two anxious watchers could not sleep For tidings heard that day.

Brave James Secord, with troubled heart, And weary crippled frame,
That bore the scars of Queenston Heights, Back to his cabin came;

For he had learned a dark design Fitzgibbon to surprise,
As with a handful of brave men At Beaver Dam he lies.

'And Boerstler, with eight hundred men, Is moving from the shore
To steal upon our outpost there, Guarded by scarce two score!

Then, wiping out, as well he may, That gallant little band,
The foe will sweep his onward way O'er the defenceless land.

Then noble Brock had died in vain—If but Fitzgibbon knew!'
And the poor cripple's heart is fain To press the journey through.

But Laura, bending o'er her babes, Said, smiling through her tears:
'These are not times for brave men's wives To yield to craven fears.

'*You* cannot go to warn our men, Or slip the outposts through;
But if perchance they let *me* pass, This errand I will do.'

She soothed his anxious doubts and fears: She knew the forest way;
She put her trust in Him who hears His children when they pray!

Soon as the rosy flush of dawn Glowed through the purple air,
She rose to household tasks—and kissed Her babes with whispered
    prayer.

To milk her grazing cow she went; The sentry at the lines
Forgot to watch, as both were lost Amid the sheltering pines.

The rising sun's first golden rays Gleamed through the forest dim,
And through its leafy arches rang The birds' sweet morning hymn.

The fragrant odour of the pines, The carols gay and sweet,
Gave courage to the fluttering heart, And strength to faltering feet.

And on she pressed, with steadfast tread, Her solitary way,
O'er tangled brake and sodden swamp Through all the sultry day.

Though, for the morning songs of birds She heard the wolf's hoarse cry,
And saw the rattlesnake glide forth, As swift she hurried by.

Nor dark morass nor rushing stream Could balk the steadfast will,
Nor pleading voice of anxious friends Where stood St. David's Mill.

The British sentry heard her tale, And cheered her on her way;
But bade her 'ware the Indian scouts Who in the covert lay.

Anon, as cracked a rotten bough Beneath her wary feet,
She heard their war-whoop through the gloom, Their steps
    advancing fleet;

But quickly to the questioning chief She told her errand grave,
How she had walked the livelong day Fitzgibbon's men to save!

The redskin heard and kindly gazed Upon the pale-faced squaw;
Her faithful courage touched his heart, Her weary look he saw.

'Me go with you' was all he said, And through the forest gray
He led her safe to Beaver Dam, Where brave Fitzgibbon lay.

With throbbing heart she told her tale; *They* heard with anxious heed,
Who knew how grave the crisis was, How urgent was the need!

Then there was riding far and near, And mustering to and fro
Of troops and Indians from the rear To meet the coming foe;

And such the bold, determined stand Those few brave soldiers made—
So fiercely fought the Indian band From forest ambuscade—

That Boerstler in the first surprise Surrendered in despair,
To force so small it scarce could serve To keep the prisoners there!

While the brave weary messenger In dreamless slumber lay,
And woke to find her gallant friends Were masters of the fray.

       *   *   *   *   *

If e'er Canadian courage fail, Or loyalty grow cold,
Or nerveless grow Canadian hearts, Then be the story told—

How British gallantry and skill There played their noblest part,
Yet scarce had won if there had failed One woman's dauntless heart!

Pictures from Canadian History for Boys and Girls

Katharine Livingstone Macpherson

Laura Secord—I

1. THE fateful 27th of May, 1813, brought ruin to the little town of Niagara. After a brave defence against great odds, the place, already in flames, was taken, and not a family but had friends among the gallant dead. The district swarmed with American troops, now more sure than ever of taking Canada. The people were really prisoners, and watched with unceasing vigilance by the besieging force.

2. In a cottage on the outskirts lived James Secord and his young wife Laura. The times were full of daring deeds, and the Secords belonged to an intensely patriotic United Empire Loyalist family. It was nearly two months since the fall of the town, and James was still only recovering from his wounds.

3. Sunrise was flooding the beautiful countryside on the 23rd of June, when Mrs. Secord entered her husband's room and carefully closed the door. Sitting by the bedside, she excitedly whispered some news she had happened to overhear from two American soldiers passing the house.

4. About twenty miles off Lieutenant Fitzgibbon, with fifty men of his Majesty's 49th Regiment, held a post. The few careless words had revealed the fact that this force was to be surprised next day by six hundred of the enemy. As no help could be sent the little garrison, it would be cut to pieces. It was a matter of desperate importance.

5. After a pause, Laura raised her head resolutely. "James," she said, "I am going to tell them." The young man looked at her for a moment without speaking. "You can't go by the road," he answered slowly. "They will see to that." "I know," was the quiet answer.

6. For a few minutes the patriotic couple talked eagerly of ways and means. The country was still but thinly settled, and the only road leading in that direction well watched. The forest, extending for miles on every side, was dense and dangerous. Wild beasts lurked in its gloomy shades, and swamps made some parts almost impassable. At length Laura rose and kissed her husband. "Good-bye," she said bravely, "till we meet again."

7. A few minutes later, hatless, and with a pail on each arm, the young woman was stopped at the meadow gate. "You can't pass here," said the sentry, shortly. Mrs. Secord put on her most engaging smile. "Can't," she returned lightly, "and what will Colonel Boerstler do without milk for his breakfast?" The man laughed, and, lowering his piece, made way for her and watched her upright figure tripping across the pasture. "Don't be long," he called sharply; "I'll be on the lookout for you!"

8. As he spoke there was a quick step on the road, and a rattle of arms caught Laura's ear. At the sound her heart bounded. It was the change of sentries, and seemed a good omen, for now her absence might not be noticed. As she proceeded, sounds of military life rose in the crisp morning air; soon the little town would awaken to its burden of sorrow. About the wide field the cows were cropping the dewy grass, while the sun touched the forest trees on the far side of the fence.

Laura Secord—II

1. MRS. SECORD chose the farthest away animal, and pushed it still nearer the fence. For a few moments there was the quick sound of milk frothing into the pail, then, with a hasty look round, she ceased work, crept past the cow, and, running a few yards, plunged into the wood. For a few minutes in terror of a musket shot to show that she was missed, the panting figure fled through the trees scarcely caring where she was going.

2. No sound, however, reached her anxious ear. As she pressed on, the brush became more dense and thorny, and the long branches of the brambles pulled at her hair and tore her face and hands. In her haste she stumbled over mossy logs, and, still trembling with excitement, had to retrace her steps again and again to find some easier way.

3. For hours the heroic woman fought her way through the jungle-like growth. Her shoes and stockings were long since worn out, and her dress torn to shreds. Her bare feet sank in the oozy swamp, or, striking against sharp stones, caused her to cry out in pain.

4. The countless trees rose on every side solemn and confusing, the dark interlacing branches almost shutting out the light. From far off now and then came the long howl of a wolf, and, once stooping to drink at a rocky spring, the horrid rattle of a snake caused her to bound back with a shriek and rush on in terror.

5. Weak and dizzy, Laura sometimes threw herself on the ground wishing to die, and again, with a prayer on her lips, sprang up, determined to push on. The day seemed endless, and yet, as the sun waned, she could have wept despairing tears. In darkness, and with no guide, she would be lost indeed.

6. Approaching what seemed to be an opening in the trees, she suddenly sprang backwards in affright. With no sound of warning, her terrified eyes were staring straight at an outpost Indian in full war-paint. With a long moan the wanderer swayed forwards, and fell fainting on the ground.

7. When she came to she found herself in a tent, surrounded by the kindly faces of white men in uniform. Half sobbing, she told her story, and was amazed to see the instant energy it produced in her hearers. Nothing could have aroused the young heroine so quickly as the way in which her brave act was received.

8. History tells how the next day Boerslier's force of Americans, marching along the road, was suddenly hemmed in by two hundred Indians at Beaver Dams, and, when Fitzgibbon's force also advanced upon them, they surrendered with scarcely a shot.

CHAPTER SIX

Louis Riel and the Meaning of Canada

Introduction

Born in 1844, Louis Riel was a Métis. The Métis were the descendants of European fur traders and Amerindian women. Riel spoke French and was a Catholic. Determined to protect Métis rights and land titles, Riel led two armed struggles, the Red River Rebellion of 1869–1870 in what is today Manitoba and the North-West Rebellion of 1885 in what is today Saskatchewan. Charged with treason for his part in the North-West Rebellion, Riel was duly convicted in 1885. The government of Sir John A. Macdonald refused to commute Riel's sentence. "He shall hang though every dog in Quebec bark in his favour," the Prime Minister grumbled and on November 16, 1885, the Métis leader was executed.

As the subject of histories, novels, poems, plays and even an opera, Riel continues to haunt the Canadian imagination. In these readings how has the depiction of Riel changed over time? How are we to explain this change? How is the depiction of Louis Riel different in the pieces by John Bourinot, a prominent nineteenth-century English-Canadian writer and intellectual, Louis Fréchette, the great nineteenth-century French-Canadian poet, and Marilyn Dumont, a Métis poet writing today? Dumont's *A Really Good Brown Girl* won the 1997 League of Canadian Poets' Gerald Lampert Award for best first collection of poetry. Prime Minister Pierre Trudeau's Riel is very different from Prime Minister John A. Macdonald's Riel. How? Why? Thinking about John Bourinot, David Duncan and Jack Bumsted, how have historians written about Riel?

The Story of Canada

J. G. Bourinot

"Is it the clang of wild-geese,
    Is it the Indians' yell
That lends to the voice of the North wind
    The tone of a far-off bell?

"The voyageur smiles as he listens
    To the sound that grows apace:
Well he knows the vesper ringing
    Of the bells of Saint Boniface.

"The bells of the Roman mission
    That call from their turrets twain.
To the boatmen on the river,
    To the hunters on the plain."

ON ALL SIDES there were evidences of comfort in this little oasis of civilisation amid the prairies. The descendants of the two nationalities dwelt apart in French and British parishes, each of which had their separate schools and churches. The houses and plantations of the British settlers, and of a few French Canadians, indicated thrift, but the majority of the French half-breeds, or *Métis*, the descendants of French Canadian fathers and Indian mothers, continued to live almost entirely on the fur trade, as voyageurs, trappers, and hunters. They exhibited all the characteristics of those hardy and adventurous men who were the pioneers of the west. Skilful hunters but poor cultivators of the soil, fond of amusement, rash and passionate, spending their gains as soon as made, too often in dissipation, many of them were true representatives of the *coureurs de bois* of the days of Frontenac. This class was numerous in 1869 when the government of Canada first presented itself to claim the territory of the Northwest as a part of the Dominion. After years of negotiation the Hudson's Bay Company had recognised the necessity of allowing the army of civilisation to advance into the region which it had so long kept as a fur preserve. The British Government obtained favourable terms for the Dominion, and the whole country from line 49° to the Arctic region, and from Lake Superior to the Rocky Mountains became a portion of the Canadian domain, with the exception of small tracts of land in the vicinity of the company's posts, which they still continue to maintain wherever the fur trade can be profitably carried on. In 1869 the Canadian ministry, of which Sir John Macdonald was premier, took measures to assume possession of the country, where they proposed to establish a provisional government. Mr. William McDougall, a prominent Canadian Liberal, one of the founders of confederation, always an earnest advocate of the acquisition of the Northwest, was appointed to act as lieutenant-governor as soon as the formal transfer was made. This transfer, however, was not completed until a few months later than it was at first expected, and the government of Canada appears to have acted with some precipitancy in sending surveyors into the country, and in allowing Mr. McDougall to proceed at once to the scene of his proposed government. It would have been wise had the Canadian authorities taken measures to ascertain the wishes of the small but independent population with respect to the future government of their own country. The British as well as French settlers resented the hasty action of the Canadian authorities. The halfbreeds, little acquainted with questions of government, saw in the appearance of surveying parties an insidious attempt to dispossess them eventually of their lands, to which many of them had not a sound title. The British settlers, the best educated and most intelligent portion of the population, believed that a popular form of government should have been immediately established in the old limits of Assiniboia, as soon as it became a part of Canada. Some of the Hudson's Bay Company's employés were not in their hearts pleased at the transfer, and the probable change in their position in a country where they had been so long masters. Although these men stood aloof from the insurrection, yet their influence was not exercised at the commencement of the troubles, in favour of peace and order, or in exposing the plans of the insurgents, of which some of them must have had an idea. The appearance of Mr. McDougall on the frontier of the settlement, was the signal for an outbreak which has been dignified by the name of rebellion. The insurgents seized Fort Garry, and established a provisional government with Mr. John Bruce, a Scotch settler, as nominal president, and Mr. Louis Riel, the actual leader, as secretary of state. The latter was a French half-breed, who had been superficially educated in French Canada. His temperament was that of a race not inclined to steady occupation, loving the life of the river and plain, ready to put law at defiance when their rights and privileges were in danger. This restless man and his half-breed associates soon found themselves at the head and front of the whole rebellious movement, as the British settlers, while disapproving of the action of the Canadian Government, were not prepared to support the seditious designs of the French Canadian *Métis*. Riel became president, and made prisoners of Dr. Schultz, in later times a lieutenant-governor of the new province, and of a number of other British settlers who were now anxious to restore order and come to terms with the Canadian Government, who were showing every disposition to arrange the difficulty. In the meantime Mr. McDougall issued a proclamation which was a mere *brutum fulmen*, and then went back to Ottawa, where he detailed his grievances and soon afterwards disappeared from public life. The Canadian authorities by this time recognised their mistake and entered into negotiations with Red River delegates, representing both the loyal and rebellious elements, and the result was most favourable for the immediate settlement of the difficulties. At this critical juncture the Canadian Government had the advantage of the sage counsels of Sir Donald Smith, then a prominent official of the Hudson's Bay Company, who at a later time became a prominent figure in Canadian public life. Chiefly through the instrumentality of Archbishop Taché, whose services to the land and race he loved can never be forgotten by its people, an amnesty was promised to those who had taken part in the insurrection, and the troubles would have come to an end had not Riel, in a moment of recklessness, characteristic of his real nature, tried one Thomas Scott by the veriest mockery of a court-martial on account of some severe words he had uttered against the rebels' government, and had him mercilessly shot outside the fort. As Scott was a native of Ontario, and an Orangeman, his murder aroused a widespread feeling of indignation throughout his native province. The amnesty which was promised to Archbishop Taché, it is now quite clear, never contemplated the pardon of a crime like this, which was committed subsequently. The Canadian Government were then fully alive to the sense of their responsibilities, and at once decided to act with resolution. In the spring of 1870 an expedition was organised, and sent to the Northwest under the command of Colonel Garnet Wolseley, now a peer, and commander-in-chief of the British army. This expedition consisted of five hundred regulars and seven hundred Canadian volunteers, who reached Winnipeg after a most wearisome journey of nearly three months, by the old fur-traders' route from Thunder Bay, through an entirely unsettled and rough country, where the portages were very numerous and laborious. Towards the end of August the expedition reached their destination, but found that Riel had fled to the United States, and that they had won a bloodless victory. Law and order henceforth prevailed in the new territory, whose formal transfer to the Canadian Government had been completed some months before, and it was now formed into a new province, called Manitoba, with a complete system of local government, and including guaranties with respect to education, as in the case of the old provinces. The first lieutenant-governor was Mr. Adams Archibald, a Nova Scotian lawyer, who was one of the members of the Quebec conference, and a statesman of much discretion. Representation was also given immediately in the two houses of the Dominion parliament. Subsequently the vast territory outside of the new prairie province was divided into six districts for purposes of government: Alberta, Assiniboia, Athabasca, Keewatin, and Saskatchewan. Keewatin is under the jurisdiction of the lieutenant-governor of Manitoba, but the other districts have an assembly and a lieutenant-governor whose seat of government is Regina, though the people do not yet enjoy responsible government. In 1896 four new provisional districts were marked out in the great northern unsettled district under the names of Franklin, Mackenzie, Yukon, and Ungava.

In the course of a few years a handsome, well-built city arose on the site of old Fort Garry, and with the construction of the Canadian Pacific Railway—a national highway built with a rapidity remarkable even in these days of extraordinary commercial enterprise—and the connection of the Atlantic sea-board with the Pacific shores, villages and towns have extended at distant intervals across the continent, from Port

Arthur to Vancouver, the latter place an instance of western phenomenal growth. Stone and brick buildings of fine architectural proportions, streets paved and lit by electricity, huge elevators, busy mills, are the characteristics of some towns where only yesterday brooded silence, and the great flowery stretches of prairie were only crushed by the feet of wandering Indians and voyageurs.

Fourteen years after the formation of the province of Manitoba, whilst the Canadian Pacific Railway was in the course of construction, the peace of the territories was again disturbed by risings of half-breeds in the South Saskatchewan district, chiefly at Duck Lake, St. Laurent, and Batoche. Many of these men had migrated from Manitoba to a country where they could follow their occupation of hunting and fishing, and till little patches of ground in that shiftless manner characteristic of the *Métis*. The total number of half-breeds in the Saskatchewan country were probably four thousand, of whom the majority lived in the settlements just named. These people had certain land grievances, the exact nature of which it is not easy even now to ascertain; but there is no doubt that they laboured under the delusion that, because there was much red-tapeism and some indifference at Ottawa in dealing with their respective claims, there was a desire or intention to treat them with injustice. Conscious that they might be crowded out by the greater energy and enterprise of white settlers—that they could no longer depend on their means of livelihood in the past, when the buffalo and other game were plentiful, these restless, impulsive, illiterate people were easily led to believe that their only chance of redressing their real or fancied wrongs was such a rising as had taken place on the Red River in 1869. It is believed that English settlers in the Prince Albert district secretly fomented the rising with the hope that it might also result in the establishment of a province on the banks of the Saskatchewan, despite its small population. The agitators among the half-breeds succeeded in bringing Riel into the country to lead the insurrection. He had been an exile ever since 1870, and was at the time teaching school in Montana. After the rebellion he had been induced to remain out of the Northwest by the receipt of a considerable sum of money from the secret service fund of the Dominion Government, then led by Sir John Macdonald. In 1874 he had been elected to the House of Commons by the new constituency of Provencher in Manitoba; but as he had been proclaimed an outlaw, when a true bill for murder was found against him in the Manitoba Court of Queen's Bench, and when he had failed to appear for trial, he was expelled from the house on the motion of Mr. Mackenzie Bowell, a prominent Orangeman, and, later, premier of the Canadian Government. Lepine, a member also of the so-called provisional government of Red River, had been tried and convicted for his share in the murder of Scott, but Lord Dufferin, when governor-general, exercised the prerogative of royal clemency, as an imperial officer, and commuted the punishment to two years' imprisonment. In this way the Mackenzie government was relieved—but only temporarily—of a serious responsibility which they were anxious to avoid, at a time when they were between the two fires: of the people of Ontario, anxious to punish the murderers with every severity, and of the French Canadians, the great majority of whom showed a lively sympathy for all those who had taken part in the rebellion of 1869. The influence of French Canada was also seen in the later action of the Mackenzie government in obtaining a full amnesty for all concerned in the rebellion except Riel, Lepine, and O'Donohue, who were banished for five years. The popularity enjoyed by Riel and his associates in French Canada, as well as the clemency shown to them, were doubtless facts considered by the leaders in the second rising on the Saskatchewan as showing that they had little to fear from the consequences of their acts. Riel and Dumont—the latter a half-breed trader near Batoche—were the leaders of the revolt which broke out at Duck Lake in the March of 1885 with a successful attack on the Mounted Police and the Prince Albert Volunteers, who were defeated with a small loss of life. This success had much effect on the Indian tribes in the Saskatchewan district, among whom Riel and his associates had been intriguing for some time, and Poundmaker, Big Bear, and other chiefs of the Cree communities living on the Indian reserves, went on the warpath. Subsequently Battleford, then the capital of the Territories, was threatened by Indians and *Métis,* and a force under Big Bear massacred at Frog Lake two Oblat missionaries, and some other persons, besides taking several prisoners, among whom were Mrs. Delaney and Mrs. Gowanlock, widows of two of the murdered men, who were released at the close of the rising. Fort Pitt, on the North Saskatchewan, thirty miles from Frog Lake, was abandoned by Inspector Dickens—a son of the novelist—and his detachment of the Mounted Police, on the approach of a large body of Indians under Big Bear. When the news of these outrages reached Ottawa, the government acted with great promptitude. A French Canadian, now Sir Adolphe Caron, was then minister of militia in Sir John Macdonald's ministry, and showed himself fully able to cope with this, happily, unusual, experience in Canadian Government. From all parts of the Dominion—from French as well as English Canada—the volunteers patriotically rallied to the call of duty, and Major-General Middleton, a regular officer in command of the Canadian militia, led a fine force of over four thousand men into the Northwest. The Canadian Pacific Railway was now built, with the exception of a few breaks of about seventy-two miles in all, as far as Qu'Appelle, which is sixteen hundred and twenty miles from Ottawa and about two hundred and thirty-five miles to the south of Batoche. The Canadian troops, including a fine body of men from Winnipeg, reached Fish Creek, fifteen miles from Batoche, on the 24th of April, or less than a month after the orders were given at Ottawa to march from the east. Here the insurgents, led by Dumont, were concealed in riflepits, ingeniously constructed and placed in a deep ravine. They checked Middleton, who does not appear to have taken sufficient precautions to ascertain the position of the enemy—thoroughly trained marksmen who were able to shoot down a considerable number of the volunteers. Later, at Batoche, the Canadian troops, led with great bravery by Colonels

Straubenzie, Williams, Mackeand, and Grassett, scattered the insurgents, who never made an attempt to rally. The gallantry of Colonel Williams of the Midlanders—an Ontario battalion—was especially conspicuous, but he never returned from the Northwest to receive the plaudits of his countrymen, as he died of fever soon after the victory he did so much to win at Batoche. Colonel Otter, a distinguished officer of Toronto, had an encounter with Poundmaker at Cut Knife Creek on Battle River, one of the tributaries of the North Saskatchewan, and prevented him from making any hostile demonstrations against Battleford and other places. Riel's defeat at Batoche cowed these Indians, who gave up their arms and prisoners to Otter. Elsewhere in the Territories all trouble was prevented by the prompt transport of troops under Colonel Strange to Fort Edmonton, Calgary, and other points of importance. The Blackfeet, the most formidable body of natives in the Territories, never broke the peace, although they were more than once very restless. Their good behaviour was chiefly owing to the influence of Chief Crowfoot, always a friend of the Canadians.

When the insurrection was over, an example was made of the leaders. Dumont succeeded in making his escape, but Riel, who had been captured after the fight at Batoche, was executed at Regina after a most impartial trial, in which he had the assistance of very able counsel brought from French Canada. Insanity was pleaded even, in his defence, not only in the court but subsequently in the Commons at Ottawa, when it was attempted to censure the Canadian Government for their stern resolution to vindicate the cause of order in the Territories. Poundmaker and Big Bear were sent for three years to the penitentiary, and several other Indians suffered the extreme penalty of the law for the murders at Frog Lake. Sir John Macdonald was at the head of the Canadian Government, and every possible effort was made to force him to obtain the pardon of Riel, but he felt that he could not afford to weaken the authority of law in the west, and his French Canadian colleagues, Sir Hector Langevin, then minister of public works, Sir Adolphe Chapleau, then secretary of state,—now lieutenant-governor of Quebec—Sir Adolphe Caron, then minister of militia, exhibited commendable courage in resisting the passionate and even menacing appeals of their countrymen, who were carried away at this crisis by a false sentiment, rather than by a true sense of justice. Happily, in the course of no long time, the racial antagonisms raised by this unhappy episode in the early history of confederation disappeared under the influence of wiser counsels, and the peace of this immense region has never since been threatened by Indians or half-breeds, who have now few, if any, grievances on which to brood. The patriotism shown by the Canadian people in this memorable contest of 1885 illustrated the desire of all classes to consolidate the union, and make it secure from external and internal dangers, and had also an admirable influence in foreign countries which could now appreciate the growing national strength of the Dominion. In the cities of Ottawa, Toronto, and Winnipeg, monuments have been raised to recall the services of the volunteers who fought and died at Fish Creek and Batoche. On the banks of the Saskatchewan a high cairn and cross point to the burial place of the men who fell before the deadly shot of the half-breed sharpshooters at Fish Creek:

> "Not in the quiet churchyard, near those who loved them best;
> But by the wild Saskatchewan, they laid them to their rest.
> A simple soldier's funeral in that lonely spot was theirs,
> Made consecrate and holy by a nation's tears and prayers.
> Their requiem—the music of the river's surging tide;
> Their funeral wreaths, the wild flowers that grow on every side;
> Their monument—undying praise from each Canadian heart,
> That hears how, for their country's sake, they nobly bore their part."

One of the finest bodies of troops in the world, the Mounted Police of Canada, nearly one thousand strong, now maintains law and order throughout a district upwards of three hundred thousand square miles in area, and annually cover a million and a half miles in the discharge of their onerous duties. The half-breeds now form but a very small minority of the population, and are likely to disappear as a distinct class under the influence of civilisation. The Indians, who number about thirty thousand in Manitoba and the Northwest, find their interests carefully guarded by treaties and statutes of Canada, which recognise their rights as wards of the Canadian Government. They are placed on large reserves, where they can carry on farming and other industrial occupations for which the Canadian Government, with commendable liberality, provide means of instruction. Many of the Indians have shown an aptitude for agricultural pursuits which has surprised those who have supposed they could not be induced to make much progress in the arts of civilised life. The average attendance of Indian children at the industrial and other schools is remarkably large compared even with that of white children in the old provinces. The Indian population of Canada, even in the Northwest territory, appear to have reached the stationary stage, and hereafter a small increase is confidently expected by those who closely watch the improvement in their methods of life. The high standard which has been reached by the Iroquois population on the Grand River of Ontario, is an indication of what we may even expect in the course of many years on the banks of the many rivers of the Northwest. The majority of the tribes in Manitoba and the Northwest—the Crees and Blackfeet—belong to the Algonquin race, and the Assiniboines or Stonies, to the Dacotahs or Sioux, now only found on the other side of the frontier. The Tinneh or Athabaskan family occupy the Yukon and Mackenzie valleys, while in the Arctic region are the Eskimo or Innuits. In British Columbia* there are at least eight distinct stocks; in the interior, Tinneh, Salish or Shuswap; on

---

*Dr. Geo. M. Dawson, F.R.S., has given me this division of Indian tribes.

the coast, Haida, Ishimsian, Kwakiool (including Hailtzuk), Bilhoola, Aht, or Nootka, and Kawitshin, the latter including several names, probably of Salish affinity, living around the Gulf of Georgia. The several races that inhabit Canada, the Algonquins, the Huron-Iroquois, the Dacotah, the Tinneh, and the several stocks of British Columbia, have for some time formed an interesting study for scholars, who find in their languages and customs much valuable archæological and ethnological lore. The total number of Indians that now inhabit the whole Dominion is estimated at over one hundred thousand souls, of whom one-third live in the old provinces.

The Story of the Canadian People

David M. Duncan

THE RED RIVER Rebellion.—To-day about half a million people dwell between Lake Superior and the Rocky Mountains, a scanty population for a land so vast. Yet what a change since confederation! Then the only occupants of the broad prairies were roving bands of Indians, a few scattered traders, and twelve thousand settlers in the valley of the Red River. Ten of these twelve thousand were half-breeds, some of Scottish descent, speaking English, others French both in origin and speech. Into this community, without warning, flocked Canadian surveyors to lay out roads and townships. The country had been handed over to Canada, and the interests of the natives were to be sacrificed. Such was the thought of the half-breed element. The presence in the colony of several Fenians and American annexationists added to the general discontent. The storm centre was the French half-breed party, the *Métis,* led by Louis Riel. Riel was the son of a white father and a half-breed mother, and had been educated in Montreal for the priesthood. Fluency of speech and magnetism of manner gave him ready control over his compatriots; unchecked ambition and extraordinary vanity blinded him to the folly of resisting the authority of the Dominion. There was no one in the colony to restrain his madness. But for the courage and tact of Donald A. Smith, acting as the agent of the Dominion government, affairs might have taken a worse turn than they did. Archbishop Taché, than whom none exerted greater influence over the *Métis,* was absent in Rome, and did not return until the frenzy of rebellion had spent itself in murder.

The news that the Hon. William McDougall was on his way to the Red River to assume the governorship was the signal for the rising. Riel and his followers seized Fort Garry, and set up the so-called "Provisional Government." McDougall was stopped at the boundary line and forbidden to enter the country. Fortunately the would-be governor obeyed, and there was every prospect of a bloodless settlement of the difficulty, when a sudden fit of madness on Riel's part precipitated a tragedy. Among some prisoners whom the latter had thrust into Fort Garry, as enemies of the "Provisional Government," was a young Ontario immigrant named Thomas Scott. This unfortunate youth, Riel picked out to be his instrument in terrorising his opponents. Court-martialled and condemned upon the charge of treason, Scott was led out before the walls of Fort Garry and shot. The news of this brutal murder raised a storm of indignation in eastern Canada. Thousands volunteered to avenge the victim, and of these seven hundred were chosen to proceed at once to the scene of rebellion. A toilsome and dangerous journey by way of Lake Superior and the fur traders' route was skilfully conducted by Colonel Garnet Wolseley. At the approach of the volunteer force all military ardour and pride of office died down within Riel's breast. He promptly fled from the scene of his transient glory to find a refuge in the United States.

The Province of Manitoba Formed, 1870.—Out of the strife of rebellion arose a new province. Even while Wolseley's force was on its way to Fort Garry, the Manitoba Act was passed by the Canadian Parliament. By this act Manitoba was admitted into confederation as a full-fledged province. The claims of the half-breeds were fully met, one million four hundred thousand acres of land being set apart for that purpose. Many of Wolseley's men remained in the new province to share in its making. The little settlement about Fort Garry was soon transformed into the populous city of Winnipeg, a monument to the foresight of that patriotic coloniser, Lord Selkirk. Manitoba drew her first governor from the far East, in the person of a distinguished Nova Scotian, Adams G. Archibald.

The Saskatchewan Rebellion, 1885.—The advent of the railway gave promise of peaceful and rapid progress, when suddenly a second rebellion broke out. To understand this new outbreak it is necessary to turn back to the close of the Red River rebellion. In settlement of the claims of Manitoba's rebellious subjects two hundred and forty acres of land were granted to each half-breed. In spite of this liberal treatment, many of the *Métis* or half-breeds, rather than remain in a province which was quickly filling up with settlers, withdrew westwards and settled upon the banks of the Saskatchewan among their near relatives, the Cree Indians. With the formation of the North-West Territories the hated civilisation began to creep up upon them once more. The rapid disappearance of the buffalo, upon which Indians and half-breeds alike depended for a living, threatened a general famine. The natural unrest of the *Métis* was increased by a fear that their lands, of which they had received no patents or title-deeds, would be snatched away by speculators. Great dissatisfaction was felt, too, with the government's method of surveying the land, which interfered with the old French plan of having all the farms fronting upon the river. If anything further were needed to provoke rebellion, it was the presence of Louis Riel, who, returning from exile, suddenly appeared upon the scene to champion once more the cause of his restless compatriots. At first Riel was moderate, and there was every reason to expect that the government, though slow to act, would eventually remove all causes of discontent, when an unfortunate encounter of armed men precipitated rebellion. Near Duck Lake, within the angle formed by the North and South Saskatchewan, a force of Mounted Police and Prince Albert volunteers, while attempting to bring in an outlying store of supplies, was met by a band of rebels and driven back with a loss of twelve men killed.

The position of the white settlers of the Saskatchewan Valley was serious. To maintain order over the wide prairies stretching from Manitoba to the Rocky Mountains there were at hand only five hundred Mounted Police. The real danger lay, not in a revolt of the *Métis*, but in the possibility of a general rising of the Indians, of whom there were over thirty thousand in the North-West. The success of the rebels at Duck Lake forced the Police and Volunteers to fall back upon Prince Albert. This point, Battleford, and Fort Pitt were left exposed to the attack of either the *Métis* or the Indians. Fortunately the tribes most to be feared, the Blackfeet, the Bloods, and the Piegans, remained quiet, only the Crees joining hands with the rebels. The most serious risings of the Indians took place near Battleford and Fort Pitt, among the followers of Poundmaker and Big Bear. The heart of the rebellion was the village of Batoche, the centre of the *Métis* settlements. Here Riel, forgetful of his overthrow at Fort Garry fifteen years before, again raised the standard of revolt.

The news of the fight at Duck Lake was the signal for a rising among the disaffected Indians. Near Battleford two murders were committed, although Poundmaker remained quiet within his reserve about thirty miles from the town. Big Bear's warriors were more lawless. Descending upon the little settlement of Frog Lake, near Fort Pitt, they disarmed and shot nine men, and carried off a number of women and children. They then moved upon Fort Pitt, a group of log-houses in the form of a square, practically defenceless. Fear of the twenty-three Mounted Police in charge of the fort kept Big Bear from attacking. The commander, Francis Dickens, a son of the famous novelist, seeing that the place could not long hold out against the enemy, withdrew his men and escaped down the river to Battleford.

When the report of the rebellion reached Ottawa, the Dominion government took prompt action. As in the case of the Red River rising, the call for volunteers met with an eager response on all sides. Distance made the transportation of troops very difficult. From Ottawa to Qu'Appelle was over sixteen hundred miles, from Qu'Appelle to Batoche, two hundred and forty. To add to the difficulty of the undertaking there were several gaps in the Canadian Pacific Railway along the north shore of Lake Superior, which necessitated the use of sleighs in transporting guns and military stores. In spite of all obstacles, within less than two months forty-four hundred men were placed in the field, all save the Winnipeg contingent being from eastern Canada.

General Middleton, commander-in-chief of the Canadian militia, who arrived at Qu'Appelle in advance of the main force, quickly formed his plans. Making the Canadian Pacific Railway the base line of his operations, he prepared to crush the rebellion in all its centres at once. Three places were in immediate danger—Prince Albert, Battleford and Fort Pitt; three relief expeditions were provided for in the plan of campaign. General Middleton was to advance from Qu'Appelle to Batoche, Riel's headquarters, Colonel Otter from Swift Current to Battleford, and General Strange from Calgary to Edmonton.

On the 6th of April General Middleton's detachment left Fort Qu'Appelle, and twelve days later reached Clark's Crossing, on the Saskatchewan, where it had been arranged to meet the steamer *Northcote* coming down the river with reinforcements and supplies. Although the steamer had not yet arrived, General Middleton divided his force, one-half on either bank, and advanced in the direction of Batoche. A few days later, as the division on the east bank was entering the ravine of Fish Creek, it came suddenly upon a strong force of the rebels under the command of Gabriel Dumont, a buffalo hunter whom Riel had chosen to be his lieutenant. In the skirmish which followed, Middleton lost ten men, the enemy eleven. Although Dumont fell back in the night, Middleton decided to await the arrival of the *Northcote*. On the

5th of May the delayed steamer arrived, and the advance was continued, two days' march bringing the force within striking distance of the rebels' headquarters. The ground before the village was found to be honeycombed with rifle-pits. Three days of skirmishing before these entrenchments wore out the patience of the volunteers, so that on the fourth day General Middleton had great difficulty in holding them. In the afternoon all restraint was thrown off, and the line, led by Colonel Williams of the Midland Battalion, swept forward at a run, drove the enemy's riflemen from their trenches, pursuing them through the village beyond. The back of the rebellion was broken, and three days later Riel gave himself up. Without loss of time General Middleton pressed on to Prince Albert, and thence to Battleford.

Ten days after leaving Swift Current, Colonel Otter halted within three miles of Battleford. Fearing that Poundmaker, although as yet not actively hostile, might be influenced to join forces with Big Bear, he decided to move in the direction of the neighbouring reserve. The Indian encampment was found to occupy the higher of two hills, beyond the ravine of Cut Knife Creek. The appearance of the volunteers upon the crest of the first hill was the signal for battle. Early in the engagement the two guns which Colonel Otter had brought with him broke down. This disaster, coupled with the superiority of the Indians in number, made it necessary to fall back in the direction of Battleford. The loss sustained in this fight was eight killed and fourteen wounded, and might have been much more serious had Poundmaker followed up his advantage by pursuing his retiring enemy.

Meanwhile General Strange had relieved Edmonton from the danger of an Indian attack, and was descending the North Saskatchewan in order to hem in Big Bear between his force and that of Colonel Otter stationed at Battleford. On the 24th of May Fort Pitt was reached. Three days later Big Bear's band was located, but was found to be too strongly entrenched to be successfully attacked. When, alarmed at the strength of the forces closing in upon them, the Indians began to retreat, Major Steele was sent in pursuit. It was a long chase over hundreds of miles of broken country. Gradually Big Bear's force was broken up, and the leader himself finally surrendered to the Mounted Police. Meanwhile, at Battleford, Poundmaker and his followers had come in and laid down their arms. With Riel, Poundmaker, and Big Bear in custody, the rebellion was at an end, and it only remained to punish the rebel leaders who had defied the authority of the Canadian government. Riel was tried at Regina, and, though ably defended, was found guilty of treason and sentenced to be hanged. Eight Indians also paid the death penalty for murder, while others were imprisoned, among the latter Poundmaker, who died in prison.

Growth of the North-West.—Although a trying experience while it lasted, the Saskatchewan rebellion was not without its good results. The Dominion government was brought to recognise the claims of the *Métis*, and did so by promptly issuing title-deeds of their lands. In recognition of their growing importance, the North-West Territories were granted representation in the Senate and the House of Commons. To preserve order and to protect the lives of the settlers scattered throughout the country, the Mounted Police force was considerably increased. But the greatest influence of the rebellion was not upon the North-West alone, but upon the whole Dominion. Eagerly the volunteers went,

> "Over dim forest and lake,
> Over lone prairie and brake,
> The clamour of battle to wake
> For kindred and country's sake
> Into the North and the Westland."

All the provinces were interested in the suppression of the revolt; their sons either shared in the fighting or were pressing to the front when stopped by the news of Riel's surrender. Common hardships upon the march, common dangers in the field of battle, and the common anxiety of friends at home made real in the hearts of Canadians the union which confederation had brought about.

Le Dernier des Martyrs

Louis Fréchette

—Mais cet homme n'a fait que défendre ses frères
Et leurs foyers.—*A mort!*—Mille actes arbitraires
Ont fait un drapeau saint de son drapeau battu. . . .
—*A mort!* . . . —Mais, songez-y, cet homme est revêtu
Du respect que l'on doit aux prisonniers de guerre:
Vous avez avec lui parlementé naguère.
—*A mort!* . . . —Mais tout rayon en lui s'est éclipsé;
Allez-vous de sang froid tuer un insensé?
C'est impossible!—*A mort!* . . . —Mais c'est de la démence;
Pour lui le jury même implore la clémence. . . .
A mort! . . . —Un peuple entier réclame son pardon;
Son supplice peut être un terrible brandon
De discordes sans fin et d'hostilités vaines. . . .
Allons!—*A mort!* il a du sang français aux veines!
—C'est ce sang qu'il vous faut? eh bien, vous avez tort:
Un martyr ne meurt pas.—*A mort! à mort! à mort!* . . .

The Last of the Martyrs

Louis Fréchette

—But this man only defended his brothers
And their homes. —*To death!*— A thousand arbitrary acts
Have made a holy flag from his beaten flag
—*To death!* . . . —But, think about it, this man is enveloped
In a respect due to prisoners of war:
You hardly spoke to him.
—*To death!* . . . —But all rays of light in him have been eclipsed;
Will you in cold blood kill a madman?
It's impossible!—*To death!* . . . —But it is because of madness
That even the jury asks for clemency
To death! . . . —An entire people beg for a pardon
His supplication is maybe a terrible brand
Discords without end and hostilities in vain . . .

Let's go!— *To death!* . . . —he has some French blood in his veins!
—It's this blood you need? well, you are wrong:
A martyr never dies. *To death!* . . . —*To death!* . . . — *To death!* . . .

Note: In a revised version of this poem, Fréchette added the following lines.
To death! To death! he has some French blood in his veins!
There is his true crime

PM/Dialogue

Pierre Trudeau

. . . with Riel

WHEN THE PRIME Minister unveiled a statue of rebel Louis Riel beside Wascona Lake in front of the Saskatchewan legislative building, Oct. 2, 1968:

Eighty-three years ago in the Mounted Police barracks in Regina, Louis Riel awaited execution as a convicted traitor. This afternoon we are assembled to unveil a monument in his honor,

No man in Canadian history suffered as many reversals of fortune during his life. He was, in turn, unofficial leader of his people, president of a provisional government, founder of the province of Manitoba, fugitive in exile, member of Parliament, outlaw, leader of another provisional government, and prisoner.

Yet it may be that none of the twists and turns in his tragic biography will be as important to the history of this country as the reversal of official and public opinion which this monument symbolizes.

We are in a beautiful garden. About us are handsome government buildings, imaginatively designed. Behind me is an important monument.

These things are evidence of the goodness of life in Canada; of our ability to combine human and physical resources to make our land rich and productive; of our talent to govern ourselves by democratic processes; of our recollection of the harshness of the frontier and its occasional injustice; of our determination to make a better life for ourselves and our children.

Yet this very setting, this very tranquility, this sense of orderliness and propriety makes me think how difficult it is for any of us to understand Louis Riel. What forces motivated this man? What social conditions lead him to believe that nothing short of rebellion would serve the cause to which he had pledged himself? How many other Riels exist in Canada, beyond the fringe of accepted conduct, driven to believe that this country offers no answer to their needs and no solutions to their problems?

How many of us understand the loneliness, the sense of futility of such a man? How many of us are willing to concede that future historians, in chronicling the events of our lives, may choose to emphasize and applaud the activities, not of the privileged majority, but of some little-known leader of an unpopular minority?

For me this is the lesson of Louis Riel. For me this is the reason why we are here.

During his life Riel aroused the fiercest passions among his compatriots, and the manner of his death was a cause of deep division throughout Canada. The controversy has not died, as we know from the stream of books, plays—and most recently an opera—which continue to be written about him. But in the perspective of eight decades of our history perhaps we can agree on the underlying themes which make an understanding of his turbulent career so important to us. "For those who do not learn from history are doomed to repeat it."

We can agree that Riel's dream of a vast, autonomous Metis nation-state in the middle of North America could never have been realized. The economic and political momentum of the two young countries which share this continent was too great to justify or to permit further fragmentation. That Riel could make his dream appear plausible to his followers is testimony to the force of his character, no doubt. More important, it indicates the bitterness of their frustration.

Both in 1879 in what is now Manitoba, and in 1885 in what is now Saskatchewan, Riel and his followers were protesting against the government's indifference to their problems and its refusal to consult them on matters of their vital interest. Questions of minority rights have deep roots in our history.

A democratic society and system of government, while amongst the grandest of human concepts, are among the most difficult to implement. In a democracy it is all too easy for the majority to forget the rights of the minority, and for a remote and powerful government to ignore its protests.

It is all too easy, should disturbances erupt, to crush them in the name of law and order. We must never forget that, in the long run, a democracy is judged by the way the majority treats the minority. Louis Riel's battle is not yet won.

That is why I suggest that we should never respond to demands for just treatment by pointing to other examples of injustice.

If a certain right is attacked or denied in one province, it is not a valid reason for refusing similar rights in another. Yet such excuses are offered, and this leads to a vicious circle in which no improvement in human liberties is possible. The rights of individual Canadians are too important to be used as bargaining counters.

Every government must accept responsibility for the rights of the citizens within its own jurisdiction. Canada as a whole suffers when any of her citizens is denied his rights; for that injustice places the rights of all of us in jeopardy.

We could find examples of rights denied or abused in many parts of Canada, but perhaps most obviously in the fields of education and language. We have a blueprint for a functional bilingual state in the report of the Royal Commission and, with the collaboration of all governments, we are beginning to build it. But it has taken us 100 years and the job is far from done.

All around us, in many foreign countries and here in Canada, we can see the disastrous results of ignoring the universal demand for human rights and freedoms. Confronted by the lessons of our own history, and the disorders of the contemporary world, we will bear a heavy responsibility if we fail to provide an adequate response.

Nor should we believe that governments alone can handle these problems. In a democracy the ultimate and essential protection for individual liberties lies within each citizen.

Only when the vast majority of citizens comes to understand and share the feelings of minorities will justice truly prevail. Only when minorities are given the opportunity not just to be heard, but to participate effectively in the democratic process through responsive political organizations, can we be reasonably certain that our society will not produce another Riel tragedy.

We pay tribute to Louis Riel as a fighter for the rights of his people. Those who share his thirst for social justice should preserve his memory in their minds and hearts.

A History of the Canadian Peoples

J.M. Bumsted

EXPANDING THE NATION, 1867–1885

Although 1 July 1867 would be celebrated a century later as the date for Canada's 100th birthday, it was in the larger sense only an interim point. The new union consisted of four provinces—Ontario, Quebec, Nova Scotia, and New Brunswick—carved from the three that had created it. Sir John A. Macdonald's government was conscious that a lot of British territory on the continent had been excluded. The new government was also quite obviously the old Canadian coalition, with a few Maritime faces. Its organization was the old Canadian departments. It used buildings erected in Ottawa for the old Province of Canada. If the new administration seemed familiar, so did many of its policies. It bought off the malcontents in Nova Scotia with better terms that were entirely financial. It started building the Intercolonial Railway along the eastern coast of New Brunswick. With the prodding of the British, the Hudson's Bay Company would sell Rupert's Land and the Northwest Territory to the new nation. Canada devoted much energy to rounding up the strays and expanding coast to coast.

In many respects, the two decades from 1867 to 1885 would focus on elaborating the myriad loose ends created by unification. There was the need to create new policies for the new Canada. In the end, too many policies continued from the older Canada, occasionally writ larger to accommodate the other provinces. The creation of new identities was even more difficult. The easiest identities to accept were the old provincial ones. Collectively, these provincial identities grew to provide one alternate vision to the national one envisioned by the founding fathers.

ADDING NEW TERRITORY

One of the earliest legislative actions of the new Canadian government in December 1867 was the passage of resolutions calling for transcontinental expansion. Most of the legislators regarded such expansion as the nation's inevitable right, a sort of Canadian version of manifest destiny. As a result, in 1868 a ministerial delegation went to London to arrange the Hudson's Bay Company's transfer of the northwest to Canada. While complex negotiations continued, the Canadian government began building a road from Fort Garry to Lake of the Woods. This was part of a proposed road and water system linking Red River with Canada. The road builders established informal connections with Dr John Christian Schultz (1840–96), the influential leader of the local faction that had been agitating for Canadian annexation for years. Nobody bothered to pay any attention to the mixed bloods who constituted the bulk of the local population of the settlement. The Canadian delegation in London finally worked out a deal for the transfer. The British government received the territory from the Hudson's Bay Company (the Canadians put up £300,000 and agreed to substantial land grants for the company) and subsequently transferred it intact to Canada.

Since the arrangements for the west were made without bothering to inform the Red River people of their import, it was hardly surprising that the locals were suspicious and easily roused to protest. The Métis were concerned on several counts. A number of racist incidents involved the road-building party. There was transparent haste on the part of the Canadian government to build a road and to send in men to survey land. This rush suggested that Canadian settlement would inundate the existing population without regard for its 'rights'. Canada made clear that it intended to treat the new territory as a colony. Furthermore, some of the road builders bought land cheaply from the indigenous peoples—land that the Métis thought was theirs. The Métis quickly perceived the Canadians as a threat to their way of life, perhaps even to their very existence. The Canadian government received a number of warnings in 1869 that trouble was brewing. The warnings came from the Anglican archbishop of Rupert's Land, Robert Machray (1831–1904); from the governor of the Hudson's Bay Company, William Mactavish (1815–70); and from Bishop Alexandre Taché (1823–94), the Catholic bishop of St. Boniface. Ottawa received all such reports with little or no interest. Subsequent events were largely a consequence of avoidable Canadian blunders and insensitivities. In colonial thralldom itself until only a few years previously, Canada had little experience in managing imperial expansion. It handled it very clumsily, and the entire nation would pay dearly for the mistakes.

In October 1869 a leader of the Métis appeared in the person of Louis Riel (1844–85), a member of a leading family in the community. His father, for whom he was named, had successfully led a Métis protest in 1849 against the Hudson's Bay Company, which had won the right to trade freely in furs. The young Riel spoke out publicly against the surveys. He then led a party that stood on the surveyors' chains and ordered them to stop. In the meantime, William McDougall (1822–1905) was on his way from Canada to assume office as lieutenant-governor of the northwest. A newly formed National Committee of the Métis resolved that McDougall should not be allowed to enter the country. The Métis made it clear that they would oppose him by force if necessary. Canada responded to the unrest by refusing to take over the territory until it was pacified. Riel escalated the conflict. In early November he and a large band of armed Métis took possession of Upper Fort Garry, the Hudson's Bay Company central headquarters. The Métis then invited the anglophone inhabitants of the settlement, most of whom were mixed bloods themselves, to send delegates to meet and coordinate policy. Riel managed to get tacit consent for the establishment of a provisional government and approval of a 'list of rights'. On 7 December he and his men surrounded Dr Schultz's store, taking Schultz and forty-eight Canadians to Fort Garry as prisoners. The next day Riel issued a 'Declaration of the People', announcing a provisional government. He declared that the people of Red River wanted to be allowed to negotiate their own entry into Confederation on the basis of the 'rights' already agreed to by the residents. William McDougall made a fool of himself with an illegal proclamation of his government—Canada having refused to take possession of the territory—and then returned home.

SITTING BULL REJECTS AMERICAN OVERTURES

[In June 1876, American General George Armstrong Custer led a frontal cavalry charge against a Sioux encampment at Little Bighorn, Montana. All the 250 soldiers involved, including Custer, were killed. The Sioux—both those involved in the battle and others—led by Chief Sitting Bull (c. 1834–90), withdrew north of the 49th parallel under the protection of Great Britain and the recently formed Royal North-West Mounted Police. This portrait of Sitting Bull was taken in 1892 (National Archives of Canada C-20038). In his memoirs, *Forty Years in Canada: Reminiscences of the Great North-West*, Colonel Sam Steele described the visit in October of 1878 to Fort Macleod by an American commission seeking to get Sitting Bull and his people to return to the United States. *Source:* S. Steele, *Forty Years in Canada: Reminiscences of the Great North-West* (Toronto: McClelland, Goodchild & Stewart, 1915):127–9.]

The day after his arrival, General Terry and General Lawrence, who accompanied him, were met at the officers' mess-room by Colonel Macleod and his officers, and received Sitting Bull and his chiefs in council. A number of American and Canadian newspapers were represented. . . . The proceedings began by Colonel Macleod stating that General Terry and his staff were present by invitation, and that the Sioux chiefs had been summoned to meet them. General Terry then addressed the chiefs, through an interpreter who, it is to be regretted, did not know even his own language and was in no manner to be compared with those who did duty at the great Blackfeet and Cree treaties. Few men of good education had opportunities of learning Sioux, consequently the fine display of oratory of some of the chiefs was cut down to laconic remarks even coarser than one sometimes heard in the magistrate's court at Fort Macleod.

The general told the chiefs that their band was the only one that had not surrendered to the United States, and that it was the desire of his government that they should return to their reservations, give up their arms and horses, and receive cattle in exchange for the money realized by the sale. In reply Sitting Bull said:

Louis Riel marshalled his forces brilliantly. A convention of forty representatives, equally divided between the two language groups, debated and approved another 'list of rights'. The convention endorsed Riel's provisional government. It appointed three delegates to go to Ottawa to negotiate with the Macdonald government. So far, so good. But in early March, Thomas Scott, a prisoner who was an Orangeman, got into trouble with Riel and his guards. A Métis court martial condemned Scott to death without offering him a chance to be heard. Riel accepted the sentence, commenting, 'We must make Canada respect us.' The 'murder' of Scott would have enormous repercussions in Orange Ontario, which was looking desper-

For 64 years you have kept me and my people and treated us badly. What have we done that you should want us to stop? We have done nothing. It is the people on your side who have started us to do these depredations. We could not go anywhere else, so we took refuge in this country. It was on this side of the country that we learnt to shoot, and that was the reason I came back to it again. I should like to know why you came here. In the first place I did not give you the country, but you followed me from one place to another, so that I had to leave and come over to this country. I was born and raised in this country with the Red River half-breeds, and I intend to stop with them. I was raised hand-in-hand with the Red River half-breeds, and we are going over to that part of the country, and that is the reason I have come over here. Here Sitting Bull shook hands with Colonel Macleod and Major Walsh. *That is the way I was raised, in the hands of the people here, and that is the way I intend to be with them. You have got ears and you have got eyes to see with, and to see how I live with these people. You see me, here I am. If you think I am a fool, you are a bigger fool than I am. This house is a medicine house. You come here to tell us lies, but we do not want to hear them. I do not wish any such language used to me, that is, to tell me such lies in my Great Mother's house. Do not say two more words. Go back to where you came from. The country is mine, and I intend to stay here, and to raise this country full of grown people. See these people here, we were raised with them.* Again he shook hands with the Mounted Police Officers. *That is enough, so no more. You see me shaking hands with these people. The part of the country you gave me you ran me out of. I have now come to stay with these people, and I intend to stay here. . . .*

The Indians . . . arose and were about to depart when the interpreter was directed by General Terry to ask: 'Shall I say to the President of the United States that you have refused the offer he has made to you? Are we to understand from what you have said that you refuse those offers?' to which Sitting Bull replied: *I could tell you more, but that is all I have to tell you. If we told you more, why, you would not pay attention to it; that is all I have to say. This part of the country does not belong to your people. You belong to the other side. This side belongs to us.*

ately for an excuse to condemn the Red River uprising. The three-man delegation from Red River, headed by Abbé Noel Ritchot (1825–1905), gained substantial concessions from the Canadian government. If honoured, they would guarantee some protection for the original inhabitants of Red River against the expected later influx of settlers and land speculators. At what the Canadians always regarded as the point of a gun, the Métis extorted the Manitoba Act of 1870. This legislation granted provincial status to a Manitoba roughly equivalent to the old Red River settlement, with 1,400,000 acres (566,580 ha) set aside for the Métis and bilingual services guaranteed. The remainder of the northwest became a territory of Canada. One of its government's principal tasks was to extinguish Aboriginal title through the negotiation of treaties with the indigenous peoples. These agreements would prepare for settlement by people of European origin.

In May 1870 the Canadian government sent a so-called peaceful military expedition to Red River. The troops occupied the province for Canada in late August, forcing Riel and his associates to flee for their lives. The Scott execution provided the Canadian government with the excuse to deny Riel and his lieutenants an official amnesty for all acts committed during the 'uprising'. Those who negotiated with Canada always insisted that such an amnesty had been unofficially promised. The result was that Louis Riel went into long-term exile instead of becoming premier of the province he had created. (An amnesty was granted Riel in 1875, on the condition that he be banished from the country for five years.) Whether the government would keep better faith over its land guarantees to the Métis was another matter.

THE STRUGGLE FOR THE WEST

Sincere efforts on the part of many in the new Dominion attempted to encourage a sense of nationhood transcending the linguistic barriers between French and English and the geographical barriers of the provinces and the regions. Nevertheless, the new Canadian nationality remained fragile, more than a bit artificial, and very racist. In addition, at least outside French Canada, it tended to express the prejudices and values of British Ontario writ large. The crucible for the new Canada, many believed, was in the vast expanse of territory west of the Great Lakes. Here its limitations were most clearly evident.

The interests of the Canadian government in the Northwest Territory, especially under Sir John A. Macdonald, were focused on agricultural settlement. This would provide both an outlet for excess eastern population and the means of encouraging the development of a truly transcontinental nation. The process of settlement pushed the Aboriginal inhabitants of the region out of the way as quickly as possible. The Canadian government negotiated a number of treaties with the First Nations. They extinguished Aboriginal titles in exchange for reserves on the most marginal and least attractive land. In August 1876, for example, the Indians of central Saskatchewan forgathered at Fort Carlton to consider the terms of the government's Treaty no. 6. The Plains Cree chief Poundmaker (Pitikwahanapiwiyin, *c.* 1842–86)

LOUIS RIEL AND HIS COUNCILLORS

This photograph shows Louis Riel at the centre of his provisional government sometime in early 1870 (National Archives of Canada C12854). In the top row, left to right, are: Bonnet Tromage, Pierre de Lorme, Thomas Bunn, Xavier Page, Baptiste Beauchemin, Baptiste Tournond, and Thomas Spence. In the middle row are Pierre Poitras, John Bruce, Louis Riel, John O'Donoghue, and François Dauphenais. In the front row are Robert O'Lone and Paul Proux.

Although Canada had not annexed Red River in December 1869 as planned, it never admitted that this government was legal. Riel (1844–85) brilliantly led the Métis resistance to Canada in 1869–70. He began as secretary of the Métis National Committee, with John Bruce as president. He took over from Bruce as president of the committee in late December 1870, and was formally elected president of the provisional government in early February. His only blunder was the execution of Thomas Scott. That mistake enabled the Macdonald government to bypass Riel and his provisional government, however, and occupy the territory by force. Scott's death also stood in the way of an amnesty for Riel and his lieutenants. The amnesty question was finally resolved in 1875 when Riel was sent into exile for five years. In the wake of this decision, he spent some time in a mental institution. He eventually ended up in North Dakota as a schoolteacher and an American citizen.

In 1885 he led a second resistance to Canada, and was eventually convicted of treason and hanged for the offence. Riel's lawyers tried to plead insanity, but Riel himself eloquently told the six-man jury that he was not insane. The jury found him guilty, but requested clemency. The Macdonald government ignored the request.

objected to the arrangement, saying that the government should be prepared to train his people as farmers and assist them in other ways after the buffalo disappeared. Nevertheless, Poundmaker signed the treaty, and three years later accepted a reserve on the Battle River. Another important Plains Cree chief, Big Bear (Mistahimaskwa, c. 1825–88), refused to sign for six years. He capitulated on 8 December 1882 when his people were starving and needed food. The following July, his small band was moved north to a reservation near Fort Pitt.

The Canadian government established the North-West Mounted Police in 1873 to act as its quasi-military agent in the west. It modelled the NWMP on the Irish constabulary. Its officers, drawn from the élites of eastern Canada, believed in a notion of public stability that associated crime and violence with the 'lower orders' and the Aboriginal peoples. The Mounties kept ahead of settlement and have always been seen as the chief instruments of a more peaceful western expansion than was true in the neighbouring United States. Certainly in Canada there was less overt violence, but this was often owing to the early exertion of state power and control.

Settlement drove the Métis, like the First Nations, to the margins. By 1885 Ontario-born settlers outnumbered the Métis five to one in Manitoba, and only 7 per cent of the population of the province was of mixed-blood origin. Many Métis drifted farther west, to the Saskatchewan Valley, where they formed small mission settlements including Qu'Appelle, Batoche, and Duck Lake. The buffalo were becoming scarce everywhere. Government surveyors caused uncertainty and fear, as they had in Red River a decade earlier. The winter of 1883–4 was particularly severe, and many Métis and Indians starved. In June 1884 Big Bear and his followers, with many others, travelled to Poundmaker's reserve to hold a big meeting. They discussed the serious state of affairs, after which some 2,000 Indians put on a thirst dance, a religious ritual. For their part, the Métis turned in despair to Louis Riel. He had apparently put his life back together after years of exile in the United States and hospitalization in 1876–8 for mental disturbance at Longue Pointe, Quebec. He became an American citizen and was teaching in St Peter's, Montana (where he had married), when a delegation from the Saskatchewan country visited him on 4 June 1884. They told him of the grievances that were burdening the peoples of the region, explained that agitation was developing against the Canadian government, and pleaded with him to return to Canada to lead them. Why Riel agreed to do so is one of the many mysteries surrounding his life. However, within a month he and his family were in Batoche. By December 1884, Riel and W.H. Jackson (secretary of the Settler's Union) had finished drafting a long petition (with twenty-five sections), which they sent to Ottawa. It concluded by requesting that the petitioners 'be allowed as in [1870] to send Delegates to Ottawa with their Bill of rights; whereby an understanding may be arrived at as to their entry into confederation, with the constitution of a free province'. Ottawa acknowledged the petition, but gave no other response.

In March 1885 events took a menacing turn. Riel's military leader, Gabriel Dumont (1836–1906), intercepted a small NWMP detachment near Duck Lake. The engagement turned into a full-fledged battle in which fatalities occurred on both sides. Riel called upon the Indians to assist him, which they did. Poundmaker's people broke into buildings in Battleford, terrifying settlers. The Cree warrior, Wandering Spirit (Kapapamahchakwew, c. 1845–85), led a band that attacked Frog Lake, killing nine. Prime Minister Macdonald determined to crush this rebellion quickly, sending an armed force under Major-General Frederick Middleton (1825–98) by way of the new Canadian Pacific Railway. The Canadian force of 800 men arrived at Batoche on 9 May. They quickly defeated Riel and about 200 Métis. The uprising was over by 12 May. Dumont and others fled to the United States. The government arrested Riel.

A formal charge of high treason, carrying the death penalty, was laid against Riel on 6 July. (Despite the fact that Riel was an American citizen, the Canadian government held with the British government that he was also a British subject, since British citizenship acquired through birth could never be renounced.) The trial began on 28 July in Regina, where feelings ran high. It was a political trial, infamously coloured in many ways by Macdonald's determination to have Riel found guilty and executed. Riel passionately denied a plea of insanity introduced by his lawyers. The jury found him guilty, but recommended mercy. Ottawa dismissed two appeals, and hanged Riel on 16 November. Poundmaker stood trial for treason and was sentenced to three years in prison. Released after a year, he died four months later. Big Bear received a similar sentence, but was released after a year and a half. Wandering Spirit was hanged.

The execution of Louis Riel had a lasting impact on Canada. In Quebec it strengthened French-Canadian nationalism and helped turn voters away from the Conservative Party, which they had supported since Confederation. On 22 November 1885, at a huge gathering in the public square in Montreal called the Champ de Mars, Honoré Mercier, the Liberal leader in Quebec, joined Wilfrid Laurier in denouncing the government action. Mercier insisted: 'In killing Riel, Sir John has not only struck at the heart of our race but especially at the cause of justice and humanity which . . . demanded mercy for the prisoner of Regina, our poor friend of the North-West.' Laurier added: 'Had I been born on the banks of the Saskatchewan . . . I would myself have shouldered a musket to fight against the neglect of governments and the shameless greed of speculators.' The two leaders disagreed over Mercier's proposal that French Canadians leave the two major parties and form one of their own. Laurier insisted that Mercier's proposal would destroy Confederation. Symbolically, French Canada took the execution of Riel to represent the final exclusion of the francophone from the west. Few spoke of the symbolic meaning of the execution of Wandering Spirit for the Aboriginal peoples.

The military defeat of the Métis and the public execution of Louis Riel in November 1885 were only part of the reason why that year (and that month) were so significant, not only in the history of the west but in the history of Canada. In November 1885 workers drove the last spike at Craigellachie in eastern British Columbia, marking the completion of the Canadian Pacific Railway. The CPR had been resurrected in 1881 as a hybrid corporation controlled by private capitalists and financed largely by the state, which, along with public subsidies, gave it about 25 million acres (10,117,500 ha) of land along its right of way. Contemporaries actively debated the question of building in advance of settlement, particularly given the inducements needed to persuade hard-headed businessmen to proceed with construction. The Macdonald government defended the railway on the grounds of national interest. Since this concept is not measurable in dollar amounts, it is impossible to know whether the price was too high. Even before the line was completed, Macdonald used it to send troops west to help suppress the Métis uprising of 1885. The construction of the CPR was a spectacular feat of engineering, partly thanks to the managerial skills of William Van Horne (1843–1915). The CPR was built chiefly on the backs of 6,500 Chinese coolie labourers especially imported for the job. Many died, and those who survived were summarily discharged when the work was completed. With the CPR finished, the Canadian government moved swiftly to limit Chi-

POUNDMAKER

Poundmaker was a Plains Cree chief who objected to the terms of the Canadian government's Treaty no. 6 with the Natives of central Saskatchewan. Although his mother was Métis, he had acquired much status when he was adopted into the Blackfoot tribe as the son of a head chief. He insisted that the government should be prepared to train the Native peoples as farmers and offer them more assistance as the buffalo herds disappeared. The suggestion was not well received by the Canadian negotiators. Poundmaker signed the treaty and accepted a reserve on the Battle River three years later. The Natives met in June 1884 on this reserve to discuss their relations with Canada, ending with a huge thirst dance in which over 1,000 dancers participated. Poundmaker tried to protect one of those involved in the ceremony from North-West Mounted Police arrest, offering himself as a hostage, but was forced to surrender the fugitive.

Poundmaker did not participate in the summons to Louis Riel, and he was unable to prevent his younger warriors from joining the Métis uprising. He eventually surrendered unconditionally and was tried for treason with Riel at Regina. He told the court that he had done everything possible to prevent bloodshed and was in custody 'because I wanted justice'. His health was broken at Stony Mountain Penitentiary after only one year of a three-year sentence, and he died soon after his release. This painting shows the surrender of Poundmaker (National Archives of Canada).

nese immigration. With the Plains Indians and their allies, the Métis, totally subjugated, Canada was open for settlement from coast to coast.

The west was to be an anglophone colony of Canada. Not only were First Nations, Métis, and Chinese cast aside as quickly as possible, but French Canadians were not expected to settle there in any substantial numbers. National consolidation was arguably complete in 1885, but much Canadian 'nationalism' still bore the distinctive mark of the Ontario WASP. Two cultures, French and English, were in firm opposition to each other, and other cultures were thoroughly marginalized. Trying to satisfy the nation's two main components would continue to be the most challenging task facing the Canadian government.

Letter to Sir John A. Macdonald

Marilyn Dumont

Dear John: I'm still here and halfbreed,
after all these years
you're dead, funny thing,
that railway you wanted so badly,
there was talk a year ago
of shutting it down
and part of it was shut down,
the dayliner at least,
'From sea to shining sea,'
and you know, John,
after all that shuffling us around to suit the settlers,
we're still here and Metis.

We're still here
after Meech Lake and
one no-good-for-nothin-Indian
holdin-up-the-train,
stalling the 'Cabin Syllables/Noun of settlement,
/ . . . steel syntax [and] / The long sentence of its exploration'
and John, that goddamned railroad never made this a great nation,
cause the railway shut down and this country is still quarrelling over unity,
and Riel is dead
but he just keeps coming back
in all the Bill Wilsons yet to speak out of turn or favour
because you know as well as I
that we were railroaded
by some steel tracks that didn't last
and by some settlers who wouldn't settle
and it's funny we're still here and callin ourselves halfbreed.

CHAPTER SEVEN

Imagining the Nation: Imperial Canada

Introduction

After Confederation in 1867, Canadians sought to define Canada, to articulate a national identity. This school of nationalism is referred to as imperialism because of its emphasis on Canada's connection to the British Empire. For obvious reasons, imperialism resonated more in English Canada than it did in French Canada. In these readings, we see imperial Canada imagined in its unofficial national anthems and a poem by the late-nineteenth and early-twentieth-century Mohawk poet, Pauline Johnson. Why did Alexander Muir's "The Maple Leaf Forever" ultimately fail to become Canada's official national anthem? The two early versions and the later official versions of "O Canada" are not just a French version and an English translation; they are different songs. What does this reveal about Canada itself? In her poem, Pauline Johnson reminds us that imperial Canada and its project of territorial expansion across the continent from sea unto shining sea, or as Alexander Muir wrote, "from Cape Race to Nootka Sound" came at a cost. What was that cost? The process of imagining Canada is an ongoing one. Shortly after the first Quebec referendum on separation in 1980, the Canadian government passed the National Anthem Act. How has the English version changed? And why does Senator Vivienne Poy want to amend the National Anthem Act? Do you agree with her arguments?

The Maple Leaf Forever

Alexander Muir, 1867

In Days of yore,
From Britain's shore
Wolfe the dauntless hero came
And planted firm Britannia's flag
On Canada's fair domain.
Here may it wave,
Our boast, our pride
And joined in love together,
The thistle, shamrock, rose entwined,
The Maple Leaf Forever.

[CHORUS]
The Maple Leaf
Our Emblem Dear,
The Maple Leaf Forever.
God save our Queen and heaven bless,
The Maple Leaf Forever.

At Queenston Heights and Lundy's Lane
Our brave fathers side by side
For freedom's home and loved ones dear,
Firmly stood and nobly died.
And so their rights which they maintained,
We swear to yeild them never.
Our watchword ever more shall be
The Maple Leaf Forever

[CHORUS]
Our fair Dominion now extends
From Cape Race to Nootka Sound
May peace forever be our lot
And plenty a store abound
And may those ties of love be ours
Which discord cannot sever
And flourish green for freedom's home
The Maple Leaf Forever

[CHORUS]

O Canada

Sir Adolphe-Basile Routhier, 1880

O Canada! Terre de nos aïeux,
Ton front est ceint de fleurons glorieux.
Car ton bras sait porter l'épée,
Il sait porter la croix.
Ton histoire est une épopée,
Des plus brillants exploits.
Et ta valeur, de foi trempée,
Protégera nos foyers et nos droits.
Protégera nos foyers et nos droits.

English translation:

O Canada! Land of our forefathers
Thy brow is wreathed with a glorious garland of flowers.
As in thy arm ready to wield the sword,
So also is it ready to carry the cross.
Thy history is an epic of the most brilliant exploits.
Thy valour steeped in faith
Will protect our homes and our rights
Will protect our homes and our rights.

O Canada

R. Stanley Weir, 1908

O Canada! Our home and native land!
True patriot love thou dost in us command.
We see thee rising fair, dear land,
The True North, strong and free!
And stand on guard, O Canada,
We stand on guard for thee.

O Canada! Where pines and maples grow.
Great prairies spread and lordly rivers flow.
Thou art the land, O Canada,
From East to Western Sea,
The land of hope for all who toil!
The land of liberty.

May stalwart sons and gentle maidens rise,
And so abide, O Canada,
From East to Western Sea,
Where e'er thy pines and prairies are
The True North, strong and free!

The Cattle Thief

E. Pauline Johnson, 1895

THEY were coming across the prairie, they were galloping hard and fast;
For the eyes of those desperate riders had sighted their man at last—
Sighted him off to Eastward, where the Cree encampment lay,
Where the cotton woods fringed the river, miles and miles away.
Mistake him? Never, Mistake him? the famous Eagle Chief!
That terror to all the settlers, that desperate Cattle Thief—
That monstrous, fearless Indian, who lorded it over the plain,
Who thieved and raided, and scouted, who rode like a hurricane!
But they've tracked him across the prairie; they've followed him hard and fast;
For those desperate English settlers have sighted their man at last.
Up they wheeled to the tepees, all their British blood aflame,
Bent on bullets and bloodshed, bent on bringing down their game;
But: they searched in vain for the Cattle Thief: that lion had left his lair,
And they cursed like a troop of demons—for the women alone were there.
"The sneaking Indian coward," They hissed; "he hides while yet he can;
He'll come in the night for cattle; but he's scared to face a *man*."
"Never!" and up from the cotton woods, rang the voice of Eagle Chief;
And right out into the open stepped, unarmed, the Cattle Thief.
Was that the game they had coveted? Scarce fifty years had rolled
Over that fleshless, hungry frame, starved to the bone and old;
Over that wrinkled, tawny skin, unfed by the warmth of blood,
Over those hungry, hollow eyes that glared for the sight of food.

He turned, like a hunted lion: "I know not fear," said he;
And the words outleapt from his shrunken lips in the language of the Cree.
"I'll fight you, white-skins, one by one, till I kill you *all*," he said;
But the threat was scarcely uttered, ere a dozen balls of lead
Whizzed through the air about him like a shower of metal rain,
And the gaunt old Indian Cattle Thief, dropped dead on the open plain.
And that band of cursing settlers, gave one triumphant yell,
And rushed like a pack of demons on the body that writhed and fell.
"Cut the fiend up into inches, throw his carcass on the plain;
Let the wolves eat the cursed Indian, he'd have treated us the same."
A dozen hands responded, a dozen knives gleamed high,
But the first stroke was arrested by a woman's strange, wild cry.
And out into the open, with a courage past belief,
She dashed, and spread her blanket o'er the corpse of the Cattle Thief;

And the words outleapt from her shrunken lips in the language of the Cree,
"If you mean to touch that body, you must cut your way through *me*."
And that band of cursing settlers dropped backward one by one,
For they knew that an Indian woman roused, was a woman to let alone.
And then she raved in a frenzy that they scarcely understood,
Raved of the wrongs she had suffered since her earliest babyhood:
"Stand back, stand back, you white-skins, touch that dead man to your shame;
You have stolen my father's spirit, but his body I only claim.
You have killed him, but you shall not dare to touch him now he's dead.
You have cursed, and called him a Cattle Thief, though you robbed him first of
    bread—
Robbed him and robbed my people—look there, at that shrunken face,
Starved with a hollow hunger, we owe to you and your race.
What have you left to us of land, what have you left of game,
What have you brought but evil, and curses since you came?
How have you paid us for our game? how paid us for our land?
By a *book*, to save our souls from the sins *you* brought in your other hand.
Go back with your new religion, we never have understood
Your robbing an Indian's *body*, and mocking his *soul* with food.
Go back with your new religion, and find—if find you can—
The *honest* man you have ever made from out a *starving* man.
You say your cattle are not ours, your meat is not our meat;
When *you* pay for the land you live in, *we'll* pay for the meat we eat.
Give back our land and our country, give back our herds of game;
Give back the furs and the forests that were ours before you came;
Give back the peace and the plenty. Then come with your new belief,
And blame if you dare, the hunger that *drove* him to be a thief."

An Act Respecting the National Anthem of Canada

HER MAJESTY, BY and with the advice and consent of the Senate and House of Commons of Canada, enacts as follows:

1. This Act may be cited as the *National Anthem Act*.
2. The words and music of the song "O Canada", as set out in the schedule, are designated as the national anthem of Canada.
3. The words and music of the national anthem of Canada are hereby declared to be in the public domain.
4. This Act shall come into force on a day to be fixed by proclamation.

Schedule

National Anthem

O Canada! Our home and native land!
True patriot love in all thy sons command.
With glowing hearts we see thee rise,
The True North strong and free!
From far and wide,
O Canada, we stand on guard for thee.
God keep our land glorious and free!
O Canada, we stand on guard for thee.
O Canada, we stand on guard for thee.

Hymne national

O Canada! Terre de nos aïeux,
Ton front est ceint de fleurons glorieux!
Car ton bras sait porter l'épée.
Il sait porter la croix!
Ton histoire est une épopée
Des plus brillants exploits.
Et ta valeur, de foi trempée,
Protégera nos foyers et nos droits.
Protégera nos foyers et nos droits.

An Act to Amend the National Anthem Act to Include all Canadians

Vivienne Poy

Honourable senators, I thank all of you who spoke in support of this amendment during the inquiry last year, senators who have indicated their support privately, as well as the many Canadians who have written to me on this issue, some of whom are assembled in the gallery today. I express my sincere thanks to Frances Wright, Jeanne d'Arc Sharp and the ad hoc committee of the Famous 5 Foundation for launching the petition to amend the national anthem last July on Parliament Hill. It is my pleasure now to speak to Bill S-39, to amend the National Anthem Act to include all Canadians.

I shall begin by outlining the specific amendment to the wording of the national anthem that I am proposing in this bill. I will then explain why I believe this change to be an appropriate one socially, linguistically and ideologically. Finally, I will address some of the critics who argue that change is not necessary or justified.

The amendment I am proposing to the national anthem is a minor one. The words "thy sons" will be replaced by the words "of us." The verse will then read: "True patriot love in all of us command." Two words will change. That is all.

I should point out that the decision to choose "of us" was not mine but was based on the public's response, discussions with linguists and music historians. According to most of the letters I received and to the experts, these two words retain the fundamental meaning of the lyric, the poetry of the line, and fit well with the music. They are also in keeping with historic tradition. I will elaborate more on this later.

There has been some confusion since I began the inquiry on this issue, so I will explain what the bill is not intended to do. It is not my intention to propose changes to the French version of the national anthem. As well, I am not proposing that a reference to God be deleted from the anthem, and I am not proposing that other seldom-sung verses of the anthem be changed. The intent of this bill is simply to update the anthem so that it is more reflective of our society today as well as inclusive of more than 50 per cent of the population.

Honourable senators may ask: Why change the anthem at all? Perhaps the best answer can be found in many letters I have received from women, and men, who have asked me to bring this bill forward.

Debates of the Senate (Hansard) 1st Session, 37th Parliament February 21, 2002.

I should like to share with honourable senators the text of a letter I received from Dr. Marguerite Ritchie in response to my inquiry on the national anthem. She reflected back to the time when she first learned the national anthem in elementary school. She wrote:

> I remember vividly my reaction on my first day of school when "O Canada!" was sung, and I knew immediately that, as a girl, I did not count for anything in Canada.

Similarly, as an impressionable teenager of 14, Catherine Clark realized the national anthem left her out. She wrote in *The Toronto Star:*

> What struck my young mind that particular Canada Day was the lyric "in all thy sons command," and the fact that our anthem didn't refer to me, or anyone of my gender.

This amendment to the anthem is not only for our generation but also for future generations of girls and boys. It was because of these children that Judith Olson, a music teacher, launched the *O Canada* Fairness Committee to change the national anthem in 1993. In her music classes, Ms Olson said that students, especially the girls, would ask her, "What about the daughters? Don't we count?"

John Goldie wrote in a similar vein, urging me to continue with this campaign, because he "has long felt embarrassed that our national anthem did not include his wife and daughter."

Another man, Donald Jackson wrote:

> I am in my 80th year and I am a veteran of World War 2. It has bothered me for some time that the words of our national anthem: "true patriot love in all thy sons command" would seem to exclude women. I feel that this part of the anthem should read: "true patriot love in all of us command." A simple change, but it would include all Canadians, not just the men of Canada.

In the letters I have received, many people say they already substitute their own words for "thy sons" when they sing the anthem. I know a number of the members of this chamber, including Senator Pearson and myself, already substitute our own words for "thy sons."

In churches such as the United Church of Canada and the Presbyterian Church, parishioners are offered an alternative inclusive wording to "in all thy sons command" in their hymnals. The best-selling modern Bible, the New International Version, has just been updated so that all parishioners feel included. For example, the word "sons" in Matthew 5:9 has been replaced by the word "children" to read "children of God," and the word "man" in Romans 3:28 has been replaced by "person" to read "a person is justified by faith." Even *Time* magazine, which only a few years ago referred to "Man of the Year" now refers to "Person of the Year." The Canadian Press stylebook notes that words such as "spokesman" and "chairman" cause resentment, understandably, when applied to women.

If our churches and media can take the lead in changing their use of language in order to make everyone feel that they belong in the community, should we not as a national community amend the language of our national anthem to include all Canadian women so that everyone can feel a sense of belonging?

Our national anthem is one of the most important symbols of Canada, and as a symbol, it represents our fundamental ideals. Although we do not often reflect on the nature of our symbols and their importance in our lives, they represent our beliefs as a society.

As Dr. Robert Birgeneau, President of the University of Toronto, wrote, the anthem is recognized as "one of our most powerful expressions of our Canadian identity."

The anthem takes on a particularly poignant meaning during international events, events such as the Winter Olympics in Salt Lake City, Utah. We have many great women athletes in our country. Should we not acknowledge them in our anthem? Last week, when Catriona Le May Doan stood on the podium after winning the first gold medal for Canada, in the 500-metre speed-skating race, should she not have been celebrated in the words of the anthem as it played for all the world to hear?

How do we define Canada as a nation on the world stage? We only have to observe the path Canada has taken since World War II and consider the last two decades since the passage, in 1982, of the Charter of Rights and Freedoms to conclude that Canada is defined by its rights culture. Michael Ignatieff wrote the following in *The Rights Revolution:* Rights are not just instruments of the law, they are expressions of our moral identity as a people.

That this form of a rights revolution has allowed for inclusiveness is to Canada's credit. Women's rights are enshrined in the Charter, as Senator Beaudoin noted in this chamber last spring. Why then should women be excluded by omission in our anthem?

Should women in Canada have less recognition than the women of Australia? The committee that examined the words of their national song in the early 1980s replaced "Australian sons let us rejoice" with "Australians all let us rejoice" before *"Advance Australia Fair"* was proclaimed officially as the national anthem in 1984.

The truth is, this simple change should have been made in the anthem before it became official in 1980. As the well-known children's entertainers Sharon, Bram and Friends wrote to me:

One might have hoped that this issue would have been recognized and addressed when the lyrics were opened up for revision in 1980.

Let us not dig in our heels on this issue now, just because we missed the boat the last time. Let us consider the words of the Honourable Mitchell Sharp, who is with us today in the gallery, who wrote to me in support of this amendment:

I was in the Pearson government that approved our national anthem and our Maple Leaf flag. I support your effort because I think it will add to the acceptability among Canadians of the words of our anthem. They will sing it with greater enthusiasm.

Many of the letters I have received are from writers, linguists, editors or educators who are sensitive to the impact of language. One writer noted that we are constantly changing our language to incorporate new words as a result of scientific, technical and social advances and that we have eliminated many racist terms over the years because we recognize that language both reflects and shapes the way we think. Nevertheless, we seem to be reluctant to acknowledge language that excludes women.

I should like to consider briefly some of the objections to this amendment.

Almost without exception, those who are opposed to an amendment to the anthem all raise the issue of tradition. Someone was reported in the media to have compared the Honourable Robert Stanley Weir's 1908 version of *O Canada!* to Shakespeare, saying it should not be changed. I agree that the 1908 version of *O Canada!* should never have been changed. According to the original text, which was first brought to my attention by Nancy MacLeod of Toronto, the lyrics of the 1908 version read as follows:

O Canada!
Our home, our native land
True patriot love thou dost in us command.
We see thee rising fair, dear land,
The True North strong and free;
And stand on guard,
O Canada,
We stand on guard for thee.

As you can see, if we return to the original lyrics of *O Canada!*, our tradition as Canadians, even in 1908, was one of inclusiveness. Ironically, the original version of 1908 was a better reflection of our times than the anthem we sing today.

You may well ask why "us" was rewritten as "sons." The earliest printed version of the anthem with "in all thy sons command" was in a song entitled, *"O Canada! Our Father's Land of Old"* for the Common School Book published in 1913. The change was then copyrighted by Weir in 1914.

We can only speculate on the reason for the rewording. Perhaps, judging by the date, it was deemed necessary to give special recognition to the sons of Canada because Canada faced the prospect of war.

Throughout the last century, Weir's version of *"O Canada!"* grew in popularity, but it was not without its competitors. At least 26 versions of *"O Canada!"* have been circulated. Ironically, the title of the 1913 schoolbook version *"Our Father's Land of Old"* was borrowed from the Richardson version of *"O Canada!"* published in 1906. Other versions began with "O Canada! Our heritage our love," "O Canada! Our fair ancestral land," and "O Canada, our country fair and free."

Weir himself changed his version of *"O Canada!"* twice, once in 1914, as I have already mentioned, and again, shortly before his death in 1926, to add a fourth verse of a religious nature to *O Canada!*. At about the same time, the Association of Canadian Clubs was one of the first groups to adopt *O Canada!* as its official song. Please note that this group, with its venerable tradition in Canada, has declared its support for the amendment I am proposing.

In 1968, the words of the Weir version were altered once again in response to the recommendations of a Special Joint Committee of the Senate and the House of Commons. It is evident, therefore, that the lyrics of *O Canada!* have never been set in stone. Changes were made.

You will all agree, the traditions of today are not the traditions of yesteryear. A little more than 80 years ago, women did not have the right to vote. Just 30 years ago, it was traditional for women to stay at home, and very few were in the professions. Twenty years ago, there were few women in non-traditional occupations or in government. It was also traditional to use racist and sexist language in a hurtful manner that would be unacceptable today. Things have changed a great deal, and I think most of you would agree with me that they have changed for the better.

Nevertheless, for those who argue that we should not diverge from the original intent of the anthem out of respect for tradition, I would agree that we should return to Justice Robert Stanley Weir's original inclusive version of *O Canada!* of 1908 and reinstate the word "us" in the lyrics of the national anthem. By so doing, we will honour the spirit of Weir's anthem.

My proposal for an amendment has also been denigrated as being a matter of political correctness. "True patriot love in all thy sons command," it is argued, refers to those who died in wartime, and an amendment would somehow diminish our recognition of men's contributions. According to Stuart Lindop of Alberta, just the opposite is true. I should like to share with honourable senators the text of a letter written by Mr. Lindop. He writes of his proposal in 1993 to his Member of Parliament, David Kilgour, to amend the national anthem to include women:

> As a veteran, a volunteer, wounded in action liberating Holland, I am very well aware of the tremendous contribution made by women to Canada's war effort in the Armed Forces, in industry, and on the home front.

He goes on to say:

> My motivation was not based on prissy, political correctness but rather to see that women, who had earned the right to be recognized, were not implicitly excluded.

I would challenge anyone to accuse Stuart Lindop, an 82-year-old veteran of World War II and a former member of the South Alberta Regiment, the only regiment to garner a Victoria Cross, of political correctness. Mr. Lindop wrote to me recently to assure me that this issue is of the utmost importance to the morale of women in the Armed Forces. He wrote:

> Subtly, one might say subliminally, doubt about one's worthiness can have a tremendous impact upon one's behaviour in a crisis situation. How about women in our various units? Their national anthem doesn't consider them worthy of mention or recognition! Perhaps the government doesn't care.

Given women's involvement in the military, in peacekeeping operations all over the world and in the conflict in Afghanistan, I would agree with Mr. Lindop that women deserve recognition in our anthem. Women's contributions to Canada, whether in the military or in civilian life, should be recognized.

Honourable senators with sons and daughters will be amused to learn that I have been told that the word "sons" in the national anthem is generic and therefore also means daughters. If that were the case, why would the word "daughter" need to exist in the English language? I certainly know that I am not a son. I suspect that it is unlikely that our daughters and granddaughters would appreciate being referred to as "sons" and "grandsons."

There are also those who denigrate this amendment as insignificant, unnecessary and a waste of time. These people are often the most vocal and long-winded in their opposition. This begs the question: If the change is so insignificant, why oppose it? Let us not waste any time in passing this bill. It is, after all, a minor change that is in keeping with today's language as well as the original historic meaning of the anthem as set out by Justice Robert Stanley Weir in 1908. So why amend the anthem? Well, why not?

The rights of women are already enshrined in section 28 of the Charter of Rights and Freedoms. Equal rights are espoused at all levels of government, in private corporations and increasingly in the home. Today's young women, who are entering so-called non-traditional occupations in record numbers, expect to be included in our national anthem.

Admittedly, there are still many injustices, inequities and barriers to overcome. This amendment will not right these wrongs, but it will signal a change that reflects the value we as a society place on equal rights for all, to everyone in Canada and to the world.

Changes in women's status in Canada have not occurred overnight. Each woman who has taken the first step across an invisible barrier has paved the way for those who follow her. In this sense, this change is just another small step that moves women forward on our long journey toward equality. As Maureen McTeer stated succinctly:

> I believe this change will reconfirm our positive role in our country's past, and our commitment to participate at all levels in the future.

Honourable senators, it is clear to me that we all have a stake in ensuring the equality of opportunity for our future generations. We need to show Canadians that parliamentarians have the will to give real meaning to equality for all Canadians.

The Honourable Sheila Finestone is in the gallery with us today. When she was Secretary of State for the Status of Women, she said:

> Equality rights are human rights—a basic principle that shapes the way we live, in good times and hard times. There is no one answer, no one action, no one player that can make equality happen. In the new century, the nations considered the leaders of the world will be those who have achieved gender equality.

Let us take one more step in the right direction, honourable senators. Let us join the leading nations of the world. I would ask that you support this amendment in the name of fairness, historic tradition, and because it is the right thing to do for all Canadians.

Honourable senators, with leave of the Senate, I wish to table letters that I have received from across Canada in support of this amendment, as well as a number of other documents relevant to this debate.

CHAPTER EIGHT

The Great War

Introduction

The First World War, or as it was known by contemporaries, the Great War, engulfed and consumed Canada from its declaration on 4 August 1914 to its conclusion on 11 November 1918. Canada participated in nearly every major battle of the war: Ypres, the Somme, Vimy Ridge, Passchendaele and Amiens. It is a Canadian, a young man from Nova Scotia, who is listed as the last Allied soldier to die in the war. He was killed by a German sniper killed at 10:58 am on the morning of November 11; the war ended two minutes later, at 11:00 am. In total, some 60 000 Canadians were killed and 173 000 were wounded. November 11 is Remembrance Day. It is a day to remember not just those who served in the Great War but to remember all the service men and women who have served their country.

The theme of remembrance, or memory, connects these readings. William Douw Lighthall was a prominent Canadian; a Montreal lawyer, he was also a historian, novelist and poet. Born in Newfoundland, E.J. Pratt studied at the University of Toronto and in 1920 joined the Department of English at Victoria College, University of Toronto. How do Lighthall and Pratt remember the war? What do they forget? David MacFarlane is a prize-winning journalist and writer from Hamilton, Ontario. His outstanding 1991 book, *The Danger Tree: Memory, War, and the Search for a Family's Past* is about the Great War, its devastating impact on Newfoundland in general and on the Goodyear family—his mother's family—in particular. MacFarlane remembers the war in a way that is different from Lighthall and Pratt. How is his work different? In a way, it is also similar. How so?

A Song of Sons

W.D. Lighthall

LIKE as a lioness, wounded for her whelp,
Britannia stands, in bleeding strong disdain,
And we for whom she bleeds, shall we not help?
Thrills there not in us her undaunted strain?
Yea, Motherland, we haste o'er ocean's tide,
Eager to fight, and perish, by thy side.

The mad werewolf that covets our estate,
And snaps his scarlet fangs, shall feel our own,
Ne'er wert thou more magnificently great,
Than when he deemed thee feeble and alone;
We haste, brave Motherland, in joy and pride,
Burning to fight and perish by thy side.

Let those mark well who think to conquer thee,
They with a might and wealth and new emprise;
Must also count, that grows o'er every sea,
And is not weak, and fast to power doth rise;
We watch fair Mother, keen o'er every tide,
Aflame to win or perish by thy side.

We shall not perish; neither yet shalt thou,
Unsilenceable is the song of truth.
Freedom fails not. Its star is on thy brow
And we bring thee the deathless gift of youth.
Yes, Motherland, we haste o'er ocean's tide,
In love to fight and perish at thy side.

Brave Triune Mother, whence we drew our blood,
Our liberty and every good we share.
Whose deeds our parents tell us. Take the flood
Of our hearts throbbing in thine hour of care.
Dear Motherland, we come, we rise like ocean's tide.
For freedom's cause of old to combat at thy side.

December 5th, 1914

Deathless

W.D. Lighthall

(Each ripe maple leaf before it falls has at the base of its stalk a fully formed next year's leaf in shape of a bud).

I
IN THE rugged limestone pasture
The old hard maple glows,
With burning tone and glory,
Like the sun in all its sunset,
In the rich Laurentian autumn
The sunset of the year.

II
At Passchendale I saw it
When the battlefield was fading,
And the roar of guns grew silent
When my life stream stopped its flowing,
I saw the old hard maple
And her fire of leaves embraced me
As my life fell off in glory,
In the sunset of the year.

III
The old hard maple glowing
With dying fire and splendor
Hid at her every leafstalk,
The perfect bud of spring,
At the root of the leaf of glory,
Of the dying leaf of splendor,
The leaf of morrow year.

IV
At Passchendale I sleep not,
Only my leaves of autumn,
My autumn leaves fell there,
In the hour of farewell splendor
In the sunset of the year,

October 30, 1917

But when they fell I died not,
For the wondrous spring was in me
And the life I gave at Passchendale
Hid the life of morrow year—
I am here.

February 3, 1918.

Design

W.D. Lighthall

IN THE fifth year of sacrifice and blood,
Mid dreams of agony and doubts of God,
And cries that screamed, again, again:
"What is the mystery of Pain?"

One morn I was awakened by a voice
Crying "Despair not, ye shall yet rejoice,

"Our life is but a sample square
Cut from a pattern vast and rare:
Could we but see the whole design,
We would not change a single line."

September, 1918.

"In Memoriam"

E.J. Pratt

I

The Dead! Upon a purple-bordered scroll
We wrote their names; then gazed awhile, and said:
"These are the Fallen; there, our honoured dead,
The silent ones in Death's vast muster roll.
This one was strong and ruddy, that one frail,
Though fleet of foot and keen. The first one met
His fate in that fierce fight at Courcelette,
The other died of wounds at Passchendale."
And thus we mused, pointing from name to name
With sad, slow count. We spoke of things like grass,
And withered leaves, and faded flowers, birth,
Old age, decay and dust, glory and fame,
And other strange mortalities that pass
At length into the all-insatiate earth.

II

Then suddenly through the mist that wrapped our sight,
An utterance fell as of great waters flowing—
Slow, but with mightier accent ever growing
Around a blazing shaft of central light:
"Fallen! There is no downward plunge. The estate
Is high. Go!—roll thy plumb-line up, and ask
Thy Master for His measures, as the task
Is one that would the heavens triangulate."
And so were compassed life's fine agonies;
By ranging hopes, and longings cut adrift
From earth's unstable shores; by faiths that spanned
Illimitable wastes and wrecking seas;
By noble strands of nature, scattered swift
From the white fingers of God's spacious hand.

Fire

David MacFarlane

A MATCH IS STRUCK, then held out between cupped hands. Necks crane forward, heads slightly twisted. One face, then another, is illumined briefly. The heads draw back and the smoke is exhaled upward. Then the flame is whisked out, well before its slender shaft of fuel is spent. For a third cigarette, a second match is required.

Three on a match is thought to be bad luck. If the injunction is something of a rarity these days, that's only because three smokers are seldom in one place at one time any more. But on the occasions that they are, the old superstition is often observed.

Today, this is a kind of gallantry, like taking off a glove when shaking hands. In the First World War, when the custom began, it was a precaution against snipers. At night, in a frontline trench, the tiny flare of a match was enough to attract the enemy's attention—sometimes from as far away as a quarter of a mile. The German marksmen had a reputation for hawk-like concentration and stubborn, sleepless patience. They squatted at the lips of observation posts or hid in the crooks of trees, peering into the darkness for hours to catch sight of a glint of moonlight on a helmet, or a shadow passing in front of a careless lantern, or the bobbing, telltale pinpoint of light that meant a few sentries were having a smoke.

Their rifle was the Mauser 98. It was actually called "the Sniper," and is considered one of the most successful bolt-action designs ever produced. It weighed nine pounds and was just over four feet in length. The caliber of its ammunition was 7.92 mm and its standard clip held five cartridges. The jacketed bullets were just over three inches long.

"Here," said a tall, sandy-haired lieutenant. He was with two Australians, accompanying them through the network of old German trenches, from Rosières back toward the Somme. It was just before dawn, late in the summer of 1918. The Canadian 102nd Battalion was under orders to link more closely with the Australians on their left, and the thirty-one-year-old lieutenant had volunteered to meet a reconnoitering party. He stopped and took a crumpled pack of Woodbines from his breast pocket. Through some mysterious oversight of Canadian Transport, the 102nd had been suffering from what their commanding officer, Colonel Fred Lister, called "a match famine" since the fifth of August. Now, with the sky growing brighter beyond Lihons and Chaulnes, it couldn't be dangerous. The lieutenant held out his smokes. "Anyone have a light?"

The Mauser 98 was a reliable, accurate weapon, and when, across a black field of mud, a match flared into visibility and a soft, round glow marked the spot where it was held in front of a man's face, the grooved thirty-inch barrel was quickly shifted into position. Lighting the second cigarette took long enough for the sniper to swing the almost imperceptible dot of yellow light into his steadying aim. The Mauser's scope had a range of almost 2000 meters, and its sights showed a circle divided in half by the horizontal line of a T. The shafts of the T did not quite intersect and the gap where the three slender lines would have met was the bull's-eye. This meant that the light of the match could be held precisely on target when it was still, and tracked within the broader periphery of the circle when it moved. The sniper curled his index finger around the trigger, touching the steel but impressing no force upon it. The extended crook of his elbow and the angle of his head ensured that the act of taking aim was always accompanied by the strong, sour odor of his armpit.

One eye was shut. His breathing was shallow and steady. As the match moved to the third smoker, he followed its passage—the end of his barrel may have shifted a quarter of an inch—and, when the match stopped, he steadied the barrel and drew a breath. He knew that the vague interruption in the darkness was a soldier's face, craned forward to the light cupped in a hand. He centered his aim on the dull glow. He had only a second before the head drew back, the match was extinguished, and his target disappeared. He tightened his index finger around the trigger, squeezing it equally from its front and two bevelled sides.

The trigger of the standard-issue Mauser required some pressure. But most experienced snipers filed the two steel pimples that acted as levers on the rifle's sear in order to quicken its action and minimize the barrel's movement during firing. Once lowered by the trigger, the sear released the cocked spring inside the bolt, which, extended to its full length, released the firing-pin. The impact ignited the shell's primer charge. Then the cordite exploded. The blast, which kicked the rifle's butt back against the sniper's shoulder with the force of a sudden shove, shot the copper-jacketed bullet through the spirals of the rifle's barrel, spinning it clockwise as it passed through the .323-inch bore. The spin kept the bullet's trajectory flat and accurate, the slight arc and the natural drift to the right compensated for by the sights. The bullet had a velocity of just under 3,000 feet per second, which meant that, from the striking of the firing-pin to the point of impact 300 yards away, less than a third of a second had elapsed. The Mauser could kill at more than 1,000 yards. At 300 yards, a bullet's weight was travelling at almost full force. Upon impact—against the right side of the young lieutenant's head, just behind the curve at the top of his ear and just below the rim of his helmet—it dimpled the flesh and, as the dimple deepened to a hole, it tore the surrounding hair and skin toward its point of entry. Skin, then bone, then brain slowed the bullet's passage, but as the bullet's velocity was reduced, it transferred its kinetic energy to the cranium. This commotion radiated out from the bullet like a shock-wave, and blasted the brain to unconsciousness before the sensation of pain had reached it from the point of entry.

Behind the bullet's deepening path a cavity opened that was many times wider than the projectile. In the case of a smaller-caliber bullet, the cavity would have closed again after a millisecond. This bullet was too big and fast for that. The impact of the Mauser's ammunition was far greater than the capacity of its target to absorb it. The cavity, widening like billiard balls on a break, would prove to be larger than the soldier's skull.

At the same time, the compression of brain, bone, blood, and skin that preceded the bullet's path was swelling the left side of the soldier's head. This bulge appeared while the spinning point of copper and lead was cutting through the midline of the brain. This was death. Pulse and respiration ceased as abruptly as if a vital strand of wires had been cut. Then the exit wound erupted. The fragments of brain and skull were drawn through the red, stellated wound. The soldier's hazel eyes began to roll back in their sockets and his lanky body began its collapse, just as the widening cavity behind the bullet's path broke out of its confines and blew his skull to pieces.

The exclusive dangers of three on a match were largely mythical. Three smokers were not necessarily a more likely target than any other number. One on a match was dangerous enough: a skilled German marksman could get off twenty-five aimed rounds a minute with the Mauser, which meant that the time it took for a soldier to strike a Swan Vesta, raise it to the oval end of his Woody or Mayo, draw a first puff, and then wave the match out was more than enough for a good sniper to take aim and fire. In these circumstances, two on a match should have been enough to have qualified for superstition. In different circumstances—if a sniper, for instance, was looking the other way when the match was struck—certainly four on a hastily shared light would have been very bad luck indeed. If the sniper was slow and the match was put out before his aim was locked on target, a huddle of four or five smokers would probably have meant that even a haphazard shot would do some damage.

But it was three on a match that was said to be bad luck, and this had as much to do with the significance of the number as with actual fact. Threes were everywhere. They still are: three meals; three wishes; three chances; three witches; three cheers; three reasons why. There's morning, noon, night; faith, hope, charity; lower class, middle class, upper class; blondes, brunettes, and redheads. Dante divided his universe into hell, purgatory, and paradise. We speak of time past, present, future. There are, according to the ancient riddle of the Sphinx, three ages of man. There are three Graces, three Furies, three bears, three rings in a circus, and three blind mice. Races begin with ready, set, go, and end with win, place, show. In folk stories, it is often the third brother who slays the dragon, wins the princess, finds the treasure. In Christian iconography, there are three crosses on Calvary, three Magi, three temptations, three denials. And there is, of course, the Trinity.

In battle, three was the natural choice for superstition. The army seemed to run—hup, two, three—on a constant and ubiquitous trichotomy. On land there was infantry, artillery, and cavalry, with separate but sequential tasks in battle. Frequently battalions were divided into three groups. For every man on sentry duty, two were allowed to rest. There were front trenches, support trenches, and rear trenches. Soldiers routinely numbered off in threes, and the number a soldier called out could mean the difference between playing cards in the reserve trench or being blown to bits in No Man's Land. Military threes were prophetic, and every soldier knew it. They packed up their troubles in their old kit bags and smiled, smiled, smiled.

The bad luck of three on a match was the perfect superstition of the First World War, for it alluded to the war's, and the number's, most potent characteristic: finality. Three is the perfect number for chances or wishes or strikes because the figure represents the beginning, the middle, and the end. Implicit in all the myths, rituals, and superstitions that surround it is the understanding that the third is always the last. After three there is nothing. But the very existence of one and two ensures that three will some day come.

In the trenches, extinguishing a match after the second cigarette was cheating the inevitable. By the last year of the war, this was all a soldier could hope to do. The count toward his death had begun the day he enlisted, and any ruse or charm that would extend the interval between beats was welcomed. And perhaps this explains why the superstition has persisted for as long as it has: our century has kept its own count and, for the lifetime of my generation, has been suspended somewhere between two and three. We keep shaking out our matches. Our grandparents were ready and our parents aimed. Now we're afraid of fire.

By the end of the war, the significance of the number three was obvious enough to the Goodyear family: after a relatively brief period of shock, what had once been unthinkable became something that had somehow always been inevitable. After the war, the number three became, for Josiah and Louisa Goodyear, as much a way of summing up who they were as seven—the number of their children—had been a way of describing themselves before it. The three dead sons paraded past their parents, and on through the century. Now, two generations later, it is difficult for me to imagine the family without them. Their deaths cast everything I would ever hear and learn about the Goodyears—their inconsequential business disputes, their uncelebrated political feuds, their adventures and tall tales, and their little-known passion for the isolated, distant island of Newfoundland—into high relief. They made everything seem important. Not that their deaths bestowed any particular meaning on events—quite the opposite. They were pointless. It's just that I come from a safe place, in the middle of a country where everything is foreign news. I live in danger of being entertained by the headlines of distant tragedies. When the wars described in newspapers and broadcast on cable television start to become prime-time abstractions to me, I think of my three great-uncles. They were ordinary men from an old, lost world. I come to them from far away. But they remind me that, in a war, death always matters more than the glorious cause that inflicts it.

Uncle Hedley may have noticed an ominous numerology on the night of August 7, 1918, although, judging from his marks in Maths, Physics, and Chemistry at

Victoria College in Toronto, and from the disastrous results of a brief real estate partnership with Roland in the spring of 1914, he was no good at arithmetic. Still, the numbers were there in front of him. By a strange quirk of fate, they were stamped in three places on the revolver he carried in his leather holster that night. It was a .455-caliber Webley Mark VI, produced in 1918. Its serial number, 332137, was stamped at the base of the six-inch barrel, in front of the steel trigger-guard, and on the rim of the revolving six-chambered magazine. Hedley couldn't have helped but notice the figures as he cleaned and loaded and checked his gun that night, preparing for what would become known as the battle of Amiens.

By August 1918, there were rumors among the troops that the end of the war was not far off. That spring, German offensives between the Marne and Amiens, and further to the north, near Ypres, had been eerily reminiscent of previous Allied offensives at the Somme and Passchendaele. After the collapse of the Russian army, the German command had been able to concentrate on the Western Front, and, with the American forces growing steadily stronger, Ludendorff and Hindenburg were convinced that the time had come for their big push. If they were going to defeat Britain and France, it was going to have to be done now. Apparently they had learned nothing from Haig's blunders. In March of 1918, as part of an extravagant southern feint, German forces had pushed through the Allied lines at the Somme. Haig, and the bulk of the British forces, were waiting uselessly further to the north.

In the confusion that followed, the French general, Foch, consolidated his position as the commander-in-chief of the Allied armies in France. Immediately he proved that he, at least, had been awake for the previous four years. In the face of the German advance, he held back his reserves. Contrary to every tenet of nineteenth-century warfare, Foch let the Germans come through. The advance won territory but it strained supply lines and consumed reinforcements. The Germans paid for every mile with appalling casualties. Then, with the restraint of a good poker player, Foch finally put down his cards. His counter-attack came on both sides of the bulge the Germans had fought their way into. It stopped the advance dead.

In the months that followed, the Germans launched offensives in Flanders, at the river Aisne, and at Rheims. In each case, they eventually choked on their own initial successes, just as they had in March at the Somme. By the summer, the war had shifted. In Germany there was talk of a compromise peace; in the German trenches there was despondency. In England, Lord Northcliffe—combining his penchant for publishing sensational half-truths with his enthusiasm for airplanes—was put in charge of dropping leaflets of propaganda over enemy lines, encouraging surrender.

By August of 1918, in the Canadian lines near Amiens, there was certainly cause for optimism. There was also cause for anxiety. The rumors of peace were welcomed, but, for the troops, hope only made each day more fateful than the one that had come before. Survival now seemed a possibility, but as the odds got better, the bets got higher and more dangerous. The thought of dying close to the end of the war was too cruel to contemplate. Superstitions and prophetic signs were everywhere, and even the most level-headed soldier found himself waiting out the long night before an attack, searching for some indication—in the stars, in his birthdate, in the number of letters in his name, in the games he played spinning the magazine of his revolver—that his luck would hold. Luck was everything, and guessing whether it was there was a pastime that may have caused Hedley Goodyear to consider the portents of a serial number while cleaning his Webley on the night of August 7. And, if he did, he could only have come up with one interpretation. The meaning of 332137 was too obvious to miscalculate: if the two represented the two wounded brothers safe in Scotland, and the one, the eldest still at home, if the seven was the sister who interrupted a mother's wish for seven sons, then it was clear enough what the threes were. And there were three of them.

Hedley sat on a groundsheet in Boves Wood, a few kilometers to the southeast of Amiens. He was surrounded by men in bedrolls and on groundsheets, sleeping outdoors or under the cover of camouflaged tents. As much as possible, noises were muffled. Lights were shielded. Everything depended on concealment. The Allied commanders—Haig, Pétain, Pershing, and Foch—had decided to counter the German offensives while the enemy was still reeling. As part of this plan, Canadian forces had been moved secretly to join the Australians near Amiens; their objective was to gain control of the railways to the east and to push the Germans back, possibly as far as the town of Roye. Hedley's commanding officer, Colonel Lister, estimated that fifty thousand men and twenty-five thousand horses were hidden in the woods. "The Canadian Corps," Lister noted in his diary, "was on the verge of the biggest operation in which it had yet been engaged and which figured as part of the most spectacular counter offensive yet launched against the Hun."

That night, Hedley wrote his farewell letter. He worked by the soft, yellow light of a hooded lantern, looking up to the chill, black sky between each sentence. There was no time for revisions. "Dearest Mother," he wrote, "This is the evening before the attack and my thoughts are with you all at home. But my backward glance is wistful only because of memories, and because of the sorrow which would further darken your lives should anything befall me in tomorrow's fray."

In the years since, copies of the page-long letter have circulated in the Goodyear family. It has been published in Newfoundland newspapers—usually on Memorial Day or on the eve of the November armistice—and once, seventy-one years and thirteen weeks after Hedley put down his pen, it was read with great dignity by the member for Bonavista-Trinity-Conception Bay on Remembrance Day in the Canadian House of Commons. The original seems to have disappeared. But the typed copies that family members keep in drawers and file-folders and scrapbooks and that the honorable member held when he rose from the Liberal benches on November 11, 1989, have been given the heading "The Last Letter of a Hero." The letter is twenty-three sentences long and concludes with a postscript. "P.S.," it reads, and instead of the expected *Please send more socks* or *Always short of fags* someone has added, "Hedley Goodyear was killed the following day, August 8th, 1918."

The letter's frequent publication was started, it seems, by E.J. Pratt. Less than two months after it was written, Pratt printed it in the Overseas Page of Victoria College's literary review, *Acta Victoriana*. He gave it the title "The Last Home Letter of Hedley Goodyear," and in his introduction Pratt wrote, "Of the thousands of farewell letters written from the trenches, few have surpassed, in noble feeling, this final message of Hedley Goodyear to his mother." Then, in a flight of rhetoric that must have floored Aunt Kate, amused a few girls in Scotland, and astounded anyone who had ever trapped young foxes out of season with my grandfather or had a few drinks in the Newfoundland Hotel with my great-uncle Ken, Pratt went on to tell *Acta*'s readers that "the sons of Josiah Goodyear were cast in heroic mould, every one of them a physical and moral giant."

I'm not sure what it is about death that brings out such extravagance in writers. Faced with something difficult and profound, the composers of eulogies often seem to choose the most windy and meaningless way of dealing with it. Pratt, who hadn't laid eyes on any member of the Goodyear family other than Uncle Hedley for more than a decade, and who had spent all of one week in Newfoundland since 1907, went on to tell his readers that Lord Northcliffe knew the Goodyears "personally" and that he had given "public testimony to their courage and resourcefulness." This was probably not absolutely untrue, but it was certainly a stretch. And it was an odd point to raise in a tribute to the one Goodyear who, educated at Ladle Cove, the Methodist College in St. John's, and Victoria College at the University of Toronto, had spent little time in Grand Falls, had no involvement in the family company, and had probably never exchanged a word with Northcliffe in his life. The "personally" has a hollow, obsequious ring to it, as if the inclusion of a celebrity's name in an otherwise ordinary obituary might make the loss seem more important. Pratt's claim that the Goodyear brothers' "devotion to their country was equalled by their love for one another" was also suspect. He couldn't have had any idea whether such a claim was true. It sounded the kind of sentimental chord that almost everyone who appeared in print felt obliged to sound in 1918. In later years, it would have surprised anyone within earshot of one of the J. Goodyear and Sons board meetings in downtown Grand Falls.

Pratt, writing from the distance of his Toronto study, seemed to be idealizing the Goodyears, if not inventing them, and this may have been why my great-aunt held Canada's great poet in such disregard. She didn't begrudge him his debt to the family or his sale of calabogus to the victims of tuberculosis on Newfoundland's coast. And it wasn't that she disagreed with him when, in describing Hedley to the readers of *Acta*, he wrote of "the high principle and absolute candour of soul that was his." She may have simply begrudged him his survival: he never enlisted, and for that reason his life was allowed to extend beyond 1918. She had little time for those who, with no experience of war, use it as an opportunity to make political hay, sell newspapers, compose moving memorials, trot out their own sensitivity—or, for that matter, write a book. I don't think she ever forgave E.J. Pratt for being indiscriminate and therefore untrustworthy in his praise of the Goodyears in general and Hedley in particular. She knew that sometimes—in the face of an untimely death, for instance—silence was best.

If not a moral giant, Hedley was certainly a moral being. He was an earnest young man, dedicated to his studies but by no means a bookworm. "His victories with Latin, the Lit., and the ladies are duly recorded," *Acta* quipped one year. "Prominent in the Literary Society," it reported upon his graduation in 1913. "An outstanding debater. During his College course he was one of the best-liked members of his class."

Hedley was also an idealist. "My eye is fixed on tomorrow," he wrote to his mother from Boves Wood on the night of August 7, 1918, "with hope for mankind and with visions of a new world."

The terrible years that passed between 1914 and 1918 are remembered today as a steady process of disillusionment. It is generally assumed that by the end of the war there wasn't a soldier in the field who believed that what he was witnessing was anything other than a tragic waste. There is truth in this—the legacy of the war's poets is that the battles of stupid old men were fought by their innocent sons, and that it was all for nothing. But there were also soldiers—Hedley Goodyear among them—who never admitted to so bankrupt a possibility. The more horrible the war and the longer it dragged on, the more necessary it was to hope that it all meant something. He couldn't bring himself to believe that the carnage was pointless, and so he invested the war with his own idealism. He paused in his writing, raised the end of the pen to his lips, thought for a moment, and then bent forward again to his paper. "A blow will be struck tomorrow," he continued, "which will definitely mark the turn of the tide. . . . I shall strike a blow for freedom, along with thousands of others who count personal safety as nothing when freedom is at stake."

It was Hedley's idealism that was responsible for his being with the Canadians in the first place. He signed up for duty with the 102nd in Toronto when it would have been perfectly natural for him to have returned to Grand Falls to enlist with the Newfoundland Regiment. After all, his nationality—as written in his own hand on the University of Toronto's registration form—was Newfoundlander.

Being from so distant a place provided him with a slight foreignness which, like the roll of his accent, distinguished him from his classmates at Victoria. It was an identity he wore easily and naturally. He spoke frequently of Newfoundland, making its innate superiority to any place else on the face of the earth a running joke with his classmates. When he closed his eyes in Toronto, in the narrow bed of his sparse little room in a boarding-house on the corner of Yorkville and Hazelton avenues, he remembered an island that had bluffs and hills and crags of rock like nowhere else he knew. It had its own colors. They were the rust of kelp, the gray of the sea, the green of forests, the black of rattling brooks. It had its own smells— salt, cut spruce, dried fish, a curl of smoke. And it had sounds which, clear as dawn, came ringing—a hammer, a shout, oars against the gunwales of a dory—across the calm blue water of a little harbor. It had its own stories and jokes and ways of doing things. And it had means of description that were as various as its weather. Newfoundland had a distinctiveness that he felt deeply and that he would never have dreamed of giving up.

And yet it was Hedley Goodyear's conviction that his country's fate was bound up with Canada's. Apparently, from the day he arrived at university, he was an ardent confederate. In the dining-hall, in common rooms, in seminars, and in debates at Hart House, he frequently argued the case for Newfoundland's joining Canada. In fact, his view on this subject—not a subject anyone else at Victoria would ever have spent much time discussing had Hedley Goodyear not constantly been bringing it up—was so well known that *Acta* took the occasional good-natured poke at him. On one occasion, ribbing him about his obsession with linking Newfoundland's fortunes more closely to Canada's, the editors even managed to include a caustic reference to Hedley's disastrous entrepreneurial fling with his older brother, Roland: "H. J. Goodyear has at last been successful in damming the straits of Belle Isle. This project, requiring six and a half million dollars, has been floated entirely on bonds guaranteed by Toronto real estate."

Uncle Hedley was a tall, sandy-haired young man. His vast black shoes were always carefully shined. His round collars were immaculate. His gray suit hung on his frame with a kind of shapeless dignity. In his academic gown, hands clutched at his lapels like a statesman, he cut an impressive figure. He was a forceful speaker and a clear, straightforward thinker, and usually, in debate, he was better informed than and twice as passionate as anyone who opposed him. He had a broad, serious face, and looked older than he was—until he smiled. Then, as he skewered his opposition on the well-turned point of his rebuttal, his expression was transformed by a boyish and mischievous grin.

"The leader of the opposition refers to Newfoundland's *manageable* public debt," he told an audience gathered for a student debate at Hart House one evening in 1913. "I fear that management is not the honorable member's strong suit, otherwise he would have *managed* to mount a more convincing argument." He moved away from the podium and took two deliberately paced steps across the polished hardwood floor. "Mr. Speaker, the public debt of Newfoundland bears over $1 million of interest annually. This, my mis-managed friend might like to know, is more than the country's combined expenditures for education, public works, fisheries, and the administration of justice and civil government." He let this sink in, looking up majestically to the leaded panes of the chamber's high, arched windows. "With managers such as these"—and here Hedley Goodyear extended an accusing finger at the opposition—"who needs natural disasters?"

No one was surprised when Hedley Goodyear chose "Newfoundland and Its Political and Commercial Relation to Canada" as the subject for his M.A. thesis. He worked at it steadily, sitting up late into the night in his room, his shirt-sleeves rolled back and his little rickety table piled with books and notes. He completed it in 1914.

It is an impassioned, well-argued paper that reads more like a speech than an academic treatise. It is polite but blunt in its assessment of England's total failure with the island. Hedley was less deferential on the subject of Newfoundland's self-inflicted catastrophes. "The backward condition of the Island," he wrote, "is not due to the inherent shiftlessness of its people, but to . . . the selfishness of business men whose best means of escaping taxation and whose surest hopes of gain lie in the submission of the people to the old order." He expressed optimism about Newfoundland's industrial potential and about the wealth of its natural resources—sounding the theme that Uncle Roland, in a somewhat less orchestrated manner, would continue to sound in railway cars and hotel rooms and in letters to the premier for the rest of his life. But Hedley knew that much was seriously wrong with Newfoundland. He dismissed the island's denominational education system as a "festering disease," raged at its poverty and low standards of health, decried the absence of local governments, and criticized the country's failure of political will. "The greatest heresy and the worst treason," he said, "is to wink at the facts." And the facts were that Newfoundland was a political, social, and fiscal disaster.

Confederation with Canada was the only option that made sense to Uncle Hedley because it had an obvious geographic, historic, and economic logic, because Canada held great promise, and because Newfoundland was in such dire straits. "The fisheries could hardly have been more neglected; fewer and less efficient transportation facilities are out of the question; a more deplorable lack of industrial development is inconceivable; and education could not have been a more sorry affair. . . ."

In his thesis, Hedley implicitly dismissed the trappings of nationalism and the pride of imagined independence. He was passionate in his pragmatism, and, never doubting his own identity as a Newfoundlander, he believed that Newfoundland had everything to gain and nothing to lose by the union. A state, he claimed, was a political arrangement; the firmer its foundations and the broader its economic base, the more likely it was to fulfil its only responsibility: securing the prosperity, health, and freedom of its citizens. Any other claim to sovereignty—however ancient the traditions, however rousing the anthem—was emptiness. "A patriot's first duty to his country," he concluded, "is to know the truth about it."

All this, apparently, was too much for Newfoundland. According to the notes of family history that Uncle Roland was constantly scribbling and that were left after his death in his trunk in Gander, Hedley's professors thought highly of the thesis. They encouraged him to publish it. They thought it would be of interest in Newfoundland. Hedley was pleased. He took up their suggestion. He hoped that he would sell enough to recover his costs.

He printed several hundred copies, bound them in handsome, soft gray covers, and shipped them to St. John's. There, no shopkeeper would carry them. Every store that Hedley approached was either owned or influenced by the merchant families of St. John's. They felt the thesis was too controversial. The little gray pamphlets remained in their cardboard boxes. Then, on the day that Hedley began his military training in Toronto—marching in Queen's Park, across the dusty road from Victoria College and from the site of what would eventually become the E. J. Pratt Memorial Library—the half-dozen boxes were shipped from St. John's to Grand Falls. Uncle Roland picked them up at Grand Falls Station. He stacked them in the loft of an old, weather-bleached shed, between the back of the Goodyears' house and the company stables. When Roland wrote Hedley to tell him this news, he addressed the letter to Private H. J. Goodyear.

The First World War presented itself to Hedley Goodyear as exactly the kind of co-operative effort and union of strengths that lay at the heart of his belief in confederation. He believed the struggle was important. The real reasons for the war were so vague and unsubstantial that it was possible for rulers, politicians, and newspapermen to lay claim to the loftiest purpose in the call to arms. And Hedley took them at their word. He was young, strong, slightly naive, and full of a student's dreams of a better world. In fact, he was a precise reflection of the forty-seven-year-old Canada. He was ready to take his place in the world. He was eager to prove his conviction to the highest of ideals.

It was time to pull together. Never doubting that he would always be a Newfoundlander at heart, he joined up with the Canadians. He rose from private, to sergeant, to lieutenant. And on the night of August 7, 1918, just before he addressed his men, he finished the letter to his mother. He wrote quickly. "I do not think for a moment that I shall not return from the field of honor, but in case I should not, give my last blessing to father, and my latest thanks for all he did for me. . . . I have no regrets and fear of tomorrow. I should not choose to change places with anyone in the world just now, except perhaps General Foch."

Before midnight on August 7, the 102nd left their position at Boves Wood. Two hours later, they reached their assembly point north of the Amiens-Roye road, at Gentelles. They waited there until just before dawn. Then, at 4:20 a.m., the Allied barrage opened up. The ground shook with it. The sky was breaking to the east and a white mist hung in the fresh, cool air.

The tanks went first. Behind them, the men crossed the shallow pools of the Luce, then headed southeast, in the direction of Roye. They flanked the road, making their way through orchards and fields of ripened corn. Shells burst in the harrowed soil. The woods were full of machine guns.

Their objectives were the Sunken Road and, beyond it, the woods at Beaucourt. The opposing fire was heavy, but they proceeded steadily. Shells screeched overhead. Bullets ripped through the air. Men cried and fell. But the battalion's discipline held. Bayonets remained fixed. The troops closed ranks on the gaps left by their casualties. The sun burnt away the mist. They moved forward.

On August 8, 1918, 110 men of the 102nd would fall in battle. And, in the remembrance of that day, the young Lieutenant Hedley J. Goodyear was numbered among the gallant dead.

But it wasn't true. He didn't die. Apparently everybody was wrong—E. J. Pratt, my Newfoundland relatives, and the editors of half a dozen newspapers. There had been an error. The postcript on the letter was incorrect. Against all odds, despite all signs, and contrary to accepted fact, his luck held. He survived the battle of Amiens without injury. Having done so, he cheerfully expected to last out the war. The worst was over.

As he had predicted, the tide had turned. Rumors ran wild. There were celebrations. Among the stores of supplies and ammunition the Canadians had captured that day were a few kegs of German beer and, amazingly, several cases of champagne. Hedley toasted his men. They hip-hip-hoorayed themselves hoarse. It was as if a wall of fear had come down within them. The gloomy anxiety they had lived with for so long disappeared in the roar of their three cheers. Things were changing, and changing quickly. Peace now seemed a possibility. The world wasn't going to end.

I learned this in Gander, not long ago. I was spending a few days there with my aunt and uncle. It was a Saturday evening, and they had worked late at their hardware store—the last of the Goodyear stores in Newfoundland. It had been a busy day for them. The store was a popular spot with Poles and Bulgarians and East Germans—Aeroflot passengers who, supposedly on their way to a winter holiday in Cuba, strolled through the security doors of the Gander airport in their sports shirts, sunglasses, and beach sandals, approached the lone, beleaguered-looking Mountie there, and, in the broken English they'd been rehearsing for hours, asked for political asylum. The coming-down of the Berlin Wall had done nothing to stem this flow; more than one thousand refugees a month arrived in Gander that winter. They were put up by authorities in the airport hotels and given meal vouchers, and they could be seen every day, walking in single file through the swirling snow along the side of the Trans-Canada Highway. They wore towels around their heads for warmth. Their arms were bare. They looked bewildered. Stunned by the cold, bleak place they'd ended up in, they were on their way into town to buy ski-jackets, hockey toques, and snow-mobile boots.

That Saturday night in Gander, after my aunt and uncle returned from their store and after our dinner, my uncle produced a cardboard box that contained a jumble of his father's—my grandfather's—possessions. It was the sort of disorganized, uninstructive collection of stuff that most people probably fear they will leave behind—old letters, ticket stubs, unused daily planners, odd cufflinks. There was a hairbrush and a meerschaum pipe. Half watching the color television, with our plates of fruitcake perched on the sofa and the arms of easy chairs, we sifted through the contents of my grandfather's box for an hour or so.

My aunt put on more coffee. A squall of snow rattled against the picture window. My uncle said, "Well, what do you know."

He pulled out a letter that had been lodged beneath a file at the bottom of the box. He looked at it closely for a few moments, and then held it out to my aunt and me. "Will you look at this."

It was a letter from Uncle Hedley to his mother. It was dated after the letter that E. J. Pratt had called his last. We couldn't believe our eyes.

It was as cheery and bright as the one that preceded it had been somber. "Dear Mother o' Mine," it began. "The last letter I wrote you was before the big show. . . . Well, the big show is over, at least as far as we know. You need have no further fear for my safety."

My aunt and I sat together on the sofa, bent over the brittle old piece of paper. "So he didn't die," my uncle said.

"It was a great day," the letter continued, "and the company to which I belong distinguished itself. There seems to be a Providence disposed to order things with justice. Strangely enough, I found myself the only officer left in the company early in the fight. When we neared our final objective, which was a wood, we found it full of the enemy. I had eight machine guns and over a hundred of the best troops in the world at my command. I ordered every gun to open up. . . . It took us ten minutes to gain superiority of fire. . . . I thought the moment opportune to charge so I gave the word and the boys went in with the bayonets. . . . I had no mercy—until they quit fighting, then I did not have the heart to shoot them. . . . But it was a great day, and we were terrible in our charge."

Reading the letter, I imagined Uncle Hedley returning to Scotland after the war was over. He would have arrived at Betsy Turnbull's door in Hawick, a bouquet of flowers in his hand and his Military Cross gleaming on the breast of his uniform. He would have taken his fiancée in his arms and, with both her feet off the ground, danced her round in circles of happiness. A month after that, back in Canada, he'd have stood in Aunt Kate's doorway, laughing at her tears and telling her that you'd think she'd never had a visit from a brother before. He'd take off his cap and undo his overcoat and tell us we'd all been mistaken. We'd got the story all wrong.

The letter was dated August 17, 1918. "Don't worry about me," it concluded, "I'm Hun-proof."

To the two Australians who were with him, it looked as if a bomb had exploded inside his head. His lanky body crumbled. Three hundred yards away, a German soldier peered over the sights of his Mauser into the darkness. He lifted the barrel from the slender crook of a dead tree. He couldn't tell if he'd hit anything. It was just before dawn. The sky was breaking over Lihons and Chaulnes. He yawned and wondered about breakfast.

It wasn't very long afterwards that the shed between the Goodyear stables and the house in Grand Falls caught fire. No one knew how it started. It may have been a wayward cinder from the blacksmith's forge, or just a carelessly tossed match. At first, smoke crept through the cracks in the boards like ivy. The smell could have been the woodstove in the house. No one heard the crackling. By the time somebody realized what was burning, it was too late. The fire was too hot to get near. The sway-backed old building was lost. Its wood was dry and the loft was stacked with cardboard boxes full of little gray pamphlets.

CHAPTER NINE

Inventing Tom Thomson

Introduction

Born in 1844 in Claremont, Ontario, Tom Thomson drowned under mysterious circumstances in Canoe Lake in Algonquin Park in 1917. Not yet forty years old when
he died, Thomson's art was—and still is—considered iconic and definitively Canadian. His landscape paintings of windswept pines, choppy northern lakes and imposing rocks inspired the Group of Seven, the Canadian art movement founded in 1920.
It has been said that had Thomson never existed he would have had to have been
invented. A clever insight, it misses the point. Thomson *was* invented. From the
moment of his death, he has been elevated, celebrated and selected not as a Canadian artist, but as the Canadian artist. One of the earliest inventions can be found
in Dr. J.M. MacCallum's 1918 essay, "Tom Thomson: Painter of the North."
MacCallum was a great patron of the arts in general and of Thomson in particular.
That invention can also be seen in the poems of Arthur Bourinot (winner of the 1939
Governor General's Award for Poetry) and George Whipple (born in Saint John,
New Brunswick, he currently lives in Burnaby, British Columbia). How is Thomson
invented by MacCallum, Bourinot and Whipple? Tom Thomson also appears in
"Death By Landscape" by Margaret Atwood. A prolific and brilliant writer, Atwood
often explores themes of survival and nature and identity. In this dark, subtle story,
she uses Tom Thomson and the Group of Seven to comment on Canada's contradictory relationship to its landscape. What is that contradictory relationship?

Tom Thomson: Painter of the North

J. M. MacCallum

WITH THE TRAGIC death of Tom Thomson in July, 1917, there disappeared from Canadian art a unique personality. Thomson's short and meteoric career, the daring handling and unusual subjects of his pictures, the life he led, set him apart. Living in the woods and even when in town avoiding the haunts of artists, he was to the public an object of mysterious interest. He lived his own life, did his work in his own way, and died in the land of his dearest visions.

It was in October, 1912, that I first met him—in the studio of J. E. H. Macdonald. The door opened and in walked a tall, slim, clean cut, dark young chap who was introduced to me as Tom Thomson. Quiet, reserved, chary of words, he interested me, for I had heard of his adventures in the Mississauga Forest Reserve. I asked Macdonald to get some of his sketches so that I might get an idea of what the country is like. This was done, and as I looked them over I realized their truthfulness, their feeling and their sympathy with the grim, fascinating northland. Dark they were, muddy in colour, tight, and not wanting in technical defects, but they made me feel that the North had gripped Thomson, as it had gripped me ever since, when a boy of eleven, I first sailed and paddled through its silent places.

The following March, at an exhibition of the Ontario Society of Artists, my attention was attracted to a picture—one of the small northern lakes swept by a northwest wind; a squall just passing from the far shore, the water crisp, sparklingly blue and broken into short, white-caps—a picture full of light, life and vigour. This picture, "A Northern Lake", the first one exhibited by Thomson, was purchased by the Ontario Government.

Autumn came again, and at last my numerous inquiries were rewarded by the information that "Tom has come home again". His hiding-place in a boarding-house I at last discovered, and found his walls covered with sketches. Half of them I borrowed to look over at my leisure, for he had sought to depict lightning flashes, moving thunder-storms, and trees with branches lashing in the wind. These sketches so interested the painter A. Y. Jackson, that he asked to meet Thomson, and ended by sharing his studio with him.

At the next exhibition of the Ontario Society of Artists, in 1914, Thomson exhibited two pictures, one of which, "A Moonlight Scene", was purchased for the National Gallery at Ottawa. As spring came on, it was arranged that the artist should go with me on a trip amongst the islands of the Georgian Bay and remain there at my summer home until August. Leaving my place, he paddled and portaged all the way from Go Home to Canoe Lake, Algonquin Park, where he was joined by Jackson, who had been painting in the Rockies. Before leaving me, we had a long talk about his work. I said to him: "Jackson has had what you have not—an academic training. He has a brighter colour sense, but he has not the feeling you have. You can learn much from him, and he from you, but you must not try to be another Jackson. Learn all you can from him, but, whatever you do, keep your own individuality."

Jackson and he camped together and painted until the snow and cold weather drove them back to the city. I awaited with some curiosity their home-coming, but the first glance at Thomson's sketches reassured me. His colour sense had broadened marvelously, but the old feeling and sympathy remained. The sketches were much higher in key, with not a trace of muddiness, but painted in clean, pure colour ranging from one end of the spectrum to the other. I felt sure that many of them had been devised simply as harmonies in colour, but I was always met with the response, "No, it is just like that". The truth of that I know now from personal experience, for I have, when camped with Thomson, frequently seen the very colours and forms to which in his sketches I had taken the most violent exception.

The group of painters of which Thomson was one soon began to be bitterly attacked by artists and newspaper critics and held up to ridicule as painting things which were untrue and impossible. Thomson lived eight months of each year in Algonquin Park, often disappearing into its recesses for a month at a time, seeing no one and being seen by no one. Only one who has so lived is in a position to attack the colour or truthfulness of his pictures. I have a sketch painted by him the spring before his death. I remember well my saying:

"I have stood for a lot, Tom, but I can't stand for this. You never saw anything like this in God's world."

"Oh, yes, that is quite like it," he replied.

"Well, what is it, anyway? What are these gray pillars here? Are they more of the pillars of cloud that led the children of Israel across the desert?"

"Those are pillars of snow. On certain winter days up here the snow hangs suspended in gray pillars up in the air."

This was news to me, but I verified it two weeks later from the lips of an old French Canadian lumber-camp foreman, who told me that these pillars were frequently seen and were gray.

Thomson painted a world of phenomena of colour and form which has not been touched by any other artist. His sketches are a complete encyclopædia of all the phenomena of Algonquin Park, and aside from their artistic merits have a historical value entitling them to preservation in the National Gallery.

Thomson painted not merely to paint, but because his nature compelled him to paint—because he had a message. The north country gradually enthralled him, body and soul. He began to paint that he might express the emotions the country inspired in him; all the moods and passions, all the sombreness and all the glory of colour, were so felt that they demanded from him pictorial expression. He never gave utterance in words to his feelings of the glories of nature. Words were not his instruments of expression—colour was the only medium open to him. Of all Canadian artists he was, I believe, the greatest colourist. But not from any desire to be unusual or to make a sensation did he use colour. His aims were truthfulness and beauty—beauty of colour, of feeling, and of emotion. Yet to him, his most beautiful sketches were only paint. He placed no value on them. All he wanted was more paint, so that he could paint others. He enjoyed appreciation of his work; criticism of its methods he welcomed, but its truthfulness was unassailable, for he had seen it. He never painted anything that he had not seen.

Sombre and gray, or gloriously golden, nature had equal appeal to him. His one criticism of his own work was "there is not enough daylight in that". He saw and painted in pure colour—colour so clean that one almost feels his pictures had been laundered. His colour is varied, brilliant and beautiful, but always dominated by the beauty of emotion. It sings the triumphant Hosannas of the joy and exaltation of nature.

Furthermore, his colour composition is beautiful. The poetry of his soul never permitted the colour, however brilliant, to be anything but harmonious. Unusual though it may be, it never jars, never brings one up with a jerk. He combined in an unusual degree the sense of design, of pattern, rhythm and decoration with the sense of composition, of character and feeling. The line and pattern—the design—but added greater beauty to nature's garb, yet nature dominated him and actuated all his work.

As has been said, Thomson had but one method of expressing himself, and that one was by means of paint. He did not discuss theories of art, technical methods nor choice of motives. He never told about marvellous scenes, of how they had thrilled and held him. He merely showed the sketch and said never a word of his difficulties or of what he had tried to express. His idea seemed to be that the way to learn to paint was to paint. He did not choose some one landscape or some one kind of landscape. All nature seemed to him paintable—the most difficult, the most unlikely subjects held no terrors for him—the confidence of inexperience it may have been. No doubt he put his own impress on what he painted, but the country he painted ever grew into his soul, stronger and stronger, rendering him shy and silent, filling him with longing and love for its beauties. His stay in the studio became shorter and shorter, his dress more and more like that of the backwoodsman. The quiet hidden strength, confidence and resource of the voyageur showed itself in the surety of handling in his work. He was not concerned with any special technique, any particular mode of application of colour, with this kind of brush stroke or that. If it were true to nature, the technique might be anything. A technique all his own, varying with the occasion, sprang into being, not as the result of any laboured thought or experiment, but because it could not be otherwise. He proved the theory that the technique should harmonize with the nature of the painting, should never overpower or dominate the idea or emotion expressed, and should appear to be the best or the only technique to adequately express the idea. However unaccustomed a technique, if, after a short acquaintance with it, one loses sight of the technique and feels only the emotion of the picture, that technique is good. Judged by these criterions, his technique is unassailable. Drawing was to him the expression of form, and form might be expressed by any method, so long as the form is true.

One would have expected that with his intimate knowledge of trees he would have loved to paint all their traceries. In the "Northern River" alone did he lavish detail on his trees and here only because it helped the pattern. In one in whom the sense of design, of decoration was so developed that is the more striking, for in his sketches and in his larger pictures he always treated trees as masses. In his painting of them he gives form structure and colour by dragging paint in bold strokes over an underlying tone. Like many other painters he felt the limitations of paint, the impossibility of expressing on a flat surface the solidity and thickness of a tree, and in some canvasses almost modelled them in paint, while in others he got the same effect by expressing them by deep grooves in the paint.

At an exhibition of some of Thomson's pictures I overheard a wellknown woman artist say, "Well! now *where* would you hang that?" She really felt the daring of the colour and of the method of execution of the picture. To the painter of the schools his work may seem daring, but it was not so to him. It was rather the joy of a boy playing with paints, intent only on expressing something which has pleasurably excited him, and all unconscious of doing anything out of the ordinary, of tackling anything unusual. Because his paintings are so striking in purity of colour and in handling they are thought to be unusual. They are unusual, in that other artists have not had the opportunity to see the same subjects or have thought them either impossible or unworthy of painting.

The northern spring radiant with hope bursting riotously forth from the grim embrace of winter always found him in the woods ready to chronicle its beauties. The awakening rivers and lakes, the earth peeping here and there through her coverlet of snow and the sunny skies afforded a wealth of ravishing colour which ever charmed his sensitive soul. The hardwood bush, budding into varied hues of pink, lavender, blue, purple, brown and black, lent itself to many harmonies.

When the beautiful white birches, and solemn stately pines were lost in the crass greens of the summer forest, his brushes were laid aside. He now began to cruise the park seeking new sketching grounds. Camped by himself, he was, to the tourist, a mysterious hermit of whose marvellous skill as a fisherman there were many tales told. To the native guides he was just as incomprehensible, "worse than any Indian", they said.

The September hardwood in its gorgeous garb of many colours; the pines, strong and grave, mourning among the forest ghosts still beautiful in their tracery against the cold blue October sky; the falling snow and biting blast, the southward migrating of wild fowl, the November heavens, chill and gray, all had response and record from him. Loath to return to the city, he lingered, painting until the forming ice warned him that he might be shut in for the winter. Then he returned to us, who were waiting to see what new thing he had brought home.

Three months of steady painting in his studio, and early March found him growing more and more restless. His fishing lures made by himself, and strung like necklaces on the wall, gradually disappeared from their accustomed place. Then we knew that his flitting time was near. One day he would say, "If I don't get up there now, the snow will all be gone."

Next day his shack would be empty.

And so his year passed by.

Thomson's knowledge of the appearance at night of the woods and lakes was unrivalled. He was wont to paddle out into the centre of the lake on which he happened to be camping and spend the whole night there in order to get away from the flies and mosquitoes. Motionless he studied the night skies and the changing outline of the shores while beaver and otter played around his canoe. Puffing slowly at his pipe, he watched the smoke of his campfire slowly curling up amongst the pines, through which peeped here and there a star, or wondered at the amazing northern lights flashing across the sky, his reverie broken by the howling of wolves of the whistling of a buck attracted by the fire. In his nocturnes, whether of the moonlight playing across the lake, or touching the brook through the gloom of the forest, or of the tent shown up in the darkness by the dim light of the candle within, or of the driving rain suddenly illuminated by the flash of lightning, or of the bare birch tops forming beautiful peacock fans against the cold wind-driven blue skies, one feels that it is nature far apart, unsullied by the intruder man.

Never was he satisfied with his own performance. Pictures were put away again and again in the spring, to be dragged forth on his return in the fall, some change made in the design or the colour, as suggested by the added observation of the year. Oftentimes he said, "Oh, no, it's not like that at all. I have been watching it again, and it is quite different."

This untiring observation, this compelling desire for truthfulness pursued him ever, making him conscious of his shortcomings and urging him on to renewed efforts. Once we had lost our way hunting for a back channel leading into the French River, when darkness and a sudden storm had forced us to camp for the night. We breakfasted in a pelting rain, tried to fish for a time, and ended by talking art, when Thomson said: "I am only a bum artist, anyway. Why, even the animals know that!" Then he added: "I had been sketching in the park and made up my mind to go farther in, two days' journey. So I decided to lighten my load by leaving my sketches to dry, and to pick them up on my way back. On my return I found that a lynx had come along and after a critical inspection of one of the sketches, had clawed it. Not satisfied with this expression of opinion, he had put his head down and chewed it."

"There's a fine picture for you, Tom," said I—"'The Art Critic'."

Down he thrust into his dunnage-bag and brought out the sketch of birches, beautiful in spite of the critic's slashing.

It has not been the fortune of any of our artists to have had during their lifetime a vogue with the Canadian public. Thomson was no exception. To the art critics of the daily press he was an enigma, something which, because beyond the pale of their experience, it seemed quite safe to ridicule. Yet in one magazine a courageous writer ventured to say, "Tom Thomson can put the spirit of Canada on a piece of board eight inches by ten inches."

The intelligent public rather liked his work, but was not quite sure whether it was the safe and proper thing to say so. He found recognition, however, among his fellow artists, who looked forward with pleasure and curiosity to see what he would show at each exhibition. It is to the credit of the Ontario Government and the trustees of the National Gallery at Ottawa that they recognized his value. He never exhibited at the Ontario Society of Artists without having one of his pictures bought for the Province or the Dominion. These will remain for succeeding generations, the ultimate arbiters of the reputation of all artists. Confidently we leave to them the fame of "Tom Thomson, artist and woodsman, who lived humbly but passionately with the wild".

Tom Thomson

Arthur Bourinot

IT WAS a gray day
with a drizzle of rain,
something of fey
in the air
as though the lake,
the islands,
the sky
were watching,
waiting,
waiting for what?
A sense of doom
in the air
with silence everywhere
as though a god
had spoken,
and then a loon laughed
and the spell was broken,
the spell was broken.
And Tom Thomson laughed
and his friends laughed
as he launched his canoe
from the dock
and paddled away
with his lures and his lines
to befool the old trout
they had lost so often
in the bay in the river
below Joe Lake Dam;
and he turned
with a wave of his hand
and was gone.
And a loon laughed
and the old trout

waited in the bay
and the sky and lake watched
but he never came
was never seen again
till his body floated
on the surface
eight days later.

What happened?
No one knows,
no one will ever know;
no one knows
except perhaps the old trout
below Joe Lake Dam
and the lake
and the islands
the loon and the sky
that watched and waited;
no one knows.
And in far off Shoreham,
A. Y. Jackson, painting again,
after a "blighty" in France
heard of the upturned canoe
on the lake
and his dreams of camping
and fishing and painting
once more with his friend
came to an end,
as all dreams come
to an end,
as all dreams come
to an end.

Legend has it in Algonquin
Tom Thomson
watches and looks
from the headland
above the bay
on Canoe Lake,
his palette and brushes
and panels in hand
painting the symphony

of the seasons
of his beloved land
he never finished;
the unfolding year,
the folding leaf,
the gathered sheaf,
the winter snow,
the bright bateaux,
painting, painting;
and the great trout
waits in the river
below Joe Lake Dam
and the loon laughs
and sky and lake watch
and only his voice is still
on land and lake
but his spirit is awake
throughout the land he loved
kindling youth to slake
their thirst in beauty.
His spirit is awake,
a torch and a token,
as though a god had spoken;
his spirit is awake,
his spirit is awake.

Tom Thomson
"There is so much to see . . . ."

George Whipple

I

Before his paintings flared out of his brush,
The accidental grandeur of burned woods
Turned him aside:
Behind the thick black cedar screen
Of time where all that changes, stilled
And verified by art, unchanging lives,
The substance of things hoped for, things unseen,
In birch white solitudes he heard—a silent call.

And always, on some always distant shore,
A light that never was, a phantom shade,
Beckoned his canoe beyond the lamplit edge
Of cities, towns.

      The charcoal hush
Of northern rivers, deep Muskoka lakes
Where deer come down to drink the lapping moon,
He caught on beaverboard. And whispered, green
Bright April breezes—1917—
Still echo spring surrenders to no fall.

II

He took his measure from the tallest spruce.
On you, beleaguered Jackpine, native harp,
The wind's gnarled language learned to reproduce
In steely arms backtwisted on black sky—
Your thunder-shaped, deep-throated silent Cry,
Spread-eagled on the west wind, strained awry,
Strengthened by strong blows, high on your scarp
He captured—rooted fast in shouts of paint.

From *Canadian Magazine*, 50, 5 (March 1918), pp 375–385.

A rangy rawboned woodsman, guide, he swore
No fealty except to art, and wore
Triumphant paths through failure, left behind
Some inner map of innocence and awe
Had led him deep within himself to find
The land's rich emptiness. He struck it big.
In motherlodes of feeling yet unmined,
In haunts of startled wilderness austere,
—A flash of certitude, a radiating force
Awakened him while others cosy slept
In borrowed castles made of borrowed blocks.
Impervious to critics' yelping tomahawks—
Nostalgia for the future made more clear
What's never missed until its found—the rocks
And trees and streams where freedom has its source.

The rough unsettled country of the mind
He caught in rugged frames—all out-of-doors,
The many scattered fragments of perhaps,
A dance of dappled mirrors on a twig
Where windy oaks reflect the leafy sun.
He salvaged day from dark and made a hole
In Time—bequeathing us the country's soul.

Intrepid distances explored his eyes
With new perspectives, forms fresh as that lake
Compacted to a ten-inch square, those rocks
And trees and streams—delicious, spare, defiant sparks
—A cause for celebration in whatever room
They shine, and more enduring than remorse
For what we never had.

One masterpiece,
Homemade, familiar friend to all, in hearts
Too long aggressively indifferent, starts
Still latent flowers, half-asleep, to sing:
Our future was the past too long assigned
To others. Now we have a voice that sees
Cantata-clear white hemlock tapestries—
Blue shadows on white arioso snow.

The joy held in suspension for long years
He tapped. Not what he saw but what he *knew*
Was there he poured upon stretched canvas, scenes
That shook between him and Algonquin Park,
While chipmunks watched him with sharp eyes.
Sometimes exhausted, on a makeshift pew
Of fallen beech, he sat beside big slathered skies,
Picked up his ukelele, plinked the ripe
Blueberry morning to its zenith, threw
Back his head and like a shaman Sioux
Sent, leaf to leaf, bright laughter which
Scared off a ruffled grouse. Then rose to pitch
His tent and build a fire, smoke his pipe.

In contemplation all remembrance dies.
The field of vision's narrowed to a cloud
Is ointments on a stick. Both humble/proud
The artist/shaman heals, and witless/wise,
Unknowing, knows. He sees by going blind
Invisible/bright objects silent/loud
As crimson on a leaf. Nor virtue, vice,
His seeing was a gift he could not give
In unpremeditated art unless he saw
Not with, but through the eye. A frightened shroud

Beneath the long-eared owl, the woodmouse shrills
At loggerheads with death . . . so, sight-unseen
Our future's past before the present dies.
Look how that yellow/blue melts into green
—An always-present mixing in our eyes!

Old forest fires flame from his right hand
To keep us warm within the city's canned-
Heat neon wilderness where thousands freeze
And turn to stone.

III

One cloudy day
In stocking cap, plaid shirt, he lit his pipe,
Shoved off from shore and paddled far away
—Into his pictures. Clutching the last straw
Of light, hands slipping from the cold
Ascending surface of the lake,
He drowned.

In jackpine solitudes
A brief encomium of moonlight sings
Above his speechless cairn. He looked and found
More than there was to see—in solemn woods
The ingrained, secret awesomeness of things.

Death by Landscape

Margaret Atwood

NOW THAT THE boys are grown up and Rob is dead, Lois has moved to a condominium apartment in one of the newer waterfront developments. She is relieved not to have to worry about the lawn, or about the ivy pushing its muscular little suckers into the brickwork, or the squirrels gnawing their way into the attic and eating the insulation off the wiring, or about strange noises. This building has a security system, and the only plant life is in pots in the solarium.

Lois is glad she's been able to find an apartment big enough for her pictures. They are more crowded together than they were in the house, but this arrangement gives the walls a European look: blocks of pictures, above and beside one another, rather than one over the chesterfield, one over the fireplace, one in the front hall, in the old acceptable manner of sprinkling art around so it does not get too intrusive. This way has more of an impact. You know it's not supposed to be furniture.

None of the pictures is very large, which doesn't mean they aren't valuable. They are paintings, or sketches and drawings, by artists who were not nearly as well known when Lois began to buy them as they are now. Their work later turned up on stamps, or as silk-screen reproductions hung in the principals' offices of high schools, or as jigsaw puzzles, or on beautifully printed calendars sent out by corporations as Christmas gifts, to their less important clients. These artists painted mostly in the twenties and thirties and forties; they painted landscapes. Lois has two Tom Thomsons, three A. Y. Jacksons, a Lawren Harris. She has an Arthur Lismer, she has a J. E. H. MacDonald. She has a David Milne. They are pictures of convoluted tree trunks on an island of pink wave-smoothed stone, with more islands behind; of a lake with rough, bright, sparsely wooded cliffs; of a vivid river shore with a tangle of bush and two beached canoes, one red, one grey; of a yellow autumn woods with the ice-blue gleam of a pond half-seen through the interlaced branches.

It was Lois who'd chosen them. Rob had no interest in art, although he could see the necessity of having something on the walls. He left all the decorating decisions to her, while providing the money, of course. Because of this collection of hers, Lois's friends—especially the men—have given her the reputation of having a good nose for art investments.

But this is not why she bought the pictures, way back then. She bought them because she wanted them. She wanted something that was in them, although she could not have said at the time what it was. It was not peace: she does not find them

Taken from *Wilderness Tips* by Margaret Atwood. Used by permission, McClelland & Stewart Ltd. The Canadian Publishers.

peaceful in the least. Looking at them fills her with a wordless unease. Despite the fact that there are no people in them or even animals, it's as if there is something, or someone, looking back out.

When she was thirteen, Lois went on a canoe trip. She'd only been on overnights before. This was to be a long one, into the trackless wilderness, as Cappie put it. It was Lois's first canoe trip, and her last.

Cappie was the head of the summer camp to which Lois had been sent ever since she was nine. Camp Manitou, it was called; it was one of the better ones, for girls, though not the best. Girls of her age whose parents could afford it were routinely packed off to such camps, which bore a generic resemblance to one another. They favoured Indian names and had hearty, energetic leaders, who were called Cappie or Skip or Scottie. At these camps you learned to swim well and sail, and paddle a canoe, and perhaps ride a horse or play tennis. When you weren't doing these things you could do Arts and Crafts and turn out dingy, lumpish clay ashtrays for your mother—mothers smoked more, then—or bracelets made of coloured braided string.

Cheerfulness was required at all times, even at breakfast. Loud shouting and the banging of spoons on the tables were allowed, and even encouraged, at ritual intervals. Chocolate bars were rationed, to control tooth decay and pimples. At night, after supper, in the dining hall or outside around a mosquito-infested campfire ring for special treats, there were singsongs. Lois can still remember all the words to "My Darling Clementine," and to "My Bonnie Lies Over the Ocean," with acting-out gestures: a rippling of the hands for "the ocean," two hands together under the cheek for "lies." She will never be able to forget them, which is a sad thought.

Lois thinks she can recognize women who went to these camps, and were good at it. They have a hardness to their handshakes, even now; a way of standing, legs planted firmly and farther apart than usual; a way of sizing you up, to see if you'd be any good in a canoe—the front, not the back. They themselves would be in the back. They would call it the stern.

She knows that such camps still exist, although Camp Manitou does not. They are one of the few things that haven't changed much. They now offer copper enamelling, and functionless pieces of stained glass baked in electric ovens, though judging from the productions of her friends' grandchildren the artistic standards have not improved.

To Lois, encountering it in the first year after the war, Camp Manitou seemed ancient. Its log-sided buildings with the white cement in between the half-logs, its flagpole ringed with whitewashed stones, its weathered grey dock jutting out into Lake Prospect, with its woven rope bumpers and its rusty rings for tying up, its prim round flowerbed of petunias near the office door, must surely have been there always. In truth it dated only from the first decade of the century; it had been founded by Cappie's parents, who'd thought of camping as bracing to the character, like cold showers, and had been passed along to her as an inheritance, and an obligation.

Lois realized, later, that it must have been a struggle for Cappie to keep Camp Manitou going, during the Depression and then the war, when money did not flow freely. If it had been a camp for the very rich, instead of the merely well off, there would have been fewer problems. But there must have been enough Old Girls, ones with daughters, to keep the thing in operation, though not entirely shipshape: furniture was battered, painted trim was peeling, roofs leaked. There were dim photographs of these Old Girls dotted around the dining hall, wearing ample woollen bathing suits and showing their fat, dimpled legs, or standing, arms twined, in odd tennis outfits with baggy skirts.

In the dining hall, over the stone fireplace that was never used, there was a huge moulting stuffed moose head, which looked somehow carnivorous. It was a sort of mascot; its name was Monty Manitou. The older campers spread the story that it was haunted, and came to life in the dark, when the feeble and undependable lights had been turned off or, due to yet another generator failure, had gone out. Lois was afraid of it at first, but not after she got used to it.

Cappie was the same: you had to get used to her. Possibly she was forty, or thirty-five, or fifty. She had fawn-coloured hair that looked as if it was cut with a bowl. Her head jutted forward, jigging like a chicken's as she strode around the camp, clutching notebooks and checking things off in them. She was like their minister in church: both of them smiled a lot and were anxious because they wanted things to go well; they both had the same overwashed skins and stringy necks. But all this disappeared when Cappie was leading a singsong, or otherwise leading. Then she was happy, sure of herself, her plain face almost luminous. She wanted to cause joy. At these times she was loved, at others merely trusted.

There were many things Lois didn't like about Camp Manitou, at first. She hated the noisy chaos and spoon-banging of the dining hall, the rowdy singsongs at which you were expected to yell in order to show that you were enjoying yourself. Hers was not a household that encouraged yelling. She hated the necessity of having to write dutiful letters to her parents claiming she was having fun. She could not complain, because camp cost so much money.

She didn't much like having to undress in a roomful of other girls, even in the dim light, although nobody paid any attention, or sleeping in a cabin with seven other girls, some of whom snored because they had adenoids or colds, some of whom had nightmares, or wet their beds and cried about it. Bottom bunks made her feel closed in, and she was afraid of falling out of top ones; she was afraid of heights. She got homesick, and suspected her parents of having a better time when she wasn't there than when she was, although her mother wrote to her every week saying how much they missed her. All this was when she was nine. By the time she was thirteen she liked it. She was an old hand by then.

Lucy was her best friend at camp. Lois had other friends in winter, when there was school and itchy woollen clothing and darkness in the afternoons, but Lucy was her summer friend.

She turned up the second year, when Lois was ten, and a Bluejay. (Chickadees, Bluejays, Ravens, and Kingfishers—these were the names Camp Manitou assigned to the different age groups, a sort of totemic clan system. In those days, thinks Lois, it was birds for girls, animals for boys: wolves, and so forth. Though some animals and birds were suitable and some were not. Never vultures, for instance; never skunks, or rats.)

Lois helped Lucy to unpack her tin trunk and place the folded clothes on the wooden shelves, and to make up her bed. She put her in the top bunk right above her, where she could keep an eye on her. Already she knew that Lucy was an exception, to a good many rules; already she felt proprietorial.

Lucy was from the United States, where the comic books came from, and the movies. She wasn't from New York or Hollywood or Buffalo, the only American cities Lois knew the names of, but from Chicago. Her house was on the lake shore and had gates to it, and grounds. They had a maid, all of the time. Lois's family only had a cleaning lady twice a week.

The only reason Lucy was being sent to *this* camp (she cast a look of minor scorn around the cabin, diminishing it and also offending Lois, while at the same time daunting her) was that her mother had been a camper here. Her mother had been a Canadian once, but had married her father, who had a patch over one eye, like a pirate. She showed Lois the picture of him in her wallet. He got the patch in the war. "Shrapnel," said Lucy. Lois, who was unsure about shrapnel, was so impressed she could only grunt. Her own two-eyed, unwounded father was tame by comparison.

"My father plays golf," she ventured at last.

"*Everyone* plays golf," said Lucy. "My *mother* plays golf."

Lois's mother did not. Lois took Lucy to see the outhouses and the swimming dock and the dining hall with Monty Manitou's baleful head, knowing in advance they would not measure up.

This was a bad beginning; but Lucy was good-natured, and accepted Camp Manitou with the same casual shrug with which she seemed to accept everything. She would make the best of it, without letting Lois forget that this was what she was doing.

However, there were things Lois knew that Lucy did not. Lucy scratched the tops off all her mosquito bites and had to be taken to the infirmary to be daubed with Ozonol. She took her T-shirt off while sailing, and although the counsellor spotted her after a while and made her put it back on, she burnt spectacularly, bright red, with the X of her bathing-suit straps standing out in alarming white; she let Lois peel the sheets of whispery-thin burned skin off her shoulders. When they sang "Alouette" around the campfire, she did not know any of the French words. The difference was that Lucy did not care about the things she didn't know, whereas Lois did.

During the next winter, and subsequent winters, Lucy and Lois wrote to each other. They were both only children, at a time when this was thought to be a disadvantage, so in their letters they pretended to be sisters, or even twins. Lois had to strain a little over this, because Lucy was so blonde, with translucent skin and large blue eyes like a doll's, and Lois was nothing out of the ordinary—just a tallish, thinnish, brownish person with freckles. They signed their letters LL, with the L's entwined together like the monograms on a towel. (Lois and Lucy, thinks Lois. How our names date us. Lois Lane, Superman's girlfriend, enterprising female reporter; "I Love Lucy." Now we are obsolete, and it's little Jennifers, little Emilys, little Alexandras and Carolines and Tiffanys.)

They were more effusive in their letters than they ever were in person. They bordered their pages with X's and O's, but when they met again in the summers it was always a shock. They had changed so much, or Lucy had. It was like watching someone grow up in jolts. At first it would be hard to think up things to say.

But Lucy always had a surprise or two, something to show, some marvel to reveal. The first year she had a picture of herself in a tutu, her hair in a ballerina's knot on the top of her head; she pirouetted around the swimming dock, to show Lois how it was done, and almost fell off. The next year she had given that up and was taking horseback riding. (Camp Manitou did not have horses.) The next year her mother and father had been divorced, and she had a new stepfather, one with both eyes, and a new house, although the maid was the same. The next year, when they had graduated from Bluejays and entered Ravens, she got her period, right in the first week of camp. The two of them snitched some matches from their counsellor, who smoked illegally, and made a small fire out behind the farthest outhouse, at dusk, using their flashlights. They could set all kinds of fires by now; they had learned how in Campcraft. On this fire they burned one of Lucy's used sanitary napkins. Lois is not sure why they did this, or whose idea it was. But she can remember the feeling of deep satisfaction it gave her as the white fluff signed and the blood sizzled, as if some wordless ritual had been fulfilled.

They did not get caught, but then they rarely got caught at any of their camp transgressions. Lucy had such large eyes, and was such an accomplished liar.

This year Lucy is different again: slower, more languorous. She is no longer interested in sneaking around after dark, purloining cigarettes from the counsellor, dealing in blackmarket candy bars. She is pensive, and hard to wake in the mornings. She doesn't like her stepfather, but she doesn't want to live with her real father either, who has a new wife. She thinks her mother may be having a love affair with a doctor; she doesn't know for sure, but she's seen them smooching in his car, out on the driveway, when her stepfather wasn't there. It serves him right. She hates her private school. She has a boyfriend, who is sixteen and works as a gardener's assistant. This is how she met him: in the garden. She describes to Lois what it is like when he kisses her—rubbery at first, but then your knees go limp. She has been forbidden to see him, and threatened with boarding school. She wants to run away from home.

Lois has little to offer in return. Her own life is placid and satisfactory, but there is nothing much that can be said about happiness. "You're so lucky," Lucy tells her, a little smugly. She might as well say *boring* because this is how it makes Lois feel.

Lucy is apathetic about the canoe trip, so Lois has to disguise her own excitement. The evening before they are to leave, she slouches into the campfire ring as if coerced, and sits down with a sigh of endurance, just as Lucy does.

Every canoe trip that went out of camp was given a special send-off by Cappie and the section leader and counsellors, with the whole section in attendance. Cappie painted three streaks of red across each of her cheeks with a lipstick. They looked like three-fingered claw marks. She put a blue circle on her forehead with fountain-pen ink, and tied a twisted bandanna around her head and stuck a row of frazzle-ended feathers around it, and wrapped herself in a red-and-black Hudson's Bay blanket. The counsellors, also in blankets but with only two streaks of red, beat on tom-toms made of round wooden cheese boxes with leather stretched over the top and nailed in place. Cappie was Chief Cappeosota. They all had to say "How!" when she walked into the circle and stood there with one hand raised.

Looking back on this, Lois finds it disquieting. She knows too much about Indians: this is why. She knows, for instance, that they should not even be called Indians, and that they have enough worries without other people taking their names and dressing up as them. It has all been a form of stealing.

But she remembers, too, that she was once ignorant of this. Once she loved the campfire, the flickering of light on the ring of faces, the sound of the fake tom-toms, heavy and fast like a scared heartbeat; she loved Cappie in a red blanket and feathers, solemn, as a chief should be, raising her hand and saying, "Greetings, my Ravens." It was not funny, it was not making fun. She wanted to be an Indian. She wanted to be adventurous and pure, and aboriginal.

"You go on big water," says Cappie. This is her idea—all their ideas—of how Indians talk. "You go where no man has ever trod. You go many moons." This is not true. They are only going for a week, not many moons. The canoe route is clearly marked, they have gone over it on a map, and there are prepared campsites with names which are used year after year. But when Cappie says this—and despite the way Lucy rolls up her eyes—Lois can feel the water stretching out, with the shores twisting away on either side, immense and a little frightening.

"You bring back much wampum," says Cappie. "Do good in war, my braves, and capture many scalps." This is another of her pretences: that they are boys, and bloodthirsty. But such a game cannot be played by substituting the word "squaw." It would not work at all.

Each of them has to stand up and step forward and have a red line drawn across her cheeks by Cappie. She tells them they must follow in the paths of their ancestors (who most certainly, thinks Lois, looking out the window of her apartment and remembering the family stash of daguerreo-types and sepia-coloured portraits on her mother's dressing table, the stiff-shirted, black-coated, grim-faced men and the beflounced women with their severe hair and their corseted respectability, would never have considered heading off onto an open lake, in a canoe, just for fun).

At the end of the ceremony they all stood and held hands around the circle, and sang taps. This did not sound very Indian, thinks Lois. It sounded like a bugle call at a military post, in a movie. But Cappie was never one to be much concerned with consistency, or with archaeology.

After breakfast the next morning they set out from the main dock, in four canoes, three in each. The lipstick stripes have not come off completely, and still show faintly pink, like healing burns. They wear their white denim sailing hats, because of the sun, and thin-striped T-shirts, and pale baggy shorts with the cuffs rolled up. The middle one kneels, propping her rear end against the rolled sleeping bags. The counsellors going with them are Pat and Kip. Kip is no-nonsense; Pat is easier to wheedle, or fool.

There are white puffy clouds and a small breeze. Glints come from the little waves. Lois is in the bow of Kip's canoe. She still can't do a J-stroke very well, and she will have to be in the bow or the middle for the whole trip. Lucy is behind her; her own J-stroke is even worse. She splashes Lois with her paddle, quite a big splash.

"I'll get you back," says Lois.

"There was a stable fly on your shoulder," Lucy says.

Lois turns to look at her, to see if she's grinning. They're in the habit of splashing each other. Back there, the camp has vanished behind the first long point of rock and rough trees. Lois feels as if an invisible rope has broken. They're floating free, on their own, cut loose. Beneath the canoe the lake goes down, deeper and colder than it was a minute before.

"No horsing around in the canoe," says Kip. She's rolled her T-shirt sleeves up to the shoulder; her arms are brown and sinewy, her jaw determined, her stroke perfect. She looks as if she knows exactly what she is doing.

The four canoes keep close together. They sing, raucously and with defiance; they sing "The Quartermaster's Store," and "Clementine," and "Alouette." It is more like bellowing than singing.

After that the wind grows stronger, blowing slantwise against the bows, and they have to put all their energy into shoving themselves through the water.

Was there anything important, anything that would provide some sort of reason or clue to what happened next? Lois can remember everything, every detail; but it does her no good.

They stopped at noon for a swim and lunch, and went on in the afternoon. At last they reached Little Birch, which was the first campsite for overnight. Lois and Lucy made the fire, while the others pitched the heavy canvas tents. The fireplace was already there, flat stones piled into a U. A burned tin can and a beer bottle had been left in it. Their fire went out, and they had to restart it. "Hustle your bustle," said Kip. "We're starving."

The sun went down, and in the pink sunset light they brushed their teeth and spat the toothpaste froth into the lake. Kip and Pat put all the food that wasn't in cans into a packsack and slung it into a tree, in case of bears.

Lois and Lucy weren't sleeping in a tent. They'd begged to be allowed to sleep out; that way they could talk without the others hearing. If it rained, they told Kip, they promised not to crawl dripping into the tent over everyone's legs: they would get under the canoes. So they were out on the point.

Lois tried to get comfortable inside her sleeping bag, which smelled of musty storage and of earlier campers, a stale salty sweetness. She curled herself up, with her sweater rolled up under her head for a pillow and her flashlight inside her sleeping bag so it wouldn't roll away. The muscles of her sore arms were making small pings, like rubber bands breaking.

Beside her Lucy was rustling around. Lois could see the glimmering oval of her white face.

"I've got a rock poking into my back," said Lucy.

"So do I," said Lois. "You want to go into the tent?" She herself didn't, but it was right to ask.

"No," said Lucy. She subsided into her sleeping bag. After a moment she said, "It would be nice not to go back."

"To camp?" said Lois.

"To Chicago," said Lucy. "I hate it there."

"What about your boyfriend?" said Lois. Lucy didn't answer. She was either asleep or pretending to be.

There was a moon, and a movement of the trees. In the sky there were stars, layers of stars that went down and down. Kip said that when the stars were bright like that instead of hazy it meant bad weather later on. Out on the lake there were two loons, calling to each other in their insane, mournful voices. At the time it did not sound like grief. It was just background.

The lake in the morning was flat calm. They skimmed along over the glassy surface, leaving V-shaped trails behind them; it felt like flying. As the sun rose higher it got hot, almost too hot. There were stable flies in the canoes, landing on a bare arm or leg for a quick sting. Lois hoped for wind.

They stopped for lunch at the next of the named campsites, Lookout Point. It was called this because, although the site itself was down near the water on a flat shelf of rock, there was a sheer cliff nearby and a trail that led up to the top. The top was the lookout, although what you were supposed to see from there was not clear. Kip said it was just a view.

Lois and Lucy decided to make the climb anyway. They didn't want to hang around waiting for lunch. It wasn't their turn to cook, though they hadn't avoided much by not doing it, because cooking lunch was no big deal, it was just unwrapping the cheese and getting out the bread and peanut butter, but Pat and Kip always had to do their woodsy act and boil up a billy tin for their own tea.

They told Kip where they were going. You had to tell Kip where you were going, even if it was only a little way into the woods to get dry twigs for kindling. You could never go anywhere without a buddy.

"Sure," said Kip, who was crouching over the fire, feeding driftwood into it. "Fifteen minutes to lunch."

"Where are they off to?" said Pat. She was bringing their billy tin of water from the lake.

"Lookout," said Kip.

"Be careful," said Pat. She said it as an afterthought, because it was what she always said.

"They're old hands," Kip said.

Lois looks at her watch: it's ten to twelve. She is the watchminder; Lucy is careless of time. They walk up the path, which is dry earth and rocks, big rounded pinky-grey boulders or split-open ones with jagged edges. Spindly balsam and spruce trees grow to either side, the lake is blue fragments to the left. The sun is right overhead; there are no shadows anywhere. The heat comes up at them as well as down. The forest is dry and crackly.

It isn't far, but it's a steep climb and they're sweating when they reach the top. They wipe their faces with their bare arms, sit gingerly down on a scorching-hot rock, five feet from the edge but too close for Lois. It's a lookout all right, a sheer drop to the lake and a long view over the water, back the way they've come. It's amazing to Lois that they've travelled so far, over all that water, with nothing to propel them but their own arms. It makes her feel strong. There are all kinds of things she is capable of doing.

"It would be quite a dive off here," says Lucy.

"You'd have to be nuts," says Lois.

"Why?" says Lucy. "It's really deep. It goes straight down." She stands up and takes a step nearer the edge. Lois gets a stab in her midriff, the kind she gets when a car goes too fast over a bump. "Don't," she says.

"Don't what?" says Lucy, glancing around at her mischievously. She knows how Lois feels about heights. But she turns back. "I really have to pee," she says.

"You have toilet paper?" says Lois, who is never without it. She digs in her shorts pocket.

"Thanks," says Lucy.

They are both adept at peeing in the woods: doing it fast so the mosquitoes don't get you, the underwear pulled up between the knees, the squat with the feet apart so you don't wet your legs, facing downhill. The exposed feeling of your bum, as if someone is looking at you from behind. The etiquette when you're with someone else is not to look. Lois stands up and starts to walk back down the path, to be out of sight.

"Wait for me?" says Lucy.

Lois climbed down, over and around the boulders, until she could not see Lucy; she waited. She could hear the voices of the others, talking and laughing, down near the shore. One voice was yelling, "Ants! Ants!" Someone must have sat on an ant hill. Off to the side, in the woods, a raven was croaking, a hoarse single note.

She looked at her watch: it was noon. This is when she heard the shout.

She has gone over and over it in her mind since, so many times that the first, real shout has been obliterated, like a footprint trampled by other footprints. But she is sure (she is almost positive, she is nearly certain) that it was not a shout of fear. Not a scream. More like a cry of surprise, cut off too soon. Short, like a dog's bark.

"Lucy?" Lois said. Then she called "Lucy!" By now she was clambering back up, over the stones of the path. Lucy was not up there. Or she was not in sight.

"Stop fooling around," Lois said. "It's lunch-time." But Lucy did not rise from behind a rock or step out, smiling, from behind a tree. The sunlight was all around; the rocks looked white. "This isn't funny!" Lois said, and it wasn't, panic was rising in her, the panic of a small child who does not know where the bigger ones are hidden. She could hear her own heart. She looked quickly around; she lay down on the ground and looked over the edge of the cliff. It made her feel cold. There was nothing.

She went back down the path, stumbling; she was breathing too quickly; she was too frightened to cry. She felt terrible—guilty and dismayed, as if she had done something very bad, by mistake. Something that could never be repaired. "Lucy's gone," she told Kip.

Kip looked up from her fire, annoyed. The water in the billy can was boiling. "What do you mean, gone?" she said. "Where did she go?"

"I don't know," said Lois. "She's just gone."

No one had heard the shout, but then no one had heard Lois calling, either. They had been talking among themselves, by the water.

Kip and Pat went up to the lookout and searched and called, and blew their whistles. Nothing answered.

Then they came back down, and Lois had to tell exactly what had happened. The other girls all sat in a circle and listened to her. Nobody said anything. They all looked frightened, especially Pat and Kip. They were the leaders. You did not just lose a camper like this, for no reason at all.

"Why did you leave her alone?" said Kip.

"I was just down the path," said Lois. "I told you. She had to go to the bathroom." She did not say *pee* in front of people older than herself.

Kip looked disgusted.

"Maybe she just walked off into the woods and got turned around," said one of the girls.

"Maybe she's doing it on purpose," said another.

Nobody believed either of these theories.

They took the canoes and searched around the base of the cliff, and peered down into the water. But there had been no sound of falling rock; there had been no splash. There was no clue, nothing at all. Lucy had simply vanished.

That was the end of the canoe trip. It took them the same two days to go back that it had taken coming in, even though they were short a paddler. They did not sing.

After that, the police went in a motorboat, with dogs; they were the Mounties and the dogs were German shepherds, trained to follow trails in the woods. But it had rained since, and they could find nothing.

Lois is sitting in Cappie's office. Her face is bloated with crying, she's seen that in the mirror. By now she feels numbed; she feels as if she has drowned. She can't stay here. It has been too much of a shock. Tomorrow her parents are coming to take her away. Several of the other girls who were on the canoe trip are also being collected. The others will have to stay, because their parents are in Europe, or cannot be reached.

Cappie is grim. They've tried to hush it up, but of course everyone in camp knows. Soon the papers will know too. You can't keep it quiet, but what can be said? What can be said that makes any sense? "Girl vanishes in broad daylight, without a trace." It can't be believed. Other things, worse things, will be suspected. Negligence, at the very least. But they have always taken such care. Bad luck will gather around Camp Manitou like a fog; parents will avoid it, in favour of other, luckier places. Lois can see Cappie thinking all this, even through her numbness. It's what anyone would think.

Lois sits on the hard wooden chair in Cappie's office, beside the old wooden desk, over which hangs the thumbtacked bulletin board of normal camp routine, and gazes at Cappie through her puffy eyelids. Cappie is now smiling what is supposed to be a reassuring smile. Her manner is too casual: she's after something. Lois has seen this look on Cappie's face when she's been sniffing out contraband chocolate bars, hunting down those rumoured to have snuck out of their cabins at night.

"Tell me again," says Cappie, "from the beginning."

Lois has told her story so many times by now, to Pat and Kip, to Cappie, to the police, that she knows it word for word. She knows it, but she no longer believes it. It has become a story. "I told you," she said. "She wanted to go to the bathroom. I gave her my toilet paper. I went down the path, I waited for her. I heard this kind of shout . . ."

"Yes," says Cappie, smiling confidingly, "but before that. What did you say to one another?"

Lois thinks. Nobody has asked her this before. "She said you could dive off there. She said it went straight down."

"And what did you say?"

"I said you'd have to be nuts."

"Were you mad at Lucy?" says Cappie, in an encouraging voice.

"No," says Lois. "Why would I be mad at Lucy? I wasn't ever mad at Lucy." She feels like crying again. The times when she has in fact been mad at Lucy have been erased already. Lucy was always perfect.

"Sometimes we're angry when we don't know we're angry," says Cappie, as if to herself. "Sometimes we get really mad and we don't even know it. Sometimes we might do a thing without meaning to, or without knowing what will happen. We lose our tempers."

Lois is only thirteen, but it doesn't take her long to figure out that Cappie is not including herself in any of this. By *we* she means Lois. She is accusing Lois of pushing Lucy off the cliff. The unfairness of this hits her like a slap. "I didn't!" she says.

"Didn't what?" says Cappie softly. "Didn't what, Lois?"

Lois does the worst thing, she begins to cry. Cappie gives her a look like a pounce. She's got what she wanted.

Later, when she was grown up, Lois was able to understand what this interview had been about. She could see Cappie's desperation, her need for a story, a real story with a reason in it; anything but the senseless vacancy Lucy had left for her to deal with. Cappie wanted Lois to supply the reason, to be the reason. It wasn't even for the newspapers or the parents, because she could never make such an accusation without proof. It was for herself: something to explain the loss of Camp Manitou and of all she had worked for, the years of entertaining spoiled children and buttering up parents and making a fool of herself with feathers stuck in her hair. Camp Manitou was in fact lost. It did not survive.

Lois worked all this out, twenty years later. But it was far too late. It was too late even ten minutes afterwards, when she'd left Cappie's office and was walking slowly back to her cabin to pack. Lucy's clothes were still there, folded on the shelves, as if waiting. She felt the other girls in the cabin watching her with speculation in their eyes. *Could she have done it? She must have done it.* For the rest of her life, she has caught people watching her in this way.

Maybe they weren't thinking this. Maybe they were merely sorry for her. But she felt she had been tried and sentenced, and this is what has stayed with her: the knowledge that she had been singled out, condemned for something that was not her fault.

Lois sits in the living room of her apartment, drinking a cup of tea. Through the knee-to-ceiling window she has a wide view of Lake Ontario, with its skin of wrinkled blue-grey light, and of the willows of Centre Island shaken by a wind, which is silent at this distance, and on this side of the glass. When there isn't too much pollution she can see the far shore, the foreign shore; though today it is obscured.

Possibly she could go out, go downstairs, do some shopping; there isn't much in the refrigerator. The boys say she doesn't get out enough. But she isn't hungry, and moving, stirring from this space, is increasingly an effort.

She can hardly remember, now, having her two boys in the hospital, nursing them as babies; she can hardly remember getting married, or what Rob looked like. Even at the time she never felt she was paying full attention. She was tired a lot, as if she was living not one life but two: her own, and another, shadowy life that hovered around her and would not let itself be realized—the life of what would have happened if Lucy had not stepped sideways, and disappeared from time.

She would never go up north, to Rob's family cottage or to any place with wild lakes and wild trees and the calls of loons. She would never go anywhere near. Still, it was as if she was always listening for another voice, the voice of a person who should have been there but was not. An echo.

While Rob was alive, while the boys were growing up, she could pretend she didn't hear it, this empty space in sound. But now there is nothing much left to distract her.

She turns away from the window and looks at her pictures. There is the pinkish island, in the lake, with the intertwisted trees. It's the same landscape they paddled through, that distant summer. She's seen travelogues of this country, aerial photographs; it looks different from above, bigger, more hopeless: lake after lake, random blue puddles in dark green bush, the trees like bristles.

How could you ever find anything there, once it was lost? Maybe if they cut it all down, drained it all away, they might find Lucy's bones, some time, wherever they are hidden. A few bones, some buttons, the buckle from her shorts.

But a dead person is a body; a body occupies space, it exists somewhere. You can see it; you put it in a box and bury it in the ground, and then it's in a box in the ground. But Lucy is not in a box, or in the ground. Because she is nowhere definite, she could be anywhere.

And these paintings are not landscape paintings. Because there aren't any landscapes up there, not in the old, tidy European sense, with a gentle hill, a curving river, a cottage, a mountain in the background, a golden evening sky. Instead there's a tangle, a receding maze, in which you can become lost almost as soon as you step off the path. There are no backgrounds in any of these paintings, no vistas; only a great deal of foreground that goes back and back, endlessly, involving you in its twists and turns of tree and branch and rock. No matter how far back in you go, there will be more. And the trees themselves are hardly trees; they are currents of energy, charged with violent colour.

Who knows how many trees there were on the cliff just before Lucy disappeared? Who counted? Maybe there was one more, afterwards.

Lois sits in her chair and does not move. Her hand with the cup is raised halfway to her mouth. She hears something, almost hears it: a shout of recognition, or of joy.

She looks at the paintings, she looks into them. Every one of them is a picture of Lucy. You can't see her exactly, but she's there, in behind the pink stone island or the one behind that. In the picture of the cliff she is hidden by the clutch of fallen rocks towards the bottom, in the one of the river shore she is crouching beneath the overturned canoe. In the yellow autumn woods she's behind the tree that cannot be seen because of the other trees, over beside the blue sliver of pond; but if you walked into the picture and found the tree, it would be the wrong one, because the right one would be further on.

Everyone has to be somewhere, and this is where Lucy is. She is in Lois's apartment, in the holes that open inwards on the wall, not like windows but like doors. She is here. She is entirely alive.

CHAPTER TEN

Labour in Canada: The Case of Cape Breton

Introduction

The Canadian memory is fundamentally one-sided. Canada's currency, for example, features our great prime ministers: John A. Macdonald, Wilfrid Laurier, Mackenzie King and Robert Borden. These men are considered nation builders. But the men and women who actually built the country—the workers who laid the railway tracks, who stood at the assembly lines and who mined tonne after tonne of coal—are not included in the pantheon of national heroes. To quote J.B. McLachlan, the subject of one the readings in this chapter, "I believe in telling children the truth about the history of the world, that it does not consist in the history of Kings and Lords and Cabinets, but consists in the history of the mass of workers, a thing that is not taught in the schools."

The 1920s and 1930s were crucial decades in Canadian labour history. The interwar years were marked by tremendous conflict in the form of strikes and set backs on the part of labour but the right of union recognition would be won. One of the greatest conflicts between labour on the one hand and capital and the state on the other was in the coal mines of Cape Breton. The leader of that protracted struggle was James Bryson McLachlan. Born in Scotland in 1869, McLachlan immigrated to Canada—to Cape Breton—in 1902 to work in the coal mines. He soon became active in the labour movement. McLachlan worked tirelessly to improve not just the wages and working conditions of coal miners but to realize his vision of a just society in which the disinherited would become the inherited. This reading comes from *J.B. McLachlan: A Biography* by David Frank. In it the author attempts to measure McLachan's life: "Did he die in defeat?" asks Frank. Why is it important to remember McLachlan? In "The Glace Bay Miners' Museum" Sheldon Currie pictures what a museum to the coal miners of Cape Breton might look like. It is a museum predicated not on the disembodied story of progress but on the embodied truth. What kind of museum does Margaret make? What is the price of coal? Currie's short story was made into a feature-length film, *Margaret's Museum*.

Epilogue *from J.B. McLachlan: A Biography*

David Frank

OUT OF THE smoke and darkness of the meeting hall, he stepped into the street. It was still daylight. There was a salt breeze in the air and a clear sky. He looked thoughtfully up the road, where a train of coal cars was creaking across the level crossing. Sounds carried crisply in the cool air, and for a moment he thought he heard bagpipes sounding in the wind. The couplings jangled, the iron wheels pounded and crackled on the frosty rails, somewhere in the background there was a ringing bell. The sounds were almost musical in the air, and he shook his head in wonder, watching for signs of a band. The train gathered speed. The sounds drifted away. There was a ringing in his ears and the pressure of burning smoke in his chest.

Then he passed through the streets of Glace Bay, through the streets where soldiers had rolled barbed wire during the strikes and mounted police had dragged men out of their homes, past the scenes of street-corner speeches and marching parades, past the union offices and the company buildings. He walked on past the churches where priests had denounced him and the moviehouses where he answered them. He continued on past the dull stockpiles of coal, the black gold that was the currency of the industrial revolution and the cause of so much heartbreak and so many struggles for his people.

McLachlan was moving slowly now, making his way home to the old farmhouse on Steele's Hill where he could command a view of the silent hills and fields above the town. He walked past the small shops and homes of his fellow citizens, past the heavy work clothes snapping on the lines in the wind, past the women watching from their windows and the children peeking around the corners at the old man marching up the hill. He was walking home to Kate, home to their daughters and sons and their neighbours, home to his favourite horse Queenie, home to the roses he loved to cultivate, home to a sunlit room on Steele's Hill. He was walking out of the anxious struggles of the past and into the everlasting present of history.

There he died, on 3 November 1937, in the bright windowed room on the side of the old farmhouse. For some time McLachlan's declining condition had been obvious to friends and family. His face was thinning, his lungs were choking, he was coughing coal dust. After his death newspapers spoke of "two years of lingering illness" and stated that "an incurable illness numbered his days on earth." McLachlan's death certificate stated his age at sixty-eight years, eight months, twenty-four days but gave no cause of death. A more specific observation was made by D.N. Brodie, one of McLachlan's oldest comrades from the days of the Socialist Party, who was a regular visitor to his bedside during his last months. Less than a week before his death Brodie wrote an urgent letter to J.S. Woodsworth concerning McLachlan's rapid deterioration: "I presume you have heard of his illness during the past year, but probably are not acquainted with details. He contracted severely bronchial trouble while in Dorchester Penitentiary some years ago for which the doctor has been treating him ever since. The past winter it developed into T.B. He is in a dying condition and may not last more than a few weeks."[1]

The funeral took place on Sunday afternoon, 7 November. The room where McLachlan died was banked to the ceiling with flowers and wreaths sent by virtually every union local in the district, as well as from the steelworkers in Sydney, other unions, and individual friends, comrades and supporters. Hundreds of people passed through the house in single file to pay their respects. Then his closest friends and family assembled for a short service. Prayers were offered by the Reverend C.R.F. McLennan of Knox United Church. He was followed by the Reverend William T. Mercer, pastor of St Luke's United Church at Dominion No. 6, who had served as the labour candidate in that summer's provincial election. Mercer pronounced McLachlan "an honest and sincere man of upstanding qualities" whose religious views were often misunderstood: "His home-loving qualities and close affection for his family were attributes of the deceased, well known to all . . . Such qualities bespoke the man he was. Though riches could have been his for the taking, he took the harder but more Christian course—the field of labour for his fellow man." McLachlan was described as "a champion of his class" and a man who "held ideals for the betterment of mankind like those of Him who went about Palestine doing good for women and children."[2]

Then the funeral procession, a mile long, carried McLachlan slowly down the hill and through the streets of Glace Bay. At the head was the coal miners' brass band from Dominion No. 6. The eight pallbearers were old friends and veterans of the local struggles: George Milley, Walter Davis, John Fortune, Alex J. McNeil, Alex McKeigan, Wesley Bond, M.A. MacKenzie, and D.N. Brodie. More than 500 miners followed on foot, and they were followed by almost 100 cars. The procession moved down the road from Steele's Hill, down Highland Street past the miners' homes, through the centre of town, past Senator's Corner, then back along Union Street and up the hill to Greenwood Cemetery.

At the graveside there were further prayers, and the band played two verses of "Nearer My God to Thee." As the family gathered around and watched, the casket was lowered into the ground, covered with flowers. There he rested, a few feet from his daughter Kate who had died so full of promise ten years earlier. In this high, secluded location on a green hillside overlooking Glace Bay, there is a measure of calm. But the Old Testament words on the polished stone remind us of the stormy life that is commemorated here: "Open thy mouth, judge righteously, and plead the cause of the poor and needy."[3]

In the pages of *The Steelworker*, the Cape Breton labour weekly published by M.A. MacKenzie that continued the traditions of McLachlan's newspapers, D.N. Brodie paid tribute to McLachlan's character and abilities and his unshakable dedication to the workers' cause. It was the kind of informed, thoughtful assessment that was rarely heard in the public press in McLachlan's own lifetime. His contributions were historic—the struggle to build the miners' union and bring the benefits of industrial unionism to all workers, the campaigns to win political influence for labour and to educate workers to their responsibilities. Brodie also singled out McLachlan's remarkable ability to plead the workers' cause, in print, on the platform, and in the small exchanges of personal interaction: "He knew the workers' thoughts, struggles, needs and aspirations, and could appreciate and present their case from his own personal experience."[4]

More followed, as those who had stood with McLachlan in various battles attempted to explain the significance of the man they had known. Alex S. McIntyre, the district vice-president in the days of the red executive in the early 1920s, described McLachlan as "a real friend of the common people and a lifelong crusader in the cause of the working class": "I never knew a more clean living, honest or sincere man. He was continually aflame with a sense of the social injustice under which the workers were laboring, and with an ever-burning zeal he strove to improve their condition." Forman Waye, the steelworkers' leader who fought alongside McLachlan in the 1923 strike and other battles, described him as "the greatest exponent of the cause of labor in the Maritime Provinces": "I came to know him as a friend whose word was his bond, as a man who was utterly fearless in fighting the tyrants who exploit the poor; and who possessed a brilliant and analytic brain that was tireless in labor's cause." A tribute signed "Coal Digger" identified "J.B." above all as a great educationalist: "The education the workers got, rank and file, whether they know it or not, during the past 30 years, will gain for them in the future as in the past, many concessions." There was even a young man's poem of farewell and dedication: "You bore the blows for us, / Forever singing of the dawn to come; / Lashing the foe to fury with the sword of truth, / You gave no ground . . ."[5]

In the pages of the Communist newspapers, such as *The Worker*, McLachlan was treated with respect: "Old Jim is gone. That grizzled old fighter who was hated and feared by the coal barons and the multimillionaires is silent and dead. His memory will be evergreen to those who fought shoulder to shoulder with him in labor's cause. When labor's history is written the name of dear J.B. McLachlan will occupy an honored place. He was a fighter for Socialism. He was an irreconcilable enemy of all those who were against the people." The *Daily Clarion* said much the same: "His great personal gifts would have brought him material ease and comfort a dozen times over if he had quit his class. But they would never have brought happiness to a heart so stoutly proletarian as Jim's—and Jim was never turned aside by bribes or frightened back by threats. A great worker, a great Canadian is gone."[6]

The labour poet Joe Wallace, who counted McLachlan as one of the influences in his own conversion to socialism at the end of Great War, described McLachlan as "the greatest Nova Scotian since the days of Joe Howe, perhaps of them all." The comparison made sense to Wallace, because he saw McLachlan as a man who struggled in his own time to extend the meaning of democracy, just as Joseph Howe had done in the early days in Nova Scotia; and both had suffered persecution by the authorities of their time. Wallace concluded with a personal recollection: "There are sand-and-sea swept roads that we will never again travel together while I drink in his salty phrases; halls where I will never again hear his voice speaking through smoke to the men and women he loved with his whole life. Jim McLachlan is dead. To some that means the passing of an almost legendary fighter in the ranks of the working-class. But to thousands of us it means in addition the passing of a dear friend."[7]

There remained difficulties arising from McLachlan's break with the Communist Party in 1936. At the funeral there was no official party representation, and a wreath from party headquarters was turned away. In the party press there were brief allusions to the late differences. *The Worker* said only that "Jim joined the Communist Party in 1922 and until stricken down with his fatal illness was an active leader of the revolutionary movement"; on the west coast, the *People's Advocate* said a little more: "He agreed with the party's policy of trade union unity but could never reconcile his political beliefs with his personal hatred of President John L. Lewis of the UMWA."[8]

In the meanwhile, had McLachlan abandoned his revolutionary views and endorsed a more moderate form of socialism? The evidence for this is not convincing, particularly in the light of the nature of McLachlan's criticism of the Communist Party, which was that the party was too moderate in its course of action at this time.[9] In his letter to Woodsworth the week before McLachlan's death, Brodie (who became a CCF MLA in 1941) noted that McLachlan "spoke of you very highly + wished he could see you again. Of course that may not be possible but I wish you could find time to write him a little letter. He would appreciate it. Whatever differences you may have had in the past—it means nothing to poor Jim now and I know he feels badly over it."[10] It is difficult to see this as anything more than a statement of personal regret, as observed by an old comrade. In addition, there are the observations of the Reverend Mercer, who officiated at the funeral; he recalled McLachlan as "a righteous man, but a Communist." During their encounters, their conversations had focused on matters of human justice and the social gospel, and Mercer recalled McLachlan presenting him with a pamphlet entitled *The Carpenter of Nazareth*. At the time of Mercer's campaign for the provincial legislature as a labour candidate in the summer of 1937, McLachlan expressed personal support— "but did not become involved for fear of hurting me, by having me associated with a Communist."[11]

Did McLachlan die in defeat? In his lifetime McLachlan could not rest easy when the outcome of so many struggles was uncertain and the revolution had not arrived. But the world was moving. The miners' union, for all its troubles, was permanently established in the coalfields, and employers in the future would not dare to challenge the miners' right to union representation. And the cause of industrial unionism, pioneered by the coal miners, was at the time of McLachlan's death gaining ground everywhere in North America. This was labour's giant step forward. In the next dozen years, hundreds of thousands of Canadian workers, millions in the United States, would join unions for the first time and win the benefits of union recognition. Ironically, the best-known leaders of this new upsurge in labour militancy included men such as John L. Lewis and Silby Barrett who had counted themselves among McLachlan's sworn enemies in the 1920s.

In Nova Scotia, the steelworkers, led by young union leaders who saw McLachlan as an inspiration, forced the provincial government to introduce the long-awaited Trade Union Act that promised workers the right to join a union and be represented by a union of their own choice. This was the first law of its kind in Canada, and over the course of the next dozen years other provinces—and in 1944 the federal government itself—would bring in similar provisions. The arrival of industrial legality, as McLachlan had warned more than once, was not the end of labour history, and it carried its own dangers of bureaucracy and complacency; but it was a victory nonetheless. What the coal miners had won for themselves in the long labour wars of the early twentieth century was now becoming the democratic right of all Canadian workers.

In political influence, too, the working class was beginning to come into its own, and industrial Cape Breton became known as one of the strongholds of working-class politics in Canada. Although Mercer's own campaign did not succeed in the summer of 1937, in subsequent elections the coal miners were victorious in electing labour candidates to the provincial assembly and Dominion Parliament. In 1938 District 26 of the United Mine Workers was the first union in the country officially to endorse the CCF, and the party quickly benefited from this alliance with the coal miners. Coal miner Clarie Gillis, a former officer of the "red" Amalgamated of the 1930s, was elected as a CCF Member of Parliament in 1940—the first CCF MP elected in eastern Canada. This was the local outcome of the united front that McLachlan had championed in his own political career, and, though party labels changed over the years, the political tradition still remained vigorous half a century later in the 1990s.

There was no doubt that the balance of power in Canadian society was changing. In the decades that followed McLachlan's death, working-class voters supported major social reforms, among them unemployment insurance, family allowances, old age pensions, and medicare. These provisions for the security of families and individuals are now counted among the rights of all Canadian citizens. For radicals of McLachlan's generation, these reforms were based on the idea that there is a shared responsibility for the social and economic welfare of the community. There were even modest advances in the direction of economic democracy, with the appearance of a form of public ownership in the coal and steel industries in the 1960s. This took place in the shadow of under-development and decline in the coal industry, and there was no transformation of the local economy. It was not the triumph of workers' control, and the available state support turned out to be an inadequate form of reinvestment. Yet, for all their defaults and disappointments, innovations in public ownership, such as the rise of the coal miners' cooperatives and credit unions, demonstrated the importance of reconciling economic development and public responsibility. These communitarian social principles, bigger than the interests of any individual or corporation, now have deep roots in the Canadian political tradition, even as they face challenges from those who would undo the progress of the past century.[12]

To be sure, the Canadian revolution had not arrived, at least not in the form that McLachlan had envisaged. Uncompromising, irreconcilable, McLachlan championed a cause that did not end in his own lifetime, and we may sympathize with the frustration of a man who was still waiting for the fulfilment of a dream of human liberation and social justice. But McLachlan was more than a dreamer, and most of his achievements were the outcome of a pragmatic labour radicalism that never lost sight of the ultimate goal of social transformation. "The world do move," he had written in 1919, and one day the disinherited would refuse to remain disinherited. Like other revolutionaries before him, he had reached the conclusion that power concedes nothing without a demand, and that numbers weigh in the balance only when united by organization and informed by knowledge. He knew, too, that in history individuals do make a difference, and McLachlan had long since identified his own mission in the service he rendered to the coal miners and to his class.

On that November day in 1937 a small boy watched as the funeral procession passed by his streetcorner. He was watching his grandfather—his "Poppa" and his namesake—travel to his final resting place. The young James Bryson McLachlan remembered it as a sad day, for he always had wonderful memories of his boyhood visits to Steele's Hill—the inspections of the barn and the fields, the lunches of fresh bread and milk and mushrooms, the warm hugs from his grandmother, and through it all the half-humorous, half-serious conversations with his grandfather.

This young McLachlan went on to spend much of his life in England as a teacher, and it would have pleased his grandfather to know that he maintained an abiding interest in literature, history, and philosophy. Half a century after his grandfather's death, the grandson shared his meditations on McLachlan's historical significance in terms that bear repeating:

> I like the idea of John the Baptist. By which I mean, that although John knew full well that he wasn't the Saviour, he also knew full well that what he was saying pointed out the only way through which salvation could be found. So it was with Gorbachev, so it was, I think, with Poppa & Hardie. None of them could, in themselves, achieve what they most dearly wanted to achieve, but they pointed to the only way by which workers could improve their lot: through unionisation & acquiring political power.
>
> And they were right, and they were successful to this degree: there doesn't exist a single democratic country in the whole world that would

dare not to look after its citizens' health & education & old age, that doesn't have at least some pretense to providing a minimum wage, that doesn't have factory acts that look after workers' safety & so on. I know of nothing that illustrates more clearly the power of the democratic system than the claim that I have just made. What's more, I marvel that these things were achieved within my own lifetime . . .

I cannot believe that the democratic process could have achieved such power if it had not been for the work like Hardie's & Poppa's. The Labour movement & the progress of democracy are very tightly intertwined indeed, so that it is, to my mind anyway, impossible to conceive of the progress of the one without the progress of the other.

History almost compels the appearance of certain sorts of people. For instance, in Athens in the 5th Century BC, people were giving up their freedom willingly to their leaders. Along came a man who taught other men to think for themselves. That was Socrates, & the world honours him to this day, though his own fellow citizens finally condemned him to death. In the 1st Century AD, a young man looked upon the fossilised form that his religion had turned into & spent 3 years preaching against it up & down what is now Israel. For his efforts, he was crucified. In medieval France, a young girl looked upon how her people were being oppressed by the English & encouraged the French armies to fight against them & win. She was burnt at the stake . . .

I am not in the least suggesting that Poppa, or even Keir Hardie, were as great as Socrates or Jesus or Joan of Arc. That they were of the same mould, however, I am sure. They were the "village Hampdens," the men of local fame. Every movement needs its disciples to propagate the word, & Poppa was certainly one of them.[13]

All this is to say that James Bryson McLachlan was a man who answered the challenges of his times. He entered history at a time when industrial capitalism was refashioning the world with its contradictory discourse of development and exploitation, prosperity and suffering, wealth and poverty. For all its achievements, so many of them fuelled by the power of coal, the industrial revolution failed to reward the working class in any way commensurate with their contribution to economic development. Under existing conditions, the wealth produced by the coal miners disappeared in the smoke and sweat of the coal country, leaving behind a ravaged social and human landscape. The world was still not redeemed from the chaos of capitalism. McLachlan was never reconciled to such a contradiction, and with all the force of his personality, he answered in the language of resistance, solidarity, and liberation.

That such a leader should emerge among the coal miners is not all that surprising. Economies based on the alienation and depletion of natural resources raise the issues of exploitation and reinvestment with special urgency. And as the historian E.P. Thompson has written, the coal miners have always been "a special case" in modern history. They have shown a stubborn difficulty in accepting such simple economic propositions as the market regulation of wages and the survival of the fittest as appropriate social ethics. Instead, they have attached great significance to such old-fashioned ideas as justice, fairness, and cooperation in human affairs and the priority of labour as a source of value. From this perspective, their history is not so much a reservoir of traditionalism and conservatism as an accumulated supply of stored cultural energy.[14]

In the world of the present it is often difficult to make out the record of perseverance, resourcefulness, and imagination that sustained those who went before us. But if the writers of history are at their work, those energies can be seen, burning still, and moments of cultural transmission and illumination will take place. Then we shall be in a position to recognize that the so-called "special case" of the coal miners is also the general case of the working people as a whole, and that the messages of empowerment and transformation that the coal miners have been delivering for the last 200 years are addressed to all citizens of the modern world. Like the coal miners, McLachlan was also a "special case," and for this reason his place in history is assured.

Notes

1. "Certificate of Death," no. 24345, issued by registrar general, Nova Scotia; D.N. Brodie to J.S. Woodsworth, 27 October 1937, Woodsworth Papers.
2. Glace Bay *Gazette,* 8 November 1937, *Daily Clarion,* 9 November 1937.
3. *Proverbs,* 31:9. The citation was meaningful to McLachlan, for it was cited in W.U. Cotton's *Sermon to the Working Class* (*c.* 1910).
4. *The Steelworker,* 6 November 1937.
5. *The Steelworker,* 6, 13, 20 November 1937.
6. *The Worker,* 4 November 1937, *Clarion,* 5 November 1937.
7. *Clarion,* 5 November 1937.
8. *The Worker,* 4 November 1937, *People's Advocate,* 5 November 1937.
9. MacEwan, *Miners and Steelworkers,* 188–93, and Mellor, *The Company Store,* 333-7. MacEwan also notes the view of McLachlan—"a rip-snortin' Bolshevik all his life"—later expressed by "one worthy" who had known him (probably Eugene Forsey).
10. Brodie to Woodsworth, 27 October 1937.
11. William T. Mercer interview, March 1980. In this interview Mercer stated that he was unaware that McLachlan had left the Communist Party and, contrary to the claim in MacEwan, *Miners and Steelworkers,* 191, that McLachlan did not participate in the 1937 campaign by preparing speeches and other materials for him.
12. For the argument that this tradition is one of the gifts of the Maritimes to Canadian democracy, see Ian McKay, "Of Karl Marx and the Bluenose: Colin Campbell McKay and the Legacy of Maritime Socialism," *Acadiensis,* vol. 27, no. 2 (spring 1998), 3–25.
13. James Bryson McLachlan [grandson] to Terry McVarish, 16 April 1993, private correspondence. This passage is quoted with the kind permission of Mr McVarish of the J.B. McLachlan Commemorative Society. Mr McLachlan died in 1995.
14. This paragraph borrows, respectfully, from a 1972 commentary by E.P. Thompson, "A Special Case," reprinted in Thompson, *Writing by Candlelight* (London, 1980), 65–76.

The Glace Bay Miner's Museum

Sheldon Currie

THE FIRST TIME I ever saw the bugger, I thought to myself, him as big as he is, me as small as I am, if he was astraddle on the road, naked, I could walk under him without a hair touching. That's the thought I had; he was coming down the aisle of the White Rose Café, looking to the right and looking to the left at the people in the booths. The size of him would kill you, so everybody was looking at him. I was looking at him too because I knew all the booths were full except mine. I was sitting in the last one, my back to the kitchen, so I could see everybody coming and going. He had a box in his hand, looked like a tool box, and I was wondering if he'd sit with me and show me what was in his box. I made a dollar keeping house for MacDonalds and came to the Bay to spend it on tea and chips and sit in the restaurant and watch the goings on. The goings on was the same old thing: girls sitting with boys and boys sitting with girls, trying to pair off to suit themselves, and making a cup of tea and chips last as long as they could so they wouldn't have to leave. It was hard to find somebody on the street. You could go to the show and sit in the dark and hope somebody would sit next to you and hold your hand, but that cost money too and hardly ever worked. It worked once for me, this fella sat beside me, and I knew it was a chance because the theatre was almost empty. I figured he saw my hair before the lights went out. I had this lovely long hair. I was lucky enough, I bought a nut bar on the way in and I gave him a piece. He took my hand. He had a huge hand. Pan shovel hands we used to call people with hands like that. We used to think you got them from loading coal with a pan shovel. My hand disappeared in his in the dark. He put his big hand on top of my knees which I was keeping together. It felt like he had taken my hand off at the wrist and moved it up to my knee. I couldn't see it and for a minute I couldn't feel it and I was sitting there looking at his big mitt and wondering if my hand was still in it. Then it started to sweat and I could feel it again. We stayed like that through two shows. We never said a word. When we came out we walked down to Senator's Corner and down Commercial Street to Eaton's where the buses stopped. We never said a word. We stood next to each other and I stared at the Medical Hall and he stared at Thompson and Sutherland. Then the bus came for No. 11 and he got on. He didn't even look out the window at me.

I was sitting alone in the White Rose because none of the boys would sit with me and none of the girls would because the boys wouldn't. For one thing I had a runny nose. They called me names and if a boy went with me they called him names.

George McNeill walked home with me from school one day—it was on the way to his house anyway—and I heard in the cloakroom next day—they had a vent between the boys cloakroom and the girls'—I heard somebody from another class say to him—"I see you're taking out snot-face these days. Don't forget to kiss her on the back of her head."

For another thing I screwed a couple of boys when I was a little girl. I didn't know you weren't supposed to, but I didn't want to anyway, and I wouldn't but this fella offered me a nickel and I never had a nickel. Then he asked if I'd do it with his cousin and I said no. But then he came to me himself, the cousin, and told me he went to the washhouse every Saturday his father was on day shift for five times and waited for him to come up and waited for him to shower and followed him to pay office and asked him for a dime, and had to promise to cut enough sticks for the week. I found out later he sold two quarts of blueberries that he stole, but he wanted to tell me a nice long story. Anyway I felt sorry for him, and he had fifty cents. So he told me to meet him up in the woods by the Scotchtown road between the bootleg pits and Rabbit Town. I didn't know then that he didn't want to walk up there with me. Anyway, I didn't really screw either one of them because they didn't know how to do it and it was too late before I could tell them, although, God knows, I knew little enough myself of the little there is to know. They didn't walk home with me either, neither one. But they told everybody I was a whore. So I was not only a whore but a snot-nosed whore. You could hardly blame the boys and girls for not sitting with me.

So I was sitting alone in the last booth at the White Rose Café when this giant of a man with a box in his hand came bearing down the aisle looking left and right, and he kept on coming until he got to my booth and saw there was nobody there but me. I remember it seemed like it got darker when he stood in front of me, he blacked out so much light with the size of him. He had on a big lumberjack shirt. I thought, when he stood there holding his box, before he said anything, I said to myself, I wish he'd pick me up and put me in his shirt pocket.

"Can I put this here on your table?" he said; he pointed his chin at his box.

"Suit yourself," I said to him awful loud. He was so big, I thought I had to yell for him to hear me.

"Can I sit down, then?" he said.

"Suit yourself again," I said. So he put his box on the table and sat down opposite me, and I could feel his knees about an inch from mine. I could feel the heat coming from his knees. I could have exploded I was so happy. But I kept my lips tight.

The waitress pounced on us right away. "Hi, snooker," she said. She was dying to find out who this fella was. So was everybody in the restaurant. I could see the ones facing me. I could feel the ones not facing me wishing they had sat on the other side of the booth. Nobody knew who he was. I just wanted to know what he had in the box.

"Something?" Kitten said, and looked at me and looked at him.

"I had something," I said.

"Would you have something else?" the man said. "I'd like to buy you a bite to eat if you don't mind." I near died. That was the first polite thing anybody ever said to me since my father got killed.

"I don't mind if I do," I said.

"Well, what is it then?" Kitten said. "What do you want?"

"I'll have a cup of tea and an order of chips," I said.

"Will you now?" Kitten said.

"Yes," I said. "I will."

"I'll have the same," the man with the box said.

"Thank you," Kitten said, and wrote it down, saying very slowly to herself like she was talking to a baby: *Two orders of chips and two orders of tea.* "That will be fine," she said, looking at me and looking at him. "I'll go see if we got any."

She went away and I looked at my little hands and I could feel my knees getting warmer and warmer. I couldn't think of anything to say. My back was cold and I thought I might start to shake if I didn't talk, but I couldn't think of anything. I looked up at him and he was looking at his hands. He had a lot to look at. Nobody said a word till Kitten came back. "Here you are," she said, "two teas and two chips. Medium rare."

We are a few chips and took the bags out of our teas and put them in the ashtray. Then he said, "Well, what do you think?"

"I think you're the biggest son of a bitch I ever saw," I said.

He looked at me then when I said that as if I just came in, and the look of him made me feel as if I just came in. I felt my back get warm, and I leaned back against the back of the booth. He started to laugh. He must of laughed for two minutes but it seemed to me two days, and it sounded like somebody playing some kind of instrument I never heard before. When he stopped, he said, "Know what I think?"

"What?" I said.

"I think you're the smallest son of a bitch I ever saw."

Then we both of us laughed for two minutes. Then we talked about the weather as if nothing happened, but I could feel the heat on my knees. After a while he said, "Well now. What's your name?"

"Margaret MacNeil."

"Well now, Miss MacNeil. It's been a pleasure meeting you. Do you come here often?"

"Every week at this same exact time," I said.

"Very well then," he said. "Perhaps we'll meet again. What do you think?"

"Suit yourself," I said.

"Okay," he said, "I will. My name is Neil Currie." Then he got up and opened the box.

When he got the box open it was full of brown sticks and a plaid bag. Bagpipes! I never seen bagpipes before. Never knew there was any. Never heard them before.

God only knows I heard them enough since. He pulled it all out of the box and started putting sticks on sticks till it was together; then he pumped it up. It snarled a couple of times, then when he had it between his arm and his ribs he came down on it with his elbow and it started to squeal, and everybody in the café either leaned out or stood up to look at the God-awful racket.

Then his fingers started jumping and it started playing something I don't know what it was. To me it sounded like a cut cat jumping from table to table and screaming like a tiger. Before you knew it the Chinaman came from the front. He didn't stop, he just slowed down to squeeze by the man and the pipes. When he got through he walked backwards a minute toward the kitchen and yelled, "Get that goddam fiddle out of here." Then two big Chinamen came out of the kitchen; I always thought Chinamen were small until I saw them two. They each had a hand of cards like they were playing cards and kept their hands so nobody could peek at them while they were out. They were just as big as Neil was, maybe bigger, and you never saw how fast two men can put one man and an armload of bagpipes out of a restaurant and into the street.

I went out after him. I took him out his box. I passed the Chinamen coming back in. They didn't do nothing to him, just fired him to the street and went back with their cards. He was sitting on the street. I helped him stuff his bagpipes in his box. Then he stood up and took the box in his hand. He looked down at me and he said, "One thing I thought a Chinaman would never have the nerve to do is criticize another man's music. If I wasn't drunk, I'd give you my pipes to hold and I'd go back in there and get the shit kicked out of me."

"Where do you live?" I said.

"I have a room down on Brookside."

"Want me to walk down?"

"Where do you live?"

"I live in Reserve."

"Let's get the bus, then. I'll see you home. Sober me up. Perhaps you could make us a cup of tea."

"Okay," I said.

"You live with your father an mother?"

"I live with my mother and grandfather. My father got killed in the pit. Come on. It's starting to rain. My brother too."

The rain banged on the roof of the bus all the way to Reserve and when we got off it was pouring and muddy all the way up to the shack where we lived. My father built it himself because, he said, he never would live in a company house. He had to work in the goddam company mine, but he didn't have to live in the goddam company house, with god only knows who in the next half. My mother said he was too mean to pay rent, but only when he wasn't around did she say it. She only said it once to his face. But he got killed. They had a coffin they wouldn't even open it.

It was dark even though it was only after seven. It was October. We had to take off our shoes and wring out our socks from walking in puddles up the lane. We didn't have a real road in. Just a track where they came with groceries and coal. We hung them down the side of the scuttle and our jackets on the oven door. "I'll get you an old pair of daddy's pants soon's mama gets out of the bedroom. You're the first one I ever saw could fit."

"You're right on time, Marg," Mama said. "I think I'll run up the Hall. Who you got here?"

"You'll get soaked."

"I know, but I better go. I might win the thousand."

"This is Neil Currie."

"Where'd you find him?"

"In the Bay."

"Are you from the Bay?"

"No. I just came."

"Where from?"

"St. Andrews Channel."

"Never heard of that. You working in the pit?"

"I was. I started but I got fired."

"You look like you could shovel. Why'd they fire you?"

"I wouldn't talk English to the foreman."

"You an Eyetalian?"

"No."

"Well, I have to run or I'll be late. Don't forget your grandfather, Margie. I hit him about an hour ago so he's about ready."

"Okay Mom. Hope you win it."

"Me too."

That was my mother's joke, about hitting my grandfather. Anytime a stranger was in she said it. He had something wrong with his lungs. Every hour or two he couldn't breathe and we'd have to pound him on the chest. So somebody had to be in the house every minute. When Mama left I got Neil the pants. "You might as well keep them," I said. "They won't fit nobody else ever comes around here." Then I went in to change my dress.

I expected to be a while because I wanted to fix myself up on my mother's makeup. It was her room, though I had to sleep in it and she had a lot of stuff for makeup. My brother slept in the other room with my grandfather. We just had the three. Where you come in was the kitchen and that's where you were if you weren't in the bedroom or in the cellar getting potatoes. But I didn't stay to fix up because I just got my dress half on when he started wailing on his bag and pipes.

I stuck my head out the door. "Are you out of your brain?" I yelled but he couldn't hear with the noise. So I got my dress all on and went out and put my hands over two of the holes the noise came out. They have three holes. He stopped. "My grandfather," I said, "you'll wake him up." I no sooner said it when the knock came. "There he is now," I said. "I'm sorry," he said. "I forgot your grandfather."

"It's okay," I said, "I think it must be time of his hit now anyway." I went in and I got the surprise of my life.

He could talk, my grandfather, but he didn't. It hurt him to talk after he came back from the hospital once with his lungs and he quit. I don't know if it got better or not because he never tried again, same as he quit walking after he got out of breath once from it. He took to writing notes. He had a scribbler and a pencil by him and he wrote what he wanted, thump me chest; dinner; beer; water; piss pot; did she win; did you pay the lite bill, then put on the lites; piece of bread; ask the priest to come; time to go now father; I have to get me thump; no, Ian'll do it. See, that's just one page. He had a whole stack of scribblers after a while. They're all here. We have them numbered.

So I went in, and I was after sitting him up in place to do his thump; you had to put him in a certain way. And he started to bang his long finger on the scribbler he had in his hand.

"Tell him to play."

"Well, Christ in harness," I said, which is what my grandfather used to say when he talked and now I always said it to tease him. "Watch your tong," he wrote me one day. "Somebody got to say it now you're dumb," I said. "If I don't it won't get said."

"Do you want your thump?" I said, and he wrote in his scribbler, "No, tell him to play." So I told Neil to play. "Isn't that lovely?" Neil said and laughed. And he played. It sounded to me like two happy hens fighting over a bean, and when he stopped and asked me if I knew what tune it was I told him what it sounded like to me and he laughed and laughed.

"Do you like the tune?"

"It's not too bad."

"Would you see if your grandfather liked it?" So I went. And he was sound asleep with his scribbler in his hands on his belly. He wrote on it: "When he comes back ask him if he can play these." And he had a list I couldn't read. Here it is here in the scribbler:

Guma slan to na ferriv chy harish achune
Va me nday Ben Doran
Bodichin a Virun
Falte go ferrin ar balech in eysgich

I took the scribbler out and showed it to Neil and he said he would. "I'll have to practice a little."

"Play some more now," I asked him. "Play that one again."

"What one?"

"The one you put him to sleep with."

"Mairi's wedding."

"Yes."

"About the bean and the chickens."

"Yes."

So he played. I was getting interested in it. My foot started tapping and my knees which I had been holding together all night fell apart. As soon as he saw that, I was sitting on a chair against the wall, he came over and came down to kiss me. I put my two feet on his chest and pushed. I was hoping to fire him across the room but nothing happened. It kept him off, but he just stayed there with his chest on my feet looking up my leg and me with a hole in my underwear.

"What's the matter with you?" he said.

I said, "Just because you play that thing don't mean you can jump me." He ran his hand down my leg and nearly drove me nuts.

"Fuck off," I said. I thought that would shock him back but he just stayed there leaning against my sneakers. He tried to take my hand but I just put the two of them behind the chair.

"I won't jump you till we're married," he said.

"Married?" I said. "Who'd marry you? You're nothing but a goddam Currie." Then he started laughing and moved back.

"And why wouldn't you marry a goddam Currie?" he said.

"Because they just come into your house, play a few snarls on their pipes, and they think you'll marry them for that."

"Well, well, well," he said. "I'll tell you what. I'll play for you every night till you're ready. And I'll make you a song of your own."

"What kind of song?"

"I don't know, we'll wait and see what I can make."

"Well, well, well," I said. "I want a song a person can sing so I'll be sure what it's saying."

"Okay, I'll make you two. One to sing and one to guess at."

"Good." I said. "If I like them. Well who knows what may happen."

"What would you like for the singing one?"

"I don't know."

"Well, what's the happiest thing in your life or the saddest?"

"They're both the same," I said. "My brother. Not the one living here now but my older brother, Charlie. We called him Charlie Dave, though Dave was my father's name. That was to tell him from the other Charlie MacNeils. There's quite a few around here. Charlie Pig and Charlie Spider. And a lot more. Charlie Big Dan. I really liked Charlie Dave."

"What happened to him?"

"He got killed in the pit with my father."

"How old was he?"

"He was just sixteen. He used to fight for me. Wouldn't let anybody call me names."

"He mustn't have been in the pit very long?"

"Not even a year. He started working with my grandfather just before he had to quit for his lungs. Then he started with my father. Then he was killed. They were both killed. He was good in school too, but he got married so he had to work. They didn't even have a chance to have their baby."

"What happened to his wife?"

"Oh, she's still around. She's nice. She had her baby. A sweet baby. They live up in the Rows. In a company house. With her mother and her sister." I started to cry then so I made a cup of tea.

So after that he came back every night and it was nothing but noise. My mother took to going out every night. When I told her he asked me to get married, she said: "That man will never live in a company house. You'll be moving out of one shack and into another."

"I can stand it," I said.

"You can stand it," she said. "You can stand it. And is he going to work?"

"He's going to look up at No. 10."

"Good," she said. "He can work with Ian. They can die together. And you can stand it. And you can live in your shack alone. Stand it, then."

The first night, after he played one of the songs my grandfather asked him, he played one he said he made for me. I loved it. It made me grin, so I kept my head down and I held my knees together with my arms.

"What's the name of it?" I asked.

"The name of it is *Two Happy Beans Fighting Over A Chicken*."

"Go whan," I said.

"Do you like it?"

"Not bad. What's the real name?"

"*Margaret's Wedding,*" he said.

"Christ in harness." I almost let go my knees.

The next night he played it again and he played another one for my grandfather. Then we went up the Haulage Road to No. 10 to get Ian. I always went to walk home with him because when he started he was scared when he was night shift to come home alone in the dark. I kept on ever since. Sometimes he had a girl friend would go. I never asked him if he stopped being scared. He never often had to try it alone. He didn't come home that night, he decided to work a double shift. So we walked back alone that night, but we took to going up together for Ian when he was night shift till Neil got the job there too and they were buddies in the pit so they worked the same shifts and came home together till we got married and moved to the Bay.

They fought like two mongrels. Miners said they never saw two men enjoy their work so much because it kept them close enough so they could fight every minute. Then on Sunday afternoon they came to our home and they sat in the kitchen and drank rum and played forty-five and fought and fought and fought.

What they fought about was politics and religion, or so they said. Ian would tell Neil that the only hope for the miner was to vote CCF and get a labour government.

"How are you going to manage that?"

"By voting. Organizing."

"When is that going to happen?"

"We have to work for it."

"The future?"

"Yes, the future."

"There's no future," Neil would say.

"There has to be a future."

"See in the bedroom, Ian. See your grandfather. That's the future."

"Well he's there. The future is there."

"He's there all right. He can't breathe, he can't talk, he can't walk. You know the only thing he's got? Some old songs in his head, that he can hardly remember, that your father hardly ever knew and you don't know at all. Came here and lost their tongues, their music, their songs. Everything but their shovels."

"Too bad you wouldn't lose yours. Have a drink and shut up."

"I will not shut up. However, I will have a drink."

He seemed so drunk to me I thought it'd spill out his mouth if he took more; but he took it. "Nothing left," he said. "Nothing. Only thing you can do different from a pit pony is drink rum and play forty-five."

Ian pointed to the cat curled up on the wood box. "Look, it's almost seven o'clock," he said. "Why don't you take that tomcat and go to Benediction since you like to sing so much. Then you can sing with him tonight. Out in the bushes. He goes out same time as you leave."

"What are you talking about?"

"You're buddies. You and the cat. You can sing near as good as he can. He's near fond of religion as you are."

"All I can say," Neil said, "is pit ponies can't go to church."

"Is that all you can say?" Ian said. "Well, all I can say is, if a pit pony went to church, that would do him some lot of good."

"Ian, you do not understand what I am talking about."

"That is the God's truth for you, Neil. Now why don't you go on the couch and have a lay down."

And that's the way Sunday afternoon and evening went. We could've been out for a walk, just as easy, and more fun.

But that second night that he came we walked down the Haulage Road, pitch black, and he sang me the song I asked him for about my brother. I sang it over and over till I knew it by heart. He sang it to me. "That's lovely," I told him.

I took him by the arm behind his elbow and slowed him down till he stopped and turned. I was crying but I told him anyway. "I'm going to get married to you." We kissed each other. Salt water was all over our lips. I think he must have been crying too. I wrote the song down in one of my grandfather's scribblers when we got back. Here it is here in this one here.

My brother was a miner
His name was Charlie David
He spent his young life laughing
And digging out his grave.

Charlie Dave was big
Charlie Dave was strong
Charlie Dave was two feet wide
And almost six feet long.

When Charlie David was sixteen
He learned to chew and spit
And went one day with Grandpa
To work down in the pit.

(chorus)

When Charlie David was sixteen
He met his Maggie June
On day shift week they met at eight
On back shift week at noon.

(chorus)

When Charlie David was sixteen
He said to June, "Let's wed"
Maggie June was so surprised
She fell right out of bed.

(chorus)

When Charlie David was sixteen
They had a little boy
Maggie June was not surprised
Charlie danced for joy

(chorus)

When Charlie David was sixteen
The roof fell on his head
His laughing mouth is full of coal
Charlie Dave is dead.

The next night when he came I told him I had to pay him back for his songs. I'd tell him a story.

"Okay," he said. "Tell me a story."

"This is a true story."

"That's the kind I like," he said.

"Okay. There was this fella worked in the pit, his name was George Stepenak, he was a Pole, they eat all kinds of stuff, took garlic in his can, used to stink. His can would stink and his breath would stink. The men used to tease him all the time, which made him cross. One day my father said. "George, what in the name of Jesus have you got in your can?"

"Shit," George said to my father.

"I know that," my father said. "But what you put on it to make it smell so bad?"

When my grandfather found out I told him a story to pay him back for the song, he wanted to tell him one. He wrote it out for him in a scribbler. Here it is here. Well he didn't write it all out, he just wrote it out for me to tell it.

"Tell about Jonny and Angie loading in '24, the roof so low they hadda take pancakes in their cans."

That's the way it went from then. Every night he'd come and play and sing. Me and my grandfather would tell or write stories. My brother even would sing when he was on day shift or back shift. But he worked a lot of night shift. That's the way it went till Neil got work. When he got work we got married as soon as he built this house. Soon as he got the job he said, "I got some land on North Street. I'll build a house before we get married. It's right on the ocean. You can hear the waves." And he did. He did. And you can see, it's no shack. He must have been a carpenter. Soon as the house was finished we got married and moved in. Him and my brother Ian were buddies by then, working the same shifts. They both got killed the same minute. I was up to Reserve keeping house for my mother when I heard the whistle, I heard the dogs howling for two nights before so soon's I heard the whistle I took off for the pit. They both just were taken up when I got there. They had them in a half-ton truck with blankets over them.

"Take them to Mama's," I said.

"We got to take them to hospital."

"You take them to Mama's, Art. I'll wash them and I'll get them to the hospital."

"Listen, snooker, the doctor's got to see them."

"I'll call the doctor."

"I can't."

"Listen, you bastard. Whose are they, yours or mine? You haven't even got an ambulance. I'll wash them, and wherever they go, they'll go clean and in a regular ambulance, not your goddam half-broken-down truck."

So he took them down to Mama's and they carried them in and put one on Mama's bed and one on the couch in the kitchen. I knew what to get. I saw Charlie Dave keep a dead frog for two years when he was going to school. I went to the Medical Hall and got two gallons. Cost me a lot. I got back as fast as I could. I locked the house before I left so's nobody could get in. Mama was visiting her sister in Bras d'Or and I didn't know when she'd be back.

When I got back, there was a bunch around the door. They started to murmur. "Fuck off," I said. "I'm busy."

To make matters worse, my grandfather was left alone all that time. He died. Choked. I took his lungs. It wasn't so much the lungs themselves, though I think they were a good thing to take, though they don't keep too well, especially the condition he was in, as just something to remind me of the doctor who told him he couldn't get compensation because he was fit to work. Then I took Neil's lungs because I thought of them connected to his pipes and they show, compared to grandfather's, what lungs should look like. I was surprised to find people have two lungs. I didn't know that before. Like Neil used to say, look and ye shall see. I took Neil's tongue since he always said he was the only one around still had one. I took his fingers too because he played his pipes with them. I didn't know what to take from Ian, so I took his dick, since he always said to Neil that was his substitute for religion to keep him from being a pit pony when he wasn't drinking rum or playing forty-five.

Then my mother came in. She went hysterical and out the door. I had each thing in its own pickle jar. I put them all in the tin suitcase with the scribblers and deck of cards wrapped in wax paper and the half empty quart of black death they left after last Sunday's drinking and arguing. I got on the bus and came home to the Bay and put in the pipes and Neil's missal and whatever pictures were around. Then I took the trunk to Marie, my friend, next door and asked her to put it in her attic till I asked for it. Don't tell anybody about it. Don't open it. Forget about it. Then I came back here and sat down and I thought of something my grandmother used to sing, "There's bread in the cupboard and meat on the shelf, and if you don't eat it, I'll eat it myself." I was hungry.

I knew they'd come and haul me off. So I packed my own suitcase, Neil's really but mine now. They came with a police car and I didn't give them a chance to even get out of the car. I jumped right into the back seat like it was a taxi I was waiting for. I just sat right in and said, "Sydney River, please." Sydney River, if you're not from around here, is the cookie jar where they put rotten tomatoes so they won't spoil in the barrel. So they put me in till they forgot about me; then when they remembered me they forgot what they put me in for. So they let me go.

My mother lived in the house all the time I was away. I told her to, to keep it for me and give her a better place to live. When I got back I told her. "You can stay here and live with me, mother, if you like."

"Thanks anyway," she said. "But I'm not feeling too good. I think I'll go back to Reserve."

"So stay. I'll look after you."

"Yes, you'll look after me. You'll look after me. And what if I drop dead during the night?"

"If you drop dead during the night, you're dead. Dead in Glace Bay is the same as dead in Reserve."

"Yes. And you'll look after me dead too, I imagine. You'll look after me. What'll you do? Cut off my tits and put them in bottles?"

I said to her, "Mother, your tits don't mean a thing to me."

By then she had her suitcase packed and she left walking. "Have you got everything?" I called.

"If I left anything," she yelled back, "pickle it."

"Okay," I said. She walked. Then she turned and yelled, "Keep it for a souvenir."

"Okay," I yelled.

I was sorry after that I said what I said. I wouldn't mind having one of her tits. After all, if it wasn't for them, we'd all die of thirst before we had our chance to get killed.

Marie came over then with the suitcase and we had a cup of tea and she helped me set things up. We had to make shelves for the jars. Everything else can go on tables and chairs or hang on the wall or from the ceiling as you can see. Marie is very artistic, she knows how to put things around. I'm the cook. We give tea and scones free to anyone who comes. You're the first. I guess not too many people know about it yet. A lot of things are not keeping as well as we would like, but it's better than nothing. Perhaps you could give us a copy of your tape when you get it done. That might make a nice item. It's hard to get real good things and you hate to fill up with junk just to have something.

CHAPTER ELEVEN

The Remarkable Mind of Harold Innis

Introduction

Born in Otterville, Ontario in 1894, Harold Adams Innis attended McMaster University. He also served in World War I. Wounded, he returned to Canada before attending the University of Chicago where he earned his Ph.D. In 1920 he joined the Department of Political Economy at the University of Toronto. He soon earned a reputation as a brilliant and original thinker. Published in 1930, *The Fur Trade in Canada* confirmed that reputation. It introduced the staples thesis, the idea that Canada's economic and political development was best understood through an analysis of its key staples: fur, fish, timber, minerals and wheat. In the conclusion to *The Fur Trade* Innis also commented on Canada's boundary in North America. In the later part of his career Innis turned his attention away from political economy and towards a consideration of time and space and empire. "A Plea For Time" is a difficult and, at times, opaque article. But in it Innis offers incredible insight into modern culture. The key to unlocking this piece lies in the title: what has happened to time and why is Innis making a plea for it? Innis died in 1952. Since his death scholars have been trying to make sense of the two Innises: Innis the staples theorist and Innis the communications theorist. The historian R. Douglas Francis finds a connecting theme between the early Innis and the late Innis. What is that theme?

Conclusion from *The Fur Trade in Canada*

Harold Innis

THE HISTORY OF the fur trade in North America has been shown as a retreat in the face of settlement. The strategic campaigns in that retreat include the Conquest of New France, the Quebec Act of 1774, the American Revolution, the Jay Treaty of 1794, the amalgamation of 1821, the Oregon Treaty of 1846, and the Rupert's Land Act of 1869. The struggle continues in the newly settled areas of the Dominion. The trade has been conducted by large organizations from the artificial and natural monopolies of New France to the Northwest Company and the Hudson's Bay Company which still occupies an important position. It has depended on the manufactures of Europe and the more efficient manufactures and cheaper transportation of England. Control of the fur trade was an index of world importance from the standpoint of efficient manufactures, control of markets, and consumption of luxuries. The shift from Paris to London of the fur trade was significant of the industrial growth of France and England—just as possession of Canada after the American Revolution was significant of the industrial limitations of the United States. The demands of the Indians for cheaper and greater quantities of goods were determining factors in the destiny of the northern half of North America. . . .

The early history of the fur trade is essentially a history of the trade in beaver fur. The beaver was found in large numbers throughout the northern half of North America. The better grades of fur came from the more northerly forested regions of North America and were obtained during the winter season when the fur was prime. A vast north temperate land area with a pronounced seasonal climate was a prerequisite to an extensive development of the trade. The animal was not highly reproductive and it was not a migrant. Its destruction in any locality necessitated the movement of hunters to new areas.

The existence of the animal in large numbers assumed a relatively scant population. It assumed an area in which population could not be increased by resort to agriculture. Limitations of geological formation, and climate and a cultural background dependent on these limitations precluded a dense population with consequent destruction of animal life. The culture was dependent on indigenous flora and fauna and the latter was of prime importance. Moose, caribou, beaver, rabbit or hare, and fish furnished the chief supplies of food and clothing. This culture assumed a thorough knowledge of animal habits and the ability of the peoples concerned to move over wide areas in pursuit of a supply of food. The devices which had been elaborated included the snowshoe and the toboggan for the winter and the birchbark canoe for the summer. This wide area contained numerous lakes and difficult connecting waterways, to which the canoe was adapted for extensive travel. Movement over this area occasioned an extended knowledge of geography and a widespread similarity of cultural traits such as language.

The area which was crucial to the development of the fur trade was the Pre-Cambrian shield of the northern half of the North American continent. It extended northwesterly across the continent to the mouth of the Mackenzie River and was bounded on the north by the northwesterly isothermal lines which determined the limits of the northern forests and especially of the canoe birch (*B. papyrifera*). The fur trade followed the waterways along the southern edge of this formation from the St. Lawrence to the Mackenzie River. In its full bloom it spread beyond this area to the Pacific drainage basin.

The history of the fur trade is the history of contact between two civilizations, the European and the North American, with especial reference to the northern portion of the continent. The limited cultural background of the North American hunting peoples provided an insatiable demand for the products of the more elaborate cultural development of Europeans. The supply of European goods, the product of a more advanced and specialized technology, enabled the Indians to gain a livelihood more easily—to obtain their supply of food, as in the case of moose, more quickly, and to hunt the beaver more effectively. Unfortunately the rapid destruction of the food supply and the revolution in the methods of living accompanied by the increasing attention to the fur trade by which these products were secured, disturbed the balance which had grown up previous to the coming of the European. The new technology with its radical innovations brought about such a rapid shift in the prevailing Indian culture as to lead to wholesale destruction of the peoples concerned by warfare and disease. The disappearance of the beaver and of the Indians necessitated the extension of European organization to the interior. New tribes demanded European goods in increasingly large amounts. The fur trade was the means by which this demand of the peoples of a more limited cultural development was met. Furs were the chief product suitable to European demands by which the North American peoples could secure European goods. . . .

The extension of the trade across the northern half of the continent and the transportation of furs and goods over great distances involved the elaboration of an extensive organization of transport, of personnel, and of food supply. The development of transportation was based primarily on Indian cultural growth. The birch-bark canoe was borrowed and modified to suit the demands of the trade. Again, without Indian agriculture, Indian corn, and dependence on Indian methods of capturing buffalo and making pemmican, no extended organization of transport to the interior would have been possible in the early period. . . .

The increasing distances over which the trade was carried on and the increasing capital investment and expense incidental to the elaborate organization of transport had a direct influence on its financial organization. Immediate trade with Europe from the St. Lawrence involved the export of large quantities of fur to meet the overhead costs of long ocean voyages and the imports of large quantities of heavy merchandise. Monopoly inevitably followed, and it was supported by the European institutional arrangements which involved the organization of monopolies for the conduct of foreign trade. On the other hand, internal trade, following its extension in the interior and the demand for larger numbers of *royageurs* and canoes to undertake the difficult task of transportation and the increasing dependence on the initiative of the trader in carrying on trade with remote tribes, was, within certain limits, competitive. Trade from Quebec and Montreal with canoes up the Ottawa to Michilimackinac, La Baye, and Lake Superior could be financed with relatively small quantities of capital and was consequently competitive. Further extension of trade through Lake Superior by Grand Portage (later Kaministiquia) to Lake Winnipeg, the Saskatchewan, Athabasca, the Mackenzie River, and New Caledonia and the Pacific coast involved heavy overhead costs and an extensive organization of transportation. But the organization was of a type peculiar to the demands of the fur trade. Individual initiative was stressed in the partnership agreements which characterized the Northwest Company. The trade carried on over extended areas under conditions of limited transportation made close control of individual partners by a central organization impossible. The Northwest Company which extended its organization from the Atlantic to the Pacific developed along lines which were fundamentally linked to the technique of the fur trade. This organization was strengthened in the amalgamation of 1821 by control of a charter guaranteeing monopoly and by the advantages incidental to lower costs of transportation by Hudson Bay.

The effects of these large centralized organizations characteristic of the fur trade as shown in the monopolies of New France, in the Hudson's Bay Company, and in the Northwest Company were shown in the institutional development of Canada. In New France constant expansion of the trade to the interior had increased costs of transportation and extended the possibilities of competition from New England. The population of New France during the open season of navigation was increasingly engaged in carrying on the trade over longer distances to the neglect of agriculture and other phases of economic development. To offset the effects of competition from the English colonies in the south and the Hudson's Bay Company in the north, a military policy, involving Indian alliances, expenditure on strategic posts, expensive campaigns, and constant direct and indirect drains on the economic life of New France and old France, was essential. As a result of these developments control of political activities in New France was centralized and the paternalism of old France was strengthened by the fur trade. Centralized control as shown in the activities of the government, the church, the seigniorial system, and other institutions was in part a result of the overwhelming importance of the fur trade.

The institutional development of New France was an indication of the relation between the fur trade and the mercantile policy. The fur trade provided an ample supply of raw material for the manufacture of highly profitable luxury goods. A colony engaged in the fur trade was not in a position to develop industries to compete with manufactures of the mother country. Its weakness necessitated reliance upon the military support of the mother country. Finally the insatiable demands of the Indians for goods stimulated European manufactures.

The importance of manufactures in the fur trade gave England, with her more efficient industrial development, a decided advantage. The competition of cheaper goods contributed in a definite fashion to the downfall of New France and enabled Great Britain to prevail in the face of its pronounced militaristic development. Moreover, the importance of manufactured goods to the fur trade made inevitable the continuation of control by Great Britain in the northern half of North America. The participation of American and English merchants in the fur trade immediately following the Conquest led to the rapid growth of a new organization which was instrumental in securing the Quebec Act and which contributed to the failure of the American Revolution so far as it affected Quebec and the St. Lawrence. These merchants were active in the negotiations prior to the Constitutional Act of 1791 and the Jay Treaty of 1794. As prominent members of the government formed under the Quebec Act and the Constitutional Act, they did much to direct the general trend of legislation. The later growth of the Northwest Company assured a permanent attachment to Great Britain because of its dependence on English manufactures.

The northern half of North America remained British because of the importance of fur as a staple product. The continent of North America became divided into three areas: (1) to the north in what is now the Dominion of Canada, producing furs, (2) to the south in what were during the Civil War the secession states, producing cotton, and (3) in the centre the widely diversified economic territory including the New England states and the coal and iron areas of the middle west demanding raw materials and a market. The staple-producing areas were closely dependent on industrial Europe, especially Great Britain. The fur-producing area was destined to remain British. The cotton-producing area was forced after the Civil War to become subordinate to the central territory just as the northern fur-producing area, at present producing the staples, wheat, pulp and paper, minerals, and lumber, tends to be brought under its influence.

The Northwest Company and its successor the Hudson's Bay Company established a centralized organization which covered the northern half of North America from the Atlantic to the Pacific. The importance of this organization was recognized in boundary disputes, and it played a large role in the numerous negotiations responsible for the location of the present boundaries. It is no mere accident that the present Dominion coincides roughly with the fur-trading areas of northern North America. The bases of supplies for the trade in Quebec, in western Ontario, and in British Columbia represent the agricultural areas of the present Dominion. The Northwest Company was the forerunner of the present confederation.

There are other interesting by-products of the study which may be indicated briefly. Canada has had no serious problems with her native peoples since the fur trade depended primarily on these races. In the United States no point of contact of such magnitude was at hand and troubles with the Indians were a result. The existence of small and isolated sections of French half-breeds throughout Canada is another interesting survival of this contact. The half-breed has never assumed such importance in the United States.

"The lords of the lakes and forest have passed away" but their work will endure in the boundaries of the Dominion of Canada and in Canadian institutional life. The place of the beaver in Canadian life has been fittingly noted in the coat of arms. We have given to the maple a prominence which was due to the birch. We have not yet realized that the Indian and his culture were fundamental to the growth of Canadian institutions. We are only beginning to realize the central position of the Canadian Shield.

Canada emerged as a political entity with boundaries largely determined by the fur trade. These boundaries included a vast north temperate land area extending from the Atlantic to the Pacific and dominated by the Canadian Shield. The present Dominion emerged not in spite of geography but because of it. The significance of the fur trade consisted in its determination of the geographic framework. Later economic developments in Canada were profoundly influenced by this background.

A Plea for Time

Harold Innis

I MUST PLEAD the bias of my special interest in the title of this paper. Economic historians and indeed all historians assume a time factor and their assumptions reflect the attitude towards time of the period in which they write. History in the modern sense is about four centuries old[1] but the word has taken on meanings which are apt to check a concern with facts other than those of immediate interest and its content is apt to reflect an interest in immediate facts such as is suggested by the words "all history proves." As a result history tends to repeat itself but in the changing accents of the period in which it is written. History is threatened on the one hand by its obsession with the present and on the other by the charge of antiquarianism. Economic history is in a particularly exposed position as is evident in the tendency to separate it from economics or to regard it as a basis of support for economics. "Knowledge of the past is at all times needed only to serve the present and the future, not to enfeeble the present or to tear the roots out of the vigorous powers of life for the future" (Nietzsche). The danger that knowledge of the past[2] may be neglected to the point that it ceases to serve the present and the future—perhaps an undue obsession with the immediate, support my concern about the disappearance of an interest in time.

Perhaps the exposed position of economic history may strengthen the urge to discover a solution of the difficulty, particularly as it becomes imperative to attempt to estimate the significance of the attitude towards time in an analysis of economic change. The economic historian must consider the role of time or the attitude towards time in periods which he attempts to study, and he may contribute to an escape from antiquarianism, from present-mindedness, and from the bogeys of stagnation and maturity. It is impossible for him to avoid the bias of the period in which he writes but he can point to its dangers by attempting to appraise the character of the time concept.

It has been pointed out that astronomical time is only one of several concepts. Social time, for example, has been described as qualitatively differentiated according to the beliefs and customs common to a group and as not continuous but subject to interruptions of actual dates.[3] It is influenced by language which constrains and fixes prevalent concepts and modes of thought. It has been argued by Marcel

Granet that the Chinese are not equipped to note concepts or to present doctrines discursively. The word does not fix a notion with a definite degree of abstraction or generality but evokes an indefinite complex of particular images. It is completely unsuited to formal precision.[4] Neither time nor space is abstractly conceived; time proceeds by cycles and is round; space is square.[5]

The linear concept of time was made effective as a result of humanistic studies in the Renaissance. When Gregory XIII imposed the Julian calendar on the Catholic world in 1582 Joseph Justus Scaliger following his edition of Manilius (1579) published the *De emendatione temporum* and later his *Thesaurus temporum* (1606) "probably the most learned book in the world."[6] With his work he developed an appreciation of the ancient world as a whole and introduced a conception of the unity of history at variance with the attitude of the church. While Scaliger assisted in wresting control over time from the church he contributed to the historical tradition of philosophy until Descartes with his emphasis on mathematics and his unhistorical temper succeeded in liberating philosophy from history. The ideal of mathematical sciences dominated the seventeenth century. It was not until the Enlightenment that the historical world was conquered and until Herder and romanticism that the primacy of history over philosophy and science was established. Historicism was almost entirely a product of the nineteenth century.[7] In geology the precise date of the earth's formation advanced by Bishop Ussher was destroyed. "The weary series of accommodations of Genesis to geology was beginning."[8] In archaeology a knowledge of earlier civilizations implied a vast extension of time. In the hands of Darwin the historical approach penetrated biology and provided a new dimension of thought for science. In astronomy time was extended to infinity. Laws of real nature became historical laws. Even in mathematics arithmetic escaped from its bondage to geometry and algebra as "the science of pure time or order in progression" (Sir William Hamilton) came into its own.

The effects on history were evident in a recognition of the limitations of the written and the printed record. Mommsen made politics proper the subject-matter of historical knowledge but in the last decades of the nineteenth century the limitations of political historiography were evident. Burckhardt and to some extent Lamprecht approached the study of civilization through fine art. The highest value of art as of all free intellectual activity was to provide release from subservience to the will and from entanglement in the world of particular aims and individual purposes.[9] Taine held that intellectual development was the moving force behind political affairs and that the classical spirit was responsible for the French Revolution.[10] Fustel de Coulanges emphasized the myth[11] as a device for studying periods before writing had developed. Worship of the dead was regarded as the inner bond uniting divergent expressions of faith.

I have attempted to show elsewhere[12] that in Western civilization a stable society is dependent on an appreciation of a proper balance between the concepts of space and time. We are concerned with control not only over vast areas of space but also over vast stretches of time. We must appraise civilization in relation to its territory and in relation to its duration. The character of the medium of communication tends to create a bias in civilization favourable to an over-emphasis on the time concept or on the space concept and only at rare intervals are the biases offset by the influence of another medium and stability achieved. Dependence on clay in Sumerian civilization was offset by dependence on stone in Babylon and a long period of relative stability followed in the reign of the Kassites. The power of the oral tradition in Greece which checked the bias of a written medium supported a brief period of cultural activity such as has never been equalled. Dependence on the papyrus roll and use of the alphabet in the bureaucracy of the Roman Empire was offset by dependence on parchment codex in the church and a balance was maintained in the Byzantine Empire until 1453. "Church and Army are serving order through the power of discipline and through hierarchical arrangement" (Metternich).[13] On the other hand in the West the bias of the parchment codex became evident in the absolute dominance of the church and supported a monopoly which invited competition from paper as a new medium. After the introduction of paper and the printing press, religious monopoly was followed by monopolies of vernaculars in modern states. A monopoly of time was followed by a monopoly of space. A brief survey of outstanding problems of time will perhaps assist in enabling us to understand more clearly the limitations of our civilization.

The pervasive character of the time concept makes it difficult to appreciate its nature and difficult to suggest its conservative influence. The division of the day into 24 hours, of the hour into 60 minutes, and of the minute into 60 seconds suggests that a sexagesimal system prevailed in which the arrangement was worked out and this carries us immediately into Babylonian history.[14] The influence persists in systems of measurement and more obviously, for example, in Great Britain where the monetary system is sexagesimal. The advantages of the sexagesimal system are evident in calculations which permit evasion of the problem in handling fractions and have been exploited effectively in the development of aviation with its demands for rapid calculations.

In a system of agriculture dependent on irrigation the measurement of time becomes important in predicting periods of floods and the important dates of the year, seed-time and harvest. A concern with time was reflected in the importance of religion and in the choice of days on which festivals might be celebrated. The selection of holy days necessitated devices by which they could be indicated and violation of them could be avoided.[15] Dependence on the moon for the measurement of time meant exposure to irregularities such as have persisted in the means of determining the dates for Easter. Sumerian priesthoods apparently worked out a system for correcting the year by the adjustment of lunar months but the difficulties may have contributed to the success of Semitic kings with an interest in the sun, and enabled them to acquire control over the calendar and to make necessary adjustments of time over the extended territory under their control.[16] With control over time kings began the system of reckoning in terms of their reigns; our present statutes defy Anno Domini and date from the accession of the king in whose reign they are enacted. Control over time by monarchies, on the other hand, in addition to the human limitations of dynastic and military power, was limited by the continuity of priesthoods and the effectiveness of an ecclesiastical hierarchy.

In Egypt and Babylonia the principal changes in nature were accompanied by appropriate rituals which were part and parcel of cosmic events. Time was a succession of recurring plans each charged with peculiar value and significance.[17] In a sense it was a biological time with a sequence of essentially different phases of life. In Egypt as in Babylonia the importance of the Nile floods and dependence on irrigation were linked with the celebration of religious festivals and the importance of determining an exact date. It is possible that the absolutism of Egyptian dynasties was dependent on the ability of kings to determine the sidereal year in relation to the appearance of the star Sirius. Recognition of the first dynasty by the Egyptians implied a recognition of time as dating from it. The joining of the two lands in Egypt apparently coincided with kingship and implied an emphasis on religious ceremony and ritual. The power of absolute kings over time and space was reflected in the pyramids which remain a standing monument to justify their confidence, in the development of mummification, a tribute to their control over eternity, and in the belief in immortality. The power of the absolute monarchy may have been weakened by the priesthood which discovered the more reliable solar year. Absolutism passed with control over time into the hands of the priesthood and checked expansion over space in the Egyptian Empire.

In Egypt the power of the absolute monarchy reflected in the monumental architecture of the pyramids and in sculpture was offset by the power of the priesthood based on a complex system of writing and the use of papyrus. The emphasis of a civilization on means of extending its duration as in Egypt accompanied by reliance on permanence gives that civilization a prominent position in periods such as the present when time is of little significance. In Babylonia the power of the priesthood was dependent in part on a mastery of complex cuneiform writing on clay tablets, and an increasing power of the monarchy on the creation of new and elaborate capitals emphasizing sculpture and architecture. Relative stability was gradually established over a long period by compromises between political and religious power. In turn the Kassites, the Assyrians, and the Persians recognized the power of the Babylonian priesthood. In Egypt the power of the priesthood checked the possibilities of political development of the monarchy and prevented effective conquest by conquerors such as the Hyksos and later the Assyrians and the Persians. Monopolies of control over time exercised by the priesthoods of Babylonia and Egypt made the problems of political organization in the Assyrian and Persian empires and indeed of later empires insuperable.

The Babylonian priesthood in its concern with time contributed to the study of astrology and astronomy by the introduction of a system of chronology at the era of

Nabonassar in 747 BC. It possibly followed the discovery that every 18 years and 11 days the moon returned almost to the same position in relation to the sun.[18] The discovery of the periodic character of celestial phenomena and the possibility of prediction gave Babylonia an enormous influence on religious cults and led to the domination of fatalism based on scientific knowledge.

The limited possibility of political organizations expanding their control over space incidental to the control of priesthoods in their monopolies of knowledge over time facilitated the development of marginal organizations such as those of the Jews in Palestine. Periods of expansion and retreat in political organization centring on Egypt or Babylonia weakened an emphasis on political organization and strengthened an emphasis on religious organization. The marginal relation to cultures with monopolies of complex systems of writing favoured the development of relatively simple systems of writing such as emerged in the alphabet of the Phoenicians and the Aramaeans. In these marginal cultures religious organization emphasized a system of writing in sharp contrast with those of Egypt and Babylonia, and in compensation for lack of success in political organization with control over space built up an elaborate hierarchy with control over time. The latter emphasized the sacred character of writing and drew on the resources of Egyptian and Babylonian civilizations to an extent obvious to students of the Old Testament. There was "no engrossment in the moment but full recognition that human life is a great stream of which the present is only the realized moment. . . . It was no accident that the supremely religious people of all time were likewise our first great historians" (W.A. Irwin). History emerged with the Hebrews as a result of the concern with time.

Contact of barbarians on the north shore of the Mediterranean with older civilizations was followed by the emergence of Greek civilization. An emphasis on problems of space incidental to a concern with conquest of territory was evident in the Homeric poems developed in the oral tradition. Geometry with its bias toward measurement and space imposed restrictions on a concern with time. The spread of a money economy strengthened an interest in numbers and arithmetic and in turn in mystery religions in conflict with the established Apollonic religion. The flexibility of an oral tradition enabled the Greeks to work out a balance between the demands of concepts of space and time in a city state. In the reforms of Cleisthenes control over time was wrested from religion and placed at the disposal of the state. The results of a balanced society were evident in the defeat of the Persians and the flowering of Greek culture in the fifth century. But such a balance was not long maintained.[19] Cleisthenes created a senatorial year with ten prytanies of 36 or 37 days in each solar year averaging 365¼ days over a period free from cycles and intercalations, but the old civil calendar sanctioned by religious observance continued. The Metonic cycle[20] of 19 years, 30 days in each month, was introduced on 25 June (Julius) 432 BC and became a norm for the accurate measurement of time. A change was made to a new senatorial year probably in the year of anarchy 404–3. When democracy was re-established the senatorial year was made to conform to the civil year.

The Callippic cycle was introduced in the first summer solstice 27–8 June 330 BC with 30 days to each month and every sixty-fourth day dropped.

The spread of writing in the latter part of the fifth and in the fourth centuries accentuated strains which destroyed Greek civilization. Following the collapse of Greece and the success of Alexander, the East was divided in the Hellenistic kingdoms. In Egypt in a new capital at Alexandria the Ptolemies attempted to offset the influence of the priesthood at Thebes and of Babylonian science by the creation of a new religion and the encouragement of research in libraries and museums. Aristotelian influence was evident in the concern with science and in developments in astronomy. The names of the planets and constellations remain as testimonials to the interest of antiquity in astronomy. Leap year was introduced in 239 or 238 BC but was later abandoned until taken up by the Romans.

After the conquest of Egypt by the Romans Julius Caesar employed Sosigenes, an Egyptian astronomer, to work out an accurate calendar and it is probably significant that the new calendar recognized the festivals of Isis and contributed to the spread of Egyptian and other religions in the Empire. Exploitation of the irregular measurement of time for political purposes[21] and demands for regularity and the power of Julius Caesar in enforcing the new calendar led to a change from the beginning of the new year on 1 March to 1 January in 46 BC, or 708 years from the date of the foundation of Rome, and to a year of 365¼ days. A fixed date of reckoning, that of the founding of the city, reflected the interest of Rome in the unique character of a single day or hour and the belief that continuity was a sequence of single moments. An emphasis on specific single acts at a unique time contributed to the growth of Roman law notably in contracts in which time is of the essence. Alternate odd months were given 31 days and even months 30 days excepting February which had 29 days but 30 every fourth year. The month following that named for Caesar, July, was called Augustus and was given the same number of days. A day was taken from February and given to August. September and November were reduced to 30 days and October and December increased to 31 days to avoid three months in succession with 31 days.

A powerful bureaucracy at Rome and at Constantinople maintained control over time. Toward the end of the third century a 15-year cycle was introduced for tax purposes and after 312 AD the Egyptian date of indiction was changed from 29 August to 1 September the beginning of the Byzantine year. As a result of the influence of astronomy each day became sacred to a planet and the liturgy of the mysteries of Mithra contributed to the substitution of the seven-day week for the Roman eight days about the time of Augustus. 25 December as the date of the birth of the sun in the worship of Mithra was replaced by Christmas Day between 354 and 360 AD.[22] Easter probably took the place of festivals celebrating Attis at the vernal equinox.[23] The Christians used 1 March as the beginning of the year following the Mosaic ordinance as to the Passover.

Following the collapse of the Empire in the West the church supported the system of dating events from the supposed year of the birth of Christ. The concern of religion for the domination of time evident in stories of the flood designed to show that a past had been wiped out and that a new era began, in the beginnings of Egyptian time, in the history of Greece and Rome continued in the Christian era. St Cyril was reputed to have drawn up a table of 95 years (five cycles of 19 years each) to be based on the accession of Diocletian in 284 AD. The base was changed to the Incarnation and the table introduced into the calendar of the West by Dionysius Exiguus in 525 AD. St Wilfrid secured adoption of the system to celebrate Easter on or after 15 March at Whitby in 664 AD in opposition to the Celtic system which allowed the celebration of Easter on the 14th and calculated the moon on a cycle of 84 years. From the time of Bede, in England the year was reckoned from the Incarnation. The system was carried by missionaries to the eastern regions of the Franks and the Incarnation became the official date in 839. Under the influence of Otto the Great it was adopted in the papal chancery in 963.[24] Use of the imperial year and indiction had apparently begun in the papal chancery in 537 and had become general practice in 550. They were never used after 781 AD.[25] Charles the Great visited Rome in that year and under Hadrian the Frankish practice of using a double form of dating documents was used, the pontifical year replacing the regnal of the emperor at Constantinople.

By at least the last quarter of the ninth century Frankish emperors reckoned from Christmas Day as the beginning of the New Year. Religious movements stimulating devotion to the Virgin Mary led to the establishment of Lady Day (25 March) as the beginning of the year in the French chancery after 1112 and in England in the latter part of the twelfth century. After the middle of the thirteenth century, possibly as a result of the study of Roman law and the increasing use of almanacs, there was a gradual return to the Roman system in which the year began on January 1. It was not until 1752 that the beginning of the year was moved from 25 March to 1 January in England.[26] The pagan form of reckoning was gradually restored by the modern state. As in Egypt and in Rome control over time by the church was emphasized by architecture notably in the enduring monuments of the Gothic cathedral.

Gregory XIII introduced a calendar reform in 1582 in which the cumulative inaccuracies of a year based on 365¼ days were corrected and 5 October reckoned as 15 October. While the Roman Catholic church exercised a dominant control over time other religions Jewish and Protestant asserted their rights notably in the determination of holidays. This division weakened the state in the creation of friction and strengthened it by compelling an insistence on unity. Significantly Protestant states grudgingly conceded the advantage of the change but it was not until 1750 that Great Britain ordered 2 September 1752 to be followed by 14 September. It was only after the overthrow of the Tsarist régime in Russia that the Julian calendar was superseded by the Gregorian.

The Christian system followed Roman religion in giving a fixed year, that of the birth of Christ, a unique position. Control over time was not only evident in chronology but also in its place in the life of the Middle Ages. Spread of monasticism and the use of bells to mark the periods of the day and the place of religious services introduced regularity in the life of the West. Sun-dials, whose usefulness was limited in the more cloudy skies of the north, gave way to water clocks and finally to devices for measuring time with greater precision.[27] The modern hour came into general use with the striking clock in the fourteenth century.[28]

Regularity of work brought administration, increase in production, trade, and the growth of cities. The spread of mathematics from India to Baghdad and the Moorish universities of Spain implied the gradual substitution of Arabic for Roman numerals and an enormous increase in the efficiency of calculation.[29] Measurement of time facilitated the use of credit, the rise of exchanges, and calculations of the predictable future essential to the development of insurance. Introduction of paper, and invention of the printing press hastened the decline of Latin and the rise of the vernaculars. Science met the demands of navigation, industry, trade, and finance by the development of astronomy and refined measurements of time which left little place for myth or religion. The printing press supported the Reformation and destroyed the monopoly of the church over time though the persistence of its interest is evident in feast days. The church recognized at an early date the threat of astronomers to the monopoly over time and treated them accordingly.

The struggle between church and state for control over time had centred about a series of measures in the states in the West and the iconoclastic controversy in the Byzantine Empire in the East. The fall of Constantinople in 1453 which followed the perfection of artillery came as a profound shock to Europe. A bulwark of opposition to the absolute supremacy of the papacy had been removed and new states became attracted to the problem of duration and to the possibility of devices which had contributed to the solution of problems of longevity in the Byzantine Empire. The experiment of the Tudors[30] had many parallels with that of the Byzantine Empire—notably the emphasis on a sort of Caesaropapism by Henry VIII in becoming head of the Anglican church, on the destruction of monasteries paralleling the iconoclastic controversy, and on the position of women on the throne in contrast with the prohibitions of Salic law. As the Tudors assumed the mantle of divine right from the papacy they laid the foundation for internal struggles for control over time evident in the contention over monopolies[31] under Elizabeth and James I, and in the absolute supremacy of parliament. The interest of parliament in time was evident in the statute of limitations, restrictions on the period for patents and copyright, the rule against perpetuity in wills, and abolition of entail. The interest of the state in the subject of mort-main has been followed by estate taxes to check control over time beyond life itself. It was not until 1774 that perpetual copyright in common law was destroyed by a decision of the courts following the refusal of Scottish courts to recognize the pretensions of English common law and London booksellers. The concern of the Crown in the problem of time and in the permanence of dynasties was evident in the choice of names for monarchs, to mention only the four Georges. A growing interest in problems of permanence of the British Empire was evident in Gibbon's *Decline and Fall of the Roman Empire*. The struggle over control of time on the Continent led the French to start a new era at the birth of the republic on 22 September 1792. Names descriptive of the seasons, such as Thermidor for the summer, were introduced. The arrangement was brought to an end in 1805 following the Concordat of 1802. Holidays determined by the church were suppressed and new holidays were created by the modern state. Economic inefficiencies incidental to the growth in numbers of religious holidays were paralleled by industrial controversies over shorter working weeks.

Weakening of control over time by the church and limited control by the state left a vacuum which was occupied by industry. The church, particularly in the monastic orders, had introduced a rigorous division of time for services following the spread in the use of clocks and the bell. But industrial demands meant fresh emphasis on the ceaseless flow of mechanical time. Establishment of time zones facilitated the introduction of uniformity in regions. An advance in the state of industrialism reflected in the speed of the newspaper press and the radio meant a decline in the importance of biological time determined by agriculture. Demands for the reform of the calendar and daylight saving schemes follow the impact of industrialism. The persistence of Easter as a movable feast points to the conservative character of time arrangements.

The demands of industry on time have been paralleled by the demands of business. Family concerns extending over generations were followed by more flexible and permanent arrangements in partnerships and corporations. Certain types of industries such as communication, particularly newspapers, were apparently suited to family control, partly because of the need for advertising and use of the same name over a long period to give an appearance of permanence where permanence and dependability were important. The length of life of corporations has been dependent on concern of management with policies affecting duration and with the character of an industry. Centennial volumes are published to reflect the element of permanency and as a form of institutional advertising. The long history of the Hudson's Bay Company was perhaps in part a result of the necessity of conducting operations extending over a period of five or six years between the date of purchase of goods and the date of the sale of furs. Periods of expansion and consolidation imply an alternative interest in time and place.

Conflict between different groups over monopolies of time hastened the intervention of the state. Devices emphasizing rapid turnover of goods, whether technological (for example, in the substitution of buses for street railways), or commercial (for example, in the introduction of pennies to secure newspaper sales and in an emphasis on changing fashions as in the case of motor cars or the publication of books by popular authors), tend to conflict with long-term investment supported by savings voluntary or compulsory, whether insurance or old age pensions. Competition between consumers' goods with rapid turnover and durable goods implies conflict within an economy and conflict between nations emphasizing the durable character of goods, such as England, and those emphasizing a less durable character, such as North America. As a result the state intervenes with policies ranging from the breaking of trusts to the devices of socialism. In fields concerned with durable goods and involving long-term investment of capital, such as railways, electric power, forests, and steel, state intervention has been marked. The ultimate steps are taken in a concern with long-term budgets and long-term capital arrangements and with five-year plans. The need for a sane and balanced approach to the problem of time in the control of monopolies, and in the whole field of interest theory and in other directions, is evident in the growth of a bureaucracy in a totalitarian state. The static approach to economic theory has been of limited assistance in meeting the problems of time.

A balanced civilization in its concern with the problem of duration or time and of extent or space is faced with several difficulties. Systems of government concerned with problems of duration have been defeated in part by biology, when dynasties fail to provide a continued stream of governing capacity, and by technology,[32] when invaders are able to exploit improvements in the methods of warfare at the expense of peoples who have neglected them. Writing as a means of communication provides a system of administration of territory for the conquerors and in religion a system of continuity but in turn tends to develop monopolies of complexity which check an interest in industrial technology and encourage new invaders. "For where there is no fear of god, it [the state] must either fall to destruction, or be supported by the reverence shown to a good Prince; which indeed may sustain it for a while, and supply the want of religion in his subjects. But as human life is short, its government must of course sink into decay when its virtue, that upheld and informed it, is extinct" (Machiavelli). A balanced concern with space or extent of territory and duration or time appears to depend on a dual arrangement in which the church is subordinate to the state and ensures that the mobilization of the intellectual resources of the civilization concerned, by religion or by the state, will be at the disposal of both and that they will be used in planning for a calculated future in relation to the government of territory of definite extent. If social stratification is too rigid and social advancement is denied to active individuals as it is in plutocracies a transpersonal power structure will be threatened with revolt.[33]

The tendency of a monopoly over time in religion to lead to an accumulation of wealth invites attacks from the state with demands for redistribution evident in the embarrassments of the church in the Middle Ages, and in the attacks on monasteries in England and in the Byzantine Empire, and in confiscation of the property of the Jews. The linking of church and state in an absolute monarchy and the accumulation of wealth may lead to revolution as it did in France and Russia. This implies a fundamental break with a concept of time increasingly out of line with the demands of a bureaucracy centring on space. The bias of communication in space or in time involves a sponge theory of the distribution of wealth which assumes violence.

It is beyond the bounds of this paper to enumerate the inventions for the measurement of time or to suggest their implications in the various developments of modern industrialism. It is concerned with the change in attitudes toward time preceding the modern obsession with present-mindedness, which suggests that the balance between time and space has been seriously disturbed with disastrous consequences to Western civilization. Lack of interest in problems of duration in Western civilization suggests that the bias of paper and printing has persisted in a concern with space. The state has been interested in the enlargement of territories and the imposition of cultural uniformity on its peoples, and, losing touch with the problems of time, has been willing to engage in wars to carry out immediate objectives. Printing has emphasized vernaculars and divisions between states based on language without implying a concern with time. The effects of division have been evident in development of the book, the pamphlet, and the newspaper and in the growth of regionalism as new monopolies have been built up. The revolt of the American colonies, division between north and south, and extension westward of the United States have been to an important extent a result of the spread of the printing industry. In the British Empire the growth of autonomy and independence among members of the Commonwealth may be attributed in part to the same development. In Europe division between languages has been accentuated by varying rates of development of the printing industry. Technological change in printing under constitutional protection of freedom of the press in the United States has supported rapid growth of the newspaper industry. Its spread to Anglo-Saxon countries has sharpened the division between English and languages spoken in other areas and in turn contributed to the outbreak of the First World War. Not only has the press accentuated the importance of the English language in relation to other languages, it has also created divisions between classes within English-speaking countries. Emphasis on literacy and compulsory education has meant concentration on magazines and books with general appeal and widened the gap between the artist concerned with improvement of his craft and the writer concerned with the widest market. The writing of history is distorted by an interest in sensationalism and war. The library catalogue reflects an obsession of commercialism with special topics, events, periods, and individuals, to mention only the names of Lincoln, Napoleon, Churchill, Roosevelt, and others.

Large-scale production of newsprint made from wood in the second half of the nineteenth century supported large-scale development of newspaper plants and a demand for effective devices for widening markets for newspapers. The excitement and sensationalism of the South African War in Great Britain and of the Spanish-American War in the United States were not unrelated to the demands of large newspapers for markets. Emergence of the comics[34] coincided with the struggle for circulation between Hearst and Pulitzer in New York. Increased newspaper circulation supported a demand for advertising and for new methods of marketing, notably the department store. The type of news essential to an increase in circulation, to an increase in advertising, and to an increase in the sale of news was necessarily that which catered to excitement. A prevailing interest in orgies and excitement was harnessed in the interests of trade. The necessity for excitement and sensationalism had serious implications for the development of a consistent policy in foreign affairs which became increasingly the source of news. The reports of MacGahan, an American newspaper man, on Turkish activities were seized upon by Gladstone and led to the defeat of Disraeli.[35] The activity of W.T. Stead in the *Pall Mall Gazette* was an important factor in the fiasco of Gordon's expedition to Egypt. While it would be fatal to accept the views of journalists as to their power over events it is perhaps safe to say that Northcliffe played an important role in shifting the interest of Great Britain from Germany to France and in policy leading to the outbreak of the First World War.

Technological advance in the production of newspapers accompanied the development of metropolitan centres. In the period of western expansion "all these interests bring the newspaper; the newspaper starts up politics, and a railroad."[36] A large number of small centres were gradually dwarfed by the rise of large cities. In turn the opinion of large centres was reflected in their newspapers and in an emphasis on differences. "No," said Mr Dooley, "They've got to print what's different."[37] Large centres became sources of news for distribution through press associations and in turn press associations became competitive with an emphasis on types of news which were mutually exclusive. The United Press became a competitor of the International News Service (Hearst) and of the Associated Press. The limitations of news as a basis of a steady circulation led to the development of features and in particular the comics and photography. Improvements in the reproduction of photographs coincided with the development of the cinema. News and the cinema complemented each other in the emphasis on instability. As a result of the struggle between various regions or metropolitan centres political stability was difficult to achieve. "It is one of the peculiar weaknesses of our political system that our strongest men cannot be kept very long in Congress."[38] While Congress was weakened the power of the president was strengthened. Theodore Roosevelt appealed to the mass psychology of the middle class and significantly gave the press a permanent room in the White House.[39] Oswald Garrison Villard claimed that "Theodore Roosevelt did more to corrupt the press than anyone else."[40]

The steadying influence of the book as a product of sustained intellectual effort was destroyed by new developments in periodicals and newspapers. As early as 1831 Lamartine would write: "Le livre arrive trop tard; le seul livre possible dès aujourd'hui, c'est un journal." The effect of instability on international affairs has been described by Moltke: "It is no longer the ambition of princes; it is the moods of the people, the discomfort in the face of interior conditions, the doings of parties, particularly of their leaders, which endanger peace."[41] The Western community was atomized by the pulverizing effects of the application of machine industry to communication. J.G. Bennett is said to have replied to someone charging him with inconsistency in the *New York Herald,* "I bring the paper out every day." He was consistent in inconsistency. "Advertisement dwells [in] a one-day world."[42]

Philosophy and religions reflected the general change. In the words of *Punch*: "It was the gradually extended use of the printing press that dragged the obscure horrors of political economy into the full light of day: and in the western countries of Europe the new sect became rampant." Hedonism gained in importance through the work of Bentham. Keynes has described his early belief by stating that he belonged to the first generation to throw hedonism out the window and to escape from the Benthamite tradition. "I do now regard that as the worm which has been gnawing at the insides of modern civilisation and is responsible for its present moral decay. We used to regard the Christians as the enemy, because they appeared as the representatives of tradition, convention, and hocus-pocus. In truth it was the Benthamite calculus, based on an overvaluation of the economic criterion, which was destroying the quality of the popular Ideal. Moreover, it was this escape from Bentham, joined with the unsurpassable individualism of our philosophy, which has served to protect the whole lot of us from the final *reductio ad absurdum* of Benthamism known as Marxism."[43] But Keynes was to conclude "we carried the individualism of our individuals too far" and thus to bear further testimony to the atomization of society. In religion "the new interest in the future and the progress of the race" unconsciously undermined "the old interest in a life beyond the grave; and it has dissolved the blighting doctrine of the radical corruption of man."[44] We should remind ourselves of Dean Inge's remarks that popular religion follows the enslavement of philosophy to superstition. The philosophies of Hegel, Comte, and Darwin became enslaved to the superstition of progress. In the corruption of political science confident predictions, irritating and incapable of refutation, replaced discussion of right and wrong.[45] Economists (the Physiocrats) "believed in the future progress of society towards a state of happiness through the increase of opulence which would itself depend on the growth of justice and 'liberty'; and they insisted on the importance of the increase and diffusion of knowledge."[46] The monopoly of knowledge which emerged with technological advances in the printing industry and insistence on freedom of the press checked this development.

The Treaty of Versailles recognized the impact of printing by accepting the principle of the rights of self-determination and destroyed large political organizations such as the Austrian Empire. Communication based on the eye in terms of printing and photography had developed a monopoly which threatened to destroy Western civilization first in war and then in peace. This monopoly emphasized individualism and in turn instability and created illusions in catchwords such as democracy, freedom of the press, and freedom of speech.

The disastrous effect of the monopoly of communication based on the eye hastened the development of a competitive type of communication based on the ear, in the radio and in the linking of sound to the cinema and to television. Printed material gave way in effectiveness to the broadcast and to the loud speaker.[47] Political leaders were able to appeal directly to constituents and to build up a pressure of public opinion on legislatures. In 1924 Al Smith, Governor of the State of New York, appealed directly by radio to the people and secured the passage of legislation threatened by Republican opposition. President F.D. Roosevelt exploited the radio as Theodore Roosevelt had exploited the press. He was concerned to have the opposition of newspapers in order that he might exploit their antagonism. It is scarcely necessary to elaborate on his success with the new medium.

In Europe an appeal to the ear made it possible to destroy the results of the Treaty of Versailles as registered in the political map based on self-determination. The rise of Hitler to power was facilitated by the use of the loud speaker and the radio. By the spoken language he could appeal to minority groups and to minority nations. Germans in Czechoslovakia could be reached by radio as could Germans in Austria. Political boundaries related to the demands of the printing industry disappeared with the new instrument of communication. The spoken language provided a new base for the exploitation of nationalism and a far more effective device for appealing to larger numbers. Illiteracy was no longer a serious barrier.

The effects of new media of communication evident in the outbreak of the Second World War were intensified during the progress of the war. They were used by the armed forces in the immediate prosecution of the war and in propaganda both at home and against the enemy. In Germany moving pictures of battles were taken[48] and shown in theatres almost immediately afterwards. The German people were given an impression of realism which compelled them to believe in the superiority of German arms; realism became not only most convincing but also with the collapse of the German front most disastrous. In some sense the problem of the German people is the problem of Western civilization. As modern developments in communication have made for greater realism they have made for greater possibilities of delusion. "It is curious to see scientific teaching used everywhere as a means to stifle all freedom of investigation in moral questions under a dead weight of facts. Materialism is the auxiliary doctrine of every tyranny, whether of the one or of the masses."[49] We are under the spell of Whitehead's fallacy of misplaced concreteness. The shell and pea game of the country fair has been magnified and elevated to a universal level.

The printing industry had been characterized by decentralization and regionalism such as had marked the division of the Western world in nationalism and the division and instability incidental to regions within nations. The radio appealed to vast areas, overcame the division between classes in its escape from literacy, and favoured centralization and bureaucracy. A single individual could appeal at one time to vast numbers of people speaking the same language and indirectly, though with less effect, through interpreters to numbers speaking other languages. Division was drawn along new lines based on language but within language units centralization and coherence became conspicuous. Stability within language units became more evident and instability between language units more dangerous.

The influence of mechanization on the printing industry had been evident in the increasing importance of the ephemeral. Superficiality became essential to meet the various demands of larger numbers of people and was developed as an art by those compelled to meet the demands. The radio accentuated the importance of the ephemeral and of the superficial. In the cinema and the broadcast it became necessary to search for entertainment and amusement. "Radio . . . has done more than its share to debase our intellectual standards."[50] The demands of the new media were imposed on the older media, the newspaper and the book. With these powerful developments time was destroyed and it became increasingly difficult to achieve continuity or to ask for a consideration of the future. An old maxim, "sixty diamond minutes set in a golden hour," illustrates the impact of commercialism on time. We would do well to remember the words of George Gissing: "Time is money—says the vulgarest saw known to any age or people. Turn it round about, and you get a precious truth—money is time."[51]

May I digress at this point on the effects of these trends on universities. William James held that the leadership of American thought was "passing away from the universities to the ten-cent magazines."[52] Today he might have argued that it had passed to the radio and television. But it is still necessary to say with Godkin in the last century: "there is probably no way in which we could strike so deadly a blow at the happiness and progress of the United States as by sweeping away, by some process of proscription kept up during a few generations, the graduates of the principal colleges. In no other way could we make so great a drain on the reserved force of character, ambition, and mental culture which constitutes so large a portion of the national vitality."[53] By culture he meant "the art of doing easily what you don't like to do. It is the breaking-in of the powers to the service of the will."[54]

If we venture to use this definition we are aware immediately of the trends in universities to add courses because people like to do them or because they will be useful to people after they graduate and will enable them to earn more money. In turn courses are given because members of the staff of the universities like to give them, an additional course means a larger department and a larger budget and, moreover, enables one to keep up with the subject. These tendencies reflect a concern with information. They are supported by the textbook industry and other industries which might be described as information industries. Information is provided in vast quantities in libraries, encyclopedias, and books. It is disseminated in universities by the new media of communication including moving pictures, loud speakers, with radio and television in the offing. Staff and students are tested in their ability to disseminate and receive information. Ingenious devices, questionnaires, intelligence tests are used to tell the student where he belongs and the student thus selected proceeds to apply similar devices to members of the staff. A vast army of research staff and students is concerned with simplifying language and making it easier for others to learn the English language and for more people to read and write what will be written in a simpler language. In the words of Santayana, "It doesn't matter *what* so long as they all read the *same* thing." Ezra Pound quotes the remark of an American professor: "The university is not here for the exceptional man."[55] Henry Adams in a discussion of teaching at Harvard summarized the problem in the remark, "It can not be done."[56] I have attempted to use the word information consistently though I am aware that the proper word is education. George Gissing has referred to "the host of the half-education, characteristic and peril of our time." "[E]ducation is a thing of which only the few are capable; teach as you will, only a small percentage will profit by your most zealous energy."[57] "To trumpet the triumphs of human knowledge seems to me worse than childishness; now, as of old, we know but one thing—that we know nothing."[58]

The relative adaptability of various subjects to mechanical transmission has threatened to destroy the unity of the university. "The University, as distinct from the technological school, has no proper function other than to teach that the flower of vital energy is Thought, and that not Instinct but Intellect is the highest form of a supernatural Will."[59] It tends to become a congeries of hardened avid departments obsessed with an interest in funds in which the department which can best prove its superficiality or its usefulness is most successful. Governments have been insensitive to the crucial significance of a balanced unity in universities and have responded to the pleas of specific subjects with the result that an interest in unity has been distorted to give that strange inartistic agglomeration of struggling departments called the modern university. The University of Oxford has recognized the threat and has set up a committee on the effects of university grants on balance in university subjects. It will probably be argued that social scientists have lost out in this race for government grants or that they should suffer for views as to the dangers of direct government intervention in the social sciences to the political health of the community. But I am afraid that just as with other subjects if the federal government should provide grants the social sciences will be on hand with the most beautifully developed projects for research that federal money can buy.

Under these circumstances we can begin to appreciate the remarks of an Oxford don who said after solving a very difficult problem in mathematics, "Thank God no one can use that." There must be few university subjects which can claim immunity or few universities which will refrain from pleading that their courses are useful for some reason or other.[60] The blight of lying and subterfuge in the interests of budgets has fallen over universities, and pleas are made on the grounds that the universities are valuable because they keep the country safe from socialism, they help the farmers and industry, they help in measures of defence. Now of course they do no such thing and when such topics are mentioned you and I are able to detect the odour of dead fish. Culture is not concerned with these questions. It is designed to train the individual to decide how much information he needs and how little he needs, to give him a sense of balance and proportion, and to protect him from the fanatic who tells him that Canada will be lost to the Russians unless he knows more geography or more history or more economics or more science. Culture is concerned with the capacity of the individual to appraise problems in terms of space and time and with enabling him to take the proper steps at the right time. It is at this point that the tragedy of modern culture has arisen as inventions in commercialism have destroyed a sense of time. "Our spiritual life is disorganized, for the over-organization of our external environment leads to the organization of our absence of thought."[61] "There is room for much more than a vague doubt that this cult of science is not altogether a wholesome growth—that the unmitigated quest of knowledge, of this matter-of-fact kind, makes for race-deterioration and discomfort on the whole, both in its immediate effects upon the spiritual life of mankind, and in the material consequences that follow from a great advance in matter-of-fact knowledge."[62] "In the long run, utility, like everything else, is simply a figment of our imagination and may well be the fatal stupidity by which we shall one day perish" (Nietzsche).

The limitations of Western culture can perhaps be illustrated by reference to the subject with which I pretend some acquaintance, namely the social sciences. Enormous compilations of statistics confront the social scientist. He is compelled to interpret them or to discover patterns or trends which will enable him to predict the future. With the use of elaborate calculating machines and of refinements in mathematical technique he can develop formulae to be used by industry and business and by governments in the formulation of policy. But elaboration assumes prediction for short periods of time. Work in the social sciences has become increasingly concerned with topical problems and social science departments become schools of journalism. The difficulty of handling the concept of time in economic theory and of developing a reconciliation between the static and dynamic approaches is a reflection of the neglect of the time factor in Western civilization. It is significant that Keynes should have said that in the long run we are all dead and that we have little other interest than that of living for the immediate future. Planning is a word to be used for short periods—for long periods it is suspect and with it the planner. The dilemma has been aptly described by Polanyi, "laissez-faire was planned, planning is not." The results have been evident in the demand for wholesale government activity during periods of intense difficulty. The luxury of the business cycle has been replaced by concerted measures directed toward the welfare state and full employment. Limited experience with the problem has involved expenditures on a large scale on armaments.

The trend towards centralization which has accompanied the development of a new medium of communication in the radio has compelled planning to a limited extent in other directions. Conservation of natural resources, government ownership of railways and hydro-electric power, for example in Canada and by T.V.A in the United States, and flood control are illustrations of a growing concern with the problems of time but in the main are the result of acute emergencies of the present. Concern with the position of Western civilization in the year 2000 is unthinkable. An interest in 1984 is only found in the satirist or the utopian and is not applicable to

North America. Attempts have been made to estimate population at late dates or the reserves of power or mineral resources but always with an emphasis on the resources of science and with reservations determined by income tax procedure, financial policy, or other expedients. Obsession with present-mindedness precludes speculation in terms of duration and time. Morley has written of the danger of a "growing tendency to substitute the narrowest political point of view for all the other ways of regarding the course of human affairs, and to raise the limitations which practical exigencies may happen to set to the application of general principles, into the very place of the principles themselves. Nor is the process of deteriorating conviction confined to the greater or noisier transactions of nations. . . . That process is due to causes which affect the mental temper as a whole, and pour round us an atmosphere that enervates our judgment from end to end, not more in politics than in morality, and not more in morality than in philosophy, in art, and in religion."[63]

Concern of the state with the weakening and destruction of monopolies over time has been supported by appeals to science whether in an emphasis on equilibrium suggested by the interest of the United States in a balanced constitution following Newtonian mathematics or in an emphasis on growth, competition, and survival of the fittest of Darwin. Attempts to escape from the eye of the state have been frustrated by succession duties, corporation laws, and anti-combine legislation. The demands of technology for continuity have been met by rapid expansion of the principle of limited liability and devices such as long-term leases guaranteeing duration but these have provided a base for active state intervention in income taxes. Little is known of the extent to which large corporations have blocked out the utilization of future resources other than in matters of general policy. A grasping price policy sacrifices indefinite possibilities of growth. A monopolist seeks expanding business at a reasonable profit rather than the utmost immediate profit.[64] Organization of markets and exchanges facilitates the determination of predictions and the working-out of calculations which in turn have their effect on immediate production as an attempt to provide continuity and stability, but limitations progressively increased as evident in business cycles and their destruction of time rigidities. The monopoly of equilibrium was ultimately destroyed in the great depression and gave way to the beginnings of the monopoly of a centralized state. The disappearance of time monopolies facilitated the rapid extension of control by the state and the development of new religions evident in fascism, communism, and our way of life.

The general restiveness inherent in an obsession with time has led to various attempts to restore concepts of community such as have appeared in earlier civilizations. The Middle Ages have appeared attractive to economic historians, guild socialists, and philosophers, particularly those interested in St Thomas Aquinas. "The cultivation of form for its own sake is equally typical of Romanticism and Classicism when they are mutually exclusive, the Romantic cultivating form in detachment from actuality, the Classicist in subservience to tradition" (Fausset).[65] It is possible that we have become paralysed to the extent that an interest in duration is impossible or that only under the pressure of extreme urgency can we be induced to recognize the problem. Reluctance to appraise the Byzantine Empire may in part be a result of paralysis reinforced by a distaste for any discussion of possible precursors of Russian government. But the concern of the Byzantine Empire in the Greek tradition was with form, with space and time. The sense of community built up by the Greeks assumed a concern with time in continuity and not in "a series of independent instantaneous flashes" (Keynes) such as appealed to the Romans and Western Christianity. "Immediacy of presentment was an inevitable enemy to construction. The elementary, passionate elements of the soul gave birth to utterances that would tend to be disconnected and uneven, as is the rhythm of emotion itself."[66] There was a "parallel emergence, in all the arts, of a movement away from a need which, whether in the ascendant or not, was always felt and honoured: the craving for some sort of continuity in form."[67] The effort to achieve continuity in form implies independence from the pressure of schools and fashions and modes of expression. In the words of Cazamian the indefinite duration of productive vitality in art and letters requires that the individual writer or reader be reinstated in the full enjoyment of his rights.[68]

Wyndham Lewis has argued that the fashionable mind is the time-denying mind. The results of developments in communication are reflected in the time philosophy of Bergson, Einstein, Whitehead, Alexander, and Russell. In Bergson we have glorification of the life of the moment, with no reference beyond itself and no absolute or universal value.[69] The modern "clerks" "consider everything only as it exists *in time,* that is as it constitutes a succession of particular states, a 'becoming,' a 'history,' and never as it presents a state of permanence beyond time under this succession of distinct cases." William James wrote: "That the philosophers since Socrates should have contended as to which should most scorn the knowledge of the particular and should most adore knowledge of the general, is something which passes understanding. For, after all, must not the most honourable knowledge be the knowledge of the most valuable realities! And is there a valuable reality which is not concrete and individual."[70] The form of mind from Plato to Kant which hallowed existence beyond change is proclaimed decadent. This contemporary attitude leads to the discouragement of all exercise of the will or the belief in individual power. The sense of power and the instinct for freedom have proved too costly and been replaced by the sham independence of democracy.[71] The political realization of democracy invariably encourages the hypnotist.[72] The behaviourist and the psychological tester have their way. In the words of one of them: "Great will be our good fortune if the lesson in human engineering which the way has taught us is carried over, directly and effectively, into our civil institutions and activities" (C.S. Yoakum).[73] Such tactlessness and offence to our good sense is becoming a professional hazard to psychologists. The essence of living in the moment and for the moment is to banish all individual continuity.[74] What Spengler has called the Faustian West is a result of living mentally and historically and is in contrast with other important civilizations which are "ahistoric." The enmity to Greek antiquity arises from the fact that its mind was ahistorical and without perspective.[75] In art classical man was in love with plastic whereas Faustian man is in love with music.[76] Sculpture has been sacrificed to music.[77]

The separation and separate treatment of the senses of sight and touch have produced both subjective disunity and external disunity.[78] We must somehow escape on the one hand from our obsession with the moment and on the other hand from our obsession with history. In freeing ourselves from time and attempting a balance between the demands of time and space we can develop conditions favourable to an interest in cultural activity.

It is sufficient for the purpose of this paper if attention can be drawn on the occasion of the 150th anniversary of a university of this continent to the role of the university in Western civilization. Anniversaries remind us of the significance of time. Though multiples of decades are misleading measures as the uniform retiring age of 65 is inhuman in its disrespect of biological differences they draw attention to a neglected factor. The university is probably older than Hellenistic civilization and has reflected the characteristics of the civilization in which it flourished, but in its association with religion and political organization it has been concerned with problems of time as well as of space. I can best close this paper by an appeal to Holy Writ. "Without vision the people perish."

Notes

1. The use of the letters AD and BC apparently dates from the eighteenth century. Hellenic rationalism might be said to have persisted for 700 years and to have been obscured for 1,200 years. "The longest period of consecutive time in human history on which we can found inductions is, upon the whole, a period of intellectual and moral darkness" (Julien Benda, *The Great Betrayal* [London, 1928]), 159.

2. History "threatens to degenerate from a broad survey of great periods and movements of human society into vast and countless accumulations of insignificant facts, sterile knowledge, and frivolous antiquarianism" (Morley in 1878). See Emery Neff, *The Poetry of History* (New York, 1947), 193.

3. P.A. Sorokin and R.K. Merton, "Social Time: A Methodological and Functional Analysis," *American Journal of Sociology* 42, 1936–37.

4. "In general, the rigidity of the Japanese planning and the tendency to abandon the object when their plans did not go according to schedule are thought to have been largely due to the cumbersome and imprecise nature of their language, which rendered it extremely difficult to improvise by means of signalled communication" (Winston Churchill).

5. R.K. Merton, "The Sociology of Knowledge," *Twentieth Century Sociology*, ed. G. Gurvich and W.E. Moore (New York, 1945), 387–8.

6. H.W. Garrod, *Scholarship, Its Meaning and Value* (Cambridge, 1946), 42.

7. Ernst Cassirer, *The Problem of Knowledge: Philosophy, Science, and History since Hegel*, trans. W.H. Woglom and C.W. Hendel (New Haven, Conn., 1950), 170–3.

8. Leslie Stephen, *History of English Thought in the Eighteenth Century* (London, 1876), 1: 458.

9. Cassirer, *The Problem of Knowledge*, 277.

10. Ibid., 251.

11. See H. Frankfort et al., *The Intellectual Adventure of Ancient Man: An Essay on Speculative Thought in the Ancient Near East* (Chicago, 1946).

12. H.A. Innis, *Empire and Communications* (Oxford, 1950).

13. Cited by Alfred Vagts, *A History of Militarism* (New York, 1937), 16.

14. See J.T. Shotwell, "The Discovery of Time," *Journal of Philosophy, Psychology, and Scientific Methods,* 1915, 198–206, 254–316. It is argued that mathematics made the use of time possible. See F. Thureau-Dangin, "Sketch of a History of the Sexagesimal System," *Osiris* 7. The Sumerian system was developed by crossing the numbers 10 and 6. Babylonian science was weak in geometry whereas the Greek science was strong. The Greeks learned the sexagesimal system through astronomy and discovered the Hindu system with a zero.

15. J.T. Shotwell, *An Introduction to the History of History* (New York, 1922), 43–4.

16. The calendar was apparently organized by Marduk and was under the control of the ruler of Mesopotamia (Frankfort et al., *The Intellectual Adventure of Ancient Man,* 181).

17. Ibid., 23–5.

18. Shotwell, *An Introduction to the History of History,* 45.

19. A new concern with time was evident in Herodotus, who presented a history "that neither the deeds of men may fade from memory by lapse of time, nor the mighty and marvellous works wrought partly by the Hellenes, partly by the Barbarians, may lose their renown." See also Thucydides' reasons for writing history.

20. See J.K. Fotheringham, "The Metonic and Callippic Cycles," *Monthly Notices of the Royal Astronomical Society* 84: 384; also B.D. Meritt, *The Athenian Calendar in the Fifth Century* (Cambridge, Mass., 1928), 72, 102, 122, 126.

21. The calendar was controlled by the college of pontifices. Of 192 days in a year on which people could be called together only 150 were left after ruling out days falling on market days, the last day of the Roman eight-day week, and days of seasonal games. An intercalary month was inserted in February every two years to bring the linear year into harmony with the solar year but in the early second century BC the pontifices obtained the right to insert it at will. The magisterial year for purposes of litigation, public contracts, and the like was changed according to their interests. These abuses were brought to an end by Caesar and the days added to the year by him as *dies fasti* were possibly intended as meeting days. See L.R. Taylor, *Party Politics in the Age of Caesar* (Berkeley, Calif., 1949), 79–80.

22. Franz Cumont, *Astrology and Religion among the Greeks and Romans* (New York, 1912), 162–5.

23. J.G. Frazer, *Adonis, Attis, Osiris: Studies in the History of Oriental Religion* (London, 1906), 200.

24. R.L. Poole, *Chronicles and Annals: A Brief Outline of Their Origin and Growth* (Oxford, 1926), 26.

25. R.L. Poole, *Lectures on the History of the Papal Chancery Down to the Time of Innocent III* (Cambridge, 1915), 38.

26. See R.L. Poole, "The Beginning of the Year in the Middle Ages," *Proceedings of the British Academy* 10.

27. A.P. Usher, *A History of Mechanical Inventions* (New York, 1929); also Lewis Mumford, *Technics and Civilization* (New York, 1934).

28. M.P. Nilsson, *Primitive Time-reckoning* (London, 1920).

29. L.T. Hogben, *From Cave Painting to Comic Strip* (London, 1949), 103ff; see also Etienne Hajnal, "Le rôle social de l'écriture et l'évolution curopéenne," *Revue de l'Institut de Sociologie,* 1934.

30. Byzantine policy also had implications for the French. The Edict of Nantes was supported by an illustration of tolerance told by Jacques Auguste de Thou (1533–1617) in *Continuation of the History of His Time,* to the effect that the Pope visited Constantinople in 526 to plead against the persecution of Arianism. See A.A. Vasiliev, *Justin the First: An Introduction to the Epoch of Justinian the Great* (Cambridge, Mass., 1950), 220–1.

31. C.H. McIlwain, *Constitutionalism, Ancient and Modern* (Ithaca, NY, 1940), 124.

32. See Benjamin Farrington, *Head and Hand in Ancient Greece: Four Studies in the Social Relations of Thought* (London, 1947).

33. N.S. Timasheff, *An Introduction to the Sociology of Law* (Cambridge, Mass., 1939), 207.

34. Coulton Waugh, *The Comics* (New York, 1947).

35. Archibald Forbes, *Souvenirs of Some Continents* (London, 1894).

36. Matthew Josephson, *The Robber Barons: The Great American Capitalists, 1861–1901* (New York, 1934), 27.

37. Cited by L.M. Salmon, *The Newspaper and the Historian* (New York, 1923), 29.

38. Brand Whitlock, *Forty Years of It* (New York, 1925), 157.

39. Matthew Josephson, *The President Makers, 1896–1919* (New York, 1940), 145.

40. Oswald Garrison Villard, *Fighting Years: Memoirs of a Liberal Editor* (New York, 1939), 151.

41. Vagts, *A History of Militarism*, 173.

42. Wyndham Lewis, *Time and Western Man* (London, 1927), 28.

43. John Maynard Keynes, *Two Memoirs* (London, 1949), 96–7.

44. J.B. Bury, *A History of Freedom of Thought* (London, 1928), 227.

45. W.R. Inge, *Diary of a Dean, St. Paul's 1911–1934* (London, 1950), 193–8.

46. J.B. Bury, *The Idea of Progress: An Inquiry into Its Origins and Growth* (London, 1920), 175.

47. William Albig, *Public Opinion* (New York, 1939), 220.

48. S. Kracauer, *From Caligari to Hitler* (Princeton, NJ, 1947), 297–8. "The camera's possibility of choosing and presenting but one aspect of reality invites it to the worst kinds of deceit" (*The Journals of André Gide*, trans. Justin O'Brien [New York, 1951], 4:91).

49. Amiel, *Journal intime*, 17 June 1852.

50. Ilka Chase, *Past Imperfect* (New York, 1942), 236. For a reference to the breath-taking feats of tight-rope walking to avoid any possible offence by the major networks see ibid., 234.

51. George Gissing, *The Private Papers of Henry Ryecroft* (London, 1914), 287.

52. Norman Hapgood, *The Changing Years: Reminiscences* (New York, 1930).

53. E.L. Godkin, *Reflections and Comments, 1865–1895* (New York, 1895), 157.

54. Ibid., 202.

55. *The Letters of Ezra Pound, 1907–1941*, ed. D.D. Paige (New York, 1950), xxiii.

56. Ibid., 338.

57. George Gissing, *The Private Papers of Henry Ryecroft*, 70.

58. Ibid., 178.

59. Henry Adams, *The Degradation of the Democratic Dogma* (New York, 1919), 206.

60. For example, the teaching that "intellectual activity is worthy of esteem to the extent that it is practical and to that extent alone . . . the man who loves science for its fruits commits the worst of blasphemies against that divinity" (Benda, *The Great Betrayal*, 121). The scholar's defeat "begins from the very moment when he claims to be practical" (ibid., 151).

61. Albert Schweitzer, *The Decay and the Restoration of Civilization* (London, 1932), 32.

62. Thorstein Veblen, *The Place of Science in Modern Civilization and Other Essays* (New York, 1919), 4.

63. John, Viscount Morley, *On Compromise* (London, 1921), 6.

64. J.M. Clark, *Alternative to Serfdom* (New York, 1948), 65.

65. E.E. Kellett, *Fashion in Literature* (London, 1931), 282.

66. Louis Cazamian, *Criticism in the Making* (New York, 1929), 72.

67. Ibid., 64.

68. Ibid., 129. The novelists Smollett, Fielding, Sterne, Richardson, Defoe, and the cockney artist Hogarth all had "an intimate connection with early journalism, sharing its time-sense as a series of discrete moments, each without self-possession, as well as its notion of the 'concrete' as residing in the particular entity or event sensorily observed" (Milton Klonsky, "Along the Midway of Mass Culture," *Partisan Review*, April 1949, 351).

69. Lewis, *Time and Western Man*, 27.

70. Benda, *The Great Betrayal*, 78–80.
71. Lewis, *Time and Western Man,* 316.
72. Ibid., 42.
73. Cited in ibid., 342.
74. Ibid., 29.
75. Ibid., 285.
76. Ibid., 295.
77. Ibid., 299.
78. Ibid., 419. For a discussion of the effects of printing on music, see Constant Lambert, *Music Ho! A Study of Music in Decline* (London, 1934).

The Anatomy of Power
A Theme in the Writings of Harold Innis

R. Douglas Francis

SINCE HIS DEATH in 1952, Harold Innis has been the subject of considerable study. Economists, historians, geographers, and communication theorists have all claimed him as one of their own, and then proceeded to examine some aspect of his thought from their own disciplinary perspectives.[1] In doing so, they have focused on one avenue of his thought, often to the exclusion of others, with the result that Innis appears fragmented in his thinking. A few Innisian scholars have looked at certain topics that appear at various times in some of his writings, such as the role of the university, but have failed to show how such topics give continuity to his thinking. To date, no one has attempted to discover any overriding themes running like leitmotifs throughout all of Innis's major works—from his first major publication, *A History of the Canadian Pacific Railway* (1923), through his economic 'staples' studies, to his later communication studies—that might show how all these studies are connected and reveal the continuity of his thought.

This paper explores one such theme in Innis's writings: the anatomy of power. Throughout his life, Innis was fascinated by what constituted power; what forces or relationships, technological or human, created power; who held power and who didn't, and why; how those in positions of power obtained and maintained their power base, and then were eventually supplanted by new power élites—what might be called the ebb and flow of power; the factors that caused old power structures to fall and new ones to arise within nation states, empires, and civilizations. The theme of power reveals a continuity and unity in Innis's thought, and in particular explains the important shift in his research interests in the early 1940s, when he abandoned his economic staple studies within the Canadian context in favour of communication studies within the context of the rise and fall of civilizations of the West, from Mesopotamia in the seventh century BC through to and including Europe and the United States in his own time. This paper will examine the power theme as it enabled Innis to explain the unique evolution of Canada as a nation on the North American continent, the dominance of the British Empire within Western civilization, and ultimately the rise and fall of that civilization. It will attempt to explain why Innis was so interested in power, and to show how that interest was in keeping with the intellectual currents of his time.

I

From an early age, Harold Innis saw power as a major factor in world politics. When, as a university student, he decided to join the army and go to war, he did so not for the reasons that most young men gave at the time—because others were joining, for glory, or because he felt compelled to fight for God, King, and Country—but because Germany had abused its power. In a letter home, explaining his decision to sign up, the young Innis wrote: 'Germany started in this war by breaking a treaty, by breaking her sealed word. Not only did she do that but she trampled over a helpless people with no warning and with no excuse. If any nation and if any person can break their word with no notice, whatever, then, is the world coming to.'[2]

Power was clearly a major theme in Innis's Ph.D. dissertation, completed at the University of Chicago and subsequently published as *A History of the Canadian Pacific Railway* (1923). Given the upsurge of Canadian nationalism immediately following the First World War, when Innis completed the study, it would have been natural for him to have seen the railroad as a noble national project, tying the country together and giving it a sense of identity and purpose. Yet he chose instead to examine its role in the matrices of power within Canada, the British Empire, and Western civilization in the late nineteenth century.[3] In essence, Innis argued that the importance of the CPR lay in the role it played in extending the sphere of influence and therefore the power of Western civilization—represented by central Canada within British North America and by the British Empire within the international context—beyond the river valleys of British North America to incorporate regions previously inaccessible, particularly the western interior. In this way the CPR enabled Canada, as a British colony, to secure control and power over the North West before the Americans were able to do so, and enabled Britain, as a major world power, to maintain a foothold in North America, and to link its vast empire together by means of an extensive communication and transportation network.

Innis viewed the building of the CPR and its role in the acquisition of the North West as the Canadian version of an imperial power struggle. It was a deliberate means by which central Canada came to dominate the hinterland of the west. And within central Canada, it was the Upper Canadian settlers who predominated. Their 'individualistic and aggressive nature' forced the new nation of Canada to expand too far too fast after 1867, before it was adequately prepared economically and financially to do so, and pitted region against region, or centre against margins, resulting in western discontent. In 1923 Innis did not foresee how this power relationship would change in the near future, despite the emergence of agrarian protest in the post-war era in the form of the Progressive movement. As he concluded in his study:

> On the whole, important as the [Progressive] movement in western Canada must become for the future development of the country, the dominance of eastern Canada over western Canada seems likely to per-

sist. Western Canada has paid for the development of Canadian nationality, and it would appear that it must continue to pay. The acquisitiveness of eastern Canada shows little sign of abatement.[4]

Thus Innis saw the railroad, the ribbon of steel, as the power link—the life blood— in the dynamic relationship between centre and margin. Within the national power structure, it bound the country together under the aegis of central Canada at the expense of the hinterland regions of the west and the east; within the context of Western civilization, the railroad was part of a vast transportation network that tied the British Empire together under British dominance at the expense of colonial hinterlands such as Canada.

What enabled the railroad to command such influence was the fact that it represented the latest and the greatest of Western technology: already, at this early stage in his thinking, Innis had come to realize that technology was power. Whoever controlled the most advanced form of technology held the superior power. In the nineteenth century, railroads were the most advanced form of technology, and Britain was the most advanced railroad nation in the world. In fact, that was the reason for Britain's position at the centre of Western civilization in the late nineteenth century. The CPR's role was to ensure Britain's continued control over British North America even after its colonies there had united in nationhood. Innis made the importance of the CPR as a source of technological power in British North America quite clear:

> The history of the Canadian Pacific Railroad is primarily the history of the spread of western civilization over the northern half of the North American continent. The addition of technical equipment described as physical property of the Canadian Pacific Railway Company was a cause and an effect of the strength and character of that civilization. The construction of the road was the result of the direction of energy to the conquest of geographic barriers. The effects of the road were measured to some extent by the changes in the strength and character of that civilization in the period following its construction.[5]

In seeing technology as power, Innis went beyond the obvious association of technology with machinery and industrialism as sources of that power to argue that technology really represented a mind set or *mentalité* within Western civilization that put power front and centre in its thinking. What is striking about his study of the CPR is the absence of discussion either of machinery or of the railroad as a form of industrialism. Instead he emphasized the political and economic factors behind the decision to build a transcontinental railroad, dwelt in detail on the construction of the main line and the addition of spur lines, and cited statistics on passenger traffic, earnings from operations, expenses, capital, and profits. The implication was that these decisions and actions reflected a way of thinking that was 'technological', that enabled those in positions of power to maintain their power.

That technological mentality measured everything in quantitative, mechanical, and mathematical terms—as profits, material values, and, most important, power—rather than human and spiritual terms. It was this 'technological mentality' that made Western civilization dominant, that gave Britain the commanding position within that civilization, and that kept Canada tied to the British Empire, and through it to Western civilization.

Such an awareness of technology as power was in keeping with the perspective of the post-1918 era.[6] The Great War, the most technologically advanced war of all time, revealed the destructive uses to which the power of technology could be put, and thus for the first time raised serious doubts about the implications of technology for civilization. The negative potential of technology came to be associated with Germany's cold, calculating abuse of the power of technology in the war. In this respect, the young Innis's condemnation of the Germans for their abuse of power was very much in keeping with the attitude of the times.

At the same time, Canadian intellectuals, like their counterparts in other Western countries, could not overlook the fact that Germany was part of Western civilization—if not its epitome. The Great War, then, was a power struggle within Western civilization, a struggle in which technology would determine which European nation—Britain or Germany—would hold the centre of power. Thus in seeing the Canadian Pacific Railroad as part of Britain's technological might, a means by which Britain extended and maintained its imperial dominance over the northern half of the North American continent, Innis was contributing to the post-war debate over the future of Western civilization: tracing the role that the technology of railroads had played in British supremacy in the nineteenth century, and by implication questioning the role that technology would play in the European power struggle in the twentieth century.

II

Having completed his study of the CPR, Innis became interested in discovering the roots of European dominance over the northern half of North America. He found it in the early fur trade and cod fisheries.[7] The staple trade not only secured first French and then British imperial control, but also established the dynamics for later American imperial dominance over Canada. As well, it established a pattern of governmental rule that determined the nature and jurisdiction of the newly created federal power when Canada became a nation in 1867. In addition, the staple trade shaped the dynamics of power between the centre, which invariably resided outside the country, and the margins represented by British North America. As Innis noted in his conclusion to the *Fur Trade in Canada* (1930): 'The economic history of Canada has been dominated by the discrepancy between the centre and the margin of western civilization. . . . Agriculture, industry, transportation, trade, finance, and governmental activities tend to become subordinate to the production of the staple for a more highly specialized manufacturing community.'[8]

Again, Innis found the source of power in technology. In the case of the fur trade, it was the superior technology of the Old World that enabled Europe to dominate over the North American hinterland. While he acknowledged the importance of the indigenous peoples of North America in enabling the early European traders and settlers to survive in the harsh climate and unfamiliar terrain of the New World, he admitted that Native cultures ultimately succumbed to the European culture because of the latter's technological superiority:

> The history of the fur trade is the history of contact between two civilizations, the European and the North American, with especial reference to the northern portion of the continent. The limited cultural background of the North American hunting peoples provided an insatiable demand for the products of the more elaborate cultural development of Europeans. The supply of European goods, the product of a more advanced and specialized technology, enabled the Indians to gain a livelihood more easily—to obtain their supply of food, as in the case of the moose, more quickly, and to hunt the beaver more effectively. . . . [But] the new technology with its radical innovations brought about such a rapid shift in the prevailing Indian culture as to lead to wholesale destruction of the peoples concerned by warfare and disease.[9]

Innis was clearly using the term 'technology' to refer to much more than iron knives, guns, and kettles. As in his study of the CPR, Innis saw the 'technical equipment' as part of a cultural matrix that put power front and centre in the European value system. Innis saw technology as a means of domination, of controlling others. In the case of the fur trade, technology had given Europeans the upper hand over the Native people, thus enabling the dynamics of centre and margin within Western civilization to work to the advantage of Europe. And when industrial technology developed in North America, it first emerged as a powerful force in the United States. Again Canada was left on the economic margin—only now it was dependent on the American, as opposed to European, imperial centre.

By the time Innis had completed his staple studies (circa 1940) he had clearly come to see Canada's marginal position in relation to the centres of power in Europe and the United States as disadvantageous, making the country dependent on external metropolitan centres, creating an economy of vulnerability, and fostering artificial growth through major government subsidies to private industries and a National Policy of high tariffs that shielded Canadian industries from international competition. Such an economy perpetuated the country's colonial position—to quote Innis's famous aphorism, 'Canada went from colony to nation to colony.' Technology as power had ensured that the centre of economic dominance would remain outside Canada's borders, leaving the country on the margin and thus powerless in the face of forces outside its control.

III

Analysts of Innis's thought have noted that it underwent a significant change around the time of the Second World War. Following his economic staples studies within a Canadian historical context he embarked on a cultural study of what Marshall McLuhan perceptively described as 'staples of the mid'[10]: the technologies of communications (stylus, papyrus, parchment, stone, clay tablets, paper, printing press) that in Innis's view had shaped the thought patterns of civilizations. This study led him to examine all the major civilizations of the West, from Mesopotamia up to and including Western Europe and the United States. While this new focus appeared to represent an abandonment of the work on Canada that he had pursued in the inter-war years, in fact it did not. His comment on Edward Gibbon's monumental *Decline and Fall of the Roman Empire,* namely that it was more a study of Gibbon's native Britain in the nineteenth century than it was of Rome, was equally true of Innis's own communication studies of ancient civilizations.[11] They had more to say about the decline of Western civilization in the twentieth century, and with Canada's role as a nation on the margin of that civilization, than they did about the past. In particular, his communication studies continued to explore the theme of power that had dominated his staple studies—only now the dominant source of power was the technology of communication.

There have been many explanations for Innis's dramatic shift in research focus. One of the most important, clearly, was the impact of the Second World War. The Great War had wounded Innis both physically and, more important, psychologically. For one thing, the war had made him more rebellious, leading him to question and challenge those in positions of power. When Innis's colleague Frank H. Underhill was threatened with dismissal from the University of Toronto in 1940–1 for challenging the views of those in political and academic authority, Innis defended him even though he disagreed with his views. His explanation of Underhill's rebelliousness revealed as much about Innis as Underhill. 'It is possibly necessary to remember,' Innis wrote to President Cody of the University of Toronto at the height of the Underhill controversy, 'that any returned man who has faced the continued dangers of modern warfare has a point of view fundamentally different from anyone who has not. Again and again have we told each other or repeated to ourselves, nothing can hurt us after this. The psychic perils of civilization mean nothing to us.'[12] That 'point of view' was one of rebelliousness against authority. Innis made the same point in a slightly different way when, in the midst of the Second World War, he recalled his permanent aversion to the bureaucrats he saw as self-important servants of distant power:

> After eight months of the mud and lice and rats of France in which much of the time was spent cursing government officials in Ottawa, I have without doubt developed an abnormal slant. I have never had the slightest interest since that time in people who were helping in the war

with a job in Ottawa or London. The contrast between their methods
of living and France made it simply impossible for me to regard them
as having anything to do with the war and I continue to look upon them
with contempt.[13]

Underhill challenged figures of authority directly and publicly; Innis challenged
them indirectly and less conspicuously, but with no less animus. His approach was
to study the source of power in societies and civilizations of the past so as to have a
better understanding of the present.

Power is an underlying theme in Innis's essay collection *Political Economy in the
Modern State* (1946), published in the immediate aftermath of the Second World War.
That the war loomed large in Innis's mind was evident in his Preface to the book.
Like the Great War, twenty-five years earlier, what the Second World War symbolized
for Innis was a power struggle within Western civilization. The difference lay in the
nature and extent of that struggle. In the Great War, the struggle had taken place
on the battlefields of Europe by means of physical force; in the Second World War,
by contrast, the site of the struggle was the mind of the general populace, and the
means was the power of communication technology. As Innis perceptively noted:

> The first essential task [of peace] is to see and to break through the
> chains of modern civilization which have been created by modern sci-
> ence. Freedom of the press and freedom of speech have been possible
> largely because they have permitted the production of words on an
> unprecedented scale and have made them powerless. Oral and printed
> words have been harnessed to the enormous demands of modern in-
> dustrialism and in advertising have been made to find new markets for
> goods. Each new invention which enhances their power in that direc-
> tion weakens their power in other directions. It is worth noting that
> large majorities in political elections accompanied the spread of the
> newspaper on a large scale in England after the sixties in the last cen-
> tury, and the spread of the radio on this continent. Swings in public
> opinion are most violent with new inventions in communication, and
> independent thought is more difficult to sustain. It is scarcely necessary
> to add, that words have carried a heavy additional load in the prosecu-
> tion of the war and have been subjected to unusual strains.[14]

Further on in his Preface Innis noted how the demands of war had increased
the demand for centralization of political power, which he saw as a danger. In one
typically cryptic comment, he linked centralization to morality and then to power:
'Extensive government expenditure and intervention and large scale undertakings
have raised the fundamental problems of morality. A friend in power is a friend lost.
A decline in morality has followed war and the growth of hierarchies in church, state,
and private enterprise. *Power is poison.*' What made power 'poisonous', Innis main-

tained, was its destructive effect on freedom of thought. 'Improvements in communication have weakened the possibility of sustained thought when it has become most necessary. Civilization has been compelled to resort to reliance on force as a result of the impact of technology on communication.[15] Here was the nucleus of Innis's interest in the technologies of communication, from ancient Mesopotamia to the present: a desire to understand the sources of power within those civilizations, the sources of challenge to that power structure, and the role of communication technology in the rise and fall of civilizations. At the roots of his new research was the old theme of power—now, however, he was seeking to understand the anatomy of power not in the economic relationship of empire and colonies but in the cultural relations between the centres and margins of civilizations based on the impact of communication technology. In particular, Innis was convinced that the centre of Western civilization in the mid-twentieth century, the United States, was in crisis, challenged by a new source of creativity and power on the margin.

Innis was looking for a pattern, or at least a convincing explanation, for the current decline of the West in the historical study of earlier civilizations. He found that pattern in the role played by the dominant medium of communication within a civilization in shaping its social structure and cultural values with the establishment of a 'monopoly of knowledge', any new creative thinking that might have allowed the civilization to flourish and continue to grow was stifled. Each form of communication technology was oriented towards either time or space—in Innis's terminology, 'time-biased' or 'space-biased'. Communication media that were durable and difficult to transport, such as stone, clay, or parchment, were time-biased, whereas those that were light and easy to transport over long distances, such as paper and papyrus, were space-biased.[16]

By 'bias' Innis meant much more than a simple preference for one type of technology or the other. He argued that civilizations oriented towards time or space created a dominant paradigm of thought—a monopoly of knowledge—that in most cases prevented counter-values or alternative social structures from emerging. As well, the principal medium of communication favoured one particular group within that civilization—the group that controlled the technology of communication—which maintained its power by preventing the emergence of any alternative communication technology that could threaten it. The oral tradition, for example, enabled the Spartan oligarchy to prevail; writing on papyrus benefited the Roman imperial bureaucracy; parchment allowed the medieval clergy and the Roman Catholic Church to monopolize knowledge in the Middle Ages; by contrast, Gutenberg's mechanical print fostered the vernacular and allowed the monarchs of nation states to consolidate their power and, through the merchant class, create vast empires.[17] The modern newspaper, a hybrid of the printed word and electronic media, particularly the telegraph, came under the control of the press lords, who in turn were pressured by charismatic political leaders and totalitarian rulers to print what they dictated.

The monopoly of knowledge enabled a civilization to maintain itself and even to achieve temporary cultural greatness, but it also led to the inevitable demise of that civilization, since it did not allow for the rise of the new ideas required for renewed growth. In essence, the civilization went into a comatose state where no rejuvenating new thought or spiritual growth could occur. At this point the civilization was open to challenge from societies on its margin that were beyond the influence of those in positions of power within the civilization. It was here, on the margin, that new technologies of communication emerged, capable of surpassing and supplanting the dominant medium of communication.

While Innis was fascinated with those who held power and the means they used to do so, he was equally interested in understanding those who challenged authority: where they came from; how they undermined the monopoly of knowledge, causing the civilization to collapse; and the means they used to establish themselves in power. Innis took a Darwinian view of the evolution of civilizations, seeing those in authority as constantly struggling to maintain their power while marginal societies outside the pale of power constantly worked to supplant them and the civilization that they represented.

In Innis's view, the truly creative thinking and the indomitable human spirit always emerged on the margins of civilization. He was just beginning to explore the material conditions and values in the marginal societies that fostered creativity and vitality as his life came to an end. As Robert Cox notes, Innis wanted to understand 'the technologies of intellectual and moral struggles.'[18] Innis discovered that these marginal societies shared a profound belief in freedom. Innis observed, in Robin Neill's words, that 'where there is liberty there is creativity; and the absence of liberty is not so much a consequence of force as of the intellectual and moral assumptions inherent in the bias of communication.'[19] Freedom flourished in a state of anomic and instability; it required conflicting ideas and open-ended debate. Power—the antithesis of liberty—required stability, security, and tyranny of thought.

Innis realized, however, that the decline of civilizations was not simply a matter of power versus freedom. Rather, he discovered a paradox: cultural creativity reached its peak in those civilizations where the power dynamics were in a state of equilibrium, not where there was an absence or weakness of power. Ironically, however, it was when a monopoly of power and the resulting stability had allowed cultural creativity to reach its height that the civilization began to decline as a result of the very power structure that had enabled it to thrive. Innis attributed the flowering of culture in fifth-century Greece to a balance between the forces of the oral and the written traditions within Athenian society, and a brief period of peace and stability among the Greek city states. The Byzantine empire reached its peak of cultural creativity because the power of the ruling élite maintained a balance between church and state, and deterred any external attacks. The tremendous creativity of the Renaissance era was due in large part to the balance of power among the emerging nation states of Europe. Yet each of these peak periods of creativity was invariably followed by a period of decline—the point when Minerva's owl took flight to a new centre of cultural creativity—because power stifled freedom and therefore the creativity essential for a civilization to sustain itself. The civilization was left vulnerable to challenges from marginal societies where new and superior technologies of communication had developed, capable of supplanting the existing dominant medium of communication and the power élite that controlled it. Thus power and creativity, authority and freedom, stood at opposite ends of the value spectrum, paralleling the centre and the margin—the sources of power and creativity respectively. Given the power of communication technologies to create a monopoly of knowledge at the centre of civilization, opposition to that monopoly would inevitably arise, it seemed to Innis, from marginal societies that initially valued freedom over power.

In the mid-twentieth century, Innis believed that Minerva's owl was once again taking flight from the centre of Western civilization in the United States. By the end of his life in 1952, he had grown cynical with regard to a civilization that had waged two wars of unparalleled destruction and was threatening to begin a third with the discovery of the atomic bomb, that had initiated a worldwide depression and that accepted, in its societies, extremes of wealth and poverty. He criticized the universities and the churches—the two institutions that should be the upholders of freedom against authority and power structures—for their failure to offer new ideas and to question the dominant paradigms of thought within the modern West.[20] Clearly, mechanized print, along with the new electronic communication technology of the telegraph and the radio (the latter Innis saw as accentuating and extending the space-bias and therefore the monopoly of mechanized print), had an iron-clad hold on Western thinking, reducing rationalism to its lowest common denominator as popular thought based on blind emotionalism.

Did he see any hope for the future? The lessons of history taught that the only hope lay in a challenge to America's imperial dominance at the centre of Western civilization from a society on the margin. Marginal forces were both internal and external. They were the new creative ideas in the minds of those individuals who were not duped or mesmerized by the prevailing ideology or dominant paradigms—those creative individuals whose spirit could not be crushed. Such human spirits, however, had to be nurtured in the bosom of a society and culture that respected and fostered creativity. Innis was too much of a realist, and materialist, to believe that new ideas developed and creative individuals emerged in a vacuum. They required a society that was not part of the existing matrix of power, not at the imperial centre. Such a society also needed to have a healthy balance of cultural values associated with time and space—what might be described as conservative and liberal values. (In Innis's view, time-biased values were traditional, hierarchical and moral (qualities of conservation), while space-biased values emphasized the present and the future, the technical, and the secular (qualities of liberalism).)

Innis believed that Canada was such a creative society. Its entire history, from the time of European exploration and settlement, had been one of marginality within Western civilization under first the French empire, then the British empire, and, more recently, the American. During the period when Europe was the centre of Western civilization, Canada was able to remain on the margin, and therefore beyond the direct dominance of imperial power, thanks to simple distance and the physical barrier of the Atlantic Ocean. Canada was not so fortunate, however, when the centre of power shifted from Europe to the United States in the twentieth century. There could be no illusion of Canadian independence from American political, economic, and cultural control. Nevertheless, through a long tradition of anti-Americanism, an association and identification with Britain offsetting the American influence, and a political ideology that incorporated both conservative and liberal values—in other words, both time-biased and space-biased values—Canada had created a society and culture different from those of the United States.

In his last publication, *The Strategy of Culture* (1952), Innis set out his concern for Canadian creativity and survival in the face of American imperial power. He also offered his belief that Canada, a country on the margin of power, had something positive to contribute to the modern world:

> The dangers to national existence warrant an energetic programme to offset them. In the new technological developments Canadians can escape American influence in communication media other that those affected by appeals to the 'freedom of the press'. The Canadian Press has emphasized Canadian news but American influence is powerful. In the radio, on the other hand, the Canadian government in the Canadian Broadcasting Corporation has undertaken an active role in offsetting the influence of American broadcasters. It may be hoped that its role will be more active in television. The Film Board has been set up and designed to weaken the pressure of American films. The appointment and the report of the Royal Commission on National Developments in the Arts and Sciences imply a determination to strengthen our position. . . .
>
> We are fighting for our lives. The pernicious influence of American advertising reflected especially in the periodical press and the powerful persistent impact of commercialism have been evident in all the ramifications of Canadian life. The jackals of communication systems are constantly on the alert to destroy every vestige of sentiment towards Great Britain, holding it of no advantage if it threatens the omnipotence of American commercialism. This is to strike at the heart of cultural life in Canada. The pride taken in improving our status in the British Commonwealth of Nations has made it difficult for us to realize that our status on the North American continent is on the verge of disappearing. Continentalism assisted in the achievement of autonomy, and has consequently become more dangerous. We can only survive by taking persistent action at strategic points against American imperialism in all its attractive guises.[21]

IV

What accounts for Innis's fascination with power? I would trace it to Innis's belief that he was on the margin of power, always looking in, so to speak, at those who held it. This was true in his personal as well as his academic life. At first glance, this statement might appear absurd. Few Canadian intellectuals have received the honours and recognition within their lifetime that Innis received. Elected president of the Royal Society of Canada, he was awarded its coveted Tyrrell Medal in recognition of his outstanding contribution to scholarship; he was the only Canadian to be chosen president of the American Economic Association; and in 1948 he was invited to give the distinguished Beit Lectures on imperial economic history at Oxford University, subsequently published as *Empire and Communications* (1950)—to name only a few of the honours and awards he received.[22]

Even so, Innis believed himself to be on the margin of power. As a farm boy, he never felt at ease in an urban setting; later as an academic, he was never comfortable with the urban power élite. As an undergraduate, coming from a poor family, he believed that he did not have the opportunities or influence that students of middle- and upper-class backgrounds enjoyed; as a graduate student at the University of Chicago, he rejected the idea of working on a dissertation topic in American, European, or international economics, as most students were doing, choosing instead to focus on Canada, a nation itself on the margin of power. In the First World War, he joined the Canadian army at a time when many university-educated Canadians were joining the more prestigious British army. He was wounded at Vimy Ridge and discharged from the army before he could distinguish himself in battle. In his subsequent academic career, he chose research topics outside the intellectual mainstream; he preferred the role of critic to that of advocate; and his writings attracted limited interest at the time of publication. He died prematurely, with no following to continue his life work. The fact that power eluded him might account for his fascination with those who did hold it, and with the role that power played in history.

In terms of intellectual context, power was much on the minds of the generation of academics writing, as Innis did, in the aftermath of the First World War, throughout the Great Depression, and in the shadow of the Second World War and the atomic bomb; for them, power politics appeared to be the dominant force in the world. The inter-war years witnessed a reaction to the optimism, sentimentalism, and romanticism of the Victorian age. Certainly the Great War brought the issue of power to the fore, making a mockery of the liberal beliefs in rationality and progress towards ultimate peace in the world. A generation earlier, Sigmund Freud had 'discovered' the irrational side of human nature. In the 1920s, idealism was giving way to realism in literature and philosophy as the urge to power underlying human actions was exposed. It was an age of debunking, of pointing out that human beings were not so noble and idealistic as some had believed them to be.

In his own writings in the inter-war years, Innis reacted against the romantic and sentimental nineteenth-century conception of history in which 'great and noble men' were depicted as the moral leaders of society; instead, he looked for the impersonal economic forces, the subconscious cultural hegemony, and the naked play of power that constituted the dynamics of history. He came to see the struggle for power as the most convincing explanation for, and hence the underlying theme in, the history of the Canadian nation state, in the dynamics of imperial and colonial relations, and in the rise and fall of civilizations.

Innis's study of the anatomy of power parallels Northrop Frye's anatomy of criticism and George P. Grant's work on the anatomy of technology.[23] All three of these important mid-twentieth-century Canadian intellectuals had at least one thing in common: a desire to get at the essence of modern thought by linking it to one central concept or theme that appeared to underlie that thought and give it form and meaning—a thread or bloodline running through the entire body of scholarship. Each of the three thinkers explored the ramifications of his central theme: Innis, the role of power in shaping societies, nations, empire, and civilizations through technology; Frye, the significance of biblical patterns in the structure of modern literature; Grant, the impact of technology on modern morals and values. In each case, that theme became their holy grail, the hidden text for which they searched in their quest for meaning in the modern world. While none found Truth, all three brought new and deeper understanding to modern thought.

The theme of power itself is very modern. Innis's fascination with power reflects Michel Foucault's writings on the subject in *Power/Knowledge* and elsewhere. Like Innis, Foucault reacted to historians' emphasis on abstract and noble concepts—for example, 'the will to knowledge'—arguing that such ideals blind historians to the reality of power throughout history. 'The history which bears and determines us,' he argued, 'has the form of a war rather than that of a language: relations of power, not relations of meaning.' In *Power/Knowledge,* he went on to explain how historians of the past tended to skirt the issue of power rather than address it directly:

> The way power was exercised—concretely and in detail—with its specificity, its techniques and tactics, was something that no one attempted to ascertain; they contented themselves with denouncing it in a polemical and global fashion as it existed among the 'others', in the adversary camp. Where Soviet socialist power was in question, its opponents called it totalitarianism; power in western capitalism was denounced by the Marxists as class domination; but the mechanics of power in themselves were never analyzed.[24]

In his fascination with power, Innis showed how modern his thinking was, offering insights that would be pursued by a later generation of historians. Here, ironically, Innis has enjoyed a power and influence that eluded him in his lifetime.

Notes

1. On Harold Innis as an economist, see Mel Watkins, 'The Staple Theory Revisited', and Ian Parker, 'Innis, Marx, and the Economics of Communication: A Theoretical Aspect of Political Economy,' in *Culture, Communication and Dependency: The Tradition of H.A. Innis,* ed. William H. Melody et al. (Norwood, NJ, 1981), 53–72 and 127–44 respectively; and Robin Neill, *A New Theory of Value: The Canadian Economics of H.A. Innis* (Toronto, 1972). On Innis's contribution to geography, see 'Focus: A Geographical Appreciation of Harold A. Innis', *Canadian Geographer* 32, 1 (1988), 63–9. On Innis as a historian, see Carl Berger, *The Writing of Canadian History* (Toronto, 1976), 85–111; William Westfall, 'The Ambivalent Verdict: Harold Innis and Canadian History', in *Culture, Communication and Dependency,* 37–52; and Frank Abbott, 'Harold Innis—Nationalist Historian', *Queen's Quarterly,* 101, 1 (Spring 1994), 92–102. On Innis and communication studies, see Paul Heyer and David Cowley, 'Introduction to Harold A. Innis', *The Bias of Communication,* reprint with a new introduction (Toronto, 1991), ix–xxviii; J. Carey, *Communication as Culture* (Boston, 1989); and D. Czitrom, *Media and the American Mind* (Chapel Hill, 1987).
2. Quoted in William Christian, *Harold Innis as Economist and Moralist* (Guelph, 1981), 2.
3. For a discussion of the importance of nationalism in the writing of Canadian history in the 1920s, see Ramsay Cook, '*La Survivance* English-Canadian Style,' in his *The Maple Leaf Forever: Essays on Nationalism and Politics in Canada* (Toronto, 1971), 141–65.
4. Harold A. Innis, *A History of the Canadian Pacific Railway* (Toronto, 1923), 294.
5. Ibid., 284.
6. For a good discussion of the First World War as a technological war, see Modris Ekstein, *Rites of Spring: The Great War and the Birth of the Modern Age* (Boston, 1989).
7. Innis discusses the fur trade in *The Fur Trade in Canada* (Toronto, 1930), and the fish trade in *The Cod Fisheries: The History of an International Economy* (Toronto, 1940). For reasons of space, I have discussed the theme of power in his study of the fur trade only, although it is also present in his study of the cod fisheries.
8. *The Fur Trade in Canada,* 385.
9. Ibid., 388.
10. Marshall McLuhan, 'The Later Innis,' *Queen's Quarterly* 60 (1953).
11. The idea is presented in Neill's *A New Theory of Value,* 16–17.
12. R. Douglas Francis, *Frank H. Underhill: Intellectual Provocateur* (Toronto, 1986), 123.
13. Quoted in Berger, *The Writing of Canadian History,* 104.
14. Harold A. Innis, *Political Economy in the Modern State* (Toronto, 1946), vii–viii.
15. Ibid., xiii–xiv.
16. The best analysis of Innis's theories on communication media is still James W. Carey, 'Harold Adams Innis and Marshall McLuhan,' *Antioch Review* 27 (Spring 1967), 5–39.
17. See Harold A. Innis, *Empire and Communications* (Oxford, 1950), and *The Bias of Communication* (Toronto, 1951), especially 'Minerva's Owl'.
18. Robert W. Cox, 'Civilizations: Encounters and Transformations', *Studies in Political Economy* 47 (Summer 1995), 20–6.
19. Neill, *A New Theory of Value,* 101.
20. See, for example, H.A. Innis, 'Discussion in the Social Sciences', *Dalhousie Review* 15 (1936), 401–13; 'The University in the Modern Tradition', in *Political Economy in the Modern State,* 71–82; 'Adult Education and the Universities,' in *The Bias of Communication,* 203–13; and 'The Church in Canada,' in *Time for Healing: Twenty-Second Annual Report of the Board of Evangelism and Social Services* (Toronto, 1947), 47–54.
21. Harold A. Innis, *The Strategy of Culture* (Toronto, 1952), 19–20.

22. There is no full-scale biography of Innis. For a biographical sketch, see Donald G. Creighton, *Harold Adams Innis: Portrait of a Scholar* (Toronto, 1957); Carl Berger, 'Harold Innis: The Search for Limits', in *The Writing of Canadian History*, 85–111; and for a personal reminiscence, Eric A. Havelock, *Harold A. Innis: A Memoir* (Toronto, 1982).

23. Northrop Frye, *Anatomy of Criticism: Four Essays* (Princeton, 1957); George Grant, *Technology and Empire: Perspectives on North America* (Toronto, 1969).

24. Michel Foucault, *Power/Knowledge: Selected Interviews and Other Writings, 1972–1977*, ed. Colin Gordon (Brighton, 1980), 114, 115–16.

CHAPTER TWELVE

From Colony to Colony

Introduction

When Arthur Lower published his famous book, *Colony to Nation*, in 1946, Canadians were already beginning to ask themselves if a master narrative of colony to nation was not, in fact, misguided. On a continent—and in a world—dominated by the United States after the Second World War, would not a narrative of colony to colony better explain Canada? That is, would Canada's history not be better understood as that of a colony of France and Great Britain to a colony of the United States?

Canada's relationship to the United States has been—and still is—a national preoccupation. Born in Reading, England in 1823, Goldwin Smith was Regius professor of modern history at Oxford University before moving to Toronto in 1871. He quickly became one of the leading intellectuals and journalists in the country. Believing the Canadian experiment a failed one, he advocated union with the United States. In his 1891 book, *Canada and the Canada Question*, he dared to ask the Canadian question. What was the Canadian question? In many ways Canadians have been asking that question—or a variation of that question—ever since. In his 2000 article on American mass entertainment and Canadian identity, David Taras asks "whether we are now so immersed in American culture that there is no longer a clear distinction between who they are and who we are?" Although less explicit, the writer Evelyn Lau also asks a variation of the Canadian question: unless we exist in the United States do we exist at all?

Canada and the Canadian Question, 1891

Goldwin Smith

WHETHER THE FOUR blocks of territory constituting the Dominion can for ever be kept by political agencies united among themselves and separate from their Continent, of which geographically, economically, and with the exception of Quebec ethnologically, they are parts, is the Canadian question . . .

Let those who prophesy to us smooth things take stock of the facts. When one community differs from another in race, language, religion, character, spirit, social structure, aspirations, occupying also a territory apart, it is a separate nation, and is morally certain to pursue a different course, let it designate itself as it can. French Canada may be ultimately absorbed in the English-speaking population of a vast Continent; amalgamate with British Canada so as to form a united nation it apparently never can . . .

From British as well as from French Canada there is a constant flow of emigration to the richer country, and the great centres of employment. Dakota and the other new States of the American West are full of Canadian farmers; the great American cities are full of Canadian clerks and men of business, who usually make for themselves a good name. It is said that in Chicago there are 25,000. Hundreds of thousands of Canadians have relatives in the United States. Canadians in great numbers—it is believed as many as 40,000—enlisted in the American army during the civil war . . . A young Canadian thinks no more of going to push his fortune in New York or Chicago than a young Scotchman thinks of going to Manchester or London. The same is the case in the higher callings as in the lower: clergymen, those of the Church of England as well as those of other churches, freely accept calls to the other side of the Line. So do professors, teachers, and journalists. The Canadian churches are in full communion with their American sisters, and send delegates to each other's Assemblies. Cadets educated at a Military College to command the Canadian army against the Americans, have gone to practise as Civil Engineers in the United States. The Benevolent and National Societies have branches on both sides of the Line, and hold conventions in common. Even the Orange Order has now its lodges in the United States, where the name of President is substituted in the oath for that of the Queen. American labour organizations . . . extend to Canada. The American Science Association met the other day at Toronto. All the reforming and philanthropic movements, such as the Temperance movement, the Women's Rights' movement, and the Labour movements, with their conventions, are continental. Intermarriages between Canadians and Americans are numerous, so numerous as scarcely to be remarked. Americans are the chief owners of Canadian mines, and large owners of Canadian timber limits. The railway system of the continent is one. The winter ports of Canada are those of the United States. Canadian banks trade largely in the American market, and some have branches there. There is almost a currency union, American bank-bills commonly passing at par in Ontario, while those of remote Canadian Provinces pass at par only by special arrangement. American gold passes at par, while silver coin is taken at a small discount: in Winnipeg even the American nickel is part of the common currency. The Dominion bank-bills, though payable in gold, are but half convertible, because what the Canadian banks want is not British but American gold. Canadians go to the American watering-places, while Americans pass the summer on Canadian lakes. Canadians take American periodicals, to which Canadian writers often contribute. They resort for special purchases to New York stores, or even those of the Border cities. Sports are international; so are the Base Ball organisations; and the Toronto "Nine" is recruited in the States. All the New-World phrases and habits are the same on both sides of the Line. The two sections of the English-speaking race on the American continent, in short, are in a state of economic, intellectual, and social fusion, daily becoming more complete. Saving the special connection of a limited circle with the Old Country, Ontario is an American State of the Northern type, cut off from its sisters by a customs line, under a separate government and flag . . .

The isolation of the different Canadian markets from each other, and the incompatibility of their interests, add in their case to the evils and absurdities of the protective system. What is meat to one Province is, even on the protectionist hypothesis, poison to another. Ontario was to be forced to manufacture; she has no coal; yet to reconcile Nova Scotia to the tariff a coal duty was imposed; in vain, for Ontario after all continued to import her coal from Pennsylvania. Manitoba and the North-West produced no fruit; yet they were compelled to pay a duty in order to protect the fruit-grower of Ontario 1500 miles away. Hardest of all was the lot of the North-West farmer. His natural market, wherein to buy farm implements, was in the neighbouring cities of the United States, where, moreover, implements were made most suitable to the prairie. But to force him to buy in Eastern Canada 25 per cent was laid on farm implements. As he still bought in the States, the 25 per cent was made 35 per cent . . .

Without commercial intercourse or fusion of population, the unity produced by a mere political arrangement can hardly be strong or deep . . .

The thread of political connection is wearing thin. This England sees, and the consequence is a recoil which has produced a movement in favour of Imperial Federation. It is proposed not only to arrest the process of gradual emancipation, but to reverse it and to reabsorb the colonies into the unity of the Empire. No definite plan has been propounded, indeed, any demand for a plan is deprecated, and we are adjured to embrace the principle of the scheme and leave the details for future revelation—to which we must answer that the principle of a scheme is its object, and that it is impossible to determine whether the object is practically attainable without a working plan. There is no one in whose eyes the bond between the colonies and the mother country is more precious than it is in mine. Yet I do not hesitate to say that, so far as Canada is concerned, Imperial Federation is a dream. The Canadian people will never part with their self-government. Their tendency is entirely the other way. They have recently . . . asserted their fiscal independence, and by instituting a Supreme Court of their own, they have evinced a disposition to withdraw as much as they can of their affairs from the jurisdiction of the Privy Council. Every association, to make it reasonable and lasting, must have some practical object. The practical objects of Imperial Federation would be the maintenance of common armaments and the establishment of a common tariff. But to neither of these, I am persuaded, would Canada ever consent; she would neither contribute to Imperial armaments nor conform to an Imperial tariff. Though her people are brave and hardy, they are not, any more than the people of the United States, military, nor could they be brought to spend their earnings in Asiatic or African wars . . . Remember that Canada is only in part British. The commercial and fiscal circumstances of the colony again are as different as possible from those of the mother country . . .

Annexation is an ugly word; it seems to convey the idea of force or pressure applied to the smaller State, not of free, equal, and honourable union, like that between England and Scotland. Yet there is no reason why the union of the two sections of the English-speaking people on this Continent should not be as free, as equal, and as honourable as the union of England and Scotland. We should rather say their reunion than their union, for before their unhappy schism they were one people. Nothing but the historical accident of a civil war ending in secession, instead of amnesty, has made them two . . .

That a union of Canada with the American Commonwealth, like that into which Scotland entered with England, would in itself be attended with great advantages cannot be questioned, whatever may be the considerations on the other side or the reasons for delay. It would give to the inhabitants of the whole Continent as complete a security for peace and immunity from war taxation as is likely to be attained by any community or group of communities on this side of the Millennium. Canadians almost with one voice say that it would greatly raise the value of property in Canada; in other words, that it would bring with it great increase of prosperity . . .

Again, Canadians who heartily accept democracy wish that there should be two experiments in it on this Continent rather than one, and the wish is shared by thoughtful Americans not a few. But we have seen that in reality the two experiments are not being made. Universal suffrage and party government are the same, and their effects are the same in both Republics. Differences there are, such as that between the Presidential and the Cabinet system, of a subordinate kind, yet not unimportant, and such as might make it worthwhile to forego for a time at least the advantages of union, supposing that the dangers and economical evils of separation were not too great, and if the territorial division were not extravagantly at variance with the fiat of Nature. The experiments of political science must be tried with some reference to terrestrial convenience. Besides, those who scan the future without prejudice must see that the political fortunes of the Continent are embarked in the great Republic, and that Canada will best promote her own ultimate interests by contributing without unnecessary delay all that she has in the way of political character and force towards the saving of the main chance and the fulfilment of the common hope. The native American element in which the tradition of self-government resides is hard pressed by the foreign element untrained to self-government, and stands in need of the reinforcement which the entrance of Canada into the Union would bring it . . .

In the present case there are, on one side, geography, commerce, identity of race, language, and institutions, which with the mingling of population and constant intercourse of every kind, acting in ever-increasing intensity, have brought about a general fusion, leaving no barriers standing but the political and fiscal lines. On the other side, there is British and Imperial sentiment, which, however, is confined to the British, excluding the French and Irish and other nationalities, and even among the British is livelier as a rule among the cultivated and those whose minds are steeped in history than among those who are working for their bread; while to set against it there is the idea, which can hardly fail to make way, of a great continent with an almost unlimited range of production forming the home of a united people, shutting out war and presenting the field as it would seem for a new and happier development of humanity . . .

Swimming Against the Current:
American Mass Entertainment and Canadian Identity

David Taras

JOHN MEISEL, A much-respected Canadian scholar and a former chairman of the Canadian Radio-Television and Telecommunication Commission, once argued that "Inside every Canadian whether she or he knows it or not, there is, in fact, an American. The magnitude and effect of this American presence in us varies considerably from person to person, but it is ubiquitous and inescapable."[1] According to Meisel, many Canadians, especially heavy TV viewers, look to the United States for their cultural orientation. Their cultural compasses point south. They watch blockbuster Hollywood movies and hit TV shows, follow American celebrities, tune in to American talk TV and newsmagazines, cheer for US sports teams and plan dream vacations in theme cities such as Las Vegas, Orlando or Nashville. These Canadians tend to have little interest in Canadian programming and don't want their tax dollars spent defending or promoting Canadian culture.

According to Meisel, the degree of infatuation with, or better still submersion into, American culture, however, often depends on one's level of education. Those who are better educated, and thus less likely to watch television, are much more likely to be consumers of Canadian culture. One can even argue that these educated Canadians form a defensive wall preventing Canadian culture from being completely overrun.

Meisel was later to alter his position, arguing that Canadian culture could survive and even flourish amid the relentless pounding surf of American images, tastes and products because there are certain constituencies whose natural allegiance is to Canadian culture.[2] They exist and find their *raison d'être* within a Canadian world. But Meisel's argument is still a chilling one. There are Canadians who inhabit media worlds that are largely American, and this, in the long run, may shape their commitments as Canadian citizens and voters.

This chapter will look at the differences between the Canadian and American media worlds. I will focus on the different structures and traditions in Canadian and American television and on the economic realities that underpin both systems. I will also compare the concentration of ownership in the Canadian newspaper industry with that found in the United States and discuss the particular problems that arise from the fact that the industry in Canada is controlled by a very few individuals and corporations. The chapter will also examine the controversy that surrounds "split runs" and what some observers see as an American assault on the Canadian magazine industry.

TV, magazines and newspapers are the central nervous systems of cultural transmission. Canadians watch on average 23 hours of television per week or, to put it differently, we spend nearly one full day out of every week glued to our TV sets. Magazines are devoured by millions of readers each week and over 5 million newspapers are sold every day in Canada. When scholars argue that Canada has a "media-constructed public sphere," they are making the point that public life in Canada, our sense of place and of society, comes to us through the mass media. If our media system fails us in some way, if our public spaces are closed off so that Canadians can't communicate with each other, then the society as a whole is weakened.

A central theme is that Canadians must come to terms with the sheer size and overwhelming power of the American media colossus. Unlike Asians or Europeans, we don't have the luxury of being able to observe the American media system from a safe and comfortable distance, and from behind the protective dikes of a different language and religion. The American system is our system as well. For better or worse, Canadians have to carve out their own identity while living within an American media bubble.

Hollywood and Canadian Broadcasting

It would be a mistake to view American network television as a distinct economic and social force. American TV networks are but spokes in much larger wheels. They are in every case part of what can only be described as huge entertainment or communication conglomerates. Disney owns ABC. General Electric controls NBC. The Fox network is part of Rupert Murdoch's giant News Corporation. Viacom, which controls Paramount Pictures, Blockbuster Video, and Simon and Schuster publishing among other companies, recently gobbled up CBS. The fledgling USA network is allied with and largely controlled by Seagram which owns Universal. And the newest kid on the block, Warner TV, is but an offshoot of AOL-Time Warner, a mammoth entertainment company that holds a large number of cable TV properties including CNN, Cinemax and HBO. American TV networks can only be understood within this wider context.

The Fox television network provides a good example of how the machinery of American television works. Fox Broadcasting is only a small part of Rupert Murdoch's News Corporation empire, an empire that includes almost all aspects of media production, distribution and publicity. The hub of the wheel is 20th Century Fox, a film and TV studio that has produced such hits as *Titanic, The Simpsons, South Park* and *The X-Files*. The distribution arm includes the TV network, a myriad of cable channels such as Fox News, a 24-hour all news channel, Fox Sports Net, and the Family Channel. In addition News Corporation owns flagship TV stations in New York, Los Angeles, Chicago, Washington, Philadelphia and Atlanta as well as in 15 other American cities, and satellite television systems in Asia and Europe. Murdoch also owns the world's largest newspaper chain, a bevy of magazines and supermarket tabloids and sports franchises such as the Los Angeles Dodgers and the LA Lakers and Kings. It would be a mistake therefore to see Fox Broadcasting as an entity that has to make money or survive on its own. Its TV programs are integrated into—are subsumed within—a larger corporate matrix.

The hit series, *The X-Files,* for instance, provides a vivid illustration of the way in which TV programs are used as a springboard for a host of other media productions and products. The program is, in effect, a brand name that is used and promoted, pumped and squeezed, by a number of arms within News Corporation. *The X-Files* has been the basis for a blockbuster movie, videos, a video game, books, various board games as well as calendars, posters, magazines and T-shirts. Murdoch's cohort of newspapers, magazines, and TV stations ensures that the program is endlessly promoted and some would argue continuously showered by favourable publicity.

The surface impression is that the major American TV networks are dying a slow death because they attract only a declining share of the audience. The explosion in the number of satellite and cable channels, competition from an increasing number of independent stations, the growing video rental market, and the Internet revolution have diverted and fragmented audiences. Where in the 1970s, the three US networks, CBS, NBC and ABC, commanded 98% of the audience, by the year 2000 their audience numbers had plunged to well below 50%. But this portrait is to some degree an optical illusion because it sees the US networks as stand-alone operations rather than as part of a wider corporate and media mix. The same companies that own the US networks also own lucrative cable franchises, and there is a great deal of cross-fertilization between network and cable operations. Disney, which owns ABC, also owns a number of cable gold mines such as ESPN, A&E and the Disney Channel. News Corporation, which owns the Fox network, also owns cable channels such as Fox News, Fox Sports Net and the Family Channel. NBC is linked with the powerful financial channel, CNBC, and to the cable and Internet broadcaster MSNBC that it owns together with Microsoft. Viacom's cable treasure trove includes MTV, Nickelodeon, Comedy Central, Showtime, Country Music Television and the Nashville Network in addition to its ownership of CBS.

When all is said and done, American TV networks have the advantage of economics of scale. With a domestic market that is roughly 10 times the size of Canada's, American TV producers have ample opportunity to recover their costs in their home market. This allows them to dominate the international market place by selling their programs at cut-rate prices. Canadian broadcasters can buy shows "off the shelf" in Hollywood for between one-fifth and one-tenth of the costs of production.[3] It is far cheaper to buy an American program than it is to produce a Canadian show from scratch.

The dominant position of US network shows is continually reinforced by the fact that Hollywood TV shows simply have more production value—they boast more production fire power—than Canadian, Australian or European programs. With budgets of $2–3 million (US) per episode or more, hit US shows can overpower the competition. They have been audience tested, have better technical quality, can afford more expensive sets, are buttressed by teams of highly paid writers and other talent, boast a cavalcade of recognizable stars, and are hyped and marketed by huge global media conglomerates that own newspapers, magazines and other media.

Canadian television is built on different foundations and has different objectives. The Canadian system is heavily subsidized by the federal government and has a crown corporation, the CBC-Radio-Canada, as one of its main engines. While American television does have a public component, the Corporation for Public Broadcasting, which controls the Public Broadcasting Service (PBS) and National Public Radio (NPR), receives far less government funding than the CBC and is heavily dependent on corporate sponsorships and membership drives.

The Canadian television system is a complex hybrid of very different options and entities. At the core is the publicly funded CBC-Radio-Canada. But there are also educational and community channels such as Now TV. TV Ontario and Radio-Quebec, which are supported by private cable operators or provincial governments. Private networks such as CTV, Global, the French-language TVA and a host of independent stations attract the lion's share of the audience. In addition there is a long picket fence of specialized cable services including such channels as TSN, Newsworld, YTV, History Television, Space: The Imagination Station, and Much Music as well as a tier of pay-per-view choices.

Even the CBC is a phalanx of networks and services. The CBC consists of the main English- and French-language TV channels, Radio One (AM) and Radio Two (FM) in both languages, Newsworld and the Reseau de L'Information, both 24-hour all-news networks, Newsworld International, which only broadcasts outside of Canada, northern services that broadcast in native languages, Radio Canada International, and a very extensive and impressive web site. The CBC remains the largest journalistic organization in Canada with almost one in five Canadian journalists working for the crown corporation. Roughly 70% of its schedule is devoted to what can be described as news and current affairs programming.

In 1997–98, the CBC had a total operating budget of $1,128 billion with two-thirds of that money coming from an annual grant from Parliament, a grant that has been reduced by approximately one-third over the last decade. The rest of the CBC's budget came from advertising, sales and other revenues. Unlike the American networks that are driven wholly by commercial imperatives and aim their programs at demographic groups that have high incomes, the CBC has a mandate geared to public needs and services. The mandate is enshrined in the Broadcasting Act of 1991 which stipulates that the public broadcaster must among other duties:

1) offer programs that are uniquely Canadian
2) "contribute to shared national consciousness and identity"
3) give expression to regional and linguistic differences as well as reflect the country's multicultural spirit
4) provide programming that "informs, enlightens and entertains."

The CBC is also the broadcaster of record, covering the major events of the Canadian political calendar. The CBC is there to cover federal and provincial elections, the opening of Parliament, federal and provincial budgets, Canada Day festivities and Remembrance Day services, and events of national significance such as the signing of the Nisga'a Treaty or the funeral for Jean Drapeau, the legendary mayor of Montreal. While commercial broadcasters may cover some of these events they are unlikely to provide the wall-to-wall in-depth coverage that the CBC does. They are leery about any kind of programming that will not draw audiences and advertisers, the bread and butter of their existence. They are more than happy to leave this kind of public affairs coverage to the CBC.

In the last decade the CBC has been wounded by budget cuts that have made it far more difficult for the public broadcaster to fulfill its mandate. With its budget having been reduced by at least one-third, the CBC has been in a continual state of disarray. Thousands of employees have been let go, stations have been closed, major projects have been shelved, shows are broadcast repeatedly and schedules have been turned inside out. All of this bleeding has made the CBC less attractive and less competitive. The CBC's audience share plummeted from almost 22% in 1984–85 to less than 10% in 1999.[4]

Perhaps the most important provisions of the Broadcasting Act, what some consider its heart and soul, are the Canadian content requirements. "CanCon" applies to television as well as radio. TV broadcasters must set aside 60% of their daily schedule for Canadian content programs. Commercial broadcasters can reduce their CanCon programming to 50% during prime time (6 P.M. to midnight). But under recent changes, they must also provide at least eight hours of Canadian drama per week in that lucrative time period. To qualify as CanCon, Canadian programs are judged according to a point system. Points are awarded based on the citizenship of key production personnel—performers, editors, writers, and so on, and on the percentage of services supplied by Canadians. In all cases the producer must be Canadian. If a program receives a score of 10 out of 10 then, in effect, the board lights up and extra CanCon time credits are awarded.

Canadian content provisions have been criticized from a number of perspectives. W.T. Stanbury, a professor of business at the University of British Columbia, believes that the imposing of CanCon requirements could be considered a violation of a citizen's right to freedom of expression.[5] His argument is that by dictating the nationality of the people that are allowed to make TV programs, the Broadcast Act has narrowed the choices available to citizens. Viewers have a right to be exposed to any and all views, and to all forms of cultural expression, to be open to the world of influences, regardless of borders and nationalities. Others argue, of course, that without CanCon commercial broadcasters in particular would have little incentive to air Canadian programs at all because they can make far more money buying programs in Hollywood than making original shows in Canada. Canadians would, in effect, be exposed to stories from across the globe but see little of our own reflection on TV.

Another problem is that CanCon as presently defined does not deal with program content. In what some see as the convoluted and twisted world of CanCon, a program can be about pollution on Australian beaches or gambling in Las Vegas and still qualify as Canadian content. The measure, the yard marker, is not whether Canadian themes or issues are being addressed but simply the citizenship of those who produce, act in or work on the program. If the TV show or film is over the high jump bar in terms of Canadian citizens, then the actual content doesn't matter. Theoretically a program could feature great Canadian divas such as Celine Dion or Shania Twain, and therefore qualify as CanCon, even though their songs might not mention Canada in any way.

Another problem is that with the advent of new information technologies, CanCon may become obsolete simply because such regulations will be impossible to enforce. In an era when all media are merging one into the other, when the telephone, cable, satellites and computer are all converging, the imposition of national standards may be impossible. For instance, it won't be long before virtually everything on the World Wide Web will be available on television. Viewers relaxing with their proverbial beer and chips will be able to access web sites from anywhere on the globe, and many of these sites will contain programming. In the new world, the defensive walls that were erected to defend cultural sovereignty are likely to come tumbling down. Some argue that CanCon's days are numbered.

The philosophy adopted by the Canadian Radio-television and Telecommunications Commission (CRTC), the body that regulates all aspects of Canada's electronic highway, is that everything should be done to make commercial broadcasting profitable. The presumption is that as broadcasters such as CTV, Global and TVA became stronger, they will spend more on Canadian programming. To ensure profits, however, governments have stepped into the breach, buttressing commercial broadcasters with subsidies, tax breaks and other advantages. It is also argued that broadcast regulations are weighted—are tilted—so that they favour commercial broadcasters.

First, commercial broadcasters are shielded to at least some degree from the full force, the full onslaught, of US network competition. Through what is known as simultaneous substitution, American TV signals are blocked, erased, when Canadian and American stations air the same programs at the same time. In fact, Canadian broadcasters often deliberately jig their schedules so that they broadcast hit series like *Frasier, E.R.* and *Friends* at the same times that the programs are being aired on American stations. Thus viewers receive Canadian feeds, and most crucially Canadian advertising, instead of signals from across the border. According to one estimate, simulcasting brings roughly $100 million annually into the coffers of Canadian networks.

Canadian broadcasters also benefit from provisions of the Income Tax Act which discourage Canadian companies from advertising on US border stations. Without this tax wall, TV stations in places like Plattsburg, N.Y., Buffalo, Detroit or Seattle, whose signals spill across the border, would draw tens of millions of dollars in advertising each year away from their Canadian competitors.

Canadian broadcasters, including the CBC, also benefit from an array of funding programs and tax breaks. The Canadian Television and Cable Production Fund (three-quarters of which comes from the federal government and the rest from the cable industry) and Telefilm Canada play a major role in launching TV and film projects. Their funding often mean the difference between life and death for a film or TV series. Without this crucial injection of capital, quite a number of important Canadian programs would never have seen the light of day. Programs such as *Cold Squad, Traders, Road to Avonlea, The Newsroom, More Tears, The City* and *Due South* among other shows were nurtured on a thick broth of public funds. Added to the mix are generous federal and provincial tax breaks that are used to offset a significant portion of labour and location costs. When all is said and done, public money often accounts for well over 50% of the costs of producing a Canadian film or TV series.

Critics argue that the existence of "hit" Canadian programs has done little to wean private broadcasters off American programming. The great irony is that the basic economics of the broadcasting industry run counter to and undermine the objectives of the federal government's policy. In order to become profitable and hence more Canadian, commercial broadcasters have first had to become more American. The bottom line is that it is far more profitable to buy shows in Hollywood—with their glitz and stars, almost guaranteed audiences and advertisers and heavy promotion in the US media—than to produce a Canadian program from scratch. Producing Canadian shows not only involves an enormous creative and financial effort, but it also entails tremendous risks. Unlike US shows that have the benefit of a large domestic market. Canadian producers have to sell their shows in the US and overseas in order to recoup their costs. And while big media empires can afford to have a number of shows that flop, a couple of big misses can be catastrophic to—can sink—a Canadian company or even a network.

While Canadian broadcasters have made great strides in terms of bringing Canadian stories to the TV screen, they also know that American shows are their proverbial meat in the sandwich. According to statistics from one Canadian network, American TV shows bring in approximately $2 in revenue for every dollar that they cost. Canadian shows bring in roughly 62 cents for every dollar that is invested.[6] The deficit with regard to Canadian programming can be put another way: an hour of Canadian drama usually costs broadcasters $200,000 in licence and rental fees. Advertising normally brings in only about $125,000 per hour.[7]

Small wonder that Canadian commercial TV showcases its US programs. In terms of audience share, which is the gold standard on which the TV industry is based, the top 20 programs in the Toronto market in spring 1998 were all big-ticket American shows.[8] If one factors in the programming from US border stations, cable channels and superstations, the harsh reality is that at least two-thirds of the shows watched by English Canadians are American. Among francophone viewers, who are sheltered by the protective cover of the French language, almost 70% of programs that they watch are Canadian. As Ivan Fecan, the president of CTV, once expressed the basic conundrum of Canadian TV: "People don't watch flags, they watch good shows."[9]

Moreover the situation may be worsening. While the explosion of new channels along the cable frontier has created many important opportunities for new initiatives, this has also led to a fragmentation of the audience. Cable channels have begun to drain viewers away from the main Canadian networks that are the main producers of Canadian television. Indeed in 1999 over 20% of the audience were glued to US and Canadian cable channels.[10] Even within the thick forest of cable offerings, the Canadian presence may be diminishing. The CRTC's decision to allow one new American cable channel in the door for every two Canadian cable services that have been established means that US cable titans such as CNN, HBO, CNBC, A&E and the Learning Channel have access to Canadian audiences.

While the Canadian television industry has had its share of successes and has emerged as an important player on the international stage, the problem of Canadians being saturated by US programs remains a serious one. In fact, to some degree the American media giants that dominate Hollywood are larger and more influential than they have ever been.

The Magazine Wars

To some degree the challenges that the Canadian magazine industry faces are the mirror image of those that have plagued Canadian television. Huge media conglomerates control much of the distribution and use magazines as part of a larger media strategy, American magazines dominate sales, and Canadian magazines are struggling to maintain their footholds in the Canadian market. The federal government, as is the case with television, has passed legislation to protect the magazine industry from the American invasion and provide subsidies to keep the industry afloat. The same drama, with the same actors—massive media empires, the federal government and a fragile vulnerable industry—is played out in a slightly different way.

American magazines, much like US TV networks, are part and parcel of the entertainment conglomerates within which they operate. AOL-Time Warner (AOL-

TW), for instance, owns a whole stable of valuable magazine properties—*Time, People, Sports Illustrated, Fortune, Life, Entertainment Weekly, In Style,* and many more. While these magazines are each expected to turn a profit, they are also promotional vehicles used to pump and spin other AOL-Time Warner media products. They cannot be seen as operating apart from Warner Brothers studios which produces blockbuster films and top-rated TV programs; cable holdings such as CNN, Cinemax and HBO; giant music labels such as Atlantic and Elektra; its impressive publishing arm, Warner Books; America Online, with its 20 million Internet subscribers; sports franchises that include the Atlanta Braves in baseball, the NHL's Atlanta Thrashers and the Atlanta Hawks in basketball, not to mention stadiums and theme parks. For instance, CNN has aggressively linked its programs and web sites with TW magazines. Its show *Sports Tonight* has been teamed with *Sports Illustrated* so that each feeds and supports the other.

In these circumstances, it's often difficult to know where journalism leaves off and self-promotion begins. When the movie *Eyes Wide Shut* was being released in the summer of 1999, *People* magazine featured the film's two stars, Tom Cruise and Nicole Kidman, on its front cover. In this case it was hard to discern whether the magazine was celebrating the release of an intriguing and sensational film, the last Stanley Kubrick epic, or whether the magazine was merely pumping a movie that had been made by Warner Brothers. Similarly when Ted Turner, a Time Warner Vice-President, is featured on *Time's* front cover because of his contributions to charity, it's not clear whether the AOL-TW publicity machine is in full throttle or play is being given to a genuine news and human-interest story.

Rupert Murdoch's News Corporation also owns a bevy of important magazines as a result of buying Triangle publications from Walter Annenberg in 1988. Murdoch's holding's include such lucrative titles as *TV Guide, Elle, Seventeen,* and the *Daily Racing Form. TV Guide* is especially valuable since it can be used to promote programs on the Fox network and channels on Murdoch's cable and satellite empire. Apparently Murdoch goes to considerable lengths to ensure that his magazines have pride of place at check-out counters and at newstands. It is difficult to compete with publications that "own" the prime magazine-buying locations.

The largest publisher of monthly magazines in the US is the Hearst Corporation. Founded by newspaper titan William Randolph Hearst, the subject of a brilliant portrayal by actor and director Orson Welles in the classic film, *Citizen Kane,* the Hearst Corporation has spread its wings into local TV and cable as well as magazines. Its mainstays include name brands such as *Cosmopolitan, Esquire, Popular Mechanics, Good Housekeeping,* and *Town & Country.* Significantly, Hearst has produced magazines and web sites that are offshoots of its cable TV properties—ESPN, The History Channel and Arts & Entertainment among others. A trip to the newsstand becomes an advertisement for other Hearst products.

Not every American magazine, of course, is part of a large media conglomerate. The prestigious Conde Nast is a company that has focused almost exclusively on the magazine business. It has specialized in upscale publications such as *Vanity Fair, Vogue, GQ, Tatler,* and *The World of Interiors* that appeal to those with money to spend on fashions, beauty products and vacations. And of course there are strong independent voices such as the *Atlantic Monthly, The New Republic,* and *The National Review* that are driven by intellectual or ideological causes.

The Canadian magazine industry is not structured in the same way as the American industry. While one company, Maclean Hunter, has a dominant position in the Canadian market producing such venerable and glossy titles as *Chatelaine, Maclean's, L'Actualite, Flare,* and *Canadian Business* among others, Maclean Hunter is a minor league player compared to its American rivals. It does not own a whole phalanx of other media properties and does not have the capacity to make inroads in the US in the same way that American magazines can flood the Canadian market.

As is the case with other Canadian publishers, Maclean Hunter believes that it is vulnerable and under attack. The problem is the relatively new practice by American magazines of producing "split-run" editions for the Canadian market. Split-runs are special Canadian editions of US publications that keep most of their American content but contain enough Canadian content to be able to qualify as a domestic publication. While *Time* and *Reader's Digest* have been allowed by special exemption to publish split-run editions because they both produced popular Canadian editions before legislation banning split-runs was put in place, it was *Sports Illustrated (SI)* that upset the apple cart when it began publishing split-run editions in 1993. Keeping their American edition largely intact, *SI* would insert articles on Blue Jays baseball or on the NHL into their "Canadian" edition. It would then use the leverage that it had as part of a megamedia corporation to undercut the advertising rates charged by Canadian magazines. Soon as many as 100 other American magazines were threatening to follow *SI*'s strategy in leaping across the border.

Fearing that Canadian magazines would be decimated by the onslaught, in 1995, the federal government moved to impose an 80% tax on the advertising revenues garnered from split-run editions. What followed was a rough-and-tumble battle between the US and Canadian governments over access by American magazines to the Canadian market. When the World Trade Organization ruled in favour of the Americans in 1997, the federal government responded by passing Bill C-55, a bill designed to limit the amount of Canadian advertising that could appear in split-runs. The American government immediately upped the ante, threatening what amounted to a full-scale trade war if Canada continued to resist the US magazine invasion. With the Americans threatening sanctions against Canadian exports of steel, apparel, wood and plastics, industries that accounted for almost $5 billion a year in exports, the Canadian government finally agreed to a compromise in May 1999. Bill C-55 was amended so that the amount of Canadian advertising that could go into split-runs would be limited to 18% of their total advertising space at the end of three years. If American magazines want to "go over the top" and attract more Canadian advertising, at least half of all of their editorial content will have to be Canadian.

Spokespeople for the Canadian magazine industry reacted to the agreement by predicting virtual doom for the industry. If all of the major US magazines that entered the country sold 18% of their ad space to Canadian advertisers (and these are often thick book-like editions swollen with ads), there would be only the thinnest of pickings left over for Canadian magazines. Brian Segal, the editor of *Maclean's,* argued that the numbers just don't add up. According to Segal, the top 13 women's magazines in the US sell a total of 19,000 pages of advertising each month. The top seven Canadian women's magazines sell 4,800 pages. With the door open to split-runs, the American magazines would be allowed to eat up 3,000 pages in a small market that previously consisted of only 4,800 pages.[11] In addition, there are concerns that much of what Canadians will read about their own country will be produced by American magazine companies. Writers for magazines such as *Time, Newsweek, Cosmopolitan* or *Fortune,* even if they are Canadian, are likely, it is argued, to see Canada through an American view-finder, unselfconsciously imposing American priorities, styles and perspectives.

Even before this last magazine war, Canadian publishers felt that they were under considerable pressure. American and foreign publications already dominate Canadian newsstands. While Canadian magazines account for some 50% of all magazine sales including those bought through subscriptions, American publications constitute 80% of all newsstand sales.[12] Canadian publishers complain about having to fight for space, of being crowded out by the sheet number and popularity of glossy US brand-name magazines.

Following its decision to water down Bill C-55, the federal government faced a deluge of criticism from not only the magazine publishers but from Canadian nationalists generally. They accused the government of buckling under US pressure, of giving up the battle without firing a shot. The federal government's response followed an old familiar pattern. The government promised to provide subsidies to Canadian magazines so that they could withstand the wave of split-run editions that everybody now expects. One is reminded of the famous saying attributed to the ancient philosopher, Thucydides: "The strong do what they can, the weak suffer what they must."

Contending with the Power of Canada's Newspaper Barons

Although the television and magazine industries illustrate some of the differences between the Canadian and American media cultures, similar patterns seem to have emerged in the politics of both industries. Huge American conglomerates dominate much of the Canadian landscape while the federal government mounts protectionist policies that provides much of the oxygen that sustains the Canadian industries. The situation with regard to newspapers is very different. What distinguishes Canadian newspapers from their American counterparts is the enormous concentration of ownership that exists in the Canadian newspaper industry. Approximately 70% of Canadian newspaper circulation is controlled by only three chains—Hollinger/Southam, Thomson and Quebecor. In the US, 75% of circulation is in the hands of 19 companies.[13] While some of the American chains are quite large and many American cities lack significant newspaper competition, no ownership group has a lock on entire provinces or segments of the market as is the case in Canada. Moreover, roughly 25% of American newspapers are independently owned, including family-run corporations like *The Washington Post* and *The New York Times,* arguably the two most powerful and influential newspapers in the United States, if not the world.[14] In English Canada, only the *Toronto Star*—a sizable media conglomerate in its own right—can be considered an independent voice. *La Presse* and *Le Devoir,* arguably the two most influential newspapers in Québec, can also be classified as being independent.

The name most identified with the Canadian newspaper industry is Conrad Black. Black, through his ownership of Hollinger/Southam, controls close to 60 Canadian newspapers including the newly founded national newspaper, the *National Post,* and most of the venerable old lions of the Canadian newspaper industry—the *Victoria Times Colonist,* the *Vancouver Sun,* the *Vancouver Province,* the *Calgary Herald,* the *Edmonton Journal,* the *Windsor Star,* the *Ottawa Citizen,* the *Gazette* (Montreal), *le Soleil* (Quebec City) and the *Halifax Daily News* among others. Black's newspapers reach approximately 2.4 million readers daily, almost 45% of total Canadian circulation.[15] His companies own all of the major dailies in five provinces—British Columbia, Alberta, Saskatchewan, Prince Edward Island and Newfoundland. Black's Canadian holdings are only part of a newspaper empire that includes such landmark publications as the *Daily Telegraph* (London), the *Jerusalem Post* and the *Chicago Sun Times.*

Black's near stranglehold on the Canadian newspaper industry has stirred considerable controversy. Black's critics argue that there is simply too much power in the hands of a single individual. They worry that Black's strong rightwing political beliefs and passions, and his penchant for lecturing journalists and politicians, are inevitably reflected in the editorial content of the newspapers that he owns. Black hires in his own image, and his publishers are well aware of what will please and what will anger their boss. Critics also point out that Black, who is a British as well as a Canadian citizen, and who spends most of his time in London as a fixture of London high society, has shown a decreasing interest in Canada and tends to see the country as little more than a backwater. But it's the sheer lack of choice, the lack of alternative perspectives, that most concerns critics of the current situation. Not only are many readers trapped in one-newspaper towns, but in many Canadian cities advertisers have to accept Hollinger/Southam rates or face the prospect of not being able to advertise in newspapers at all.

Observers are also concerned that while the *National Post* has offered competition to the *Globe and Mail* on the national level, thus adding to the editorial choices available to readers, Black has created a two-tiered system within his media empire. While the *National Post* has been made into a flagship newspaper which pays competitive salaries and gives writers a great deal of space for their articles and columns, the fear is that it has reduced other papers in the chain to minor league status. The *National Post* often takes the best stories away from papers like the *Calgary Herald* or the *Halifax Daily News,* reducing them to reporting strictly local news or to news "lite" accounts of stories that receive greater play in the *Post.* Papers in the farm system are becoming less distinctive as they are forced to fit a "cookie-cutter" mold dictated by head office. Part of the model requires them to cut costs by hiring young reporters at reduced salaries, doing less investigative work and using more wire service copy. In the end, local newspapers have been weakened: some would say that they have been reduced to hollow shells.

Supporters of Conrad Black would dispute every one of these charges. They would argue that Black is one of the few businessmen who had actually invested in the newspaper business in the last decade. The *National Post* has added to the mix of views available to newspaper readers, and as a national newspaper it has contributed to and strengthened awareness of Canadian arts and culture. And far from having weakened local papers, Black has saved quite a number of papers from extinction. Some papers were in critical condition before Black provided the financial oxygen that they needed to survive.

His supporters also contend that while he has strong—even fierce—political views, he does not meddle in editorial policy. And even if he did, a newspaper baron such as Black has far less influence in shaping public opinion today than was true in the heyday of American newspaper titans such as William Randolph Hearst or Walter Annenberg. They were able to flex raw political muscle by supporting some political leaders while ignoring or damning others. While the extraordinary nature of Black's power is seen as potentially dangerous by some, its also true that satellites, cable and the Internet have expanded horizons so that readers have access to a cacophony of news choices and views. They are not dependent on newspapers, in fact far from it. At the click of a mouse, readers can literally be almost anywhere on the globe. Moreover, there is speculation that newspapers will soon become an endangered species because new information technologies will drastically cut into their advertising and readership.

Those who believe that Black has a grip on too much power are also disturbed by the fact that other newspaper owners seem to share Black's staunch conservative views. Quebecor owns the Sun Media Corporation, with its fleet of tabloid newspapers in Toronto, Calgary, Edmonton, Winnipeg, and Ottawa. It also owns *Le Journal de Montreal,* which has the second largest circulation in Canada, the *London Free Press* and a smattering of other newspapers in Quebec and the Maritimes. Sun President and CEO, Paul Godfrey, a former elected politician, is a rock ribbed conservative. The *Suns'* rough-and-tumble reporting of and fascination with car crashes, celebrities, sports heroes and women's bodies belies an editorial slant that is unabashedly right of centre. The *Suns* are continually cheerleading for many of the same causes that have become the grist for the *National Post*'s editorial mill.

Critics can also gain little comfort from the editorial positions taken by the *Globe and Mail,* which is owned by the giant Thomson Corporation. The *Globe* is the *National Post*'s deadly rival in the battle to remain Canada's national newspaper, and the two seemed locked in a contest for many of the same readers—upscale, business-oriented consumers. Although the *Globe* often focuses on charting social trends and is not afraid to ruffle the feathers of Ottawa politicians of every stripe, its editorial views tend to fall in line with those of the business community. The *Globe*'s establishment credentials, its dark grey respectability, are hard to miss.

The issue is not that almost all newspapers tend to be conservative in their editorial policies. If newspapers were all left-leaning or liberal the question would be the same: are readers being given the full range of views that they need in order to make informed judgments about the nature of communities in which they live? Some observers believe that for all of the controversy about ownership, citizens are being provided with a rich smorgasbord of views and perspectives. Owners realize that readers will simply not read newspapers that continually take positions that irritate them, or that fail to provide them with the "spite and spit" that they expect from their newspapers. With so many other media to choose from, newspapers can be easily abandoned. Others claim that Canadians are getting a thin diet of views and have little choice in what to digest.

The structure of the newspaper industry differs considerably from that of television and magazines. Where Canadian television viewers and magazines readers are effectively part of a wider North American market in which Canadian content is a cherished and protected resource, newspapers remain one of Canada's great nationalizing institutions. While American news stories and American wire service copy are part of any newspaper, a national and local focus predominates. Hence newspapers play a critical role in offsetting the integrating power, the north-south gravitational pull, of other media. The future of Canadian cultural sovereignty is likely to be linked at least to some degree with the future of newspapers.

Conclusion

Canadians and Americans largely inhabit the same media universe. As a result, American images, products, priorities and values have become part of the way that Canadians see the world. The American experience as conveyed through the lens of the mass media has also become part of our experience. Yet a distinct, successful and powerful media tradition has taken root in Canada. Institutions like the CBC, *Maclean's,* the *Globe and Mail,* CTV and *La Presse* are part of the fabric of Canadian life. While each of these institutions is likely to face difficult challenges in the years ahead, especially as new information technologies begin to scramble, reorient and displace the old media, they each have established traditions and loyalties that will not easily be erased.

The issue perhaps is whether a distinct Canadian media system could stand on its own if it were not propped up by protectionist legislation, subsidies and tax breaks. Historically there have been two schools of thought on this question. One school believes that the Canadian media system is strong and vibrant enough to withstand any and all pressures from south of the border. If the protectionist walls were removed, Canadian media industries would still draw audiences and readers and produce distinctive and creative Canadian programs and magazines. Canadians will inevitably turn to their own cultural products, turn to images that reflect their identity and concerns. The more pessimistic position is that without protectionist barriers, the American invasion—the American conquest—would even be more complete than it is today. Canadians are simply, to use Pierre Trudeau's famous analogy, "lying in bed with an elephant." Even if the elephant is a friendly elephant, it still has the capacity to crush anyone who gets too close. Some feel that the elephant has already rolled on top of us, doing a great deal of damage to prospects for Canadian cultural independence.

The two media systems described in this article live in conflict and symbiosis with each other. They are not mutually exclusive at least from the Canadian point of view. Living with and measuring our own sense of self against the values of American mass culture has long been one of the defining characteristics of being a Canadian. Scholars such as Seymour Martin Lipset argue that Canada emerged in part as a conservative reaction to and rejection of the values of the American Revolution.[16] The question posed by John Meisel is whether we are now so immersed in American culture that there is no longer a clear distinction between who they are and who we are?

Notes

1. John Meisel, "Escaping Extinction: Cultural Defence of an Undefended Border," in David Flaherty and William McKercher, eds., *Southern Exposure: Canadian Perspectives on the United States* (Toronto: McGraw Hill Ryerson, 1986), 12.
2. John Meisel, "Extinction Revisited: Culture and Class in Canada," in Helen Holmes and David Taras, eds., *Seeing Ourselves: Media Power and Policy in Canada* (Toronto: Harcourt Brace Canada, 1996), 249–56.
3. See W.T. Stanbury, "Canadian Content Regulations: The Intrusive State at Work." *Fraser Forum* (August 1998), 49.
4. See *Report of the Mandate Review Committee—CBC, NFB, Telefilm* (Ottawa: Minister of Supply and Services Canada, 1996) and Canadian Broadcasting Corporation. *Annual Report 1997–98: A Summary.*
5. Stanbury. "Canadian Content Regulations," 7.
6. Liss Jeffrey, "Private Television and Cable," in Michael Dorland, ed., *The Cultural Industries in Canada: Problems, Policies and Prospects* (Toronto: Lorimer, 1996), 245.
7. Stanbury, "Canadian Content Regulations," 50.
8. Jacquie McNish and Janet McFarland, "Izzy Asper Ascends to TV's Throne," *Globe and Mail* (August 22, 1998), B5.
9. Quoted in Susan Gittens, *CTV: The Television Wars* (Toronto: Stoddart, 1999), 333.

10. Canadian Media Director's Council, *Media Digest 1997–98,* 19.
11. Brian Segal quoted in Heather Scoffield, "Publishers Greet Split-run Deal with Dismay," *Globe and Mail* (May 27, 1999), B4.
12. "Canada's Magazines," *Globe and Mail* (May 27, 1999), B1.
13. Gene Roberts, "Conglomerates and Newspapers," in Erik Barnouw et al., *Conglomerates and the Media* (New York: The New Press, 1997), 72.
14. Gene Roberts, "Conglomerates and Newspapers."
15. Statistics drawn from Tim Jones, "That Old Black Magic," *Columbia Journalism Review* (March–April 1998), 40–43.
16. Seymour Martin Lipset, *Continental Divide: The Values and Institutions of the United States and Canada* (Toronto and Washington: C.D. Howe Institute and National Planning Association, 1990).

America

Evelyn Lau

ON THE FIRST day of the month that his book was officially on the stands in America, the young Canadian writer rushed to the street and bought every magazine he thought might contain an excerpt, a review, or at least a mention of his book. *Esquire, GQ, The New Yorker, Vogue* . . . he tore the pages in his haste to find the books section, the entertainment page, and "New and Noteworthy." There was nothing in the major publications, and it wasn't until he had reached the bottom of the pile that he found a single review of his book. It was featured in a splashy broadside with unreadable graphics and photographs of scruffy twenty-somethings with canary or pumpkin-coloured hair, brandishing electric guitars. It was a rave review, describing his stories as "plangent," but it failed to cheer him up—he could not imagine a regular reader of such a magazine standing in a bookstore lineup, purchasing a work of literature.

He called his publisher's publicity department to find out what had gone wrong. "I can't believe *GQ* hasn't called to request an interview," he said.

"Well, we did the usual mail-out," the publicist said. "The book's just come out, I'm sure that over the next few months you'll see plenty of reviews in the small magazines. You know, literary magazines sometimes take a year to publish reviews."

"Maybe *GQ* will want to do something after I've gotten some attention elsewhere. Isn't that how it works? After I've launched the book in New York, and visited a few other cities. What are your tour plans for me, anyway?"

The publicist was silent for a moment. The young writer heard the long-distance seconds ticking away in the precious, wasted silence; the publisher had a special block on their telephone line that kept out prospective collect calls from their authors. "As you know, things have changed with the company since you first signed with us. Your editor left for another house, and the staff at the publicity department has completely turned over as well. I'm afraid that the budget we've been given for your book won't allow for a tour."

The writer, who had nursed a hiatus hernia for the last several years—it had developed shortly after he'd published his first book—felt the acid rise in his chest in a hot suffusing column. His heart began to beat faster, and his temples pulsed in unison. Whenever he became angry he could not speak, his throat snagged on every word.

"They said—everyone there said, everyone I spoke to—said I'd be coming. That I'd go on tour. Everyone kept saying. 'When you're in New York, you'll meet so-and-so, you'll have dinner at such-and-such a restaurant, you'll launch your book—'"

"It's not written into your contract."

"No, but I was *told*—"

"I'm sorry, there's nothing we can do about it. The publisher might reconsider if something major happened. For example, if your book ended up with a front page review in *The New York Times,* or if someone bought film rights for six or seven figures."

Both of them knew this would never happen. He heard the sour edge of amusement in the publicist's voice. He said, "Thanks a *lot*," and hung up the phone. He sat for a while on his couch, rubbing his sternum, looking around the small, boxy apartment where he worked, lived and slept. It was all he could afford with his Canadian royalties; it was a far cry from the palatial homes of some American writers, whose book sales had the opportunity of being at least ten times as large as their colleagues' to the north.

After a few minutes his breathing slowed, and he picked up the phone and called the publicist back to apologize, so she would not harm his chances by doing even less for his book than she was already doing.

A few days later, the publicist called the writer, her voice full of cheer. "I've got good news for you!"

"What?" *Front page of The New York Times . . .*

"We've had another look at your budget, and we've decided we can put you on a bus to Seattle, since it's not too far across the border from you. You'll do a reading, and some interviews. Isn't that wonderful?"

"A bus."

"We'll also put you up for two nights," she continued. "You'll stay in the hotel we always use."

The publishing company had money, which they did not spend on their literary authors but lavished on their authors whose books promised commercial success. They had just published an exposé of the Hollywood film industry by a well-placed executive, for whom they had rented billboards all along Sunset Boulevard depicting his face and the cover of his book.

The young writer consoled himself with the thought that at least he would have a decent place to sleep, and he planned to order lavish meals from room service which he would charge to the publisher.

When the greyhound bus rolled to a stop in front of the Customs office, the young writer elbowed past the other passengers to the front of the line. This way, he reasoned, the officer would see the line of twenty or so exasperated, weary travellers behind him and wave him through quickly. To his surprise, his plan worked, and he stepped jauntily outside to wait by the conveyor belt for the others behind him to clear Customs. It was a crisp Spring day and he shivered a bit in his thin sweater, watching the American and Canadian flags snap side by side above a duty-free store across the highway. On other occasions this proximity to America the land where the unlikeliest people could attain wealth, fame and sex—had brought romantic tears to his eyes, but not this time. He was cold, and wished he was back inside the Customs office. Eventually the bus driver pulled up to the exit and he and others were able to climb aboard, but they still had to wait for several other passengers to be cleared.

At the front of the bus, a man who looked to be in his mid-thirties, with pallid skin and a goatee, struck up a conversation with the elderly woman sitting across the aisle from him. "The last time I crossed the border I was going to see my grandparents, and the guy went through all my bags. He kept asking all these questions. I was going to visit my grandparents, for God's sake!"

The woman clucked sympathetically. "This time I'm visiting my daughter and her husband. I was just in the hospital, not for anything serious. I'd been having these pains. It turned out to be a bruised rib and a hiatus hernia, that's all."

"I'm twenty-five," the man announced. "And I have ulcers. The doctor thought it might be bacteria, but they did a gastroscopy and found nothing. So it's stress induced. I have a hernia too, and gastritis. All this at my age!" he added, half in horror, half boastfully.

The writer looked wearily out the window. He was twenty-four years old, and his body was falling apart. He too had ulcers, and had had to drink a thick, nauseating cup of barium which he then watched travel haltingly down his insides on a monitor in the X-ray room where he lay on a metal table. Seeing his live, mortal organs contract ghostily on the screen had made him aware of his own vulnerability. Lately he had taken to lying awake at night and worrying about posterity— would his work survive him, and if so, for how long? Books went out of print so rapidly these days, and more and more books were being published every season, more already in the last century than in all the years previously, since the beginning of time. Why would anyone chose to read him? He was only adding to the impossible clutter in libraries and bookstores, remainder bins where even books by famous, dead authors sold for two dollars or less. Already he had given a reading where a bright-eyed college girl, clutching one of his books for him to sign, had confessed, "Actually, I didn't buy it full price. Your publisher was clearing its warehouse, and I bought a huge box off hardcover books for twenty dollars. I was so *happy* to find your book among the others!"

The bus was quiet for the next half hour, except for the occasional rustle of plastic snack wrappers, and someone who was biting into an apple with loud, cracking noises that made the writer's own teeth—weak and, in the words of one amazed dentist, "phenomenally eroded" from night-time gnashing and grinding—ache sympathetically. At last the couple who had held up the bus came on board. They were black, and they both wore suits in an extraordinary shade of banana. The man looked like a pimp in his wing-tip shoes. "Sorry about that, ladies and gentlemen," the man said, raising his hand, lurching forward as the bus driver gunned the motor and the bus hastened, behind schedule, into America.

As he had anticipated, his hotel was magnificent. An enormous arrangement of flowers scented the lobby—lilies, paintbrushes and the branches of a flowering quince, which made him think of that famous short story, "The Japanese Quince." The floors and counters were marble, and the furniture covered in silk. A bellhop took him up to his room, a 900 square-foot suite with exposed brick walls and two fireplaces. Unaccustomed to so much space, the young writer took a long time to unpack, constantly forgetting one item or another in the bedroom or the living room and needing to retrace his steps—something that never required more than a few steps in any direction in his own apartment.

He liked hotel rooms, especially when they were expensive. He loved the televisions with their fifty channels, their remote controls, their wide screens across which a more attractive version of the world shimmered. At home he owned only a small television he had bought at a drugstore, and which did not include either a converter or a remote. In hotel rooms across Canada he had sat transfixed in front of late-night Chinese movies with hilarious subtitles, American talk shows where men and women with bad hair and mottled skin screamed accusations of infidelity at each other, Japanese music shows where diminutive young men pranced around singing outmoded Western pop songs, real estate channels showing split-level houses on spacious lots selling for prices he could never hope to afford . . . unless he made it big in America.

When he picked up the phone to order from room service, he noticed that the receiver smelled faintly but distinctly of the cologne that the guest who had stayed there the night before had used. He was pleased by his own observation, and wrote it down on a piece of hotel stationery so that he might use it later in a story. He was less pleased when, at 5:45 the next morning, two hours before he intended to wake up, the alarm that the previous guest had set and then not bothered to turn off began blipping into his ear—but he reached over to the pad of paper conveniently at his bedside, and wrote that down too.

The morning was occupied with interviews: a radio host whose eyes watered with boredom as they talked, an exquisitely pretty television reporter who laughed insincerely at his jokes, a male journalist from a literary paper who wore black eyeliner and white face powder. A photographer walked him around the block and photographed him in the rain. The young writer wore a dark suit, and was uncomfortable. At home, when he was working he wore a bathrobe with toast crumbs down its front, or sometimes only his underwear. For public appearances he put on sharp, well-cut suits which nonetheless made him feel like a car salesman, a fraud.

His afternoon was free, and a man from the publicity firm who represented the publisher in Seattle drove him around the city for an hour. The publicist had pop eyes that made the young writer think of hard-boiled eggs yet he bragged about his sexual exploits with women. Years ago he had bought a house cheaply and had recently sold it for nearly four times what it was worth. All the women he dated, he claimed, wanted to marry him. Soon he would quit the firm and start a company of his own, but first he would take a long holiday in a warm climate. The writer could not help feeling jealous as he was driven past the commodious homes on the west side, with their emerald lawns, skylights, and staircases which spiralled elegantly behind floor-to-ceiling living room windows.

The reading was scheduled for that evening. The writer went back to his room, took off his suit, watched three talk shows and ordered room service in his sweatpants, put the suit back on, drank a glass of wine for courage, and went down to the lobby at the appointed hour to meet the publicist who would take him to the bookstore. He was nervous about the reading, and his throat was doing funny things in anticipation. When he saw the publicist standing with two other people who turned curiously towards him, he squeaked out, "Hello," in a falsetto voice. Appalled, he swallowed furiously and managed a more subdued greeting as he shook their hands, and then gave him a series of cartoons he had drawn of naked young men with tattooed penises.

The restaurant Fleming had chosen was divided into two levels, and the young writer followed the waiter down a set of stairs to their table by the window. Fleming followed behind him, and he felt the older writer's eyes on his back as they descended, and when he turned to manoeuvre into his chair he saw Fleming watching him as closely as if he were an object he had been asked to describe. Fleming even looked at his shoes, not as though they were on the feet of his lunch companion, but as though he were looking at them in a store window, judging their price, durability and attractiveness. When the young writer was a child he had thought he was the most observant person in the world, that no one was as capable as he was of seeing what others tried to hide about themselves. Now he understood that this was a talent all writers shared to one degree or another. He had to hold himself still under Fleming's gaze. What was the other writer observing about him that caused the corners of his mouth to tilt slightly, secretively, upwards? Was the young writer as naked to other writers' eyes as he liked to think they were to his? He knew he could never be comfortable among other writers, particularly those whose company he coveted. He would see them watching him, and dread the clarity of their observations, and he would see that they knew this, and felt themselves to be watched in turn. . . .

There was a balcony outside their window, and when the sun came out it passed through the railings and landed in bars of yellow across Fleming's face. It was the first time the young writer had seen him in daylight at this proximity, and he was struck by the other man's dissipation. When Fleming propped his chin in his hand he looked like a wizened, cynical monkey, the sleeve of his tweed jacket tightening and puckering over what was a thin, unmuscular arm. His teeth were the colour of English salad cream, and the decay of his breath could be smelled clear across the table. This was oddly stirring, because Fleming was unaware of it, and his eyes were self-assured and boastful above his open, dead mouth.

Fleming immediately lit a cigarette. The young writer tried to lean away from the smoke but it wafted unerringly into his face. Even second-hand smoke disturbed his hernia, set it spasming in his chest so that he could actually feel the sphincter at the base of his esophagus fluttering, and he knew that as a result of these hours with Fleming he would be coughing and nauseated during the bus ride home. Perhaps he would even have to throw up in the narrow, jerking bathroom at the rear of the vehicle. This was the price he was willing to pay for the man's company.

"I've seen some of the press from Canada," Fleming said as their entreés arrived. "You're doing very well for your age I mean, of all the people born in the year that you were born, you're the first writer out of the gate. You've already secured a place among the five people born in that year who will become major writers."

Why then, the young writer thought, am I so afraid? Even now, sitting with Fleming a mere arm's length away, their imminent separation was more real to him than the moment they were sharing. Did he feel his hold on his career, on life itself, to be so tenuous?

"I'm not doing nearly as well as you," he said.

"Oh well, it'll happen. You'll be up to your ears in money before you know it," Fleming said nonchalantly. "The book I'm working on now, I've already been paid half of a six-figure advance. *High* six figures."

The young writer swallowed a forkful of asparagus that seemed to burn his gullet. Outside a high wind blew above the street, and the flowers in their clay pots on the balcony railing fluttered like butterflies. Fleming talked about the only things that seemed to interest him—advances, royalties, and famous people in the publishing industry. He knew people whose bylines often appeared in magazines with circulations a hundred times larger than those of Canadian literary magazines. In some way the young writer had never thought of these authors as real people whose first names could be bandied about over a meal. He mentioned a story he had admired in a recent issue of *The New Yorker,* and Fleming said, "Oh right, the guy who wrote that was at a party I gave last summer. Lots of writers came"—and he named several, the sound of their very names causing the young writer's heart to skip faster. He had to force himself to sit back in his chair; his body was canted forward so sharply with his interest that he was leaning halfway over the table towards the other writer.

"His wife was just awful," Fleming continued. "She was in a bad mood, and she'd had a few drinks, and she went around telling everyone what an awful party it was. Finally she came up to me and snapped, 'I just hate parties like this. Nobody talks to you unless you're famous!'" Fleming grinned, and leaned back in his chair. He looked satisfied, as if the wife's complaint had been a compliment, confirming that his party had indeed been a success.

They lingered over lunch, nursing martinis, until the older writer laid a gold credit card over the bill and it was time to go to the bus station. While they stood on the curb outside the restaurant, waiting for the valet to drive up in Fleming's car, the young writer looked at the older writer's face in the gusting wind. The flesh was loose enough on his bones that it blew slightly on his face as though anchored only here and there—around the eyes, nose and chin—while the rest of it flapped independently. He half expected his face to suddenly blow off like a detached sail, revealing Fleming's actual face beneath.

The young writer sat in a plastic chair in the bus depot, waiting for the Greyhound to pull in at its designated berth. Around him were candy bar and Snapple machines, video terminals, unhappy people who wore several layers of clothing and had lined, dirty faces sunk between their stooped shoulders. He sat there wondering what sort of life Fleming would return to that afternoon. Did he have a family, a woman he loved? Were any of his friends not famous, nor well-connected? The young writer had extended an invitation for Fleming to visit him in Vancouver, but the older man had said a polite, "Will do," with his body already half turned away from him, into the wind. Did he consider what he had to be enough?

The young writer did not know. He felt a sadness disproportionate to the situation, as though he were mourning the loss of someone to whom he had been close. Once again all he had left was his own work, which waited for him now that his tour of America was over.

CHAPTER THIRTEEN

Vive Le Québec Libre: French-Canadian Nationalism in the 1960s

Introduction

As long as there has been a Quebec there has been a Quebec nationalism. Quebec has its own memory and its own myths and Canada means something quite different to French-speaking Quebeckers. In the 1960s many Quebec nationalists embraced separatism: only Quebec's separation from Canada and the achievement of national independence would preserve the French language in North America. Born in 1922, the charismatic, passionate, energetic and brilliant René Lévesque was a powerful Quebec cabinet minister from 1960 to 1966 in the Liberal government of Jean Lesage. Always a fierce and proud Quebecker, Lévesque embraced the separatist option in the 1960s and tried to convince the Quebec Liberal Party to make Quebec's independence part of its policy platform. When he failed he broke with the party and in 1968 he formed the Parti Québécois, a political party dedicated to realizing Quebec's independence through democratic means. A chapter from his memoirs, "A Country That Must Be Made" deals with his decision to leave one party and create another one. Although he was elected premier in 1976, Lévesque failed to convince Quebeckers to support independence in the 1980 referendum. He died in 1987. Of course, Lévesque was not the only Quebecker to embrace separatism in the 1960s. Solange Chaput Rolland, a prominent intellectual, writer and journalist, concluded after travelling across Canada, that her country was not Canada but Quebec. The Quebec playwright and poet, Michèle Lalonde, wrote "Speak White" in 1968. It was performed at the Nuit de la Poésie in March 1970—a self-consciously nationalist event that attracted many French-speaking writers—and published in 1974. What does Lalonde mean by speak white?

A Country That Must Be Made

René Lévesque

HOW LONG IT seemed, that aisle dividing the immense auditorium of the Château Frontenac, down which I walked in quitting the Liberal Party. From one row to the next, I recognized a throng of familiar faces. Some discreetly made friendly little signs, but most, feeling the eyes of the party vigilantes upon them, acted as though I had ceased to exist. Only Gérin-Lajoie dared cross the psychological barrier and step forward with outstretched hand to say good-bye. This pause allowed me to realize that a handful of accomplices had followed and that I wouldn't be completely alone at the exit.

As foreseeable as it had become, this departure cost me something. I recognized members from every region in Quebec along with certain workmates who had crossed over to the opposition with me, remembering all those successes and failures we had shared! We had covered a lot of ground from April, 1960, to October, 1967, and now it was the parting of the ways. I felt a twinge in my heart. As far as the party was concerned, I was frankly relieved to be leaving it. I had never been a real partisan. Maybe I should say straight off that I believe I could never be a party man, no more Péquiste than Liberal. For me any political party is basically just a necessary evil, one of the instruments a democratic society needs when the time comes to delegate to elected representatives the responsibility of looking after its common interests. But parties that last generally age poorly. They have a tendency to transform themselves into lay churches with power to loose and to bind and can turn out to be quite insupportable. In the long run sclerosis of ideas sets in and political opportunism takes over. Every new party should, in my opinion, write into its statutes a clause anticipating its disappearance after a certain time, perhaps after a generation, certainly no longer. If it goes on past this, no matter how much plastic surgery it undergoes to restore its beauty, one day it will be nothing more than a worn-out old thing blocking the horizon and preventing the future from breaking through.

In any event, that's how I had come to see the Liberal Party. There was nothing traumatic about it; I wasn't breaking up with my family, just an old, outmoded party fallen into sterility. It had used me as long as I had seemed profitable to it, and I had used the platform and other means it provided to realize or at least to advance things I believed in. We were quits, all the more so because right up until the last moment I had followed the fundamental rule that requires every member to work loyally within the party framework as long as his conscience will permit.

From *Memoirs* by René Lévesque. Used by permission, McClelland & Stewart Ltd. The Canadian Publishers.

In the normal line of things I had first tried out my ideas on my Laurier riding association, where the sovereignty-association project went down with the greatest of ease, almost unanimously. That surprised me, but it moved me even more. For this neighbourhood assembly, made up of good souls who boasted no more than their title as ordinary citizens, my plan was a question of common sense as well as a perspective on the future that the party should not hesitate to underwrite. In no time, interdictions and threats of excommunication would begin to ring in their ears, and I was sure that many of them would resign themselves to make due apology and request absolution, but for the meantime what could be more encouraging than this spontaneous adhesion by a hundred or so Québécois simply following their reason and their instinct.

Once this stage was passed, the project was officially out in the open, together with the names of those who had worked so hard to articulate it. There could be no doubt that they would be subjected to continuous pressure, or that certain of them would find themselves plunged into a cruel dilemma: either a dive into these untried waters or the very legitimate hope of a more certain and accelerated career.

Nothing guaranteed that a final examination of the project wouldn't reveal risks or weaknesses that hadn't been anticipated clearly enough. That's the reason Robert Bourassa gave for leaving us. At the decisive moment he discovered that the monetary question (which, in all fairness, was to remain one of his most deepseated obsessions right up to 1976) hadn't been scrutinized thoroughly enough for him. Then, one of the very last, Yves Michaud withdrew, almost bringing tears to our eyes with his evocation of the Rocky Mountains, a part of his patrimony it seemed to him as impossible to abandon as his urge to go there one day seemed improbable to the rest of us.

After the usual editorial cacophony, I drew fire from the big guns. Lesage proclaimed that never—and this time a "never" as solid as rock!—would he accept to direct a separatist organization. Eric Kierans let it be known that it was him or me, and that if it was me, he'd leave, slamming the door. Nothing was more predictable than this reflex from an Anglophone who was more Canadian than Québécois. Back when he'd been accused of being the "marionette" of the chief suspect, hadn't he rushed to clear his name? Quebec still wasn't capable of going it alone, he explained, curiously, and even if that changed, he'd still be against the idea! It was the natural slope of his mind, and it ultimately led him to Ottawa, where Trudeau made short work of him.

Opposed by both the leader and the president of the party, I didn't stand much chance. Right up to the eve of my departure, however, I had hoped we would have a proper debate and that perhaps with our skeleton crew of supporters we might rally, say, 10 per cent of the vote. For that, they'd have had to accept a secret ballot. Not only did they refuse to hold one, but as I entered the auditorium I saw Lesage sitting right next to the microphone, on the lookout for trouble. According to rumours circulating in the corridors, it wasn't what I said that was going to be discussed, but my head, and apparently it wasn't even going at a very good price. So when my right to speak to the group one last time was recognized, I expressed myself approximately as follows.

> I want to thank those who have at least allowed our proposition to become a full-fledged motion so that you can see what it says. But I know it has no chance of being studied on its own merits. Without holding anything against those who want to make a scarecrow of it, I think that one day they will see they were wrong. Now all that remains for me to do is to leave, taking with me my share of our common memories and the regret that things had to end this way.

I had left in a deathly silence. Two hours later I found myself in another room whose walls seemed ready to burst. Several hundred exuberant people were crowded in there, young people mostly, making an infernal racket. I couldn't hear myself think and was struck by the fact that even without the delirium the same spirit of spontaneous adhesion was there as with the crowd in my riding association. Carried by this current, I promised that things wouldn't stop there.

It was a bold impulse. If it meant anything more than words in the air, such a promise could only signify one thing—a new political commitment. Scarcely demobilized, was I going to re-enlist so quickly? And so completely? They wanted me as provisional leader of a provisional group that intimated I should take over the no less provisional committee that had just been established. They wanted me, first because I was the most widely known of the bunch, and then because I had started the ball rolling. My acts were catching up with me. "Bah!" I said to myself, wasn't I resigned to go on till 1970 anyway? I would just cross the floor from the Liberal benches to that particular purgatory the House reserves for independent members, that was all.

But it was most urgent to consolidate the provisional before it frittered itself away, as it was eminently likely to do if we didn't take care. In a few weeks we were ready to give birth to a new movement, not a party, just a simple gathering with a minimum of very supple controls to keep it as open and welcoming as possible. That way we would have time to wait for a response that only the population as a whole was capable of supplying. Would it be, as Claude Ryan wrote in *Le Devoir*, the end of a "time of ambiguity"? Or would it be the little "separatist adventure" without a future that other journalists disdainfully foresaw?

The best way to see the situation more clearly was obviously to make public the text that had stirred up such a fuss and which the Liberal Party had buried so hastily it remained largely unknown. Without it, in fact, the name we had given ourselves—Mouvement Souveraineté-Association, or MSA to its friends—risked returning to limbo.

A small book, *Option Quebec*, was soon ready for the press and was launched early in 1968. Working at that speed, in order to bring the weight up to the respectable level required of a serious book, we had to devote more than half our 173 spacey pages to various appendices that mainly reproduced commentaries or statements of support signed by personalities who added a precious dose of credibility to our project.

One of these was none other than Jacques Parizeau. He had already been thinking of joining us when he was called to give a conference at Banff. He prepared his commentary on the transcontinental, the great empty spaces of the Prairies undoubtedly giving him extra inspiration. The text he stepped out of the train with, entitled "Quebec-Canada: A Blind Alley," remains one of the most cruelly exact portraits of the non-sense of the Canadian nation. On the one hand are nine provinces for whom, despite many historical and political differences, belonging together must inevitably exclude "a degree of decentralization that can only be ruinous. . . . As for Quebec, whatever could be offered would necessarily fall short, sooner or later, of what it wants, no matter how generous these propositions might seem at the outset. The answer lies in recognizing frankly that we are faced with two different societies, that efficient economic policies for one are not necessarily efficient for the other because values are different, and that there is no need to sacrifice efficiency for the larger society to accommodate the smaller one, which is likely in any case to be dissatisfied with the compromise."*

It was this same absurdity, seen by the economist under his specialized angle, that we attacked in the two "official" chapters of our thin volume. We locked in hand-to-hand combat with our adversaries, who hadn't hesitated in laying the stick to us at the same time as they dangled a few pale greenhouse carrots before the noses of the Quebec people, like the "biculturalism" that came out of the Laurendeau-Dunton report, which enticed a lot of nationalists whose appetites were modest. Daniel Johnson, for example, who had felt considerable pressure from the De Gaulle affair, made this the occasion to put a good deal of water in the wine of his "Equality or Independence." This slogan, as strong as it was politically sinuous, could be interpreted, according to the needs of the moment, either in the sense of global equality between two distinct nations, or else as so-called cultural equality between two so-called founding peoples. The Quebec Premier took the federal bon-ententist bait: "I have made a sort of bet," he declared, "on the future of Canada in a renewed federalism that rests on cultural duality. . . ."† His vocabulary was sadly outdated and erratic, and a later premier would try to freshen it up a little by daring to use the term cultural "sovereignty" . . . with the same amazing results!

The basis of these snares and delusions was and still is, for our obstinate ostriches, nothing less than the mirage of a bilingual Canada upon which Messrs. Trudeau and Company so shrewdly built their careers. Weren't there to be more and

---

*This and the following excerpts from *Option Quebec* can be found in René Lévesque, *An Option for Quebec* (Toronto, 1968).

†*Le Devoir*, December 1, 1967.

more French employees behind federal wickets? Weren't our minorities outside Quebec learning to let themselves be cuddled by Ottawa as never before despite or because of the fact that they were on the road to extinction?

"And now," I wrote on December 3, 1967 (and would write again today), "how can they get out of this situation? By obtaining, as a host of honest folk and others who are not so honest persist in imagining, advantages comparable to those already enjoyed by Anglo-Québécois? That would mean starting immediately with as good schools, from elementary to university, for minorities that are not well off, are often widely scattered, and, except for New Brunswick, do not make up even half the percentage of Anglophones in Quebec. And what would this incredible effort result in? In launching workers trained in French culture into a marketplace and a climate that is exclusively English. Or more probably in sending them here to Quebec as soon as they graduated (at least that much would be gained).

"In short, what they would like to substitute for the indispensable emancipation of Quebec is the pale shadow of a pious impossibility."

It was based on those assumptions that I had entitled my manifesto "A Country That Must Be Made." The eminently simple theme that I developed in twenty pages or so has had a reception that has always surprised me. For twenty years now it has been a political option that has never ceased to hold favour in many hearts, as well as in the polls. I may be a bad judge, but it seems to me that such persistency is significant. At the very least it shows that the idea is very much alive, even if the firemen of the status quo continue to do all they can to douse the fire under the ashes. Rereading it again for the first time in a long while, I tell myself, I can still live with that, and even, presumptuously, that the day will come when we will finally end up with something of the kind. It's up to the reader to judge.

We Are Québécois

If there is one thing time has never ceased to confirm progressively, it's the permanent truth of the identification I state in my title.

> That means first and foremost, and if need be exclusively, that we are attached to this one corner of the earth where we can be completely ourselves, this Quebec, the only place we have the unmistakable feeling, "here we can be really at home."
>
> Being ourselves is essentially a matter of keeping and developing a personality that has survived three and a half centuries. At the heart of this personality is the fact that we speak French. Everything else depends on this one essential element and follows from it or leads us infallibly back to it.

Then, having evoked the history that made us who we are and gave us the will and stubborn hope that permit us to survive and grow, the manifesto continued:

Until recently in this difficult process of survival we enjoyed the protection of a certain degree of isolation. We lived a relatively sheltered life in a rural society in which a great measure of unanimity reigned, and in which poverty set its limits on change and aspiration alike.

We are children of that society, in which the *habitant,* our father or grandfather, was still the key citizen. We are also heirs to a fantastic adventure—that early America that was almost entirely French. We are, even more intimately, heirs to the group obstinacy which has kept alive that portion of French America we call Quebec. . . .

This is how we differ from other men and especially from other North Americans, with whom in all other areas we have so much in common. This basic "difference" we cannot surrender. . . .

It wasn't that there weren't plenty of opportunities to lose it. I had only to recall the waves of forced abdications that the other provinces and some of the American states had been forced to accept in difficult times, without counting internal exile, uprootings, assimilations. . . .

For a small people such as we are, our minority position on an Anglo-Saxon continent creates from the very beginning a permanent temptation to self-rejection, which has all the attractions of a gentle downward slope ending in comfortable submersion in the Great Whole. . . .

The only way to overcome the danger is to face up to this trying and thoughtless age and make it accept us as we are, succeeding somehow in making a proper and appropriate place for ourselves. . . . This means that we must build a society which, while it preserves an image that is our own, will be as progressive, as efficient, as "civilized" as any in the world.

In fact there are other small peoples who are showing us the way, demonstrating that size is in no way synonymous with maximum progress among human societies. . . .

But I was obliged to confess that we hadn't dared give ourselves this country of our own. We were always claiming that we were building it piece by piece, by means of partial recuperations of power, by statutes that were more or less "special" in tax matters, in social security, in the field of immigration, and in controlling the main instruments of mass culture (radio, television, cable-diffusion). And while we clutched in vain at these disjointed pieces, justice continued to be dislocated, corporate competency fragmented, and our financial networks troubled. Consequently, it was no great merit on my part to arrive at this common-sense conclusion:

Order must be re-established in the chaos of a governmental structure created at a time when it was impossible to foresee the scientific and technical revolution in which we are now caught up, the endless changes it demands, the infinite variety of things produced, the concentration of enterprises, the crushing weight that the greatest of these impose on individual and collective life, the absolute necessity of having a state able to direct, co-ordinate, and above all humanize this infernal rhythm.

It required no great insight to trace the ceaseless see-saw of the Byzantine federal-provincial regime I had been involved in and to show that such an objective was simply a dream in the context of Canadian institutions.

From a purely revisionist point of view, our demands would seem to surpass both the best intentions displayed by the "other majority" and the very capacity of the regime to make concessions without an explosion. . . .

If Quebec were to begin negotiations to revise the present frame of reference, it would soon fall back on the old defensive struggle, the enfeebling skirmishes that make one forget where the real battle is, the half-victories that are celebrated between two defeats, the relapse into divisive federal-provincial electoral folly, the sorry consolations of verbal nationalism, and, above all—this must be said, and repeated, and shouted if need be—above all the incredible squandering of energy which certainly is for us the most disastrous aspect of the present regime. . . .

So many years later, in seeing what has passed, and in attending the most recent constitutional hagglings, wouldn't one have to admit that this description wasn't far from what we actually had to live through, or rather, what we inflicted upon ourselves? Wouldn't one have to admit also that it was below our dignity? By 1967 our people had already found the strength to catch up a distance that they would never have believed possible. From then on, our rising generations have had the same chance to be educated and skilled as young people in other advanced societies. In certain sectors of social planning and even in economic life, Québécois have quickly crossed obstacles that place them in the avant-garde in Canada, if not in the whole continent.

From all that, then, from the repeated failure of federal-provincial negotiations to the revelation of our striking new maturity, one could draw only one conclusion:

. . . Quebec must become sovereign as soon as possible.

Thus we finally would have within our grasp the security of our collective "being" which is so vital to us, a security which otherwise must remain uncertain and incomplete.

Then it will be up to us, and us alone, to establish calmly, without recrimination or discrimination, the priority for which we are now struggling feverishly but blindly, that of our language and culture.

Only then will we have the opportunity, and the obligation, to use our talents to the maximum in order to resolve without further excuses or evasions all the great problems that confront us [as well as] the form and evolution of the political structures we must create for ourselves. . . .

In other words, we had to take into our own hands the entire liberty of Quebec and affirm our right to the essential content of independence and the full control of each and every one of our principal decisions. In this way we would be rejoining one of the two major currents of our times: that of national emancipation. It would be, in fact, a double emancipation that might take place. The Anglo-Canadian majority would also at the same stroke be rid of constraints that our presence imposed upon it, would be free to reorganize its own institutions, and free to prove to itself that it really wanted to preserve a society distinct from that of the United States.

And if this is the case there is no reason why we, as future neighbours, should not voluntarily remain associates and partners in a common enterprise, which would conform to the second great trend of our times: the new economic groups, customs unions, common markets, etc.

Here we are talking about something which already exists, for it is composed of the bonds, the complementary activities, the many forms of economic co-operation within which we have learned to live. Nothing says that we must throw these things away; on the contrary, there is every reason to maintain the framework. If we destroyed it, interdependent as we are, we would only be obliged sooner or later to build it up again, and then with doubtful success. . . .

We are not sailing off into uncharted seas. Leaving out the gigantic model furnished by the evolution of the Common Market, we can take our inspiration from countries comparable in size to our own—Benelux or Scandinavia—among whom co-operation is highly advanced, and where it has promoted unprecedented progress in the member states without preventing any of them from continuing to live according to their own traditions and preferences.*

To sum up we propose a system that would allow our two majorities to extricate themselves from an archaic federal framework in which

---

*I had used two sentences from John Kenneth Galbraith as an epigraph: "There certainly exists a tendency which impels peoples to form ever-larger economic groups. But one sees in the world no equivalent tendency toward more extended political units." Time has confirmed this judgement made in 1967.

our two very distinct "personalities" paralyse each other by dint of pretending to have a third personality common to both.

This new relationship of two nations, one with its homeland in Quebec and another free to rearrange the rest of the country at will, would be freely associated in a new adaptation of the current "common-market" formula, making up an entity which could perhaps—and if so, very precisely—be called a Canadian Union.

I was persuaded, need I say, that such a change would really be *the* solution. But I was nevertheless aware of the extreme difficulty of the enterprise. According to a maxim of Gramsci, which has become one of a few favourite mottos of mine, "Pessimism of the intelligence; optimism of the will."

The first half made me guess the fright that would seize many people at the thought of leaving a political dwelling that a very long habitation had almost made sacred. Indeed, this old house of "Confederation" constitutes one of the last vestiges of those ancient certainties that our times are constantly stripping us of. Without foreseeing the extent of the phenomenon or the quite extravagant excesses it would lead to, I knew that at the moment of decision certain people would fasten onto the status quo with that kind of panic energy that betrays more fear of the new than reasonable attachment to the old.

As for optimism of the will, it made me bet on that moment, despite the foregoing, because it would be a time "when courage and calm daring become the only proper form of prudence that a people can exercise in a crucial period of its existence. If it fails at these times to take the calculated risk of the great leap, it may miss its vocation forever, just as a man does who is afraid of life."

Hoping with all my heart to have been mistaken in that last sentence, this is what I continue to believe.

My Country, Canada or Quebec

Solange Chaput Rolland

I SHALL END this diary by noting the similarities between French and English societies both subjected to cultural, economic, and political pressures. *Vis-à-vis* the U.S.A., English Canada does not exist politically; economically it offers to the Americans some good possibilities for investment which allow them to reaffirm their strength on this continent.

Vis-à-vis English Canada, French Canada has no political power either, but the economic development of our province rests on English and American capital. Thus, French and English Canadians are satellites of the Americans and we are both in danger of becoming more and more Americanized. The only difference between our two nations is that we in Quebec hold desperately to our identity, while English Canada does not yet fully understand the meaning of one. But our two national weaknesses do not make a political force. If years ago we had only studied our qualities instead of harping on our respective faults, Canada would probably not be a more united nation; but least it would have more strength to fight American pressures and to convince Canadians not to seek radical answers to difficult and long-standing problems.

Here I must confess that I am not very good at adopting a constitutional or juridical language to speak about our Canadian crisis. But I must say that even if the true spirit of the B.N.A. Act signed in 1867 did not allow for the presence of two political nations in Canada, it is no longer possible in 1967 to ignore the two branches of the Canadian tree. Quebec is not and never will be a province *comme les autres,* because four million human beings live, think, speak, and fight in a political and cultural climate completely different from that of the nine other provinces. Even when Donald Creighton, the high priest of constitutional matters, writes in arrogant anger, 'French-Canadian nationalism could be carried to the point at which English Canada would finally decide in disgust and indignation that it had had enough,' English Canada will still have to face the fact that we have survived, we are the second-largest majority in Canada, and we have the right to speak in our own country.

Since Quebec forms a society in constant evolution, her needs in 1967 cannot be fulfilled by a constitution ratified one hundred years ago. As long as Quebec will be compelled to act as a province, there will be tensions between our provincial government and the federal one, and within a few months we will come to a constitutional impasse endangering the life of the whole nation. Yes, independence for Quebec would be the ideal solution for those of us tired of not being able to feel at home in our own country. But English Canada is not ready to fight alone against the American giant; and Quebec is no more ready to assume alone the destiny of four million people, because these four million French Canadians have chosen to dream their fate rather than work to better it in their everyday lives.

This is why, if English Canada can never be my country because it refuses to accept my language and culture and refuses to share with me Canada's future, Quebec therefore is *ma patrie*. But Quebec is not yet a country. My own compatriots have not so far created structures for our political, cultural, and economic independence. If I analyse the failures of our societies, I cannot resist pointing out that we form two worlds in agony. An independent Quebec that in twenty years could no longer assume its liberty would die in the arms of irate Americans furious at being obliged to add our problems to theirs. And an English Canada economically weak could not survive if it were cut in two by Quebec's secession. In consequence, French and English Canadians who, for the sake of superiority, revenge, or racial prejudices refuse to accept the reality of our collective weaknesses will, tomorrow, be held responsible for Canada's death.

Yes, I am pessimistic, but I defy my reader to live for months among people who have nothing much in common and to come out of this experience without being morally bruised. Like all French-Canadian nationalists, I would love to write firmly that my country is Quebec, but again I face the problem that Quebec as a country does not exist. And I will not create it with words of anger, with dreams, with love or hatred; I will not invent a country by refusing to live in step with an Anglo-American rhythm, by justifying my hunger for freedom, or by seeking revenge because Ottawa has refused to give what I considered vital. Quebec will become a country only when the whole nation wants it . . .

I begin to suspect that the best solution for problems confronting us for years to come might be to adopt a special status that will eventually lead us to the concept of associate states modelled on the Federation of Switzerland. I already hear the loud protest of my English-speaking friends who will accuse me of wanting too much too quickly. But I feel that the time is ripe to ask for too much and very quickly. If English Canada does not give Quebec a more important place in the constitution, then yes, we will run to an independence for which neither French nor English Canada is prepared. I have no intentions of blackmailing anyone with these remarks; I have studied some facts and I simply give them their logical evaluation.

When I began this diary I stated: 'What I will write about Canada will not change Canada.' How little did I know on that night of February 1966 how much my trip would transform me. More than my publishers and my readers, I am fully conscious that the task of inventing solutions to unify a country divided into ten republics is too much for a single human being. I am also aware that though I have tried to remain serene and objective, I have probably not reported all I have heard and seen, nor have I been able to study extensively the imperatives for each province. But for more than six months, I have looked in all sincerity for a common denominator between French and English Canadians, and I have not found one.

Consequently, I have come back to my land, *ma Terre-Québec,* more *Québécoise* than *Canadienne,* because I have learned harshly, with pain and anguish, that to remain true to my past, to my culture, to my language, and to the very French individual that I have become, I must live in Quebec, in a Quebec that one day may yet become my *country.*

Speak White

Michèle Lalonde

Speak white
it is so lovely to listen to you
speaking of Paradise Lost
or the anonymous, graceful profile trembling in the sonnets of Shakespeare

We are a rude and stammering people
but we are not deaf to the genius of a language
speak with the accent of Milton and Byron and Shelley and Keats
speak white
and please excuse us if in return
we've only our rough ancestral songs
and the chagrin of Nelligan

speak white
speak of places, this and that
speak to us of the Magna Carta
of the Lincoln Monument
of the cloudy charm of the Thames
or blossom-time on the Potomac
speak to us of your traditions
We are a people who are none too bright
but we are quick to sense
the great significance of crumpets
or the Boston Tea Party

But when you really speak white
when you get down to brass tacks
to speak of Better Homes and Gardens
and the high standard of living
and the Great Society
a little louder then speak white
raise your foremen's voices
we are a little hard of hearing

"Speak White" by Michele Lalonde, translated by D.G. Jones. Reprinted by permission of the translator.

we live too close to the machines
and only hear our heavy breathing over the tools
speak white and loud
so we can hear you clearly
from Saint Henri to Santo Domingo
yes, what a marvellous language
for hiring and firing
for giving the orders
for fixing the hour to be worked to death
and that pause that refreshes
and bucks up the dollar

Speak white
tell us that God is a great big shot
and that we're paid to trust him
speak white
speak to us of production, profits and percentages
speak white
it's a rich language
for buying
but for selling oneself
but for selling one's soul
but for selling oneself

Ah
speak white
big deal
but for telling about
the eternity of a day on strike
for telling the whole
life-story of a nation of caretakers
for coming back home in the evening
at the hour when the sun's gone bust in the alleys
for telling you yes the sun does set yes
every day of our lives to the east of your empires
Nothing's as good as a language of oaths
our mode of expression none too clean
dirtied with oil and with axle grease
Speak white
feel at home with your words
we are a bitter people

but we'd never reproach a soul
for having a monopoly
on how to improve one's speech

In the sweet tongue of Shakespeare
with the accent of Longfellow
speak a French purely and atrociously white
as in Viet Nam, in the Congo
speak impeccable German
a yellow star between your teeth
speak Russian speak of the right to rule speak of repression
speak white
it's a universal language
we were born to understand it
with its tear-gas phrases
with its billy-club words

Speak white
tell us again about freedom and democracy
We know that liberty is a Black word
as misery is Black
as blood is muddied with the dust of Algiers or of Little Rock

Speak white
from Westminster to Washington take turns
speak white as on Wall Street
white as in Watts
Be civilized
and understand our conventional answer
when you ask us politely
how do you do
and we mean to reply
we're doing all right
we're doing fine
we
are not alone

We know now
that we are not alone.

CHAPTER FOURTEEN

Pierre Trudeau and the Re-Definition of Canada

Introduction

If René Lévesque represented one face of Quebec nationalism, Pierre Trudeau represented the other. Born in Montreal in 1918, he grew up in a wealthy family. He attended the best schools and in the summer months he went to the exclusive Taylor Statten Camps in Algonquin Park. He completed his law degree at the Université de Montréal in 1943 and later studied at Harvard, the École libre des sciences politiques in Paris and the London School of Economics. Returning to Montreal in 1949, Trudeau worked closely with the journal *Cité Libre*, first published in 1950. As its name suggests, *Cité Libre* offered an outlet to intellectuals and writers for the free exchange, the give and take, of ideas and arguments and opinions about politics, nationalism and the future of Quebec. Trudeau's article, "New Treason of the Intellectuals" first appeared in *Cité Libre* in 1962. What was the new treason of the intellectuals?

In 1965 Trudeau entered the Liberal government of Lester Pearson. He was quickly appointed to the Cabinet as Minister of Justice. When Pearson resigned in 1968 Trudeau replaced him as Leader of the Liberal Party and Prime Minister of Canada, a position he would hold—with a brief interruption from the spring of 1979 to February of 1980—until 1984. He was selected as Leader of the Liberal Party in part because he was a French Canadian with strong federalist views. In 1980 he helped the "Non" side to victory in the Quebec referendum. This speech, delivered at the Paul Sauvé Arena in Montreal at the height of the referendum, was one of the most passionate of his career. In it he responded to a desperate René Lévesque who had questioned his middle name: "His name is Pierre Elliott Trudeau and that is the Elliott side taking over," Lévesque asserted, "and that's the English side, so we French Canadians in Quebec can't expect any sympathy from him." Trudeau's vision of bilingualism and multiculturalism inspired a generation of young Canadians who came of age during his long tenure in office. Catherine Annau, a documentary film maker from Toronto, was one of the many young Canadians inspired by Trudeau. In this personal essay she looks at what Trudeau meant to her and her generation. In addition to this essay, Annau directed the critically acclaimed National Film Board documentary, *Just Watch Me,* which investigates the impact of Trudeau on the 1970s generation. Trudeau died in 2000.

New Treason of the Intellectuals

Pierre Trudeau

*The men whose function it is to defend all eternal and impartial values,
like justice and reason, and whom I call the intellectuals (les clercs),
have betrayed this function in the interests of expediency . . . . It has been above all
for the benefit of the nation that the intellectuals have perpetrated this betrayal.*

Julien Benda

The Geographic Approach

It is not the concept of *nation* that is retrograde; it is the idea that the nation must necessarily be sovereign.

To which the champions of independence for Quebec retort that there is nothing at all retrograde about a concept that has brought independence to India, Cuba, and a multitude of African states.

This argument postulates the equation: independence equals progress. Independence, they insist, is good in itself. And to confound the enemy they fire back the aphorism "Good government is no substitute for self-government."

Their frequent recourse to this battle-cry (which is invariably misquoted—but do we all have to speak English?) indicates the extent of the Separatists' muddled thinking. Self-government does not mean national self-determination. (This is not a matter of showing off one's linguistic brilliance; we have to know what we are talking about when we raise the cry for Quebec's independence.) Let us not confuse these two ideas.

That self-government is a good thing—or, more precisely, that a trend toward so-called responsible government is in general a trend toward progress—I want to concede at the outset of this article. I have too often denounced Union Nationale autocracy in Quebec and Liberal and Socialist paternalism in Ottawa to be suspect on that score. I have always maintained that the people of Quebec would never approach political maturity and mastery of their future so long as they failed to learn by experience the mechanisms of really responsible government. To this end they must thrust aside both the ideologies that preach blind submission to "the authority delegated by God" and those that have us running to Ottawa every time there is a difficult problem to solve.

From *Federalism & the French Canadians* by John T. Saywell, ed. (Toronto, MacMillan, 1968).

But what I was calling for then was "liberty *in* the city," observes G.C. What we must have today, he says, is "liberty *of* the city," that is to say, the absolute independence of the French-Canadian nation, full and complete sovereignty for *la Laurentie.* In short, national self-determination. Marcel Chaput writes:

> Since the end of the Second World War, more than thirty countries, formerly colonies, have been freed of foreign tutelage and have attained national and international sovereignty. In 1960 alone seventeen African colonies, fourteen of them French-speaking, have obtained their independence. And now today it is the people of French Canada who are beginning to rouse, and they, too, will claim their place among free nations.

Indeed, Mr. Chaput hastens to admit that French Canada enjoys rights these people never did. But it does not have complete independence, and, according to him, "its destiny rests, in very large measure, in the hands of a nation foreign to it."

The confusion is utter and complete.

Practically all these "thirty countries, formerly colonies" are states in the same way that Canada is a state. They have acceded to full sovereignty just as Canada did in 1931. In no way are they nations in the sense that French Canada might be a nation. Consequently, putting the independence of Quebec into this particular historical context is pure sophistry.

The State of India is a sovereign republic. But there are no fewer than four languages officially recognized there (which include neither English nor Chinese nor Tibetan nor the innumerable dialects). There are eight principal religions, several of which are mutually and implacably opposed. Which nation are we talking about? And just what independence should we take as an example?

The State of Ceylon embraces three ethnic groups and four religions. In the Malay Federation there are three more ethnic groups. The Burmese Union arrays half a dozen nationalities one against the other. The Indonesian Republic comprises at least twelve national groups, and twenty-five principal languages are spoken there. In Viet Nam, besides the Tonkinese, the Annamese, and the Cochinchinese there are eight important tribes.

In Africa the polyethnic nature of the new states is even more striking. The frontiers of these countries simply retrace lines marked out years ago by the colonialists, according to the fortunes of conquest, exploration, and administrative whimsy. Consequently, members of one tribe, speaking the same language and sharing the same traditions, have become citizens of different states, and these states are barely more than conglomerations of distinct and rival groups. A sample of what this can lead to can be seen in the former Belgian Congo. But if we examine Ghana, the Sudan, Nigeria, or almost any other ex-colony, there, too, we find the same kind of ethnic complexity. In French West Africa, for example, the population consisted of ten scattered tribes; nevertheless, France found it convenient to divide them up into eight territories. And the course of history is at present transforming these territories into sovereign states. In vain may we look there for nation-states—that is to say, states whose delineations correspond with ethnic and linguistic entities.

As for Algeria, which our *Indépendantistes* are always holding up as an example, there is no doubt what kind of state she is seeking to become. Besides inhabitants of French, Spanish, Italian, Jewish, Greek, and Levantine origin, in this particular country we must count Berbers, Kabyles, Arabs, Moors, Negroes, Tuaregs, Mazabites, and a number of Cheshire cats. Of the disputes, notably between Kabyles and Arabs, we are far from having heard the end.

Finally, as far as concerns Cuba, endlessly discussed by the Separatists as a pattern to be followed, it's all obviously pure cock-and-bull. This country was sovereign under Batista and it is sovereign under Castro. It was economically dependent before and it still is. Democratic self-government was non-existent there yesterday and it is still non-existent there today. So what does that prove? That Castro is not Batista? To be sure; but Hydro-Québec under René Lévesque is not Hydro under Daniel Johnson. A lot of good that argument does for the Separatists.

What emerges from all this is that promoting independence as an end good in itself, a matter of dignity for all self-respecting peoples, amounts to embroiling the world in a pretty pickle indeed. It has been held that every sincere anti-colonialist who wants to see independence for Algeria ought also to want it for Quebec. This argument assumes that Quebec is a political dependent, which shows very poor knowledge of constitutional history; but even if it were, logically speaking one would then have to say that every Quebec Separatist should advocate independence for the Kabyles, or, to give an even better example, independence for twenty-five million Bengalis included in the State of India. Should the Separatists try to take the wind out of my sails by saying that they would indeed like to see this independence for Bengal, I would ask why they would stop there in the good work; in Bengal ninety different languages are spoken; and then there are still more Bengalis in Pakistan—What a lovely lot of separations that would be!

To finish this particular discussion with the aphorism we started with, I am, in the light of all this, tempted to conclude that "good government is a damned good substitute for national self-determination," if one means by this last term the right of ethnic and linguistic groups to their own absolute sovereignty. It would seem, in fact, a matter of considerable urgency for world peace and the success of the new states that the form of good government known as democratic federalism should be perfected and promoted, in the hope of solving to some extent the world-wide problems of ethnic pluralism. To this end, as I will show later, Canada could be called upon to serve as mentor, provided she has sense enough to conceive her own future on a grand scale. John Conway wrote, of true federalism, "Its successful adoption in Europe would go a long way towards ensuring the survival of traditional western civilization. It would be a pity, if, in Canada, so young, so rich and vigorous and plagued with so few really serious problems, the attempt should fail."

Further on the subject of federalism, it would seem well understood that President Wilson, that great champion of the "principle of nationality," in no way intended to invite nationalist secessions, but sought rather to ensure the right of nationalities to a certain amount of local autonomy within existing states.

Moreover, it is quite wrong to insist, as our advocates of independence often do, that the principle of nationality is an internationally recognized right, and sanctioned by the United Nations. Rather than adopting Wilson's equivocal pronouncements, and finding themselves faced with a new wave of plebiscites and secessions echoing the post-World-War-I period, the U.N. has preferred to talk—citing Article I of the Charter—of the right of "peoples" to self-determination. The term "peoples," however, is far from being identical with "ethnic groups."*

The Historical Approach

If the idea of the nation-state is hard to justify in terms of the evolution of anti-colonialism in recent years, how does it look in the light of history as a whole?

At the threshold of time there was man, and also, no doubt, in keeping with man's very nature, that other undeniable fact called the family. Then, very soon, the tribe appeared, a sort of primitive community founded on common customs and speech.

Now the history of civilization is a chronicle of the subordination of tribal "nationalism" to wider interests. No doubt there were always clan loyalties and regional cohesions. But thought developed, knowledge spread, inventions came to light, and humanity progressed wherever there was intermingling of tribes and exchange between them, gathering impetus through commerce and the division of labour, the heavy hand of conquests (from Egypt and China down to the Holy Roman Empire),

---

*It is obvious that the language of politics is riddled with pitfalls. The word "nation," or "nationality," from the Latin "nasci" (to be born), denotes most often an ethnic community sharing a common language and customs. The Japanese nation. It is in this sense that we speak of the "principle of nationality" leading to the "national state" or "nation-state." But sometimes the reverse is the case, where the state, originally made up of a number of ethnic communities, comes to think of itself as a nation; then the word is understood to mean a political society occupying a territory and sharing customs in common over a considerable period of time. The Swiss nation. In Canada, as I will explain later, there is, or will be, a Canadian nation in so far as the ethnic communities succeed in exorcising their own respective nationalisms. If, then, a Canadian nationalism does take form, it will have to be exorcised in its turn, and the Canadian nation will be asked to yield a part of its sovereignty to a higher authority, just as is asked, today, of the French-Canadian and English-Canadian nations. (For a discussion of the vocabulary of this subject, see p. 4 of a remarkable essay by E.H. Carr in Carr et al., *Nations ou Fédéralisme* [Paris, 1946].)

and the drive of the militant religions (from Buddhism on through Christianity to Islam).

Finally, after more than sixty-five centuries of history, with the breaking down of the rigid social structure of the Middle Ages, the decline of Latin as the mark of the learned man, and the birth of the cult of individualism, the modern idea of "nation" began to develop in Europe. The displacement of the Church by national Churches, the rise of the *bourgeoisie,* mercantilism for the protection of territorial economies, outrages committed against certain ethnic groups such as the Poles, the Jacobin Revolution, the relentless fervour of Mazzini, the domination of poor nations by industrialized ones like England: so many factors helped fan the flame of nationalist aspirations, leading to the setting up of one national state after another. The countries of Latin America revolted against Spain. Italy and Germany fought their wars of unification. The Greeks and the Slavs rebelled against the Ottoman Empire. Ireland rose against Great Britain. In short, all of Europe and a great deal of the New World took fire. The era of wars of nationalism, starting in Napoleon's day, reached its peak with the two world wars. And so it is that we have entered a new age, the nations now indulging their vanity in the possession and use of nuclear arms.

Some seven thousand years of history in three paragraphs is, of course, a little short. I will have more to say on the subject later, but for the time being it will suffice to keep three things in mind.

The first is that the nation is not a biological reality—that is, a community that springs from the very nature of man. Except for a very small fraction of his history, man has done very well without nations (this for the benefit of our young bloods, who see the slightest dent in the nation's sovereignty as an earth-shaking catastrophe).

The second is that the tiny portion of history marked by the emergence of the nation-states is also the scene of the most devastating wars, the worst atrocities, and the most degrading collective hatred the world has ever seen. Up until the end of the eighteenth century it was generally the sovereigns, not the nations, who made war; and while their sovereigns made war the civilian populations continued to visit each other: merchants crossed borders, scholars and philosophers went freely from one court to another, and conquering generals would take under their personal protection the learned men of vanquished cities. War killed soldiers, but left the various civilizations unhindered. In our day, however, we have seen nations refusing to listen to Beethoven because they are at war with Germany, others boycotting the Peking Opera because they refuse to recognize China, and still others refusing visas or passports to scholars wishing to attend some scientific or humanitarian congress in a country of differing ideology. Pasternak was not even allowed to go to Stockholm to accept his Nobel Prize. A concept of nation that pays so little honour to science and culture obviously can find no room above itself in its scale of values for truth, liberty, and life itself. It is a concept that corrupts all: in peace time the intellectuals become propagandists for the nation and the propaganda is a lie; in war time the democracies slither toward dictatorship and the dictatorships herd us into concentration camps; and finally after the massacres of Ethiopia come those of London and Hamburg, then of Hiroshima and Nagasaki, and perhaps more and more until the final massacre. I know very well that the nation-state idea is not the sole cause of all the evils born of war; modern technology has a good deal to answer for on that score! But the important thing is that the nation-state idea has caused wars to become more and more total over the last two centuries; and that is the idea I take issue with so vehemently. Besides, each time a state has taken an exclusive and intolerant idea as its cornerstone (religion, nationhood, ideology), this idea has been the very mainspring of war. In days gone by religion had to be displaced as the basis of the state before the frightful religious wars came to an end. And there will be no end to wars between nations until in some similar fashion the nation ceases to be the basis of the state.* As for inter-state wars, they will end only if the states give up that obsession whose very essence makes them exclusive and intolerant: sovereignty. Now—to get back to the subject—what worries me about the fact that five million Canadians of French origin cannot manage to share their national sovereignty with seven million Canadians of British origin, beside whom they live and who they know, in general, have no fleas, is that this leaves me precious little hope that several thousand million Americans, Russians, and Chinese, who have never never met and none of whom are sure the others are not flea-ridden, will ever agree to abdicate a piece of their sovereignty in the realm of nuclear arms.

The third observation I would draw from the course of history is that the very idea of the nation-state is absurd. To insist that a particular nationality must have complete sovereign power is to pursue a self-destructive end. Because every national minority will find, at the very moment of liberation, a new minority within its bosom which in turn must be allowed the right to demand its freedom. And on and on would stretch the train of revolutions, until the last-born of nation-states turned to violence to put an end to the very principle that gave it birth. That is why the principle of nationality has brought to the world two centuries of war, and *not one single* final solution. France has always had its Bretons and Alsatians, Britain its Scots and its Welsh, Spain its Catalans and Basques, Yugoslavia its Croats and Macedonians, Finland its Swedes and Lapps, and so on, for Belgium, Hungary, Czechoslovakia, Poland, the Soviet Union, China, the United States, all the Latin American countries, and who knows how many others. As far as the more homogeneous countries are concerned, those that have no problems of secession find themselves problems of accession. Ireland lays claim to the six counties of Ulster; Indonesia wants New Guinea. Mussolini's nationalist Italy, when it was done with the *irredentas*, turned to

---

*See Emory Reeves, *A Democratic Manifesto* (London, 1943), p. 43, and also, by the same author, *The Anatomy of Peace* (New York, 1945).

dreams of reconquering the Roman Empire. Hitler would have been satisfied with nothing less than the conquest of the entire non-Aryan world. Now there is something for Quebec's Separatists to sink their teeth into: if there is any validity to their principles they should carry them to the point of claiming part of Ontario, New Brunswick, Labrador, and New England; on the other hand, though, they would have to relinquish certain border regions around Pontiac and Temiskaming and turn Westmount into the Danzig of the New World.

So the concept of the nation-state, which has managed to cripple the advance of civilization, has managed to solve none of the political problems it has raised, unless by virtue of its sheer absurdity. And, where civilization has pushed ahead in spite of all, it is where the intellectuals have found the strength within themselves to put their faith in mankind before any national prejudice: Pasternak, Oppenheimer, Joliot-Curie, Russell, Einstein, Freud, Casals, and many others who have replied: *E pur si muove* to the *raison d'état*.

"Man," said Renan, "is bound neither to his language nor to his race; he is bound only to himself because he is a free agent, or in other words a moral being."

Listen, too, to what Father Delos has to say:

> What we must know is whether Man is intended to fill a predetermined role in history, whether history encompasses Man, or whether Man possesses innate powers which transcend all historical forms of culture and civilization; the question is whether it is not a denial of Man's dignity to reduce him to mere identification with any particular mass of humanity.

The Origin of Nationalism

Absurd in principle and outdated in practice as it may be, the idea of the nation-state has enjoyed extraordinary favour, and still does. How can it be? That is what I would like to explore next.

The birth of the modern state can be fixed near the end of the fourteenth century. Until then the feudal system was sufficient to maintain order in Europe, where the means of communication were limited, economy and trade were essentially local, and where, consequently, political administration could remain very much uncentralized. But as trade spread and diversified, as each political-economic unit demanded a broader base and better protection, and as kings found the means of giving free rein to their ambitions, the *bourgeois* classes allied themselves with their reigning monarchs to supplant the powers of feudal lords and of free cities by strong and unified states. In 1576 Jean Bodin ascertained that the new and essential characteristic of these states was "sovereignty," which he described as the *suprema potestas* over its citizens and subjects, unlimited under the law.

For a few centuries absolute monarchy remained master of these sovereign states. But they were not yet nation-states, because their frontiers remained a family matter, in the sense that their locations were shifted according to the fortunes of marriage and of war between the various reigning families. Nationalities were taken so little into account that Louis XIV, for example, after having annexed Alsace, made no attempt to forbid the continued use of German there, and schools for the teaching of French were introduced only twenty years later.

Individualism, scepticism, rationalism, however, continued to undermine the traditional powers. And the day came when absolute monarchy, in its turn, was obliged to step aside to make way for the *bourgeoisie,* its ally of earlier days. But as the dynasties disappeared, there was already a new cohesive agent at work to fill the vacuum and head off a weakening of the state: popular sovereignty, or democratic power.

Democracy indeed opened the way, first to the *bourgeoisie* and much later to all classes, by which all could participate in the exercise of political power. The state then appeared to be the instrument by which eventually all classes—that is to say, the entire nation—could assure peace and prosperity for themselves. And quite naturally all wished to make that instrument as strong as possible in relation to other states. Thus nationalism was born, the child of liberal democracy and the mystique of equality.

Alas, this nationalism, by a singular paradox, was soon to depart from the ideas that presided at its birth. Because the moment the sovereign state was put at the service of the nation it was the nation that became sovereign—that is to say, beyond the law. It mattered little then that the prosperity of some meant the ruin of others. Nations historically strong, those that were industrialized first, those that had inherited strategic or institutional advantages, soon came to see the advantages of their situation. Here rulers closed ranks with the ruled, the haves with the have-nots, and they set out together as a body, in the name of the nationalism that bound them together, to line their pockets and feed their vanity at the expense of weaker nations.

Expansionist nationalism then began to bestow fancy titles upon itself: political Darwinism, Nietzschean mysticism, the white man's burden, civilizing mission, pan-Slavism, Magyarization, and all the other rubbish by which the strong justify their oppression of the weak.

In all these cases the result was the same. Nations that were dominated, dismembered, exploited, and humiliated conceived an unbounded hatred for their oppressors; and united by this hatred they erected against aggressive nationalism a defensive nationalism. And so a chain of wars was ignited that keeps bursting into flame all over the planet.

It is into the depths of this world-wide nationalist phenomenon that we must delve in examining the sub-sub-species Quebec of the subspecies Canada. The Seven Years' War saw the five great powers of Europe deployed against each other in accordance with a complicated system of alliances and compacts. France and Russia fought on the side of Austria, while England aligned herself with Prussia. But while Louis XV lent support to Marie Thérèse with his armies and his money, in the hope of broadening French influence in Europe, Pitt sent to Frederick II plenty of money and a small number of soldiers. These he sent off with English fleets to vanquish France in India and America, and to lay the foundations of the most formidable empire the world has ever known. We know the rest: by the Treaty of Paris, Canada, among others, became English.

At this period the English were already the most nationalist of nationalists. The whole country, proud of its political and economic superiority, unanimously favoured the planting of the flag in the most far-flung lands. This nationalism was necessarily cultural, too; to English eyes they bestowed a priceless favour on the undeserving countries they colonized: the right to share the Anglo-Saxon language and customs. And then, despite having so effectively and admirably built up the cult of civil liberties at home in England, they gave not the slightest thought to the protection of minority rights for others.

From the moment of delivery of the Royal Proclamation of 1763, the intention was obvious: the French Canadian was to be completely assimilated. In 1840 Durham, while "far from wishing to encourage indiscriminately [these] pretentions to superiority on the part of any particular race," none the less considered that assimilation was simply "a question of time and mode."

Throughout this period, Canadians of British origin would have considered it an indignity to be in any inferior position. So they invented all kinds of stratagems by which democracy was made to mean government by the minority.

Generations passed. Hopes of assimilating the French Canadians dimmed to a flicker (although right up to 1948, immigration laws continued to favour immigrants from the British Isles over those from France). But English-speaking Canadians have never given up their condescending attitude to their French-speaking fellows, even to this day.

At Ottawa and in provinces other than ours, this nationalism could wear the pious mask of democracy. Because, as English-speaking Canadians became proportionately more numerous, they took to hiding their intolerance behind acts of majority rule; that was how they quashed bilingualism in the Manitoba legislature, violated rights acquired by separate schools in various provinces, savagely imposed conscription in 1917, and broke a solemn promise in 1942.*

In Quebec, "where they had the money if not the numbers, our Anglo-Canadian fellow-citizens have often yielded to the temptation of using without restraint the

---

*André Laurendeau has just written with great clarity an account of how, with the plebiscite of 1942, the state became the tool of Anglo-Canadian nationalism, and of how that state took advantage of French-Canadian numerical weakness to divest itself of pledges it had made (*La Crise de la conscription* [Montreal, 1962]). A tale even more shameful could be told of how, during the same war and with similar inspiration, the vengeful powers of the state were turned against the Japanese-Canadian minority.

means at their command." This was how, in politics, Anglo-Canadian nationalism took on the form of what André Laurendeau has so admirably named the "cannibal-king theory" (*théorie du roi-nègre*). Economically, this nationalism has been expressed essentially in treating the French Canadian as *un cochon de payant*. Sometimes, magnanimously, they would go as far as putting a few straw men on boards of directors. These men invariably had two things in common: first, they were never bright enough or strong enough to rise to the top, and second, they were always sufficiently "representative" to grovel for the cannibal-king's favours and flatter the vanity of their fellow-tribesmen. Finally, in social and cultural matters, Anglo-Canadian nationalism has expressed itself quite simply by disdain. Generation after generation of Anglo-Saxons have lived in Quebec without getting around to learning three sentences of French. When these insular people insist, with much gravity, that their jaws and ears aren't made for it and can't adapt themselves to French, what they really want to get across to you is that they will not sully these organs, and their small minds, by submitting them to a barbarous idiom.

Anglo-Canadian nationalism produced, inevitably, French-Canadian nationalism. As I have said before, speaking of the roots of our nationalism and the futility of its tendencies:

> Defeated, occupied, leaderless, banished from commercial enterprise, poked away outside the cities, little by little reduced to a minority and left with very little influence in a country which, after all, he discovered, explored and colonized, the French Canadian had little alternative for the frame of mind he would have to assume in order to preserve what remained of his own. So he set up a system of defense-mechanisms which soon assumed such overgrown proportions that he came to regard as priceless anything which distinguished him from other people; and any change whatever (be it for the better or not) he would regard with hostility if it originated from outside.

"Alas," I added, "the nationalists' idealism itself has been their downfall. 'They loved not wisely but too well.'"*

The Conflict of Nationalisms in Canada

We must accept the facts of history as they are. However outworn and absurd it may be, the nation-state image spurred the political thinking of the British, and subsequently of Canadians of British descent in the "Dominion of Canada." Broadly speaking, this meant identifying the Canadian state with themselves to the greatest degree possible.

---

*In *The Asbestos Strike* (Toronto: James, Lewis & Samuel, 1974), p. 7—Ed.

Since the French Canadians had the bad grace to decline assimilation, such an identification was beyond being completely realizable. So the Anglo-Canadians built themselves an illusion of it by fencing off the French Canadians in their Quebec ghetto and then nibbling at its constitutional powers and carrying them off bit by bit to Ottawa. Outside Quebec they fought, with staggering ferocity, against anything that might intrude upon that illusion: the use of French on stamps, money, cheques, in the civil service, the railroads, and the whole works.

In the face of such aggressive nationalism, what choice lay before the French Canadians over, say, the last century? On the one hand they could respond to the vision of an overbearing Anglo-Canadian nation-state with a rival vision of a French-Canadian nation-state; on the other hand they could scrap the very idea of nation-state once and for all and lead the way toward making Canada a multi-national state.

The first choice was, and is, that of the Separatists or advocates of independence; an emotional and prejudiced choice essentially—which goes for their antagonists too, for that matter—and I could never see any sense in it. Because either it is destined to succeed by achieving independence, which would prove that the nationalism of Anglo-Canadians is neither intransigent, nor armed to the teeth, nor so very dangerous for us; and in that case I wonder why we are so afraid to face these people in the bosom of a pluralistic state and why we are prepared to renounce our right to consider Canada our home *a mari usque ad mare.* Or else the attempt at independence is doomed to failure and the plight of the French Canadians will be worse than ever; not because a victorious and vindictive enemy will deport part of the population and leave the rest with dwindled rights and a ruined heritage—this eventuality seems most unlikely; but because once again French Canadians will have poured all their vital energies into a (hypothetically) fruitless struggle, energies that should have been used to match in excellence, efficacy, and persistence a (hypothetically) fearsome enemy.

The second choice, for the multi-national state, was, and is, that of the Constitutionalists. It would reject the bellicose and self-destructive idea of nation-state in favour of the more civilized goal of polyethnic pluralism. I grant that in certain countries and at certain periods of history this may have been impossible, notably where aggressive nationalism has enjoyed a crushing predominance and refused all compromise with national minorities. Was this the case in the time of Papineau and the *patriotes?* I doubt it; but the fact remains that the upshot of this "separatist" uprising was an Act of Union which marked a step backward for minority rights from the Constitutional Act of 1791.

As a matter of fact, this second choice was, and is, possible for French Canadians. In a sense the multi-national state was dreamed about by Lafontaine, realized under Cartier, perfected by Lauriet, and humanized with Bourassa. Anglo-Canadian nationalism has never enjoyed a crushing predominance and has never been in a position to refuse all compromise with the country's principal national minority; consequently, it has been unable to follow the policy perhaps most gratifying to its arrogance, and has had to resign itself to the situation as imposed by the course of events.

The first of such events was the Quebec Act, passed under the shadow of the American Revolution. Then there were the terrible dark days—three-quarters of a century of them—when Canadians of British origin knew there were fewer of them than of French Canadians. As Mason Wade says of the Loyalists: "They were badly scared men, who had lived through one revolution in America and dreaded another in Canada." Eventually, it was the constant threat of American domination that—like it or not—obliged Anglo-Canadian nationalism to take cognizance of the French-Canadian nation; it would have been virtually impossible otherwise to reunite the remaining colonies of British North America.

In actual fact, Anglo-Canadian nationalism has never had much of an edge. Those among French Canadians who have had the acumen to realize it—the Constitutionalists, as I call them—have naturally wagered on the multi-national state, and have exhorted their compatriots to work for it boldly and eagerly. But those who could not see it have never ceased in their fear of a largely imaginary adversary. Among these are, first, the assimilated converts and boot-lickers who have given in to the idea that French Canada is already dead, and that the Anglo-Canadian nation-state is rising triumphant over its remains; these, though, are insignificant in number and even more so in influence, so I am writing them off as a force to be reckoned with. Secondly, there are Separatists and nationalists of all shapes and sizes baying after independence, who devote all their courage and capabilities to stirring up French-Canadian nationalism in defiance of the Anglo-Canadian variety. These are incessantly promoting what Gérard Pelletier has very aptly called "the state-of-siege mentality." Now, recalling something I once wrote, "the siege was lifted long ago and humanity has marched ever onward, while we remain stewing steadily in our own juice without daring even once to peek over the edge of the pot."

If Canada as a state has had so little room for French Canadians it is above all because we have failed to make ourselves indispensable to its future. Today, for example, it would seem that a Sévigny or a Dorion could perfectly well leave the federal cabinet, as a Courtemanche did, without causing irreparable damage to the machinery of government or the prestige of the country. And, with the sole exception of Laurier, I fail to see a single French Canadian in more than three-quarters of a century whose presence in the federal cabinet might be considered indispensable to the history of Canada as written—except at election time, of course, when the tribe always invokes the aid of its witch-doctors. Similarly, in the ranks of senior civil servants, there is probably not one who could be said to have decisively and beneficially influenced the development of our administration as has, for example, an O.D. Skelton, a Graham Towers, or a Norman Robertson.

Consequently, an examination of the few nationalist "victories" carried off at Ottawa after years of wrangling in high places will reveal probably none that could not have been won in the course of a single cabinet meeting by a French Canadian of the calibre of C.D. Howe. All our cabinet ministers put together would scarcely match the weight of a bilingual cheque or the name of a hotel.

To sum up, the Anglo-Canadians have been strong by virtue only of our weakness. This is true not only at Ottawa, but even at Quebec, a veritable charnel-house where half our rights have been wasted by decay and decrepitude and the rest devoured by the maggots of political cynicism and the pestilence of corruption. Under the circumstances, can there be any wonder that Anglo-Canadians have not wanted the face of this country to bear any French features? And why would they want to learn a language that we have been at such pains to reduce to mediocrity at all levels of our educational system?

No doubt, had English-speaking Canadians applied themselves to learning French with a quarter the diligence they have shown in refusing to do so, Canada would have been effectively bilingual long ago. For here is demonstrated one of the laws of nationalism, whereby more energy is consumed in combating disagreeable but irrevocable realities than in contriving some satisfactory compromise. It stands to reason that this law works to greatest ill effect in respect to minority nationalisms: namely, us.

Let me explain.

The Sorry Tale of French-Canadian Nationalism

We have expended a great deal of time and energy proclaiming the rights due our nationality, invoking our divine mission, trumpeting our virtues, bewailing our misfortunes, denouncing our enemies, and avowing our independence; and for all that not one of our workmen is the more skilled, nor a civil servant the more efficient, a financier the richer, a doctor the more advanced, a bishop the more learned, nor a single solitary politician the less ignorant. Now, except for a few stubborn eccentrics, there is probably not one French-Canadian intellectual who has not spent at least four hours a week over the last year discussing separatism. That makes how many thousand times two hundred hours spent just flapping our arms? And can any one of them honestly say he has heard a single argument not already expounded *ad nauseam* twenty, forty, and even sixty years ago? I am not even sure we have exorcized any of our original bogey men in sixty years. The Separatists of 1962 that I have met really are, in general, genuinely earnest and nice people; but the few times I have had the opportunity of talking with them at any length, I have almost always been astounded by the totalitarian outlook of some, the anti-Semitism of others, and the complete ignorance of basic economics of all of them.

This is what I call *la nouvelle trahison des clercs:* this self-deluding passion of a large segment of our thinking population for throwing themselves headlong—intellectually and spiritually—into purely escapist pursuits.

Several years ago I tried to show that the devotees of the nationalist school of thought among French Canadians, despite their good intentions and courage, were for all practical purposes trying to swim upstream against the course of progress. Over more than half a century "they have laid down a pattern of social thinking impossible to realize and which, from all practical points of view, has left the people without any effective intellectual direction."

I have discovered that several people who thought as I did at that time are today talking separatism. Because their social thinking is to the left, because they are campaigning for secular schools, because they may be active in trade union movements, because they are open-minded culturally, they think that their nationalism is the path to progress. What they fail to see is that they have become reactionary *politically.*

Reactionary, in the first place, by reason of circumstances. A count, even a rough one, of institutions, organizations, and individuals dedicated to nationalism, from the village notary to the Ordre de Jacques Cartier, from the small businessman to the Ligues du Sacré-Coeur, would show beyond question that an alliance between nationalists of the right and of the left would work in favour of the former, by sheer weight of numbers. And when the leftists say they will not make such an alliance until it is they who are in the majority, I venture to suggest once again that they will never be so as long as they continue to waste their meagre resources as they do now. Any effort aimed at strengthening the nation must avoid dividing it; otherwise such an effort loses all effectiveness so far as social reform is concerned, and for that matter can only lead to consolidation of the *status quo.* In this sense the alliance is already working against the left, even before being concluded.

In the second place, the nationalists—even those of the left—are politically reactionary because, in attaching such importance to the idea of nation, they are surely led to a definition of the common good as a function of an ethnic group, rather than of all the people, regardless of characteristics. This is why a nationalistic movement is by nature intolerant, discriminatory, and, when all is said and done, totalitarian.* A truly democratic government cannot be "nationalist," because it must pursue the good of all its citizens, without prejudice to ethnic origin. The democratic government, then, stands for and encourages good citizenship, never nationalism. Certainly, such a government will make laws by which ethnic groups will benefit, and the majority group will benefit proportionately to its number; but that follows naturally from the principle of equality for all, not from any right due the strongest. In this

---

*As early as 1862, Lord Acton was already writing thus: "The nation is here an ideal unit founded on the race. . . . It overrules the rights and wishes of the inhabitants, absorbing their divergent interests in a fictitious unity; sacrifices their several inclinations and duties to the higher claim of nationality, and crushes all natural rights and all established liberties for the purpose of vindicating itself. Whenever a single definite object is made the supreme end of the State—the State becomes for the time being inevitably absolute." John Dalberg-Acton, *Essays on Freedom and Power* (Glencoe, 1948), p. 184.

sense one may well say that educational policy in Quebec has always been democratic rather than nationalistic; I would not say the same for all the other provinces. If, on the other hand, Hydro-Quebec were to expropriate the province's hydro-electric industries for nationalistic rather than economic reasons, we would already be on the road to fascism. The right can nationalize; it is the left that socializes and controls for the common good.

In the third place, any thinking that calls for full sovereign powers for the nation is politically reactionary because it would put complete and perfect power in the hands of a community which is incapable of realizing a complete and perfect society. In 1962 it is unlikely that any nation-state—or for that matter any multi-national state either—however strong, could realize a complete and perfect society; economic, military, and cultural interdependence is a *sine qua non* for states of the twentieth century, to the extent that none is really self-sufficient. Treaties, trade alliances, common markets, free trade areas, cultural and scientific agreements, all these are as indispensable for the world's states as is interchange between citizens within them; and just as each citizen must recognize the submission of his own sovereignty to the laws of the state—by which, for example, he must fulfil the contracts he makes—so the states will know no real peace and prosperity until they accept the submission of their relations with each other to a higher order. In truth, the very concept of sovereignty must be surmounted, and those who proclaim it for the nation of French Canada are not only reactionary, they are preposterous. French Canadians could no more constitute a perfect society than could the five million Sikhs of the Punjab. We are not well enough educated, nor rich enough, nor, above all, numerous enough, to man and finance a government possessing all the necessary means for both war and peace. The fixed per-capita cost would ruin us. But I shall not try to explain all this to people who feel something other than dismay at seeing *la Laurentie* already opening embassies in various parts of the world, "for the diffusion of our culture abroad." Particularly when these same people, a year ago, seemed to be arguing that we were too poor to finance a second university—a Jesuit one—in Montreal.

To this third contention, that sovereignty is unworkable and contradictory, the Separatists will sometimes argue that, once independent, Quebec could very well afford to give up part of her sovereignty on, for instance, re-entering a Canadian Confederation, because then her choice would be her own, a free one. That abstraction covers a multitude of sins! It is a serious thing to ask French Canadians to embark on several decades of privation and sacrifice, just so that they can indulge themselves in the luxury of choosing "freely" a destiny more or less identical to the one they have rejected. But the ultimate tragedy would be in not realizing that French Canada is too culturally anaemic, too economically destitute, too intellectually retarded, too spiritually paralysed, to be able to survive more than a couple of decades of stagnation, emptying herself of all her vitality into nothing but a cesspit, the mirror of her nationalistic vanity and "dignity."

The Younger Generation

What French Canadians now in their twenties will find hard to forgive in people of my generation a few years from now is the complacency with which we have watched the rebirth of separatism and nationalism. Because by then they will have realized how appallingly backward French Canada is in all fields of endeavour. What! they will say to the intellectuals, you did so little writing and so little thinking and yet you had time to ruminate over separatism? What! they will say to the sociologists and political scientists, in the very year that men were first put into orbit you were replying gravely to inquiries on separatism that in your opinion, perhaps, yes, one day, no doubt, possibly. . . . What! they will say to the economists, with the western world in its age of mass production striving, by all kinds of economic unions, to reproduce market conditions already enjoyed within such large political unions as the United States and the Soviet Union, how could you, in Quebec, have looked on with satisfaction at a movement whose aims would have reduced to nil any common market for Quebec industry? What! they will say to the engineers, you could not even manage to build a highway that would survive two Canadian winters and you were pipe-dreaming of a Great Wall all the way around Quebec? What! they will say to the judges and lawyers, civil liberties having survived in the province of Quebec thanks only to the Communists, the trade unions, and the Jehovah's Witnesses, and to English and Jewish lawyers and the judges of the Supreme Court in Ottawa,* you had nothing better to do than cheer on the coming of a sovereign state for French Canadians? Finally they will come to the party politicians. What! they will say, you, the Liberals, spent twenty-five years growing fat on sovereignty filched from the provinces; you, the Conservatives, alias Union Nationale, subjected Quebec to two decades of retroactive, vindictive, discriminatory, and stultifying laws; and you, of the Social-Democratic-cum-New-Democratic Party, in the name of some obscure sort of federal *raison d'État,* had sabotaged the *Union des forces démocratiques* and thereby snuffed out any glimmer of hope for Quebec's radicals; and you all discovered, all of a sudden, that Quebec must have more independence, some of you to the point of becoming avowed Separatists?

I venture to predict that among these young people of such acid criticism there will be one called Luc Racine, who will be a little sorry that he once wrote as follows in *Cité libre:* "If today's youth has turned to separatism, it is not from indifference to

---

*Seven times in the last decade alone, beginning in 1951, the Supreme Court in Ottawa has reversed the decisions of the Court of Appeal of the Province of Quebec, decisions which would have spelled disaster for civil liberties: the Boucher case (seditious libel); the Alliance case (loss of union certification); the Saumur case (distribution of pamphlets); the Chaput case (religious assembly); the Birks case (compulsory religious holidays); the Switzman case (padlock law); the Roncarelli case (administrative discretion). At the moment of going to press we learn that yet an eighth case can now be added to this list: the case of *Lady Chatterley's Lover.*

the great problems facing humanity, but from the desire to concentrate its efforts on conditions that are within its power to change." Because by then he will understand that a given people, at a given moment in their history, possess only a given amount of intellectual energy; and that if a whole generation devotes the greater part of that energy to imbecilities, that generation, for all practical purposes, will indeed have shown its "indifference to the great problems facing humanity." (I would lend a word of advice to Racine, however: that in 1972 he not take it into his head to talk about nationalism as a form of alienation, because my friend André Laurendeau will once again feel compelled to fly to the defence of his forebears, protesting that in 1922 Abbé Groulx deserved our complete respect.)*

So much for that. But how does it happen that separatism enjoys such a following *today* among the younger generation? How is it, for example, that so many young people, responding to *Cité libre*'s editorial "Un certain silence," have declared themselves for separatism?

Pelletier has pointed out that, having preached—through *Cité libre*—systematic scepticism in the face of established dogmatism, and having practised it as regards most of our traditional institutions, we should hardly be surprised if a new generation should turn it against one of the establishments we ourselves have spared: the Canadian state.

This has some validity at the psychological level; but it fails to explain the reactionary direction of their dissension.

For my part, I would think there would be some analogy to be found in the democratic impetus that gave birth to the various nationalisms in Europe a century or two ago. The death of Duplessis marked the end of a dynasty and of the oligarchy it had fostered. The advent of liberal democracy to the province bore promise of power for all classes henceforth. But in practice the newly self-conscious classes have found most roads to a better life blocked: the clergy clings to its grip on education, the English continue to dominate our finances, and the Americans intrude upon our culture. Only Quebec as a state would appear to belong unquestionably to French Canadians; and the fullest power for that state is therefore highly desirable. Democracy having declared all men equal within the nation, so all nations should enjoy equality one to another, meaning in particular that ours should be sovereign and independent. It is predicted that the realization of our nation-state will release a thousand unsuspected energies, and that, thus endowed, French Canadians will at last take possession of their rightful heritage. In other words, there is sup-

---

*An emotional allusion to an emotional rejoinder by Laurendeau, *Le Devoir*, March 3, 1961. This soul of refinement, one of the fairest-minded men I know, who shares with Bourassa the privilege of being the favourite target of the Separatists (who, logically enough, will not allow that nationalism could be anything but separatist), rarely speaks of nationalism without betraying, in some little detail, a blind spot. Thus it was that in an otherwise excellent editorial (*Le Devoir*, January 30, 1962), he put forth the ridiculous idea of a "moral conscription of French Canadians." What! Mr. Laurendeau? Conscription!?

posed to be some sort of creative energy that will bestow genius on people who have none and give courage and learning to a lazy and ignorant nation.

This is the faith that takes the place of reason for those who are unable to find a basis for their convictions in history, or economics, or the constitution, or sociology. "Independence," writes Chaput, "is much more a matter of disposition than of logic. . . . More than reason, we must have pride." That is the way all those dear little girls and young ladies feel, who like to put it in a nutshell thus: "Independence is a matter of dignity. You don't argue about it; you feel it." Isn't that the sort of thing that many poets and artists say? Jean-Guy Pilon writes:

> When the day comes that this cultural minority, hitherto only tolerated in this country, becomes a nation unto itself within its own borders, our literature will take a tremendous leap ahead. Because the writer, like everyone else in this society, will feel free. And a free man can do great things.

Now it would seem that Chaput is an excellent chemist. What I would like to know, though, is how the energies set in motion by independence are going to make him a better one; he need show us nothing else in order to woo us into separatism. As for his book, it bears the mark of an honest and dedicated man, but it destroys itself with one of its own sentences: "To hope that one day, by some sort of magic, the French-Canadian people will suddenly reform and become as one body respectful of the law, correct in its speech, devoted to culture and high achievement, without first becoming imbued with some inspiring ideal: this is a dangerous aberration." So Chaput rejects magic, but counts on an inspiring ideal as the way of salvation for our people. As if reform, correctness of speech, culture, and high achievement—*all of which are already accessible to us under the existing Canadian constitution*—were not in themselves inspiring ideals! And in what way is the other ideal he proposes—the nation-state—any more than a kind of magic called forth to fill in for our lack of discipline in pursuing the true ideals?

It would seem, too, that Pilon is a good poet. I would like him to tell me—in prose, if he likes—how national sovereignty is going to make him "a free man" and "capable of doing great things." If he fails to find within himself, in the world about him and in the stars above, the dignity, pride and other well-springs of poetry, I wonder why and how he will find them in a "free" Quebec.

No doubt bilingualism is attainable only with some difficulty. But I will not admit that this should be any insurmountable hurdle to men who call themselves intellectuals, particularly when the language they carp over is one of the principal vehicles of twentieth-century civilization. The day of language barriers is finished, at least as far as science and culture are concerned; and if Quebec's intellectuals refuse to master another language than their own, if they will recognize no loyalty but to their nation, then they may be renouncing forever their place among the world's intellectual élite.

For men of intellect the talk about energy set in motion by national independence means nothing. Their function, particularly if they come from a milieu where sentiment takes the place of reason and prejudice the place of understanding, is to think, and then think some more. If their intellectual pursuits have led to a dead end, there is only one thing to do: turn around and go back. Any attempt at escaping through intellectual hocus-pocus is contemptible; as Arthur Miller has said in *L'Express*, "The task of the real intellectual consists of analyzing illusions in order to discover their causes."

True enough, but for people in general it is another matter. Nationalism, as an emotional stimulus directed at an entire community, can indeed let loose unforeseen powers. History is full of this, called variously chauvinism, racism, jingoism, and all manner of crusades, where right reasoning and thought are reduced to rudimentary proportions. It could be that in certain historical situations, where oppression was intolerable, misery unspeakable, and all alternative escape routes blocked, it was nationalism that sparked the subsequent break for freedom. But the arousing of such a passion as a last resort has always had its drawbacks, and the bad has invariably gone hand in hand with the good. This bad has almost always included a certain amount of despotism, because people who win their freedom with passion rather than with reason are generally disappointed to find themselves just as poor and deprived as ever; and strong governments are necessary to put an end to their unrest.

I was in Ghana during the first months of her independence. The poets were no better, the chemists no more numerous, and, on a more tangible level, salaries were no higher. Since the intellectuals were unable to explain to the people why this should be, they distracted their attention to some obscure island in the Gulf of Guinea which needed to be "reconquered." To this end a large slice of this economically destitute state's budget was earmarked for the army—which ultimately served to put the parliamentary opposition in jail.

A similar thing has happened in Indonesia. This former-colony-turned-state, which is only barely succeeding in governing itself and has yet to achieve prosperity, has called its people to arms to liberate its territories in New Guinea. Now these territories do not belong to it for any reason whatever, neither of race, nor language, nor geography. Nevertheless, I have met, in Quebec, men of radical convictions who—through inability to reason in any terms other than of national sovereignty—consider the operation justified. The State of Quebec can count on these men one day, when, unable to improve social conditions for her people, she sends them off to win "her islands" in Hudson Bay. Already the Honourable Mr. Arsenault is preparing us for this glorious epic. And Lesage stands ready with his applause.

Most fortunately, the backbone of our people entertain fewer illusions on such subjects, and show more common sense, than do our intellectuals and *bourgeoisie*. The province's large trade unions have pronounced themselves categorically against separatism. They are well aware of the powers latent in mob passion; but, rightly, they shrink from setting in motion a vehicle with faulty steering and unsound brakes.

In short, those who expect to "release energies" by independence (or the feeling of independence) are playing the sorcerer's apprentice. They are resolving not one single problem by the exercise of reason; and in stirring up collective passions they are engaging an unpredictable, uncontrollable, and ineffective mechanism. (It will be noted that I am talking here primarily of energies supposedly to be released *by* independence; about the energies behind the *origins* of today's separatism, I had something to say in *Cité libre* of March 1961, p. 5. But on that, Messrs. Albert and Raymond Breton offer in the present issue by far the most serious study ever made on the subject.)

As a final argument, certain young people justify their flirtation with separatism as a matter of tactics: "If the English get scared enough we'll get what we want without going as far as independence." This tactic has already provoked concessions of purely symbolic value for French Canadians: one slogan ('The French Canadians deserve a New Deal'), two flags (Pearson—Pickersgill), a few new names for old companies (e.g., La Compagnie d'électricité Shawinigan), several appointments to boards of directors, and a multitude of bilingual cheques (Diefenbaker). *De minimis non curat praetor,* but all the same I must confess that the flap among English-speaking politicians and businessmen is funny to see. It bears witness certainly to a guilty conscience for their own nationalistic sins. But that could have its repercussions, too. There is nothing meaner than the coward recovered from his fright. And I would like to think that then French Canada would be bolstered by a younger generation endowed with richer assets than their nationalistic passion.

The Future

If, in my opinion, the nation were of purely negative value, I would not be at such pains to discredit a movement that promises to lead the French-Canadian nation to its ruin.

The nation is, in fact, the guardian of certain very positive qualities: a cultural heritage, common traditions, a community awareness, historical continuity, a set of mores; all of which, at this juncture in history, go to make a man what he is. Certainly, these qualities are more private than public, more introverted than extroverted, more instinctive and primitive than intelligent and civilized, more self-centred and impulsive than generous and reasonable. They belong to a transitional period in world history. But they are a reality of our time, probably useful, and in any event considered indispensable by all national communities.

Except to pinpoint ourselves in the right historical perspective, then, there is not much to be gained in brushing them aside on the ground that the nation of French Canadians will some day fade from view and that Canada itself will undoubtedly not exist forever. Benda points out that it is to the lasting greatness of Thucydides that he was able to visualize a world in which Athens would be no more.

But the future with which we should concern ourselves here is the one we are building from day to day. The problem we must face squarely is this: without back-sliding to the ridiculous and reactionary idea of national sovereignty, how can we protect our French-Canadian national qualities?

As I have already said earlier in this article, we must separate once and for all the concepts of state and of nation, and make Canada a truly pluralistic and polyethnic society. Now in order for this to come about, the different regions within the country must be assured of a wide range of local autonomy, such that each national group, with an increasing background of experience in self-government, may be able to develop the body of laws and institutions essential to the fullest expression and development of their national characteristics. At the same time, the English Canadians, with their own nationalism, will have to retire gracefully to their proper place, consenting to modify their own precious image of what Canada ought to be. If they care to protect and realize their own special ethnic qualities, they should do it within this framework of regional and local autonomy rather than a pan-Canadian one.

For the incorporation of these diverse aspirations the Canadian constitution is an admirable vehicle. Under the British North America Act, the jurisdiction of the federal State of Canada concerns itself with all the things that have no specific ethnic implications, but that have to do with the welfare of the entire Canadian society: foreign affairs, the broader aspects of economic stability, foreign trade, navigation, postal services, money and banking, and so on. The provinces, on the other hand, have jurisdiction over matters of a purely local and private nature and those that affect ethnic peculiarities: education, municipal and parochial affairs, the administration of justice, the celebration of marriage, property and civil rights, and so forth. Nevertheless, in keeping with the fact that none of the provincial borders coincides perfectly with ethnic or linguistic delineations, no provincial government is encouraged to legislate exclusively for the benefit of a particular ethnic group in such a way as to foster a nation-state mentality at the provincial level. On this point the record of Quebec's treatment of its minorities can well stand as an example to other provinces with large French, German, Ukrainian, and other minorities.

I have no intention of closing my eyes to how much Canadians of British origin have to do—or rather, undo—before a pluralist state can become a reality in Canada. But I am inclined to add that that is *their* problem. The die is cast in Canada: there are two main ethnic and linguistic groups; each is too strong and too deeply rooted in the past, too firmly bound to a mother-culture, to be able to engulf the other. But if the two will collaborate at the hub of a truly pluralistic state, Canada could become the envied seat of a form of federalism that belongs to tomorrow's world. Better than the American melting-pot, Canada could offer an example to all those new Asian and African states already discussed at the beginning of this article, who must discover how to govern their polyethnic populations with proper regard for justice and liberty. What better reason for cold-shouldering the lure of annexation to the United States? Canadian federalism is an experiment of major proportions; it could become a brilliant prototype for the moulding of tomorrow's civilization.

If English Canadians cannot see it, again I say so much the worse for them; they will be subsiding into a backward, short-sighted, and despotic nationalism. Lord Acton, one of the great thinkers of the nineteenth century, described, with extraordinarily prophetic insight, the error of the various nationalisms and the future they were preparing. Exactly a century ago he wrote:

> A great democracy must either sacrifice self-government to unity or preserve it by federalism. . . . The co-existence of several nations under the same State is a test, as well as the best security of its freedom. It is also one of the chief instruments of civilization. . . . The combination of different nations in one State is as necessary a condition of civilized life as the combination of men in society. . . . Where political and national boundaries coincide, society ceases to advance, and nations relapse into a condition corresponding to that of men who renounce intercourse with their fellow-men. . . . A State which is incompetent to satisfy different races condemns itself; a State which labours to neutralize, to absorb, or to expel them is destitute of the chief basis of self-government. The theory of nationality, then, is a retrograde step in history.

It goes without saying that if, in the face of Anglo-Canadian nationalism, French Canadians retreat into their own nationalistic shell, they will condemn themselves to the same stagnation. And Canada will become a sterile soil for the minds of her people, a barren waste prey to every wandering host and conquering horde.

I will say it once again: the die is cast in Canada. Neither of our two language groups can force assimilation on the other. But one or the other, or even both, could lose by default, destroying itself from within, and dying of suffocation. And accordingly, by the same law of retribution and in just reward for faith in humanity, victory is promised to the nation that rejects its nationalistic obsessions and, with the full support of its members, applies all the powers at its command to the pursuit of the most far-reaching and human ideal.

By the terms of the existing Canadian constitution, that of 1867,* French Canadians have all the powers they need to make Quebec a political society affording due respect for nationalist aspirations and at the same time giving unprecedented scope for human potential in the broadest sense. (On pages 98–9 of his book, Mr.

---

*This was what I had in mind when I wrote—referring to the younger Separatists—something that annoyed a great many people: "They . . . are tilting headlong at problems which already had their solution a century ago" (*Cité libre*, December 1961, p. 3).

Chaput proposes sixteen items of economic reform which could be undertaken by an independent Quebec. Except for the first, which would abolish taxes levied by Ottawa, all these reforms could be undertaken under the present constitution! On pages 123–4, Mr. Chaput outlines, in seven items, the measures by which an independent Quebec could ensure the protection of French-Canadian minorities outside Quebec. None of these, except the declaration of sovereignty itself, would be any more accessible to an independent Quebec than it is to present-day Quebec.)

If Quebec became such a shining example, if to live there were to partake of freedom and progress, if culture enjoyed a place of honour there, if the universities commanded respect and renown from afar, if the administration of public affairs were the best in the land (and none of this presupposes any declaration of independence!) French Canadians would no longer need to do battle for bilingualism; the ability to speak French would become a status symbol, even an open sesame in business and public life. Even in Ottawa, superior competence on the part of our politicians and civil servants would bring spectacular changes.

Such an undertaking, though immensely difficult, would be possible; it would take more guts than jaw. And therein, it would seem to me, is an "ideal" not a whit less "inspiring" than that other one that has been in vogue for a couple of years in our little part of the world.

For those who would put their shoulders to the wheel, who would pin their hopes for the future on the fully developed man of intellect, and who would refuse to be party to *la nouvelle trahison des clercs*, I close with a final word from the great Lord Acton:

> Nationalism does not aim either at liberty or prosperity, both of which it sacrifices to the imperative necessity of making the nation the mould and measure of the State. Its course will be marked with material as well as moral ruin, in order that a new invention may prevail over the works of God and the interests of mankind.

Speech at the Paul Sauvé Arena, Montreal, Quebec, May 14, 1980 (TRANSLATION)

Pierre Trudeau

MR. CHAIRMAN

(Applause)

Thank you. Thank you very much. Thank you very much.

(Applause)

No, no. Thank you very much.

(Applause)

Mr. Chairman, fellow Canadians.

(Applause)

First of all, I want to thank you for this warm welcome. I think it is obvious by this immense gathering—it is obvious that these are historic moments.

There are very few examples in the history of democracy of one part of a country choosing to decide, for itself and by itself, whether, YES or NO, it wants to be part of the country to which it has always belonged. There are very few occasions when this has happened in the history of democracy. And I believe that all those here this evening, all those who have worked for the NO in this province for over a month, will be proud to reply when when our children and perhaps, if we are lucky our grandchildren, ask us in twenty or thirty years:

You were there in May 1980. You were there when the people of Quebec were asked to decide freely on their future. You were there when Quebec had the option to stay in Canada or to leave. What did you do in May 1980—"No, that was our answer."

(Applause)

I should like to ask you this evening to reflect on the question that is asked of us, and on the consequences of the answers we may give to these questions.

Allow me—perhaps for the last time before going to the polls-allow me to remind you of the essence of the question. There are two issues involved:

The first is the sovereignty of Quebec, and that is defined in the question itself as: the exclusive power to make its laws, levy its taxes and establish relations abroad in other words, sovereignty.

And while we in this room answer NO, in other rooms in other parts of the province, there are people who answer YES; who truly and honestly want sovereignty.

I share your opinion: this is the false option; an option that means, as Jean Chrétien said, that we will no longer send Quebec MPs to govern us in Canada; an option that means independence; an option that means the separation of Quebec from the rest of the country.

To this our answer is NO.

But it is not to those who are for or against sovereignty that I wish to address my remarks this evening.

After the referendum, I hope we will continue to respect one another's differences; that we will respect the option which has been freely chosen by those who are for or against independence for Quebec.

(Applause)

In this question, therefore, there is sovereignty and there is everything else.

Everything else is a new agreement. It is equality of nations. It is at the same time economic association. It is a common currency. It is change through another referendum. It is a mandate to negotiate.

And we know very well what they are doing, these hucksters of the YES vote.

They are trying to appeal to everyone who would say YES to a new agreement. YES to equality of nations. YES at the same time to association. YES at the same time to a common currency. YES to a second referendum. YES to a simple mandate to negotiate.

It is those who say YES through pride of because they do not understand the question, or because they want to increase their bargaining power, and to those among the undecided who are on the brink of voting YES, to whom I am addressing myself this evening, because what we have to ask ourselves is what would happen in the case of a YES vote, as in the case of a NO vote.

And it is the undecided, those who are on the YES side through pride, or because they are tired and fed up, who, in these last few days, must be addressed.

So let us consider this. The Government of Canada and all the provincial governments have made themselves perfectly clear.

If the answer to the referendum question is NO, we have all said that this NO will be interpreted as a mandate to change the Constitution, to renew federalism.

(Applause)

I am not the only person saying this. Nor is Mr. Clark. Nor is Mr. Broadbent. It is not only the nine premiers of the other provinces saying this. It is also the seventy-five MPs elected by Quebecers to represent them in Ottawa

(Applause)

who are saying that a NO means change. And because I spoke to these MPs this morning, I know that I can make a most solemn commitment that following a NO vote, we will immediately take action to renew the Constitution and we will not stop until we have done that.

And I make a solemn declaration to all Canadians in the other provinces, we, the Quebec MPs, are laying ourselves on the line, because we are telling Quebecers to vote NO and telling you in the other provinces that we will not agree to your interpreting a NO vote as an indication that everything is fine and can remain as it was before.

We want change and we are willing to lay our seats in the House on the line to have change.

This would be our attitude in the case of a NO vote.

Mr. Lévesque has asked me what my attitude would be if the majority of Quebecers voted YES.

I have already answered this question. I did so in Parliament. I did so in Montreal and in Quebec City. And I say it again this evening: if the answer to the referendum is YES—I have said it clearly in the House of Commons—Mr Lévesque will be welcome to come to Ottawa, where I will receive politely, as he has always received me in Quebec City, and I will tell him that there are two doors. If you knock on the sovereignty-association door, there is no negotiation possible.

(Applause)

Mr. Lévesque continues to repeat, "But what about democracy—what would you do if a majority of the Quebec people voted YES? Would you not be obliged, by the principle of democracy, to negotiate?"

No indeed!

It is like saying to Mr. Lévesque, "The people of Newfoundland have just voted 100 percent in favour of renegotiating the electricity contract with Quebec. You are obliged, the name of democracy, to respect the will of Newfoundland, are you not?"

It is obvious that this sort of logic does not work.

The wishes of Quebecers may be expressed through democratic process, but that cannot bind others—those in other provinces who did not vote to act as Quebec decides.

So by that reasoning, Mr. Lévesque, there will be no association. Now, if you want to speak, if you want to speak of sovereignty, let me say that you have no mandate to negotiate that, because you did not ask Quebecers if they wanted sovereignty pure and simple.

You said: Do you want sovereignty on the condition that there is also association?

So, with no association, you have no mandate to negotiate sovereignty; you do not have the key to open that door, and neither do I.

(Applause)

I do not have that mandate either, because we were elected on February 18, scarcely a couple of months ago—for the specific purpose of making laws for the province of Quebec.

So don't ask me not to make any, don't ask me to give full powers to Quebec.

(Applause)

On the other hand, if Mr. Lévesque, by some miracle, and it truly would be a miracle, knocked on the other door, saying: I have a mandate to negotiate, and would like to negotiate renewed federalism then the door would be wide open to him, and I would say: you did not have to go to the trouble of holding a referendum for that; if it is renewed federalism you want, if that is what you wish to negotiate, then you are welcome.

But is it really possible that Mr. Lévesque would say that, because what are the YES supporters saying?

The YES supporters are saying—and I asked Mr. Lévesque this a couple of weeks ago: What will you do if the majority votes NO? What will you say then? Will you respect the will of the people, or will you claim that a NO vote does not mean as much as a YES vote, and that a NO does not count for the moment, but that another referendum needs to be held?

I asked Mr. Lévesque that, and this was his answer: We will not refuse a few crumbs of autonomy for Quebec, but we will still be going around in circles.

Mr. Lévesque, if the people of Quebec vote NO, as I believe they will

(Applause)

won't you say that since the people have rejected sovereignty-association, it is your duty to be a good government and put an end to the status quo on which you place so much blame, and to join us in changing the Constitution.

Mr. Lévesque told us: we will still be going around in circles.

Well, that should enlighten all those who intend to vote YES in order to increase Quebec's bargaining power, all those who intend to vote YES out of pride, and all those who intend to vote YES because they are fed up.

If Mr. Lévesque does not want renewed federalism even if the people note NO, then, clearly, if the people vote YES, he is going to say:

"Renewed federalism is out of the question."

For my part, I will say: Sovereignty-Association is out of the question.

(Applause)

Which means that we have reached an impasse and those who vote YES must realize right now that a YES vote will result in either independence, pure and simple, or the status quo—that is what the YES option boils down to: the independence of Quebec, the separation of Quebec, or else the status quo, no change, because Mr. Lévesque refuses to negotiate.

That's what we have to say to the YES side: if you want independence, if you vote YES, you won't get independence because you made it conditional on there being an Association, an Association being achieved along with independence.

If you want Association, your YES vote doesn't mean anything because it is not binding on the other provinces, which refuse to join in an association with you. And if you vote YES for a renewed federalism, your vote will be lost as well, because Mr. Lévesque will still be going around in circles.

So you see, that is the impasse that this ambiguous, equivocal question has led us into, and that is what the people who are going to vote YES out of pride, that is what they should think about.

Voting YES out of pride means that we are putting our fate in the hands of the other provinces, which are going to say NO, no association, and then we will have to swallow our pride and our YES vote.

And those who are saying YES in order to get it over with, YES to break away, Yes to get negotiations started, they read in the question itself that there will be a second referendum, and then maybe a third, and then maybe a fourth. And that, my friends, that is precisely what we are criticizing the Parti Québecois government for; not for having want Independence—that is an option we reject and we're fighting it openly.

But what we are criticizing the Parti Québecois for is for not having the courage to ask: INDEPENDENCE, YES or NO?

(Applause)

YES or NO?

(Applause)

You, the supporters of the NO side, you know the divisions this referendum has caused. You have seen the divisions it has caused with families. You have seen the hatred it has created between neighbours. You know it has widened the generation gap. You know that the deep suspicion and mistrust between supporters of the YES side and those of the NO side will last for a long time to come.

You know what kind of trial the referendum is. Well, you have been told by the Parti Québecois government that there will be other referendums and you know that the hatred, the differences, the enormous waste of energy in Quebec will go on and on. Well, we are saying NO to that. NO, it will not go on.

(Applause)

Here is a party whose goal was separation, then independence, then sovereignty, then Sovereignty-Association, and then they even said that Sovereignty-Association was only for the purposes of negotiation. Here is a party that, in the name of pride, said to Quebecers: Stand up, we are going to move on to the world stage and assert ourselves.

And now, this party, on the point of entering the world stage, gets frightened and stays in the wings. Is that pride? Should we use that as a reason to vote for a party that tells us it will start all over again if the answer is YES, that there will be another referendum?

Well, that is what we are criticizing the Parti Québecois for—not having the courage to ask a clear question, a question a mature people would have been able to answer, really a simple question: DO YOU WANT TO LEAVE CANADA, YES OR NO?

NO:

(Applause)

Well, it's because the Parti Québecois knew how the vast majority of Quebecers would answer the question: DO YOU want to stop being Canadians. The answer would have been NO and that is why it has failed to enter the world stage.

Well, we know there is a clear answer, there is an unambiguous answer and that answer is NO. That answer is NO to those who want, as Camil Samson, I think said, to take our heritage away from us and from our children.

The answer is NO to those who advocate separation rather than sharing, to those who advocate isolation rather than fellowship, to those who—basically—advocate pride rather than love, because love involves challenges coming together and meeting others half-way, and working with them to build a better world.

So then, one must say, leaving that whole convoluted question aside, one must say NO to ambiguity. One must say NO to tricks. One must say NO to contempt, because they have come to that.

I was told that no more than two days ago Mr. Lévesque was saying that part of my name was Elliott and, since Elliott was an English name, it was perfectly understandable that I was for the NO side, because, really, you see, I was not as much of a Quebecer as those who are going to vote YES.

That, my dear friends, is what contempt is. It means saying that there are different kinds of Quebecers. It means that saying that the Quebecers on the NO side are not as good Quebecers as the others and perhaps they have a drop or two of foreign blood, while the people on the YES side have pure blood in their veins. That is what contempt is and that is the kind of division which builds up within a people, and that is what we are saying NO to.

Of course my name is Pierre Elliott Trudeau. Yes, Elliott was my mother's name. It was the name borne by the Elliotts who came to Canada more than two hundred years ago. It is the name of the Elliotts who, more than one hundred years ago, settled in Saint-Gabriel de Brandon, where you can still see their graves in the cemetery. That is what the Elliotts are.

My name is a Quebec name, but my name is a Canadian name also, and that's the story of my name.

Since Mr. Lévesque has chosen to analyse my name, but let me show you how ridiculous it is to use that kind of contemptuous argument.

Mr. Pierre-Marc Johnson is a Minister. Now, I ask you, is Johnson an English name or a French name?

And Louis O'Neill—a former Minister of Mr. Lévesque's and Robert Bruns, and Daniel Johnson, I ask you, are they Quebecers, yes or no?

And, if we are looking at names, I saw in yesterday's newspaper that the leader of Quebec's inuit, the Eskimos, they are going to vote NO. Do you know what the leader's name is? His name is Charlie Watt. Is Charlie Watt not a Quebecer? These people have lived in Quebec since the Stone Age; they have been here since time immemorial. And Mr. Watt is not a Quebecer?

(Applause)

And, according to yesterday's newspaper, the chief of the Micmac Band, at Restigouche, the chief of fifteen hundred Indians—what is his name? Ron Maloney. Is he not a Quebecer? The Indians have been there for a good two thousand years. And their chief is not a Quebecer?

My dear friends, Laurier said something in 1889, nearly one hundred years ago now, and it's worth taking the time to read these lines: "My Countrymen," said Laurier, "are not only those in whose veins runs the blood of France. My countrymen are all those people—no matter what their race or language—whom the fortunes of war, the twists and turns of fate, or their own choice, have brought among us."

All Quebecers have the right to vote YES or NO, as Mrs. De Santis said. And all those Nos are as valid as any YES, regardless of the name of the person voting, or the colour of his skin.

(Applause)

My friends, Péquistes often tell us: the world is watching us, hold our heads high; the world is watching us, the whole world is watching what is happening in our democracy. Let's show them we are proud.

Well, I just received what is apparently the last pamphlet that will be put out by the YES committee. Go pick it up somewhere. I recommend it. It's a historic document.

It's a historic document because we find, all through this pamphlet, expressions such as NEGOTIATE SERIOUSLY—A QUEBEC PROJECT—A BETTER CONTRACT WITH THE REST OF CANADA—AN ASSOCIATION BETWEEN EQUALS—NEGOTIATIONS—ANOTHER REFERENDUM.

We don't once find the word SEPARATISM. We don't find the word INDEPENDENCE, either. We don't find the word SOVEREIGNTY. We don't find, not even once, the term SOVEREIGNTY-ASSOCIATION.

That's what pride is!

That's what deceiving the public is. And I don't know what historians will say about those who lacked courage at this historic turning point, but I know that they will be hard on those who sought to deceive the public and who say, in this last pamphlet—who say this: Some would have you believe that the question deals with separation. That's false.

That's false. Your question is about SOVEREIGNTY. Take a stand, you PQ supporters. Show us your true colours. Are you for independence?

(From the floor: NO)

No. We are against independence. Of course the world is watching us. The world will be a bit astonished by what it sees. I admit, because in today's world.

(Applause)

you see, things are unstable, to say the least. The parameters are changing, to use a big word. And that means that there is fire and blood in the Middle-East, in Afghanistan, in Iran, in Vietnam, that means that there is inflation which is crippling the free economy; that means that there is division in the world; that means there is perhaps a third of the human race which goes to bed hungry every night, because there is not enough food and not enough medicine to keep the children in good health.

And that world is looking at Canada, the second largest country in the world, one of the richest, perhaps the second richest country in the world.

(Applause)

A country which is composed of the meeting of the two most outstanding cultures of the Western world: the French and the English, added to by all the other cultures coming from every corner of Europe and every corner of the world. And this is what the world is looking at with astonishment, saying: These people think they might split up today when the whole world is interdependent? When Europe is trying to seek some kind of political union? These people in Quebec and in Canada want to split it up?

(From the floor: NO)

they want to to take it away from their children.

(From the floor: NO)

they want to break it down? NO. That's what I am answering.

(Applause—NO, NO, NO)

I quoted Laurier, and let me quote a Father of Confederation who was an illustrious Quebecer: Thomas D'Arcy McGee. The new nationality—he was saying—is thoughtful and true; nationalist in its preference, but universal in its sympathies; a nationality of the spirit, for there is a new duty which especially belongs to Canada to create a state and to originate a history which the world will not willingly let die.

Well, we won't let it die. Our answer is: NO, to those who would kill it.

(Applause)

(Prime Minister repeats in French last part of D'Arcy McGee quotation)

We won't let this country die, this Canada, our home and native land, this Canada which really is, as our national anthem says, our home and native land. We are going to say to those who want us to stop being Canadians, we are going to say a resounding, an overwhelming NO:

(NO—Applause)

The Sphinx

Catherine Annau

I AM A CARD-CARRYING member of the Trudeau generation. Those of us born in the 1960s were too young to vote for Pierre Elliott Trudeau. All we got to do was grow up with him.

The way I see it, if the 1970s belonged to Trudeau and my optimistic adolescence, then the 1980s belonged to the men in dark suits and the reality of adulthood. Our new prime minister Brian Mulroney, speaking to bankers in New York City in 1984, declared that "Canada is now open for business" and enjoined the Big Boys to buy up the country. During the Mulroney years, venerable national institutions were dismantled or cut back to the bone. A new mantra of "privatization" and "deficit reduction" was chanted from sea to shining sea. The new guard informed us that we had been "overprotected" and that from now on we Canucks had to face the harsh realities of the real world.

But by the early 1990s our American conquerors, having snagged all the free toiletries and towels they could, checked out—leaving us to stumble through what were the worst economic times since the 1930s. Brian Mulroney, so confident and imperious early in his reign, now stood helplessly amid the wreckage of the Meech Lake and Charlottetown accords. Despite this would-be nation builder's best efforts to make his mark on history, the situation in Quebec had actually deteriorated. The place cards had been tossed, the chairs had been put on the tables and the party was definitely over.

The dismal climate of the early 1990s made it hard to remember that Canada hadn't always been this way. I grew up in Toronto in the 1970s, in what is now known as the heyday of Canadian nationalism. Both my parents were immigrants. My father left Hungary in 1945, just ahead of Stalin's legions, and came to Canada in 1951, the same year as my British-born mother. My parents met on a blind date in 1952. I came on the scene in 1965, with my two sisters following in 1968 and 1970. My childhood was a mosaic of cultural influences, from my Hungarian grandmother's hazelnut cookies to a well-worn collection of Enid Blyton's books to hanging out at the local mall.

Like many who had come before me, I searched for a Canadian identity. I found mine in Trudeau's vision of a Canada that was one country, two languages, many cultures. Looking back, I realize that Trudeau's idea of Canada was so pervasive it might have been an additive in our drinking water. Between the Participation propaganda I was fed in elementary school, my French classes, and my parents' endless enthusiasm for the new Canada, I became a Trudeauite by osmosis. It may seem naïve, but it worked for me. It made a neat fit with my particular linguistic and cultural pedigree.

A thoroughly modern Canadian, I embraced learning French because for me a bilingual Canada *was* Canada. Only much later, in my thirties, did I come to realize how fully I had bought into Trudeau's vision. A keener I might have been, but I truly believed that learning to speak French was about saving the country.

At sixteen, I plastered the walls of my North Toronto bedroom with posters stolen off construction hoardings during visits to Quebec City and Montreal. The posters served as teen wallpaper, but they also reminded me of the romance and adventure of the exotic other world only a few hours down the road from boring Toronto. I spent hours lying on the living room floor of my girlfriend Gill's house, memorizing the lyrics to songs by Québécois folk-rockers Harmonium, smoking clove cigarettes, and blissfully dreaming of having a French-Canadian boyfriend.

So intoxicated were Gill and I by the promise of Québécois culture that we even took a vacation to Quebec City in the dead of winter. To sanctify the memory, I'd love to say this trip was when I met my French-Canadian dream lover. But the truth was anything but romantic. The weather was so cold we spent less time on the Plains of Abraham than the fifteen minutes the actual battle lasted, then spent two hours in a café just inside the walls of the old city desperately trying to warm up. The only men we met belonged to the middle-aged lonely-hearts crowd. Still, our dream of French Canada persisted.

In the midst of all my teenage angst, one thing was certain. P.E.T. was my hero, and there was no way the country was going to fall apart under his watch. So, for me, the 1980 referendum drama came and went without much surprise. In 1982, after Canada got its own Constitution, I remember my father coming home from Ottawa where he'd been on business, bearing gifts of constitutional memorabilia. He had booklets from the swearing-in ceremony, first-day-issue stamps, and copies of the Constitution Act for my sisters and me. I wasn't excited by these souvenirs so much as puzzled. By his own admission, my father had stumbled upon the ceremony and scarcely seen it across the sea of heads and umbrellas on Parliament Hill. As for the document itself, which had been so long fought over and was, with its Charter of Rights and Freedoms, a truly magnificent achievement, it seemed somewhat underwhelming: a rather ugly bureaucratic booklet notable only for the bad design typical of so many government publications. The excitement around the 1980 referendum I had understood—the visuals were better; the ideas easier to grasp. This I could not. It wasn't until our geography became explicitly linked to constitutional accords that I began to sense that this poorly packaged document would prove to fascinate politicians far more than had the 1980 Referendum ever did.

In the fall of 1985, as I headed from Toronto to Montreal for my first year at McGill, the issue of separation seemed to me to be pretty much dead. And as politically inclined as I was, the prospect of finally living in the city I had so long ideal-ized preoccupied me much more. Once there, I relished walking through the Pla-teau on my way to the university and hearing French being spoken all around me. Frustrated by my slow progress at speaking French, in the summer of 1988 I jour-neyed up to Chicoutimi to take part in the federal government's Second Language Bursary program. Politics seemed very far away as we watched French-Canadian movies and learned about French-Canadian culture and lived with French-speaking families. I even began to dream in French.

But in June 1990, still at McGill and now in the middle of my History M.A., I woke up. My buddies and I had decided to take in the annual Saint-Jean-Baptiste parade. Standing on the curb at Jeanne Mance and Sherbrooke, we watched as the colourful floats celebrating great moments in Quebec history gave way to chants of "Le Québec aux Québécois!" The air became, literally and metaphorically, stifling. As we drifted back to our apartments we felt like strangers in our own country, as if we were guest workers or tourists, and not particularly welcome ones at that. Upon graduation, fed up with a Canada that now promised neither economic nor politi-cal stability, many of my peers left to seek their dreams south of the border, in the country of cohesive myth and seemingly endless opportunity.

Where, I felt like screaming, was my Canada in all of this? Where was Trudeau's Canada, the dream I'd grown up believing in? And where was Trudeau himself? With his walk in the snow in 1984—the one that took him all the way back to his Art Deco mansion in Montreal—we had lost a vision of ourselves as stylish and sophisticated. Meanwhile, the constitutional revisionists had blanketed the country in a profound sense of ennui. Occasionally, Trudeau would emerge to remind us of what we could be, what we might achieve, and what we were on the point of losing. With his accus-tomed flair he spoke out against Meech Lake, calling Mulroney and his companions "pleutres," and in the process sending the French and English media alike scurry-ing for their dictionaries. The old gunslinger showed he still had it. In 1992, at the eleventh hour, he issued a blistering attack on Charlottetown from the Montreal res-taurant La Maison Eggroll, reminding us all that there was a larger vision at stake. He had not lost the ability to surprise and astonish us.

In 1995, Trudeau gave us perhaps the greatest surprise of all—he said nothing. Canada faced yet another Quebec referendum and the possibility of disintegration. Perhaps he was bullied into silence by his political heirs who thought they could handle things, or perhaps he'd simply had enough. But those of us looking for some-one to defend the country found the house lights down and the stage empty.

I can't emphasize enough how deeply the close call of 1995 shook me. In my mind I stood stunned amid the discarded "Oui" posters and "Non" balloons, the wrapping-paper remains of the second Quebec referendum in my lifetime. It felt like a bloodletting. This wasn't politics in the abstract; it was my home, my family, my neighbourhood that was at stake. My lovers, my friends, my trains, and my trails. It was the country of my parents' new beginnings, the country that had shaped me.

This near-death experience, witnessed via television, galvanized me to begin work, first in my own head and by 1997 at the National Film Board, on what would become my film, *Just Watch Me: Trudeau and the 70s Generation*.

After graduation I had returned to Toronto, where through good luck and good timing I found myself working in film as a researcher. With hindsight, it seems obvious that I would one day make a documentary about bilingualism, Trudeau, and my generation. But at the time the subject didn't seem quite sexy enough, and I was too busy learning the ropes and paying my dues.

The promise of Trudeau's Canada, I realized, wasn't just part of my autobiography, it was the story of a whole generation of Canadians. Despite his contradictions and his failures, Trudeau encouraged us to believe in a Canada that was bilingual and multicultural, a nation that recognized French Canadians had suffered discrimination, and that sought to right those wrongs. He allowed us to see ourselves as an open, tolerant, intellectual, and romantic people. This is what I believed then and what I believe now, and no amount of smooth talking from men in dark suits is going to convince me otherwise.

I met Pierre Elliott Trudeau only once, and to tell the truth, it was something of a let down. The occasion was the Toronto relaunch of *Cité libre* in the winter of 1998. Since I had just begun the research for my NFB film, attending a reception with the man himself seemed propitious. So, on a cold, snowy, January evening my producer Gerry Flahive and I trekked down to Metro Hall. The room held a veritable Who's Who of the English-Canadian cultural and intellectual establishment—of about thirty years ago. At age thirty-two, I was perhaps the youngest person in the room and began to feel as if I'd crashed a bad party.

Suddenly klieg lights illuminated the podium, a receiving line was formed, and we all filed past the guest of honour. We were each given ten seconds to express our admiration and gratitude and get out of the way. My exchange with the Great Man was for all intents and purposes banal. He barely spoke and I was struck by how old and shrunken he seemed. A far cry from the last time I'd seen him on television, vigorously paddling a canoe. As I shook his hand, however, a slight smile crossed his lips and a distant twinkle could be discerned in his eyes. But there was no mistaking this for the Trudeau of my youth. That man had vanished. Like the era he had dominated.

Yet during those few brief seconds, I understood why Trudeau continues to captivate us. He showed us a Canada greater than the mere sum of its parts. His vision may have faded and the two solitudes may continue to divide us, perhaps now more than ever, but it still has the power to inspire us. I know this to be true, and I know Lucky Pierre knows it too. I saw it in his eyes.

CHAPTER FIFTEEN

Anne of Green Gables and Commodification of Canada

Introduction

Canada is a country of regions. Although an imperfect and imprecise definition, Canada's regions are most often defined by geography and political boundaries: the Atlantic provinces, Quebec, Ontario, the prairie provinces, British Columbia and the north. Regions are both real places and states of mind. In chapters 13 and 14 we saw how Quebec is a real place that can be located on a map and how Quebec is a state of mind: *je suis Québécois*. In this chapter we turn our attention east to Prince Edward Island and its most famous native daughter, the fictional character Anne, from Lucy Maud Montgomery's 1908 novel, *Anne of Green Gables*. Although the PEI-born Montgomery would publish 22 novels, some 500 short stories and over 500 poems, her most famous work remains her first: *Anne of Green Gables*.

Anne Shirley is a red-haired, freckle-faced little orphan girl who is adopted by an elderly Island couple who want a boy to help with the farm work. But the spunky, lovable Anne quickly wins their hearts and, for that matter, has been winning hearts ever since. Translated into several languages—including Polish and Japanese—and made into musicals, movies and television shows, *Anne of Green Gables* is now more than a book and Anne is more than a fictional character. Both are commodities. The area around Cavendish, PEI, where Montgomery was raised, is now an important tourist destination and tourism is crucial to the Island economy. Every summer, thousands of people from across Canada and from around the world, make their way to Green Gables, the farm that once belonged to cousins of Montgomery's grandfather and inspired the setting for *Anne of Green Gables*. Acquired by the Government of Canada in 1937, Green Gables is part of Prince Edward Island National Park. Green Gables is at once unique (rooted in a specific place and time, it would not make sense to replicate it in, say, downtown Los Angeles) and generic (opening with an interpretive centre and closing with a gift shop that sells an endless array of Anne products, from the obligatory Anne of Green Gables fridge magnets to the very odd Anne of Green Gables finger and toe nail clippers, it conforms to an international formula, to the logic of modern tourist destinations everywhere).

A figure from a specific region, Anne has national and international appeal. In her article, Tara Nogler looks at the "Anne thing" in Japan. Why does Anne strike a resonant chord in Japan? What are people—not just Japanese people—buying when they buy Anne? How has Prince Edward Island turned regional stereotypes of simplicity and innocence into a tourist economy? In May 2000 Laura Robinson—then a professor of English at the Royal Military College in Kingston and now a professor of English at Nipissing University in North Bay—delivered an academic paper at an academic conference. It became a national and international story. Did Robinson say that Anne was gay? If not, why the outrage?

Snapshot: **My Life as Anne in Japan**

Tara Nogler

AS A SHY yet excitable redhead growing up on Prince Edward Island, I vividly recall my first viewing of the musical production at age four, an experience marked by my parents' frantic attempts to keep me in my seat. *Anne of Green Gables* was one of the first novels I read. At age thirteen, I was hired by a company named 'Anne and I on P.E.I.' to play the red-haired Anne Shirley during the summer tourist season in Cavendish. Playacting Anne, I attended birthday parties and weekend picnics and was interviewed on radio to promote the company. I had my picture taken with tourists, many of them Japanese. Even with the language barrier, my introduction to the Japanese love of Anne was memorable. I vividly recall a young Japanese woman clinging to my body, crying and sobbing uncontrollably: at thirteen, a powerful if somewhat disconcerting experience.

In April 1996, by then a university student, I noticed a classified advertisement in Charlottetown's *The Guardian* newspaper:

Employment opportunity:

Applications are being accepted for employment as 'Theme Park Hosts' with Canadian World in Ashibetsu, Japan. Successful Candidates will portray Anne, Diana, Gilbert and Miss Stacy. Acting experience required.

Even though I no longer harboured illusions of grandeur concerning my acting ability, I took my cue from my encouraging mother and made the call to Charlottetown's City Hall.

Three weeks later, I was on a plane bound for Sapporo, the capital city of Hokkaido, the north-eastern island of Japan. Much like Anne Shirley upon her arrival at Bright River Station, I was transported to a different world, one that would be my adoptive home for little more than six months. The intense shock of the time change after an eighteen-hour trip, combined with my apparent deafness in one ear (a result of the shift in altitude), lack of sleep, water, and nutrition, not to mention the language barrier, all combined to produce what must have seemed a countenance of stunned semi-catatosis. My anxiety was somewhat allayed by my good-humoured translator/guide/boss, Hiromi Fukada, who slipped in a CD with 'The Vapors.' To the tune of 'I Think I'm Turning Japanese,' we departed from Sapporo's Narita Airport.

On the drive to Ashibetsu City, we stopped at the local Seven-Eleven for my first moment of local culture. While the layout was much like that of North-American convenience stores, there was a mid-sized water tank with live octopus, squid, and other sea urchins. One refrigerated aisle was lined with rice balls, of a variety of shapes and sizes, labelled in one of the four Japanese alphabets. Another section was devoted to snack foods—different combinations of rice crackers, dried and smoked seafood, and trail mixes with mini-dried fish mixed in with peanuts, raisins, and coconut. The walls surrounding the store were lined with a plethora of refrigerated drinks, many of which, as I later learned, were iced teas, coffees, and high-powered sports drinks with names such as 'Pocari Sweat.' The stop produced the desired effect: I had my glimpse of Japanese junk-food culture.

Our destination was Canadian World in Hokkaido, one of many theme parks in Japan dedicated to cultural and national figures. Presenting Canada through a nineteenth-century lens, Canadian World had opened its gates in 1991.[1] Upon entering the park, guests received a 'Canadian' passport, which mapped out the park's terrain and in which they could collect stamps from each of the 'countries.' The theme park spanned one hundred acres, each of the six areas labelled as a 'country.' Avonlea spanned the largest area and served as the main attraction of Canadian World, housing an exact replica of Green Gables. The house was built using the blueprints of the original located in Cavendish, P.E.I.; even the kitchen utensils were placed strategically to reflect the original. Across the way was Diana Barry's house, where guests could rent period clothing and have their pictures taken posing with Anne amid the natural scenery. It was not uncommon to see Japanese women enter sporting long, lacy, and extravagant dresses with petticoats, even in the heat of summer, bearing everything from parasols to Anne dolls. Behind Diana's house was the Haunted Wood, where guests could take a long hike, and Lovers' Lane, which led up to Terra Nova, a large chalet that housed a gift shop, an art gallery, a large collection of antique organs and other musical instruments, and a traditional English-style tea-room. Across a field of sunflowers was Orwell School, where Miss Stacy—or myself, on her days off—conducted hourly basic English lessons.

My life as Anne Shirley involved greeting guests, conducting tours, posing for photographs with tourists and for promotional and advertising shoots, doing interviews for various television shows, and performing skits from *Anne of Green Gables*. My average daily schedule looked like this:

6–7:00 a.m.   Wake up and prepare for work.

7:30 a.m.   Catch Canadian World bus at Maple Heights, Kamiashibetsu.

8:00 a.m.   Arrive at Canadian World 'Parliament' (main office).

8:00–8:25 a.m. Get into costume, prepare make-up, braid hair, etc.

8:25 a.m.   Attend staff meeting with three big bosses and office staff. Greetings, prayers, and debriefing session on the day's events.

8:45 a.m.	Walk to the front gates of Canadian World with four fellow Canadian actors.
9–10:00 a.m.	Greet guests entering the park; pose for pictures, etc.
10:00 a.m.	Walk from front gate through Bright River Station, past clock tower, to Avonlea and Green Gables.
11:30 a.m.	Have lunch.
12:20 p.m.	Walk to Terrase Dufferin to make appearance and attend the lunchtime performance shows; once or twice a week, do weekly performance or skit of scenes from the play.
12:50 p.m.	With Miss Stacy and Diana, take bus to Orwell School-house for 1:00 p.m. English conversation lessons.
2:00 p.m.	Leave Orwell School and return to Green Gables or Colts to converse with guests.
2:30 p.m.	Go to Mrs Lynde's Restaurant for 'Teatime with Anne,' to socialize with guests and discuss Canada and Island life and culture.
3:00 p.m.	Return to Green Gables for pictures, pictures, and more . . .
4:45 p.m.	Return to main entrance to bid farewell to guests.
6:00 p.m.	Return to Parliament (main office) and change.
6:20 p.m.	Take bus back to Kamiashibetsu.
6:45–7:00 p.m.	Arrive home.

While this schedule made up my regular daily routine, there was some room for spontaneity.[2] To guests, I was 'Akage no An chan,' literally translated, 'Anne of Red Hair child.' As Anne, I went wherever my 'Anne spirit' took me. That meant trekking over to Diana Barry's house, where guests paid to dress up in nineteenth-century period clothing, complete with 'Anne' paraphernalia: parasols, wigs, hats, and make-up. As Anne, I ran down to Terrase Dufferin, a strip of restaurants and cafés styled after Old Quebec, featuring 'Canadian' cuisine and gift shops on the bank of 'The Lake of Shining Waters,' in front of which buskers and performers displayed their talents to an eager audience. Still as Anne, I also enjoyed horseback riding, picnicking, or canoeing in the Lake of Shining Waters on quiet days. Sometimes I was able to steal away to the First Aid Station for a lunchtime nap.

During the busy months of June to August, we routinely welcomed up to two thousand Japanese guests per day, including five to ten tour buses with high school girls or Anne clubs from across Japan. As the only 'Anne' working in the park, I was in high demand. Along with four other Canadians who played Diana, Miss Stacy, and other characters from the novel, I felt an experience akin to the 'Mickey Mouse' phenomenon in the United States. As Anne, I was the star of the show, for visitors did not always remember the other characters in the novel, many having been exposed to the film versions or to *Animé,* a popular, condensed pocketbook version of the story.[3]

Within its beautiful nature setting, the park served as site for various Canadian rituals, most notably the Western wedding. Surrounded by immaculate gardens, there was a church in which many Japanese couples had Christian weddings performed after their traditional Shinto wedding. Many young women devoted to Canadian culture saw the Christian wedding as an act designed to bring good luck or good fortune. This practice of the double wedding, a recent trend, seemed more common with couples from Honshu, the most densely populated central island of Japan. Similarly, Anne was most popular in the biggest cities such as Tokyo and Osaka, as city dwellers are drawn to Anne's longing for innocence, simplicity, and beauty in nature. In this way, the appeal of Hokkaido was obvious: natural beauty, scenery, and serenity were marketed as avidly as Anne Shirley herself. Historians and literary scholars, including Douglas Baldwin in 'L.M. Montgomery's *Anne of Green Gables:* The Japanese Connection' and Yoshiko Akamatsu in 'Japanese Readings of *Anne of Green Gables,*' have documented that this desire for nature and innocence explains aspects of Anne's appeal to the Japanese. Canadian life amid beautiful natural scenery and surrounded by mountains (reminiscent of the Canadian West) provided an ideal setting. Not only was the climate similar to Canada's, Hokkaido being subject to climatic extremes and unpredictable weather, but there was little boundary between the park itself and the surrounding wildlife, with foxes and rabbits wandering freely in the park.

The natural setting of Canadian World was not only part of the park's allure; it also became, like the many Anne products in the gift shops, a marketable product. From bags of lavender bearing the title, 'Anne's Lavender Dreams' to dried and pressed flowers and squash from the Craft Village botanical and vegetable gardens, some of the best-selling products came from nature and were used to sell an image of Canada to the Japanese consumer. The products ranged from Anne beanbag dolls to Anne wines and beers, Anne-shaped chocolates, cookies, and candy, and T-shirts bearing the mysterious misprint *Anne of Green Gavole.* When I was touring Osaka, we went to a 'Canadian Bakery' that was selling 'Anne cakies,' a sweet white donut with red bean paste in the middle. Part of our work involved preparing, organizing, and packaging various products to be sold at gift shops in the park and, on a larger scale, at shops in various urban centres. Some of my most vivid memories involve afternoons spent at Green Gables, with friends and fellow workers, separating and packaging bundles of lavender, clover, chives, and other natural products while guests passed through and took our pictures.[4]

In my Anne costume I was a cultural ambassador for Prince Edward Island, but also a promoter of products. Besides my work at the theme park, my position required my participation on many promotional tours and trips across Japan. On my travels, I visited Osaka, Tokyo, Kobe, Asahikawa, and Obihiro. These trips involved non-stop activity. For example, on a five-day trip to Osaka, we spent each day meeting with newspaper and magazine companies (fourteen in one day), appearing on television talk and game shows and at cultural events and department stores, and signing autographs. On these tours, I did television promotions and photography shoots to promote Canadian World and commercial Japanese products, attended business meetings with various company officials (major tourist and commercial companies), and handed out promotional flyers. As Anne, I was constantly in the public eye.

The Japanese fascination with cultural authenticity extended beyond the material trappings of Green Gables and its household products to us as Canadians—foreigners and representatives of Canadian culture. One incident in particular encapsulates for me this pursuit of authenticity, when a television crew for a Tokyo talk show came to do a profile of Canadian World. The hosts were two women in their twenties with cutesy, bright-coloured attire, short skirts, pigtails, and high-heeled boots. I had a short interview with one of the hosts and then gave a tour of the house. While the sight of Anne's room evoked sighs and great enthusiasm, a good portion of the tour was spent in the kitchen where the two hosts fawned over each and every item, from meat grinder to washboard, spoon to broom, wood-stove to wrought-iron pots. Everything was 'authentic' in the words of the hosts!

In the afternoons, Mrs Lynde's Restaurant provided the setting for 'Teatime with Anne,' a period reserved for socializing, during which the guests had an opportunity to test their recently learned English phrases and ask me questions about my life in Canada.[5] While I was asked the typical questions ('What does P.E.I. look like?' 'How many kindred spirits do you have?'), I was also frequently asked questions that seemed odd to me (though commonplace and acceptable to many guests): 'Is that your real hair?' 'What's your blood type?' 'How many teeth do you have?' 'What colour is the roof of your mouth?' 'How many toes do you have?' (The list goes on.) As Anne, I had my hair examined, my skin touched and gawked at, my breasts touched, and my nose tweaked on a daily basis. When I greeted guests, their typical first reaction would involve excited exclamations of *kawaii* ('cute'), followed by *Shashin?* ('May I take a picture?'). While I was often the exotic object of the visitor's gaze, I was also looking in on Japanese culture. The obsession with cuteness and the perfect body image—even more pervasive than in North America—remains a forceful memory. It seemed that Anne's biggest fans were the teenage girls and women in their early twenties who embodied sweetness with their ponytails, short skirts, high-heeled shoes, and 'Hello Kitty' backpacks.

In 'my life as Anne,' certain incidents and experiences stand out. While my promotional tours across Japan gave me insight into Japanese pop and traditional culture, I also visited a live volcano and the hot springs that are reputed to be ancient forms of therapy in Japan and are abundant in the mountains of Hokkaido. Yet my most profound human experience occurred on my visit to Kobe. In 1995, an earthquake had killed nearly 6,000 people and left more than 300,000 homeless; in May 1996, when I visited, people were still picking up the broken pieces of devastation. On the edge of central Kobe, set along a land-filled port, were tents and shelters, temporary housing for the victims of the earthquake. During our stay, we spent a day at an orphanage with children whose parents had been killed in the earthquake. Many of the younger children had never heard of Anne, while others knew her only through the *Animé* cartoon that was popular at the time. Whether or not they knew Anne or the story, however, these children embraced us literally with open arms. I left that orphanage feeling a mixture of sadness, frustration, compassion, yet also of hope and gratitude for the light that shone in their eyes. While I certainly cannot fathom the very real sense of loss and isolation these children must have felt, I could not help but draw connections to Montgomery herself, orphaned as a child, whose adult work weaves the thematic threads of orphans who attempt to forge identities and homes in foreign communities.

I met people who shared their love for L.M. Montgomery and Anne Shirley, as well as sharing their homes and traditions, taking me inside their rich cultures. In Osaka, I visited numerous ancient Shinto and Buddhist shrines and participated in a traditional Japanese tea ceremony, complete with the kimono and obi, conducted by a Shinto priestess. Japan provided for me a stage for exploring my identity and culture. Just as Anne's fictional character negotiates personal spaces of identity in a new home, so did I, and I will always remember the sound of Japanese girls calling out, 'Hello An Chan,' as I walked by in my Anne costume, an exotic attraction in Hokkaido's Avonlea.

Notes

1. The park shut down in 1998 when it was bought out by the City of Ashibetsu. It is now run as a government amusement park. I later learned that Japan housed such theme parks as German World, Spanish World, Dutch World, and American World, among others.
2. Traditional Japanese (Obon, Candle Art, and Cherry Blossom) festivals and celebrations often commanded special celebrations in the park.
3. The renowned Japanese animator-director team of Hayao Miyazaki and Isao Takahata collaborated on the original *anime* screen adaptation of *Akage no An* (1979), while Miyazaki illustrated and produced several picture-book classics, including *Akage no An (Anne of Green Gables)*, vols 1–5, videocassettes (1992) and *'Akage No An': Tokuma Anime Ehon ('Anne of Green Gables': Tokuma Animé Picturebook)* (1996), abbreviated and illustrated versions of *Anne of Green Gables* for children. For a detailed discussion, see Timothy Craig, *Japan Pop!*
4. At one point, we had small bushels of lavender and chives hanging from the ceiling across the whole first floor of Green Gables. Also, during the weeks preceding Halloween, we carved and painted pumpkins, which were sold at the main entrance to the park.
5. Commercial culture played upon this obsession with North American culture, using popular English words and phrases to sell products. It was not uncommon, for example, in a department store, to see a large stock of clothing items with words such as 'happy,' 'beautiful,' 'I Love You' printed on them in a variety of colours and textures. Popular cultural icons ranged, at the time, from Michael Jackson to Elvis Presley to The Carpenters.

Did Our Anne of Green Gables Nurture Gay Fantasies?
Or has a professor had too many sips of Marilla's cordial?

Hanneke Brooymans

ANNE OF GREEN GABLES' love wasn't exclusively for Gilbert, it turns out?

The irrepressible carrot-topped heroine of Canadian author Lucy Maud Montgomery's novels also had lesbian desires and life-long love affairs with at least three women, contends Laura Robinson, a professor at Royal Military College in Kingston.

"Anne's most intense relationships are with Diana Barry, Katherine Brooke and Leslie Moore," said the diminutive academic, her own curly red locks pulled back in a bun. "In each, Anne displays an unbearable longing or desire, and there is some obstacle in the path of their love. The obstacle is finally overcome, only for their love to be trampled upon by the triumph of compulsory heterosexuality, usually for the sake of plot."

Robinson presented her ideas Thursday at the Congress of the Humanities and Social Sciences in a paper entitled *Bosom Friends: Lesbian Desire in L.M. Montgomery's Anne Books.*

She doesn't go as far as to say Anne is a lesbian, but even the suggestion of lesbian tendencies doesn't go over well with everyone.

At Greenwoods' Small World bookstore, Cindy Ewanus sells the popular Anne series, in which the heroine marries Gilbert and has seven children. Ewanus's initial response to the idea that Anne would have lesbian desires was laughter followed by a heartfelt "Good grief!"

"I suppose you can read anything into anything if you want to," she said, admitting she had never heard the theory before.

She wasn't sure how this new perspective on Anne might affect sales of the book.

"If anything it will probably boost sales because people will want to read it to find out what they missed the first time. I just don't know how this will affect sales in Japan."

Montgomery's emphasis on relationships between women are probably modeled after her own experiences, said Robinson.

"She had a lot of intense female friendships. She loved deeply her cousin, Frede, and grieved so much for years and years after she died."

None of these relationships were sexual, though, and Montgomery was married. She did have an encounter with a woman who expressed lesbian desires towards her, though.

In her journals, Montgomery tells of a young teacher named Isobel who became infatuated with her, stalked her and confessed to wanting to kiss her and sleep with her. Montgomery didn't know how to cope with this, but stated emphatically in her journal, "Faugh! I am not a Lesbian."

Yet, even after her experience, she continued to describe deep, involved relationships between the women in her books, while the men occupied marginal roles, said Robinson.

Labeling the desires as lesbian helps challenge assumptions that everything and everyone in society is heterosexual, she said.

The media's response to her paper is a bit of a puzzle to Robinson, since she says the ideas aren't new in academic circles. "Academics are very comfortable with queer theory, I think. People are open to it."

"Big Gay Anne":
Queering Anne of Green Gables and Canadian Culture

Laura M. Robinson

IN MAY 2000, at the annual meeting of the Congress of the Humanities and Social Sciences Council of Canada in Edmonton, Alberta, one paper titled, "Bosom Friends: Lesbian Desire in L.M. Montgomery's Anne Books," drew almost-unbeliev-able media attention, which is fairly unusual for an academic paper in the humanities. What intrigued the media and troubled the general public (not to mention some academics) was the connection the paper made between Canadian children's writer, L.M. Montgomery, her feisty flame-haired heroine, Anne, and lesbianism. The media claimed that I, the author of the controversial paper, declared Anne to be a lesbian. In actuality, I examined Montgomery's Anne books for their treatment of the ideology of compulsory heterosexuality. Regardless of the original argument, the backlash from the media and the public over my perceived research has become its own phenomenon which invites inquiry. Why did people care so much? Why is the public so deeply invested in maintaining a particular view of a literary character? To answer these questions, I will examine what happens when someone challenges the sacred "innocence" of a Canadian icon, and I will suggest that what underwrites the response is not only the need to protect a massive tourist industry but also a ho-mophobia that belies Canada's cherished self-image as a leader in human rights and tolerance. Jostle a red-haired literary character who represents the nation, and the nation's true colours spill forth in a mix of defensiveness and outrage.

A Brief History

First, I will give a small history of the moment, also charted to a degree by Cecily Devereux in "Anatomy of a 'National Icon': Anne of Green Gables and the 'Bosom Friends' Affair."[1] On 12 May 2000, I was contacted, along with the other two panellists in my conference session on Montgomery, by *Ottawa Citizen* reporter, Tom Spears. The "send-to" line of his email contained the names of all three panellists, so I took him at his word that he wanted to cover the entire session.[2] Naively delighted that a reporter was interested in my research, I sent a copy of the requested paper and another paper I was presenting at the same conference. Devereux states that she refused to send her paper, and I do not know if the third panellist, Kate Lawson, did. I did not anticipate nor did I invite the type of reportage or the reactions to my work. By the time I arrived in Edmonton, 24 May, the day before my paper, Spears was attempting to track me down. I blithely chatted with him on the phone the morning of my presentation, 25 May, completely unaware of the headlines on page three of the *Ottawa Citizen* that day: "'Outrageously sexual' Anne was a lesbian, scholar insists" (*Ottawa Citizen,* 25 May 2000, A3). Indeed, it was a producer at CBC Newsworld, calling to set up an interview, who let me know about the article, which scooped my presentation. I only spoke to two reporters that first day: an *Edmonton Journal* reporter who came to my talk and the *Ottawa Citizen* reporter, in addition to the CBC Newsworld producer. The Walkerton water crisis, real and important news, rightfully usurped my spot on Newsworld. Even though the tragedy in Walkerton[3] occurred at the same time, the media would not let go of the "lesbian Anne" story. Some of the media who contacted me were the *Ottawa Citizen, Edmonton Journal,* CBC Newsworld, *Saturday Night* magazine, *Maclean's* magazine, *Globe and Mail, National Post,* CBC Radio Toronto, CBC Radio Ottawa, CBC Radio PEI, CFRB Radio, Talk 460 Radio, QR77 Calgary, and a Japanese magazine. They bombarded my voicemail at the Royal Military College where I worked, they called the secretary of the English Department, they emailed, and they somehow got hold of my unlisted telephone number. The story also appeared in the *Boston Globe,* across Canada in the Southam papers, in *Frank* magazine, on the CNN website, on Swedish and Japanese websites as well as dozens of North American ones, and on radio shows in more places than I know. Letters condemning my work and, most disturbingly, me personally, arrived from Winnipeg; Brandon, Manitoba; Vancouver; Providence, Rhode Island; Austin, Texas; Rancho Palos Verdes, California; Lethbridge, Alberta; and Gatineau, Quebec;[4] I also received some supportive letters and emails from Kingston, Saskatchewan, Toronto, and Montreal. Friends and acquaintances from across the country called and emailed. Unprepared for the hostility and quite distressed, I stopped answering the phone or responding to any questions.

Even as a Montgomery scholar accustomed to enthusiastic Anne fans, I was stupefied by the impassioned response. Most Canadians are familiar with freckle-faced, red-haired Anne, whether they have read the books or not. What is striking is the general public's engagement with this news story, particularly the need to deny the findings of an academic paper the public and most of the media had not read. Spears' initial article is not that misleading, but the headlines give my research a spin that sets it on the edge. Rather than claiming Anne's "outrageously sexual" lesbianism,[5] my paper is an examination of the female friendships in the Anne of Green Gables series, questioning heterosexist assumptions about Anne. If one reads the novels from a perspective that does not assume that everyone is heterosexual until proven otherwise, one can see that, even if she wanted to, Anne could not be a lesbian. While Anne has passionate female friendships, particularly with Leslie Moore when Anne is in her late twenties, and Montgomery's language to describe them verges on the erotic, Anne can never be a lesbian because compulsory heterosexuality always intervenes, both in terms of generic constraints (a wedding has to form the ending) and social constraints (as one faction of the public debate foolishly yet somewhat insightfully argues, lesbians did not exist in 1908). Regardless, Montgomery's novels call attention to other possibilities that cannot be pursued and therefore highlight the extent to which heterosexuality is not simply a natural way of being but is, rather, rigidly enforced. The paper has since undergone major revisions and was published by the academic journal, *Canadian Literature*. The feedback from the conference session was what one would expect: no outrage, no upsets. One question about compulsory heterosexuality provoked a small discussion about my paper specifically. No one seemed disturbed because academics, the audience for whom the paper was intended, are accustomed to queer theory, even if they do not agree with its tenets. One colleague gave me rather backhanded support by saying, "no offense, but it seems so obvious."

Antimodern Anne

The media spin and resulting public outcry salaciously exposed and quickly silenced an alternative voice, most notably a voice that spoke about the possibility of alternative sexualities and thus an alternative version of Canadian tradition. While the media gave voice to my supposed work for two and a half weeks, the way they did showed the danger of attempting to cast a critical, particularly a queer, eye on cherished Canadian institutions, such as Anne. The massive backlash reveals a concern about "innocence" which should be challenged; it works to defend a prosperous Canadian industry predicated on antimodernism; and it promotes an unquestioned homophobia. As Devereux points out, Canadians have invested much in the sanctity of Victorian-era Anne as a national icon ("Anatomy"). At the same time, however, an alternative view, as distorted and ridiculous as it seemed, still managed to make itself heard.

Anne is undeniably a Canadian icon, and the media portrayal of my work disturbed Canadian complacence. People's responses to Anne's "innocence" being questioned is, in part, a result of the massive tourist industry that, by its singular focus on money-making, actually undermines the very innocence it touts and purports to protect. In *The Quest of the Folk*, Ian McKay explores the social construct of "the folk" in Nova Scotia, arguing that "the folk," rather than any real, historical entity, is a discourse promulgated by "twentieth-century modernity (urbanization, professionalization, and the rise of the positive state) and the antimodernism that arose as a response to it"(39). He suggests that a focus on innocence was integral for establishing a sense of "folk" in the period of 1920–1950 Nova Scotia,[6] which then supports a booming tourist industry:

> Innocence discerned the essence of the [Nova Scotian] society. The province was essentially innocent of the complications and anxieties of twentieth-century modernity. Nova Scotia's heart, its true essence, resided in the primitive, the rustic, the unspoiled, the picturesque, the quaint, the unchanging: in all those pre-modern things and traditions that seemed outside the rapid flow of change in the twentieth century. (30)

This innocence was embodied in the simple, commonsense people and their culture: the folk. Moreover, McKay contends, "Nova Scotia came to be defined more and more unequivocally as a 'therapeutic space' removed from the stresses and difficulties of modern life" (31). McKay's analysis can easily be extrapolated to Prince Edward Island, a smaller maritime province very similar to Nova Scotia, with arguably an even greater reliance on its tourism industry. McKay explains the impact of tourism on Nova Scotia's cultural life: "It made possible a fully commercialized antimodernism, which (paradoxically) entailed simultaneously celebrating the premodern, unspoiled 'essence' of the province and seeking ways in which that essence could be turned into marketable commodities within a liberal political and economic order" (35). The irony is palpable: Anne is touted as a symbol of innocent premodernism in order to support a boisterous tourist industry embodying the very capitalist principles of twentieth-century modernity that it denigrates. Moreover, the tension between the rural and urban, the simple and complicated, and inevitably, the heterosexual and the homosexual is required by the tourist industry and the public in order to have a therapeutic space, an "innocence," an escape. My purported examination of Anne effectively blurred the lines between these clear-cut oppositions, and the media and the public scrambled to set the oppositions up again.

Rural Innocence Disrupted

The spin the newspapers gave my research clearly establishes me as some sort of demonic antagonist disrupting the purity of sweet Anne. The first story in the *Ottawa Citizen* claimed, "Laura Robinson pitches the traditional view of Anne off a red sandstone cliff" (25 May 2000: A3). The traditional imagery of PEI clashes with the violence of Anne being hurled from a cliff. Anne's pastoral innocence is also highlighted by two academics in another *Ottawa Citizen* article: David Staines says, "I see her [Anne] as a beautiful depiction of a young girl, an orphan with an elderly farm couple from PEI"; and Mary Rubio's own "childhood in rural Indiana was like Anne's" (26 May 2000:A7). This newspaper story works to set up the rural as the ideal. The implication in this story is that if Anne is a beautiful depiction from a farm or if her childhood is like one in rural Indiana, then she cannot be gay (read: decadent, urban, complicated, and so on). The *Edmonton Journal* fell into the same trap by asking "has a professor had too many sips of Marilla's cordial?" (26 May 2000: A3). A Montgomery fan will realize that Marilla's cordial was not, in fact, cordial, but alcohol, resulting in Diana's drunkenness. The implication here is that the researcher must be drunk, again setting up a tension between urban decadence and pastoral, rural innocence.

The media presented the story in such a way as to suggest that the innocence of Anne is threatened, not just by alcohol-imbibing researchers prone to violence, but by befuddled academics who lack the commonsense of the folk. The very loquacious Rex Murphy decries the illogic of academia: "By this logic, we have to face it, folks: Anne, the pig-tailed, freckle-faced gamine of Green Gables, was a street-hustling drug pimp, with a habit longer than daylight in Colombia and more connections than the new Air Canada" (*Globe and Mail*, 2 June 2000: A13). Murphy's attempt at humour rests on irony, juxtaposing a new version of Anne against what she inarguably represents to all Canadians: the innocent, rural (rather than "street-hustling") icon that allows us escape from the trials of modern life.

The need to re-establish order required not only that my argument be simplified to labelling Anne a lesbian, but also that Anne be quickly re-categorized as heterosexual. The *Daily News* headline proclaimed, "Readers: Anne is Straight" (31 May 2000:3). The *Ottawa Citizen* shouted, "Anne a Lesbian? Poppycock!" (26 May 2000: A7). Readers felt a need to explain the context of *Anne of Green Gables:* "The characters were written in more innocent times, said many callers [into The *Daily News* poll], when women were more free to express devotion to each other" (*Daily News*, 31 May 2000:3). An article in the *Boston Globe* marvelled at the outcry, crediting it to the fact that so many people still care about Anne: "Indeed, almost incredibly in this age of nipple rings and the unlike-a virgin pop chart descendants of Madonna, dreamy Anne of Green Gables remains an idol for millions of girls and young women around the world" (10 June 2000: A01). Each story constructs a simplistic opposition: rural, innocent (and therefore heterosexual) Anne opposes urban, modern (gay) culture.

The Anne Industry: Big Gay Anne

But why did people care so much? Why did the media run with the story, even in the face of traumatic and important concurrent news, such as the Walkerton crisis? The media spun the story in such a way as to create the outrage and responses; it poked at the nation's tender spot: Canadian tourism predicated on the notion of Canadian innocence and premodernity. Undeniably, L.M. Montgomery's books have been integral to Prince Edward Island and Canadian tourism. The Anne books have been translated into over a dozen languages. Carole Gerson cites the 63 *Anne of Green Gables* books and spin-off books listed in the 1999–2000 *Books in Print* (Gerson 17; see also Devereux "Canadian Classic," 12). Devereux is one of many critics who lists some of the Anne and Montgomery merchandise: alongside dolls, a wristwatch, and teas is "potting soil, seeds, maple syrup, tea sets, prints and posters, rugs, curtains, pins, hair accessories, lollipops, Christmas balls, puzzles, furniture, aprons, sculptures, house signs, stained-glass windows, soap, cookies, chocolates and potato chips" (Devereux, "Classic Canadian" 13; see also Gammel 6). The "Heirs of Montgomery, Inc" established the "Anne of Green Gables Licensing Authority," now jointly owned by the province of Prince Edward Island and the "Heirs" due to a legal battle in the 1990s. This "Authority" oversees and mandates approval for the various products that bear Montgomery's or Anne's name or image, and royalties are paid to "The Heirs of L.M. Montgomery, Inc." An Ontario corporation, "The Heirs" applied in 1990 for the trademark and received rights in 1993, which arguably had a devastating effect on the cottage industry in Prince Edward Island. All Anne and Montgomery products must now submit to approval by the Authority or face legal action.[7]

The irony is thick. The outraged public defended Anne's "innocence," insisting that she is removed from the urban, decadent concerns of twentieth- and twenty-first-century modernity. Yet, what is really at stake here is, in part, a profitable tourist industry and an economic cash cow. In almost all of the news stories, the media presented the tourist industry as threatened by the claims that Anne is a lesbian. What needed to be protected were economic interests, a manifestation of modernity that seems at odds with pre-modern Anne. The *Edmonton Journal* reporter asked a bookstore owner how the claims of the academic paper will affect sales: "If anything it will probably boost sales," the bookstore owner replied, "because people will want to read it to find out what they missed the first time. I just don't know how this will affect sales in Japan" (26 May 2000: A3). Similarly the *Globe and Mail* reported that "Heavy-hitters in the Anne-based tourism industry in PEI reacted with sputtering denial" (31 May 2000:A1, A5). The *Ottawa Citizen* quoted a professor of Japanese history, John Brownlee who focused on the export value of Anne: "Anyone who floated a lesbian Anne theory in Japan, the world's biggest importer of Anne, would encounter pure disbelief" (26 May 2000: A7). The *Boston Globe* brought front and centre the concerns of the tourist industry: "Besmirch Anne and you besmirch Prince Edward Island, at least in the minds of businessfolk and officials presiding over the pint-sized province's $207 million tourist industry, half of it attributable to Anne. Hundreds of thousands of tourists flock to the various "Anne Sites," such as Montgomery's birthplace and the real-life Green Gables, now a national park" (10 June 2000: A01).

The PEI minister of tourism, Greg Deighan, waded into the media frenzy when he "dismisse[d] the whole idea, saying there's no substance to back the claim. Deighan also sa[id] it's typical of some reports out of Toronto and Ontario which try to make Atlantic Canada look bad" (CBC.ca (31 May 2000)). Don MacPherson highlights the assumptions underlying the minister's dismissal:

> Deighan noted that the implication of lesbianism on the part of a Prince Edward Island icon could affect the province's tourism industry. It was quite clear that he viewed homosexuality as, well, wrong.
>
> The unfortunate thing about the whole debate is that Deighan is, in part, correct. PEI tourism could suffer as a result of this issue . . . not because of people who reject a literary icon, but because of Islanders' vehement and sadly vocal opposition to lifestyles that are accepted all over the world. Prince Edward Island is not in danger of becoming known as the home of Big Gay Anne, but of developing a reputation as a haven for homophobia.
>
> Say good-by to several thousand dollars, Mr. Deighan.
> *Island Edition* (5 June 2000)

Homophobia: On the Need to Queer the Folk

In raising the key issue of homophobia, MacPherson also underlines the fact that the outcry cannot be attributable to economics alone. Gay people might also have significant disposable income and take holidays. The greater issue is ideological. What the "Bosom Friends Affair," to borrow Devereux's phrase, also reveals is the unthinking heterosexism that belies Canada's notion of itself as a fair, liberal, and just society, a world leader in peace-keeping and human rights. The assumptions that emerged in the media were blatantly homophobic. The belief that I "besmirched" or "attacked" Anne by (reportedly) calling her a lesbian reveals that "lesbian" is regarded as derogatory. The bland belief that lesbianism did not exist in 1908, or in rural PEI, or in Japan, or in young girls' relationships reveals how effective the heteropatriarchy has been in erasing from history traces of lesbianism and in indoctrinating citizens into notions of women's (not to mention East Asians) asexuality. The assumption that homosexuality is less innocent, more decadent than heterosexuality is almost laughable in the face of a daily onslaught of media images and stories about violent or pornographic or abusive heterosexuality. Indeed, Montgomery's readers are quite comfortable discussing Anne's repressed love for Gilbert. It is not sexuality itself but specifically lesbianism that is the problem.

But why? Why did Canadian readers care so much to respond? I have argued that they needed to protect their cherished view of Anne as premodern innocent in order to maintain the tourism industry, but more is going on. Why does that cherished view of Anne require her to be heterosexual? My original paper, and the revised version, examines what theorist Adrienne Rich calls compulsory heterosexuality, or the extent to which heterosexuality is a rigidly-enforced ideology and not a natural way of being. Most importantly, Rich argues that compulsory heterosexuality reinforces patriarchy by naturalizing the dominance of men and the submission of women. The ideology of compulsory heterosexuality needs to erase lesbians from history, and to divide women from each other and keep them in competition in order to maintain patriarchal dominance. If we place Anne on what Rich has called the lesbian continuum, effectively blurring the line between women who sexually desire women and all women who love and support women, then Anne's love for girls and women potentially disrupts the foundations of patriarchy by suggesting alternatives to heterosexual coupling. The media's representation of Anne as a lesbian plunged the fundamental beliefs of Canadians into cold water, and Canadians emerged sputtering and protesting, struggling to protect their view of both patriarchal ideology and the capitalist economics that emerges from and reinforces it as biologically natural and thus innocent commonsense. Little did they know that in their accusations of my "shoddy scholarship"[8] and their continued and vehement protests, they were actually proving my point: heterosexuality is a compulsory *ideology*. Look at what happens when it is challenged.

Notes

Small sections of this paper have been modified from my articles "ACCUTE and the Media: Bosom Friends?" and "Bosom Friends: Lesbian Desire in L.M. Montgomery's Anne Books."

1. Devereux proposes to examine what she terms "The Bosom Friends Affair" to determine what it is that Canadians hold so dear, but she does not succeed in explaining what this is; she simply states that the Anne ruckus underlines "the real importance of Montgomery's heroine in English Canada" (41–42). Both Devereux and Gavin White attempt to show the flaws in my conference paper, at the time unpublished and not in circulation (as far as I know). Academics, like the general public, were not immune to the desire to shut down the possibility for other voices (see also Robinson "ACCUTE and the Media: Bosom Friends?").

2. I later found out from Noreen Golfman, the then-president of the Association of Canadian College and University Teachers of English, that Spears had contacted her to get a copy of my paper. She told him that he would have to ask me. By the time he contacted me, he used the ruse of being interested in all three papers.

3. The town of Walkerton, Ontario had E.coli in its water system, causing many individuals to become ill and several deaths. The news of this tragedy hit mainstream media on 24 May 2000. The Anne story was followed regardless, suggesting that the content of this story captivated readership-hungry editors; it was not simply a slow news week.

4.. Sadly, because of copyright laws, I am not able to use these letters unless I seek the permission of the letter-writers or their heirs, which I am in no hurry to do. The general sense of them, all written by women, is that the world is going to hell in a handbasket. Women felt a need to write to me to explain that they are not lesbians, that I was perverted, and that the gay community does not benefit from my work. The overwhelming emotional tenor of all the letters is sputtering outrage and hostility.

5. Indeed, the words "outrageously sexual," lifted from my article, were originally used to describe the language of *one* passage in *one* of the eight novels. At no point did I describe the character Anne as "outrageously sexual," as the headline led readers to believe: "'Outrageously sexual' Anne was a lesbian, scholar insists."

6. McKay's study largely keeps to this time frame, but in his final chapter on the postmodern folk, he suggests that the quest for the folk in support of a tourist industry is still operative in postmodern Nova Scotia.

7. In July of 1999, the "Heirs of Montgomery, Inc" brought a lawsuit against Sullivan for withholding royalties; the Sullivan vs. "Heirs" lawsuits and counter-lawsuits are still ongoing. Similarly, in March 2000, they launched a lawsuit against Avonlea Traditions, a merchandising company, for withholding payments to the "Heirs." These are only two examples of the fierce legal battles. When Irene Gammel uses the phrases "fiercely contested arena," "hotly disputed," and "highly contested and litigated arena" within four sentences in a discussion about the contemporary legal battles over the multimillion dollar Montgomery industry, she is not overstating the case (Gammel 6).

8. This is a quotation from one of the letters to the editor, *Ottawa Citizen* (27 May 2000: A13), that represents an often-repeated idea in the discussions of my so-called claims.

Works Cited

Devereux, Cecily. "Anatomy of a 'National Icon': Anne of Green Gables and the 'Bosom Friends' Affair" in *Making Avonlea: L.M. Montgomery and Popular Culture*. Ed. Irene Gammel. Toronto: University of Toronto Press, 2002: 32–42.

——. " 'Canadian Classic' and 'Commodity Export': The Nationalism of 'Our' *Anne of Green Gables*." *Journal of Canadian Studies* 36.1 (Spring 2001): 11–28.

Gammel, Irene. "Making Avonlea: An Introduction" in *Making Avonlea: L.M. Montgomery and Popular Culture*. Ed. Irene Gammel. Toronto: University of Toronto Press, 2002: 3–13.

Gerson, Carole. *Anne of Green Gables* Goes to University: L.M. Montgomery and Academic Culture. *Making Avonlea: L.M. Montgomery and Popular Culture*. Ed. Irene Gammel. Toronto: University of Toronto Press, 2002: 17–31.

McKay, Ian. *The Quest of the Folk: Antimodernism and Cultural Selection in Twentieth Century Nova Scotia*. Montreal: McGill-Queen's University Press, 1994.

Rich, Adrienne. "Compulsory Heterosexuality and Lesbian Existence" in *The Lesbian and Gay Studies Reader*. Eds. Henry Abelove, Michele Aina Barale, David M. Halperin. New York: Routledge, 1993: 227–254.

Robinson, Laura M. "ACCUTE and the Media: Bosom Friends?" *ACCUTE Newsletter* (June 2000): 37–39.

——. "Bosom Friends: Lesbian Desire in L.M. Montgomery's Anne Books." *Canadian Literature* 180 (Spring 2004):12–28.

White, Gavin. "Falling out of the Haystack: L.M. Montgomery and Lesbian Desire." *CCL: Canadian Children's Literature* no. 102 vol. 27.2: 43–59.

CHAPTER SIXTEEN

The Prairies Imagined and Real

Introduction

The three prairie provinces—Manitoba, Saskatchewan and Alberta—are obviously real. The soil, the climate, the rivers, the foothills: all are tangible features of a physical geography. But the prairie west is also an imagined geography; it is an invented place at the same time as it is a real place. As Doug Owram points out in his book, *Promise of Eden: The Canadian Expansionist Movement and the Idea of the West, 1856-1900,* that process of inventing the west began in the 19th century. Why and in what ways did the expansionist movement—that movement that encouraged Canada's western expansion—construct the west? The idea of an imaginary landscape as distinct from but related to an objective landscape can be seen in western Canadian fiction and non-fiction. Di Brandt is a poet. Born in 1952 to Mennonite farmers, she received her PhD from the University of Manitoba in 1993. "This land that I love, this wide wide prairie" is about the land and what it means to Brandt; it is also about "us" and what "we" mean to the land. Can you locate a connecting thread between the expansionist movement and today's agricultural practices?

New Worlds to Conquer:
The Opening of the Expansionist Campaign, 1856–57

Doug Owram

IN 1850 SIR GEORGE SIMPSON wrote Chief Factor Donald Ross of Norway House to tell him the good news that 'H.M. Government has put an extinguisher on the agitation respecting the Company's rights and management.[1] Simpson's comment accurately summed up the conclusion of the attacks on the Hudson's Bay Company by Alexander Isbister and others. For all the doubts that had been raised concerning the future of the Hudson's Bay territories, British policy indicated that it was still felt that the North West would remain a fur trading empire for the immediate future and that the company was best suited to rule over the area. Both the Colonial Office and the British House of Commons had, after investigation, given the company a vote of confidence.

In Canada there had been even less reaction to the challenges to the Hudson's Bay Company. The only official Canadian involvement had been through the office of Lord Elgin, the Governor-General; and even that had been in response to a British request and favourable to the company. A few editorials by the Toronto *Globe* and letters from retired fur traders, while stirring interest in a few people, could hardly be said to have transformed the Canadian attitude to the vast region that lay to the north and the west. Over the next few years the occasional article or book was written on the company or the lands over which it ruled, but these elicited little response from the public.

This lack of interest did not last. Beginning in 1856 a new debate developed on the future of the Hudson's Bay territories, and, in contrast to the 1840s, this one aroused widespread Canadian interest. By the time it was over the company had lost any hope of retaining its exclusive position in the North West: Vancouver Island, its symbol of vindication a few years before, was taken away from it and raised to the status of a crown colony; the company's application for a renewal of the exclusive right to trade was refused; and, potentially most important of all, in 1857 a Select Committee of the British House of Commons accepted in principle Canada's 'just and reasonable wishes' to annex the North West.[2] By the end of the decade the debate on the Hudson's Bay Company had ended, because everyone, including its own officials, accepted the impending end of the fur trade empire.

From the Canadian perspective, the most noticeable characteristic of this successful assault on the position of the Hudson's Bay Company was the extremely small number of individuals who acted as its spearhead. In the later 1850s less than fifteen people formed the core of the movement that led Canada to assert its right to the region. This small group comprised those individuals who continually spoke or wrote of the potential of the West and of the crucial need for Canadian expansion. Together they were very quickly able to effect a profound shift in public and official opinion.

Perhaps the most committed of all these early expansionists was Allan Macdonell. His father, Alexander, had been in the employ of Lord Selkirk and it is possible that Macdonell first developed his interest in the North West through this connection. His belief in the potential of the West predated that of most other Canadians, and through the 1840s he had been involved in fruitless schemes to tap the wealth of the vast Canadian Shield north of Lake Superior. In 1851 the forty-three-year-old Macdonell took inspiration from the works of the British pamphleteers to apply for a Pacific railroad charter. The Canadian legislature, while it had granted somewhat dubious charters in the past, found Macdonell's proposal unacceptable. Undaunted by this rejection, he tried again in 1853 and 1855 only to be turned down both times. In August 1856 he began a series of letters to the editor of the Toronto *Globe* under the pen name of 'Huron' in support of Canadian interests in the North West. He was also the driving force behind the North-West Transportation. Navigation and Railway Company, the first substantial commercial attempt to reopen trade with the region.[3] In his enduring enthusiasm and endless schemes Macdonell did much to arouse interest in the possibilities of the North West, even though the company he initiated encountered difficulties making a profit.

Closely associated with Macdonell in the North-West Transportation Company was William Macdonell Dawson. As Dawson's middle name implies, he was connected with the same large clan of Highland Scots as was Macdonell. Until 1857 Dawson was an employee of the Crown Lands Department and used his official position to urge an expansionist policy on the government.[4] His two brothers, Aeneas Macdonell Dawson and Simon James Dawson, were soon to become committed to the vision of Canadian expansion and to use their considerable talents to support that policy.

Linked with the schemes of Macdonell and Dawson was a man who had long ago expressed his hostility to the Hudson's Bay Company. Captain William Kennedy had not changed his views since he had written the public letter to Elgin in 1848, and in his numerous articles and speeches he encouraged a favourable image of the North West and a hostile view of the Hudson's Bay Company. In 1857 he went to Red River and with his brother, Roderick, attempted to convince the residents of that isolated settlement to support Canadian expansion.[5]

Another person who had been interested in the North West from the 1840s was the powerful editor of the Toronto *Globe*, George Brown. The letters to his paper from 'Huron' in 1856 caught his attention and he soon became one of the most consistent advocates of Canadian expansion. A distrust of the monopolistic Hudson's Bay Company and a fervent enthusiasm for the spread of British institutions gave the movement a particular appeal to Brown. His commitment was further deepened by two factors which had little to do with the North West. First, his brother, Gordon, was involved with Macdonell and Dawson in the North-West Transportation Company and the fortunes of the Brown clan thus to some extent rested on Canadian expansion. Secondly, it was apparent to Brown that the annexation of the North West would imply a constitutional alteration for Canada and hence, he hoped, a political system that would ensure the dominance of English Canada and the Reform party.

Brown was joined in his enthusiasm for the North West by thirty-four-year-old William McDougall, who had previously been a Clear Grit and thus a political opponent of Brown. By 1857, however, the two movements of Reform and Clear Grit had effectively merged, and McDougall had abandoned his own newspaper, the *North American,* and merged it with the *Globe.* In 1857 he was on Brown's staff and it is possible that some of the editorials on the West in this period were written by him. In capturing the energies and abilities of Brown and McDougall, the expansionist movement gained two of its most powerful propagandists. Both were leaders within the Reform party and their influence would help to bring that party to a position of official support for the annexation of the North West as early as 1858.[6]

While the Reform party contained some of the most vociferous supporters of expansionism, the issue was not a partisan one. Within government circles Philip M. Vankoughnet, President of the Executive Council and a future Commissioner of Crown Lands, lent his support to the campaign for expansion as early as September 1856.[7] Other individuals within the government also came to advocate expansion and ensured that the Liberal-Conservatives of John A. Macdonald accepted the idea of expansion, albeit more cautiously.

The efforts of these prominent men were paralleled by more obscure figures. Typical of this group was Alfred R. Roche, another employee of the Crown Lands Department, who had been one of the first to express the new interest in the North West.[8] It is likely that he was the author of the numerous letters sent to the Montreal *Gazette* under the signature of 'Assiniboia,' thus performing a role in that paper similar to the one played by Macdonell in the Toronto *Globe.*

Perhaps the most important of all Roche's efforts on behalf of Canadian expansion was the key role he played in bringing the Canadian government to assert its historical and legal claims to the Hudson's Bay territories. In 1857 the British government appointed a select committee of the House of Commons to investigate all matters concerning the Hudson's Bay Company. The Canadian government appointed Chief Justice William Draper as its representative before the committee. At the time of his appointment Draper knew nothing of the question and admitted that he had 'the whole thing to study.'⁹ The men who guided these studies were none other than William Dawson and Alfred Roche, and whatever tinges of expansionist thought coloured Draper's testimony before the committee can be attributed to them.¹⁰ Moreover, Roche accompanied Draper to London and gave his own testimony before the committee. If Draper presented the position of the Canadian government, Roche represented the Canadian expansionist movement. Overall, he was a central figure in the early phase of expansionism and only his tragic drowning in 1859 has caused him to be noticed less than the rest.

Other individuals became associated with the expansionist movement in these years, though their primary participation would come later. Surveyors Alexander Russell and John Stoughton Dennis, both of the Crown Lands Department, seemed to catch the expansionist spirit which pervaded that organization. The rising railway engineer, Sandford Fleming, fresh from the construction of the Toronto Northern, began to consider the possibilities of even more ambitious railway projects. Alexander Morris, thirty-two-year-old son of the well-known Canadian politician, William Morris, wrote a pamphlet depicting an optimistic future for an expanded Canada.¹¹ In the coming years all of these men would have a great deal to do with the North West.

The expansionist campaign was effective only because it appealed to widespread hopes and fears within the Canadian community. In the 1840s attacks on the Hudson's Bay Company had aroused little interest in Canada. By 1856, however, when the issue was again raised, conditions had changed in such a way as to make the idea of expansion seem both desirable and necessary. The first half of the 1850s had brought tremendous growth in Canada. The economic dislocation that had accompanied the British shift to free trade in 1846 had given way to prosperity. The successful conclusion of a reciprocity treaty with the United States in 1854 and the beginning of the Crimean War the same year increased the market and demand for Canadian timber and foodstuffs. Immigration and a high natural birth rate continued to increase the population, and Canada West, which received the bulk of that immigration, surpassed Canada East early in the decade. By the middle of the decade Canadians had become accustomed to a degree of prosperity that few would have thought possible even a few years before.

The great symbol of Canadian prosperity was the railroad. The passage of the Guarantee Act of 1849 which, under certain conditions, provided a government guarantee for railway bonds, enabled years of schemes to assume more concrete form. Through the 1850s railways spread across the Canadian countryside at an amazing pace and within a decade the province's total railway mileage increased from 66 to 2066. Canadians enthusiastically welcomed the orgy of construction with its dizzying effects on society, economy, and, all too often, on politics. The same faith in technology and progress that had so marked the British pamphleteers of the 1840s was abundantly present in Canada. Individual cases of profiteering and jobbery did not alter this fact. Thomas Keefer's dictum, first written in 1849, that 'as a people we may as well . . . attempt to live without books or newspapers, as without Railroads,' was still accepted in 1856.[12]

Of course, the reality of the railroad could never match the myth, but its arrival did have a profound effect on Canada. Goods could be transported more easily and cheaply and patterns of trade conformed to the lines of the railway. This, in turn, encouraged the dominance of those urban centres which had been able to attract railway depots. Industrial firms sprang up to service the new technology and this further aided the growth of these urban centres.[13] Most important of all, the railway expanded the horizons and the ambitions of Canadian manufacturers and entrepreneurs.

The optimism of the decade and the enthusiasm for railways were, in part, recognition that recent events signalled a new stage in Canadian development. It was hoped and believed that the progress of the early fifties would continue into the future. A new periodical, the *Canadian Journal of Science, Literature and History*, reflected the mood of 1856 when it saw fit to open its first volume with an eulogy to Canadian progress, past and future: 'The advancement of Canada in commercial and agricultural prosperity during recent years, is without parallel in the history of the British Colonies; and there is abundant reason for believing that it is even now only on the threshold of a career of triumphant progress.[14] The Brantford *Courier* expressed the same theme a few months later when it stated that 'the prospect of Canada was never better or more encouraging than at the present moment.[15] The development of Canada meant that the world would soon have to think of it as more than a backwoods colony, and then both Canadians and others would realize, as Alexander Morris put it, that 'her destiny is a grand one.'[16] A sense of immediacy overlay such thoughts and many confidently asserted that this destiny would become apparent in the near future.

Canada was outgrowing its previous status as a frontier colony. While this fact was a point of pride, it also forced Canadians to consider the implications of the changes that were taking place. A means had to be found to ensure that the transition from the frontier economy and society was smooth and successful. The problem was that Canada's past growth had depended to a large extent on the existence of an untapped frontier. Immigration from Europe and the settlement of the wilderness had been the basis of trade and prosperity. Canada, like the United States, had experienced and been shaped by the New World's peculiar economic resource, free land. Now, however, at the very time when the benefits of past growth were being felt, this resource was becoming scarce.

On 14 September 1855 the *Globe* noted that the last 'wild' land in the western peninsula of Canada West had been sold. With this sale Canadians were threatened with a new and possibly crucial factor—confinement. The problem was that for all the vastness of the Canadian territory the amount of suitable agricultural land was relatively limited. The great Canadian Shield arched over the province and severely limited the northward extension of settlement; with the settlement of the western peninsula the only place left to go was on to that shield. The implications of this fact were not encouraging. Joseph Cauchon, as Commissioner of Crown Lands, noted in 1856 that the western peninsula had been the scene of the greatest settlement of public lands. His argument that their sale did not signal the end of the Canadian settlement frontier was only partly successful, for, as he admitted, the remaining lands 'are not equal in climate nor in general fitness for cultivation to the western peninsula of Upper Canada.' What was fit for settlement was limited and before long, it appeared, 'the desirable lands in the sections described will be insufficient to meet the evident demand.'[17] The message was clear. It was only a matter of time before Canada ran out of wild land suitable for agriculture and when this happened its most powerful inducement to the immigrant would disappear. The worries expressed by Cauchon were firmly grounded in land sales. In 1856 some 140,520 acres of public land were sold in Canada West; in 1857 this figure dropped to 122,119 acres and by 1863 to 91,069.[18] Canada's settlement frontier had collided with the natural barrier of the shield.

It is doubtful that the later 1850s and early 1860s brought severe population pressure to Canada. There were still large areas of vacant land in the province in the hands of private individuals. Canada, however, needed not only land but an abundance of it. If it was to attract immigrants from Europe and prevent its own population from emigrating to the United States, it had to be able to offer a surplus of good land at nominal prices. By the later 1850s it could no longer do so, and more and more people, both European immigrants and Canadians, began to look to the United States. Cauchon concluded bluntly that 'they will continue to do so, much to the loss and injury of the Province,' unless lands can be found to compete with those available in the United States.[19]

Concerns for the future focused not only on settlement but on commerce. For more than a generation Canadian commercial schemes had centred on the St Lawrence—Great Lakes transportation network. The hopes for this trade artery had been badly shaken by the British shift to free trade, but by the early 1850s the faith in the system had been rekindled with a new rhetoric based on free trade and access to American markets. Unfortunately, the rhetoric could not disguise the weakness of the system. In spite of the reciprocity treaty, trade figures by the middle of the decade made it clear that the traffic of the St Lawrence system accounted for only a minute percentage of American trade.[20] If the great transportation system on which so much had been expended was ever to contribute to the further growth of the province a means would have to be found to increase the flow of goods through it.

The feeling that Canada had, for better or worse, come to turning point in its development was general to all regions of the province. There were certain areas, however, where this was felt more strongly than others. In two quite different regions, the city of Toronto and the Ottawa Valley, the hopes and fears for the future were felt with a special acuteness. Equally important were geographical and commercial factors which drew the attention of men in these areas to the upper Great Lakes and beyond. It is perhaps not surprising that the origins of much of the Canadian interest in the Hudson's Bay territories can be traced to these two centres.

Toronto, perhaps more than any other city in Canada, had felt the benefits of prosperity in recent years. When the town of York had become the city of Toronto in 1834 the total population had been only 9252. By 1851 the city had reached a figure of slightly over 30,000; the next decade, with the aid of the railway, would bring Toronto to a population of nearly 45,000 and give it ideas of competing with Montreal for the position of Canada's primary urban centre.[21] The residents of the 'Queen City of the West' had reason to feel proud of their city and its record of accomplishments. They were also anxious to ensure that the future would be as bright as the past.

Toronto, even more than Canada as a whole, had grown because of its ability to exploit an expanding western hinterland. The filling of the western peninsula thus posed serious questions concerning Toronto's future development. George Brown was one of many Torontonians who sensed the potential problems implicit in the closing of this settlement frontier. 'While congratulating ourselves on the rapid growth of the city,' he wrote in August 1856, 'it behoves us to consider well the circumstances that have produced that expansion.' The circumstances were many but Brown warned that one stood out above all the others—the progressive expansion and settlement of the western peninsula. That expansion had reached its limit and possibly so had Toronto's: 'Unlike the cities of Lake Michigan, our back country is comparatively limited, and unlike the cities of the south shore of Lake Erie, we have as yet no commerce with the distant states and territories of the United States to pour its riches into our laps.'[22] George Brown's enthusiasm for expansion has often been seen to derive from his adhesion to a frontier-based Reform party.[23] This enthusiasm, however, came not simply from the frontier but also from the city. It was the city of Toronto, not the farmer of the western peninsula, which had to find room for further growth if it was 'ever to rise above the rank of a fifth-rate American town.'[24]

It was natural that when Toronto began to cast about for a new frontier it should turn to the north and west. For a decade explorations had been carried out under the direction of the Geological Survey of Canada in the regions north of lakes Huron and Superior. The results had encouraged several mining companies to attempt to tap the wealth of the area.[25] In 1855 the completion of the Northern railroad to Collingwood gave the city direct access to the upper lakes and, potentially, control of any development in the area. The same factors which had led to this interest would soon lead to a call for the exploration of a more distant and vast potential hinterland for Toronto.

The communities situated in the Ottawa Valley were subjected to the same forces as Toronto but in a slightly different way. Toronto's aspirations were based on a desire to maintain its dominant position in Canada West. The Ottawa Valley, however, in the 1850s was a relatively remote hinterland—tributary to the St Lawrence system and the city of Montreal. If Toronto found its hinterland too small for its grand ambitions, the communities in the Ottawa Valley realized that, except for the timber trade, they had no back country at all. In fact, the settlement of such counties as Lanark and Renfrew reflected the population pressure which was forcing agricultural settlement on to marginal land. These counties were on the edge of the shield and residents of the area had to fight a stubborn and often rocky land in order to make a living.

The geographical position of the valley did offer at least the possibility of an escape from current conditions. In 1854 Thomas Keefer pointed to another, more specific application for the power of the railway. All that had to be done, he noted, was to 'burst the narrow belt between the upper Ottawa settlements and the broad expanse of Lake Huron' and a new and much more vast hinterland of the upper Great Lakes would become tributary to the valley.[26] Keefer's idea was not new and earlier plans to use either railway or canal had come to nothing. Two years later, however, such talk seemed much more meaningful. The government, concerned for the future of the St Lawrence system, sent an engineer, Walter Shanly, to investigate the feasibility of constructing either a canal or a railway between Georgian Bay and the Ottawa River.[27] The government's apparent interest in the long-standing idea encouraged a commercial speculation which stretched from the town of Perth down the valley to the city of Montreal. Through the early months of 1856 discussion raged as to the possibilities and implications of such a project as writers sought new adjectives to describe the numerous beneficial results that would come in its wake. Few, if any, of the citizens of the Ottawa Valley opposed the idea.

The trade possibilities of such a development were such that politicians dependent on votes from the region soon found it useful to give their support to the scheme. Philip Vankoughnet, running for a position on the newly elective Legislative Council in the autumn of 1856, was no exception. Speaking to a crowd of electors in September, Vankoughnet restated the traditional themes, pointing to the potential trade from Chicago and the Great Lakes. This trade alone would, if made to flow through the Ottawa Valley, give wealth to the region. Vankoughnet, however, did not stop with the possibilities of the American trade. There was no reason, he pointed out, to remain dependent on another nation as 'there was a great west to Canada as well as the United States.' That west, if only Canadians acted to open it, would provide an even greater and more certain source of wealth for the Ottawa Valley. It would also lead, inevitably, to that almost mythical source of wealth, Asia. Vankoughnet's speech called forth visions of the 'products of China and the East, journeying down the Ottawa valley, and the Gulf of St Lawrence on their way to Europe.'[28] Here was a hinterland large enough to satisfy even the most ambitious residents of the valley.

This vision of a vast new hinterland captured the imaginations of a number of people in the region, and before long the Ottawa Valley became a centre of expansionism rivalled only by Toronto. The town of Perth, for instance, was the first community outside of Toronto to adopt a public resolution calling for the annexation of the North West.[29] Various newspapers in that and other communities along the valley emulated the Toronto *Globe,* in tone if not in influence, in their insistence on immediate expansion. The spirit generated in 1856 was to have an influence for some time to come. Over the next several years such counties as Lanark and Renfrew were to have close associations with the expansionist movement. Alexander Morris and William McDougall both sat as members for the area. Other individuals— Charles Mair, Charles Napier Bell, and a future mayor of Winnipeg, Thomas Scott— hailed from the region. Years of discussion in their home towns had instilled an attraction for the West in all of them.

While Toronto and the Ottawa Valley were centres of expansionist sentiment interest in the North West was not confined to these regions. There was a provincial as well as a regional dimension to interest in the idea of expansion. A combination of pride in achievements to date and concern for the future led a good many Canadians to conclude that failure to expand would result in stagnation. Canada was outgrowing its boundaries; if room for Canadian energies was not found, the colony would sink into obscurity. The old Province of Canada was no longer sufficient for these energies, and, as the *Globe* put it on 10 December 1856, Canadians were 'looking about for new worlds to conquer.'

What gave the expansionist movement its power was a fusing of enthusiasm for the North West with a recognition of the crucial position Canada had reached. In a speech before the Toronto Board of Trade in December 1856, William Kennedy made the connection between the two explicit in order to show the importance of the campaign he and others were waging. Kennedy pointed out that since 1849 he had tried to arouse interest in the North West but had never had any real success. What had changed since then was neither the condition of the West nor the rule of the Hudson's Bay Company but the circumstances of the Province of Canada: 'But great progress has been made since then in railways, and other public works, and another aspect was given to the subject. Canadians now saw that the comparatively small fragment of this continent which they occupied would soon be both too narrow and too short for them, too small a field on which to exercise and develop their new born energies. It was the most notable work for the Canadians of the present day to undertake to bring within the pale of civilization the larger half of the North American continent, a country containing 270 millions of acres.'[30] The *Globe* echoed Kennedy's comments. Referring to Macdonell's unsuccessful bids for a transcontinental railway charter, it concluded that 'the circumstances of the country have materially changed' and urged acceptance of his latest application.[31]

Only possession of the North West could ensure that these changes would be allowed to continue to the benefit of Canada. The sheer size of the West encouraged Canadians to think that its development would allow them to rival the tremendous growth of the United States. In recent years Canadians had looked with envy on the flow of immigrants to the American mid-west while Canada backed onto the shield. The United States was a nation with seemingly infinite room for expansion and the

Canadian desire for the North West was, in part, a desire to emulate the American experience. As Cauchon's 1856 report clearly revealed, a shortage of good land in Canada meant that it could not compete with the United States for immigrants; the report noted, as well that 'it is in the valleys of the Red River, the Assiniboine, and the Saskatchewan that such lands are to be found.'[32]

Agricultural settlement, however, was but a means to a wider end. As the references to the United States imply, Canadian expansionists were primarily concerned with the commercial implications of an expanding frontier. The tone was set by the North-West Transportation, Navigation and Railway Company, chartered in 1858 for the purpose of 'participating in the important and lucrative trade' which was thought to exist in the North West. The fur trade would provide the initial market but it was assumed that other markets would develop, giving 'an unlimited extent to Canadian industry, and to British commerce.'[33] The details of agricultural settlement were only vaguely conceived and even then were portrayed in terms of the production of goods for sale and as a market for eastern manufacturers. Expansionism did not contain any images of an Arcadian utopia such as ran through the American idea of the frontier.[34] Trade would precede settlement. The Canadian expansionist movement was essentially an attempt to increase the hinterland of such centres as Toronto and, more generally, to provide an extension for the great trade artery of the St Lawrence.

As was fitting for such a movement the potential for trade was almost invariably put in terms of the benefits that would accrue to the east. The concept of a vast agrarian empire, which emphasized the prosperity awaiting the farmer, had not yet developed. The editorials, speeches, and pamphlets of the first years of expansionism concentrated on the exploitation of a hinterland for the sake of a homeland. It was to the people of this homeland, Canada, that expansionist rhetoric was directed, not to those who might seek a livelihood in the hinterland. The North West was to be, in the words of the *Globe*, the 'back country' which Canada wanted.

The most dramatic, if still remote, expression of this commercial orientation was the idea of a transcontinental railroad system. Even the cautious William Draper expressed the hope that he would live 'to see the time, or that my children may live to see the time when there is a railway going all the way across the country and ending at the Pacific.'[35] Allan Macdonell reprinted his 1851 prospectus in his pamphlet on the North-West Transportation Company as an obvious indication of the ultimate goal of that firm.[36] George Brown reminded his readers in late 1856 that 'through British territory lies the best route for the Atlantic and Pacific Railway.'[37] No matter how remote the accomplishment or vague the conception, the transcontinental railway was always an integral part of Canadian expansion. Only with visions of such a railway was it possible to imagine a means whereby the vast North West could be developed and governed.

There were two alternate ways in which it was thought the railway would contribute to Canadian commerce. The first envisioned a hinterland carved out of the North West, supplying the railway with produce and returning eastern goods to the

398 - Chapter Sixteen

West. The other went beyond the North West in its search for wealth and looked, as had Synge, to the markets of Asia. The two ideas were not mutually exclusive for any railroad could serve both functions, but they did reflect different ideas as to the ultimate worth of the North West. It is indicative of the still limited faith in that region that, in the late 1850s and early 1860s, any transcontinental railroad was seen almost exclusively in terms of the Asian trade. As John Ross, the president of the Grand Trunk, said to the British select committee: 'the construction of a railroad is an important subject, apart entirely from the opening of the country through which it would pass.'[38] Ross was not an expansionist, but his comment did not bring forth any expressions of disagreement from those who were.

As a means of access to Asia, as a commercial hinterland and eventual settlement frontier, expansionists in 1856 and after looked to the North West as a potential answer to Canada's hopes and fears. The strength of the expansionist movement and the ability of a small number of individuals to influence public and official opinion was the result of various developments which made access to a large hinterland seem essential. Canada was at a crossroads. This fact had been sensed independent of the North West. The North West, however, made clear the choice that existed. In developing or not developing this region Canadians would make the choice 'whether this country shall ultimately become a Petty State, or one of the Great Powers of the earth.'[39]

Armed with varied arguments and supported, at least half-heartedly, by the Canadian government, the expansionists set out to convince the British government that the vast territory in question should be ceded to Canada by the Hudson's Bay Company. The company had faced challenges before and on those occasions it had employed its vast power, prestige, and political influence to shrug off such attacks. There seemed no reason for it not to do the same with the obviously self-interested expansionist criticisms. Canadian expansionists, however, while they could not deny the selfish side of their campaign, argued that their commercial aims, unlike those of the Hudson's Bay Company, were complementary to other goals. The religious, humanitarian, and imperial themes of the 1840s had not been forgotten and it was not difficult to find reasons to justify the Canadian desire for the North West.

The first step for Canadians was to convince themselves that the act of expansion had some foundation in law. Canadians had often condemned the United States for its seizure of additional territory and were thus sensitive to charges they were adopting similar methods. Very quickly, the expansionist movement came to the convenient conclusion that there was no comparison between its aims and the American experience. Canada, it turned out, already owned the North West territory.

The legal claim to the territory was first detailed by Joseph Cauchon in the summer of 1857, though the ideas can be traced back to John McLean's writings in the 1840s.[40] While Cauchon signed the document in his capacity as Commissioner of Crown Lands, it is probable that the actual arguments were organized by William Dawson.[41] Canada's claim to the North West was based on the clause of the Hudson's

Bay Company charter that excluded from its grant the territory of any Christian prince or state. Cauchon turned to the colonial era to argue that New France had comprised everything in North America above the British colonies in New England. The battle of the Plains of Abraham and subsequent cession of New France meant that Canada was the heir to these colonial claims.[42] Thus, in rather audacious fashion, Canada laid legal claim to the Hudson's Bay territories.

The exact boundaries of this extended Canada were uncertain. Draper, acting on instructions from the Executive Council, laid claim to all the territory south of the 'barren grounds' as far west as the Rocky Mountains.[43] The Toronto Board of Trade was less modest in its assertion of Canadian rights and claimed 'the whole region of country, extending westward to the Pacific Ocean, and northward to the shores of Hudson Bay.'[44] Whatever the actual extent of the claim, the fact remained that the legal fiction of territorial rights derived from New France allowed Canadians to covet the North West without any feeling of guilt. The expansionists argued that the officials of the Hudson's Bay Company were 'simply squatters' on Canadian land.[45]

The attacks on the Hudson's Bay Company were not confined to legal arguments. Expansionists turned to the ideas of Isbister and others in order to lay not only a legal but a moral claim for the transfer of the region to Canada. There was, however, a significant change in the rhetoric by the later 1850s. In the 1840s the assumption had been that the West would remain unsettled for some time to come and the primary concern was therefore a missionary one for the Indian. By 1857 the impulse was commercial and based on the belief that the region would quickly be opened up to civilization. This shift in assumptions drew attention from the Indians, those representatives of the wilderness, to the Red River settlement, that 'brave little colony of Britons' in the centre of the continent.[46]

It is true that some concern for the Indian population persisted. In England the Aborigines Protection Society continued to act as a lobby for what it perceived to be the interests of the Indian.[47] In Canada the occasional editorial by the *Globe* referred with concern to the Indian population and various individuals continued to call for aid to the native. But generally the exponents of expansionism in the fifties paid relatively little attention to the native population. This may have been because of at least a vague awareness that the plans to open the west were potentially harmful to the Indian. Allan Macdonell and others tried to convince the public that the release of the fur trade from the hands of a monopoly would ensure that the Indian was no longer 'compelled to submit to such terms as the Company may impose' and would thus benefit.[48] Men with a much more creditable background as humanitarians than Macdonell were not so certain. Even Isbister, pressed on the matter during the hearings of the British select committee, answered only that 'I should not like to express a very decided opinion on that point.'[49]

The decreased concern for the Indian was more than compensated for by a strong interest in the European and half-breed settlers of Red River. In shifting its focus the humanitarian motivation behind expansionism moved from a missionary concern for the native to a political movement aimed at aiding 'British subjects' who were currently 'vassals in a galling state of dependence on their lords of the company.'[50] Canada, as Macdonell wrote to the *Globe* on 30 September 1856, had a duty to stand 'between the oppressor and the oppressed.'

Expansionists argued that it was natural for Canada to be especially concerned with the plight of the Red River settlers, for their position was simply a more extreme example of what the Hudson's Bay Company had done to Canadians. Both groups had been hurt by the evil effects of monopoly. The Hudson's Bay Company was, in the words of the Toronto Board of Trade, 'injurious to the interests of the country so monopolised and in contravention of the rights of the people of the British North American Provinces.'[51] The company was harmful to Canada, and for that matter the British Empire, in that it opposed any attempt to develop the territory under its rule. Restating the arguments of the 1840s, expansionists claimed that the company deliberately sought to keep the territory a wilderness in order to preserve the fur trade. The progress of Minnesota, directly south of the Red River settlement, was both evidence of what could be accomplished and what the company had failed to accomplish. To fail to develop such a resource was to weaken the power and potential of the whole British Empire.

The Hudson's Bay Company was not just a passive obstacle to Canadian aspirations. Like Fitzgerald in 1849, Canadian expansionists explained the previous lack of knowledge of the region with a conspiratorial theory of Hudson's Bay Company policy. The company, it was said, had deliberately wrapped the country in a 'deep, thick veil of obscurity and darkness.'[52] Macdonell charged that it had perpetuated a false image of the North West as a region of 'barren lands, swamps, and granite rocks' in an attempt to make people believe the country was 'unfitted for civilization, and debased by nature from ever benefitting by its humanising efforts.'[53]

This conspiracy theory created a filter through which evidence about the company and the North West was viewed. The expansionists tended to suspect anyone who made negative comments on the North West to be a part of the conspiracy to keep the region a wilderness. The result was a strong selectivity in the use of source material. Increasingly the value attached to such material tended to be determined by its conclusions rather than the other way around. One of the more understandable examples was shown in the Canadian response to Sir George Simpson's attempt to explain away his earlier writings on the territory. His denigration of the land and the soil were seen as further proof of the company's willingness to distort the truth in its own interests. As the Montreal *Gazette* commented on Simpson's testimony: 'he must expect that people will be very ready to impute bad motives, for his change of opinion just at this particular time.'[54] Simpson was particularly vulnerable, but henceforth any person who undertook the task of defending the Hudson's Bay Company ran the risk of finding himself accused of being part of the conspiracy against the people of Red River and Canada.

The varied forms of the expansionist attack on the position of the Hudson's Bay Company left that company without any real defence. In earlier years there had been little question that the economy of the North West would remain based on the fur trade. Given that assumption, it was argued that monopoly was a necessary, if unfortunate, expedient in order to prevent the abuses and disorder that accompanied competition. By 1857, however, the assumptions were quite different. Canadians were now talking of opening the territory to settlement and, in spite of the vague nature of such statements, they proved irresistible. The company found it impossible to defend the mercantile empire in an era of free trade and the idea of a fur trade preserve in the face of agricultural settlement.

Even the representatives of the company dared not deny the desirability of opening the region. Edward Ellice, deputy governor of the Hudson's Bay Company, was suspicious of Canadian designs, but even he was forced to admit that if any of the company's powers were harmful to settlement they ought to be taken away.[55] Expansionists, of course, argued that the very existence of the company charter was a hindrance to settlement. In order to maintain its reputation as an honourable and patriotic firm the Hudson's Bay Company had to support the principle of development. In so doing it undercut its very reason for existence—the fur trade.

The Hudson's Bay Company was vulnerable because expansionists couched their arguments in terms of universally desirable principles. The opening of the West was to be in the name of progress and that progress would be to the benefit of the whole Empire and, for that matter, all of humanity. At the same time, as the basic legal claim put forward by Cauchon indicates, expansionists also looked to the particular interests of Canada. The specific right of Canada to participate in the development of the North West was seen to be as important as the principle of opening it for settlement. Any scheme that would have left the North West in other hands was rejected outright. In 1863 a reformed, newly progressive, and seemingly repentant Hudson's Bay Company received little sympathy from Canadian expansionists because, no matter how progressive, it did not represent Canadian aspirations.[56]

In order to assert Canada's particular claim on the North West, expansionists turned to history. Long after the fall of New France, it was argued, Canadians had been present in the North West. Various companies operating out of Montreal had competed with the Hudson's Bay Company for the wealth of the region. Then, in 1821, the merger of the North West Company and the Hudson's Bay Company had brought that Canadian presence to an end. In the climate of the 1850s this amalgamation took on a new and sinister significance. The natural course of history was said to have been diverted by the schemes of a tyrannical monopoly. The North West Company, for its part, assumed almost mythical stature as a symbol of the past that had been wrenched unjustly from Canada.

The main figure in this interpretation of events was Allan Macdonell. In his series of letters to the *Globe* he continually hammered home the theme that Canada had at one time had a direct and lucrative involvement in the North West. Not just a few traders in Montreal but 'Canada at large was benefitted by the trade,' he argued, 'for the wealth it brought back was freely flung back to circulate through those various industrial pursuits' associated with it.[57] Macdonell's argument was soon picked up by others, including George Brown. At a public meeting in Toronto in August 1857 Brown called on his listeners to remember the 'immense traffic' of the 'hardy voyageurs.' The earlier wealth supposedly generated by the North West Company served as proof that 'every citizen of Canada is deeply interested in the opening up of settlement and commerce of those vast regions now held in the iron grasp of the Hudson's Bay Company.'[58]

In contrast to the years before 1821, the period after had left the wealth of the North West in the hands of what Alexander Morris termed 'a Company of London merchants.'[59] In spite of Canadian faith in the Empire, the Hudson's Bay Company, for all the benefits it conferred on Canada, might as well have been, as Alfred Roche termed it, 'a foreign body.'[60] In 1821 this foreign company had severed all connection with Canada and made Hudson's Bay the main route of commerce between the North West and Europe. The expansionist distrust of the Hudson's Bay Company obscured the very real transportation problems which had led to this change of route. Rather, the switch to the bay was seen as a deliberate attempt to alter the course of history and to prevent Canadian influence in the region. From the time of the merger, 'no merchant trading along the St. Lawrence witnessed the imports for the west, nor the exports therefrom.' The Hudson's Bay Company closed the Superior route and the trade of the west was deliberately 'kept a secret from rising generations in Canada.' As a result, the wealth of the West, previously flowing into Canada, went instead to those 'who have never contributed one farthing to the revenues of this country.'[61]

George Brown saw evidence that this conspiracy against Canada continued even in the face of the expansionist campaign. In 1856 rumours spread that a contingent of troops was to be sent to Red River by the British government. When the government decided, not surprisingly, to use the normal route through Hudson's Bay, Brown charged that the company had used its influence to prevent the use of the Superior route. 'It is beyond a doubt,' he concluded, 'that the troops could be transported with the utmost ease by that route; yet they are to be sent round by the frozen waters of Hudson's Bay, that the secrets of the Company may be kept.'[62]

The deliberate diversion of trade and the destruction of Canada's participation in the North West trade was, expansionists felt, sufficient to condemn the Hudson's Bay Company. But there was much more to it than that. Expansionists made the North West Company much more than a commercial organization. In their writings it became a specifically Canadian company, symbolizing Canadian enterprise and initiative. Its destruction by the Hudson's Bay Company thus also came to represent the destruction of the spirit of progress in the West. The difference in the two companies was apparent in their records in the opening of the West before 1821. 'The Canadian North West Company were everywhere in advance of their rivals,' and while the Hudson's Bay Company rested timidly on the shores of the bay these Canadians explored half a continent.[63]

Had the North West Company continued in existence, expansionists argued, this adventurous and progressive attitude eventually would have led to the opening of the West. Expansionists read into the North West Company their own goals and as such created a myth of it as the precursor of Canadian civilization. Macdonell told the Canadian Select Committee on the Hudson's Bay Territories that had the merger not taken place 'there is no doubt that the route via Lake Superior would by this time have been navigable all the way to the Saskatchewan.' William Dawson painted an inspiring, if romantic, picture of what might have been had the course of history been allowed to proceed unimpeded. The Fort William of the early nineteenth century, he stated, contained all 'the features of an embryo city, in strange contrast with the desolate and decaying loveliness which the blight of an illegal monopoly has thrown over it today.' Instead of this scene it should have been 'the entrepot of the trade of half a continent.'[64] Much more had been lost in 1821 than the profits of the fur trade.

The myth of the North West Company significantly reinforced Canada's claim to special rights in the North West. The West had all along been the means by which Canada might escape from the confines of the shield. In deliberately obstructing that development the Hudson's Bay Company had retarded Canadian growth and limited Canadian prosperity. The company was thus the enemy not only of the Indian and Red River settler but also of Canada. Expansionists were determined, now that the plot had been uncovered, that Canada's rightful destiny would no longer be blocked by a monopolistic trading company.

No conflict was thought to exist between these particular Canadian interests and the claims of the British Empire. From the time of Synge the closing of such a vast region had been seen as a hindrance to the development of the Empire and of civilization, and it continued to be so viewed. 'The time has come,' said Alexander Morris, 'when the claims of humanity and the interests of the British Empire, require that all the portions of this vast empire which are adapted for settlement should be laid open to the industrious emigrant.'[65] Canada, unlike the Hudson's Bay Company, would act not only in its own interests but in the name of progress.

While the opening of the West was for the benefit of the whole Empire, expansionists feared that only they clearly recognized this. They were, in fact, suspicious of the British government's ability to come to any objective conclusion on the whole question. In the same way that it was thought that Canada embodied the spirit of the North West Company, it was feared that at least the ruling circles in Britain had been tainted by the presence of the Hudson's Bay Company. The Canadian decision to send Draper to England was in part based on the fear that the British government would not take Canadian aspirations into consideration.[66] As the proceedings unfolded, expansionists were convinced that these precautions had been only prudent: 'Without the presence in London of some one to speak in our behalf the Committee would have been a sham; things would have "been made pleasant" for the Company; an unconditional renewal of the Charter would have been granted and we would have been sold.'[67]

This sort of bias on the part of the British government was not thought to be confined to the current round of hearings. Expansionists pointed to the stifling of attacks against the company in 1849 as proof that the British government could not or would not see the company for what it was. The refusal of the Colonial Secretary, Earl Grey, to act on Isbister's petition led Macdonell to ask in a rather far-fetched analogy whether 'the history of North America recall any ominous warning to deter that nobleman from pursuing his own selfish views?'[68] When it came to questions involving the Hudson's Bay Company, the British government seemed blind not only to the dictates of progress but also to the lessons of history. 'If history is of any value,' warned the *Globe* on 24 June 1857, 'even folly and infatuation must be made to hear the witnesses of the past.' The attitude of the British to date, however, led inevitably to the conclusion that it was 'in a mere death like sleep.'

The British government seemed unable to comprehend the dangers that the Empire faced. It delayed acting against a monopoly which, if removed, would have assured the Empire a great future. Canada, for its own sake and for the sake of the Empire, must force action if Britain would not. Its history gave it a right to the North West and its future seemed dependent on the region. It could not afford to stand by and watch an ignorant or corrupted mother country sacrifice its future. From 1857 on, Canada increasingly arrogated to itself the role of trustee of the North West in the name of the British Empire and civilization.

There was a certain expediency underlying the often shifting rhetoric of imperial and Canadian interests in the North West. When it came to matters of funds to develop the region, for instance, Canadians were quite willing to emphasize imperial interests. At the same time they continued to insist that whoever paid for that development it must ultimately be controlled by Canada. Beneath this expediency, however, a grandiose and significant idea was beginning to emerge. Many Canadians began to sense that the potential of the North West not only guaranteed future Canadian prosperity but would also eventually alter in a fundamental way the relationship of the colony and the mother country.

At least since the 1720s when Bishop George Berkeley had written his famous and fatalistic line, 'Westward the course of empire takes its way,' the idea that power naturally moved westward from old seats of civilization to new had been commonplace. In the eighteenth and nineteenth centuries, at least in the English-speaking world, the word 'empire' as used by Berkeley implied the British Empire. Canada, as Britain's loyal offspring in the New World, liked to think of itself as the eventual successor to the mother country. Unfortunately, as Canadians were aware, that renegade daughter of the Empire, the United States, also had pretensions in this direction. And in the face of the tremendous growth of their neighbour to the south a good many Canadians might have concluded, as did one writer, that 'against such advantages possessed by the neighbouring states it seemed idle to compete.'[69] With a mixture of envy and fear Canadians noted the growing power of the United States, a power which might truly one day outstrip that of Britain.

As interest in the North West developed expansionists began to argue that there was no reason to assume the United States would inherit the British mantle. Alexander Morris, who developed the theme in the most detail, argued that if Canadian energy and vitality was focused on the vast potential of the North West, then British North America, not the United States, would be the scene of the 'new Britannic Empire on these American shores.'[70] If Canada was allowed to expand into the North West, it would continue to mature 'as surely as the child becomes the man, or the feeble sapling becomes the sturdy monarch of the forest.' With growth, its relationship to Britain would be transformed. Canada, not the United States, would ultimately inherit the British position as the centre of the English-speaking world. The British Empire would, of course, remain, for the connection with Britain 'will not be rudely severed.' The British North American confederation would remain true to British principles, 'reflecting the great parent country from which their inhabitants have mainly sprung, and rising to power and strength under her guiding influence.'[71] While the Empire would remain, however, the power relationships within it would inevitably shift and, ultimately, Canada would become the 'keystone of its strength.'[72]

Given these potential results of expansion it is not surprising that the North West took on an importance far greater than most hinterlands. In the future it was thought possible that the West would be the basis of power for the whole British Empire. This theme had been present in the writings of the British pamphleteers of the 1840s. Unlike the British pamphleteers, however, Canadian expansionists like Alexander Morris saw in their province the seed of an empire in its own right: 'With two powerful colonies on the Pacific, with another or more in the region between Canada and the Rocky Mountains, with a railway and a telegraph linking the Atlantic with the Pacific and absorbing the newly-opened and fast-developing trade with China and Japan . . . who can doubt of the reality and the accuracy of the vision which rises distinctly and clearly-defined before us, as the Great Britannic Empire of the North stands out in all its grandeur.'[73]

In the 1850s this vision of a future Canadian empire was still very hazy. The nature of any empire was undefined and the achievement of imperial status reserved for an unspecified and distant future. Nevertheless, the rising importance of the North West in the minds of Canadian expansionists was clearly revealed when people like Alfred Roche could predict that Canada would 'become a mightier empire in the West than India has ever been in the East.'[74] Over the next few years, as Canadians grappled with the implications of expansion, such statements would become more common and possess a sense of immediacy which was still lacking in the 1850s.

Almost from the beginning the expansionist movement in Canada saw the North West as a means to empire. Given the enormous implications of this fact, it is perhaps understandable that expansionists insisted that the particular rights of their province be recognized. It is also understandable that their campaign should have met with such success and led the Canadian government to lay claim to the region.

Notes

1. Public Archives of Canada (PAC), Charles Bell Papers, Simpson to Ross, 17 Dec. 1850
2. Great Britain, House of Commons, *Report from the Select Committee on the Hudson's Bay Company*, 1857, iii-iv
3. Donald Swainson, 'The North-West Transportation Company: Personnel and Attitudes,' Historical and Scientific Society of Manitoba, *Transactions*, series III, no 26 (1969–70), 59–77, 66–7
4. *Ibid.*, 66
5. A.C. Gluek, Jr, *Minnesota and the Manifest Destiny of the Canadian Northwest* (Toronto 1965), 225
6. J.M.S. Careless, *Brown of the Globe: The Voice of Upper Canada, 1818–1859* (Toronto 1959), 1, 235
7. *Gazette*, Montreal, 9 Sept. 1856
8. Roche, 'A View of Russian America, in connection with the present war,' Literary and Historical Society of Quebec, *Transactions*, vol. IV, part IV (Feb. 1856), 263–328
9. PAC, John A. Macdonald Papers, vol. 209, Draper to Macdonald, 25 Jan. 1857
10. *Ibid.*, Draper to Macdonald, 8, 19, 21 Feb. 1857
11. On Russell and Dennis, see *Canadian Almanac and Repository of Useful Knowledge*, 1857, p. 35; Alexander Morris, *Nova Britannia* (Montreal 1858)
12. Keefer, *Philosophy of Railroads* (Toronto 1849), 32
13. J.M.S. Careless, *The Union of the Canadas: The Growth of Canadian Institutions* (Toronto 1967), 144–5
14. 'Preliminary Address,' Jan. 1856, p. 1
15. Cited in *Gazette*, 4 Sept. 1856
16. 'Excerpts from an Essay by Alexander Morris,' *Canadian Journal of Science, Literature and History*, Sept. 1855, p. 353
17. *Annual Report of the Commissioner of Crown Lands*, 1856, pp. 44–5
18. *Ibid.*, 1856, p. 6; 1857, p. 7; 1863, p. 7
19. *Ibid.*, 1856, p. 43
20. Province of Canada, *Journals of the Legislative Assembly*, 1857, app. 2; see also S. McKee, Jr. 'The Traffic of the Middle West,' *Canadian Historical Association Annual Report*, 1940, pp. 26–35, 34.
21. Population figures are from Peter Goheen, *Victorian Toronto, 1850 to 1900* (Chicago 1970), 49, and D.C. Masters, *The Rise of Toronto, 1850–1890* (Toronto 1947), 53.
22. *Globe*, Toronto, 28 Aug. 1856
23. Chester Martin, *'Dominion Lands' Policy* (Toronto 1973), xx; F.H. Underhill, 'Some Aspects of Upper Canadian Radical Opinion in the Decade before Confederation,' *Canadian Historical Association Annual Report*, 1927; George W. Brown, 'The Grit Party and the Great Reform Convention of 1859,' *Canadian Historical Review*, XVI, 3 (Sept. 1935), 245–65
24. *Globe*, 13 Dec. 1856. See, on Brown's metropolitanism, J.M.S. Careless, 'The Toronto *Globe* and Agrarian Radicalism, 1850–67,' *Canadian Historical Review*, XXIX, 1 (March 1948), 14–39.
25. Morris Zaslow, *Reading the Rocks: The Story of the Geological Survey of Canada* (Toronto 1975), 50–2
26. Keefer, *Montreal and the Ottawa* (1854), in *Philosophy of Railroads and Other Essays*, ed. H.V. Nelles (Toronto 1972), 76
27. The *Annual Report of the Department of Public Works*, 1859, contains Shanly's report.
28. *Gazette*, 9 Sept. 1856
29. PAC, Records of the Governor General, G20, vol. 383, 'Petition of the Inhabitants of Lanark and Renfrew,' 17 March 1857

30. *Globe*, 4 Dec. 1856
31. *Ibid.*, 19 Dec. 1856
32. *Annual Report of the Commissioner of Crown Lands*, 1856, p. 43
33. Allan Macdonell, *The North-West Transportation, Navigation and Railway Company: Its Objects* (Toronto 1858), 7, 10
34. Henry Nash Smith, *Virgin Land* (New York 1950), and Leo Marx, *The Machine in the Garden* (New York 1964), both discuss this theme at some length.
35. Great Britain, *Select Committee*, 'Minutes of Evidence,' 218
36. Macdonell, *North-West Transportation . . . Company*, app.
37. *Globe*, 10 Dec. 1856
38. *Select Committee*, 'Minutes of Evidence,' 7
39. *Journals of the Legislative Assembly*, 1857, app. 17, 'General Remarks'
40. McLean, *Twenty-Five Years Service in the Hudson's Bay Territory* (London 1849), 321
41. Macdonald Papers, vol. 209, Draper to Macdonald, 8 Feb. 1857
42. *Journals of the Legislative Assembly*, 1857, app. 17
43. *Select Committee*, 'Minutes of Evidence,' 212
44. Alexander Begg, *History of the North-West* (Toronto 1894), I, 309
45. *Select Committee*, app. 8; comment by William Dawson
46. *Globe*, 13 Dec. 1856
47. Aborigines Protection Society, *Canada West and the Hudson's Bay Company* (London 1856), 6
48. *Globe*, 2 Sept. 1856; letter from 'Huron'
49. *Select Committee*, 'Minutes of Evidence,' 123
50. *Gazette*, 6 June 1857
51. *Globe*, 4 Dec. 1856
52. Alexander Morris, *The Hudson's Bay and Pacific Territories* (Montreal 1859), 7
53. *Globe*, 2 Sept. 1856
54. 24 March 1857
55. *Select Committee*, 'Minutes of Evidence,' 339
56. PAC, Sir Edward Watkin Papers, vol. 2, Watkin to Head, 24 July 1863
57. *Globe*, 19 Aug. 1856; letter from 'Huron'
58. *Ibid.*, 26 Aug. 1857
59. Morris, *Hudson's Bay*, 13
60. *Select Committee*, 'Minutes of Evidence,' 249
61. Macdonnell, *North-West Transportation . . . Company*, 8
62. *Globe*, 6 May 1857
63. *Journals of the Legislative Assembly*, 1857, app. 17
64. *Select Committee*, app. 8, pp. 388, 402
65. Morris, *Hudson's Bay*, 13
66. Instructions to Draper cited in Begg, *History of the North-West*, I, 310–12
67. *Gazette*, 23 June 1857
68. *Globe*, 30 Sept. 1856; letter from 'Huron'
69. Charles Bass, *Lectures on Canada* (Hamilton 1863), 14
70. Morris, *Hudson's Bay*, 39
71. Morris, *Nova Britannia*, 45–6
72. Bass, *Lectures on Canada*, 45
73. Morris, *Hudson's Bay*, 56
74. Roche, 'A View of Russian America,' 310. Note that this quotation is used by Morris in *Nova Britannia*, 55.

This Land that I Love, This Wide Wide Prairie

Di Brandt

IT IS IMPOSSIBLE for me to write *the land*. This land that I love, this wide wide prairie, this horizon, this sky, this great blue overhead, big enough to contain every dream, every longing, how it held me throughout childhood, this great blue, overhead, this wide wide prairie, how it kept me alive, its wild scent of milkweed, thistle, camomile, lamb's-quarters, pigweed, clover, yarrow, sage, yellow buttercup, purple aster, goldenweed, shepherd's purse, wafting on the hot wind, hot clods of dirt under our bare feet, black, sun soaked, radiating heat, great waves of heat standing in the air, the horizon shimmering, flies buzzing endlessly, wasps, bees, cicadas under the maple trees, dripping with sap, the caragana hedges brushing the air lazily, heavy, golden with blossoms, the delirious scent of lilacs in bloom, hot pink begonias, marigolds, sweet peas, spider queens, wild yellow roses, crimson zinnias, baby's breath, the cool fresh smell of spruce, jack pine, elms gracefully arching overhead, asparagus, cucumber, radishes, onions, peas, beans, corn, raspberries, strawberries, chokecherries, gooseberries, blackberries, yellow currants, red currants, rhubarb, wild yellow plum, crab apples, Japanese cherries, canteloupe, watermelon. It was heaven, the prairie was, the gift of its bounty accepted easily by us, her children, running barefoot all summer, through the garden, the fields, our feet hating the constriction of shoes in the fall, the return to school desks and books and sweaty silence. The hot dry smell of wheat during harvest, the sexy smell of our own skin, bellies, thighs. The call of crows, killdeer, sparrows, kingbirds, barn swallows, robins orioles, nuthatches, woodpeckers, blue jays, mourning doves, the surprise of toads, little frogs, earthworms after rain. The bellow of cows, the cool wet nuzzle of calves' noses, the grunt and snuffle of huge pink sows wallowing in dirt, the squeal of newborn piglets, soft newborn kittens in the barn. How I loved you, how I loved you, how I love you still.

This stolen land, Rupert's Land, Métis land, Indian land, Cree land. When did I first understand this, the dark underside of property, colonization, ownership, the shady dealings that brought us here, to this earthly paradise? Our thousand acres of prime black farm dirt, waving with wheat, barley, flax, oats, corn, alfalfa, and later, sugar beets, buckwheat, yellow rapeseed, corn. Our many fields patched together painstakingly, passionately, laboriously by our father, with devoted help from our mother, field by field, bank loan by bank loan, from a single field and two-room shack in the 1940s, shortly after the war, into a large, modern farm in the '60s and '70s, debt-free, fully mechanized, flourishing. Was it the time our mother searched through our winter drawers for underwear and stockings to give to the Native woman who walked across the fields from her camp, with outstretched hands, to our door? Who was she, we pestered our mother, where did she come from? Why does she need to ask us for things? Was it the time I read about our Canadian history, in Grade Six, where I first heard about the Hudson's Bay Company, Rupert's Land, the Selkirk Settlers, the Métis Rebellion? And later, in Mennonite history class, I heard about our own arrival as a people, a contingent of Mennonites a thousand strong, from Ukraine, by ship and the Red River wagon, to what became known as the West Reserve, near the U.S. border, in the newly formed province of Manitoba in 1875. (Was it then I began to doubt the purity of our fathers' pacifist stance, refusing to fight in the war, choosing instead to go to CO camp in northern Manitoba to cut timber, or even, in some cases, enduring imprisonment, a betrayal of our *Privilegium,* our Charter of Rights granted by the Governor General of Canada in 1873, which included "exemption from any military service" [Zacharias 30], our fathers refusing to defend the land with their bodies, their hands, yet clearly benefitting from the territorial struggles that created Canada?)

It was something else, it was something unspoken, invisible yet tangible, in the air, in the vibrations of the rich black prairie soil under our feet, a memory, lingering in weeds, in grassy ditches, on the edges of fields, a wildness, a freedom, faint trace of thundering herds of buffalo and men on horses, whooping joyfully, dangerously, reining them in for the kill, unbroken prairie, sweet scented, rustling, chirping, singing, untamed, unsubdued, stretching to the wide horizon, women and children sitting around a campfire, the smell of woodsmoke in the air, the incessant beating of drums. There was no getting hold of this memory, this ghost, this whiff of another world, another way of life, no way to see it or understand it, and yet it was there, in the wind, calling to us, plaintive, grieving, just beyond the straight defined edges of our farms, just outside the firm rational orderliness of our disciplined lives. I spent many hours during adolescence following its scent, alone, escaping the house and yard, tracing its outline, its beckoning shadow in the clouds, in bushes, in forgotten bits of prairie near creeks or bogs, in our twenty acres of pasture out back behind the yard, still unbroken grassland, buzzing with crickets and grasshoppers and flies, redolent with wildflowers and cowpies and sage.

There was another memory, too, hidden in my blood, my bones, that sang out from me sometimes in that place of newly broken prairie, an older memory, of a time when the women of my culture had voices and power and freedom, and their own forms of worship, across the sea, out on the green hills under the moon, in the Flemish lowlands of northern Europe, a sturdy peasant life, deeply rooted, before the persecutions, the Inquisition, the burning times, the drowning times, the hanging times, before we became transients, exiles, hounded from one country to the next, seeking refuge from wrathful authorities who couldn't stand our adult baptisms, our democratic communities, our disloyalties to the Pope and king. Before the violence of the persecutions got internalized in our psyches, before we began inflicting them on each other, the same violent subjugations of body and spirit the Inquisitors visited upon us, only we did it secretly, in our homes, we did it to our young children, so no one would see us, we did it to our adolescents, with ritual beatings and humiliations, so they would have no voice, no will, no say of their own, we kept the women bound with rules of humility and obedience, as servants to the masters, their husbands, who owned all the land, owned everything, who went to church with head held high, proud in their democratic brotherhood, proud in their tyrannical lives at home.

The first time I participated in an Aboriginal ceremony near Winnipeg, a few years ago, in the bush, under the full moon, I had such a strong sense of recognition coursing through me. I remember this, I remember this, my body sang, I remember when we gathered, my women ancestors, around fires like this one, surrounded by trees, not so many centuries ago, before we were made to tremble under the wrath of God, the vengeful One, and his long-armed, heavy-handed privileged henchmen, our bishops and fathers. I remember when worship meant laughter and dancing and lovemaking under the moon, carelessly, instead of sternly remembering the torture of a god, and fearing the night, and obeying our husbands, and sitting still in church.

This man's land, owned and ploughed and harvested by men. And the women kept as servants and slaves. When did I first understand this, that the women had no place, no voice of their own in the Mennonite farm village economy, even though they worked as hard as the men, keeping huge gardens, and weeding and canning all summer long, and cooking and sewing and cleaning year round, for us all? Was it the time my father ostentatiously brought out the black farm book, where he kept his accounts and his field notes, after dinner, and announced it was time for our brother to begin learning about how the farm was run, and my sister Rosie and I crowded round, full of curiosity, and he sent us to help our mother do the dishes instead? (Was it then I began to hear the hypocrisy of our fathers' endless talk of religious community and anti-hierarchy and brotherhood?) Was it the time we joined the 4H sugar beet club, and our dad said, no, only boys can grow sugar beets, and he sent us to pull weeds in our brother's acre all summer instead? (I always loved the weeds more than the cultivated plants, they were prettier, wilder, they smelled nicer, I admired the way they kept coming back, insisting on their right, their place on the prairie.) And at harvest time our brother had a record yield and made a lot of money, several hundred dollars, and when we complained about the unfairness of it, our dad ordered our brother to pay us for our labour and he gave us each a dollar. (It still sticks in my throat.) Was it the many times we watched our mother swallow her disappointment, her disagreement, her own wishes, her needs, in deference to our father? And later, there were calves, entire fields, a series of new motorcycles and trips across the country, a half share in a new pickup truck for our brother, and for us, five cents a pound for picking raspberries and strawberries all morning in the summer heat, if there were customers for them, which came, on a good day, to thirty-five cents in our pockets. And strict rules about how we could spend it and where we could go. And eventually, a half share in the entire farm for our brother. And for us, disapproval, endless disapproval, for our women's bodies and dreams, going off to the city to find our own lives, with no parental support.

When the Governor General Lord Dufferin visited the Mennonite settlements on the West Reserve in 1877, two years after their arrival en masse from Ukraine, he found, as historian William Schroeder tells it, a beautifully decorated arbour in which three young Mennonite girls in lace kerchiefs were serving hot lemon-seasoned tea, surrounded by flower bouquets wrapped with poetic lines of welcome, in German, hung on little pine trees. After listening to the Mennonite bishop's welcoming speech, His Excellency addressed the gathering of a thousand or so new immigrants thus:

> Fellow citizens of the Dominion, and fellow subjects of Her Majesty: I have come here today in the name of the Queen of England to bid you welcome to Canadian soil . . . You have left your own land in obedience to a conscientious scruple . . . You have come to a land where you will find the people with whom you associate engaged indeed in a great struggle, and contending with foes whom it requires their best energies to encounter, but those foes are not your fellow men, nor will you be called upon in the struggle to stain your hands with human blood—a task which is so abhorrent to your religious feelings. The war to which we invite you as recruits and comrades is *a war waged against the brute forces of nature,* but those forces will welcome our domination, and reward our attack by placing their treasures at our disposal. It is a war of ambition—for we intend to annex territory after territory—but neither blazing villages nor devastated fields will mark our ruthless track; our battalions will march across the illimitable plains which stretch before us as sunshine steals athwart the ocean; the rolling prairie will blossom in our wake, and corn and peace and plenty will spring where we have trod. (Schroeder 104–5; italics mine.)

Schroeder does not specify how the Mennonites received His Excellency the Lord Dufferin's speech, so liberally sprinkled with military metaphors. I imagine they grimaced and recoiled from this language, reminiscent as it must have been of recent persecutions suffered at the hands of the Russian military, and other military persecutions before that. Still, the weird, contradictory combination of warfare and husbandry, conquest and cultivation of land (and convenient blanking out of its earlier inhabitants), the schizophrenic attitude toward the prairie he articulated is a deadly accurate description of Mennonite farming practice in Manitoba as I knew it, growing up in Reinland.

How come, I remember asking my dad, if the wheat is poisoned by the red stuff you've sprayed on it before seeding, to kill bugs, poisoned enough so we can't taste handfuls of it anymore as it gets poured into the seeder troughs, how come it won't poison us later when it grows new plants, too? Every year throughout the '50s and '60s (while the U.S. and U.S.S.R. were building bombs) there were new pesticides, new herbicides, bigger machines, fancier equipment to disseminate them more quickly, efficiently, every year the chemicals became more poisonous, as the weeds became hardier to withstand them, as the pesticide companies and seed companies grew larger to sustain and control this burgeoning market. My father scoffed at safety measures against pesticides. He remembered spraying DDT all over his bare arms, before it was banned, to ward off flies. And look at me, he'd chortle, healthy as an ox. He was annoyed at new spraying restrictions as they arose. He died of cancer at age sixty-one. My brother, who is forty-seven, recently quit farming and left the community in desperation due to environmental illness, surely caused by exposure to pesticides. (And that was the end of Elm Ridge Farm, my father's thousand-acre dream that we sacrificed so much of our lives for, his carefully stitched-together playing field, so unsolid after all, scattered back into the hands of strangers.) Here is how Harvey Janzen, my brother, describes his symptoms in a recent letter from Calgary, Alberta, where he is being treated by a doctor specializing in chemical sensitivities.

> My weakened body had begun to react to fumes besides farm chemicals like automobile exhaust, commercial cleaners, fabric dyes, glues, ink, paint, perfumes, and scented personal care products. My body reacts instantly when exposed to these. Different fumes will cause different symptoms to occur. Fatigue and exhaustion is usually the end result. I have done very little driving during the past year due to fatigue and loss of muscle control. Driving is also affected by loss of vision due to cataracts in the lenses of both of my eyes.

In a little more than a hundred years, my fellow countrymen and women, we have managed to poison the land and our food sources and our own bodies so drastically as to jeopardize the future of all life in this country. The birch trees in the Pembina Hills close to our farming village, which we used to visit every fall to admire their flaming orange colours before the onset of winter, are dying. The rivers are being choked with reeds and fungi because of fertilizer run-off into the water systems. Many, many people in south central Manitoba, in the heart of Mennonite farmland, are dying of cancer, MS, pneumonia, leukemia, all of them victims of damaged immune systems and, indisputably, environmental pollution. There are very few birds now, very few frogs, toads, gophers, foxes, deer, very few wildflowers and prairie grasses left. It is the same in other farming communities across the nation. And elsewhere in this province, the forests and lakes are being ravaged by the pulp and paper and mining industries. It is the same in other provinces and countries across the globe.

In all those years of listening to preachers preach to us, every Sunday, in the Mennonite village churches, endlessly exhorting us to repentance, to a more ethical life, not once did I hear a single one of them talk about the land, except to pronounce gleefully that we "shall have dominion over it," a special permission, a decree from God, though, on the other hand, paradoxically, we should not go to war to defend it. Not once, in all those lists of sins, fornication and lust and desire and whatnot that we were endlessly warned against, did I hear one of them talk about an ethical practice of land ownership or address in any way the politics of gender and race, the politics of chemical intervention, the dangers of pesticides and herbicides and chemical fertilizers, and later, the implications of genetic manipulation of seeds and livestock for the land and the creatures in it and our own bodies. (When I became a vegetarian at age twenty and began cooking organically, my father said, "You're trying to sabotage my farm.")

This is why I weep, sitting on my wooden veranda in Winnipeg, not far from the Forks, where the Red and the Assiniboine Rivers meet, on a beautiful tree-lined street canopied by great green elms, on this beautiful July evening, in this prairie landscape that is still heaven, still paradise on earth, despite the volatile weather, the bugs, the mosquitoes, the endangered earth and air, because I remember, somewhere my body still remembers, when it wasn't so, when this beautiful land was unconquered, unsubdued, unbroken, when the people of this land tried to live in harmony with its shifts and rhythms instead of in violent conquest over it, when the creeks and ditches were filled with frogs and meadowlarks and red-winged blackbirds and butterflies and wild clover and bees instead of sprayed grass, when the fields were grazing grounds for wild herds of buffalo and antelope and deer instead of straight hard rows of chemically altered grain.

There is regret in me, regret I feel deeply, sharply, here in my belly, sometimes, so I can hardly breathe, for this slow dying prairie, how she lost her stupendous wildness, forever, around the time my great-grandparents came to settle the dispossessed Native territories, to break them, to plant their rich farms and gardens, that I am so grateful for, so sad about. It is why I cannot write *the land,* because I am torn inside over it, my helplessness in the face of such massive destruction, my ongoing love for the prairie, how her beauty still catches my throat, her power, majesty, so much bigger than we are, there is still time to turn it around, to save the land, undo its massive poisoning, the scent of prairie on the hot wind, calling out to me, my love, *eck lev dee, ni-mi-ta-ten,* I'm sorry, *ki-sa-ki-hi-tin,* I love you.

Sources

Schroeder, William. *The Bergthal Colony,* revised edition (CMBC Publications, 1986)
Zacharias, Peter D. *Reinland: An Experience in Community.* (Reinland Centennial Committee, 1976)
Cree translations by Emily Munroe

CHAPTER SEVENTEEN

Canada: A Northern Country

Introduction

Canada is a northern country. It has been said so often—in art, in literature, in history and in tourism promotion—that we take it for granted. Canada's north has been called one of its defining facts. But where exactly is the north? Where does the south end and the north begin? Is it north of 60°, that is, is it the Yukon, the Northwest Territories and Nunavut? Or is it also much farther south, in, say, cottage country north of Toronto? The north is a region defined by geography—although where the boundary should be marked is a matter of debate—and it is a national symbol. It is part of how Canadians see themselves and of how Canada projects itself to the world. In this classic essay, first published in 1966, the historian Carl Berger examines the origins of Canada's northern identity. F.R. Scott (1899–1985) was a legal scholar and a highly acclaimed poet. Inspired by a 1946 train trip through northern Ontario, from Quebec to Saskatchewan, the poem "Laurentian Shield" explores Canada's northern identity and its northern destiny.

Two of Canada's most brilliant thirty-something poets—Karen Connelly and matt robinson—also address Canada's northernness, but in a very different way. Winner of the 1992 Governor General's Award for Non-Fiction, Connelly's country, "this white frozen world," is a much darker place than Robert Stanley Weir's "true north strong and free." matt robinson—who received the 2000 Petra Kenney International Poetry Prize and the 2000 Writer's Federation of New Brunswick Poetry Prize—writes an anthem that is likewise very different from Weir's "O Canada." In "trees in ice" he self-consciously re-thinks Scott's "Laurentian Shield." What does robinson mean when he writes, "with apologies to f.r. scott"? Canada is a northern country, isn't it?

The True North Strong and Free

Carl Berger

Hail! Rugged monarch, Northern Winter, hail!
Come! Great Physician, vitalize the gale;
Dispense the ozone thou has purified,
With Frost and Fire, where Health and age reside,—
Where Northern Lights electrify the soul
Of Mother Earth, whose throne is near the Pole.

Why should the children of the North deny
The sanitary virtues of the sky?
Why should they fear the cold, or dread the snow,
When ruddier blood thro' their hot pulses flow?

. . .

We have the Viking blood, and Celtic bone,
The Saxons' muscled flesh, and scorn to groan,
Because we do not bask in Ceylon's Isle,
Where Heber said, that 'only man is vile'.

. . .

But we, as laymen, must get down to earth,
And praise the clime which gave our nation birth.
Kind Winter is our theme.

William Henry Taylor,
Canadian Seasons. Spring:
Summer: Autumn: Winter:
with a Medley of Reveries in Verse and Prose
and Other Curios (Toronto, 1913)

EVERYBODY TALKS ABOUT the weather and the climate: seldom have these been exalted as major attributes of nationality. Yet from the days of the French explorers, who often remarked that the future inhabitants of northern America must necessarily be as hardy as their environment, to John Diefenbaker's invocation of the northern destiny of the nation, detached observers and patriotic spokesmen alike have fixed upon the northern character of Canada as one of the chief attributes of her nationality. Canadian national feeling, like the nationalist impulse in other countries, has expressed itself in myths and legends about the past and anticipations of noble mission in the future, as well as in distinctive economic and international policies. Such myths and symbols nourish and sustain the emotional taproot of nationalism, and impart to it an intellectual content which itself has an attractive power. The purpose of this paper is to describe the elements and savour the texture of one such recurrent theme in Canadian nationalist thought which flowered in the half century after Confederation and which is, in muted form, still with us—the idea that Canada's unique character derived from her northern location, her severe winters, and her heritage of 'northern races.'

The True North, Strong and Free

In the rhetoric of the day, Canada was the 'Britain of the North', 'this northern kingdom', the 'True North' in Tennyson's phrase, the 'Lady of the Snows' in Kipling's. 'Canada is a young, fair and stalwart maiden of the north.'[1] 'The very atmosphere of her northern latitude, the breath of life that rose from lake and forest, prairie and mountain, was fast developing a race of men with bodies enduring as iron and minds as highly tempered as steel.'[2] Canada was the 'Young giant nation of the North', the 'Young scion of the northern zone'; her people, 'Our hardy northern race'; her location, those 'Stern latitudes.'[3] These images denote not merely geographical location or climatic condition but the combination of both, moulding racial character. The result of life in the northern latitudes was the creation and sustenance of self-reliance, strength, hardness—in short, all the attributes of a dominant race. 'Northern nations always excel southern ones in energy and stamina, which accounts for their prevailing power.'[4] In the north 'the race is compelled by nature to maintain its robust attributes, mental and physical, whereas in more sunny countries like Africa and Australia the tendency of the climate is toward deterioration.'[5] 'A constitution nursed upon the oxygen of our bright winter atmosphere', exclaimed Governor General Dufferin, 'makes its owner feel as though he could toss about the pine trees in his glee . . .'[6] Just as 'northern' was synonymous with strength and self-reliance, so 'southern' was equated with degeneration, decay, and effeminacy. Our 'bracing northern winters', declared the *Globe* in 1869, 'will preserve us from the effeminacy which naturally steals over the most vigorous races when long under the relaxing influence of tropical or even generally mild and genial skies.'[7] Moreover, it was believed that liberty originated among the tribes of northern Europe and was dependent upon those very characteristics which the northern environment called forth. Canada, then, was not only the true north, but also strong and free.

In origin, ideas about the relationship between climate and the character of 'races' and their institutions were rooted in myths and stereotypes in classical, medieval, and renaissance Europe, most of which viewed the southern Mediterranean peoples as gay, lively, and individualistic, and the northerners as stupid and dull bar-barians.[8] The first coherent Canadian statement of the idea of the northern race came from an associate of the Canada First Movement who was also a Fellow of the Royal Society of Northern Antiquaries of Copenhagen, Robert Grant Haliburton. Lamenting the fact that Confederation had been created with as little excitement among the masses as if a joint-stock company had been formed, he asked, 'Can the generous flame of national spirit be kindled and blaze in the icy bosom of the fro-zen north?' Convinced that the indispensable attribute of a nation, a 'national spirit', was the product of slow growth unless stimulated by a violent struggle, the memory of a glorious past, or the anticipation of a bright future. Haliburton added to the Canada First spirit the contention that Canada's future as a dominant nation was secure because of its northern character. 'We Are the Northmen of the New World', his lecture to the Montreal Literary Club in 1869 on the men of the north and their place in history was the seedbed of the northern race idea. Ironically, Haliburton's poor health compelled him to spend his winters in tropical climates, where he de-voted himself to ethnological and anthropological investigations. In 1887 he discov-ered the existence of a race of pygmies in North Africa.

Haliburton's declaration that Canadians were a northern race was expressed in the language of science and the rich imagery of romantic history. 'Our cornfields, rich though they are, cannot compare with the fertile prairies of the West, and our long winters are a drain on the profits of business, but may not our snow and frost give us what is of more value than gold or silver, a healthy, hardy, virtuous, dominant race?' The peculiar characteristic of the new dominion, he asserted, 'must ever be that it is a Northern country inhabited by the descendants of Northern races.' This claim to dominance rested on two assumptions: firstly, the hardy northern races of Europe are attracted to Canada. The British people themselves are 'but a fusion of many northern elements which are here again meeting and mingling, and blending together to form a new nationality'. This new nationality must comprise at once 'the Celtic, the Teutonic, and the Scandinavian elements, and embrace the Celt, the Norman French, the Saxon and the Swede'. Secondly, to Haliburton, the climate it-self was a creative force. 'Is it climate that produces varieties in our race or must we adopt the views of some eminent authorities of science, who hold that the striking diversities now apparent in the languages, temperament, and capacities of nations, must have existed *ab initio*? The Mosaic chronology must be rejected and the period of man's life on earth must be extended to millions of years.' 'If climate has not had the effect of moulding races, how is it that southern nations have almost invariably been inferior to and subjugated by the men of the north?'

The stern climate would preserve in their pristine vigour the characteristics of the northern races and ensure that Canada would share the destiny of the northmen of the old world, who destroyed Rome after it 'had become essentially Southern in its characteristics.' Those northmen were not barbarians but the carriers of the germ of liberty. 'On investigating the history of our laws and of the rise of civil and political liberty in Europe', Haliburton found them rooted in the elemental institutions of the northmen. 'Almost all the Northern nations had similar systems of regulating the rights of property and the remedies of wrongs. Their laws were traditions called by them their *customs,* an unwritten code which still exists in England where it is known as the Common law, . . . [and] it is a remarkable fact that wherever these unwritten laws have been preserved, civil and political liberty has also survived.' In Canada, 'the cold north wind that rocked the cradle of our race, still blows through our forests, and breathes the spirit of liberty into our hearts.'[9] Thus, because of the climate and because Canadians are sprung from these men of the north—the 'Aryan' family, Canada must be a pre-eminent power, the home of a superior race, the heir of both the historical destiny of the ancient Scandinavians and their spirit of liberty.

In the exuberant optimism of Canada First nationalism, Haliburton took the Canadian climate—since the days of Voltaire's famous disparagement, the symbol of sterility, inhospitality, and worthlessness—and turned it into the dynamic element of national greatness. Though he was to break with Haliburton over the issue of Canadian independence, to the end of his days the irrepressible Colonel Denison could boast that 'We are the Northmen of the new world.'[10] Charles Mair, too, thought that 'whilst the south is in a great measure a region of effeminacy and disease, the north-west is a decided recuperator of decayed function and wasted tissue.'[11] And William Foster, in his address on the new nationality in 1871, said that 'The old Norse mythology, with its Thor hammers and Thor hammerings, appeals to us,—for we are a Northern people,—as the true out-crop of human nature, more manly, more real, than the weak marrow-bones superstition of an effeminate South.[12] It is no accident that members of this youthful and intellectual nationalist group should appeal to what Mair, in his poem on Foster's death, called 'the unconquered North', that they should extol Alexander Morris's vision of 'the Great Britannic Empire of the North', or that they should be remembered a generation later as exponents of the northern destiny of Canada. Their most practical achievement in politics was the agitation for Canadian acquisition of the northwest territory, the importance of which they contended had been obscured by tales of ice and snow falsely broadcast by Hudson's Bay Company officials to protect their fur domain from settlement.

Climatic or Racial Determinism?

While Haliburton's address included much that was to receive progressive elaboration by others, such as the notion that French and English were, in racial terms, one people, it contained an ambivalence that was to become more obvious as the idea of the northern race became enmeshed in a popularized Darwinism. This dichotomy was simply between an optimistic, idealistic meliorism which took climate as moulding desirable qualities irrespective of the racial origins of the people, and a scientific determinism which saw racial capacities as fixed, or changeable only to a limited degree. Haliburton avoided such subtleties by implying that all future immigration into Canada would consist of those races already inured and adapted to the northern environment. Later, more pessimistic writers were to see the climate as a 'barrier' to certain kinds of immigrant, rather than as an agency for totally transforming them. This dualism can be best illustrated by considering two different versions of the idea.

A most forceful statement of the view that assumed the complete malleability of character was made in 1877 by another Nova Scotian, Charles R. Tuttle. A self-educated schoolteacher who later made a career of journalism in Winnipeg and the United States, Tuttle produced a large number of now forgotten books including an imposing two-volume history of Canada. In this history he expressed the optimistic opinion that the institutions, soil, and climate of Canada would determine the character of the people. The immigrants, he wrote, come from the monarchical countries of Europe, 'ignorant, rude, and unmannerly', but their character is transformed, they become self-reliant, and exhibit a 'manly independence', under the influence of British institutions and the 'broad rivers, boundless prairies, high mountains, and pathless woods.'[13]

In Tuttle, a romantic ruralism was mixed with the conviction that man's capacity for improvement was infinite and, in a favourable environment, inevitable. Where he saw the 'ignorant, rude, and unmannerly' being formed into independent and hardy yeomen by the natural features of the country and British institutions, more pessimistic observers, while not denying the potent influence of environment, nevertheless emphasized rather the inherent and unchangeable aptitudes of the 'northern races'. That the northern climate constituted a national blessing because it excluded 'weaker' races was the persistent theme of the writings and orations of the Canadian imperialist George Parkin. A native of New Brunswick, Parkin was one of the most forceful and idealistic spokesmen of the Imperial Federation League, Principal of Upper Canada College during the late 1890s, and subsequently one of the organizers of the Cecil Rhodes scholarship trust. Heavily influenced by the social Darwinism of the time, and acknowledging his debt to the historian Buckle for the idea of climatic influence upon the life of nations, Parkin called the Canadian climate 'one of our greatest blessings'. The 'severe winter climate of Canada', he said, 'is perhaps the most valuable asset that the country has.' A temperature of twenty degrees below zero which he found at Winnipeg 'seemed to give an added activity to people's steps and a buoyancy to their spirits.' The climate necessitates vigorous effort; 'it teaches foresight; it cures or kills the shiftless and improvident; history shows that in the long run it has made strong races.'

Where Tuttle viewed the capacity for self-government as the product of the environment, Parkin contended that fitness for self-government was itself the inherent function of the northern races. Without race vanity, he asserted, we may attribute to the Anglo-Saxon race a unique aptitude for self-government. The special importance of the Canadian climate, therefore, was not merely that it sustained the hardy character of the stronger races, but that it also constituted, in Darwinian terms, 'a persistent process of natural selection.' The northern winters ensured that Canada would have no Negro problem, 'which weighs like a troublesome nightmare upon the civilization of the United States'; and it seemed that nature itself had decreed that Canada would have no cities 'like New York, St Louis, Cincinnati, or New Orleans which attract even the vagrant population of Italy and other countries of Southern Europe.' 'Canada,' Parkin emphasized, 'will belong to the sturdy races of the North-Saxon, and Celt, Scandinavian, Dane and Northern German, fighting their way under conditions sometimes rather more severe than those to which they have been accustomed in their old homes.' The climate 'is certain, in short, to secure for the Dominion and perpetuate there the vigour of the best northern races.'[14]

The Advantages of Northernness

To recapitulate and detail the elements of this concept is to indicate the basis of its credibility and the nature of its appeal. First of all, the very fact of northernness connoted strength and hardihood, vigour and purity. 'Strength and power', ran the familiar refrain, 'have ever been with the Northern peoples.'[15] In the struggle for existence, the northern conditions called forth the virtues of self-reliance and strength: only the fittest survived. On the other hand, the 'south' conjured up the image of enervation, of abundance stifling the Victorian values of self-help, work, and thrift, of effeminacy, of voluptuous living, and consequently of the decay and degeneration of character.

A whole series of desirable national characteristics were derived from Canada's northern location. It was implied that northern peoples expressed their hard individualism in an individualistic religion, stripped of the gorgeous luxuries congenial to southern Catholicism. The climate said Parkin, imparts 'a Puritan turn of mind which gives moral strenuousness.'[16] A Methodist clergyman and editor, who attended the American centennial exhibition in 1876 and saw a representative collection of European paintings, reported his disgust with the Catholic art of the south, a reaction he attributed to the lax morals of the 'Latin' races. 'I must', he wrote, 'record my protest against the sensuous character of many of the foreign paintings, especially of France, Austria, and Spain. In this respect they are in striking contrast with the almost universal chaste and modest character of the English and American pictures, and those of Rothern [sic, Northern] Europe. I attribute this difference partly to the only partial moral restraints of the Roman Catholic religion, and partly to a survival, in the old Latin races, of the ancient pagan characteristics which created the odious art and literature, and social corruptions of the effete and dying Roman Empire.'[17] These impurities, of course, were due to much else besides climate, but the clear, cold, and frosty air itself seemed an insulation against lax morality. Another clergyman found in the Canadian winter the impulse to cultural and mental improvement. The winter 'is prophetic . . . of a race, in mind and body and moral culture, of the highest type.' Applying to Canada the remarks that Sir Charles Dilke had made in reference to Scotland, the Reverend F.A. Wightman cited with approval the opinion that the '"long winters cultivate thrift, energy and fore-thought, without which civilization would perish, and at the same time give leisure for reading and study. So the Scottish, the Icelanders, the Swedes, and the northern races generally, are much better educated than the Latin and southern races.'"[18]

The Canadian winter was not only considered to be conducive to mental improvement: in maintaining physical health and stimulating robustness, according to one of the foremost Canadian physicians of the day, it was unsurpassed. A belief in the healthful qualities of the climate was expressed in much of the literature on the northern theme, but it was left to a surgeon at the Hôtel-Dieu in Montreal to impart to this idea the authority of medical knowledge and statistical proof. William Hales Hingston had studied medicine at McGill and Edinburgh, as well as Berlin, Heidelberg, and Vienna; in 1854 he began practice in Montreal and was for many years surgeon at the largest hospital in Canada and a professor of clinical surgery at the Montreal School of Medicine. In 1884 Hingston published a series of papers under the title, *The Climate of Canada and its Relation to Life and Health.* Employing statistics provided by the surgeons at British and American army stations, he ascertained that as one passed northward the salubrity of the climate increased, that the ratios of mortality from digestive, respiratory, and nervous disorders decreased in a northward progression. After considering practically every known malady from diarrhoea to dysentery, consumption to cataract, he emphasized that there are no diseases indigenous to the country. The dry air and cold winter, moreover, are decided recuperators of disease. 'Indeed,' he concluded, 'in considering the few diseases which here afflict humanity relatively to elsewhere, we have great reason to be thankful to the All-powerful Controller of the seasons as of our fate. . . . He keeps us in health, comfort and safety.' If only such pernicious social habits as intemperance could be avoided, the climate was most 'favourable to the highest development of a hardy, long-lived, intelligent people'; the tendency 'is unmistakably in favour of increased muscular development'; 'the future occupants of the soil will be taller, straighter, leaner people—hair darker and drier and coarser; muscles more tendinous and prominent and less cushioned . . .' These future occupants of the soil will be, emphatically, a '*Canadian* people', for the distinct nationalities of Europe will blend here into a homogeneous race, the predominating characteristics of which will be determined 'after the fashion described by Darwin as the struggle for existence.' To this people 'will belong the privilege, the great privilege, of aiding in erecting, in what was so lately a wilderness, a monument of liberty and civilization, broader, deeper, firmer, than has ever yet been raised by the hand of man.'[19] There was much in Hingston's book—description of the variety of the climate, reflections on social habits, and the straight faced observation that those frozen to death display on their visages a look of contentment achieved only by successful religious mystics—but its central burden was that the northern location will breed a distinctive, superior, and healthy people.

It seemed that scarcely any advantages accruing to Canada from the winter season went unnoticed or unsung. The winter snow covers and protects fall crops; the frost acts as a solvent on the soil, ploughing the ground and leaving it in springtime 'completely pulverized'; the cold freezes newly-killed livestock and preserves them for market. It makes possible the commercial activity of lumbering, for the 'frost makes bridges without a cent of cost; the snow provides the best roads', 'the whole face of the country being literally Macadamized by nature.' Winter makes possible sleighing, tobogganing, snowshoeing, and skating. 'Jack Frost effectually and gratuitously guards us on three thousand miles of our northern coast, and in this he does us a distinct service, greatly relieving national expenditure and contributing much to our sense of security.'[20]

A Basis for Racial Unity

While Canada's northernness implied these desirable national advantages, in its second aspect it underlined the fundamental unity of the French and British Canadians. According to most definitions of nationality offered in the late nineteenth century, a nation was held together by the ties of race, religion, and language, as well as by a general similarity in political and social institutions. The very existence of the French Canadians, however, and the 'racial conflict' and disunity their distinctive social and religious institutions helped to engender, seemed to belie the contention that Canada was a nation.

But the French Canadians, by the very facts of their colonization, settlement, and multiplication, had demonstrated their fitness to cope with the inhospitable northern environment. The stern climate and the winds of winter were uniform on both sides of the Ottawa River. The 'geographical contour of our Country', said F.B. Cumberland, Vice-President of the National Club of Toronto, 'assists by creating a Unity of Race. Living throughout in a region wherein winter is everywhere a distinct season of the year, inuring the body and stimulating to exertion, we are by nature led to be a provident, a thrifty, and a hardy people; no weakling can thrive among us, we must be as vigorous as our climate.' Through the 'natural selection' of immigration, only the northern races, including the 'Norman French', have settled here, and what selective immigration has effected 'nature is welding together into Unity and by this very similarity of climate creating in Canada a homogeneous Race, sturdy in frame, stable in character, which will be to America what their forefathers, the Northmen of old, were to the continent of Europe.'[21]

It was argued, moreover, that 'there is no real or vital difference in the origin of these two races; back beyond the foreground of history they were one.'[22] This identification of the common racial origin of both the British and French Canadians rested on the results of the research of genealogists, like Benjamin Sulte and Cyprien Tanguay, who had inquired into the origins of the original immigrants to New France. Between 1871 and 1890 Tanguay compiled no less than seven volumes of his *Dictionnaire généologique des familles canadiennes* and demonstrated that the majority of

French Canadians were descended from immigrants who had come from Brittany and Normandy. The 'French Canadian type', declared Sulte, 'is Norman, whether its origin be pure Norman, mixed Norman, Gascon or French-English.'[23] Since the Normans themselves were descendants of the Scandinavian invaders of the ninth and tenth centuries who had gone to conquer Britain, it could be claimed that both British and French were a northern race, or at least that both contained elements of the northern strains. It is an interesting fact, asserted the historian William Wood, 'that many of the French-Canadians are descended from the Norman-Franks, who conquered England seven hundred years before the English conquered La Nouvelle France, and that, however diverse they are now, the French and British peoples both have some Norman stock in common.'[24]

That the 'Norman blood' was a positive unifying force in Canada was emphasized by George Bourinot in his constitutional histories, and in 1925 G.M. Wrong, Professor of History in the University of Toronto, told the Canadian Historical Association that 'There is in reality no barrier of race to keep the English and French apart in Canada: the two peoples are identical in racial origins.'[25] As late as 1944, Abbé Arthur Maheux, Professor of History at Laval University, after condemning those 'people who think along the lines of blood, so being Hitlerites without knowing it', pointed out that 'the Norman blood, at least, is a real link between our two groups.' The French people, the Abbé explained, 'is a mixture of different bloods: the Gaul, the Briton, the Romans, the Norman each gave their share. The same is true with the English people, the Celt, the Briton, the Roman, the Saxon, the Dane, the Norman each gave their share of blood. It is easy to see that the elements are about the same and in about the same proportions in each of these two nations. Both are close relatives by blood from the very beginning of their national existences. And both Canadian groups have the same close kinship.'[26]

A Rationale for Anti-Americanism

The Canadian people were thus not only collectively a superior race, but their 'northernness' was constantly compared to the 'southernness' of the United States. The third use of the idea was a vigorous statement of the separateness of the two countries. When the annexationists asked 'why should the schism which divided our race on this continent 100 years ago, be perpetuated? . . . What do we gain by remaining apart?' and answered their own question by saying that 'Union would be the means of ultimately cementing the Anglo-Saxon race throughout the world,'[27] the usual retort was to deny that the Republic was an Anglo-Saxon country and to elaborate Canadian virtues derived from its northernness against the degeneration of 'the south.' While the northern climate of Canada was both moulding the northern elements and rejecting weaker, southern immigration, thus creating a homogeneous race, the southern climate of the United States was sapping the energies of even those descendants of vigorous races at the same time that it was attracting multitudes of the weaker races from Southern Europe, in addition to providing a hospitable home to the large Negro element. This destruction of the homogeneity of the Republic was regarded as 'diluting' its strength, as a species of 'deterioration.' This was because the southern immigrants were neither formed by a hardy climate in their homeland nor forced to adapt to one in the States. In Canada, Principal Falconer of the University of Toronto reassured his readers, 'the rigour of the northern climate has been, and will continue to be, a deterrent for the peoples of Southern Europe.'[28] Our climate, contended Parkin, excludes the lower races, 'squeezed out by that 30 or 40 degrees below zero.' Canada attracts 'the stronger people of the northern lands. That is the tendency to squeeze out the undesirable and pump in, as Kipling says, . . . the strong and desirable.' 'We have an advantage, this northern race, of a stern nature which makes us struggle for existence.' The 'submerged tenth', the weaker members of even the stronger races, are also excluded, and hence Canada does not suffer from the American labour troubles. Labour problems are unknown in Canada partly because of the abundance of land and partly because the 'Canadian winter exercises upon the tramp a silent but well-nigh irresistible persusasion to shift to a warmer latitude.' The United States itself thus serves as a 'safety-valve' for labour questions in the Dominion. The climate 'is a fundamental political and social advantage which the Dominion enjoys over the United States.' It ensures stability and ordered development as well as superiority.[29]

North = snow

Northernness and Liberty

The notion of strength and superiority inhering in the quality of northernness included a fourth, and perhaps the most important, element of the general idea. Expressed in the words of Emerson, it was that 'Wherever snow falls, there is usually civil freedom.'[30] Not only did the northern climate foster exactly those characteristics without which self-government could not work, but it was held that, historically, the 'germs' of the institutions of liberty originated among the northern peoples and that northern races, inured by centuries of struggles with the elements and acquaintance with these institutions of self-government, enjoyed a superior capacity for governing themselves. Liberty itself depended upon self-reliance, a rugged independence, instilled by the struggle for existence. Thus to the equation of 'northern' with strength and the strenuous virtues, against 'southern' with degeneration and effeminacy, was added the identification of the former with liberty and the latter with tyranny.

Because 'liberty' was itself somehow the major stimulant to 'progress', the comparison was often made in terms of progress and regression. In a book review, the editor of the *Canadian Methodist Magazine* contrasted the result of Anglo-Saxon development in North America with that of the Latin races in South America. 'On the one side,' he wrote, 'a forward motion of society and the greatest development of agriculture, commerce and industry; on the other, society thrown backward and plunged to grovel in a morass of idle, unproductive town life, and given up to officialism and political revolutions. In the North we have the rising of the future, in the South the crumbling and decaying past.'³¹ Wherein, asked a pamphleteer, lies the secret of such marvellous progress? 'It springs largely from the fact that the country was peopled by the Anglo-Saxon race. . . . When Rome was overshadowing the nations of Southern and Central Europe with its greatness, in the cheerless, uninviting north, a people was undergoing hardy discipline, on land and sea, in constant strife and endless foray, which produced a nobler type of manhood than Rome. . . . It is from these fearless freemen of North Germany, England is indebted in a large measure for her political liberties.'³²

The idea that it was in the north 'that the liberties of the world had their birth' was sustained by the political science of the day. Influenced by the 'comparative politics' of E.A. Freeman in England and H.B. Adams in the United States, the constitutional and political writings of George Bourinot detailed the operations of the Teutonic germ theory in Canada. In biological analogy, freedom was a 'seed', a 'germ', which originated in the tribal assemblies of the ancient Scandinavians, was transplanted to England and subsequently to New England, and then to Canada by the migration of descendants of these Teutonic races. Wherever the favoured race appeared, its early institutional life was repeated and amplified because 'freedom' was in 'the blood.' Conversely, southern non-Teutonic peoples were either 'untutored' in self-government but were educable, or were incapable of governing themselves altogether. In the bracing climate of the north, so resembling freedom's original home, liberty, it was thought, would flourish in a purer form.³³

It was this identification of liberty with northernness that gave such force to the anti-American emotion that Canadian, or 'British', liberty was far superior to the uproarious democracy of the United States. It was a charge taken directly from pessimistic American racists. The 'new immigration' coming from southern and southeastern Europe became the object of concern and then dread in the late 1880s, partly because it coincided with political and social disturbances arising from the transition from an agrarian to an industrial civilization. It was thought that this immigration not only destroyed the homogeneity of the American people, but also threatened the very existence of Anglo-Saxon leadership and Anglo-Saxon values. Commenting editorially on an article by Henry Cabot Lodge, the chief immigration restrictionist in the Senate, the *Empire* agreed that the old-stock families in the United States were losing their hold, that immigration and the multiplication of 'the dregs of the old world population' were increasing too rapidly for assimilation. 'The Anglo-Saxon element, the real strength of the nation, is not proportionally as influential now as it once was.'³⁴ Even earlier, Goldwin Smith feared that 'the Anglo-American race is declining in numbers; . . . The question is whether its remaining stock of vitality is sufficient to enable it, before it loses its tutelary ascendancy, to complete the political education of the other races.'³⁵ What Smith viewed with apprehension, others relished in the conviction that Canada was preserved from such a fate. 'Take the fact that one million two hundred thousand people passed through Ellis Island into the port of New York last year. Who were they,' asked Parkin, 'Italians, Greeks, Armenians, Bulgarians, the Latin races of the South. People unaccustomed to political freedom, unaccustomed to self-government, pouring in. . . . They did not come to Canada.'[36] In Canada, because of the climate, there were no Haymarket riots, no lynchings, no assassinations of public men. 'The United States', declared the *Dominion Illustrated* in 1891, 'are welcome to the Hungarians, Poles, Italians and others of that class; they are, as a rule, wretchedly poor, make very poor settlers, and bring with them many of the vices and socialistic tendencies which have caused much trouble to their hosts already. Renewed efforts should . . . be made by our government to induce more of the hardy German and Norwegian races to remain here.'[37]

The Imperialism of the Northern Race

For the imperialist the idea of the northern race had an importance which transcended its purely Canadian application. It supported the notion of the tutelary role of the stronger races in extending order and liberty to southern peoples who, either because of their climate alone, or because of their inherent weakness, could neither generate progress unassisted nor erect the institutions of self-government. Imperialists like Parkin had an immense pride in their native Canada: it alone, of all the Dominions, lay above the forty-fifth parallel. Because of the vigour implied in its northernness, Canada could exercise within the imperial framework a dynamic influence on the future, perhaps even exceeding that of the homeland. Because of the inevitable deterioration that was creeping over the urbanized and industrialized Englishman, cut off from the land, Canada was to be a kind of rejuvenator of the imperial blood. For all their rhetoric about the citizens of Canada regarding South Africa or Australia as their own country, this notion of northernness bolstered their feeling of a unique connection between Canada and Britain.

The imperial role of Canada depended on the character of the race, and it was with 'character' that imperialists like Parkin and Kipling were most concerned. Their apprehensions that the character of the imperial race had deteriorated, that the instinct of adventure and self-sacrifice which had been the motive force of imperial expansion had decayed, were coupled with the pervasive fear that the race was becoming 'soft', that it no longer manifested 'hardness'—hardness meaning not callousness but the stoical acceptance of the strenuous life and the performance of duty irrespective of rewards. It was this concern that lay at the bottom of their advocacy of a manly athleticism, their praise for what seemed to some a martial arrogance, and their exhortations to uplift the weaker races, not so much because they believed that the weaker races could be transformed but because the imperial race's assumption of the burden was in itself a test and an exaltation of their race's 'character'. The motive was as much self-regeneration as altruism. The northern race idea is subtly related to this concern, at least psychologically. In Canada, said Kipling, 'there is a fine, hard, bracing climate, the climate that puts iron and grit into men's bones.'[38]

In moulding character this climate was a permanent fixture, unlike an abundance of free land. It instilled exactly those characteristics upon which the imperialists themselves placed the most value—hardness, strenuousness, endurance—so vital to dominance.

The aspect of northernness was associated with the historic imperialism of the northern races. The British Isles were conquered by the northmen, who transmitted to the Anglo-Saxons their love of the sea as well as their genius for self-government. 'The English came to America', wrote the secretary of the Navy League in Quebec, 'in obedience to the same racial sea-faring instincts that led their ancestors to England itself.'[39] One of the reasons for British primacy, explained another historian, was that 'our northern climate has produced a race of sailors and adventurers from the days of the Vikings to the present, inured to all the perils of the sea and the rigours of climate.' The Icelandic sagas, he continued, 'are an interesting part of the native literature of our race, which owes much of its hardihood and enterprise to the admixture of northern blood.'[40] The celebrations of 1892 and 1897 of the voyages of Columbus and Cabot deepened interest in the Norsemen who had preceded both of them, an interest sometimes associated with the arguments of the navalists in the Navy League. Like liberty, the 'seafaring instincts' were racial properties. Parkin said that imperial expansion was not haphazard but the inevitable result of 'racial instincts' as well as national necessities. The mind which viewed expansive and hardy racial character as northern products saw the Norse voyages as something more than interesting details at the beginning of Canadian history books. 'Though nothing came of these Norse discoveries,' wrote Charles G.D. Roberts, 'they are interesting as the first recorded contact of our race with these lands which we now occupy. They are significant, because they were a direct result of that spirit of determined independence which dwells in our blood.'[41]

Moreover, this northernness of the imperial race was connected with the notion of the tendency of world power to shift northward as the phases of evolution proceeded. Parkin, who confessed finding confirmation and amplification of his own beliefs in Benjamin Kidd's *Social Evolution,* must have read with approval Kidd's prediction that northward the march of Empire makes its way:

> The successful peoples have moved westwards for physical reasons: the seat of power has moved continuously northwards for reasons connected with the evolution in character which the race is undergoing. Man, originally a creature of a warm climate and still multiplying most easily and rapidly there, has not attained his highest development where the conditions of existence have been easiest. Throughout history the centre of power has moved gradually but surely to the north into those stern regions where men have been trained for the rivalry of life in the strenuous conflict with nature in which they have acquired energy, courage, integrity, and those characteristic qualities which contribute to raise them to a high state of social efficiency. . .[42]

Especially after 1890, the northern-race concept was frequently explained in the language of a popularized social Darwinism which imparted to it a scientific credibility surpassing in authority either vague rhetoric or poetic allusions. Parkin often employed the terminology of evolutionary science when expressing the notion, but it was left to an obscure writer in a university magazine to place the idea in the general context of 'The Theory of Evolution'. Beginning with a curt dismissal of the Mosaic account of creation as 'a mixture of Hebrew folk-lore and Christian teaching', he stated that 'man himself does not stand apart from the rest of living things as a separate creation, but has had a common origin with them and is governed by the same laws.' One of these laws is the progressive evolution of man which accompanied his migration from the tropical to the northern zones. 'The most primitive type of man at present existing is the Negro, who, like the Apes most nearly allied to Man, is essentially a tropical animal, and does not flourish in cold countries.' 'As the negro race, however, spread, it gradually reached the temperate regions, and here the struggle with Nature became fiercer and the whole civilization underwent development and a higher type of man—the yellow or Mongolian race was evolved.' This race, which included the Red Indians, Peruvians, Chinese, and Japanese, also came into contact with a more vigorous climate, either by expanding northward, or meeting the Ice Age as it moved southward. The result was progressive evolution: 'the struggle for the necessities of life, the need for bravery, endurance, and all the manly virtues, reached its climax, and the highest type of man was evolved—the Nordic type or white man, whose original home was on the fringe of the ice-sheet.' Subsequently, from Scandinavia and Russia, the Nordic race conquered Britain and temperate Europe. From this capsule history, 'as determined by zoological methods', the writer drew several 'comforting conclusions as to the future of Canada.' For one thing, the Canadian must be 'the conquering type of man', and this included the 'French-speaking fellow countrymen who, so far as they are of Norman descent, belong to the same race.' Moreover, the 'Nordic man is essentially an arctic animal and only flourishes in a cold climate—whilst in a warmer region be gradually loses virility and vitality. So that from a zoological point of view the outlook is bright for Canada.'[43]

The Northern Myth in Canadian Art

The image of Canada as a northern country with a strenuous and masterful people was reinforced and sustained in the novels, travelogues, and works of scientific exploration that abounded in the period. The adventure stories centering on life in the isolated Hudson Bay posts and the exploits of the lonely trapper had long been the staple themes of the novels of Robert M. Ballantyne and the boys' books of J. Macdonald Oxley. But after 1896, when the northwest became the locus of immigration and investment, imaginative writers found in that region not only a picturesque setting and indigenous historical incidents and themes but also an area which a large number of their readers had never experienced. Certainly it is significant that a number of the best-selling writers in the decade before the First World War, Ralph Connor, Robert Service, and William Fraser, not only set their works in the northerly setting but also lived there.

The very titles of these books are indicative of their focus: Agnes Laut's story of the fur-trader, *Lords of the North* (1900), and her history—*Canada, the Empire of the North* (1909); Gilbert Parker's *An Adventure of the North* (1905); H.A. Cody's life of Bishop Bompas, *An Apostle of the North* (1905); Ralph Connor's many manly novels set in the northwest, like *Corporal Cameron* (1912) with its inevitable blizzard; travelogues like Agnes D. Cameron's description of her journey through the Athabasca and Mackenzie River region of the Arctic, *The New North* (1909); chronicles of exploration, J.W. Tyrrell's *Across the Sub-Arctics of Canada* (1897), and Vilhjalmur Stefansson's *My Life with the Eskimo* (1913). In 1926, a literary critic complained that the 'whole of Canada has come to be identified with her northernmost reaches', and in 'modern folk-geography Canada means the North.'[44]

This image was strengthened by the paintings of the 'national movement' in Canadian art, the Group of Seven. While some of the most characteristic work of men like A. Y. Jackson and J.E.H. Macdonald was done in the post-war decades, it was during the years before 1914 that their nationalism was inspired and their determination made to express the essence of Canada through her landscape. Some of them were directly influenced by a Scandinavian art exhibition in 1912 which 'impressed them as an example of what other northern countries could do in art'. A member of the group admitted that in their minds Canada was 'a long, thin strip of civilization on the southern fringe of a vast expanse of immensely varied, virgin land reaching into the remote north. Our whole country is cleansed by the pristine and replenishing air which sweeps out of that great hinterland. It was the discovery of this great northern area as a field of art which enticed and inspired these painters.' But the north—with its sparkling clear air and sharp outlines which could never be apprehended with the techniques of Old World art—was much more than a field of art: it was the mirror of national character. After a trip into the Arctic with A.Y. Jackson, Lawren Harris reported that 'We came to know that it is only through the deep and vital experience of its total environment that a people identifies itself with its land and gradually a deep and satisfying awareness develops. We were convinced that no virile people could remain subservient to and dependent upon the creations in art of other peoples . . . To us there was also the strange brooding sense of another nature fostering a new race and a new age.' Though they displayed a variety of personal styles and attitudes, the group was united in the effort to portray the rugged terrain of the Canadian Shield and the changing seasons in the northern woods. While present in J.E.H. Macdonald's *The Solemn Land* (1921) and other early works, the theme of northernness culminated in A.Y. Jackson's *The North Shore of Baffin Island* (c. 1929) and Lawren Harris's *Bylot Island* (1930) both of which exude the crystalline cold and seem themselves to be a part of the stark northern wastes.[45]

The Northern Theme in Retrospect

In retrospect, the northern theme, as it was expressed in the first half-century after Confederation, must be regarded as a myth, for not only did the observations it exalted conflict with objective appraisal, but its primary, intellectual assumptions became suspect. While it rested on the truism, confirmed by modern human geography, that certain climates are stimulating to human exertion, it too frequently glossed over the variety of climatic regions within Canada, and it tended to identify the whole country with that region of it which contained the fewest of her people. It was related and sustained, moreover, by the ebullient faith in the progress of the northwest, in the lusty but mistaken hopes of the wheat-boom years that the northern zone would become the home of millions of happy yeomen. The northern theme also assumed a racist aspect, holding that the capacity for freedom and progress were inherent in the blood of northern races. Not only was this belief progressively undermined by modern anthropological scholarship, but the identification of the Teutonic race with the spirit of liberty appeared especially specious after the First World War. In addition, the appeal of the northern-race idea was limited in the post-war period because its main usefulness had been to underline the differences between Canada and the United States. In the 1920s the focus of nationalist thought shifted, and one of its dominant preoccupations came to be the definition of Canadian character in terms of North American experience, to emphasize the similarities between Canada and the United States.

Intellectual styles change but the permanent facts they seek to interpret and render meaningful do not. As long as there exists a nationalist impulse in Canada the imagination of men will be challenged by the very existence of the fascinating north. Though racism and crude environmentalism have now largely been discredited, the effort to explain Canadian uniqueness in terms of the north has not. As late as 1948, Vincent Massey found several differences between the United States and Canada, such as 'the air of moderation in Canadian habits' to be derived from climate and race:

> Climate plays a great part in giving us our special character, different from that of our southern neighbours. Quite apart from the huge annual bill our winter imposes on us in terms of building construction and clothing and fuel, it influences our mentality, produces a sober temperament. Our racial composition—and this is partly because of our climate—is different, too. A small percentage of our people comes from central or southern Europe. The vast majority springs either from the British Isles or Northern France, a good many, too, from Scandinavia and Germany, and it is in northwestern Europe that one finds the elements of human stability highly developed. Nothing is more characteristic of Canadians than the inclination to be moderate.[46]

Apart from the muted tone, these observations do not really differ in substance from the remarks made in ringing rhetoric and with scientific certainly in the late nineteenth century by George Parkin, who was, incidentally, Massey's father-in-law.

Very different, however, and of high political potency, was the emotional appeal to the Canadian northern mission evoked by John Diefenbaker in the election of 1958. Seizing upon a theme which his native northwest had inspired in poets and nationalists since Confederation, he declared, suitably enough at Winnipeg, that 'I see a new Canada'—not orientated east and west, but looking northward, responding to the challenges of that hinterland, its energies focused on the exploration and exploitation of the Arctic—'A CANADA OF THE NORTH!' To this compelling theme, which runs so persistently through Canadian nationalist thought since the days of D'Arcy McGee, Canadians responded eagerly and with conviction.[47]

On a more sober and scholarly plane, but not less pungent and appealing, is another recent exposition of the northern theme articulated by a president of the Canadian Historical Association, W.L. Morton, also a native of the northwest. In an address delivered in 1960, Professor Morton fixed upon Canada's 'northern character', her origins in the expansion of a northern, maritime frontier, and her possession of a distinctive, staple economy, as factors which explained a substantial aspect of her development, her historical dependence upon Britain and the United States, the character of her literature, even the seasonal rhythm of Canadian life.[48]

The concept of Canada as a northern nation, like the idea that the unique character of the United States was shaped by the westward movement, is as important for understanding the intellectual content and emotional appeal of nationalism as it is for explaining the objective determinants of historical development. From the time of Benjamin Franklin, Americans saw 'the west' not so much as a geographical fact but as a symbol, around which they grouped the leading tenets of their nationalist faith—that their movement westward was carrying the American further and further away from effete Europe, that 'the garden' would become the home of an independent yeomanry in which alone reposed true Republican virtue, that the frontier was a safety valve which kept social conditions in the new world from ever approximating those in decadent, classridden Europe. Like the American symbol of the west, the Canadian symbol of the north subsumed a whole series of beliefs about the exalted past, the national character and the certain future. Unlike the American frontier of free land, however, the north itself was inexhaustible: as A.R.M. Lower has recently reminded us, it is a perpetual breath of fresh air.

If Canadian nationalism is to be understood, its meaning must be sought and apprehended not simply in the sphere of political decisions, but also in myths, legends, and symbols like these. For while some might think that Canadians have happily been immune to the wilder manifestations of the nationalist impulse and rhetoric, it seems that they too have had their utopian dreamers, and that they are not totally innocent of a tradition of racism and a falsified but glorious past, tendencies which have always been the invariable by-products of nationalism. For by its very nature, nationalism must seize upon objective dissimilarities and tendencies and invest them in the language of religion, mission, and destiny.

Notes

1. William Pitman Lett, *Annexation and British Connection, Address to Brother Jonathan* (Ottawa, 1889), p. 10.
2. Walter R. Nursey, *The Story of Isaac Brock* (Toronto), 1909, p. 173.
3. Joseph Pope, *The Tour of Their Royal Highnesses the Duke and Duchess of Cornwall and York through the Dominion of Canada in the Year 1901* (Ottawa, 1903), p. 259; Hon. George W. Ross, *The Historical Significance of the Plains of Abraham, Address Delivered Before the Canadian Club of Hamilton, April 27th, 1908* (n.p., n.d.), p. 18; *The Canadian Military Gazette*, xv (January 2, 1900), p. 15; Silas Alward. *An Anglo-American Alliance* (Saint John. N.B. 1911).
4. G.D. Griffin, *Canada Past, Present, Future, and New System of Government* (n.p. 1884), p. ii.
5. George Parkin, address to the Canadian Club and Board of Trade in Saint John, N.B., reported in *The Daily Telegraph*, Saint John, N.B., *March 6, 1907*. Clipping in *Parkin Papers, vol. 82 (Public Archives of Canada, hereinafter PAC)*.
6. William Leggo, *History of the Administration of the Earl of Dufferin in Canada* (Toronto, 1878), p. 599.
7. *Weekly Globe*, April 2, 1869.
8. For a fascinating sketch of these myths see J. W. Johnson, "'Of Differing Ages and Climes'". *Journal of the History of Ideas*, XXI (Oct.–Dec., 1960) pp. 465–80.
9. R. G. Haliburton, *The Men of the North and their place in history. A Lecture delivered before the Montreal Literary Club, March 31st, 1869*, (Montreal, 1869) pp. 2, 8, 16.
10. Clipping from *The Globe*, December 8, 1904, in *Denison Scrapbook 1897–1915*, p. 167. *Denison Papers* (PAC).
11. Charles Mair, 'The New Canada: its natural features and climate.' *Canadian Monthly Magazine*, VIII (July, 1875), p. 5.
12. *Canada First: A Memorial of the late William A. Foster* (Toronto, 1890), p. 25.
13. Charles R. Tuttle, *Popular History of the Dominion of Canada*, 2 vols., Boston 1877 and 1879, vol. 1, p. 28.
14. G. R. Parkin, *The Great Dominion, Studies of Canada*, London, 1895, pp. 25, 211–15: 'The Railway Development of Canada'. *The Scottish Geographical Magazine* (May, 1909), p. 249, reprint in *Parkin Papers* vol. 66 (PAC), address to Canadian Club and Board of Trade in Saint John. New Brunswick, reported in *The Daily Telegraph*, March 6, 1907. Clipping in *Parkin Papers*, vol. 82 (PAC).
15. Edward Harris. *Canada, The Making of a Nation* (n.p., ca 1907), p. 7.
16. G.R. Parkin, *The Great Dominion*, p. 216.
17. W.H. Withrow, 'Notes of a Visit to the Centennial Exhibition', *Canadian Methodist Magazine* (December, 1876) p. 530.
18. Rev. F.A. Wightman, *Our Canadian Heritage, Its Resources and Possibilities* (Toronto, 1905), p. 46.
19. W.H. Hingston, *The Climate of Canada and its Relation to Life and Health* (Montreal, 1884). pp. xviii, 94, 126–7, 260, 263, 265–6.
20. Wightman, *Our Canadian Heritage*, pp. 280, 44–5; J. Sheridan Hogan. *Canada, An Essay: to which was awarded the first prize by the Paris Exhibition Committee of Canada* (Montreal, 1855). pp. 53–4.
21. F.B. Cumberland, 'Introduction', *Maple Leaves: being the papers read before the National Club of Toronto at the 'National Evenings', during the Winter 1890–1* (Toronto, 1891), pp. vii–viii.
22. Wightman, as cited, p. 221.
23. Benjamin Suite, *Origin of the French Canadian. Read before the British Association, Toronto, August, 1897* (Ottawa, 1897), p. 14. See also his essay of 1897. 'Défense de nos Origines' in *Mélanges historiques*. compiled by Gérard Malchelosse, vol. 17 (Montreal, 1930).

24. *The Storied Province of Quebec, Past and Present,* W. Wood (ed.) vol. 1 (Toronto, 1931), p. 3.
25. G.M. Wrong, *The Two Races in Canada, a Lecture delivered before the Canadian Historical Association, Montreal, May 21st, 1925* (Montreal, 1925), pp. 4–5.
26. Abbé Arthur Maheux, *Canadian Unity: What Keeps Us Apart* (Quebec, 1944), pp. 22, 23, 25.
27. *Canada's Future! Political Union With the U.S. Desirable* (1891), pp. 2–3.
28. Principal R.A. Falconer. 'The Unification of Canada', *University Magazine,* VII (February, 1908), pp. 4–5.
29. George Parkin, 'Canada and the United States on the American Continent', reported in *Yarmouth Herald,* March 3, 1908. Clipping in *Parkin Papers,* vol. 84, (PAC): *The Great Dominion,* p. 214.
30. Cited in Charles and Mary Beard, *The American Spirit, A Study of the Civilization of the United States* (New York, 1962), p. 173.
31. *Canadian Methodist Magazine* (December, 1898) pp. 566–7.
32. Silas Alward, as cited, pp. 8–10.
33. See especially, J.G. Bourinot, *Canadian Studies in Comparative Politics* (Montreal, 1890).
34. *The Empire,* January 24, 1891.
35. *The Week,* January 1, 1885.
36. G. Parkin, in *Yarmouth Herald,* March 3, 1908.
37. *Dominion Illustrated,* VI (April 11, 1891).
38. Cited in *Canadian Methodist Magazine* (June, 1899), p. 536.
39. William Wood, *The Fight for Canada* (Boston, 1906), p. 33.
40. Rev. W.P. Creswell, *History of the Dominion of Canada* (Oxford, 1890), pp. 11, 15.
41. Charles G.D. Roberts, *A History of Canada* (Boston, 1897), p. 3.
42. Benjamin Kidd, *Social Evolution* (London, 1895), pp. 61–2.
43. E. W. MacBride, 'The Theory of Evolution', *The McGill University Magazine,* 1 (April, 1902), pp. 244–62.
44. Lionel Stevenson, *Appraisals of Canadian Literature* (Toronto, 1926), pp. 245–53.
45. R. H. Hubbard, *The Development of Canadian Art* (Ottawa, 1964), p. 88; L. Harris, 'The Group of Seven in Canadian History'. *Canadian Historical Association Report* (1948) pp. 30, 36–7.
46. Vincent Massey, *On Being Canadian* (Toronto, 1948), pp. 29–30.
47. Peter Newman, *Renegade in Power: The Diefenbaker Years* (Toronto, 1964), p. 218.
48. W.L. Morton, 'The Relevance of Canadian History' in *The Canadian Identity* (Toronto, 1961), pp. 88–114.

Laurentian Shield

F.R. Scott

Hidden in wonder and snow, or sudden with summer.
This land stares at the sun in a huge silence
Endlessly repeating something we cannot hear.
Inarticulate, arctic,
Not written on by history, empty as paper,
It leans away from the world with songs in its lakes
Older than love, and lost in the miles.

This waiting is wanting.
It will choose its language
When it has chosen its technic.
A tongue to shape the vowels of its productivity.

A language of flesh and of roses.

Now there are pre-words,
Cabin syllables,
Nouns of settlement
Slowly forming, with steel syntax,
The long sentence of its exploitation.

The first cry was the hunter, hungry for fur,
And the digger for gold, nomad, no-man, a particle;
Then the bold commands of monopoly, big with machines,
Carving their kingdoms out of the public wealth;
And now the drone of the plane, scouting the ice,
Fills all the emptiness with neighbourhood
And links our future over the vanished pole.

But a deeper note is sounding, heard in the mines,
The scattered camps and the mills, a language of life,
And what will be written in the full culture of occupation
Will come, presently, tomorrow,
From millions whose hands can turn this rock into children.

From *The Collected Poems of F.R. Scott.* Reprinted with the permission of William Toye, literary executor for the Estate of F.R. Scott.

I Kneel To Kiss The Ice

Karen Connelly

On a day grayer than a bitter sea
I return from the ocean.
My heart red and bitter
    as an ant, so obedient, so familiar,
    dragged by simple time into the habits of blood,
       twitching into and out of shadows,
       twitching to sister-skin,
          my body drawn like an insect
          to this sweet sick dirt.

I return to this country,
    so huge, but nothing grand.
The great trees here entomb me.
Snow angels haunt the air.
The plane burns down the runway
    long silver flame
    trembling.
Trembling, already I am up to my chin
in gravel and poplars, pines,
already surrounded.

The ghosts loom out of the snow
    like fantastic birds
       dancing
       all plume and pierce of talons
       striking, driving into skin,

touching, as lovers touch,
    or warriors in ancient battles,
    the way a murderer grasps weaker flesh

mothers touch their husbands,
who touch their daughters,
in turn, brothers, sisters,
those elaborate battles of small blood,
those memories of a dead dog
and a dead woman who left me
alone in the blue-green world
this white frozen world,
this country
trees, rocks, sky

and streets, the voice of my friend
in her attic of masks and paint:

>this is the city where something
>is always about to happen
>and never does—

streets I stumbled down
laughing, crying, the two words blur,
I dance down the pavement and my feet sting
I had to be born somewhere
I had to be born

the eternal surprise

and I am touched idiotically
by snow, the memory
of my five-year-old soul
believing deeply in diamonds
under the streetlights, blanketing
all the fields, the talcum of seraphs.

I come home
hating this language,
these words, my stories,
my eyes, hands, wishing
only to forget the clamour
inside that has brought me here
again

trolls sleep under
the pink bridge of my tongue
I kiss my mother's cheek
I reach to kiss the sky
Sticky pine sap is on my chin
I have been holding trees
I kiss the door of an old house

I slip down to the creek
on the edge of the city
and kneel to kiss the ice

my lip bleeds a little

I am not surprised.

She Returns to the Farm

Karen Connelly

Irse es morir un poco.—Aita
To leave is to die a little.

Volver es una pesadilla. Odio volver.—Noemi
To return is a nightmare. I hate returning.

I come back to an empty field,
    gray stones, warm blood beating
    through animals that no longer remember
        the smell of my skin.
And white, scapes of snow so white that my face
    is alone with them, my eyes turn to frost,
    my jaws stiffen from wind and weeping.

I have forgotten how to speak.
I cannot explain the hands that do not reach,
    the feet that walk wordless into the woods.
There is nothing here but fields and freezing steers
    and the sharp new teeth of stars.
I find the frost-plumed ribs of an old horse.
The coyotes cackle in the valley.
Even the trees, so keen and naked, are cruel.

Only the snow is not dangerous.
I touch it with my bare hands.
It is violet-skinned and cold.
I want the numbness gnawing my fingers
    to mean forgiveness

    but like the skin of a dead lover,
        the snow feels nothing,
            offers no signs.

anthem

matt robinson

no, this great canadian novel doesn't open in
   the beginning of the month of november. and there
are no faces, cold-scarred and dust-blinded
   by the winter's sweeping violence. no, instead

   i sing of the great asphalt plains.
glistening hard and black, smooth and clean;
save for the leaked rainbow-kaleidoscope swirls.

and the moon is just another streetlight, a slightly faded
   or obscured illumination—not a reasoning of tides, of
the cresting waves that lament and steal husbands
   and fathers from their work. removed, it glows while

   i sing of the great asphalt plains.
numbered neatly. divvied up for the new-age
settlers. this, a new tundra below the tree line.

and only a suburb, (all sidewalk concrete and lawn ornament
   beautiful, all junior high school crush linear),
greets the morning dawn. our not even close to log cabin
   dwelling has indoor plumbing, a central vac.

trees in ice

matt robinson

(with apologies to f. r. scott . . .)
loveliness
is a form—
(all) cruelty.

branching limbs snap
under
the weight of
falling mercury.

CHAPTER EIGHTEEN

Hockey: Our Game

Introduction

Part of Canada's sense of itself as a northern country is hockey. After all, hockey is a northern game. And it's our game, to borrow Ken Dryden's phrase. The classic Canadian image of kids playing hockey on a frozen pond is featured on the five-dollar bill. These readings focus not on hockey as a sport but on hockey as "our game," as a part of the Canadian memory. "If there's a goal that everyone remembers," to quote The Tragically Hip, "it was back in ol' 72." Indeed, Paul Henderson's series-winning goal in game 8 of the 1972 Summit Series between Canada and the Soviet Union remains a national moment, a moment that, for a variety of reasons, captures what it means to be Canadian. In his article, Neal Earle examines the important place Team Canada 1972 occupies in Canadian popular culture. David Adams Richards, one of Canada's greatest novelists, adores the game of hockey. In *Hockey Dreams: memories of man who couldn't play,* Richards writes about growing up on the Miramichi River in northern New Brunswick and what hockey meant—and means— to him.

Hockey as Canadian Popular Culture
Team Canada 1972, Television and the Canadian Identity

Neil Earle

IT IS COMMONPLACE to assert that ice hockey signifies something about Canadian popular culture, indeed, about Canadian culture as a whole. Yet what it might signify has not been explored at any length by scholars. The 1972 Canada-Soviet series can serve as a useful model to probe certain questions. How does electronic technology impact upon a mass audience? Is there a bardic function for television? Only recently has popular culture theory become advanced enough to attempt an analysis of these questions. In *Canada Learns to Play: The Emergence of Organized Sport, 1807–1914*, Alan Metcalfe tells us that G.M. Trevelyan wrote the social history of 19th-century Great Britain without once mentioning the most famous Englishman of his time, the cricket champion W.G. Grace.[1] If Canada were substituted for England, Donald Creighton for Trevelyan, and Foster Hewitt or Wayne Gretzky for W. G. Grace, we would be going some distance towards framing the theme of this study, namely ice hockey in Canadian culture as perceived through the codes and aesthetics of electronic technology.

Hockey and television still seem inseparably linked in the popular imagination. On 7 October 1992, the Canadian Broadcasting Corporation (CBC) presented a televised documentary of the 1972 international hockey series between Team Canada and the former Union of Soviet Socialist Republics (USSR), a program that explored the lyricism and the menace that suffuses hockey at most levels. Later that winter hockey announcer Danny Gallivan, for years the eloquent and elegant voice of the Montreal Canadiens, died. On 28 February 1993, hockey's dark side was further probed by another CBC "hybrid drama" involving the career of former Toronto Maple Leaf Brian "Spinner" Spencer. The theme was a "life cursed by violence" both on and off the ice.[2] But it is the Canada-Soviet Series of September 1972 that offers an especially useful paradigm for a study of "our game" on two levels: first, the series occasions reflection on the cultural nexus of the great national pastime; and second, electronic technology was sufficiently developed by 1972 to allow a fairly sustained probe into some of its codes and structures. Especially interesting is mass technology's capacity to transform play into a form of collective drama.

Popular culture theory provides the methodological tools to study systematically the game that—for good or for ill—has helped define Canadians.[3] While no irrefutable thesis has yet come to light as to why hockey looms so large in the Canadian popular imagination, Americans have long known what we were about. "Canadians value hockey so highly," wrote the authors of *The Social Significance of Sport: An Introduction to the Sociology of Sport,* that "it has been called Canada's culture."[4] If hockey broadcasts and telecasts have long been a recognizable staple of Canadian popular culture, the question about what it signifies is less clear. This article blends the insights of such theorists as Horace Newcomb, John Fiske, and Paul Rutherford with the observations of players and keen followers of the game such as Ken Dryden, Michael Novak, Jack Ludwig and Doug Beardsley. "Technology," taught Martin Heidegger, "is a way of revealing."[5] Remarkably, in September 1972 at least 12 million Canadians gathered around their television sets and radios to hear the animated voice of hockey broadcaster Foster Hewitt exclaim "Henderson has scored for Canada!"[6] The question remains: what did this electronic national drama signify?

For 27 days in September 1972 Canadian television was the matrix for a sports event that has become an enduring folk memory, a cultural text. For once, disparate notions of class, ethnicity and gender were welded into a rare Canadian moment. Millions of adult Canadians reserve hallowed psychic space, not just for Pearl Harbor or the assassination of President John Kennedy, but also for the memory of Paul Henderson's winning goal in Game Eight of the 1972 Canada-Soviet series. Is this hockey as mythos, the arena as locus for a technologically driven actuality drama? One could respond that if hockey is just a game in Canada, then the Rockies are just hills on the prairies. The game, like the mischievous "puck" itself, has the ability to ricochet and career unexpectedly in and out of the Canadian experience. Rick Salutin, in preparing his 1977 play *Les Canadiens,* was astonished to hear a sportswriter for the *Montreal Star* relate how the enduring success of the city's celebrated franchise had been seen by many as a ritualistic act of revenge for the Plains of Abraham. Wayne Gretzky's move to the United States in 1988 during the Prime Ministership of Brian Mulroney was a cultural signpost to an era, as was the refusal of Ontario's Eric Lindros to play for the Québec City *Nordiques* in the aftermath of the Meech Lake constitutional crisis. The transcendence attached to the 1972 series is further attested to by the fact that both President Nikolai Podgorny and Premier Alexi Kosygin were in the audience that September night in the Luzhniki Arena in Moscow when the Soviet team won their hometown opener over Team Canada.[7] Students of sport, especially as it pertains to popular culture, have elaborated upon its myth-making potential. Michael Novak is one of the few analysts willing to penetrate through to hockey's mystical core:

> What is the basic underlying myth dramatized in hockey? One can't help noticing hockey's speed, its teamwork, its formal plays, its violent contact and exceptionally hot temper tantrums . . . and finally the exhilaration of slapping a tiny rubber puck into a narrow, low net. . . . The game is played on ice. Its symbolic matrix lies in the lands of snow, blizzards and dark, freezing nights. . . . One gets suggestions of an Ice Age

once again smothering the planet. One senses the sheer celebration of hot blood holding out against the cold, the vitality of the warm human body, of exuberant speed rejoicing in its own heat, of violence and even the sight of red blood on white ice as a sign of animal endurance. . . .[8]

Novak's study of our gender-biased yet pervasive national pastime applies to Canada, even though we are not his prime focus: "Hockey celebrates the heat and passion of survival. Take the worst, accept and conquer. Give as well as get. Take it to them. If hockey is, with chess, the national sport of Russia, let the world recognize the fierce resolve of people toughened by their climate; let them remember Stalingrad."[9]

Doug Beardsley's personalized account of the game, *Country on Ice,* argues that in Canada hockey is played for its own sake, for the fact that almost every Canadian has been touched by its mystery and mystique. It is noteworthy, too, that hockey is a sport played with equal relish on both sides of the Ottawa River. Ice hockey has been called the "common coin" of Canada. Roch Carrier's tender and moving short story *The Hockey Sweater,* for example, touched both solitudes. It is hard to forget the impact of Maurice "the Rocket" Richard on French and English Canadians in the period just after World War II. Hockey as our authentic "national anthem" may indeed weave one of the few imaginative strands in a huge country with a diverse population.[10] Jack Ludwig offers anecdotal evidence for the significance of hockey as a Canadian badge of identity on the international scene. At Munich, where over 300 expatriates gathered to watch Canada lose 7 to 3 in the series opener, an Australian flung out this challenge to a disappointed Canadian: "Aye, mate, isn't this your game. . . . What's going on losing to the Ruskies?"[11]

Yet at home it was televised hockey that had elevated the game into a national preoccupation. Canadian content is (except during players' strikes) alive and well on prime time each April to June, as the Stanley Cup playoff series skate their seemingly interminable way across the nation's television screens. Broadcast historian Paul Rutherford offers this perspective:

Hockey on television was an actuality broadcast. The broadcasters adjusted to the rhythms and routines of the game itself. . . . The experience wasn't all that different from being in the arena. . . . The camera's role was always to focus on the puck, providing close-ups around the nets or when the action got heavy and personal, say, on the boards or in the corners. . . . The first producer of hockey was Sydney Newman who hadn't any real experience with the sport. After watching a game he told two old pros that it would be easy to cover—it was really like ballet. . . .[12]

Rutherford argues further that television and hockey seemed to be made for each other: "The audience for hockey grew to about 3.5 million English Canadians and around 2 million French Canadians. . . . The success of hockey, first on CBC and later on CTV, had no counterpart in the United States, until the birth of ABC's "Monday Night Football" in 1970. . . . Many people experienced hockey only via the television set or the radio."[13]

Television is suited to the game's strengths. Hockey is a transition game—everyone gets a chance to play, and it is one of the few games where players can change "on the fly." Crucially, the spectators are very much part of the action in the confined, enclosed arena; they are close to the ice surface. This serves to heighten the intensity of crowd reactions, reactions which the cameras and microphones—in that relatively small space—can easily amplify. It is not extravagant to assert a parallel between televised hockey's participatory dynamic and the presentational and affective aspects of Greek and Shakespearean drama, the Odeon and the "wooden O." Add to this the distinctive pacing and "rhythm" of a hockey game, the changing mood and psychological tempo created by the switches in focus from the team to the individual player and back again, and one is offered aesthetic spectacle "par excellence." An excerpt from a game narrated by Danny Gallivan in the early 1960s is illustrative:

> The Hawks regrouping behind their own line coming out over centre. Beliveau STEALS the puck, takes a shot right on the short side and Hall was there to stymie him with a scintillating save . . . Cournoyer now CUTTING IN on goal, trying to get right IN FRONT . . . ANOTHER SHOT . . . the Canadiens really firing the puck around with authority . . . Lemaire WINDS UP, Beliveau takes a poke at it . . . COURNOYER A REAL SPINNERAMA . . . THEY BANG AWAY AT IT, THEY BANG IT IN! and the Montreal Forum crowd goes crazy.[14]

Hockey's speed and intensity played well to the myth of a rough, tough game demanding skill, effort, commitment, endurance. "It was the Canadian game because we had created it. . . . It suited a land in which the winter always loomed so large," explains Rutherford. "Even more the game fitted an image of Canadian manhood."[15] If there is no Canadian Stalingrad or Marathon, might not the Stanley Cup playoffs and the international Canada Cup competitions form an imaginative substitute? Ward Cornell, a broadcaster from the 1960s, expressed one aspect of hockey's overweening maleness: "We're tough, rugged guys from the North," he expostulated half-jokingly to Rutherford.[16] The element of catharsis encouraged the "juvenile" facets of the game ("Stand your ground, don't back down from a fight!"), the ugly primitivism that led inevitably to the outcries and protests against hockey violence. "Canadian seamen of long professional foulmouth careers would sound like Little Lord Fauntleroy at any NHL practice session. . . . To be a man in Canada is to *fight*. The sweetest hero this side of heaven is someone like Derek Sanderson, who isn't really very good at fighting, but fights nevertheless, because getting beaten shows much more macho than skating away."[17]

Yet, hockey reflects another part of the male sensibility that televised hockey magnifies and transmits. This aspect is its most redeeming cultural feature and lies close to the core of the hockey mystique. This was and *is* the game's evocation of a peculiarly Canadian paradisiacal myth, the appeal to "the boy inside the man," a myth that intelligent students and players of the game have captured. Ken Dryden is a former goal-tender in the National Hockey League. One of the photographs in Dryden's *Home Game: Hockey and Life in Canada* is simply and tellingly entitled "Icons." It features a small square photograph of the Montreal Forum scoreboard imposed upon a two-page spread of boys in toques and sweaters playing shinny (the unstructured form of hockey) on a slough in St. Denis, Saskatchewan.[18] The picture brilliantly captures hockey's imaginative hold over millions of Canadian males.[19] The image of the boy with his hockey stick on the outdoor pond evokes something distinctive—"the true north strong and free," a myth that, as we shall see, can be enhanced by technology. What Dryden elsewhere characterized as "the voice in my head" was an electronic imprint. The alchemy of electronic technology thus made possible in televised hockey a synchronization of the mythopaic and the mechanical. A flooded driveway became a locus of myth:

> It was Maple Leaf Gardens filled to wildly cheering capacity, a tie game, seconds remaining. I was Frank Mahovlich or Gordie Howe. I was any-one I wanted to be, and the voice in my head was that of Leafs' broad-caster Foster Hewitt: ' . . . there's ten seconds left, Mahovlich, winding up at his own line, at center, eight seconds, seven, over the blueline, six—he winds up, he shoots, he scores!' It was a glorious fantasy, and I always heard that voice. It was what made my fantasy seem almost real. For to us, who attended hockey games mostly on TV or radio, an NHL game, a Leafs game, was played with a voice. If I wanted to be Mahovlich or Howe, if I moved my body the way I had seen them move theirs and did nothing else, it would never quite work. But if I heard the voice that said their names while I was playing out the fantasy, I could believe it. Foster Hewitt could make me them.[20]

This is the romance of hockey; play as idyll. The mysterious bonding of millions of Canadian males to "the game" traces back to the pond, the slough, the indoor rink; to the iced driveway, to the time when they, in their youthful fantasies, were Gordie Howe or Bobby Orr or Wayne Gretzky. Here is hockey's cultural core, the central explanation for its mystical attraction for prime ministers and pipe-fitters, for Nobel Prize winners and new immigrants. This beguiling innocence mitigates and helps neutralize the inherent sexism and violence of the game.

On 28 September 1972 both Ken Dryden and Foster Hewitt were on hand when 12 million Canadians—not all of them male—heard the most memorable lines in Canadian sports history: "Cournoyer has it on that wing. Here's a shot. Henderson makes a wild stab for it and falls. Here's another shot. Right in front. They score!

Henderson has scored for Canada."[21] Televised hockey is superb participatory drama, complete with the requisite heroic, antiheroic, and otherwise transcendently significant leading characters. Keith Cunningham believes that sport resembles sacred time:

> There is a festival time in the soul. We dress ourselves up and jump from profane time, time as linear continuation, 9 to 5, week in week out, into sacred time. In sacred time, as Mircea Eliade has called it, we enter the flight of mythic fantasy. We enter again the old tales, we live again the high adventure of the soul. Everything becomes fluid in a shifting landscape; we are Hercules as much—or as little—as our existential selves. We are here and we are there.[22]

Sacred time is re-emphasized in the ritual aspects of sport, as in, for example, the lighting of the Olympic torch. Cunningham links the mythos of sport to drama:

> Always at issue is man's relation to Being. Is he going to remain a dreamer in the cavern, repeating the round of illusions and pleasure-principle fantasies forever, or is he going to recognize the dynamic patterns behind the scenes which govern his own life. . . . The drama is itself a symbol, unfolding in time. . . . The dramatic hero, like the dream ego, acts as our magic double, inhabiting the compressed underworld of the drama, subjected to trials and experiencing incredible delights for our sake. [Drama] immerses us in the emotional experience of growth through crisis.[23]

Drama, argues Cunningham, is an acting out, a symbolic participation in ritual. As such, ice hockey's values of actuality and involvement provide an experience with the potential to "wound us with knowledge." In September 1972 technology created an electronically centred national drama, a conclusion attested to by recent developments in popular culture theory.

Many theorists of popular culture refuse to ascribe a mere passive or negative role to the television audience. John Fiske, for example, sees culture-making as a social process. Fiske differentiates popular culture from mass culture. In popular culture, he asserts, the people themselves actively engage in shaping social meanings from the products offered by the consumer society. A hockey stick is a product of mass culture, but a hockey stick advertised by Mario Lemieux becomes an artifact of popular culture. People, in effect, invest mass commodities with socio-cultural meanings. In Fiske's term, "meanings meet."[24] The public, as consumers of mass culture, give mass-produced items a meaning that they "decode" from the product. Semioricians speak about "the phenomenon of duplicity," a larger possibility of meanings than is connoted by the obvious, intended meaning.[25] Thus, for an item of mass culture—a three piece suit, a pair of blue jeans, or a Canadiens sweater—to become a significant item of the popular culture, a process of mediation must take place. In the Fiskean analysis, the consumer is engaged in cultural production, in giving an artifact of mass culture a meaning which will assure it a place in the public imagination.[26] Just as millions of teens had their "favourite Beatle" in the 1960s, so millions of Canadians have been able to identify with Maurice "the Rocket" Richard, Ted "Teeder" Kennedy, Gordie Howe, Bobby Hull, Bobby Orr, Wayne Gretzky, and Doug Gilmour.

One could thus argue that Canadians are involved in a form of collective myth-making when watching hockey telecasts. The mass audience polyvalently "decodes" the game. On one level, there is a fairly straightforward hero-worship dynamic at work. Yet there are hidden duplicities as well. Some enjoy the "we're rough, tough guys from the North" message; hence, hockey's violence has never hurt its ratings. Others more likely enjoy the social segmentation noted by Rutherford. ("Where are all the women?" said one wife to her husband during her first game at Maple Leaf Gardens.) Then, as the wrestling phenomenon illustrates, excess possesses its own appeal. The striking uniforms, the crowd noises, the body checks—these aspects of excess throw into bold relief conventional notions of decorum, propriety and law and order. Hockey's very physicality is part of its appeal. Ice hockey thus represents a multifaceted, rich and duplicitous text, rooted in rural signifiers, the symbolic re-call of simpler, more innocent days when life was fresh and bright and bracing and friendship seemed forever. Here are aspects of a northern pastoral that in Canada (at least until fairly recently) was not all myth. Is this hockey's *sanctum sanctorum*, a locus of that elusive intangible, "the true north strong and free"?

In 1972, then, "meanings met." The series with the USSR stirred potent cultural signifiers. Ken Dryden felt it and wrote at the time: "[A]s far as the vast majority of Canadians are concerned, this series was not conceived in a spirit of brotherhood and understanding but as a means of putting down the Russians and asserting our claim to hockey supremacy."[27] The mass audience across Canada functioned as an imaginative sensorium capable of being "wounded with knowledge," of experiencing Aristotelian tragic pity and fear as well as moments of transcendence. In September 1972, the codes and aesthetics of television gave a heightened dramatic spin to a moment of high nationalist tension: an imaginative echoing, metaphorically, of the Greek-Persian wars.[28] In September 1972, Canadian television tapped the latent myth-making inherent in all sport:

> Sports (offers) cohesion and identity, the mythic model. Because of the powerful visibility of such a model, it has always been used as far more than either entertainment or cultural unifier. It is quickly transformed into a vehicle for cultural values, and we translate the playing field into an image for "real life." The virtues of practice, hard work, dedication, desire, competitive spirit, fair play, "good sportsmanship," and a host of other commodities are pointed out to generation after generation of young people. The language of the games, the initiations into rituals,

the formalities of winning, are transformed into mystical moments. Sport is hallowed as holy text.[29]

Some 15 million Canadians shared in the vicarious climax when Henderson scored for Canada. Many were to watch the last game at home, at work or at school as—in some cases—television sets were brought into classrooms by excited teachers aware that a moment of Canadian history was being made. Scott Young remembered the excitement the series generated in the country: "Nothing to match the excitement of this series had ever happened in Canada; rarely anywhere in any sport. The last time Canada had beaten the Soviets at hockey was in the world championships of 1961. . . . Nine years of regular beatings later, Canada said to hell with it and withdrew from world competition. . . . The ultimate . . . then and now, is for world championships to be decided by the best against the best; the best, in Canada's terms, meaning professionals."[30]

Ken Dryden also caught the embedded nationalist agenda:

> The talk all through the summer of 1972 was about the series. And because Canada was the best and sure to win, Canadians couldn't wait for the series to begin. It would be a glorious "coming out" party, a celebration of us. This gave to it a more fundamental dimension. For though much may be special about Canada, surrounded as it is historically and geographically by countries that are bigger, richer, more powerful, whose specialness seems more obvious, we cling to every symbol. A game is a game. But a symbol is not. We had to win this series.[31]

Dryden is right; symbols are important. The team's name—"Team Canada"—was rife with meaning, cast in a form that would be easily translatable into both French and English, thus fitting the bilingual ethos of the times. Little wonder that the 2 September 1972 opening night at the prestigious Montreal Forum resembled, in restrospect, the first act of a national drama. Phil Esposito, the rugged goal-scorer from the Boston Bruins, was almost manic about the need to win the opening event: "It was only a ceremonial face-off, but I had to win that draw. . . . I mean, I had to win that draw! This guy didn't even try and it really aggravated me. . . . I remember I drew the puck back and put up my hand like, wow, we won the first face-off!" The tension was contagious: "At that same moment, sounding a little surprised himself, Foster Hewitt, who had in his lifetime described thousands of games, was telling his nation-wide audience, 'I can't recall any game that I've ever been at where you can just feel the tension. And it keeps building up.'"[32]

The opening moments exploded with emotional energy and harbingers. Esposito scored for Canada after the first 30 seconds, Paul Henderson six minutes later. But in the next 53 minutes, recalled Dryden, "Team Canada's players, its fans, Canadians, could feel everything slipping away."[33] After such an explosive start the Soviets doggedly fought back to win 7–3. It was the worst of all possible scenarios:

Team Canada humbled in one of the holy of holies of Canadian hockey, the Montreal Forum. The nightmarish spectacle that was to engage the entire nation for the next few days was launched.

As the continued fascination with "horror" movies reveals, popular culture is pleasurable even (perhaps especially) when it takes on nail-biting intensity. After the first game, Canadian coach Harry Sinden commented: "A little piece of all of us died today." Scott Morrison captures perfectly that mingled feeling of exhilaration and apprehension as the second game opened two nights later in Toronto: "The best players the NHL was allowed to assemble playing under the name Team Canada had been soundly beaten, and their pride had been deeply wounded. So, when they stepped on the ice that night for a second game in Toronto, they weren't playing for a doubting nation, but mostly for themselves. As a team."[34]

The nation-wide audience knew that according to the tried and true rhythm of play-off hockey, this second game would be crucial. The feeling in Maple Leaf Gardens was palpable. The cameras framed a bright red maple leaf on the television screens of the millions who watched: "There existed in historic Maple Leaf Gardens that night more stifling pressure than excitement . . . though the support of the fans was staggering. In conservative Toronto, where the fans are generally quite reserved . . . on this night they stood as one and chilled the air singing the national anthem. But there also remained a sharp sense of trepidation, of apprehension. This sense no longer pertained to what the opposition would bring, but the home team."[35]

The cameras and commentary were relaying "bardic television," functioning as an electronic stage bringing together viewers from the Atlantic and Pacific coasts. It superbly transmitted tragic pity and fear. Once again the Chorus-like presence of Foster Hewitt accentuated the strained emotion. A hapless Team Canada felt the sting of tragic reversal: after Game One a solid majority of their countrymen condemned them for refusing to shake hands with the Soviets, a convention of international hockey. That night, however, Maple Leaf Gardens was the venue for the spectacle of redemption: Team Canada won 4–1. It was to be their most decisive victory of the series.

Television's superb "theatre of the ether" synergized ice hockey, Team Canada and the electronic aesthetic in a transcendent moment. Peter Mahovlich's short-handed goal at 6:47 of the third period incarnated Novak's words:

> One imagines that in every human life is cocooned an ideal form, the ideal beauty of which the human race is capable. . . . Imagine that we walk through our days on hidden tracks, in cycles round and round, and at foreordained moments we are lifted out of the ordinary sphere and allowed momentarily in the eternal "time of the heroes". . . . In the sacred time of sports, the time of the heroes occasionally breaks through. No one dictates the moment. It comes when it comes. . . . One experiences a complete immersion in the present, absorption in an in-

stantaneous and abundant now . . . life in a different mode from that of the life we normally lead in time. . . . [36]

Mahovlich scored as the Soviets, with a one-man advantage, were pressing hard. Paul Henderson would never forget it: "I can still see that goal. . . . He was one-on-one with the defenceman (Evgeny Poladyev), and when he got to the blue line he faked the slapshot, pulled in the puck and froze the defenceman. Then he just barged through and reached around Tretiak to tuck the puck behind him. It was an absolutely incredible goal. That one put the icing on the cake for us. It was short-handed and put us ahead 3–1."[37]

Yet, the redemptive drama that unfolded in Game Two was only a prelude to the theatre of the absurd that would characterize Games Three and Four. Professional hockey's crude commercialism emerged in full force, beginning with the public squabble about the exclusion of superstar Bobby Hull, who had signed with the Winnipeg Jets of the rival World Hockey Association. The National Hockey League, which supplied most of the roster for Team Canada, refused to let him play despite urgent pleas from Prime Minister Trudeau. The internal team squabbles went public and a few of the highly touted stars found that relative newcomers like Bobby Clarke and J.P. Parise were out-playing them and getting more ice time as a result. Thus a fractious Team Canada was forced to endure the irony of superstar Bobby Hull watching his brother Dennis play in Winnipeg. Game Three was a heartbreaking encounter. The Canadians gave up two leads on brilliant shorthanded goals by the Soviets—scoring while Team Canada had the one-man advantage. Team Canada was thankful to skate away with a 4–4 tie. A feeling of impending doom was intensifying as Game Four loomed in Vancouver.

The ambivalence about Team Canada that was building up across the country is best expressed in theatrical terms: the footlights were definitely down; the spectators were very much part of the action, and they were angry. One of the dimensions of popular culture is the pleasurable opportunity sometimes presented to vent feelings of rage or frustration at an object of disapproval. Sneering at politicians or at inane commercial advertisements on television are classic examples. Oppositionality—having it both ways—is an earmark of the popular. The mass audience treasures its freedom to pick and choose, to mediate between alternatives, to have it both ways.

On 8 September 1972, the Vancouver fans chose revenge. The feverish fourth game in British Columbia saw Team Canada crushed 5–2. Worse, it was a loss Team Canada perhaps made inevitable by drawing two rather silly minor penalties in the first 10 minutes. The "home" part of the series had ended with the Soviets holding a commanding 2-1-1 lead. The final four games were to be played in Moscow. Ken Dryden later related: "It seemed as though it had all slipped beyond us." Then came an unusual chain of events. First, the players, seared by the reaction of the Vancouver fans, steeled their determination and decided to "win it for themselves."[38] Second, what Horace Newcomb has called "the aesthetics of television" began to emerge as a factor in its own right. According to Newcomb, "The central symbol of television is the family . . . a tightly knit circle." The perennially popular situation-comedy for-mat is television's stock in trade: "The smallness of the television screen has always been its most noticeable physical feature. It means something that the art created for television appears on an object that can be part of one's living room, exist as furni-ture. It is significant that one can walk around the entire apparatus. Such smallness suits television for intimacy; its presence brings people into the viewer's home to act out drama."[39] Television, claims Newcomb, has a bias for intimacy: "Television is at its best when it offers us faces, reactions, explorations of emotions registered by hu-man beings. The importance is not placed on the action, though that is certainly vital as stimulus. Rather, it is on the reaction to the action, to the human response."[40]

Not action but reaction—an interesting thesis. That wild night in Vancouver did not end with Team Canada's loss. Something else happened. Television beamed the spectacle of a totally believable Phil Esposito—his "sad-eyed, washed-out face, bathed with the sweat of the world," in Dryden's words—speaking "heart to heart" with the Canadian public. Esposito, who had emerged as the unofficial leader of Team Canada, had his moment of personal angst captured in close-up by the camera as waves of frustration convulsed his countrymen. Yet, Esposito treated the audience to what television does so effectively, some would say too effectively: the personalizing and humanizing of a complex, mass spectacle: "To the people of Canada, we're try-ing our best. . . . The people boo us. We're all disappointed, disenchanted. I can't believe people are booing us. If the Russians boo their players like some of our Ca-nadian fans—not all, just some—then I'll come back and apologize. We're com-pletely disappointed. I can't believe it. We're trying hard. Let's face facts. They've got a good team. We're all here because we love Canada. It's our home and that's the only reason we came."[41]

The "intimate" medium was about to transform the 30-odd players of Team Canada into "our guys," an embattled little family up against life's bewildering com-plexities and letdowns. This was what television had been transmitting and celebrat-ing for decades: the surrogate families of *Star Trek* and *The Beachcombers,* of *A Gift to Last* and *Upstairs, Downstairs.* Audiences identified with the tight little worlds of the Plouffes and the Bunkers, the Kings of Kensington and the Waltons.

If there was intimacy there was also *continuity,* the second of Newcomb's televisual aesthetics. Prime time's dynamics helped make Team Canada as familiar as extended family: Clarke and Cournoyer, Henderson and Ratelle, Esposito and the Mahovlich brothers. Heroes are often found in defeat, as the reputations of Winston Churchill, Charles de Gaulle and John Diefenbaker can attest. The shrill voice of Foster Hewitt crackling across the ether from the grim and dour Soviet capital for the last four games thus deepened the element of participatory drama. In Ken Dryden's words, those scratchy transmissions over the pole came embedded with their own dramatic intensity, "momentous with distance . . . never certain of getting through."[42]

Canadians watching the telecast of 22 September 1972 from Moscow, by now were involved in something deeper than sport. There was an element of heroic daring in the fact of a middle power contending with the largest national land mass in the world, a nuclear-armed superpower at the time, for hockey supremacy. The dénouement would be played in a capital that had refused to yield before Napoleon and Hitler. Who were the Canadians to think they could redeem themselves in such a place?[43] The very audacity of the attempt seemed heroic. The fight had to be played out to the final seconds, according to the prescribed codes of sport. If this was not Newcomb's "mythic model," then what was?

Team Canada lost their first game in Moscow 5–4. Yet the Canadians "were adjusting, adapting, experimenting . . . now able to break up the Soviets' intricate passing plays." Thus, Game Six was do-or-die for Team Canada, a spiritual *ne plus ultra*. They chose to "do." Game Six produced the first Canadian victory since that seemingly long-ago night in Toronto. It was noted for something else as well; a particular piece of infamy that starkly reflects hockey's darker side. Canada's Bobby Clarke purposely set out to "tap" and thus sabotage the speedy Russian Kharlamov's ankle. Years later Clarke was only mildly repentant: "It's not something I would've done in an NHL game, at least I hope I wouldn't. But that situation . . . at that stage in the series, with everything that was happening, it was necessary."[44]

"With everything that was happening"—if there was little grace in Clarke's confession there was admittedly some in his candour. For by now these were obviously more than just hockey games; the whole experience had been lifted beyond sport.[45] The series was pointing to something beyond itself, something primal, something of hockey's own elemental origins. The juvenility and sexism, the Odysseus-like cunning and calculated cruelty—hockey's eternal dark side was always present though somehow counterbalanced by a sense of transcendence. The 3,000 plus fans who flew to Moscow to shout "Da, Da Canada; Nyet, Nyet, Soviet" testified to that. So did Bobby Orr's desire to sit behind the bench as a supporter, his bad knees making it impossible for Sinden to play him. Another quiet piece of heroism could be seen when players of the calibre of Stan Mikita and Rod Seiling waited patiently for ice time that hardly ever came.

All added to the drama. The telecasts revealed more and more of the pride as well as the insecurity welling up from deep inside the psyche of a young nation at a "coming out party" with the whole world watching. "They were Russia. We were Canada," Harry Sinden recalled. The attitude was: "I'm playing for . . . every Canadian in the world who ever put on skates and thought about being the best in the world, if only in his dreams."[46] The emotional intensity of this electronic drama stunned all the participants. "Some of them [the players] after that series were never the same," Tony Esposito related years later.

After Team Canada pulled together for a 4–3 victory in a wild stick-swinging Game Seven to tie the series, the stage was set for the final resolution, the eighth and final game of the series. "The game was broadcast on both CBC and CTV. All other programming came to a stop. Canada's population in 1972 was 21.8 million. On this Thursday afternoon, a work day, 7.5 million watched."[47] Foster Hewitt had been saying "Hello Canada!" for decades, but it never seemed to resonate with such meaning before. For, in an amazing moment of postmodern reflexivity, it was Foster Hewitt "playing" Foster Hewitt that added to the sense of other-worldliness that last night in Moscow. The aura lingers even today. As a sporting phenomenon that ended in an incredible display of the power of the television aesthetic and of the mythos of sport, the Canada-Soviet series is unique. It carried the freight of multiple, embedded meanings.

The last four games no doubt evoked another shared folk memory. There was the weighted sociological meaning of over four decades of small-town families huddled around the radio as Foster Hewitt's voice came crackling from one of the few big cities in Canada at the time. From the 1930s to the 1960s it was Foster Hewitt who had provided, for millions of Canadian boys, the electronic voice in their heads:

> How old were we when we first heard the nasal, rasping voice of Foster Hewitt's "He shoots! He scores!" coming at us over the airwaves? [Foster Hewitt] . . . convinced me that the world of the imagination was where I wanted to be. . . . Sitting by the fire having supper or doing the dishes. On the farm. In a tiny fishing village. No other game has been such a force in bringing our country together. A Canadian boy's dreams were nurtured by Foster Hewitt. . . . To steal a famous baseball announcer's axiom: "Nothing happened until he said so."[48]

On 28 September 1972, 12 million Canadians heard that voice say that they were the best in the world at the game of hockey. It was a unique Canadian epiphany. A Soviet coach commented years later: "We do not have the spirit to draw on that these Canadians do." To him, the Canadian players had "a light that cannot be put out. . . . You defeat them sometimes, but you discourage them never."[49] What was the source of that light? Was it money and commercialism? Was it the male physicality and exclusiveness? Or perhaps it was something much deeper—the intensification and celebration of a collective myth as enhanced by electronic technology.

The national fervour unleashed across the country was unprecedented in modern, peacetime Canada and beyond. "Muscovites saw them everywhere," the *Toronto Sun* reported on the 3,000 Canadians who had travelled to Moscow, "Walking hand in hand through the Gum department store. Singing Da, Da, Canada—Nyet, Nyet, Soviet; waving their little Canadian flags in the lineup which occasionally stretched for a mile outside Lenin's tomb."[50] Back home, Ontario Education Minister Tom Wells intervened to allow half a million elementary and secondary school students in the province to watch or listen to the final game in school auditoriums or cafeterias. A *Toronto Star* survey "failed to find a single school where students would not get the chance to follow the game."[51] On 29 September, the day after the final victory, the *Globe and Mail* led with "From Russia With Glory." Colin McCullough's report from the USSR interestingly profiled "The fans who discovered their own nationality in Moscow":

The games have been splendid of course . . . [b]ut the series produced more than hockey scores. For one thing, a lot of Canadians discovered their nationality. Had any of them ever before stood up and loudly sung O Canada, even the high notes, with tears running down their cheeks? They did it at the Palace of Sports at Lenin Central Stadium, and it was because of Canada, not hockey. . . . In the hotels and in the streets, the factory worker from Hamilton felt quite comfortable discussing hockey on the Moscow subway with Seagram's president Edward Bronfman of Montreal or any other available Canadian.[52]

The *Halifax Chronicle-Herald* reported that the federal election campaign of 1972 had "ground to a standstill" for the last act of the drama.[53] Frank Moores, then Premier of Newfoundland, invited all members of the victorious Team Canada to spend a week's holiday hunting and fishing at government expense, while at the other end of the country, British Columbia leader Dave Barrett exulted: "The French couldn't do it [i.e. conquer Moscow], the Germans couldn't do it; now Canada has done it and they had better get out of town before it starts snowing."[54] The *Calgary Herald,* whose front page on 28 September pictured a crowd of Calgarians watching the game in a downtown department store, a scene "undoubtedly repeated in stores, offices and living rooms across the country," recorded how actor William Hutt, declaiming King Lear at Stratford, Ontario, paused dramatically during the storm scene, to announce the score to the 2,000 students in his audience.[55]

Hockey, for all its regrettable "male-only" encodements, its violence and occasional juvenility, serves as a primal source of identity-reinforcement for Canadians. It is rooted in a paradisiacal locus of the imagination, drawing upon the game's rural, northern signifiers. Playing hockey on the ponds that dot the frozen landscape for many appears to be nothing less than a Canadian rite of passage, a vital part of the acculturation process. It began in the backyards and on the rivers, continues in the arenas and indoor stadiums, and injects into the growing-up process something Canadians do that is distinctive, something no one else does with quite the same intensity and devotion: "firewagon hockey."[56]

If the 1972 series was a Canadianized form of the Persian-Greek Wars, and Foster Hewitt—to stretch the metaphor—was our electronically relayed Homer with a microphone, then television served as national theatre. The tiny screen became the locus for "the time of heroes." Television's bias for intimacy helped enshrine one of those rare shared moments of collective national myth, an electronically catalyzed national drama.

In 1972 television superbly transmitted the poetry of hockey, its lyricism and its menace. Paul Henderson's game-winning goal in Game Seven is illustrative. With four Soviet players close around him at the centre line, he somehow scooped up the bouncing puck and pulled away with the Russians in hot pursuit. Moving in over the Soviet line he had one defenseman draped around him as he began to fall. Incredibly, he was able to squeeze away a shot at the Russian goaltender and bear the Soviet goalie from an almost impossible angle. Finally, he and the Soviet defender slid gracefully out of camera range together, a freeze-framed tribute to the poetry of hockey and of television.

To watch that goal is to see incarnated Novak's sense of northern hardiness wresting narrow victory against the primitive elements of ice and snow, a Canadian *corrida* set against the inhospitability and bleakness of the landscape. A game nurtured amid the eternal mountains, lakes and prairie that make up Canada—scenes of both lyricism and menace—does indeed fulfill Novak's celebration of "hot blood holding out against the cold." Through hockey Canadians characteristically celebrate a delight in speed, skill and gracefulness of form in the face of a bleak and often unforgiving environment.

The 1972 series lives on in the popular imagination. It demonstrated as never before or since that televised hockey, perhaps the most characteristic artifact of Canada's popular culture, points to a desire for something essential about Canadians as a northern people. Winter, with its abstract black and white patterns, its long shadows and desolation, has nurtured—perhaps to their surprise—a nation of mythmakers after all.

Notes

1. C.L.R. James quoted in *Canada Learns to Play: The Emergence of Organized Sport, 1807–1914,* by Alan Metcalfe (Toronto: McClelland and Stewart, 1987), 9.
2. Barbara Righton, "Waking up 'The Spin,'" *TV Times: Vancouver Sun* (February 26, 1993), 2.
3. Donald Macintosh and Donna Greenhorn, "Hockey Diplomacy and Canadian Foreign Policy," *Journal of Canadian Studies,* 28, 2 (Summer, 1993), 96–112. The authors construct the thesis that it was concern for Canada's prestige on the international level that was a prime springboard for the 1972 series.
4. Barry D. McPherson, James E. Curtis and John W. Loy, *The Social Significance of Sport: Introduction to the Sociology of Sport* (Champaign: Human Kinetics Books, 1989), 21–23. Unfortunately the authors do not expand on that statement.
5. Martin Heidegger, *The Question Concerning Technology* (New York: Harper and Row, Publishers, 1977), 12.
6. Scott Morrison, *The Days Canada Stood Still: Canada vs USSR* (Toronto: McGraw Hill, 1989), 14. Morrison, a sports reporter for the *Toronto Sun,* is President of the Professional Hockey Writers' Association. His book is a valuable resource for the series not the least because of the interviews conducted with the help of his colleague Pat Grier. The interviews amount to as thorough a personal retrospective as we presently have from the principals involved with Team Canada 1972.
7. Ibid., 135.
8. Michael Novak, *The Joy of Sports: End Zones, Bases, Baskets, Balls and Consecration of the American Spirit* (New York: Basic Books, Inc., 1976), xii, 94–96.
9. Ibid.
10. Doug Beardsley, *Country on Ice* (Winlaw: Polestar Press, 1987), 26. Morrison, *The Days Canada Stood Still,* 220. A key organizer of the series, Alan Eagleson, shared his reflections on his reception in Montreal upon arrival from Moscow. He was overwhelmed by excited spectators crowding the train station, and "everyone talking about the series, and all of it in French."

11. Jack Ludwig, *Hockey Night in Moscow* (Toronto: McClelland and Stewart, 1972), 46. Ludwig's engaging and frank account is a valuable reference for anyone studying the 1972 series as a cultural signifier. His string of colourful recollections still have a ring of "having been there" over 20 years later.
12. Paul Rutherford, *When Television Was Young: Prime-Time Canada, 1952–1967* (Toronto: University of Toronto Press, 1990), 242–43. Rutherford is an indispensable source for anyone analyzing television's impact upon Canadians in its early years. He is generally fair and objective, both on the issue of "Canadian content" and on the subject of the medium itself.
13. Ibid., 245.
14. Beardsley, *Country on Ice*, 24–25. Perhaps more attention needs to be paid to the aesthetics of hockey announcing as a cultural form. Hewitt and Gallivan's styles are the best places to start.
15. Rutherford, *When Television Was Young*, 248.
16. Ibid., The loquacious Howie Meeker, another of the game's intense analysts and a television commentator of note, opened up all kinds of possibilities for postmodern students of ideology in a personal interview at Maple Leaf Gardens in November 1991. "Boy, it's rough," Meeker told the writer, "We play it hard. I tell you it's free enterprise. . . . [It] reflects the countries it's played in . . . it's a reflection of the free market system."
17. Ludwig, *Hockey Night in Moscow*, 41–42. Of course Ludwig happily provides evidence of this Canadian equation of manliness and hockey in his gripping series of vignettes sprinkled through his account of the 1972 series: Wayne Cashman playing with a serious gash in his tongue; Serge Savard likewise afflicted with a hairline fracture; the 6'8" (on skates) Peter Mahovlich charging over the boards, stick at the ready, to rescue a beleaguered Alan Eagleson in the final game.
18. Ken Dryden and Roy MacGregor, *Home Game: Hockey and Life in Canada* (Toronto: McClelland and Stewart, 1989), 4–5.
19. This seems to apply to many women as well. One thing that surprised me at a University of Toronto graduate seminar on hockey was how all the women accepted hockey's "boy inside the man" mythos as more than compensating for its physicality. "Well, it's a rough game played by rough people," was a common response.
20. Ken Dryden, *The Game: A Thoughtful and Provocative Look at a Life in Hockey* (Toronto: Harper and Collins, 1983), 67–68.
21. Morrison, *The Days Canada Stood Still*, 15.
22. Keith Cunningham, "Myths, Dreams and Movies: Exploring the Archetypal Roots of Cinema," *The Quest: A Quarterly Journal of Philosophy, Science, Religion and the Arts* 5, 1 (Spring 1992), 30. The linkage between film and television, though not absolute, is clear enough for our purposes.
23. Ibid., 33, 35.
24. John Fiske, *Reading the Popular* (London: Unwin Hyman, 1990), 2, 84.
25. Terence Hawkes, *Structuralism and Semiotics* (Berkeley: University of California Press, 1977), 68. Roland Marchand, *Advertising the American Dream: Making Way for Modernity, 1920–1940* (Berkeley: University of California Press, 1985), 235–38, 270, 154–55.
26. John Fiske, *Television Culture* (London: Routledge, 1987), 14.
27. Ken Dryden with Mark Mulvoy, *Face-Off at the Summit* (Toronto: Little, Brown, 1973), 65.
28. CBC television production, "Summit on Ice" (7 October 1992). Earnest testimonials to this deduction were not lacking in this telecast: "It wasn't a game, it wasn't a series," Phil Esposito declaimed to an interviewer, "it was our society against their society." Alan Eagleson, a key organizer, stated: "In those days, the Soviet Union was the . . . home of Communism, the enemy of democracy." Serge Savard speculated on what a Canadian defeat would mean: "It was like the . . . Communist country sending the world a message that our system was better than yours."
29. Horace Newcomb, *TV: The Most Popular Art* (New York: Anchor Press, 1974), 193.
30. Scott Young, *Hello Canada! The Life and Times of Foster Hewitt* (Toronto: Seal Books, 1985), 172.

31. Dryden and MacGregor, *Home Game*, 202. Dryden's summation of the series in Chapter Five has a fine postmodern ring in its title, "No Final Victories."

32. Ibid., 204–5.

33. Ibid.

34. Harry Sinden, *Hockey Showdown: The Canada-Russia Hockey Series* (Toronto: Doubleday, 1972), 8. Morrison, *The Days Canada Stood Still*, 65–66.

35. Ibid., 64–65.

36. Novak, *The Joy of Sports*, 130, 131.

37. Morrison, *The Days Canada Stood Still*, 69.

38. Ibid., 94, 97, 102.

39. Newcomb, *TV: The Most Popular Art*, 261, 245.

40. Ibid., 245–46.

41. Morrison, *The Days Canada Stood Still*, 95.

42. Dryden and MacGregor, *Home Game*, 194.

43. The military analogy was also seized upon by Jack Ludwig, as noted in his comments after the game opener: "Not only had the headlines in the Montreal papers been of a size and blackness one associated with a World War, but the metaphors used in the days that followed were frequently derived from World War I and World War II. Ypres was invoked. Dieppe, Dunkirk." (*Hockey Night in Moscow*, 45.)

44. Morrison, *The Days Canada Stood Still*, 151, 167.

45. CBC. "Summit on Ice." By now Team Canada was, in a Cunningham phrase, "out of the body and flying." Yvan Cournoyer considered the experience "Better than ten Stanley Cups." Paul Henderson testified "Almost every day of my life a Canadian will come up to me and shake my hand and say, 'Thank you for one of the greatest thrills of my life.'" Ron Ellis ruminated "Folks alive at the time can remember where they were and what they were doing," while Ken Dryden speculated darkly before the last game on the chances of being "the most hated man in Canada" if his team had lost. The Soviet participants were equally enthralled: "It will never again be the same as it was in '72. The series with Canada was an historic affair," said Boris Mikhailov.

46. Harry Sinden, *Hockey Showdown*, 15.

47. Dryden and MacGregor, *Home Game*, 1940.

48. Beardsley, *Country on Ice*, 19–20.

49. Ibid., 36.

50. Douglas Creighton, "Canadian unity at peak in Moscow," *Toronto Sun*, 30 September 1972, 19.

51. "500,000 in Metro Schools may be watching hockey," *Toronto Star*, 28 September 1972, 2.

52. Colin McCullough, "The fans who discovered their own nationality in Moscow," *Globe and Mail*, 29 September 1972, 1.

53. "Feared winter of discontent: Hockey win helped campaign—Trudeau," *Halifax Chronicle-Herald*, 29 September 1972, 3.

54. "Giant Welcome for Team Canada: They'll return as conquering heroes," *Vancouver Sun*, 29 September 1972, I–2.

55. "Canadians flip as Russians slip—WE'RE THE CHAMPS," *Calgary Herald*, 29 September 1972, 1. The article also mentions how Québec Premier Robert Bourassa telegrammed to Team Canada that "[y]our teamwork and your determination to win has earned you the admiration of Quebeckers and all Canadians."

56. Trevor Brown, a Jamaican-born mathematics professor at York University, attests to hockey's significance for today's youth, and immigrant youth in particular. Brown's son enjoys informal league hockey every Saturday night at Chesswood Arena in northern Toronto. The team includes Vietnamese and Trinidadian immigrants and has at times involved both Jewish and Arabians. "Hockey is far more than a puck and a stick to a youngster living in Canada," says Brown. "It is a ceremony, a ritual, an almost mystical rite. . . . The playing of the game credentials a boy and makes him an authentic Canadian." (Personal communication, 16 November 1993.)

Hockey Dreams:
Memories of a Man Who Couldn't Play

David Adams Richards

I WAS FIVE thousand miles away from home, in the middle of the mountains of British Columbia, in the middle of winter. On a reading tour, in 1989, I was going from town to town while the snow fell, covering up the small roads along the mountain passes.

I was billeted at different houses, and would often find myself in a strange little village, at a stranger's house at midnight. And since I'm a night person I found myself sitting in uncomfortable positions reading cookbooks at one o'clock in the morning.

One of the people who billeted me, I did become quite fond of. He was a man who had moved here with his wife from the United States a number of years before, during the "back to the land" movement. He was very kind to me, although I disagreed with him on the back to the land movement itself. And nothing he told me did anything but reinforce my bias.

But I gave him the greatest compliment I could. I told him he reminded me of my friend Stafford Foley—a boy I grew up with, way back in the Maritimes. Both of them were quite small men, with a great kind-heartedness.

I left his house on a Thursday morning to go to another village, some 40 miles away where I had a reading.

"If you ever need a place to stay again—" he said, "at any time—look me up." He handed me his telephone number.

I told him I would.

It had been snowing for four days. The snowflakes were as big as sugar cookies.

By Thursday night I found myself in an untenable position. It was one of those nights when I wanted to be anywhere but where I was. I had been with my new host fifteen minutes, and already a tense discussion had taken place.

I was honour bred. I knew I could no longer stay in his house. But where would I go? It was after ten at night. The roads were all blocked.

I telephoned my little back-to-the-land friend some 40 miles away. "You have to come and get me," I whispered.

"Now?" he said.

"If you don't mind. You wouldn't have a skidoo or something?"

"No, I have no skidoo—I'd have to take the car."

"Car is fine—I like a car—"

"But it's snowing—"

"Yes."

"What happened?"

"It would be better if you just came and got me as quickly as possible—" I said.

"If I go over the mountain pass—I won't be found until next spring—"

(long pause)

"I know, I know, but desperate circumstances call for desperate measures. That's a chance I'm willing that you take." I sighed.

I said my goodbye to the host, and stood outside the house with my suitcase. The man looked out the window at me now and again, as I waited for my friend, and closed the curtains when I glanced back at him.

Snowstorms were different in this part of Canada. But it was still Canada, dark and gloomy.

It had all started because of a thought I shared that evening. I had thought at supper, that from this part of the world—at this very time of year, in 1961 the Trail Smoke Eaters had left for their long and famous journey. This is what I had told my host. I had happened to mention that journey. The trip to Europe. The idea of hockey versus the dratted ice hockey.

He had come here from Britain in 1969. He had read my books. He thought we'd be kindred spirits, bred of the same bone. And he said, "My good God man—that sounds a bit nationalistic."

It wasn't so much Trail, it was the World Juniors. I was talking about their fight against the Russians at suppertime.

"Didya see when the lad from Big Cove smucked the Russian in the head—set him on his ass?" I asked.

He looked at me as if I might be rather subhuman.

Well, it wasn't so much the World Juniors—it was Team Canada. It was the Summit Series of '72. It was—

"Good God man. I thought you were a novelist," he said.

"Novelist shmovelist—" I said.

So here I was outside waiting, as the snow poured down out of the gloom. But it was too late to turn back.

After an hour I saw the headlights of my friend's compact car coming down the street.

My heart leaped with joy. And in I got.

We turned about and started back into the gloomy night, the windshield wipers on high and visibility almost zero. And besides that my ears popping off every time we went up and down a hill.

"What happened?" he said, finally. "Didn't the reading go as planned?"

"No no—it went all right—for a stormy night. Some showed up—well three or four snowshoed in. I gave a pretty good reading—got to know them all on a first-name basis."

(silence)

"Well—what was the problem?"

"An age old problem," I said seriously.

"Oh yes," he said, looking at me and not understanding, "an age old problem." He smiled gently. "What age old problem is that, David?"

(I know when people finally address me as "David" I am about to make a fool of myself. That I have once again crossed the line from rational human being to something else. So I knew I had to answer him as impassioned and as sincerely as possible. So he would know he had not risked his life for nothing.)

"That son of a bitch doesn't like hockey," I said.

I began to think then that I would go back home, to my childhood home, and see the place again where we went sliding. Where we played hockey on the river. I would make the pilgrimage, for it had to be made.

I would smell the flat ice and the smoke over the dark, stunted trees again. I would visit the place where Michael grew up, and poor Tobias, and see the old lanes we all played road hockey on. Paul and Stafford and Darren and all of us.

But they would be ghosts to me now. Almost everyone was gone. The laughter against the frigid, blue skies would have all disappeared, evaporated like the slush under our boots in 1961.

I found myself somewhere in Northern Ontario, later in the month. I forget the name of the town. It was one of those reading tours where somehow you no longer know where you are.

Again I was billeted. The woman kept a bed-and-breakfast of some kind. I was given a small room at the back of the house. There was a hockey game that night. I don't remember who was playing—it may have been Montreal. It may have been Edmonton. It may have been anyone.

I could hear, far away, the shouts of the crowd, the sound of the announcer. And I left my room and began to look for the TV.

The woman met me in the kitchen.

"Are you hungry?"

"No—I can hear a game coming from somewhere—I just thought someone might be watching it."

"Oh," the woman said. "That's Burl."

"Burl?"

"My husband," she said. "We don't live together anymore—he lives downstairs and I live upstairs. He's downstairs."

"Oh," I said. "Downstairs."

"So if you want to go on downstairs and watch the game—"

"Well—I don't want to intrude."

"Burl? Intrude on Burl? Burl don't mind."

I went back into my room and sat on the edge of the bed fidgeting. There was a great roar. Perhaps Roy had made a fantabulous save. Maybe Burl wouldn't mind.

The wind howled. I could see a streetlight far away from the small window next to my bed.

Things in hockey were changing every day. Canadians and Russians were now playing on the same lines, in arenas all across the United States. The two greatest Canada Cups had already taken place—and within six years it would be called "the World Cup." (I didn't know that then of course.)

Everything was changing. But not so much for *our* benefit—yet we pretended that it was. We still pretended that the NHL was ours. It was always one way to get along. That's what Canadians were like.

Suddenly I felt nostalgic. It would be good to catch the last few periods of a game. I left my room, opened the basement door and tiptoed down.

Then I caught myself. What would I do if I was sitting watching a hockey game and a stranger came tiptoeing around the corner?

I knocked on the side of the wall. No one answered. I hesitated and then walked into the room.

Sideways to me was a man, sitting on the leather couch in his underwear, with a pint of beer between his legs, staring at the television.

"G'day?"

I thought he looked over at me, and nodded.

So I sat down on the chair near the couch and began to watch the game.

It seemed as if Burl had been relegated to a kind of subterranean prison life. There were no windows in the basement, but he had curtains up. He had a huge bar, with two barstools, and a clock that told the time backwards. Above the bar was a picture of himself with a tiny bass, and under the picture his signature, and the words *bass master.* In the picture he was smiling as if he knew in his heart he wasn't a real bass master.

I was beginning to get comfortable. It seemed as if Burl and I would get along.

Suddenly something happened in the game, and we both started yelling at the television. Then roared at the obvious cheap shot someone made.

Burl shook his head. I shook my head. Burl got up and went to the fridge and taking out a beer, opened it. He turned about and started back. I was watching the television and grinning. Suddenly, he stopped. He turned. He looked down. He stared at me as if he had never seen me before.

"Who the Christ are you?"

"David," I said.

"David—David who?—what are you doing here?"

"You know—watching the game here—if you don't mind?"

"Where in hell are you from?"

"The Maritimes—"

"The *Maritimes*—what in the living name of God gives you the right to travel up from the Maritimes?"

"I don't know—"

I began to get a little flustered. He was standing in his underwear with a pint of Molson, and his little bass master photograph on the wall. He turned about, and there in his chair was a man from the Maritimes watching the game.

However, he could understand one thing. He could understand *why* I wanted to watch it. It was only a shock initially because I was watching it in *his* house.

Once I explained why that had to be, he was satisfied. Although, he did not offer me a beer.

Later, I even got to talk about my feelings on the game. How there are two *theirs* in the game, and how *our* game doesn't seem to count anymore. How one *their* is the product of business interests in the States—how we think it is *their* game; and how the second *their* is one that is strangely joined to the first *their*. The second *their* is the European *their*. How European ice hockey is supposedly more *moral* and *refined* than *our game* is. How we need European ice hockey to teach us a lesson. And that both of these *theirs* are linked in trying to defeat the *our* in hockey.

How probably this has already been done. How the huge arenas in the States and the lack of hockey in Hamilton attest to this, more than any of the false promises, or our pretence of still controlling our game does.

Maybe he didn't understand what I said. But he probably did. He probably already knew all of what I was saying before I said it. He understood Henderson's goal and what it meant. He understood when I spoke about my childhood friends, Michael and Tobias, and Stafford, and the game we played on the river in 1961. Because he himself had played those games too.

And of course I always spoke of Stafford Foley when I spoke of hockey. I thought of him on September 28, 1972. I thought of him twenty years later to the day.

September 28, 1992, I was at home in Saint John watching the news when they announced the anniversary of Henderson's goal. It put the hosts at a loss. They did not know how to approach it—as a human interest story or a noteworthy date in history. Finally it seemed that the best way to acknowledge to their audience that it was an anniversary of perhaps the most famous goal ever scored by a Canadian was to be whimsical and remote about its significance.

They laughed as if they didn't want to be known as the ones to credit this as serious historical information. What relevance would Canadians attach to it "now"? one of the announcers asked. And then added that her sport was baseball. You see, she was only pretending to be indifferent. But no one is indifferent to hockey in our country, and so it was a self congratulatory indifference—one that looked out at her audience and said, "I have risen above the game you wish me to celebrate as mine."

Without a doubt in my mind, the franchises in the United States need this reaction from us to exist. If they did not have it—if it was for one moment decided that the game was ours—there would be no lights on in St. Louis before there were lights on at Copps Colosseum. Winnipeg would not be going the way of Quebec.

It was 1984 and I was writer-in-residence at a university in New Brunswick. The Canada Cup was on. The night before, Team Canada had beaten the Russians in overtime to advance to the finals.

In the former Soviet Union, the game against the Russians was on tape delay. All night, all day long, the phone was ringing at the Canadian Embassy in Moscow to ask what the final score was, who won the game. I knew who had won the game. I had watched it live. I wanted to celebrate. I wanted to talk about how exciting it was. I knew no one in Fredericton, however, except for certain English professors. And, as admirable as English professors tend to be, they were a different breed than I.

I went into the common room and poured myself a coffee and sat down—waiting for the arrival of someone to talk to. A young female professor from Newcastle Creek entered the room. She was a nice lady, and had met me once at the president's house. She'd once made the remark that she didn't see how anyone would be able to live without reading Henry James.

As she sat there I glanced at her. *Go on,* I said to myself, *Ask her—she's from Newcastle Creek—Newcastle Creek for God's sake. She'd have cut her teeth on hockey.*

I made a stab at my coffee with a stir-stick and looked about. Twice I went to the door and looked down the hall to see if anyone else was coming.

Finally I could stand it no longer. Turning to her I ventured, "Did you see the game last night?"

"Pardon?"

"Did you see the hockey game?"

"We don't have a television," she said.

"Oh, what's wrong?" I said. "Is it broken?"

Then I thought that maybe she and her husband had a fight over a program and someone had thrown the television through the wall—I know people who do that, so I thought—well she was from Newcastle Creek, so I'd better be discreet.

"We don't approve of television," she said.

There was an awkward silence.

I looked about, mumbled something to myself. "Right in front of the net—they score."

I too was from New Brunswick, I too had cut my teeth on hockey. I too remember sitting in front of an ancient black-and-white television watching the small figures of men gliding up and down the ice. I remembered the Richard riot, and how even then I thought it was ugly.

But I had entered, for the first time, another realm, where a woman from Newcastle Creek who may or may not have grown up on salt cod and moose meat could tell me that she disapproved of television and not be a fundamentalist. Could tell me that I wasn't alive until I read Henry James and believe it.

"My husband was up early—to listen to the radio so he could hear the score," she said.

"Oh," I said. I smiled. I had misjudged her. Forever I would be sorry for it.

"Yes," I said. "Did he find out?"

"Yes—he's heartbroken."

"No," I said, "not heartbroken—we won—Canada won 3–2."

She looked at me, as if I really was such a country bumpkin. And I suppose when considering it, I have been looked at like this almost all my life over something or other.

"But we were going for the Russians," she said.

"No," I said.

I had the same tone as a man might who had just learned that the *Titanic* had sunk or Passchendaele had cost us thousands of men for 50 yards of mud.

Hearing my tone, the tone of a person bleeding, maybe she felt as if she had won a moral victory.

"Well, we both hate Gretzky you see." Her accent now turned slightly British. "Why?"

"Oh, he's just such a Canadian." She smiled.

"You hate greatness or just Canadian greatness?" I asked.

In a way, Canadians have been asking this question all of their lives. And while asking this question they have been running to outsiders for the answer.

In a way my learned friend's stance embodies the notion of the intelligentsia that hockey is a part of what is wrong with our country.

Of course I know this about my country. I have known it since Stafford Foley used to debate the merits of Alex Delvecchio in a room at the tavern, as if he could turn back the clock and make, with the original six, everything right with the world again and with himself.

It was, by some rascals, rather smart-alecky to cheer for the Russians. I remember this all too well.

It was December 31, 1975—all day I waited. Red Army was playing Montreal. I was in Victoria with an acquaintance. He was extremely adept (or he thought he was) at taking the opposite position—the educated, therefore contrived, outrageous part. And so he "wished" to cheer for the Russians. He felt *no one else* would be doing this. (He would only have to listen to one CBC commentary to realize how Canadians bent over backwards to kiss the Russian behinds in order to be fair.)

I shouted at him, told him if he had only known the dozens of minutes of un-recognizable penalties that were given to our amateurs in Sweden and Czechoslovakia over the years he'd feel different. Or if he had only known the hundreds of thousands of dollars that Hockey Canada had given to the Russians to help their sport, he may change his mind.

He stared at me, as if I had not just said something wrong. It went well beyond this. It was as if I had demonstrated the kind of unfair sportsmanship he was ridiculing. "My Good God man—get a hold of yourself; it's only a game—you're frightening the house guests."

What was under attack was simply fear of a lack of Canadian identity. And he, a learned man whose father was a poet, connected to a university, did not wish to have anything to do with the sport that could make us feel—even manhandle us into feeling—Canadian. It was supposed to be done another way; I suppose a more *civilized* way. (Also it was the elitist idea that the ideal of Soviet life was one that hinged on working-class fairness.)

For most people who talk this polemic against hockey as a point of identity there is a certain degree of cant, of wrong-headedness. Besides, part of this kind of conceit hinges on the identity crisis itself. Because some of us continue to believe that Canadians are famous for nothing except hockey. Therefore they argue that Canadians must be greater than what they are famous for.

My answer to that has always been yes and no. And hockey, when you know what it says about us as a people, proves it.

So we sat in silence, he and I, in a little room on that long ago New Year's Eve. Montreal did not win that game as we all know. They tied Red Army 3–3, after outplaying them and outshooting them by a margin of 4–1. Tretiak, who the Czechs always seemed mystified by our inability to score against, saved them—and Dryden was in net for us.

Dryden never played that well against the Soviets, but all in all, well enough.

I remember at one point during that game Guy Lafleur stickhandling at centre ice, and mystifying three Russian players. It comes back to me time and again when I am lectured, usually by university professors, on how the Europeans taught us finesse, and how shameful I am not to record that. I will and do record the Russians' greatness. But, my son, they did not teach us finesse.

Finesse in the age of Orr and Lafleur?

Finesse in the age of Lemieux and Gretzky? In the age of Savard (Denis) or a hundred others?

I was in Australia in 1993, at a literary festival. It is a wonderful country and has a rugby league and Australian rules. In some way (this is exaggerated) the difference between these two kinds of rugby is the same as the difference between ice hockey and hockey.

I was sitting with a writer from the Czech Republic and a woman who worked for Penguin Books. The writer from the Czech Republic and I had an interesting conversation about Australia and how it compared to our countries. All of a sudden he gave a start, and he said, "Oh—you are *Canadian*—I thought you were an American—so mister Canadianman tell me—who is the greatest hockey player in the world today?"

"Gretzky or Lemieux—I'm not sure which," I replied.

"Gretzky or Lemieux—Gretzky or Lemieux—bahhh! What about Jagr—?"

"Who?" the young woman from Penguin asked.

"Jagr—Jagr—the greatest to ever exist."

"Great, no doubt," I said. "Definitely a great asset to the Penguins—but not the greatest who ever lived—he isn't even the greatest of his era—he isn't even the greatest for the Penguins."

"Pardon me?" the woman from Penguin said.

"The Penguins would be nothing without him," my Czech acquaintance said.

"I agree—he is great—but Lemieux is far greater—anyway the Penguins might get rid of them both within the next few years. I am very cynical about it."

"Who are they?" the woman from Penguin said.

She made a stab. "So what do you think of Kundera?" she said to the Czech gentleman after a moment's silence.

"Kundera—what team does he play for?" the Czech writer asked, and winked my way.

The sales representative from Penguin excused herself and did not come back to the table. Her meal got cold. This is true, and I feel badly about this now (a little).

Earlier that day in Melbourne, I needed a pair of shoes for this particular dinner. I went with my wife and son to a shoe store near our hotel. In this store one of the salesmen was a young Russian immigrant. He was fairly new to his job, and new to Australia.

He told me that the one thing he missed was hockey. He mentioned Larionov and Fetisov—he asked me if Fetisov had retired. I was never a big fan of Fetisov (except when he got punched in the head by Clarke) but I understood that his hockey talk was more than a sales pitch. And even if it were only a sales pitch *it worked*. For how many customers could he have used it on in Melbourne?

Years before, in my home town I got drunk one night with a boxer off a Russian ship. We liked each other very much. We talked two things—hockey and boxing. The only thing I can say is that all through the evening this partisan Russian who lived fifteen miles from Leningrad never once mentioned hockey as "ice hockey."

Ah but the game is lost boys, the game is lost. To go on about it, at times, is like a farm boy kicking a dead horse to get up out of a puddle.

But still, some horses are worth a kick or two. And if it is good and even noble to have sport, and if hockey is *our* sport, and if we can make the claim that we play hockey better than any other country—if we can make that claim, without having to listen to apologies about why we made it—then who speaks for *us,* as a HOCKEY nation, when three-quarters of our NHL teams are in the states, and 324 of our players as well?

It is not America's fault, maybe not even ours. Perhaps it is just the nature of the economic beast. And a few years back—in the dark age of Mulroney, when we spoke about selling out our culture, what great ballet were we thinking of—what great ballet had we already let go?

CHAPTER NINETEEN

Multiculturalism: Policy

Introduction

By any measuring stick, Canada is the world's most multicultural country and Toronto is the world's most multicultural city. It is part of how Canadians define themselves: one nation, two languages, many cultures. In point of fact, Section 27 of the 1982 Charter of Rights and Freedoms explicitly states, "This Charter shall be interpreted in a manner consistent with the preservation and enhancement of the multicultural heritage of Canadians." Canada's policy of multiculturalism—as stated in the 1988 Canadian Multiculturalism Act—did not fall out of the sky, fully formed. Rather, it came out of Canada's history. From the very beginning, Canada has been forced to imagine identities big enough and protean enough to accommodate French Canadians and English Canadians, Catholics and Protestants.

J.M.S. Careless and Irving Abella are historians. In very different ways, both scholars examine the origins of Canada's commitment to ethnic pluralism. Where and in what does Maurice Careless locate the origins of multiculturalism? In his 2000 presidential address to the Canadian Historical Association, Irving Abella argues that the new Canada—that is, "the humane, decent, culturally diverse nation it is today"— was made, in part, by Canadian Jews. Change did not come from the top-down, it was insisted upon from the bottom-up.

Canadian Multiculturalism Act

An Act for the Preservation and Enhancement of Multiculturalism in Canada

Whereas the Constitution of Canada provides that every individual is equal before and under the law and has the right to the equal protection and benefit of the law without discrimination and that everyone has the freedom of conscience, religion, thought, belief, opinion, expression, peaceful assembly and association and guarantees those rights and freedoms equally to male and female persons;

And whereas the Constitution of Canada recognizes the importance of preserving and enhancing the multicultural heritage of Canadians;

And whereas the Constitution of Canada recognizes rights of the aboriginal peoples of Canada;

And whereas the Constitution of Canada and the *Official Languages Act* provide that English and French are the official languages of Canada and neither abrogates or derogates from any rights or privileges acquired or enjoyed with respect to any other language;

And whereas the *Citizenship Act* provides that all Canadians, whether by birth or by choice, enjoy equal status, are entitled to the same rights, powers and privileges and are subject to the same obligations, duties and liabilities;

And whereas the *Canadian Human Rights Act* provides that every individual should have an equal opportunity with other individuals to make the life that the individual is able and wishes to have, consistent with the duties and obligations of that individual as a member of society, and, in order to secure that opportunity, establishes the Canadian Human Rights Commission to redress any proscribed discrimination, including discrimination on the basis of race, national or ethnic origin or colour;

And whereas Canada is a party to the *International Convention on the Elimination of All Forms of Racial Discrimination,* which Convention recognizes that all human beings are equal before the law and are entitled to equal protection of the law against any discrimination and against any incitement to discrimination, and to the *International Covenant on Civil and Political Rights,* which Covenant provides that persons belonging to ethnic, religious or linguistic minorities shall not be denied the right to enjoy their own culture, to profess and practise their own religion or to use their own language;

Statutes of Canada, 35-36-37 Elizabeth II, Chap. 31 Assented to 21 July 1988.

And whereas the Government of Canada recognizes the diversity of Canadians as regards race, national or ethnic origin, colour and religion as a fundamental characteristic of Canadian society and is committed to a policy of multiculturalism designed to preserve and enhance the multicultural heritage of Canadians while working to achieve the equality of all Canadians in the economic, social, cultural and political life of Canada;

Now, therefore, Her Majesty, by and with the advice and consent of the Senate and House of Commons of Canada, enacts as follows:

Short Title

1. This Act may be cited as the *Canadian Multiculturalism Act . . .*

MULTICULTURALISM POLICY OF CANADA

3. (1) It is hereby declared to be the policy of the Government of Canada to

   (a) recognize and promote the understanding that multiculturalism reflects the cultural and racial diversity of Canadian society and acknowledges the freedom of all members of Canadian society to preserve, enhance and share their cultural heritage;

   (b) recognize and promote the understanding that multiculturalism is a fundamental characteristic of the Canadian heritage and identity and that it provides an invaluable resource in the shaping of Canada's future;

   (c) promote the full and equitable participation of individuals and communities of all origins in the continuing evolution and shaping of all aspects of Canadian society and assist them in the elimination of any barrier to such participation;

   (d) recognize the existence of communities whose members share a common origin and their historic contribution to Canadian society, and enhance their development;

   (e) ensure that all individuals receive equal treatment and equal protection under the law, while respecting and valuing their diversity;

   (f) encourage and assist the social, cultural, economic and political institutions of Canada to be both respectful and inclusive of Canada's multicultural character;

   (g) promote the understanding and creativity that arise from the interaction between individuals and communities of different origins;

   (h) foster the recognition and appreciation of the diverse cultures of Canadian society and promote the reflection and the evolving expressions of those cultures;

   (i) preserve and enhance the use of languages other than English and French, while strengthening the status and use of the official languages of Canada; and

(j) advance multiculturalism throughout Canada in harmony with the national commitment to the official languages of Canada.

(2) It is further declared to be the policy of the Government of Canada that all federal institutions shall

(a) ensure that Canadians of all origins have an equal opportunity to obtain employment and advancement in those institutions;

(b) promote policies, programs and practices that enhance the ability of individuals and communities of all origins to contribute to the continuing evolution of Canada;

(c) promote policies, programs and practices that enhance the understanding of and respect for the diversity of the members of Canadian society;

(d) collect statistical data in order to enable the development of policies, programs and practices that are sensitive and responsive to the multicultural reality of Canada;

(e) make use, as appropriate, of the language skills and cultural understanding of individuals of all origins; and

(f) generally, carry on their activities in a manner that is sensitive and responsive to the multicultural reality of Canada.

IMPLEMENTATION OF THE MULTICULTURALISM POLICY OF CANADA

4. The Minister, in consultation with other Ministers of the Crown, shall encourage and promote a coordinated approach to the implementation of the multiculturalism policy of Canada and may provide advice and assistance in the development and implementation of programs and practices in support of the policy.

5. (1) The Minister shall take such measures as the Minister considers appropriate to implement the multiculturalism policy of Canada and, without limiting the generality of the foregoing, may

(a) encourage and assist individuals, organizations and institutions to project the multicultural reality of Canada in their activities in Canada and abroad;

(b) undertake and assist research relating to Canadian multiculturalism and foster scholarship in the field;

(c) encourage and promote exchanges and cooperation among the diverse communities of Canada;

(d) encourage and assist the business community, labour organizations, voluntary and other private organizations, as well as public institutions, in ensuring full participation in Canadian society, including the social and economic aspects, of individuals of all origins and their communities, and in promoting respect and appreciation for the multicultural reality of Canada;

(e) encourage the preservation, enhancement, sharing and evolving expression of the multicultural heritage of Canada;

(f) facilitate the acquisition, retention and use of all languages that contribute to the multicultural heritage of Canada;

(g) assist ethno-cultural minority communities to conduct activities with a view to overcoming any discriminatory barrier and, in particular, discrimination based on race or national or ethnic origin;

(h) provide support to individuals, groups or organizations for the purpose of preserving, enhancing and promoting multiculturalism in Canada; and

(i) undertake such other projects or programs in respect of multiculturalism, not by law assigned to any other federal institution, as are designed to promote the multiculturalism policy of Canada.

(2) The Minister may enter into an agreement or arrangement with any province respecting the implementation of the multiculturalism policy of Canada.

(3) The Minister may, with the approval of the Governor in Council, enter into an agreement or arrangement with the government of any foreign state in order to foster the multicultural character of Canada.

6. (1) The ministers of the Crown, other than the Minister, shall, in the execution of their respective mandates, take such measures as they consider appropriate to implement the multiculturalism policy of Canada.

(2) A Minister of the Crown, other than the Minister, may enter into an agreement or arrangement with any province respecting the implementation of the multiculturalism policy of Canada.

7. (1) The Minister may establish an advisory committee to advise and assist the Minister on the implementation of this Act and any other matter relating to multiculturalism and, in consultation with such organizations representing multicultural interests as the Minister deems appropriate, may appoint the members and designate the chairman and other officers thereof.

"Waspishness" and Multiculture in Canada

J.M.S. Careless

IN DEALING WITH the British component in the Canadian multicultural heritage, one runs into problems of definition at the very start. Just who were the "British-Canadians", historically speaking? Canadians whose origin lay in the British Isles, presumably; yet this wide category not only covers the three different national communities of English, Scots, and Irish, but also two notably divergent kinds of Irish, the mainly Northern Protestants and the Southern Catholics; and let us not forget the Welsh either. The Southern Irish, besides, might not thank you for the description "British", although probably at the time of their main nineteenth-century influx into Canada many of them would then have accepted it. Still, at least all these settlers from Britain could be described as English in a broad linguistic sense? Scarcely the Gaelic-speaking Scots Highlanders, or many of the Irish and Welsh! The major British immigrant groups, in fact, could be no less nationally, religiously and to a great extent linguistically distinct and separate among themselves as share in one collective British category.

But apart from the foregoing caveats, can British-Canadians even be loosely defined as those who emigrated to this country from the British Isles? What of the United Empire Loyalists whose arrival after the American Revolution from the former Thirteen Colonies did much to shape the very outlines of a British Canada? They certainly regarded themselves as British—as loyal British Americans in contradistinction to traitorous American rebels—but they included sizeable numbers of German origin, not to mention Dutch or Gaelic Scottish, while those of English stock among them had often been well settled in America for a century or more. Then, too, what of the many migrants from the United States who followed in the wake of the Loyalists and who continued to enter in waves or in trickles onward to the present? They have generally fitted readily into the English-speaking community; their descendants have largely come to consider themselves, and be considered, part of the British-Canadian segment. Yet like the Loyalists—or even more so—they stemmed from a considerable variety of ethnic backgrounds. Some of them, including those New Englanders who had settled in Nova Scotia even before the Loyalists, had been out of Britain since the days of the *Mayflower;* others in later migrations had not had British forebears in the first place. In short, the British-Canadian heritage has sprung from a fairly heterogeneous community of peoples, and however the term "British" be used as a convenient label, it should always convey the evident fact of ethnic variety, not some willfully imagined racial or cultural monolith.

We might be better off, indeed, to talk of "British Americans" in order to refer to this prominent and historically dominant culture group in Canada. One can recognize, however, that by now some short-forms such as "BRAMs" is not too likely to replace "WASPs", White Anglo-Saxon Protestants, as a popular catchword to denote their powerful presence. True, WASP is an American transfer of terminology that does not wholly fit the Canadian situation, like a good many American transfers. For it is obvious that the Canadian British were by no means all Anglo-Saxons or Protestants in themselves. Nevertheless, their ruling élites were pre-eminently Protestant, and their ethnic values tended to exalt presumed "Anglo-Saxon" stock, tradition and character—whose excellence other breeds should properly endorse, and whose admirable guidance in Canada they thus should surely follow. Hence in a figurative if none too friendly way, these other breeds might conceivably figure British-Canadian WASPs as living high on the national tree in strong, well-defended nests, ready to sting any who rose up to challenge them. Besides, if they were not exactly banded black and yellow, they sometimes wore striped old school ties as emblems of their influential kinships, usually got more than those below, and sought commonly and combatively to maintain their sway. Though this insect analogy is a partial myth, it does still suggest a sense of WASPishness quite widely perceived by those outside the British-Canadian ethic segment; and it does express the fact that this significant group, for a long time the actual majority of the Canadian population, is still clustered in many of the top controlling sectors of the Canadian society and economy.

Accordingly, WASPs and WASPishness seem very indicative words to use in examining the British-Canadian share in the heritage of a multicultural and bilingual Canada. In particular, there is much historic evidence that WASPishness also had as one of its leading features the desire or expectation that other cultures in Canada should eventually assimilate; that everyone should and would in the long run become just like *us,* absorbed in One Canada, which would turn out to be remarkably WASPlike. Here an identification with American WASPism does look valid, for in that country emphasis on "think American" and "the American way" traditionally have meant that immigrant outsiders should adopt the standards and outlook of the possessing native WASP elements and become assimilated to them. So in Canada, too, WASPishness has frequently seemed to mean assimilation and uni-culture, not the acceptance and development of multicultural heritage.

But *has* WASPishness in Canada really worked out in such a way? Has the British-Canadians' contribution to multiculturalism essentially been that negative: to deny it, oppose it, and strive against it? I do not think so. Whatever the WASPish aims and desires for dominance and absorption, which assuredly have been present, I would contend that in the larger reach of history, the British-Canadian element has actually operated (if often unwittingly) to found and develop a multicultural environment. This did not emerge by accident, though some of it did by necessity. But the essential point is that the British-Canadian community, being multicultural itself in many respects, served to foster a multi-cultural heritage. It was not as WASPish as it tried to be. That, then, is what the rest of this paper seeks to illustrate: the ways in which, in Canada—unlike in the United States—our own British-Canadian WASPs contributed all but inevitably to the growth of ethnic pluralism and the patterns of popular multicultural existence.

In the first place, ethnic identity is often powerfully buttressed by religious distinction. One need not labour this general, worldwide proposition, illustrated by the historic role of Greek Orthodoxy in many Slavic nations, Roman Catholicism in Latin countries, national Protestant churches in northern Europe, or Hinduism, Islam and Buddhism in Asian lands. The much more specific proposition contained here is that in British-dominated Canada—for all its ascendant Protestantism—the legal and constitutional guarantees given to Roman Catholic inhabitants provided through the course of history a built-in basis for ethnic differentiation. Whether these rights were sufficiently fair or full as granted is not under consideration now. What matters instead is that, from the Quebec Act in the eighteenth century to the Ontario separate school laws during the nineteenth, the public aid and recognition awarded to Roman Catholic communities in varying degrees across the country meant that church and state were never as constitutionally separated as in the United States; that a principle of state-supported religious division was acknowledged here, behind which cultural distinctions could shelter and maintain themselves. Plainly, this was of great consequence for French-speaking Canada, for the Catholic Irish who otherwise formed part of English-speaking Canada; and who is to say that Italians or Portuguese in Ontario today do not find the separate school of positive value in preserving their own ethnic identity?

Unquestionably these religious supports for ethnic differentiation have not applied equally and everywhere to the whole range of distinctive culture groups in Canada; although their example has proved capable of extension well beyond the situations out of which they originally emerged. Yet religious minority rights, as granted within a mostly British Canada, meant that its Roman Catholic elements came historically to occupy a much stronger position, politically and socially (if not necessarily economically) than their counterparts long did in the neighbouring United States. In that republic, Irish Catholics until far into the present century were attacked by nativist WASPs as posing an alien menace of papistry and state-church connection to American religious liberty and equality, as were German Catholics, Polish Catholics, Italian Catholics and others in turn. Assuredly the same sort of charges were recurrently and vehemently raised among Protestant British-Canadians; but the situation and the rules of the system were different. Between the Quebec Act of 1774 and Confederation in 1867 the Canada that was so largely led by WASPs enacted a series of special religious entitlements; whether or not it did so reluctantly, for plain expediency, or through political bargaining. In consequence, Canadian WASPism was constantly to be qualified by Catholic co-recipients of power in its very midst. (Notably we had our first Catholic Prime Minister, Sir John Thompson, in 1892: a long time before John Kennedy's presidency in the United States). And so the British-Canadian heritage came to incorporate a potential pattern for future plu-ralism, based on the state-established religious rights initially confirmed for French-Canadian or Irish-Catholic communities.

In the second place, Canada's long-enduring British colonial connection (which British-Canadians generally upheld and which only gradually disappeared) was not, I would argue, necessarily a barrier to multicultural development, but in many ways a positive encouragement. There is indeed a certain popular assumption that if only Canada had had a nice clean break from its British imperial past, perhaps featured by a formal pronouncement of independence, things would be much bet-ter for everyone, especially the non-WASP elements. Perhaps so: I do not seek to examine the whole complex case here; but rather to point out that in ex-colonial countries that do "begin anew", that declare clear-cut independence and a fine fresh start, cultural minorities often are the first to get it in the neck. The mass of citizens are supposed to conform to some new national pattern, generally that of an ascen-dant uni-culture, to be taught, imposed, and required with patriotic fervour. For di-vergences from this national norm are seen as dangerous, if not treasonous; above all, if independence comes accompanied by violence and revolutionary explosion. And least of all, then, is there time and place for those who would cherish and con-serve a differing older heritage, especially one imported originally from outside.

But Canada, historically, has been linked with the other side of revolution: the continuing, conserving side. This other side of the American Revolution produced the Loyalists who helped to shape British Canada, by defending legal colonial insti-tutions and traditional ways. The French-Canadians who faced the British Conquest of 1760 (and that decidedly was a revolution for them) similarly expressed their own desire to conserve what had grown up out of their earlier colonial heritage. And since, as it is often stated, Canada thereafter advanced gradually to national status by evolutionary rather than revolutionary stages, older modes and patterns were adapted rather than disrupted or discarded. Our constitution consequently has been one of the oldest, unbroken forms of government in the world. Our ties with a trans-atlantic past were maintained, and not replaced by self-consciously new political and cultural designs. We did not, as did revolutionary America, look with distrust on whatever was not truly American or indigenous to the New World—what ever that might be. I think it is not without significance, indeed, that our federal parliamen-tary buildings, symbols of the Canadian political entity, would be Victorian British adaptations of the Gothic tradition of medieval Europe, whereas the American re-public largely took up an idealized neo-classicism for its own young national and state capitols.

The upshot of all this is, that if it was right and desirable for French and British to retain old heritages, so it would be for other ethnic groups who later joined them in Canada. There was no revolutionary patriot tradition in this resolutely colonial country which said "you must be born again." Granted, the two older Canadian groups still might display alarm over incoming alien elements as dilutants of their own heritages; but they had no overall moulding pattern to impose instead. For the French, on the whole, the immigrant tide might best go away, or at least move beyond their cherished native patrimony of the St. Lawrence, westward into British Canada. For the British, "foreign" newcomers should no doubt adopt a duly British-Canadian way of life: but just what was this Canadian way? Actually, it *was* there; an historic pattern of gradual adaptation and of conserving change which over time did work to integrate immigrants as Canadians, without cutting off old roots. Yet that was hard to conceptualize or present as an explicit ideal. And so—very much because Canada had emerged but slowly out of British colonialism, without definite proclamation of some overriding new national model—ethnic pluralism based on the continued recognition of past cultural traditions was itself enabled slowly to develop with the increasing influx of non-British, non-French peoples into this country.

The long-lasting colonialism of British-Canadians, (a willing colonialism that was seen essentially as a guarantee against absorption by the mighty United States) was thus an influential, long-term factor that made for a multicultural environment in Canada. Of course, the British-Canadians also talked glowingly of the greatness of the British "race"—of its Law and Liberty, its Parliament and Empire. In that regard, particularly in the later nineteenth and earlier twentieth centuries, they went through an effusion of sentimental, racist-sounding imperialism—though this, as has been effectively noted, was also an expression of an incipient British-Canadian nationalism striving to promote Canada as the brightest jewel in the worldwide British imperial diadem.[1] None the less, they still had to accept the truth that the vast empire they lauded was composed of many races, creeds and colours; and why should not Canada be so comprised itself? If the great ideal was globe-girdling variety, all within a frame of free British institutions, then it was logically difficult not to accept such a pattern within Canada, too. The very "empire-consciousness" of the British-Canadian habit of mind, plus its almost instinctive anti-American leanings, impelled it on into our present era to assert as presumed fact that continental European immigrants were freer to live their own lives and carry on their own customs within the flexible, British-derived Canadian system, than they were within a monolithic American nationality that sought to make everyone conform to it. The Canadian British may have really wanted to see assimilation; but their own imperial heritage brought them, at policy levels, to affirm the mosaic (actually arising in the Canadian West) as superior to the American premise of the melting-pot. Imperialism consequently also pointed towards multiculturalism in Canada.

This—to underline the point—was very much the British form of imperialism, arguably more ready to accept multicultural existence in its holdings than were Spanish, French or perhaps Czarist Russian empires. Such cultural tolerance certainly did not preclude political mastery or economic exploitation; but the fact remained that British imperialism on the whole considerably permitted ethnic differences within a common political power structure; and this often recognized fairly extensive special minority rights, from the Quebec Act (a striking imperial departure in its eighteenth-century day) to the Morley-Minto reforms in early twentieth-century India. I would hazard the proposition that some of this historic imperial procedure inevitably left a mark on the British-Canadians. They came to develop in Canada a nation-state that was based on a common political and economic power structure, but with wide internal diversity—not cultural unity.

Beyond doubt, the French-Canadians also had more than a little to do with this national result. They successfully resisted varied attempts to deny their own cultural existence, largely through gaining a share of control of the political structure itself. Thus they ensured the persistence of dual, legally recognized cultures in Canada. (And where there are two such chartered ethnic partners, call them Founding Peoples or not, it is hard to avoid three, four or more in some degree: let alone to ignore the native peoples forever, who, oddly enough, just might have some claim to being Founding Peoples themselves). In any event, as for the French-Canadians, however much they had to strive to gain or extend their cultural rights, it is important also to recognize that the British-Canadians by no means simply stood in opposition to that determined effort. There were those among the latter element who consistently sought a partnership of the dual peoples in Canada, who looked for a common pattern of parliamentary institutions, within the British imperial model, to hold the two big cultural communities together. That concept did not always work out; it was not always sincerely pursued; but the intention and the endeavour can be repeatedly documented through history. In fact, the aim in Canada when our present federal union was erected in the 1860s was essentially to create a "political nationality", which—it was said by leading spokesmen for Confederation—would include four much older nations: the French, the English, the Irish, and the Scots.

What else was this but a recognition at a crucial stage in Canadian development of the idea of ethnic plurality within political unity? One can see it visually, moreover, in the original Canadian ensign after Confederation, which carried emblems of the four peoples on its field—or in the still existent arms of the City of Montreal, again emblazoning the rose, lily, thistle and shamrock. Small things, possibly; but culturally indicative. Admittedly, also, the symbolic emblazoning, thus, of four culture-groups hardly proves a readiness to add Italian, German, Polish and further armorial bearings to some Canadian coat of arms that would nearly have to rival the other kind of Canadian Shield in monumental size. No, all that needs to be suggested here is that, if in our past not just two charter peoples, but four component ethnic communities could be seen as co-existing within one overall self-governing entity, then it would be the more difficult in the future to deny that other ethnic groups might similarly come to co-exist within the national frame. Certainly a once-large and powerful British-Canadian majority might want, and even expect, to retain its ascendancy as a collective body. Yet that very collectivity had in its own heritage not the principle of the bloodstream nation as a unified folk, but that of the political nation embracing several folk.

Furthermore, from initial settlement until well into the later nineteenth century, the British elements who came to Canada widely lived under what might almost be described as tribalized, as well as localized, conditions. Scots and Irish in particular tended to settle in ethnic blocks in the earlier colonies of British North America: no less than did Icelanders or Ukrainians on the western plains thereafter. From the Scottish Highlanders of Cape Breton to the Lowlanders on the Huron Tract, from the Catholic Irish of Montreal or Ottawa to the Ulstermen of Toronto or Hamilton, there were close-bonded ethnic communities all across English-speaking Canada. Moreover, while persons of English origin tended to congregate less (though some still did so) they did not form the greatly preponderant sector in the total British-Canadian collectivity that they constituted in Great Britain itself. There was a different British mix here. Aside from the leading cities—or until English migrants became by far the largest component of the British influx in the early twentieth century—the British stocks in Canada were markedly weighted on the side of the Scots and Irish. And these were peoples strongly oriented to clan and extended family relationships who had often functioned within quite parochial environments at home. They consequently created their own ethnic mosaic in this country, even if it was far less multiple and varied than is our present one.

Note, too, that in so doing these incomers still remained acceptably British in a British colony. In the United States, WASPs might come to denounce the immigrant trait of ethnic hiving as un-American, a threat to the established Anglo-Saxon integrity and conformity of the republic. But Canada in history (at least beyond New France) grew up with this accepted degree of ethnic, or almost tribal, diversity. The original Loyalists had exhibited it themselves. The real test of collective conformity for colonial Canada was loyalty to Crown and empire. In this regard some of the Catholic Irish might at times arouse suspicions of harbouring disloyal Fenian sentiments over Ireland's wrongs; but in politics in general they complied readily enough. A nineteenth-century Canadian might thus be a Saint John Loyalist or immigrant Irish timber driver, a Lunenberg schoonerman of German ancestry or an American merchant who had first settled into Victoria during the Cariboo gold boom of the 1860s: as long as their British loyalty was duly manifest, other differences could be lived with. In short the uniting pattern of "British" collectivity could best be found (much like that of the British empire itself) in group, clan, or familial ties to the ultimate headship of the Crown. And the Crown was especially venerated when it was worn by an emphatically family figure, Victoria, the Queen-Mother.

Once more a comparison with the United States is instructive. There, the Revolution had established the Sovereign People, of which each citizen, ideally, formed an equal part. But in Canada, the people were self-governing yet not sovereign. The Sovereign was both an individual and a symbol, distant but almost mystical in the reverence it could inspire. Under that monarchical form, to which all owed allegiance, British subjects could and did retain their own local differences and distinctions as members of varied organic cultural or ethnic units; whether as upholders of the Orange Order, the St. George or St. Andrews Society, or as good Irish Catholics who still rendered—as their clergy taught—due obedience to a heretic monarch in those things which were Caesar's.

I do not mean to paint some nostalgic romantic picture of medieval order and contentment under a benign regal sway in bygone Canada. The aim is merely to indicate that the British-Canadian pattern of authority and political perception then favoured the maintenance of group identities and even their exclusiveness, while the American promoted the merging and conforming of groups within a would-be egalitarian society.[2] The former bonussed internal differences without at all opposing the liberty either of individuals or communal units; the latter underwrote democratic equality for all, but, theoretically at least, on the basis of mass conformity within the Sovereign People. Theory and perception do not always work out in practice and conduct; nevertheless, they have their powerful influences. Hence it is still my contention here that the British-Canadian experience, as it developed into a major Canadian heritage, had within it strong propensities that made for the continued growth of multiculturalism in this country. Whereas in the United States, it is only quite recently that its people have awakened to the fact that not everyone becomes assimilated; that the problem of ethnicity remains of vital significance, not merely for blacks and Chicanos, but for a wide assortment of other cultural elements as well.[3]

Coming closer to the present in Canada, one should observe that succeeding waves of British immigrants, from before the First World War up to the 1970s, could by and large no longer be described as tribalized or parochial in their make-up, arriving as they did from a highly industrialized and urbanized British society. The same of course, had long been true for those who came and still come here from the United States. Moreover, it is quite a time since we have had stalwart peasants in sheepskin coats arriving from continental Europe, and most recent Caribbean or Asian immigrants to Canada have not been simple agriculturalists either. Yet, to revert to the British-Canadian element, what matters chiefly is the heritage which they had already built up well before the present era of our modern, urban, industrial Canada—prior to the final withering away of the British empire, and the cosmopolitan (yet equally regional) condition in which this country and the world now finds itself. The British-Canadian component has today changed vastly; and not least from now becoming but one more of the minorities in the total Canadian population, large and potent as it does remain.

Where is WASPishness today? In its would-be assimilative aspects we still hear from it: from those who still talk of One Canada to which no "hyphenated-Canadians" need apply, from self-styled Loyalists in Ontario, New Brunswick or Alberta who are not the U.E.L.'s of yesteryear; from those who think it would be so patriotic and simple—as indeed it would—if we all spoke English, thought English, and conformed to one hundred per cent Canadianism—without saying what is in that hundred-proof bottle! It is seen also in attacks on the creeping menace of bilingualism in high places (how slow can you creep?), and at least in some of the alarmed reactions to the immigrants' presence in our cities, when they are held to foster poverty, crime and violence in the same way the Irish were as immigrants, back in the 1850s.

There is, no less, the other side to WASPishness which I have endeavoured to set forth here. And in my view this comprehends a much more vital and significant part of the historic British-Canadian heritage: its empirical acceptance of diversity, thereby affording factual consent if not intellectual approval to ethnic variety; its manifest record of acknowledging minority rights and internal community differences under law; and the sense it has repeatedly shown, however tacitly, that within a common political allegiance, regional and ethnic differences can be maintained and protected—so that the resulting integration, not unification, of the various component groups in Canada can serve each or all together as the best means of their living and growing within a free society. This last may be preaching; but I seek to preach. I do believe that the British-Canadian heritage has something to offer all Canadians that is not just represented by power or wealth. Nor is it the case that French-Canadians and many other Canadian groups have always appreciated the value of live-and-let-live; even though they may assuredly have suffered as minorities themselves. In truth, minorities need to practice tolerance, accept differences, resist their own internal conforming pressures no less than do majorities. Now that the British-Canadians have also become a minority in our present state of multiculturalism perhaps they may assert as much. That side of WASPishness is worth marking and remembering, at any rate.

Endnotes

1. Berger, Carl. *The Sense of Power: Studies in the Ideas of Canadian Imperialism, 1867–1914.* (Toronto, 1970), *passim* and especially Chapter 10.
2. Careless, J.M.S. "Limited Identities in Canada," *Canadian Historical Review.* (Toronto), Vol. I, No. 1, March 1969, pp. 4–6.
3. Glazer, N. and Moynihan, D.P., ed. *Ethnicity: Theory and Experience.* (Cambridge, 1975), Introduction especially.

Jews, Human Rights, and the Making of a New Canada

Irving Abella

PICKING A TOPIC for this address, as most of my predecessors have observed, is almost as difficult as writing it. After much reflection, and after many false starts, a whole series of events came together which would choose my subject for me. I remembered Judith Fingard's dazzling presidential speech two years earlier in Ottawa in which she showed that the personal history of the historian was crucial to the choice of his or her area of research. Then I was informed that the Royal Society would join us in our sessions and had selected human rights in Canada as their theme.

As well, the year 2000 marks several important anniversaries in my family. Exactly 75 years ago this week, my father arrived in Halifax, a bewildered 15 year old from Eastern Europe escaping the bitter pogroms and vicious anti-Semitism that would soon engulf his world and destroy it. He loved his new country, and despite the antipathy directed towards him and other Jews during the first part of his life here, he watched a new and better Canada take shape before his eyes. He worked hard every day of his life to make sure that this country would not regret allowing him in.

Twenty-five years later, exactly 50 years ago this month, another child arrived at Pier 21 in Halifax. This little 4 year old was born in a displaced persons camp in Germany, the daughter of survivors of concentration camps who had lost everything—friends, fortune and family, including a 2 year old child—to the murderous Nazis. They were determined to do well in their new home, and they succeeded brilliantly. Today that little girl sits on the Court of Appeals of Ontario, though I must admit that when I married her, Rosie Silberman was still a lowly law student.

So it all came together. Human rights, Jews, the holocaust: the new Canada versus the old; anti-Semitism and xenophobia; the year 2000. When and why and how did Canada change from the benighted, nativist nation it was a generation or two ago, to the humane, decent, culturally diverse nation it is today? And finally, in support of the Fingard law, when I was elected, the resident CHA historian and secretary, Don Wright, reminded me that I was the first Jewish president in the 73-year history of the Canadian Historical Association.

And so I chose as my topic: Jews, Human Rights, and the Making of a New Canada.

The Canada of the first half of the last century and particularly from the 1920s through the 1940s was a foreboding place for Jews, as it was for most immigrants. Closed to most of the world by racist immigration laws that divided the peoples of the world into preferred and (mostly) non-preferred, Canada was a country permeated with xenophobia, nativism and anti-Semitism. The Jew was the pariah of Canadian society, demeaned, denounced and discriminated against.

For Canadian Jews in these years, quotas and restrictions were a way of life. According to a 1938 study by the Canadian Jewish Congress, few of the country's teachers and none of its school principals were Jewish. The banks, insurance companies and the large industrial and commercial interests, it charged, also excluded Jews from employment. Department stores did not hire Jews as salespeople. Jewish doctors could not get hospital appointments, and when one Jewish doctor, Sam Rabinovich, was hired as an intern at the Montreal hospital, the other interns went out on strike, along with other doctors, closing the hospital for a week until Rabinovich was fired.[1]

If the Jew experienced difficulty finding a job or getting an education, finding a place to live or to vacation was even harder. Increasingly, restrictive covenants were placed on various properties prohibiting their sale to Jews, and at beaches and resorts throughout the nation, signs were springing up that banned Jews. So-called swastika clubs of young hoodlums were formed to intimidate Jews and keep them away from "restricted" beaches. The threat of violence was so great that Jewish leaders took the unusual step of warning the community "not to hold large gatherings in any portion of the city where such a gathering is liable to arouse the animosity of certain classes of the non-Jewish population."[2] Indeed, so threatening did the situation appear that a Jewish member of the Ontario legislature warned his co-religionists: "Unless something is done quickly then Jewish people may well meet the same fate in Canada that the Jews are meeting in Germany . . . No fire is so easily kindled as anti-Semitism. The fire is dormant in Canada, it has not yet blazed up, but the spark is there. Germany is not the only place with prejudice."[3]

Why was Canada so anti-Semitic? There are various reasons. To some extent the massive anti-Semitic propaganda of the Nazis had its impact. Some were taken in by it and by such American hate mongers as Henry Ford, Father Coughlin, Gerard L. K. Smith and dozens of others. It was also a time of depression and the search for scapegoats invariably ended at a Jewish doorstep. Jews were also publicly seen and denounced as troublemakers. The prominence of Jewish names in the left-wing movement seduced many gullible or malevolent Canadians into believing that most Jews were Communists. Obviously, many others hated Jews for religious reasons.

---

1 Canadian Jewish Congress Archives, Montreal, (CJC). Files on Anti-Semitism, 1934–1939.

2 Ibid.

3 Toronto *Star,* 24 April 1933.

Much of the anti-Semitism in Quebec and in fundamentalist areas of western Canada originated from religious teachings. Jews had killed Christ, had refused to repent or convert to Christianity and, therefore, were damned.

In addition, many Canadians were reacting to the three decades of almost un-limited immigration. The rapid rise of nativism in the 1920s came out of a concern for the type of Canada that these millions of uneducated, illiterate aliens would pro-duce. For many, the Jew, since he tended to live in cities and therefore was the most visible of immigrants, symbolized this mongrelization. Anti-Semitism to many, there-fore, was simply an extreme form of Canadian nationalism. Also, many immigrants, particularly from Eastern Europe, had brought over traditional anti-Semitic phobias. An anti-Jewish tradition of many generations could not be dissolved overnight.

All of these were factors contributing to the anti-Semitism that permeated Canada in these years. One factor, however, stands out, and that was a feeling amongst many Canadians, especially the opinion-makers—the politicians, academ-ics, writers, businessmen and journalists who set the tone for a society—that the Jew simply did not fit into their concept of Canada. Their's was to be a country of home-steaders and farmers. Despite what the Jews were doing in Palestine at the time—turning a desert green—few Canadians felt that Jews could make successful agricul-turalists. Those immigrants who did not farm were expected to go into the woods, or mines or smelters, or canneries, or textile mills, or join the construction gangs needed to build and fuel the great Canadian boom. And most Canadians felt that Jews did not fit this pattern, that they were city people, in a country attempting to build up its rural base, that they were peddlers and shopkeepers in a country that wanted loggers and miners. They were seen as a people with brains in a country that preferred brawn, as a people with strong minds in a country that wanted strong backs.

What is most astonishing about this anti-Semitism is how few and powerless were Canadian Jews at this time. They made up just over 1 per cent of the population and had no political or economic clout. Clearly they could be seen as a threat only by the paranoid. Equally surprising was the silence of the churches in the face of this fright-ful and oppressive anti-Jewish feeling.[4]

Perhaps Canada's attitude was best symbolized by its treatment of a young, bril-liant law student who arrived back in Canada in the 1930s fresh from an outstand-ing academic record at Harvard. His applications to teach at the universities of Manitoba and Toronto were rejected because he was Jewish. He found it difficult to rent a home in Toronto because many areas of the city were restricted. His wife, a trained cosmetician, was turned away by Eaton's because she was Jewish. To survive he agreed to write head-notes for court cases for a law journal at 50¢ a piece. Even-

---

4 Alan Davies and Marilyn Nefsky. *How Silent Were the Churches? Canadian Protestantism and the Jewish Plight during the Nazi Era*, (Waterloo, 1997).

tually he was hired by the University of Toronto but only after the head of the law department wrote a bizarre letter to a doubting president testifying that though the young man was a Jew, he was nonetheless "a loyal British Subject, loyal to our institutions and traditions . . . [who] . . . will not disgrace the university . . . [and who has] . . . sworn on a bible before witnesses that [he is not] a member of any subversive movement."[5]

And this is how Bora Laskin finally began an academic career that would eventually lead, in a newer, different Canada, to the chief justiceship of the Supreme Court.

The University of Toronto was not alone. As Gerald Tulchinsky has shown, most universities were determined to limit their Jewish student enrolments and to keep their faculties free of Jews.[6] And they succeeded. Most notorious of all was McGill. For years it was an open secret that standards of admissions were far higher for Jewish applicants than for anyone else. And from the university's point of view, for good reason. As principal Sir Arthur Currie warned, so many Jews would qualify for admission that there would scarcely be any room for non-Jews. McGill, he cautioned, would become the Yeshiva University of the North. His own Dean of Arts, R.A. Mackay, was even more brutal. Jews, he said, "are of no use to this country . . . [because] their traditions and practices do not fit in with high civilization in a very new country."[7] It was this attitude that explains Canadian university behaviour during the refugee crisis of the 1930s and 40s.

Of the tens of thousands of Jewish intellectuals, scientists, writers, and artists driven out of German universities and schools, only a tiny handful, perhaps a dozen, found jobs in Canadian academic institutions. Though some Canadian professors supported the movement of Jewish scholars to Canada, most were indifferent or aggressively hostile. Indeed, a past president of the Canadian Historical Association praised the government for its restrictionist policy and warned that if the policy became more flexible, Canadian universities would be flooded with Jews. What would happen, he asked, to the country's graduate students if Canada allowed in European Jewish academics? There would be no jobs for them, he charged, since the Jews would have taken them all.[8]

5 Irving Abella, "The Making of a Chief Justice: Bora Laskin, The Early Years" in *The Cambridge Lectures 1989*. F.E. McArdle ed. (Montreal, 1990): 164.

6 Gerald Talchinsky. *Branching Out: The Transformation of the Canadian Jewish Community* (Toronto, 1998).

7 McGill University Archives. Mackay to Jenkins. 23 April 1926.

8 National Archives of Canada (NAC). R.J. Manion Papers, MG 27-III B7, G.F.G. Stanley to Manion, 21 December 1938.

At the annual Conference of Canadian Universities in 1939, a session was held to discuss the plight of the refugee intellectual. The chair of the meeting, a distinguished Canadian scientist, reassured his audience that they need not be concerned; no sacrifice would have to be made by them. Rather a resolution was unanimously passed calling on the government not to admit any refugee who might take a job from a Canadian and demanding that all those refugees already in the country on temporary permits who could only find jobs "for which other Canadians might be qualified" be deported.[9] This resolution was passed in May of 1939, just three months before the Nazis marched into Poland.

With the onset of war, if Canadian attitudes towards Jews changed at all, it was for the worse. Fully half of the Canadian people, according to a Gallup poll in 1943, indicated that they wanted no more Jews in the country. At about the same time, Maurice Duplessis was campaigning through Quebec waving a copy of a document, which he charged showed that the federal government had made a deal with the International Zionist Brotherhood, a fictitious group, to settle 100,000 Jews in Quebec in return for campaign funds for Liberal candidates.[10] Duplessis was decisively elected.

Even the end of the war brought no respite for Canadian Jews. Discovery of the Nazi barbarities against the Jews, and the graphic horrors of the Holocaust detailed by newspapers, magazines, and newsreels in theatres across Canada did not lessen anti-Semitic feelings. Rather, it seemed to exacerbate them. According to all the opinion polls, anti-Jewish feeling actually rose in Canada between 1945 and 1948. Indeed a notorious Gallup Poll in 1946 indicated that Canadians preferred almost any kind of immigrants, including Germans, to Jews. Almost 50% of those questioned were opposed to any further Jewish immigration to Canada.[11]

Nevertheless it is clear that by 1948, attitudes in Canada were beginning to change. Mackenzie King had retired; the venomous Frederick Blair, the xenophobic Deputy Minister of Immigration, was dead. And new leaders with new ideas and expanded visions began moving into positions of power. Many felt that Canada's hour of opportunity had finally arrived. With most of the world's economies still devastated, Canada was on the brink of becoming a genuine world power. All she needed was more people. Thus Canada's immigration doors were flung open and over the next decade, over a million and a half newcomers poured through, including thousands of Jews, most of them survivors of death camps.

By 1948 as well, the pervasive anti-Semitism of earlier years had receded. Obviously, the horrors of the Holocaust shocked many Canadians; others were caught up

---

9 CJC, Constance Hayward, Report on National Conference of Canadian Universities. May 1939.

10 Irving Abella and Harold Troper, *None Is Too Many: Canada and the Jews of Europe, 1933–1948* (Toronto, 1982), chapter 6.

11 CJC, Canadian Institute of Public Opinion News Service Releases, 1946–7.

in the dramatic struggle of the Jews in Palestine to create their own state. Though official Canadian policy was to support the British attempts to forcibly blockade Jewish refugees from entering Palestine, it seemed that a large number of Canadians sympathized with the plucky struggle of the beleaguered Jews in the Holy Land.

It was at this propitious moment that Canadian Jewish leaders chose to launch an all-out offensive against discriminatory practices in Canada.

This was not the first time such an attempt had been made. In the late 1930s, the Canadian Jewish Congress had set up a committee called the Joint Public Relations Committee (JPRC) with the cooperation of another Jewish communal organization, the B'nai B'rith, to deal with discrimination against Jews in employment. But its strategy was fatally flawed. It was decided to approach firms that discriminated in a "social, friendly manner." As the Chair of the committee put it: "By personal contact and conversation with various employers, a great deal of constructive work can be done."[12] This strategy was simply a continuation of the quiet diplomacy used by the Congress in its vain efforts to get the Canadian government to allow Jewish refugees into Canada. Predictably the strategy proved hopeless. The enveloping anti-Semitism of the period had been too powerful to be pierced.

But the JPRC persevered and believed that if it could not compel employers to end their discriminatory behaviour, at least it could embarrass them by publicizing their conduct. And as it turned out, amongst the worst offenders was the Government of Canada. So deeply embedded was anti-Semitism in the National Selective Service, the government's employment agency, that even war industries starved for workers would regularly reject Jewish applicants. NSS officials stubbornly refused to refer Jewish workers to various munitions plants, prompting even the non-partisan Canadian Legion at the behest of the Congress to pass a resolution demanding the elimination of discriminatory practices in war industries. Only then did the Director of the Service, after a meeting with Jewish leaders, issue a directive that the Service must stop its discriminatory behaviour at once. The directive, however, had little effect, and NSS officials continued their behaviour until the end of the war.[13]

Nor did the Congress have much success in its campaigns to prohibit discriminatory signs and advertisements or to stop the anti-Semitic abuse by government officials. In a well-publicized incident a Jewish landlord complained to a Toronto city official that he had been called a "dirty Jew" by a municipal employee. The official's response was: "Well then, don't be a dirty Jew." When Congress complained to the mayor, it was told that being called a dirty Jew "doesn't necessarily make you one." Even worse, it was reported that the Mayor of the City of Toronto had referred to one of his aldermen as "a dirty Jew." Congress leaders attempted to meet the mayor.

---

12 CJC, Minutes, Plenary Session, 1936.

13 CJC, Discrimination in Employment files, 1940–5.

His response: "I have no more respect for Jews than Hitler has." The mayor was easily re-elected.[14]

In 1943, angered by a decision of the Port Elgin Council to revoke the licences of all hotels and tourist homes that admitted Jews as guests, a Liberal member of the Ontario Legislature introduced a bill to bar discrimination in housing and accommodation. The Congress campaign to support the bill was joined by the newly created Canadian Council of Christians and Jews whose leader, the Reverend Claris Silcox of the United Church, wrote Ontario Premier George Drew: "It is no use fighting Nazism abroad and condoning it in Ontario, nor it is any use throwing stones at Quebec for its anti-Semitism while we encourage it in our province."[15]

For once the campaign against discrimination had some success. Concerned about the real threat of the CCF, Drew's minority Conservative government introduced the Racial Discriminatory Act that prohibited the publication and display of discriminatory signs and symbols. Unfortunately it provided for few sanctions and was largely ignored.

But it was as far as the Drew government was prepared to go. Supported by the Toronto *Globe* and the *Telegram,* who argued that anti-discrimination laws were a threat to free speech and would lead Canada down the path of dictatorship, for the rest of his tenure as premier, Drew refused to meet any Jewish lobby groups.

By 1946 the Congress was ready to try again. As Jewish soldiers were returning from overseas they found the same old restrictions barring their way. In a much publicized incident, a veteran was fired from his salesman's job in a Toronto hardware store when it was discovered he was Jewish. "I would lose customers," the storekeeper explained. Others found that skating rinks, swimming pools, golf clubs and hotels refused them admission despite their heroic efforts on behalf of their country.[16]

Outraged that this kind of behaviour was perfectly legal, the Congress organized a protest march of various ethnic and religious groups from City Hall to the Icelandia Skating Rink, which had refused to remove its signs restricting admission to Gentiles. As a result of the march, the coverage of it by the Toronto *Star,* and a meeting with Congress officials, the Toronto Police Board ruled that licences of public places were subject to cancellation if the licence holder discriminated against any minority. This was the first of many victories for the Jewish Public Relations Committee and for its new partner, the aggressive Jewish Labour Committee. Its 50,000 feisty members would provide the backbone to the Congress' political lobbying.

The partnership was not a happy one. The JPRC, composed of middle class businessmen and professionals, never felt comfortable with the combative trade unionist leaders of the Jewish Labour Committee. The former preferred a cautious

14 CJC, Files on Anti-Semitism, 1939–45.

15 Public Archives of Ontario (PAO). Drew Papers, RG 3, Box 434, File 74–6, February–March, 1943.

16 CJC, Files on Anti-Semitism, op. cit.

492 — Chapter Nineteen

approach; the latter believed in the words of its director Kalman Kaplansky that "you have to be nasty and noisy if you want to get anything done."[17] But in the end, both submerged their differences and joined together to fight the battle for human rights.

The campaign was given a boost by J. Keillor Mackay of the Supreme Court of Ontario who ruled in 1945 that the restrictive covenant clause barring the sale of property to Jews and others was not in the public interest and therefore illegal. Though the case worked its way through the courts for another five years before the Supreme Court gave a definitive judgement, the first blow against discrimination had been struck. Others would soon follow.

A massive publicity campaign was launched by Jewish organizations. Led by two activists, Saul Hayes and Ben Kayfetz, the JPRC conducted a survey documenting many hundreds of cases where race, nationality, or religion had prevented someone from getting a job. Speakers and literature were sent to various groups across the country encouraging them to lobby for the removal of discriminatory laws. Institutes for race relations were founded and the National Film Board and the CBC were persuaded to develop supportive films and programmes.[18] Meanwhile the Jewish Labour Committee distributed thousands of pamphlets, published newsletters and articles, and lobbied extensively amongst labour leaders and politicians. Between the two organizations, hundreds of thousands of Canadian households were reached.[19]

A national poll in 1947 reported that 64% of Canadians were in favour of removing discriminatory hiring policies. Yet the Ontario government was not convinced. It rejected any attempts to introduce new legislation on the grounds that discrimination in Ontario was so negligible that it warranted no corrective action.

Only days after rebuffing opposition attempts to present anti-discriminatory bills to the House, the Ontario government suffered a grievous blow. Ben Kayfetz had approached a journalist, Pierre Berton, to write an article on discrimination in Canada. Entitled "No Jews Need Apply," it appeared in *Maclean's Magazine* in November of 1948, and did for Canada, and specifically Ontario, what the movie "Gentlemen's Agreement" had done a year earlier for American audiences south of the border. Berton concluded that discrimination in the province was so widespread that only legislation could change it. The research for the article was done primarily through test cases. Berton had one woman call for advertised jobs using the name Greenberg. She then called back using the name Grimes. Of 47 calls, Greenberg got 17 interviews, while Grimes got 41. In 21 cases Greenberg was told the job was filled, though a week later most of the jobs were still being advertised. Berton then followed up by contacting the firms. He wrote that most would never hire a Jew over a Gen-

---

17 Interview, Kalman Kaplansky, June 1982.

18 Herbert Sohn, "Human Rights Legislation in Ontario; A Study of Social Action," unpublished Ph.D. thesis, University of Toronto (1975), chapter 1.

19 Arnold Bruner, "Citizen Power: The Story of Ontario Human Rights Legislation," *Viewpoints* 3 (1981): 5.

tile, since the "Jewish temperament" was not conducive to employment among Gentiles, while others simply said that Jews "don't know their place," and they would never knowingly hire a Jew. Finally, one munitions plant manager was insulted by Berton's allegation, proudly arguing that of 1700 employees, 2 were Jews.[20] Berton concluded that anti-Semitism was as strong as ever in Canada, especially in professions such as nursing, engineering, banking, university teaching, and judging. There were only two Jewish judges in the entire country.

Using the article as ammunition, the Jewish community increased its pressure on both federal and provincial governments to pass legislation to deal with the problems uncovered by Berton. Their case was strengthened by newspaper coverage of a number of disturbing incidents taking place in Ontario. A Black woman was rejected from a nurses' training programme in the Owen Sound General Hospital. Other Blacks reported they could not find jobs as nurses anywhere in Canada. A Black war veteran and community leader in Hamilton was refused entry to a public dance because officials felt it "would be bad for business."[21] Lamely, the Ontario government claimed it could do nothing since "you cannot legislate tolerance." Discrimination, the province's Attorney General claimed, could not be eradicated by statute. It would "have to erode gradually, on its own."[22]

Worse for the Ontario government, attention was now focused on the town of Dresden, where it was reported that 4 of town's 5 restaurants would not serve Black nor would the hotels allow Blacks as guests. Though Dresden was important to Black history as the burial place for the man thought to be the model for the protagonist of *Uncle Tom's Cabin,* and had been a haven for Blacks escaping slavery, it was in the 1950s little different from any town in the southern US. Blacks were excluded socially and economically from town life: barbershops, beauty salons, taverns and pool halls refused admission and service to all Blacks.

By now the campaign of the Jewish community was gaining important new allies. Various church and service groups offered their support, as did the Association of Civil Liberties, an important legal organization. Its most significant convert, however, was the new Premier of Ontario, Leslie Frost. A pragmatist, Frost was far more sympathetic to the objectives of the Jewish community than had been his predecessor George Drew. Frost was also very much aware of the changing demography in Ontario. The province was becoming increasingly less British, as the post-war boom was bringing tens of thousands of immigrants from Southern and Eastern Europe. And they were settling in the cities of the province, not on its farms. At the same time, the number of trade unionists had increased by some 65% in a decade. The new Canada was beginning to take shape.

---

20 *Maclean's Magazine,* November 1948.

21 CJC, Files on Anti-Semitism, op.cit.

22 Sohn, op. cit. p. 11.

Frost was keenly aware that he was leading a new Ontario whose votes his rural-based Conservative party would be hard-pressed to attract. But he was equally aware that many elements of his own party were adamantly opposed to the changes proposed by the Jewish lobby groups. As well, he had heard that any new legislation might increase tensions amongst Protestants, Catholics, and Jews. His initial instinct was to eschew legislation and to move slowly, to allow the majority to voluntarily treat all minorities fairly rather than to enjoin them to do so by law.

Meanwhile members of both the JPRC and the Jewish Labour Committee were unrelenting in their lobbying. They arranged for delegations to meet the Premier and his Cabinet colleagues; they spoke at hundreds of meetings across the country, they planted articles in the press, they met editorial boards; they distributed pamphlets; they embarked on letter-writing campaigns and they arranged for talks on radio and to various service clubs of prominent speakers who supported their views. One of these, Senator Wayne Morse (a Republican from Oregon), spoke so passionately and persuasively on the Trans-Canada network of CBC radio in favour of fair employment legislation that it had a real impact on one of his listeners, the Premier of Ontario, Leslie Frost.[23]

By 1951 it was clear that the lobbying had made a real difference. Most Ontario newspapers were now in favour of anti-discrimination legislation, as were many city councils across the province. And so it seemed was Premier Frost. He arranged a quick meeting with the Jewish and Civil Liberties organizations and told them secretly that he would be enacting an anti-discrimination law in the next session of the House.[24]

Three weeks later, in the Speech from the Throne, the Government of Ontario announced its intention of introducing a fair employment practices act, which would bar discrimination in hiring because of the race, creed, colour, nationality, ancestry, or place of origin. It was a remarkable piece of legislation and the historians who have written about it (particularly James Walker and Ruth Frager and Carmela Patrias) have described it as one of the Jewish community's great victories in this country.[25] But more would follow. There would be no let-up in the Jewish groups' activities. They would act as watchdogs of the legislation to ensure that there would be no backsliding.

Of course employment discrimination did not disappear in Ontario, but the Act marked the beginning of an era in which discrimination was no longer acceptable.

---

23 Ben Kayfetz, "On Community Relations in Ontario in the 1940s," *Canadian Jewish Studies* 2 (1994): 60.

24 Ibid.

25 Carmela Patrias and Ruth Frager, "'This is our country, these are our rights': Minorities and the Origins of Ontario's Human Rights Campaigns," *Canadian Historical Review* 82/1 (March 2001): 1–35; James Walker, "The Jewish Phase in the Movement for Racial Equality in Canada," in *Heritage in Transition: Essays in Canadian Jewish Studies*, Irving Abella and Joseph Levy eds. (McGill-Queen's University Press, forthcoming).

Both the JPRC and the Jewish Labour Committee saw the legislation as the "thin edge of the wedge." Once the Ontario government had admitted that discrimination in employment was unjust and immoral, how could it be condoned in other areas such as housing?

Predictably, the moment the Act had passed the human rights groups around the JPRC began lobbying for a fair accommodations practices law. And Dresden became the focus for the struggle. So outrageous was the anti-Black behaviour of many of the town's businesses, that a huge lobby led by the Jewish Labour Committee was mounted to compel the government to introduce legislation preventing discrimination in housing and service. And in March of 1954, the Frost government introduced just such a bill in the Ontario legislature.

One final item remained on the community's agenda: to create, as the director of the Jewish Labour Committee described it in 1954, one department "which could administer the [anti-discrimination] laws, establish contact with the public at large and be in charge of educational programmes."[26] Such a human-rights commission had been established by the Socialist government of Saskatchewan in 1947, and the activists in Ontario believed it was time to create one in their province.

For the next few years the JPRC, the Jewish Labour Committee, and the Association for Civil Liberties and their allied organizations made this campaign their highest priority. In 1956 they submitted a lengthy brief to the government outlining the need for a human-rights commission and outlining its powers. In response, the Ontario government created the Ontario Anti-Discrimination Commission.

However, not satisfied with the limited powers of this commission, human rights advocates demanded one with, in Kaplansky's words, "real teeth." And it was clear that such a commission was necessary. Studies sponsored by the Congress indicated that discrimination in hiring and housing was still widespread. A private study commissioned by Tom Eberlee, the personal assistant to the Premier, produced similar results. Finally in 1962 the government created the Ontario Human Rights Commission, many of whose powers were those recommended in the brief of the Canadian Jewish Congress five years before.

The victory was now largely complete. Though obviously racism and discrimination would not disappear, there were now in place mechanisms and legislation to protect minorities. With both anti-discrimination statutes and human rights commissions successfully established, not only in Ontario but in most provinces, the human rights lobby could move onto other issues.

Thus, by the 1960s, Canada had turned the corner. For Jews, as well as for this country's other minorities, that decade was a watershed. Before it existed the old Canada, parochial, nativist, exclusionary; beyond it a new Canada was taking shape, a Canada of diversity, colour, vibrancy, a Canada of open minds rather than closed

---

26 CJC, Survey of Group Relations in Canada, Kalman Kaplansky: 3–5.

doors, a Canada in which Jews and other ethnic groups were quickly becoming part of the Canadian mainstream, and were seen as part of the solution rather than as part of the problem.

The decade began with Canada finally repealing its odious racist immigration laws and opening itself up to all the world's nations, and it closed with a government commitment to implement an official policy of multiculturalism. And it was in the 1960s that all of the barriers, restrictions and quotas against Jews crumbled, one by one, sector by sector. At long last, after 200 years in the country, the Jewish community would be able to play out its dreams and become an integral part of the very same Canadian society that had excluded it for so long. It was, said an observer, a social earthquake, demolishing creaky, outmoded customs and institutions and creating a new Canadian society largely unrecognizable to Jews of a previous generation. It was in these years, recalled the long-time director of the Canadian Jewish Congress, Saul Hayes, that Canadian Jews finally became "white."[27]

And with reason. The elevation of Louis Rasminsky to Governor of the Bank of Canada in 1961 indicated that Ottawa would no longer be, in the words of a former British High Commissioner Joe Garner, the most "anti-Jewish capital city" he had ever encountered. The breakthrough meant that the "Ottawa men" would now include Jews, as they would soon include women. A few years later, Herb Gray became the first Jew since Confederation to sit in a federal cabinet, and David Lewis the first to lead a national political party. In that decade as well, hospitals finally began accepting Jewish doctors and major law firms began hiring their first Jewish lawyers. And of course, the universities dropped their quotas and restrictions, best symbolized by the appointment at the University of Alberta of Max Wyman as Canada's first Jewish university president.

Hayes, Kaplansky and Kayfetz and all the other intrepid men and women in the human rights trenches of the 1940s and 50s had succeeded far better than they realized. They had helped set the table not only for Jews, but for other minority groups as they made their way in Canadian society, a path made easier because of Jewish activists of a previous generation.

Of course the battle for human rights in Canada is not yet won. Racist, homophobic, and xenophobic attitudes still manifest themselves too often, and much remains to be done. Yet who can deny that today's Canada is a far better place, and that its minorities better integrated thanks in large part to the trail-blazing efforts 50 years ago by the Canadian Jewish Congress and the Jewish Labour Committee.

---

27 Interview, Saul Hayes, June 1980.

CHAPTER TWENTY

Multiculturalism: Practice

Introduction

Canada's commitment to multiculturalism is real. It is embodied in the primary law of the land, the Charter of Rights and Freedoms. But multiculturalism as policy and multiculturalism as practice can mean two different things. In other words, if multiculturalism is real, racism is also real. Lawrence Hill is a novelist. But in 2001 he published *Black Berry, Sweet Juice: on being black and white in Canada,* a memoir about growing up with a black father and a white mother, about coming into his own and finding his racial identity in a mixed-race family. Among other things, he interrogates what he calls The Question. What is the question? And how does it work to create insiders and outsiders? Shani Mootoo grew up in Trinidad, in a family of mixed Indian and Nepalese roots. When she was 19 she moved to Canada to study at the University of Western Ontario; she eventually moved to Vancouver. In this story, she captures something of the loneliness, isolation and broken expectations of the immigrant experience. What does having a garden of her own symbolize? Tamara Vukov is an academic. Her article, "Performing the Immigrant Nation at Pier 21" studies Pier 21 in Halifax, Nova Scotia. From 1928 to 1971 Pier 21 served as the point of entry into Canada for over one million immigrants, refugees and war-time evacuees. It is now a National Historic Site. What does Vukov mean by the phrase, performing the immigrant nation? What is remembered at Pier 21? What is forgotten?

The Question

Lawrence Hill

CANADIANS HAVE A FAVOURITE pastime, and they don't even realize it. They like to ask—they absolutely have to ask—where you are from if you don't look convincingly white. They want to know it, need to know it, simply must have that information. They just can't relax until they have pinpointed, to their satisfaction, your geographic and racial coordinates. They can go almost out of their minds with curiosity, as when driven by the need for food, water, or sex, but once they've finally managed to find out precisely where you were born, who your parents were, and what your racial make-up is, then, man, do they feel better. They can breathe easy and get back to the business of living.

I don't have the math background of, say, an actuary, but I can manage the following calculation. I am forty-four years old. Since about age ten, I have been asked "So what are you, anyway?" and all its variations. ("Where are you from?" "Yes, but where are you really from?" "Yes, but where were your parents born?") That's thirty-four years I've been fielding The Question.

Let's assume I have been asked The Question once a day over these past thirty-four years. 34 x 365 = 12,410. But that would be an underestimation because it fails to factor in the two years I lived in Quebec. During those two years, I was most certainly asked The Question five times per day. *("D'où viens-tu?" "Quelles sont tes souches?" "Tes parents sont de quel pays?")* An extra four times per day for two years in Quebec City would add on another 2,920 questions. 12,410 + 2,920 = 15,330.

That, ladies and gentlemen, is the absolute minimum number of times Canadians have asked me either "Where are you from?" or *"D'où viens-tu?"* or any of the multitudinous variations.

Minelle Mahtani, whose doctoral thesis at the University of London examined identity among mixed-race Canadian women, tells a story of how she was walking alone one day in Toronto's St. Lawrence Market area, when someone tapped on her shoulder. Minelle turned around to find a woman who seemed motivated by a particular urgency—she had obviously been watching Minelle and just had to know where she was from.

"Ah," you may say, "but it's just curiosity. What's wrong with people being curious?"

I am a patient man. So patient that my children can confidently remove a chocolate chip cookie right from the edge of my fingers, or raid my dish of French vanilla ice cream and leave nothing but the cloudy bowl, and still know that I won't lose my cool. But even this patience was exhausted some time around the 5,000 mark of the 15,330 questions I have faced.

What is wrong with The Question? Nothing at all—when it is asked at the right time, when it results from a genuine interest in you as a person, and when the person asking the question actually accepts the answer.

Let's dissect the interrogation process. Imagine me at a party, sipping mineral water. A stranger walks up.

STRANGER: "Do you mind my asking where you are from?" [This is code for "What is your race?"]

ME: "Canada." [This is code for "Screw off."]

STRANGER: "Yes, but you know, where are you *really* from?" [This is code for "You know what I mean, so why are you trying to make me come out and say it?"]

ME: "I come from the foreign and distant metropolis of Newmarket. That's Newmarket, Ontario. My place of birth. [Code for "I'm not letting you off the hook, buster."]

STRANGER: "But your place of origin? Your parents? What are your parents?" [Code for "I want to know your race, but this is making me very uncomfortable because somehow I feel that I'm not supposed to ask that question."]

This exchange is like the opening of a chess game. The first few moves are pretty standard: White moves Pawn to King Four, Black responds with Pawn to King Four, White answers with Knight to King Bishop Three, and Black answers with Knight to King Bishop Three. From this point on, the possibilities multiply.

I can give a teaser, such as "My parents came up from the States," which frustrates the questioner, who really wants to know my parents' racial background.

I can give it all up and explain that I have a black father and a white mother.

I can invent an answer, such as "My father is a White Russian and my mother is an Ethiopian Jew."

Or I can turn the question around, as in "Why are you asking me this?"

And that is the nub of the issue. Why am I always asked that question? Why do people need to know the answer so desperately?

Have you ever noticed that black people rarely put other people of any race through the ringer like this? That's because many of them have been asked The Question more times than they care to count. They're sophisticated enough—by virtue of their own experiences—to understand that many people resent this line of interrogation.

Is it truly innocent? Can The Question be chalked up to basic curiosity? I don't think so. Children are the most innocent and curious of all human beings, yet they never hammer me with these questions. As a rule, adults aren't all that curious about other people. With me, they are generally interested in just one thing: my ancestry.

Do you suppose that—15,330 times in thirty-four years—strangers will ask an indisputably white Canadian with a traditional Anglo-Canadian accent where he is from, where he was born, or where his parents were born? Absolutely not. Strangers will assume that he is a true Canadian, and leave that part of his identity unmolested. The offence-causing kernel at the centre of this line of interrogation is its implication: "You are not white, you don't look like me, so you're clearly not Canadian." It also suggests "Since you're clearly not Canadian, and I am, I am within my rights to ask you just exactly where you're from."

We grow up learning that certain questions are off-limits in polite conversation. Any properly socialized Canadian knows, by the teenage years at the latest, that it would be considered grossly impolite to walk up to strangers and ask how much money they make, how they vote, whether they believe in God, or whether they sleep with men, women, or both. These questions are deemed intrusive. But to my way of thinking, they are eminently preferable to "Where are you from?" After all, what is wrong with asking what people do or think? But to ask what they *are*, and to presume to know at least part of the answer—that they are not white and therefore are not Canadian—is very different.

Digging into someone's identity—especially a stranger's identity—is tricky business. Hell, people can spend top dollar on psychotherapists to figure out their own identities and still fall short of satisfaction. When I wake up in the morning, stumble to the mirror, and brush my teeth, I'm certainly not saying to myself, "Hello, black man, how are you today?" Nor am I saying, "Hello, white and black mixup, what are you doing today?"

Obviously, the blackness and the whiteness within me are reflected back at me by society. But I don't care to have my identity boiled down to race. My identity may, at any given time, comprise a hundred elements.

I suppose the reason many of us mixed-race people find The Question offensive is not just that it makes assumptions, which are often false, about our identity, but because it attempts to hang our identity on one factor: our race.

*

Not everybody I interviewed had the same take on this issue. Interestingly, two of the strongest opposing views came from young men, both in their twenties, university-educated, and living in southern Ontario.

Stefan Dubowski, of Hamilton, told me The Question doesn't bother him. When he is asked about his background, he just says he is part Ukrainian, part Barbadian. "Then we get into a discussion of what they thought I was. I've had Armenian, Egyptian, Pakistani, East Indian . . . It's just a question of curiosity. I've been asked so many times. If I got mad about it every single time, I'd just be this really angry person. I certainly don't feel any anger about it when people ask me about it, but my back does go up when I read it on an application form or on a government census."

Tyson Brown, who was raised in Burlington and now lives in Toronto, said he takes The Question as an opportunity to educate people about issues of mixed race and blackness. "I say, 'I'm mixed, African Canadian and white Canadian.'" Tyson emerged from a largely white high school to embrace his black identity completely as a young man. He read black literature, listened to black music, wore funky black clothes, dated black women, and chose to immerse himself completely in the black student community at York University. Later, he lived with his girlfriend for a year in Barbados, and there the constant references to his race grated on him. "They called me 'red man' the whole time I was there," he complained.

However, my brother, Dan, described The Question as a painful experience, especially during childhood. "I was definitely asked that question a lot. And a lot of times, when I said part black, or half black, people would then decide to argue with me and tell me that no, I wasn't, 'cause I didn't look black enough. I can remember it happening a lot when I was a boy, at summer camp. When I went up to camp for the first time, I was sitting on the bus with this kid who was probably a year or two older than I was. And this kid was saying, 'You're not. You can't be.' So there I was arguing with him about this."

Like Dan, most of the people I interviewed—and virtually all of the women—expressed impatience with constant questions about their racial background.

Karyn Hood, of Toronto, said, "People think I'm everything under the flipping sun, and it drives me insane. I get North African, Moroccan, Italian, Sicilian, Greek, Spanish, Jewish . . . Whenever I meet someone, I know it's going to be 'What are you? What background are you?' I usually try to put it to bed with one answer: 'My father is West Indian, my mother's Irish Canadian.' It's annoying. But life's a puzzle, and they want to know how you fit into their world." Karyn resents being perceived as "exotic," cultivates friendships in the black community, and prefers to date black men. "You can't live in two worlds. You have to make a choice. Saying you're white isn't really an option. So this makes it clear to people. If there's any doubt, that's the choice I'm making."

Natalie Wall, of Toronto, concurred. "I've been asked what I am so many times. It is the rudest question in the world. It's the basest form of labelling I've ever seen. People on the street are always guessing. 'You're Spanish, right? Indian? What the hell are you?' I tell them I'm Canadian. 'But where are you from?' 'Canada.' 'What about your parents?' 'My mom is from Nova Scotia, my dad is from Trinidad.' 'So what are you?' 'Black.' I get a surprised look. 'You *are*?'"

Jazz Miller, of Toronto, is so sick of The Question that when people ask her what she is, she has taken to answering "aardvark." "It is designed to embarrass the person asking the question. There's always a little bit of nervous laughter."

Aaron Cavon, who has a white father and a black mother, was a graduate student at Dalhousie University when I interviewed him. He said people always look astonished when he says that The Question irritates him and he won't answer it. He described the attitude of the questioner as unconsciously aggressive, a stance that suggests the person being questioned is inferior. Underneath The Question, Aaron argued, is this unarticulated belief: "It's not necessary for me to explain my origins, but it's necessary for you to tell me who you are." He told me, "The assumption behind The Question is, 'I'm just white. You are the person who answers the question because you are the one who is unknown.'"

Sara, one of my anonymous interviewees, fumed as she recalled the numerous times she had dealt with The Question.

"Sometimes I'm very rude. I don't give much information. I might just say, 'I'm from here.' Some days, if I don't feel like it, I just say, 'Africa.' And they're happy, not realizing that Africa's a continent and that there are fifty-two countries in it. It's just what they want to hear. They want to place you somewhere because it makes them feel comfortable, helps them compartmentalize you.

"Where the hell are they from? No one's from here unless they're First Nations peoples. But they're trying to make you feel strange. It's a displacement. They're just trying to let you know that you don't belong . . . They are not coming from a position of intelligence, asking those questions. White privilege doesn't operate from a level of consciousness. It operates from a position of privilege. Because they're privileged, they don't have to think about stuff. They really don't. Does it mean that they're not well intentioned? These can be people you love dearly, you know? But that's the way the world is. They're operating from a position of belligerent white privilege, and they don't have to look at stuff and think about stuff. So they ask these reckless questions."

A Garden of Her Own

Shani Mootoo

A NORTH-FACING balcony meant that no sunlight would enter there. A deep-in-the-heart-of-the-forest green pine tree, over-fertilized opulence extending its midriff, filled the view from the balcony.

There was no window, only a glass sliding door which might have let fresh air in and released second- or third-hand air and the kinds of odours that build phantoms in stuffy apartments. But it remained shut. Not locked, but stuck shut from decades of other renters' black, oily grit and grime which had collected in the grooves of the sliding door's frame.

Vijai knew that it would not budge up, down or sideways. For the amount of rent the husband paid for this bachelor apartment, the landlord could not be bothered. She opened the hallway door to let the cooking lamb fat and garlic smells drift out into the hallway. She did not want them to burrow into the bed sheets, into towels and clothes crammed into the dented cream-coloured metal space-saver cupboard that she had to share with the husband. It was what all the other renters did too; everyone's years of oil—sticky, burnt, over-used, rancid oil—and of garlic, onions and spices formed themselves into an impenetrable nose-singeing, skin-stinging presence that lurked menacingly in the hall. Instead of releasing the lamb from the husband's apartment, opening the door allowed this larger phantom to barge its way in.

Vijai, engulfed, slammed the door shut. She tilted her head to face the ceiling and breathed in hard, searching for air that had no smell, no weight. The husband was already an hour late for dinner. She paced the twelve strides, back and forth, from the balcony door to the hall door, glancing occasionally at the two table settings, stopping to straighten his knife, his fork, the napkin, the flowers, his knife, his fork, the napkin, the flowers. Her arms and legs tingled weakly and her intestines filled up with beads of acid formed out of unease and fear. Seeing a smear of her fingerprint on the husband's knife, she picked it up and polished it on her T-shirt until it gleamed brilliantly, and she saw in it her mother's eyes looking back at her.

*

Sunlight. I miss the sunlight—yellow light and a sky ceiling miles high. Here the sky sits on my head, heavy grey with snow and freezing rain. I miss being able to have doors and windows opened wide, never shut except sometimes in the rainy season. Rain, rain, pinging on, winging off the galvanized tin roof. But always warm rain. No matter how much it rained, it was always warm.

And what about the birds? Flying in through the windows how often? Two, three times a week? Sometimes even twice in a single day. In the shimmering heat you could see them flying slowly, their mouths wide open as if crying out soundlessly. They would actually be flicking their tongues at the still air, gulping and panting, looking for a window to enter and a curtain rod to land on to cool off. But once they had cooled off and were ready to fly off again, they could never seem to focus on the window to fly through and they would bang themselves against the walls and the light shade until they fell, panicked and stunned. I was the one who would get the broom and push it gently up toward one of these birds after it looked like it had cooled off, and prod, prod, prod until it hopped onto the broom and then I would lower it and reach from behind and cup the trembling in my hand. I can, right now, feel the life, the heat in the palm of my hand from the little body, and the fright in its tremble. I would want to hold on to it, even think of placing it in a cage and looking after it, but something always held me back. I would put my mouth close to its ears and whisper calming shh shh shhhhs, and then take it, pressed to my chest, out the back door and open my hand and wait for it to take its time fluffing out right there in my open hand before flying away.

But here? There are hardly any birds here, only that raucous, aggressive old crow that behaves as if it owns the scraggly pine tree it sits in across the street. This street is so noisy! Every day, all day and all night long, even on Sundays, cars whiz by, ambulances and fire trucks pass screaming, and I think to myself thank goodness it couldn't be going for anyone I know. I don't know anyone nearby.

Too much quiet here, too shut off. Not even the sound of children playing in the street, or the sound of neighbours talking to each other over fences, conversations floating in through open windows, open bricks. Here even when doors are open people walk down hallways with their noses straight ahead, making a point of not glancing to even nod hello.

Oh! This brings all kinds of images to my mind: the coconut tree outside my bedroom brushing, scraping, swishing against the wall. Green-blue iridescent lizards clinging, upside down, to the ceiling above my bed.

And dinner time. Mama's voice would find me wherever I was. "Vijai, go and tell Cheryl to put food on the table, yuh father comin home just now." Standing in one place, at the top of her meagre voice she would call us one by one: "Bindra, is dinner time. Bindra, why you so harden, boy? Dinner gettin cold. Turn off that TV right now! Shanti, come girl, leave what you doin and come and eat. Vashti, go and tell Papa dinner ready, and then you come and sit down." Sitting down, eating together. Talking together. Conversations with no boundaries, no false politeness, no need to impress Mama or Papa.

But that's not how it was always. Sometimes Papa didn't come home till long after suppertime. Mama would make us eat but she would wait for him. Sometimes he wouldn't come for days, and she would wait for him then too.

But there were always flowers from the garden on the table. Pink and yellow gerberas, ferns, ginger lilies. That was your happiness, eh Mama? the garden, eh? And when there were blossoms you and I would go outside together. You showed me how to angle the garden scissors so that the plant wouldn't hurt for too long. We would bring in the bundle of flowers and greenery with their fresh-cut garden smell and little flying bugs and spiders, and you would show me how to arrange them for a centrepiece or a corner table or a floor piece. The place would look so pretty! Thanks for showing that to me, Mama.

Mama, he's never brought me any flowers. Not even a dandelion.

I don't want him to ask how much these cost. Don't ask me who sent them. No one sent them; I bought them myself. With my own money. My own money.

He's never given me anything. Only money for groceries.

Late. Again.

I jabbed this lamb with a trillion little gashes and stuffed a clove of garlic in each one with your tongue, your taste buds in mind. I spent half the day cooking this meal and you will come late and eat it after the juices have hardened to a candle-wax finish, as if it were nothing but a microwave dinner.

I want a microwave oven.

Mama, why did you wait to eat? If I were to eat now would you, Papa, he think I am a bad wife? Why did you show me this, Mama?

I must not nag.

*

Vijai remained sleeping until the fan in the bathroom woke her. It sputtered raucously, like an airplane engine starting up, escalating in time to fine whizzing, lifting off into the distance.

Five-thirty, Saturday morning.

She had fretted through most of the night, twisting, arching her body, drawing her legs up to her chest, to the husband's chest, rolling, and nudging him, hoping that he would awaken to pull her body into his and hold her there. She wanted to feel the heat of his body along the length of hers, his arms pressing her to him. Or his palm placed flat on her lower belly, massaging, touching her. He responded to her fidgeting once and she moved closer to him to encourage him, but he turned his naked back to her and continued his guttural exhaling, inhaling, sounding exactly like her father.

Eventually Vijai's eyes, burning from salty tears that had spilled and dampened the pillow under her cheek, fluttered shut and she slept, deep and dreamless, until the fan awakened her.

When the sound of the shower water snapping at the enamel tub was muffled against his body, she pulled herself over to lie in and smell his indentation in the tired foam mattress. She inhaled, instead, the history of the mattress: unwashed hair, dying skin, old and rancid sweat—not the smell she wanted to nestle in. Neither would the indentation cradle her; she could feel the protruding shape of the box-spring beneath the foam.

She debated whether to get up and thanklessly make his toast and tea, or pretend not to have awakened, the potential for blame nagging at her. She slid back to her side of his bed, the other side of the line that he had drawn down the middle with the cutting edge of his outstretched hand. Vijai pulled her knees to her chest and hugged them. When the shower stopped she hastily straightened herself out and put her face inside the crack between the bed and the rough wall. Cold from the wall transferred itself onto her cheek, and layers upon layers of human smells trapped behind cream-coloured paint pierced her nostrils.

Vijai was aware of the husband's every move as she lay in his bed. Water from the kitchen tap pounded the sink basin, then attacked the metal floor of the kettle, gradually becoming muffled and high-pitched as the kettle filled up. He always filled it much more than was necessary for one cup of tea, which he seldom drank. The blow dryer. First on the highest setting, then dropped two notches to the lowest, and off. The electric razor. Whizzing up and down his cheek, circling his chin, the other cheek, grazing his neck. Snip, snip and little dark half-moon hairs from his nostrils and his sideburns cling to the rim of the white sink basin. Wiping up, scrubbing, making spotless these areas, and others, before he returns, are her evidence that she is diligent, that she is, indeed, her mother's daughter.

At this point in the routine she always expects a handsome aftershave cologne to fill the little bachelor apartment, to bring a moment of frivolity and romance into the room. In one favourite version of her memories, this is what normally happened in her parents' bedroom at precisely this point. But the husband would only pat on his face a stinging watery liquid with the faintest smell of lime, a smell that evaporated into nothingness the instant it touched his skin.

She held herself tensely, still in the crack between the bed and the wall, as he made his way into the dark corner that he called the bedroom. The folding doors of the closet squeaked open. A shirt slid off a hanger, leaving it dangling and tinkling against the metal rod. Vijai heard the shirt that she had ironed (stretched mercilessly tight across the ironing board, the tip of the iron with staccato spurts of steam sniffing out the crevice of every seam, mimicking the importance with which her mother had treated this task) being pulled against his body and his hands sliding down the stiff front as he buttoned it.

Then there was a space empty of his sounds. The silence made the walls of her stomach contract like a closed-up accordion. Her body remained rigid. Her heart sounded as if it had moved right up into her ears, thundering methodically, and that was all that she could hear. She struggled with herself to be calm so that she could know where he was and what he was doing. Not knowing made her scalp want to unpeel itself. Then, the bed sagged as he kneeled on it, leaned across and brushed his mouth on the back of her head. His full voice had no regard for her sleep or the time of morning. He said, "Happy Birthday. I left twenty dollars on the table for you. Buy yourself a present."

The thundering subsided and her heart rolled and slid, rolled and slid, down, low down, and came to rest between her thighs. She turned over with lethargic elegance, as if she were just waking up, stretching out her back like a cat, but the apartment door was already being shut and locked from the outside.

*

The streets here are so wide! I hold my breath as I walk across them, six lanes wide. What if the light changes before I get to the other side? You have to walk so briskly, not only when you're crossing a wide street but even on the sidewalk. Otherwise people pass you and then turn back and stare at you, shaking their heads. And yet I remember Mama telling us that fast walking, hurrying, was very unladylike.

I yearn for friends. My own friends, not his, but I'm afraid to smile at strangers. So often we huddled up in Mama's big bed and read the newspapers about things that happened to women up here—we read about women who suddenly disappeared and months later their corpses would be found, having been raped and dumped. And we also read about serial murders. The victims were almost always women who had been abducted from the street by strangers in some big North American city. Mama and Papa warned me, when I was leaving to come up here, not to make eye contact with strangers because I wouldn't know whose eyes I might be looking into or what I was encouraging, unknowingly. It's not like home, they said, where everybody knows everybody.

No bird sounds—there are not quite so many different kinds of birds here. Yes, Papa, yes, I can just hear you saying to stop this nonsense, all this thinking about home, that I must think of here as my home now, but I haven't yet left you and Mama. I know now that I will never fully leave, nor will I ever truly be here. You felt so close, Papa, when you phoned this morning and asked like you have every past year, how was the birthday girl. You said that in your office you often look at the calendar pictures of autumn fields of bales of hay, lazy rivers meandering near brick-red farmhouses, and country roads with quaint white wooden churches with red steeples, and you think that that's what my eyes have already enjoyed.

"It's all so beautiful, Papa," I said, and knowing you, you probably heard what I wasn't saying. Thanks for not pushing further. I couldn't tell you that he is working night and day to "make it," to "get ahead," to live like the other men he works with. That he is always thinking about this, and everything else is frivolous right now, so we haven't yet been for that drive in the country to see the pictures in the calendars pinned on the wall above your desk. He doesn't have time for dreaming, but I must dream or else I find it difficult to breathe.

At home the fence around our house and the garden was the furthest point that I ever went to on my own. From the house, winding in and out of the dracaenas and the philodendrons that I planted with Mama many Julys ago, feeling the full, firm limbs of the poui, going as far as the hibiscus and jasmine fence, and back into the house again. Any further away from the house than that and the chauffeur would be driving us! And now? Just look at me! I am out in a big city on my own. I wish you all could see me. I wish we could be doing this together.

Papa, you remember, don't you, when you used to bring home magazines from your office and I would flip through them quickly looking for full-page pictures of dense black-green tropical mountains, or snow-covered bluish-white ones? Ever since those first pictures I have dreamt of mountains, of touching them with the palms of my hands, of bicycling in them, and of hiking. Even though I never canoed on a river or a big lake with no shores, I know what it must feel like! I can feel what it is to ride rapids like they do in *National Geographic* magazines. Cold river spray and drenchings, sliding, tossing, crashing! I still dream of bicycling across a huge continent. I used to think, if only I lived in North America! But here I am, in this place where these things are supposed to happen, in the midst of so much possibility, and for some reason my dreams seem even further away, just out of reach. It's just not quite as simple as being here.

This land stretches on in front of me, behind me and forever. My back feels exposed, naked, so much land behind, and no fence ahead.

Except that I must cook dinner tonight.

What if I just kept walking and never returned! I could walk far away, to another province, change my name, cut my hair. After a while I would see my face on a poster in a grocery store, along with all the other missing persons. The problem is that then I wouldn't even be able to phone home and speak with Mama or Papa or Bindra and Vashti without being tracked and caught, and then who knows what.

Well, this is the first birthday I've ever spent alone. But next time we speak on the phone I will be able to tell you that I went for a very long walk. Alone.

I think I will do this every day—well, maybe every other day, and each time I will go a new route and a little further. I will know this place in order to own it, but still I will never really leave you.

Mama, Papa, Vashti, Bindra, Shanti.
Mama, Papa, Vashti, Bindra, Shanti.
Mama, Papa, Vashti, Bindra, Shanti.

*

Twenty-four years of Sundays, of eating three delightfully noisy, lengthy meals together, going to the beach or for long drives with big pots of rice, chicken and peas, and chocolate cake, singing "Michael Row Your Boat Ashore," and "You Are My Sunshine," doing everything in tandem with her brother and sisters and Mama and Papa.

This particular characteristic of Sundays was etched deeply in her veins. (Not all Sundays were happy ones but recently she seems to have forgotten that.)

It would be her twenty-fourth Sunday here, the twenty-fourth week of marriage.

The only Sunday since the marriage that the husband had taken off and spent in his apartment was six weeks ago, and since he needed to spend that day alone Vijai agreed to go to the library for at least three hours. Before she left the house she thought she would use the opportunity to take down recipes for deserts, but once she began walking down the street she found herself thinking about rivers and mountains. She bypassed the shelves with all the cooking books and home-making magazines and found herself racing toward valleys, glaciers, canoeing, rapids and the like. She picked up a magazine about hiking and mountaineering, looked at the equipment advertisements, read incomprehensible jargon about techniques for climbing.

After about forty minutes, not seeing herself in any of the magazines, she became less enthusiastic, and eventually frustrated and bored. She looked at her watch every fifteen minutes or so and then she started watching the second hand go around and counting each and every second in her head. When three hours had passed she remembered that she had said at least three hours, and she walked home slowly, stopping to window-shop and checking her watch until an extra twenty minutes had passed.

The strength of her determination that they not spend this Sunday apart warded off even a hint of such a suggestion from the husband. What she really wanted to do was to go for the long drive up to a glacier in the nearby mountains. That way she would have him to herself for at least five hours. But he had worked several twelve-hour shifts that week and needed to rest in his apartment.

She went to the grocery store, to the gardening section, and bought half a dozen packages of flower seeds, half a dozen packages of vegetable seeds, bags of soil, fertilizer, a fork and spade, a purple plastic watering can, and a score of nursery trays. She brought it all home in a taxi. Enough to keep her busy and in his apartment for an entire Sunday. She was becoming adept at finding ways to get what she wanted.

He never asked and Vijai did not tell that from her allowance she had paid a man from the hardware store to come over and fix the balcony sliding door. She stooped on the balcony floor scooping earth into nursery trays. He sat reading the newspaper, facing the balcony in his big sagging gold armchair that he had bought next-door at a church basement sale for five dollars. She was aware that he was stealing glances at her as she bent over her garden-in-the-making.

*

I wore this shirt, no bra, am stooping, bending over here to reveal my breasts to you. *Look at them! Feel something!*

I might as well be sharing this apartment with a brother, or a roommate. She feels his hands on her waist, leading her from behind to the edge of his bed. Her body is crushed under his as he slams himself against her, from behind, grunting. She holds her breath, taut against his weight and the pain, but she will not disturb his moment. She hopes that the next moment will be hers. She waits with the bed sheet pulled up to her chin. The toilet flushes and, shortly after, she hears newspaper pages being turned in the sagging five-dollar gold armchair.

Later, deep-sleep breathing and low snoring from the bedroom fills the apartment, dictating her movements. She sits on the green-and-yellow shag carpet, leaning against the foot of the husband's armchair, in front of the snowy black-and-white television watching a French station turned down low enough not to awaken him. Something about listening to a language that she does not understand comforts her, gives her companionship in a place where she feels like a foreigner. She is beginning to be able to repeat advertisements in French.

Performing the Immigrant Nation at Pier 21: Politics and Counterpolitics in the Memorialization of Canadian Immigration

Tamara Vukov

On the last Canada Day of "Canada's Century" and the millennium (July 1, 1999), Halifax's Pier 21, historic point of arrival for over one million immigrants from 1928–1971, became the site of a national memorialization of Canadian immigration. A private initiative that received significant funding from the Canadian government and the Chrysler Corporation, the Pier 21 memorial promises "to do for Canada and Canadians what Ellis Island has done for the United States" (*Pier 21* 2000). Yet, as Gérard Noiriel reminds us, national narratives of immigration history are never innocent, for they are always implicated in and tied to the politics of nationality at work in a given moment (Noiriel 1996).

This paper explores what it is precisely that Pier 21 does for Canada and "Canadians," examining how it produces a celebratory founding myth of the immigrant nation. Pier 21's opening ceremonies offered a performance of the immigrant nation as a spectacular "fairytale" of immigrant inclusion (see below, Abella 1999). In the latter part of the paper, I pursue some of the critical implications of the institutional "forgetting" of the settler legacies of ethnic and racial exclusion that have been and continue to be central to Canadian immigration policy. In order to do so, I focus on a site of contestation that offers a provocative counterpolitics of memorialization to the official histories produced at Pier 21: that of Canadian independent, intercultural video productions of the 1990s by such artists as Richard Fung, Leila Sujir, and Paul Wong.

The permanent exhibition at the Pier 21 centre, entitled "The Immigration Experience," promises to "trace the physical and emotional journey" of immigrants at Pier 21. Installed in the former Pier 21 immigration-processing centre, the exhibit is organized around a series of iconic, dramatized moments in the immigrant journey that visitors re-enact. At the start of the visit, guests are given a Pier 21 passport to be stamped at each station in the "journey." Filled with imaginative multimedia displays and creative design elements, the vividness and pathos of the journey through Pier 21 is recreated through the exhibition narrative of reenactment, the life-size cutout figures of different immigrant "types" complete with listening stations

From *International Journal of Canadian Studies*, 26, Fall 2002 by Tamara Vukov. Copyright © 2002 by International Council for Canadian Studies. Reprinted by permission.

for their oral histories, and the immigration hall benches equipped with speakers broadcasting new immigrant voices and sounds. The Bronfman "In-Transit Theatre" entrance is designed like the deck of a ship, and inside, a spectacular holographic film called "Oceans of Hope" recounts the story of immigration at Pier 21 through the figure of an immigration officer in a tone of epic melodrama.

Once passports are properly stamped at each stage of the route, visitors complete the journey by boarding a stationary CN Rail car with projections of the Canadian countryside in the windows, recreating the train journey immigrants undertook from the pier. In each train compartment, videotaped oral histories of Canadian immigrants are projected. Stepping off the train, visitors face a wall-sized video mosaic of diverse faces and origins projected over Canadian landscapes to the accompaniment of the national anthem.

As I follow the journey and get my passport stamped along the way, one particularly curious element in the exhibit strikes me. Passing through the "Crossing the Atlantic" section of the exhibit, a large wall of statistics and graphs chart the "Waves of Immigration" that Pier 21 received. The charts and graphs show how British immigration constituted by far the largest group (1,252,435 according to the chart), over half of all immigrants that passed through Pier 21. Mention is made of the world events that determined who came to Canada, from "economic cycles, war, oppression—as well as government policy and individual choice." Yet no mention is made of how government policy systematically regulated the preferential inclusion of British and Northern European immigrants (Kelley and Trebilcock 1998, 326–329). References to mistreatment and exclusions occasionally surface in the testimonies and oral histories through the individualized voices of personal experience, but they are largely absent from the main exhibition narrative and statistical displays. Such questions are contained within the melodrama of individual struggle and overcoming, rather than being posed as matters of systematic policy.

One tiny, out of the way section, "Barriers to Immigration," does mention the history of racial restrictions of Africans, Chinese, Indian, and Jewish immigration, as well as the deportation of political radicals and the medically unfit. Located in an out of the way corner outside the dominant spatial flow of much of the exhibit, the text naturalizes and elides the exclusionary settler colonial structures of Canadian immigration in the following terms: "Until 1961, immigration policies favored immigrants who would *blend into the existing population*" (emphasis added). The text then quickly jumps to the progressive new point system introduced in the 1960s that "opened the door to immigration from all over the world." The passage narrative culminates in the customs station, and I watch the lineup of visitors perform their immigration interviews and get their passport cheerfully stamped under the "Welcome to Canada" sign. Needless to say, no deportations are reenacted, and no one is interrogated or refused entry.

Pier 21's Opening Ceremonies:The Spectacle of the Open Door

The Pier 21 Society was initiated in 1988 as a "non-profit volunteer organization" made up of a consortium of "private citizens" from the governmental, business, and cultural sectors. It modeled its project very explicitly on the Ellis Island Immigration Museum,[1] the museum that opened in New York City in 1990 to commemorate the most famous point of entry for over 12 million immigrants to the United States from 1892–1954. Sitting in the shadow of the Statue of Liberty, the Ellis Island Immigration Museum sought to enshrine this iconic gateway as "the symbol of America's immigrant heritage" and "golden door," strongly influencing the eventual formulation and design of Pier 21. The Pier 21 Society's goals were two-fold: firstly, transforming Pier 21 into a permanent exhibition and learning resource centre, and secondly, " . . . interpret[ing] the immigration experience of those who came through Pier 21, and recognizing the important role immigration has played and continues to play in forming our Canadian identity" (*Pier 21* 2000).[2]

In June of 1995 at the Halifax G7 summit, Prime Minister Jean Chrétien announced the donation of $4.5 million in government funding for the establishment of a "permanent monument" to Canada's immigrants. The funding consisted of moneys from all three levels of government: $2.5 million from the federal government, and the rest from the Nova Scotia provincial and the Halifax municipal governments. In what has become a standard neoliberal governmental tactic in the funding of public culture, the other half of the operating budget came from private corporate sponsorships. Chrysler Canada donated $250,000 for the construction of the Chrysler Canada Welcome Pavilion, in what Chief Executive Officer William C. Glaub called a "permanent and living testament to freedom and to Canada" ("Chrysler Canada" 2000). However, such funding strategies also follow a long-standing tradition of Canadian government and corporate sector collaboration in the business of immigration, through joint efforts and policies to attract (historically shifting definitions of) "desirable immigrants." Most notable given its major historical involvement in Canadian immigration as one of the largest importers and transporters of immigrant labour (and party to the 1925 Railways Agreement), Canadian National Rail's (CN) donation of $150,000 to Pier 21 was accompanied by a good deal of local media fanfare. Part of the donation went towards the recreated CN railcar complete with a pulsating floor that culminates the immigration exhibition, along with a second restored 1937 railcar for display outside the entrance to Pier 21 (*Passages*). The strategy for corporate sponsorship was also notable in the way that it linked various themes and sections of the exhibition to particular corporate sponsors. Canada Trust sponsored one section of the exhibit dealing with the historical role of volunteers at Pier 21. A range of corporate bodies (Sobey's, Nesbitt Burns) have underwritten different parts of the exhibit and national narrative. In this way, the national narrative of immigration offered at Pier 21 became a distinctly promotional and commodified one.

The focal point of the Pier 21 spectacle was the 1999 Canada Day opening ceremonies. Hosted by Hana Gartner of the Canadian Broadcasting Corporation (the CBC), the opening ceremonies were broadcast nationally and drew thousands of visitors, many of them so-called "Pier 21 alumni," who had themselves immigrated through Pier 21. Enactments of remembrance, testimony, and affect were abundant throughout the day. Their continual repetition and circulation was crucial to the performance of the celebratory nation-building narrative of immigration dramatized at Pier 21. As Senator Al Graham declared, "We can hear their voices. We can feel their strengths. The walls behind us whisper" (Jeffrey and Duffy 1999). Proclaiming the opening of the "permanent monument to immigrants," Prime Minister Jean Chrétien delivered a live video-relayed national address in which he offered the following somewhat less than nuanced analysis of Canada's settler colonial history: "Canada Day is important for the values that we share. We had first the natives who were here before the French and the English, and after that people came from all over the world to build this nation . . . Here in Canada we are all equal."[3]

At the peak of the ceremony, a specially commissioned Pier 21 musical anthem was performed, proclaiming, "Oh Canada, behind these dockyard walls, there's freedom to dream . . . And here on this day, a new life has begun, when we first set foot on Pier 21."[4] President Ruth Goldbloom pronounced that, "as one of the greatest symbols of Canada's national heritage, Pier 21 is a tribute to immigrants, a living icon in the hearts and minds of Canadians, the heartbeat and pulse that makes up Canada."[5] The ceremony was closed with the ceremonial placing of puzzle pieces over images of Pier 21 immigrants so as to complete a jigsaw Maple Leaf flag, in a rather literal display of the founding myth of the multicultural Canadian mosaic. Gartner proclaimed: "As the pieces of our puzzle show, we are one Canada. It doesn't matter where you are from, we are one people. Pier 21 is a testament to this. Canada's front-door is now officially open."[6]

Yet another pinnacle moment of the opening day took place in the prelude to the official ceremony, when an early morning on-ship reenactment took place performed by 160 former war brides reliving their arrival at the pier (Duffy 1999). The ceremonial landing of the navy's HMCS Preserver recreated the 1945–1947 arrivals of 48,000 war brides predominantly from the British Isles and Western Europe, along with their (continually emphasized) 22,000 children. Escorted ashore by young men dressed in wartime uniforms and paraded into the opening ceremonies with romantic tribute, the sentimental tone of national love that accompanied the war brides' performance of sexual citizenship confirmed the extent to which immigration practices are bound up with "the ideology of (white) women as the reproducers of the nation" (Mohanty 1991, 26–27).

Yet perhaps the most fascinating component of the celebrations was the avid and active participation of approximately 6,000 people in the opening day ceremonies. Many were (less eminent) Pier 21 "alumni" or relatives of those who had arrived at Pier 21 (including soldiers who had embarked from Pier 21 to fight in World War II). It was among these participants that the sheer intensity and affective power of recognition—recognition of immigrant struggles and pasts clearly not often or consistently available to many of the participants—was most strongly evident and at times very movingly displayed. It was also here that the active interpellation of affect, personal memory, and ritualized testimony into the national narrative proved to be most complex, contradictory, and potent. Such families as the Leegwater's of Pictou County actively participated in the sentimental staging and reenactments of the day. Having donated the suitcases with which they arrived at Pier 21 to the exhibit display case, the Leegwater's posed for the media as they watched a National Film Board film of their 1952 arrival and immigration processing (Jeffrey and Duff 1999, A2). Some were more hesitant and uncomfortable with the media attention, while others strongly played into the media spectacle as journalists scrambled to find Pier 21 immigrants to rehearse the stories of their passages and arrival to Canada. This was only one layer in the larger interpellation of immigrant testimony at Pier 21, which includes the oral history component of the exhibition and archives, along with the "Calling All Memories" project (the videotaped oral history archives initiated as a joint project between the CBC and Pier 21).

The extensive local, national, and international media coverage of the war bride reenactment and the opening ceremonies were key components in the wider spectacle of Pier 21, popularly diffusing this promotional rendition of the nation's history both nationally and internationally. A strategic and "innovative" broadcast partnership was struck between Pier 21 and the CBC, resulting in live coverage of the opening ceremonies and several co-productions that were broadcast on Canada Day ("CBC Television" 2000). Most of the other national media coverage combined the testimony of local immigrants who arrived through the pier with Pier 21's own promotional rhetoric, as in such headlines as "A Pier Into the Past" (directly reiterating the Pier 21 slogan) (Jeffrey and Duffy 1999) or "Where History's Soul Remembers" (Toughill 1999).

One of the few articles to circulate widely in the national media coverage of Pier 21 that even alluded to the thorny question of Canada's exclusionary history reveals how the implications of that history tended to be managed and contained. Ontario Court of Appeal Justice Rosalie Abella delivered a speech at the inaugural dinner of the Pier 21 opening that was widely cited and reprinted throughout the ceremony and the media, particularly with respect to the emotional nature of the speech that drew tears around the room. Abella is well known as an influential figure in the shaping of Canadian public policy, particularly for her role as the head of the 1984 Royal Commission on Equality of Employment (known as the Abella Commission) that led to the Employment Equity Act of 1986.

Abella arrived at Pier 21 as a four-year old Jewish D.P. (displaced person) in 1950, her family having attempted to get into Canada for several years. Although he had worked as a lawyer for displaced persons in Germany, as an immigrant, her father was barred from practicing law in Canada. These tales of hardship constituted the backdrop to Abella's immigrant paean, as she recounted the significance of Pier 21:

> The story of Canada is the story of immigrants, and Pier 21 is their proud celebratory symbol . . . Every immigrant who landed at Pier 21 has two stories—the story they came from and the story they started when they landed in Canada . . . There was one thought attached to every immigrant who set foot here: gratitude. This country is full of tenaciously grateful immigrants and their descendants who bloomed in Canada's field of opportunities . . . This triumvirate of opportunity, generosity, and idealism is what Pier 21 stands for—Canada's best self. It is *the Canada that let us in,* the Canada that took one generation's European horror story and turned it into another generation's Canadian fairytale (Abella 1999). (Emphasis added)

In this way, Abella's speech offered a literal articulation of Pier 21's fairytale of inclusion. Yet, unaddressed and unspoken in this story's circulation in the media is the fact that, a few years prior to Abella's arrival in 1950, her family was likely unable to enter due to the systematic anti-Semitism informing Canadian immigration policy of the day.[7]

When fragments of Canada's exclusionary history did surface in the Pier 21 celebrations, they tended to be contained within a rags-to-riches class narrative of progress and triumph against the odds. Tales of immigrant hardship and the real exclusion recounted in stories such as Abella's served to create melodramatic tension and affective force. The stories of prominent and successful immigrants and their class achievements were promoted as emblematic of the immigrant experience and the glory of Canada as a nation.

While virtually all of the national media closely reproduced such celebratory myths of Pier 21,[8] one of the few pieces of mainstream media coverage to offer a more critical and less celebratory assessment surfaced outside the national press in a *New York Times/International Herald Tribune* article. The headline points to the selectivity at work in the celebratory founding myth of Pier 21: "Canada Celebrates Immigrants, but Which Ones?" With a distinct tone of American condescension, it goes on to legitimately criticize the Pier 21 project for its selective focus on an era of predominantly European immigration to the exclusion of contemporary non-European immigration (De Palma 1999).

Founding Myths of Inclusion: National Celebration, Terms of Recognition and the Politics of Immigrant Affect in Settler Nationalism

According to Anne McClintock, "nationalism is a theatrical performance of invented community" (McClintock 1995, 375). If founding myths of Canadian immigration have long served to imagine and enforce the bounds of the settler nation (Anderson 1983), the Pier 21 opening ceremonies constituted a striking contemporary performance of the immigrant nation through the institutional practice of memorialization. In interrogating the links between such founding myths and the contemporary politics of immigration, it is worth considering Bonnie Honig's claim with respect to the United States that "the myth of an immigrant America serves to renationalize the state and reposition it at the centre of any future . . . politics" (Honig 1998, 17). Similarly, Pier 21 spectacularizes national history and dramatizes immigrant inclusion in seeking to recuperate immigrant energies in this recentering of the nation-state.

At first glance, such founding national myths of immigration hold out the promise of liberal pluralism and the allure of recognition of the immigrant roots of the nation (Taylor 1992), particularly in contradistinction to nations or versions of national history that deny their immigrant pasts and constitution in favour of a homogenized historical narrative.[9] Without downplaying its political significance or affective power however, it is crucial to interrogate the strategic terms of recognition, when it is offered and how it is performed, in settler nations where "the commemoration of origins is an essential element of strategies of political consensus" (Noiriel 1996, 7). Such strategies demand interrogation regarding the function and circulation of these celebratory founding myths of immigration, by locating the specific and critical role they play in national narratives of settler nations—nations borne of settler colonialism and the dispossession of native peoples. In the so-called "new world," any retrospective mythology of a primordial or pastoral rootedness in the land is foreclosed or "interrupted" by colonial settlement (unlike for instance, French national narratives based on "a fable of primordial, continuous Frenchness," Noiriel 1996, vii). Instead, settler nations anchor their mythical origins in the romance of immigration as a historical euphemism for settler colonialism.

According to Honig, such a founding mythology is often expressed through xenophilia, the mythic inclusion of the "iconic immigrant who once helped build this nation and whose heirs might contribute to the national future" (Honig 1998, 1). Xenophilia plays a crucial role in settler nations, not just as an arbiter of pluralist recognition and multiculturalism, but as a discourse closely bound up with the strategic interests of nation-building (from founding settler narratives to economic nationalism and population growth). Such xenophilia is closely implicated in a "bootstraps" narrative of class achievement that serves to both flatter the nation's self-image of tolerance and opportunity, and to distinguish the merits of the "deserving,

hard-working immigrant" from anxieties around its mirror-image: the lazy or dangerous immigrant/refugee who is a drain on the system. As Honig cautions, such
xenophilic performances are inextricably linked and interdependent on their necessarily xenophobic opposite.[10] She argues that "the iconic good immigrant who
upholds American liberal democracy is not accidentally or coincidentally partnered
with the iconic bad immigrant who threatens to tear it down" (Honig 1998, 3).

The national memorialization that Pier 21 performs "for Canadians" functions
through certain highly selective iconic moments of xenophilia, while glossing over
and suppressing the history and continued social relations of xenophobia that are
still central to the regulation of Canadian immigration. It spectacularizes a selective
version of immigration history into a celebratory nationalism. For example, a *Toronto
Star* editorial entitled "Wave the Flag for Canadian Mosaic" answers my opening question of what Pier 21 does for Canadians rather candidly:

> The opening of [this] shrine . . . will help raise national consciousness
> about the centrality of immigration to the story of Canada. Pier 21
> should do for Canada what Ellis Island has done for America-romanti-
> cize and idealize immigration, and put poetry around it (Siddiqui,
> "Wave the Flag" 1999).

This insistence on romantic idealism as way to frame immigration history is crucial. By embedding a celebratory narrative of immigration into the popular construction of the nation, a highly selective version of national identity and history is produced. In this way, the memorialization of this site sanctifies the following narrative
of the nation, as displayed in a front-page headline of the *Toronto Star*: "On Pier 21
Canada opened its doors, and a nation walked in" (Schiller 1999). Such a figuring
of immigration history suggests a nation that has been externally preconstituted, in
effect naturalizing the exclusionary structures of past immigration policy by celebrating a mythical "openness" of the nation to whomever enters its "doors." Indeed, the
image of the "open door" presents a strongly domestic and domesticated image of
the immigration selection process and bureaucracy. This obscures the ongoing reality that the "doors" of the nation have never been open to everyone, and the practices and exclusions that are formative to Canadian immigration are forgotten or
effectively erased.

In this sense, the public memorialization of Pier 21 serves to both imagine and
manage the bounds of a national narrative of immigration through which the founding myth of the settler nation is produced. Such practices of memorialization offer
a rich site from which to examine the active performance and governance of
memory and forgetting in the official historical narrative of Canadian immigration.
They are clearly informed by Ernest Renan's classic formulation of memory and forgetting as the source of the nation. For Renan, projects of nationhood impose a
structural necessity of "forgetting" selective aspects of the violence at the heart of

state formation, along with the suppression of disruptive historical memory in the forging of national "unity"—or "unity through brutality" as Renan puts it (Renan 1882, 11, 14).

Pier 21 also faithfully articulates Renan's linkage of history with the essence of the nation. To cite the famous passage: "A nation is a soul, a spiritual principle. Two things constitute this soul or spiritual principal. One lies in the past, one in the present" (19). The main promotional slogan of Pier 21 proclaims it to be "Canada's National Historical Soul." Pier 21 literature continually circulates such claims: "[immigration] enriched our social and cultural landscape and uplifted the very soul of the nation forever!" (*Pier Into Our Past* 1999). All of the promotional literature closes with the invocation to visit Pier 21 as a way to "start you national historic soul searching." In this way, Pier 21's institutional articulation of the national soul positions immigration as the core essence of the settler nation.

This evocation of the national "soul" as central to the memorialization of Pier 21 clearly implies an affective if not a spiritual project. Indeed, affect was central to the staging of Pier 21, it constituted its very *mise-en-scène*. It is through the affective elements of spectacle that the links between institutional or official histories and subjective memories of the nation were sought and regulated. In the opening ceremonies, an affective linking of immigration with utopian nation-building and historical progress was repeatedly articulated through Pier 21's celebratory structure of feeling (Williams 1977). Pier 21's other key slogan encapsulates this deployment of national history as a matter of nation-building: "Pier into our past, and see the future of Canada." Yet, if Renan is to be taken seriously, such affective investments in the national "soul" require forgetting as much as they do remembrance.

The Pier 21 exhibition is rife with dramatizations of this affect. A typical case among myriad examples: "If these walls could speak, they would tell powerful stories of fear and anticipation, tears and laughter, of those seeking a new life and the promise of a future in this country" (*Passages* 1999). The resolution of such public displays of immigrant affect is channeled through melodramatic national feeling. In staging such a celebratory structure of feeling, the more traumatic aspects of immigrant affect are subsumed into sentimental nationalism and the drama of individual struggle.

In this way, immigrant dreams, memory, and senses become microcosms of the nation. Immigrant affect is strategically mobilized towards national(ist) feeling. As Pier 21 publicity puts it, "Every immigrant must dream boldly, risk, and dare to create a new life. To achieve greatness, a nation must be equally bold in its dreams. Pier 21 is a testament to Canada's profoundly emotional immigration experience" (*Pier 21* 2000). By staging a fairytale of inclusion, the memorialization of Pier 21 provokes "sentimental experiences of the nation through contact with its monumental media" (Berlant 1997, 43). National melodrama was also the privileged genre for the popular memorialization of the settler nation in the media. "Canada's newest museum is a place where ghosts come alive and memories whisper out loud, a place of pain and nightmares and hope beyond measure. They call it the National Historic Soul" (Toughill 1999).

This insistence on *celebration* as the means of memorializing Canadian immigration history requires an institutionalized forgetting of Canada's settler colonial legacy and exclusionary immigration practices. The traumatic silences resulting from such exclusionary structures, palpable in many immigrant testimonies, are subsumed by the celebratory impulse of Pier 21. Traumatic immigrant histories are thereby resolved through a progress narrative that recapitulates the glory of the nation.

Ultimately, the compulsory celebration of Pier 21 demands a regulated performance of remembrance in which *gratitude* becomes the obligatory affective response. As recent works on the role of testimony in public culture show (Berlant 1997, Fortier 2001), the public compulsion to testify and the call to manifest one's national allegiance is disproportionately directed at those who, in the very act of being called to testify or remember, are already marked as alien or suspect of non-allegiance. The very terms of immigrant recognition and inclusion then, are set by this obligatory call to demonstrate and perform one's patriotic allegiance.[11] In the governmentalized terms of recognition offered at the Pier 21 ceremonies, compulsory gratitude was the emblematic affective marker of immigrant patriotism.

The insistent rhetoric of gratitude, dreams and a new life, constantly recited by iconic immigrants and "Pier 21 Alumni" such as Abella, serves to usurp the political silences and traumatic histories underlying such affective expression. In these compulsory performances of immigrant gratitude, the requisite suppression of traumatic immigrant memory is institutionally aligned with the official "forgetting" of systematic national exclusions. Celebratory nationalism and liberal multiculturalism constitute the exclusive and highly regulated frameworks through which immigrant memory is acknowledged, governed and recognized in public culture. In exchange for this limited and regulated recognition, gratitude is upheld as a pledge of national allegiance for immigrants to perform. Such interpellations of immigrant gratitude are further embedded in a whole series of rearticulations of "place" that the opening of Pier 21 inaugurated.

Les Lieux de Mémoire: Memorialization as Performance and Practice of Place

The official practice of memorialization is an institutional project that effects a redefinition of place. Here I invoke Doreen Massey's critique of the traditional notion of "place" as a fixed and enclosed, bounded entity (Massey 1995, 53). Massey reformulates "place" to refer to the provisional convergence and intersection of social relations in a particular material location (63). Memorialization is a public practice that seeks to link specific interpellations of social memory with particular places, sites, and historical moments. It entails the designation of a physical place or monument as a repository for particular forms of memory. This social practice links material markers with practices of affective remembrance (such as testimonials or pil-

grimages) for the purposes of a specific institutional and/or national project. It re-
defines and designates the memorialized site as a new *place*—a new place that channels particular social and cultural meanings or performances of historical memory.
Such practices of memorialization mediate between the institutional and the subjective, and between national history and personal memory.

Several layers of social relations converge in the Pier 21 memorial as a particular rearticulation of place. The memorialization of the Pier is motivated by clear
national imperatives in the redefinition of this site. Like the Ellis Island museum,
Pier 21 legitimates its national memorial status through the claim that 1 in 5 Canadians can trace their lineage through the Pier. Indeed, both museums have or are
developing interactive genealogy database projects, including ships' passenger lists
and immigration interview archives. In this way, the Pier 21 project seeks to reconstruct itself as a site of national genealogy for the settler nation.

In addition to the nationalist agenda, there is a local economic agenda of urban "renewal" at work in the creation of a tourist attraction in the context of a larger
redevelopment and "upgrading" of the Halifax waterfront over the past decade,
spearheaded by the Halifax Waterfront Development Corporation. Halifax Mayor
Walter Fitzgerald noted at the opening ceremonies that the Pier 21 project was "the
cornerstone of the revitalization of the city's south end" (Jeffrey and Duffy 1999).
This was effected in the context of a regional Maritime economy that has been decimated through the decline and closure of traditional industries such as mining and
fishing. The federal government has responded to this economic decline and its own
neoliberal withdrawal of social spending in part by funding and promoting heritage
and tourist industries. The rearticulation of place at work in Pier 21 thereby plays
into an economic progress narrative of the urban regeneration and gentrification of
the Halifax waterfront (McClean 2001).[12]

The memorialization of Pier 21 also seeks to incite performances of pilgrimage,
rearticulating the site as a "national shrine" (as it was described by much of the media). Pilgrimages invoke both a physical and affective journey that links the memorialized place with a practice of affective remembrance. Pier 21's promotional literature repeatedly conjures such a journey, promising to "trace the physical and
emotional journey of immigrants and refugees" (*Pier Into Our Past* 1999). At a time
of national uncertainty with respect to the competing claims of Québec, First Nations
sovereignty, and regional decentralization, along with the increasingly alarmist association of multiculturalism with fragmentation and threats to "social cohesion," Pier
21 also responds to the federal government imperative of building unity, of the need
to construct places of national pilgrimage as a unifying practice. As an institutional
as well as a physical and affective practice of place, the pilgrimage to Pier 21 thereby
interpellates (grateful) immigrants as Canadian citizens.

Pier 21's articulation of place crucially implies a practice of *borders,* linking the
physical borders of the nation to the liminal spaces of national identity. This articulation of the institutional to the subjective is achieved through the dramatization of

the "First Steps" on Pier 21 (as the first steps in the nation). The Pier 21 theme song is only one of repeated instances in which the "first steps" are dramatized. The romanticization and mythification of this transformational moment is effected through the testimonial focus on sensation and memory. The affective component of this construction of place is continually evoked, not only through explicit appeal to national memory, but to a vocabulary of senses, tastes, smells (memories of the smell of Pier 21, the first food tasted, etc.) staged as the moment of arrival into nationhood.[13] The first steps in the new land are mythologized and retracted as a threshold moment, a crossing of borders that signals a ritual of national becoming.

If there is one critical function that Pier 21 serves as a particular construction of place then, it is in the image of the national gateway as both a marker of physical geography and national identity. The gateway and border as a place of passage is constantly linked to the iconic moment of assimilation and national becoming. Pier 21 becomes a gateway to a federalist construction of national identity and citizenship. As the title of a *Macleans' Magazine* column by Peter C. Newman announces, "Pier 21: the place where we became Canadians" (Newman 1996). This is effected through the continual focus on the physical passage through Pier 21 as a romanticized moment of passage from an old life to a new life, from old world to new, mythologizing the moment of arrival into nationhood. Based on the strictures of celebratory nationalism, the narrative of this passage becomes a narrative of national progress, of leaving behind old world oppression, for a new, better life. Rooted in this official state nationalism, Pier 21 offers an institutional articulation of immigrant citizenship as a xenophilic and celebratory myth of national inclusion.

The Closed Door and the Writing on the Wall: The Politics of Forgetting and the Counterpolitics of Canadian Intercultural Video

While sites of memory (*les lieux de mémoire*) are often framed as attempts to "block the work of forgetfulness" (Nora 1984, xxxv), the regulation of memory enacted through official practices of memorialization simultaneously produce "les lieux mémoire" as sites of a strategic and highly regulated forgetting. I want to pursue this question of institutionalized forgetting in the celebratory memorialization of Pier 21, a forgetting that Renan argues is so central to the forging of national "unity." Given that Canada has never just opened its doors and let a nation walk in, as proclaimed in Pier 21's fairytale of inclusion, what are some of the implications of this selective national memory? And what is strategically forgotten?

By historically locating the key narrative of immigration mythology in the era of 1928–71 as the exhibit does, and by geographically locating Canada's national historic soul in Halifax, Pier 21 centres this narrative of the nation on white European immigration.[14] This historical distancing strategy obscures the ongoing structures of systematic exclusion in contemporary immigration policy at the same time that it distances its prior history. In framing this period as a story of Canadian nation-building, of a "Pier Into Our Past" that shows the "future of Canada," the racial and ethnic legacies of immigration history are also recapitulated in the imagining of the future nation. This founding myth simultaneously naturalizes and "forgets" the legacies of settler colonialism and exclusionary social structures in the national project of immigration. It tells a federalist tale of unity that glosses First Nations perspectives on the roots of Canadian immigration in colonial settlement, as well as the specificities and complexities of immigration dynamics for French Canada and the nation-building narratives of Québec. Through this staging of a xenophilic myth of inclusion, the memorialization of Pier 21 as the nation's gateway obscures the xenophobic exclusions that have been and continue to be central in defining the borders of the nation.

It is worth noting here that comparative analyses of memorials addressing the specificities of immigration to Québec remain to be conducted. For instance, in 1998, Parks Canada established a memorial to Canadian immigration at Grosse Île, Québec, the quarantine station for the main port of entry to Canada in an earlier wave of immigration, and the site of a large-scale typhus epidemic that resulted in the death of thousands of predominantly Irish immigrants in 1847.[15] In the summer and fall of 1997, the Musée de la Civilisation in Québec City held a major exhibition entitled "Des Immigrants Racontent." The exhibition focused on immigrant integration into Québec society, reflecting a predominant theme through which immigration tends to be framed in Québec.

Recent works by First Nations artists such as Mohawk artist Shelley Niro have also strongly challenged the very terms of settler practices of memorialization. In a November 2002 exhibit entitled "Memory Keepers," Niro reframes the Statue of Liberty, not as a celebratory symbol of freedom, but as a marker of settler colonization and brutal displacement that brought neither liberty nor freedom to her people. Over an image of the iconic statue that oversees Ellis Island, Niro superimposes her own response: "in my culture, there are no monuments, no man-made structures, no tourist sites; one visits, burns tobacco, says a prayer" (Smoke-Asayenes 2002).

While space for the contestation of the dominant national narrative was marginal at the actual physical site of Pier 21, I want to consider an alternative site, a representational rather than a material site, where a critical counterpolitics of national memory and a counternarrative of immigration's role in the nation is being articulated. Through the works of such artists as Richard Fung, Leila Sujir, and Paul Wong, Canadian independent video productions of the 1990s and 2000s have evolved as a critical ensemble of sites through which the exclusionary histories obscured and buried by Pier 21's celebratory structures of feeling are directly confronted and explored in terms of their implications for the nation's imagining of itself. I close by briefly considering how the video practices of these three artists offer a challenging dialogue with and contestation of the founding narratives of immigration espoused at Pier 21.

The works of these artists can be situated within a broader tradition of intercultural cinema and politically committed art video that distinctively emerged in the context of Canadian and Québécois independent video production in the 1980s and 1990s (Gale and Steele 1996). In *The Skin of the Film,* Laura Marks defines intercultural cinema as an emergent genre of film and video largely based in the practices of diasporic, First Nations, and migrant populations in the West. Suggesting a form that cannot be confined to a single culture, intercultural works are often short (due in part to production and funding constraints), formally experimental, often with a distinctly activist bent, that confront the particular crisis arising from the political discrepancy between official national histories and the personal and collective memories of marginalized and racialized communities. As Marks puts it, "Intercultural cinema moves backward and forward in time, inventing histories and memories in order to posit an alternative to the overwhelming erasures, silences, and lies of official histories . . . that result from public and personal amnesia" (Marks 2000, 25). In this way, intercultural cinema is rooted in acts of historical excavation, interrogating the official archive, mining the gaps and silences of recorded national history.

Marks argues that intercultural cinema often employs *recollection-images*[16]—visual images, songs, material artifacts, and sensory experiences that index forgotten histories, histories that have been silenced or erased in the official historical archive (Marks 2000, 37, 50; Deleuze 1989, 47–50). Since they cannot directly represent these pasts precisely because the conditions for their direct representation have been politically thwarted or destroyed, recollection-images bear the traces of buried events, occasioning a confrontation between that which has not been represented in official histories and the private memories of disenfranchised communities. They are often the basis for imaginative reconstruction and the creative generation of forgotten histories in response to the challenge of representing suppressed pasts for which the official modes of representation have been destroyed or denied.

Fung, Sujir, and Wong use intercultural cinema as a way to confront the buried histories of Canadian immigration, the kind precisely glossed over by Pier 21. As space does not permit the kind of fully developed analysis of the complex repertoire of images and themes each of the videos offers, I focus on one particular recollection image each artist employs in a much larger and more complex aesthetics of countermemory, an image that in each case directly confronts the silences wrought in the official historical narrative of Pier 21. In short, these videos constitute a representational site of Canadian immigration history that produces a counterpolitics of national memorialization. Given the challenges that Noiriel notes immigrant populations tend to face in "leaving their own visible trace or forging their own 'places of memory'" (Noiriel 1996, 8), it is ironic yet somehow telling that these traces are located in a representational site of recollection images rather than a physical place replete with material markers of memory, such as Pier 21.

Leila Sujir's *Dreams of the Nightcleaners* (1996) employs a unique experimental narrative to delve into the links between historical and family secrets as they play out for three women whose lives have been indelibly shaped by the history of South Asian immigration to Canada, along with the ongoing racism confronted by these communities today in immigration, labour, and cultural practices. The video explores how the untold and buried stories of the past reappear, how history repeats itself and its exclusionary legacies. It also considers how immigrant dreams seek to create new stories out of these haunting pasts and the haunted present.

One of the characters, Jeanne, quite literally undertakes an act of historical excavation, seeking to understand how the history of exclusionary early twentieth century immigration policies echoes in the present, and how it has shaped her life and the life of her deceased Indian husband. Rummaging through the past, Jeanne scrolls through archival microfilm of newspaper headlines on anti-Asiatic parades and the White Canada policies of immigration. Amidst quotes from Mackenzie King's Report on Oriental Immigration that decreed the 1908 Direct Passage Ruling as a policy of exclusion towards South Asians (Kelley and Trebilcock 1998, 147–150), Jeanne declares, "It's still the same story now, the same things people are saying . . . [we] are finding out how the past is haunting the present, the same stories being repeated again and again."

Out of the perpetual scrolling images of anti-Asian newspaper headlines on the screen, an electronically recreated image of the ship called the Komagata Maru suddenly floats up off the screen and enters the room inhabited by Jeanne. It acts as a recollection image of the infamous ship that challenged the Direct Passage Ruling in 1914 and was forced to turn back after two months moored in the Vancouver harbour-carrying over 300 Indian passengers back with it (Kelley and Trebilcock 1998, 150–152). This electronic likeness is reconstructed in order to speak a suppressed history, reactivating the legacies of these exclusionary policies and reanimating the past to trace their continued operation in the present. In this way, *Dreams of the Nightcleaners* confronts the celebratory official history of Canadian immigration with the countermemories of those who bear the brunt of what the film's narrator/storyteller calls the "times of public darkness, where the cameras have not gone." In response to the suppression of an official repertoire of images of this buried event, the video resourcefully employs such recollection images as the electronic flying Komagata Maru to create the traces of a shadow history of the nation that the official historical narrative of Pier 21 structurally evades.[17]

Perhaps the starkest way to foreground the very questions that Pier 21 works to suppress is to contrast this so-called "front door" and gateway to the nation with what would by implication be its back door. During the same summer as the opening of Pier 21, this implied back door was the site of a xenophobic counterpart to the xenophilic spectacle of Pier 21: the media panic surrounding the landing of almost 600 Fujian Chinese refugees on the shores of British Columbia (Lai 2000). How can we understand the celebratory narrative of inclusion that played out on the nation's east coast in relation to the inflammatory xenophobia incited on the west coast? In other words, what are the links between xenophilia and xenophobia in the politics of national memory?

A telling picture emerges when one sets Pier 21's Sobey's Wall of Honour against its shadow counterpart on the West Coast: the Victoria Immigration Building, one of the primary gateways of East and South Asian immigration. At the entrance of Pier 21, the Sobey's Wall of Honour, like the American Immigrant Wall of Honour at Ellis Island, stands as a memorial vehicle for the inscription of personal histories into officially sanctioned national history. For $200, individuals and families can have their names installed on the Wall of Honour at the entrance of Pier 21, answering the Pier 21 slogan "If these walls could talk" in a promotional register.

But which walls speak and which walls are silenced in the politics of national memorialization? In his 1996 independent video *Dirty Laundry*, Toronto-based videomaker Richard Fung delves into the legacies of the Chinese Exclusion Act (1923) (Kelley and Trebilcock 1998, 203–204). The video opens with historical footage of a Canadian Pacific Railway train entering a mountain tunnel, the CPR constituting the very locus of the "national dream" as well, of course, as a monumental product of migrant labour. Layered over this image of movement is a voiceover by historian Nayan Shah (Shah 2001) that reveals the project of historical excavation about to unfold: "Historical memory is full of mythologies, so its not necessarily a matter of selecting which are the good and the bad ones, or which is the one truth and all others false. It is a matter though of discovering which mythologies aren't allowed to speak because of the ways in which conventional history has been written . . . " The video goes on to retrace a kind of counter-memorialization of Canadian immigration history by offering a lineage of dates of exclusionary legislation and practices: from the 1885 and 1923 Chinese Exclusion Acts, to the 1903 introduction of the Head Tax, to the 1885 criminalization of sodomy and such sexual "vices" as homosexuality and prostitution. These pieces of legislation were all used as tactics for the exclusion of Asian immigrants. Their narrative juxtaposition in the video serves to emphasize the close links between sexuality, labour, race and ethnicity in the exclusionary practices and legacies of Canadian immigration.[18]

In one of several critical recollection images in the video, Fung reveals the words of Chinese immigrant detainees furtively etched on the walls of the Victoria Immigration Building in the detainment cells, words recounting the mistreatment and racism they faced in seeking to enter one of Canada's other gateways where the doors were not so open. "What crimes have I committed? Why am I locked up here like a prisoner?" These secret inscriptions form a stark counterpoint to the official inscriptions of the Sobey's Wall of Honour.[19]

Confronting the contemporary politics of Canadian immigration, Paul Wong's *Prisoner's Lament* (2000) is a provocative two-minute video produced for an anti-racist campaign by the Canadian Race Relations Foundation. The campaign has been broadcast as a series of television commercials since 1999, which in itself is suggestive of the strategies alternative video artists such as Wong are adopting to insert themselves into more "mainstream" media sites and formats. A densely layered video montage, *Prisoner's Lament* intersperses close-ups of Canadian high school students who came to Canada as refugees speaking of their hopes and dreams. These mini-testimonials are overlayed with images of historical newspaper headlines suffused with anti-immigrant and specifically anti-Asian sentiments (in a similar aesthetic strategy to Sujir), layered onto media images of the 1999 Fujian Chinese refugees being led into detention by immigration agents. The connecting thread of the video is a haunting recollection image, a song of lament sung by some of the women detainees:

> To come to this far away land, we suffered and risked our lives. In this civilized country, I could not have imagined that we would end up being treated this way. You saved us to be locked up in your prisons. Is this your justice? I do not understand. How could I not be sad? We are shuffled from here to there, days and nights turn into months. We know no peace. My tears never stop. What is the crime? I do not understand.

As a recollection-image of the refugee's detainment, the prisoner's lament stands in stark contrast to much of the mainstream media representation of the migrant's landing, which in many respects strongly recapitulated the historical legacy of anti-Asian racial panics on the West Coast.[20] By layering anti-immigrant headlines from these past historical events over the images of the detainees being led away in chains. Wong effectively foregrounds the continuity between these historic and current events. Whereas much of the mainstream media evacuated all traces of the refugees' subjectivity by framing the event strictly in terms of the panic it raised for the (far from neutrally coded) "Canadian public," the prisoner's lament counters this dominant suppression by evoking the impact and recounting the event from the perspective of the refugees themselves through their own available forms of affective expression. As a stark counter-image to the national narrative celebrated the same summer at Pier 21 (the self-proclaimed "front door" of the nation), it offers a very different and far less celebratory trace of the history and current politics of Canadian immigration (at the so-called "back door").

Among the most significant and revealing of the links between official narratives of immigration history and the current politics of nationality, the founding myth of the open front door and the closed back door was central to Citizenship and Immigration Minister Elinor Caplan's introduction of the new *Immigration and Refugee Protection Act*, Bill C-11, in February of 2001. As echoed in the title's correlation of immigration with protection, this restrictive act constructs immigration as a security risk. Many argue that this overemphasis on "closing the back door" codifies an alarmist criminalization of immigration into official policy (Canadian Council of Refugees 2001), partially in response to the panic mobilized around the Fujian Chinese refugee landings.[21] As noted in the overview of Bill C-11: " . . . the proposed immigration and Refugee Protection Act and its regulations carry a dual mandate: closing the back door to criminals and others who would abuse Canada's openness and generosity while opening the front door to genuine refugees and to the immigrants the country needs" (*Bill C-11* 2001). This statement is telling in its structural linkage of the xenophilia of the open front door (as a strategic national interest) to the xenophobia of the closed back door.

Perhaps most hauntingly of all given the current political context, the prisoner's lament in Wong's video eerily echoes the words inscribed on the walls of the Victoria immigration Building portrayed in Fung's video. "What crimes have I committed? Why am I locked up here like a prisoner?" How can we think about the Sobey's Wall of Honour in relation to the recollection images of the detainee inscriptions and the prisoner's lament? In contrast to the memorialization of Pier 21 and its Wall of Honour, Fung reveals in *Dirty Laundry* that the Victoria Immigration Building was demolished in 1977, and its walls only speak through remaining archival photographs and Fung's video. Yet, ultimately, these walls also speak volumes about the celebratory founding myths and the ongoing exclusionary politics of Canadian immigration.

Notes

The author wishes to thank Chantal Nadeau. Monika Kin Gagnon, and Mario DeGiglio-Bellemare for their astute comments and generous critical engagement with the substance of this article. I also want to acknowledge the support of the Fonds Québecois de la Recherche sur la Société et la Culture during the period in which this article was prepared for publication.

1. Ellis Island Immigration Museum. Statue of Liberty-Ellis Island Foundation. June 26, 2000. <www.ellisisland.com> and <www.ellisisland.org>.
2. "About Pier 21 Society". *Pier 21*. Ed. Erez Segal. June 21, 2000. Pier 21 Society. June 26, 2000. <http:www.pier21.ns.ca/about.html>. For the most recent version of the Pier 21 website, see <www.pier21.ca>.
3. Jean Chrétien. Address. Pier 21 Opening Ceremonies. Halifax. 1 July 1999.
4. Lennie Gallant. Michelle Campagne, Connie Kaldor and James Keelaghan. *Pier 21*. Musical Performance. Pier 21 Opening Ceremonies, Halifax. 1 July 1999.
5. Ruth Goldbloom. Address. Pier 21 Opening Ceremonies. Halifax. 1 July 1999.
6. Hannah Gartner. Address. Pier 21 Opening Ceremonies, Halifax. 1 July 1999.
7. Under Director of Immigration Frederick Blair, it was designed to keep out all "undesirables" (basically any non-British or white American), particularly Jews at the height of the explosive refugee crisis that culminated in the Holocaust and World War II. This exclusionary history is amply documented by Irving Abella (Abella's husband) and Harold Troper in *None Is Too Many: Canada and the Jews of Europe, 1933–1948*. Furthermore, the Abella Commission's findings clearly demonstrated the ongoing nature of employment discrimination in Canada as historically rooted in its exclusionary legacy.
8. One segment of the CBC Gartner-hosted special "Welcome Home to Canada" did explicitly address the racialized past of Canadian immigration through the stories of Gim Wong and the Uppal brothers, second generation Chinese and Indo-Canadian men respectively. Yet the implications of these powerful stories are contained in two ways: by stressing the successes and achievements

of these men (hence reinforcing a "bootstraps" narrative of overcoming), and by locating these stories in the distant (pre-World War Two) past. Similarly, one *Toronto Star* article also explicitly addresses the racialized history of immigration policy, only to similarly distance it in the era prior to the policy reform of the 1960s (Schiller 1999).

9. See, for instance, Noiriel on French national amnesia about the massive historic role played by immigration in the formation of the French nation (Noiriel 1996).

10. Some argue that xenophilic conjunctures in which "pro-immigration" economic nationalist positions are strongest also occasion some of the most virulent expressions of xenophobia (Biles 1999).

11. More recently, in the post-September 11th (2001) climate, the extremely limited nature of this recognition is all the more evident in the highly intensified and sometimes violent call for non-Western immigrants, particularly North American Muslims, to testify to and declare their patriotic allegiance (see Fortier 2001).

12. Pier 21 had been used as an artistic venue by local artists for exhibition and studio space, as well as a refuge for squatters and the homeless (Peck 1994). Yet promotional literature continually claims that Pier 21 is a former abandoned shed.

13. This emphasis on the physicality of senses, smells, and tastes strategically mobilizes the heightened sense memory that accompanies intercultural migration. As Marks shows, cinematic narratives of migration also tend to rely on sense memories of native cultures to evoke a physical sense of home for diasporic communities. Yet in this case, the sense memories of arrival in Canada are emphasized to evoke a sense of national becoming (for instance, the taste of the white bread served to immigrants on their train rides from Pier 21, from which derives the Italian Canadian idiomatic slang of *mangiacake* to denote Canadians).

14. For a critique of the racist whitewashing at work in Pier 21's myth of immigration and its elision of Black Nova Scotian history in particular, see Walcott (2001). Yet even within the strictures of the European immigrant narrative that Pier 21 offers, there is a continual managing and silencing of the cleavages and exclusions that have stratified British, white American, and North and West Europeans settlers as preferred immigrants, while Jewish, South and East Europeans were defined as non-preferred and were at various times and to different degrees excluded from immigration. Indeed, the cohesion of whiteness that defines Canadian national identity requires such suppressions. Such policies as the Railways Agreement of 1925 demand further critical analysis in this regard (Kelley and Trebilcock, 194–199, 210).

15. For more on Grosse Île and the Irish Memorial National Historic Site of Canada, see http://www.parkscanada.gc.ca/parks/quebec/grosseile/en/frame_online_visit_e.htm.

16. The concept of recollection-images is drawn by Marks from Deleuze's work on cinema, which itself is influenced by Bergson's theory of sensation and memory.

17. To date, the only official markings of this incident are two memorial plaques in Vancouver, near the Gateway to the Pacific and at the Ross Street Gurdwara. The Komogata Maru incident was the subject of a documentary directed by Ali Kazimi entitled "Passage from India" (1998). It was produced as one episode of the 52-part television series on Canadian immigration entitled "A Scattering of Seeds: The Creation of Canada," produced by Lindalee Tracey and Peter Raymont. A feature film project on the Komagata Maru is also in development, to be directed by Deepa Mehta (see http://www.komagatamaru.com/).

18. Indeed, the association of undesirable immigration with sexual degeneracy is a deep-rooted one. Valverde has shown how fears of immigration and sexual excess were linked in social purity campaigns against national degeneration (108). Reciprocally, Roberts has shown how the evolving social categories of sexual deviancy (from sexual "promiscuity," prostitution, to homosexuality) became a central focus of deportation practices in early twentieth century Canadian immigration policy.

19. A similar politics of memorialization vis-à-vis European and Asian immigration to the United States resulted in the establishment of the Angel Island Immigration Station as a monument to Asian immigration in San Francisco in the 1970s. The walls of the station, containing similar inscriptions of predominantly Chinese and Japanese detainees, remain standing and have been transcribed into books of poetry. Angel Island, however, is vastly underfunded relative to Ellis Island, and is the subject of a revitalisation campaign as it has fallen into disrepair. See <http://www.aiisf.org/>.

20. Several researchers are conducting comparative media analyses of the historical media coverage of the 1914 Komagata Maru crisis and the 1999 media coverage Fujian Chinese refugee landings. For instance, Biles notes strong connections between the two conjunctures, particularly with respect to the rhetorical imagery of racial panic mobilized in metaphors of immigration as an invasion or flood.

21. In the interim since this paper was first written, the xenophobic panic that followed the September 11th, 2001 terrorist attacks in the United States have rapidly accelerated the push to implement the most restrictive impulses behind the Bill, particularly with respect to security and detention provisions. The new Immigration and Refugee Protection Act came into effect on June 28, 2002.

22. Fung notes that the archival photographs exist due to a historian who happened to learn of the demolition plans and documented the walls before they were demolished. Pier 21 was, in fact, the last standing immigration shed in Canada.

Bibliography

Abella, Irving and Harold Troper. *None is Too Many: Canada and the Jews of Europe, 1933–1948.* Toronto: Lester & Orpen Dennys, 1982.

Abella, Rosalie. "A Refugee's Triumphant Return to Pier 21." *Toronto Star* 1 July 1999: A13.

Anderson, Benedict. *Imagined Communities: Reflections on the Origin and Spread of Nationalism.* 1983. London: Verso, 1991.

Angel Island Immigration Foundation Station. Angel Island Foundation. July 15, 2000. <http://www.aiisf.org/>.

Berlant, Lauren. *The Queen of America Goes to Washington City. Essays on Sex and Citizenship.* Durham & London: Duke University Press, 1997.

Biles, John. "A Ship Off the Old Block: A Comparison of Popular Reaction to the Komagata Maru and the Arrival of Chinese Refugee Claimants in 1999." Association of Canadian Studies Annual Conference. Congress of the Social Sciences and Humanities (Quebec City, Quebec). May 25, 2001.

Bill C-11. Immigration and Refugee Protection Act Overview. Citizenship and Immigration Canada. Government of Canada. June 2001. <http://www.cic.gc.ca/english/about/policy/c11-overview.html>.

"CBC Television and the Pier 21 Society Form Strategic Partnership to Provide A Living Testament to Canada's Immigrants." *Pier 21.* Ed. Erez Segal. June 21, 2000. Pier 21 Society. June 26. 2000. <htp://www.pier2l.ns.ca/cbc-pier2l -release.html>.

Canadian Council of Refugees. "Bill C- 11: New Immigration Bill Information Sheets." July 27, 2001. *Canadian Council of Refugees.* January 30, 2002. <http://www.wcb.net/~ccr/infosheets. PDF>.

"Chrysler Canada Becomes Major Sponsor of Pier 21 Project." *Pier 21.* Ed. Erez Segal. June 21, 2000. Pier 21 Society. June 26. 2000. <http://www.pier2l.ns.c/pr/essrelease-june23. html>.

Deleuze, Gilles. *Cinema 2: The Time Image.* Minneapolis: U of Minnesota, 1986.

De Palma, Anthony. "Canada Celebrates Immigrants, but Which Ones?" *New York Times* 2 July 1999, final ed.: A4.

Duffy, Peter. "War Brides Recreate Arrival." *Halifax Mail-Star* 2 July 1999: Al.

Fortier, Anne-Marie. "Multiculturalism and the New Face of Britain." Conference. Centre d'Études Ethniques de l'Université de Montréal. 13 décembre 2001. Department of Sociology, Lancaster University. January 28, 2002. <http://www.comp.lancs.ac. uk/sociology/soc095af. htm#_ednref22>.

Gale, Peggy and Lisa Steele, eds. *Video re/View.* Toronto: Art Metropole and V-Tape, 1996.

"History Key in Holiday Celebration." *Halifax Mail Star* 2 July 1999: A1.

Honig, Bonnie. "Immigrant America? How Foreignness 'Solves' Democracy's Problems." *Social Text* 56 (16.3, Fall 1998): 1–17.

Jeffrey, Davene and Peter Duffy. "A Pier Into the Past: Families relive experiences at immigration shed." *Halifax Mail Star* 2 July 1999: A1–2.

Kelley, Ninette and Michael Trebilcock. *The Making of the Mosaic: A History of Canadian Immigration Policy.* Toronto: U of Toronto P, 1998.

Lai, Larissa. "Asian Invasion versus the Pristine Nation: Migrants Entering the Canadian Imaginary." *Fuse* 22.2 (September 2000): 30–40.

Marks, Laura U. *The Skin of the Film: Intercultural Cinema, Embodiment, and the Senses.* Durham: Duke UP, 2000.

Massey, Doreen. "The Conceptualization of Place." *A Place in the World?* Ed. Doreen Massey and Pat Jess. Oxford: Oxford UP, 1995.

McClean, Edel. "Voices from the Margin: Social Exclusion and Urban Regeneration in Halifax, Nova Scotia." Association for Canadian Studies Annual Conference. Congress of the Social Sciences and Humanities (Quebec City, Quebec). May 26, 2001.

McClintock, Anne. *Imperial Leather: Race, Gender, and Sexuality in the Colonial Conquest.* New York: Routledge, 1995.

Mohanty, Chandra. *Third World Women and the Politics of Feminism.* Indianapolis, Indiana UP, 1991.

Newman, Peter C. "Pier 21: The Place Where We Became Canadians." *Maclean's Magazine* 22 July 1996: 56.

Nora, Pierre, ed. *Les lieux de mémoire.* Paris: Gallimard, 1984.

Noiriel, Gérard. *The French Melting Pot: Immigration, Citizenship, and National Identity.* Trans. Geoffrey de Laforcade. Minneapolis: U of Minnesota Press, 1996. Translation of *Le Creuset Français: Histoire de l'Immigration XIXe-XXe siècles.* Paris: Seuil, 1988.

Passages 1.4 (May 1999). Halifax: Pier 21 Society, 1999.

Peck, Robin. "Ghosts: Sculpture Photographed at Pier 21." *C Magazine* 4 (Spring 1994):18–25.

Pier 21. Ed. Erez Segal. June 21, 2000. Pier 21 Society. June 26, 2000. <http://www.pier21.ns.ca>.

Pier Into Our Past and See the Future of Canada. Pamphlet. Halifax, Pier 21 Society, 1999.

Renan, Ernest. "What is a Nation?" *Nation and Narration.* Ed. Homi Bhabha. 1882. Trans. Martin Thom. London: Routledge, 1990. 8-22.

Roberts, Barbara. *From Whence They Came: Deportation from Canada, 1900–1935.* Ottawa: U of Ottawa P, 1988.

Schiller, Bill. "On Pier 21, Canada Opened its Doors and a Nation Walked In." *Toronto Star* 23 Jan. 1999, metro ed.: A1.

Shah, Nayan. *Contagious Divides: Epidemics and Race in San Francisco's Chinatown.* American Crossroads; 7. Berkeley: University of California Press, 2001.

Siddiqui, Haroon. "A Tribute to our Investment in Immigrants." *Toronto Star* 27 June 1999.

——————. "Wave the Flag for Canadian Mosaic." *Toronto Star* 1 July 1999: A14.

Smoke-Asayenes. Dan. "In Memorials: Memory Keepers." rabble.ca. *22* November 2002. http://www.rabbie.ca/news_full _story. shtml?x *17187*&url.

Taylor, Charles. *Multiculturalism and The Politics of Recognition.* Princeton: Princeton University Press. 1992.

Toughill. Kelly. "Where History's Soul Remembers." *Toronto Star* 1 July 1999: A3.

Valverde, Mariana. *The Age of Light, Soap, and Water: Moral Reform in English Canada, 1885–1925.* Toronto: McClelland & Stewart, 1991.

Walcott, Rinaldo. "Remaking History." *This Magazine* November/December 2001: 28–29.

Williams, Raymond. "Structures of Feeling." *Marxism and Literature.* London: Oxford University Press, 1977. 128–135.

CHAPTER TWENTY-ONE

First Nations

Introduction

Native Canadians are not one more ethnic group among many. To quote Jerry Ducharme, the main character in "The Seventh Wave," a short story by the native writer Jordan Wheeler, "We're not ethnic, we're aboriginal." But what does it mean to be Aboriginal? That question informs the following readings by George Sioui and Thomas King. There is no one answer. George Sioui is a Huron-Wyandot traditionalist, a historian and a former Dean of Academics at the Saskatchewan Indian Federated College. To be Aboriginal is to be part of what Sioui calls "the Indian problem." Towards settling "the problem," towards building a better foundation for Aboriginal-non-Aboriginal relations in Canada, Sioui goes back to the beginning, to contact. Why? Thomas King is a writer, essayist and professor. Of Cherokee, Greek and German descent, King was born and raised in California; he earned his PhD at the University of Utah and is now a professor of creative writing at the University of Guelph. He delivered the 2003 Massey Lectures. "Borders" comes from his 1993 short story collection, *One good story, that one.* It is most obviously a story about the artificiality of the Canadian-American border to a Blackfoot woman; what other borders does the story interrogate?

The Stadaconan Contribution to Canadian Culture and Identity

George Sioui

I AM A HURON and a Canadian Indian. I am well aware that my nation originates in part from the Wendat of present-day Ontario and that the name "Huron" was given by the French to the Wendat as a way to belittle, negate and ultimately, dispossess them. However, I am able to fully assume the history that made me and my people what we are today, that is, Hurons. That name allows us to see the whole picture of where we have been, where we are and where we want to go. To me, Huron means being Canadian in a uniquely profound way, a sacred way. Being a Huron means being directly related to the Stadaconans, the people who were there before Quebec City existed, just like the rocks, the trees and the Saint-Charles and Saint-Lawrence rivers. The Stadaconans were those of my ancestors who, in 1535, gave Jacques Cartier a cradle, a name and a spirit for the country he fancied he had discovered: Kanatha.

I guess my dear reader already has a sense that if asked to talk or write about "Aboriginal Contributions to Canadian Culture and Identity," I can really get going. I will use the opportunity to share with my fellow Canadians some of my secret Huron knowledge about what the most ancient Canadians, the Stadaconas, did in order to help create a country that would, from then on, have to include Cartier's people and, as they already knew, so many other Europeans. I use the words "have to" because the French and others (such as the Basques) showed clear signs, by 1535, that they were going to keep coming here, many to stay. We knew this from at least two of our own Stadaconan youth who had been deceitfully captured by Cartier the year before and brought back home to Stadacona in 1535 on Cartier's second voyage.

At this point, some readers may object that the Huron, reputed to have come from (what is now) Ontario to (what is now) Quebec about 115 years later (1650), when their country was definitively destroyed "by the Iroquois," cannot claim to be ethnically related to the Stadaconans. I would answer that recent archaeological findings have confirmed our "coming to Quebec" in 1649–1650. It was, in fact, a return home for many of our families who had their roots as Stadaconans, but had had to flee from their ancestral "Quebec" lands as a result of the first impact of the French and European invasion in Cartier's time. More than any other Amerindian group, the Huron of today, though few in number, carry the heritage of the Stadaconans, just as they are the principal carriers of the spiritual and intellectual heritage of many of the great Iroquoian (or Nadouek) peoples and confederacies who have disappeared: the Tionontati or Tobacco, the Attiwandaronk or Neutral, the Erié or Cougars, the Wenro, the Susquehanna, the Hochelaga and others.

Cartier first used the word "Canada" in his log book in 1535, on his second voyage, to designate both the town of Stadacona (now Quebec City) and the country whose centre it was, which extends approximately from Trois-Rivières to l'Ile-aux-Coudres. The previous year, Cartier's three ships had entered the Gulf of the Saint Lawrence and had encountered two groups of Amerindians: Mi'kmaq (Micmacs) and Stadaconans. These people possibly journeyed far away from their homes with other people from "Canada." The Stadaconans camped at present-day Gaspé and were catching lots of fish and smoking them.

On Friday, July 24, 1534, Cartier had a large cross made and planted at the entrance of the bay of Gaspé, carrying the inscription: "Vive le Roi de France." Donnacona, whom Cartier will identify a year later (September 8, 1535) as the "Seigneur du Canada," paddled up to Cartier's ship with three of his sons. This historically important moment was described in some detail by Cartier. First, we learn that the Stadaconan leader and his people did not come as close to the French as they had during the initial days of this one-week encounter. Rather, Donnacona's canoe remained at a distance while he addressed the French to explain to them that, as Cartier understood, "all the land is his" and that his people opposed the making and the planting of that object, which the French call a cross and collectively worship. (We know from many early sources that Aboriginal people were then able to and, in fact, did enforce their strict prohibition that the Europeans should not cut even a twig or to take anything from their land without their permission.) We also learned that even though very far away from their homes and immediate country, these first Canadians shared territorial rights and, therefore, land stewardship with the Mi'kmaq. Also importantly, we learned that these Frenchmen, far from being affected by this defensive act against their intrusion, had a subterfuge ready to use that was intended to make the Native people understand that the French did not believe they had to respect the political order that Native peoples had already established on their lands. At the end of Donnacona's harangue, which Cartier found lengthy, he showed the Stadaconan leader an axe, feigning a wish to barter it for a bearskin that the Chief wore. The latter, moved by this gesture, came closer to the French ship, "believing he was going to get [the axe]." Upon this, one of the sailors grabbed the Stadaconans' canoe, which allowed two or three Frenchmen to get into it and force two of Donnacona's sons to climb into Cartier's boat. Fear of French arms and the vulnerability of the women and children present may have been a factor in the lack of Stadaconan resistance to the treacherous act of the French, to whom the Aboriginal people had given no motive whatsoever to conduct themselves in such underhanded manner.

The French, on board their ship, made "a great show of love" for their two captives in presence of their people gathered in many canoes in the bay of Gaspé. Cartier, then, responded to Donnacona's speech about the cross and about Aboriginal "ownership" of the land by explaining (again deceitfully) that the cross was only meant to be a landmark for future visits, which they intended to make soon, and that, at any rate, they would then bring with them all sorts of gifts, of iron and otherwise, for Donnacona's people. This, of course, meant that the French, despite the strange way they had acted by seizing Donnacona's sons, still felt that they had to pay for using the land and, furthermore, had to account to the Aboriginal people for that use and for their presence. The Stadaconans considered all the components of this new necessary relationship: the love and solicitude the French showed for their two captured "Sauvages;" their promise to bring them back soon; and the strategic knowledge about the French these two young men would bring back. The Stadaconans, then, decided that they would, in time, be able to control and contain those newcomers. They showed themselves to be happy enough about everything. They even promised that they would not cut down the cross. Thus ended, on July 24, 1534, this prelude to France's Canadian adventure.

Over the next year they spent in France, Cartier's two Stadaconan captives, Domagaya and Taignoagny, studied the French in order to understand their motives and their aims and devised their own Aboriginal strategy. Most certainly, the two young men, probably drawing maps, had spoken to Jacques Cartier and other French about their "Kanatha," that is, their "chief town," which was Stadacona (present-day Quebec City). Little did they know that the French would use this descriptive word as the name of a country, an actual "Kingdom" called "Canada." Nor could the two Stadaconans imagine that their father, Donnacona, had been made a European-style monarch in this new land, which the French fancied and planned to conquer (steal). Certainly, these two sons of an important Aboriginal Headman could not have foreseen that their father, too, would soon be deceitfully and forcefully captured by Cartier and his men on May 3, 1536, and would die in France less than two years afterwards, sick and mortally sad for his lost people and country.

However, much happened before Donnacona's capture that is very significant to the Stadaconan contribution to Canada's culture and identity. As promised, Cartier did return on a second voyage the following year. Cartier's three ships left Saint-Malo on May 19, 1535. Taking advantage of their two Amerindian guides' knowledge of the geography of the two coasts from the entrance of the gulf right up to Montreal (Hochelaga) and beyond (Cartier is explicit about that knowledge and assistance), the French took their time to reconnoitre (they, of course, said "discover") the country, where they met inhabitants in every part.

The French were intent on visiting three "countries," namely, Canada, Saguenay and Hochelaga. Cartier's account and other evidence (including our own oral tradition) indicate that Donnacona's sons, already well trained in the region's geopolitics, had reasoned that such an exploratory plan, still to be approved by leading

Stadaconan Councils and their allies, could potentially develop into an eventual alliance between their people and the French. They first took the French to Canada, where Donnacona, their father and major leader, lived. Donnacona was a man whose authority the French already knew extended at least as far east as Gaspé.

Cartier and his people believed that during their year spent in France, Taignoagny and Domagaya had become naturally imbued with a sense of French cultural and religious superiority in relation to their own people, and would, therefore, once back home in Canada, be perfectly prepared to help the French conquer their land and peoples. To Cartier's dismay, the attitude of the two young men changed radically from the moment they set foot on their own soil once again. Understandably, that evening and night of September 8, 1535, was one spent in intense discussion and long-awaited revelations about the French and their land. The Aboriginal people of the region had, by this time, been aware of and mystified by the Europeans for almost four decades.[1]

Fixated on the idea of finding a passage to the Orient, its gold and its other riches, the French were determined to visit Hochelaga and, at a later date, Saguenay, another very rich "kingdom," according to the two Stadaconan captives and guides. During the trip back, the Stadaconans had agreed that they would lead the French to Hochelaga. However, Donnacona and other council leaders did not think the time was appropriate. Not only was the season too advanced to travel much more, but there were also strict protocols to be learned and observed regarding the laws of a particular territory, the respect to be paid to its leaders, customs of different Aboriginal nations, the advance notice to be sent to another country that one wished to visit, and many other things to be aware of.

The French had only been in "Canada" for six days when on September 14, they began pressing their two former captives to lead them to Hochelaga. On the next day, Taignoagny, whom Cartier resented more than he did Domagaya, informed the French captain that the Headman Donnacona was annoyed to see the French constantly bearing arms, to which Cartier replied that he (Taignoagny) knew very well that this was the way in France and that he would, therefore, let his men bear arms. Still, the Stadaconans remained cheerful and optimistic that they would eventually find common ground and make the French see their real interests, which meant using the friendship that was being offered them to create a larger, more affluent and powerful society from uniting the two peoples.

On September 16, Donnacona and 500 of his people (roughly the population of the town of Stadacona) approached Cartier's two main boats anchored in the harbour of the Saint Charles River. The leaders entered Cartier's boat to once again try to impress on the French that they should not navigate towards Hochelaga (Montreal) at this time (they, of course, thought of another time, likely the following spring). Taignoagny, once again acting as the spokesman for the Stadaconans, withdrew his offer to guide Cartier, stating that his father, Donnacona, did not wish him to go because the Headman had said, "la rivière ne valait rien" (the river forebode nothing good). The French explorer answered that his mind was set to go anyway, adding that should Taignoagny change his mind and agree to accompany them as he had promised, he would receive gifts and attention from the French that would make him happy. At any rate, Cartier explained, his aim was only to make a quick trip to see Hochelaga and then return to Canada. Taignoagny remained firm in his refusal to go and the visit ended.

The next day, the Stadaconans staged a very sensitive and solemn effort to make the French reconsider their plan to go to Hochelaga and, mostly, to appreciate the great solidarity that would result from uniting their two peoples. They attempted this by actually marrying Jacques Cartier to the highest-ranking of their marriageable young women. To this day, an account other than Cartier's own has never been presented to Canadians about this very meaningful event in their country's history.

I have personally witnessed wedding ceremonies and other similar ceremonies still practised by Canadian Aboriginal peoples whose spiritual ways are almost identical to ours. I will take the reader through Cartier's account of what happened to him, the young maiden and the people of Canada that day. First, we are told that the people of Stadacona walked up to the French boats at low tide with large quantities of eels and other fish, as gifts for the French. Then, there was much chanting and dancing, which usually occurred at such visits, Cartier said. What Cartier did not see, at this point, was that these particular songs and dances were preparatory to a specific ceremony that was about to take place. As well, the abundant quantities of fish and the prevailing feasting atmosphere that was described, indicate that the whole town (very likely with many guests and visitors from neighbouring places) was present for a very important event—a ceremony ordained after much praying, chanting, council-making and, quite likely, fasting, under the highest spiritual leadership.

Then, the Agouhanna (a title carried by Donnacona, which implies very high stature in society) had his people (likely, the other leaders) stand to one side and drew a circle on the sand, inside of which he had Cartier and his own principals stand. Donnacona then made a long speech in front of the, thus, reunited French and Stadaconans. While he spoke, the headman "holds the hand of a girl of about ten to twelve years old" whom, after finishing speaking, he presented to the French captain. At this point, all of Donnacona's people began to "scream and shout, as a sign of joy and alliance." Now, the fact that Cartier accepted the girl was affirmed by the loud, festive reaction of the throng. At any rate, was not Cartier and all of these Frenchmen, in the eyes of the Amerindians, much too long deprived of normal social relations, including those of a man with his wife, or a woman's companionship, as sadly seen in their disorderly behaviour and appearance? Could so many negative traits in the present state of their intercultural relations not be modified by beginning to create a normal human life, a society around those angry, rude, rowdy strangers?

Following this ceremony, two younger boys were given to Cartier in the same official way, upon which the Stadaconans made similar demonstrations of joy.[2] Cartier then officially thanked Donnacona for these presents. Finally, a crucial detail was given by Taignoagny: the "girl" (in Aboriginal cultural terms, she is a *young woman*) ceremonially given (again, in the Aboriginal social frame of reference, that gift was a wife) to Jacques Cartier was "Lord Donnacona's sister's own daughter." This, in the matrilineal system of these Huron-Iroquoians, meant that the young woman was called "my daughter" by Donnacona, and that she belonged to the same clan as he does, as opposed to his own children, who belonged to their mother's clan.

Thus, that young woman was the highest, as well as the purest, gift that could possibly have been offered to the first man among these Frenchmen. The Stadaconans probably thought, given these gifts and a chance to establish a normal life in this new land, who would care about an oppressive monarch back in problem-ridden France and about the lifelong odious obedience that was owed him; this land was Donnacona's, this was a pure and abundant, free country, this was Canada. Most surely and naturally, there was a burning desire in many French hearts present to make that Canadian way of thinking their own.[3] Unfortunately, of course, it was, for that time, impossible. It was almost entirely a matter of religious prejudice.[4]

Cartier had his human gifts "put on board the ships." He gave no details about what occurred to the three young Stadaconans thereafter, except that the "older girl," had, three days later, fled the ship and that a special guard had been arranged so that the two boys would not do likewise. When finally "found" by Donnacona and her own family, the young woman explained that she had escaped because "the pages had beaten her," and not, as the French contended, because her own people had tried to make her (and the two boys) leave the French. Cartier showed reluctance to take the young woman back until, he said, the Stadaconan leaders (her family) begged him to do so. (To them, at least, Jacques Cartier and she were husband and wife.) She was accompanied to the ship by her father and other relatives. Nothing further is said about her.

Cartier tells us that Taignoagny said to him, after the bride-giving ceremony, that these three human presents had been given in order to keep the French from going up to Hochelaga. I have already presented my reasoning, based on the available evidence which includes my own culturally informed perception, about the Stadaconans' motives for trying their hardest to create unifying bridges between themselves and the French. At any rate, I believe Cartier's blinding obsession about going to Hochelaga is self-evident. The last-ditch attempt of the Stadaconans to make him stay, on the next day, and the strange but accurate warning that he received about having to prepare for wintering right away, are further proof of Cartier's fool-hardiness and spite toward his Aboriginal hosts, friends and benefactors.

On September 18, 1535, the Stadaconans, again attempting to avert misfortune from the French, turned to supernatural forces. Cartier described how this was acted out before his eyes. First, three men clothed themselves in black and white fur (Cartier disparagingly says dog skins) and wore long horns on their heads. The three men hid in a canoe and, momentarily, rose up as their craft approached the boats.

The spirit-being in the middle began to make a "marvellous" speech directed at the French, even though the three "devils" never even took notice of the French, as they floated past the French boats. The canoe was steered back to shore. Upon arriving, the three beings dropped to the bottom of the canoe, as though they had died. They were then carried to the woods in the canoe by Donnacona and other men. Every single Stadaconan followed their leaders into the forest and disappeared from sight. Then began a half-hour "predication" by the three spirit-beings. At the end of this, Taignoagny and Domagaya came out of the woods and, after the Catholic way they had observed, walked towards the French, their hands joined as if in prayer. "Showing great admiration," they advanced with their eyes lifted towards the sky and pronounced the words "Jesus, Maria, Jacques Cartier," as though (my interpretation) asking for protection for Cartier and his men. At that moment, the French captain, seeing their grave countenance and having witnessed their "ceremonies," inquired "what the matter was, what new things had occurred." The two young men answered that there was "pitiful news," that nothing foreboded well ("il n'y a rien de bon"). When pressed further by Cartier, his two usual interpreters told him that Cudouagny (likely the Great Spirit for the Stadaconans and possibly the Hochelagans) had spoken in Hochelaga and, through the three spirit impersonators mentioned above, had announced that there would be so much ice and snow that they (the French) would all die. (Actually, 25 sailors died of sickness and hardship over the winter. At one point, Cartier himself became quite certain that all, including himself, would die. We will later see how they were saved.)

To be sure, Cartier made light of the Stadaconans' way of trying to make him stay and to persuade his companions to start preparing for their first Canadian winter. "Go tell your messengers that your god Cudouagny is a fool who does not know what he talks about," retorted Cartier amid laughter from all the French who were there. "If you just believe in Jesus, he will keep you from the cold," added a sailor. As a way of restoring balance in the communication, the two youths then diplomatically asked Cartier whether he had had Jesus' word on the matter, to which the captain curtly replied that his priests had asked him (Jesus) about it and learned that the weather was going to be all right. Taignoagny and Domagaya gave many thanks to Cartier for this exchange and returned to fetch from the woods their own townsfolk who, as Cartier detected, could not conceal their disillusion, even amidst their cheers, shouts, chants, dances and other expressions of joy.

The next day, on September 19, Cartier's smaller vessel left for Hochelaga. The round trip lasted 24 days, during which the rest of his men, back in Stadacona, mostly used their time bracing for imagined attacks from the Stadaconans. As for them, the Stadaconans continued to demonstrate the same goodwill and humanity toward their strange visitors, bringing them victuals and waiting for their visits, which were, in fact, quite infrequent. Because the French did not visit very often, they began suffering from a lack of fresh food, especially meat and fish.

The rest of the story of Cartier's second voyage to Canada is better known. In brief, things soon turned very bad for the French, as foreseen by the Stadaconans.

From mid-November, the cold was brutally felt by the ill-prepared Frenchmen. From December, the whole crew was hit hard by scurvy. By mid-February, eight sailors were dead. By mid-April, 25 had succumbed to the scourge and another 40 were dying; of 110, "there were not three healthy men," wrote Cartier. "We were so overtaken by the said disease," confided the explorer, "that we had almost lost all hope of ever returning to France."[5]

Most readers will already know that people stopped dying in Cartier's fort thanks to a remedy (very likely, the white cedar) that the Stadaconans gave the French and taught them how to prepare. The credit for this human solicitude and actual salvation from sure catastrophe, however, was entirely given to God, the Europeans' God. The surviving crewmen, further strengthened by the fresh meat and fish that the Amerindians brought them every day, got better so rapidly that in less than three weeks, they were ready to set sail for France. However, as many readers must also know, they did not depart from Canada before realizing a very pressing dream: that of capturing Donnacona, Domagaya and Taignoagny, along with two other prominent leaders and two other young Stadaconans, one of whom was another pubescent girl. To succeed in laying his hands on these people, especially the headmen, Cartier had to act his wiliest and also use force, as he proudly recounted in his journal. We know that ten Stadaconans, probably all belonging to Donnacona's direct immediate family, were in possession of the French when they left for France on May 6, 1536. Among them were Donnacona, Taignoagny, Domagaya, two other chiefs, another girl "of about ten," (almost certainly) Cartier's Canadian wife and his two given sons, and lastly, two other persons of unknown gender or age.

One of Cartier's promises made to appease the Stadaconans after so callously and treacherously stealing their leaders was that he would bring back all ten of their people "in ten or twelve moons" (as, in fact, he had done with his first two captives). When he finally came back, without his captives, five years later and was asked by the Stadaconans what had become of their Agouhanna and other people, Cartier, still his deceitful self, replied that Donnacona had died and was buried in France (which was factual), but that all the others had remained there, where they were now married and had become "grands Seigneurs" (great Lords). We know from Cartier's own chronicle that eight more of his captives had died by then (French archival sources confirm that they all died within two years), except a girl of about 10 (at the time of her capture).

This time, in August 1541, the French arrived in Canada to find an Aboriginal population in a state of virtual panic. Diplomacy was still present, but was mostly dictated by fear. The French had brought heavy weaponry and were ready for any eventuality. They were here to create a French colony. The Canadians' country would be theirs, for civilized Europeans were not bound to virtues practised by "Savages."

However for now, the task proved too great, support from France was not quite sufficient and the enmity of the First Peoples was too overwhelming. Cartier's third and last voyage ended in failure. However, the French (and Basque) presence in the Laurentian region increased year by year, drawn to the wealth of fur and fish.

Hochelaga and Saguenay endured, but Canada's peoples, directly and forcibly affected by the European invasion (not just the sheer human pressure, but also, and mostly, by the everpresent, devastating new epidemic diseases), had to seek refuge, which archaeology in the last few decades has revealed (again confirming our own traditional belief), that they mostly found among the Wendat of present-day Ontario (in the Lake Simcoe-Georgian Bay area). According to leading archaeologists,[6] it is more likely that the original Canadians joined the Wendat Confederacy in the last decades of the 16th century, becoming its Nation of the Rock (maybe in remembrance of Stadacona: the place of the Big Standing Rock[7]).

Conclusion

No foundation can forever rest on lies, especially lies rooted in racial prejudice. While it is necessary to find the reasons and to understand why the French, like many Europeans at the time, perceived reality and other peoples as they did and acted with corresponding spite and inhumanity, it is equally necessary to help today's heirs to that ancient society (which means most of us, in greater or smaller measure) shed any lingering thinking and behavioural patterns related to that inheritance. We are long past the time when Europeans came here needing new places and new conditions for a renewed lease on life. However, after providing the same "Canadian" generosity and contributing the very best of themselves and what they have, our Aboriginal peoples are still being deceived, mistreated and visibly destroyed as peoples in this great, rich and powerful country. One can take the Stadaconans' history of contact with Europe and, thereafter, non-Aboriginal Canada, and apply it exactly to the historical and present-day experience of any other Canadian Aboriginal group or nation. After all the political, social, academic and religious rhetoric, the very real fact remains that Canada, born in 1534 with an Aboriginal spirit, given an Aboriginal name in 1535 and tenderly cared for in an Amerindian cradleboard by the people of Stadacona, has seen, and caused, its Aboriginal peoples to waste away during its 468 years of existence, while everyone else who has come here has, as Jacques Cartier and his men were, been cared for, healed and found a new life. Can we now stop saying that this was, and will continue to be, the price to pay for a true civilization, until Canada's "Indian problem" has been settled?

In this essay, I have mainly wanted to suggest to my readers and fellow Canadians that a better understanding of the way things happened in their country at the beginning of the contact between Aboriginals (the first Canadians) and Europeans is necessary if one is to also understand why all Canadians are still collectively afflicted by an immense incapacity to empathize, communicate and construct as we should, the kind of secure, happy future that we all desire for our children and their descendants. As an Aboriginal historian, I believe an ignorance of history is the major reason for the glacial indifference of mainstream society that is still felt by most of my Aboriginal fellow citizens and is known and denounced by many non-

Aboriginal Canadians and others, and is the major reason so much impedes us collectively to tackle and conduct our many common affairs in normal, empathetic, intelligent ways.

Finally, I am grateful for this opportunity to write about our peoples—their very many important past, present and, maybe especially, potential future contributions to our great and dear country's culture and identity. I also wish to greet and thank my readers for their time.

Long live my country, Canada!

Notes

1. Two centuries or so after the Vikings ceased coming to the region, vivid memories of them were certainly still present. However this time, these newcomers behaved in very different, much more aggressive ways than had their Norse predecessors.
2. With a high-ranking young wife given to him by the first Headman of the land and two young boys, one of whom was Donnacona's own son, did Cartier not have prime human material with which to start up a very good life in "Canada?" The Stadaconans certainly thought he did.
3. The "ensauvagement" of the French "coureurs des bois" probably was the most marking trait (and simultaneously the one most damned by the religious authorities) in French-Indian relations throughout the next two centuries. It produced Canada's Métis nation.
4. Cartier exhibited his deep European religious conditioning and unfeelingly uttered a very dark sentence regarding the original Canadians when, pondering what little he knew about their spiritual beliefs, he simply wrote: "One must be baptized or go to hell."
5. Since mid-November, the Stadaconans also had lost about 50 people. Cartier, reflecting the knowledge of his epoch, could and did blame the "Canadians" for his people's sickness. Today's science, however, informs us that, rather, the Stadaconans' disease was caused by the Europeans' presence, because they were beginning to be struck down by "contact epidemics."
6. For sources, readers may consult my book *Huron-Wendat. The Heritage of the Circle* (Vancouver: University of British Columbia Press, 1999).
7. Because of the imposing rocky promontory it presents, Quebec has historically been called "Canada's Gibraltar." I encourage readers to consult a remarkable book on Quebec City, published in 2001 by Les Presses de l'Université Laval: *Québec, ville et capitale,* a volume in the *Atlas historique du Québec,* which is edited by Serge Courville and Robert Garon.

Borders

Thomas King

WHEN I WAS TWELVE, maybe thirteen, my mother announced that we were going to go to Salt Lake City to visit my sister who had left the reserve, moved across the line, and found a job. Laetitia had not left home with my mother's blessing, but over time my mother had come to be proud of the fact that Laetitia had done all of this on her own.

"She did real good," my mother would say.

Then there were the fine points to Laetitia's going. She had not, as my mother liked to tell Mrs. Manyfingers, gone floating after some man like a balloon on a string. She hadn't snuck out of the house, either, and gone to Vancouver or Edmonton or Toronto to chase rainbows down alleys. And she hadn't been pregnant.

"She did real good."

I was seven or eight when Laetitia left home. She was seventeen. Our father was from Rocky Boy on the American side.

"Dad's American," Laetitia told my mother, "so I can go and come as I please."

"Send us a postcard."

Laetitia packed her things, and we headed for the border. Just outside of Milk River, Laetitia told us to watch for the water tower.

"Over the next rise. It's the first thing you see."

"We got a water tower on the reserve," my mother said. "There's a big one in Lethbridge, too."

"You'll be able to see the tops of the flagpoles, too. That's where the border is."

When we got to Coutts, my mother stopped at the convenience store and bought her and Laetitia a cup of coffee. I got an Orange Crush.

"This is real lousy coffee."

"You're just angry because I want to see the world."

"It's the water. From here on down, they got lousy water."

"I can catch the bus from Sweetgrass. You don't have to lift a finger."

"You're going to have to buy your water in bottles if you want good coffee."

There was an old wooden building about a block away, with a tall sign in the yard that said "Museum." Most of the roof had been blown away. Mom told me to go and see when the place was open. There were boards over the windows and doors. You could tell that the place was closed, and I told Mom so, but she said to go and check anyway. Mom and Laetitia stayed by the car. Neither one of them moved. I sat down on the steps of the museum and watched them, and I don't know that they ever said anything to each other. Finally, Laetitia got her bag out of the trunk and gave Mom a hug.

I wandered back to the car. The wind had come up, and it blew Laetitia's hair across her face. Mom reached out and pulled the strands out of Laetitia's eyes, and Laetitia let her.

"You can still see the mountain from here," my mother told Laetitia in Blackfoot.

"Lots of mountains in Salt Lake," Laetitia told her in English.

"The place is closed," I said. "Just like I told you."

Laetitia tucked her hair into her jacket and dragged her bag down the road to the brick building with the American flag flapping on a pole. When she got to where the guards were waiting, she turned, put the bag down, and waved to us. We waved back. Then my mother turned the car around, and we came home.

We got postcards from Laetitia regular, and, if she wasn't spreading jelly on the truth, she was happy. She found a good job and rented an apartment with a pool.

"And she can't even swim," my mother told Mrs. Manyfingers.

Most of the postcards said we should come down and see the city, but whenever I mentioned this, my mother would stiffen up.

So I was surprised when she bought two new tires for the car and put on her blue dress with the green and yellow flowers. I had to dress up, too, for my mother did not want us crossing the border looking like Americans. We made sandwiches and put them in a big box with pop and potato chips and some apples and bananas and a big jar of water.

"But we can stop at one of those restaurants, too, right?"

"We maybe should take some blankets in case you get sleepy."

"But we can stop at one of those restaurants, too, right?"

The border was actually two towns, though neither one was big enough to amount to anything. Coutts was on the Canadian side and consisted of the convenience store and gas station, the museum that was closed and boarded up, and a motel. Sweetgrass was on the American side, but all you could see was an overpass that arched across the highway and disappeared into the prairies. Just hearing the names of these towns, you would expect that Sweetgrass, which is a nice name and sounds like it is related to other places such as Medicine Hat and Moose Jaw and Kicking Horse Pass, would be on the Canadian side, and that Coutts, which sounds abrupt and rude, would be on the American side. But this was not the case.

Between the two borders was a duty-free shop where you could buy cigarettes and liquor and flags. Stuff like that.

We left the reserve in the morning and drove until we got to Coutts.

"Last time we stopped here," my mother said, "you had an Orange Crush. You remember that?"

"Sure," I said. "That was when Laetitia took off."

"You want another Orange Crush?"

"That means we're not going to stop at a restaurant, right?"

My mother got a coffee at the convenience store, and we stood around and watched the prairies move in the sunlight. Then we climbed back in the car. My mother straightened the dress across her thighs, leaned against the wheel, and drove all the way to the border in first gear, slowly, as if she were trying to see through a bad storm or riding high on black ice.

The border guard was an old guy. As he walked to the car, he swayed from side to side, his feet set wide apart, the holster on his hip pitching up and down. He leaned into the window, looked into the back seat, and looked at my mother and me.

"Morning, ma'am."

"Good morning."

"Where you heading?"

"Salt Lake City."

"Purpose of your visit?"

"Visit my daughter."

"Citizenship?"

"Blackfoot," my mother told him.

"Ma'am?"

"Blackfoot," my mother repeated.

"Canadian?"

"Blackfoot."

It would have been easier if my mother had just said "Canadian" and been done with it, but I could see she wasn't going to do that. The guard wasn't angry or anything. He smiled and looked towards the building. Then he turned back and nodded.

"Morning, ma'am."

"Good morning."

"Any firearms or tobacco?"

"No."

"Citizenship?"

"Blackfoot."

He told us to sit in the car and wait, and we did. In about five minutes, another guard came out with the first man. They were talking as they came, both men swaying back and forth like two cowboys headed for a bar or a gunfight.

"Morning, ma'am."

"Good morning."

"Cecil tells me you and the boy are Blackfoot."

"That's right."

"Now, I know that we got Blackfeet on the American side and the Canadians got Blackfeet on their side. Just so we can keep our records straight, what side do you come from?"

I knew exactly what my mother was going to say, and I could have told them if they had asked me.

"Canadian side or American side?" asked the guard.

"Blackfoot side," she said.

It didn't take them long to lose their sense of humor, I can tell you that. The one guard stopped smiling altogether and told us to park our car at the side of the building and come in.

We sat on a wood bench for about an hour before anyone came over to talk to us. This time it was a woman. She had a gun, too.

"Hi," she said. "I'm Inspector Pratt. I understand there is a little misunderstanding."

"I'm going to visit my daughter in Salt Lake City," my mother told her. "We don't have any guns or beer."

"It's a legal technicality, that's all."

"My daughter's Blackfoot, too."

The woman opened a briefcase and took out a couple of forms and began to write on one of them. "Everyone who crosses our border has to declare their citizenship. Even Americans. It helps us keep track of the visitors we get from the various countries."

She went on like that for maybe fifteen minutes, and a lot of the stuff she told us was interesting.

"I can understand how you feel about having to tell us your citizenship, and here's what I'll do. You tell me, and I won't put it down on the form. No-one will know but you and me."

Her gun was silver. There were several chips in the wood handle and the name "Stella" was scratched into the metal butt.

We were in the border office for about four hours, and we talked to almost everyone there. One of the men bought me a Coke. My mother brought a couple of sandwiches in from the car. I offered part of mine to Stella, but she said she wasn't hungry.

I told Stella that we were Blackfoot and Canadian, but she said that that didn't count because I was a minor. In the end, she told us that if my mother didn't declare her citizenship, we would have to go back to where we came from. My mother stood up and thanked Stella for her time. Then we got back in the car and drove to the Canadian border, which was only about a hundred yards away.

I was disappointed. I hadn't seen Laetitia for a long time, and I had never been to Salt Lake City. When she was still at home, Laetitia would go on and on about Salt Lake City. She had never been there, but her boyfriend Lester Tallbull had spent a year in Salt Lake at a technical school.

"It's a great place," Lester would say. "Nothing but blondes in the whole state."

Whenever he said that, Laetitia would slug him on his shoulder hard enough to make him flinch. He had some brochures on Salt Lake and some maps, and every so often the two of them would spread them out on the table.

"That's the temple. It's right downtown. You got to have a pass to get in."

"Charlotte says anyone can go in and look around."

"When was Charlotte in Salt Lake? Just when the hell was Charlotte in Salt Lake?"

"Last year."

"This is Liberty Park. It's got a zoo. There's good skiing in the mountains."

"Got all the skiing we can use," my mother would say. "People come from all over the world to ski at Banff. Cardston's got a temple, if you like those kinds of things."

"Oh, this one is real big," Lester would say. "They got armed guards and everything."

"Not what Charlotte says."

"What does she know?"

Lester and Laetitia broke up, but I guess the idea of Salt Lake stuck in her mind.

The Canadian border guard was a young woman, and she seemed happy to see us. "Hi," she said. "You folks sure have a great day for a trip. Where are you coming from?"

"Standoff."

"Is that in Montana?"

"No."

"Where are you going?"

"Standoff."

The woman's name was Carol and I don't guess she was any older than Laetitia. "Wow, you both Canadians?"

"Blackfoot."

"Really? I have a friend I went to school with who is Blackfoot. Do you know Mike Harley?"

"No."

"He went to school in Lethbridge, but he's really from Browning."

It was a nice conversation and there were no cars behind us, so there was no rush.

"You're not bringing any liquor back, are you?"

"No."

"Any cigarettes or plants or stuff like that?"

"No."

"Citizenship?"

"Blackfoot."

"I know," said the woman, "and I'd be proud of being Blackfoot if I were Blackfoot. But you have to be American or Canadian."

When Laetitia and Lester broke up, Lester took his brochures and maps with him, so Laetitia wrote to someone in Salt Lake City, and, about a month later, she got a big envelope of stuff. We sat at the table and opened up all the brochures, and Laetitia read each one out loud.

"Salt Lake City is the gateway to some of the world's most magnificent skiing.

"Salt Lake City is the home of one of the newest professional basketball franchises, the Utah Jazz.

"The Great Salt Lake is one of the natural wonders of the world."

It was kind of exciting seeing all those color brochures on the table and listening to Laetitia read all about how Salt Lake City was one of the best places in the entire world.

"That Salt Lake City place sounds too good to be true," my mother told her.

"It has everything."

"We got everything right here."

"It's boring here."

"People in Salt Lake City are probably sending away for brochures of Calgary and Lethbridge and Pincher Creek right now."

In the end, my mother would say that maybe Laetitia should go to Salt Lake City, and Laetitia would say that maybe she would.

We parked the car to the side of the building and Carol led us into a small room on the second floor. I found a comfortable spot on the couch and flipped through some back issues of *Saturday Night* and *Alberta Report*.

When I woke up, my mother was just coming out of another office. She didn't say a word to me. I followed her down the stairs and out to the car. I thought we were going home, but she turned the car around and drove back towards the American border, which made me think we were going to visit Laetitia in Salt Lake City after all. Instead she pulled into the parking lot of the duty-free store and stopped.

"We going to see Laetitia?"

"No."

"We going home?"

Pride is a good thing to have, you know. Laetitia had a lot of pride, and so did my mother. I figured that someday, I'd have it, too.

"So where are we going?"

Most of that day, we wandered around the duty-free store, which wasn't very large. The manager had a name tag with a tiny American flag on one side and a tiny Canadian flag on the other. His name was Mel. Towards evening, he began suggesting that we should be on our way. I told him we had nowhere to go, that neither the Americans nor the Canadians would let us in. He laughed at that and told us that we should buy something or leave.

The car was not very comfortable, but we did have all that food and it was April, so even if it did snow as it sometimes does on the prairies, we wouldn't freeze. The next morning my mother drove to the American border.

It was a different guard this time, but the questions were the same. We didn't spend as much time in the office as we had the day before. By noon, we were back at the Canadian border. By two we were back in the duty-free shop parking lot.

The second night in the car was not as much fun as the first, but my mother seemed in good spirits, and, all in all, it was as much an adventure as an inconvenience. There wasn't much food left and that was a problem, but we had lots of water as there was a faucet at the side of the duty-free shop.

One Sunday, Laetitia and I were watching television. Mom was over at Mrs. Manyfingers's. Right in the middle of the program, Laetitia turned off the set and said she was going to Salt Lake City, that life around here was too boring. I had wanted to see the rest of the program and really didn't care if Laetitia went to Salt Lake City or not. When Mom got home, I told her what Laetitia had said.

What surprised me was how angry Laetitia got when she found out that I had told Mom.

"You got a big mouth."

"That's what you said."

"What I said is none of your business."

"I didn't say anything."

"Well, I'm going for sure, now."

That weekend, Laetitia packed her bags, and we drove her to the border.

Mel turned out to be friendly. When he closed up for the night and found us still parked in the lot, he came over and asked us if our car was broken down or something. My mother thanked him for his concern and told him that we were fine, that things would get straightened out in the morning.

"You're kidding," said Mel. "You'd think they could handle the simple things."

"We got some apples and a banana," I said, "but we're all out of ham sandwiches."

"You know, you read about these things, but you just don't believe it. You just don't believe it."

"Hamburgers would be even better because they got more stuff for energy."

My mother slept in the back seat. I slept in the front because I was smaller and could lie under the steering wheel. Late that night, I heard my mother open the car door. I found her sitting on her blanket leaning against the bumper of the car.

"You see all those stars," she said. "When I was a little girl, my grandmother used to take me and my sisters out on the prairies and tell us stories about all the stars."

"Do you think Mel is going to bring us any hamburgers?"

"Every one of those stars has a story. You see that bunch of stars over there that look like a fish?"

"He didn't say no."

"Coyote went fishing, one day. That's how it all started." We sat out under the stars that night, and my mother told me all sorts of stories. She was serious about it, too. She'd tell them slow, repeating parts as she went, as if she expected me to re-member each one.

Early the next morning, the television vans began to arrive, and guys in suits and women in dresses came trotting over to us, dragging microphones and cameras and lights behind them. One of the vans had a table set up with orange juice and sandwiches and fruit. It was for the crew, but when I told them we hadn't eaten for a while, a really skinny blonde woman told us we could eat as much as we wanted.

They mostly talked to my mother. Every so often one of the reporters would come over and ask me questions about how it felt to be an Indian without a coun-try. I told them we had a nice house on the reserve and that my cousins had a couple of horses we rode when we went fishing. Some of the television people went over to the American border, and then they went to the Canadian border.

Around noon, a good-looking guy in a dark blue suit and an orange tie with little ducks on it drove up in a fancy car. He talked to my mother for a while, and, after they were done talking, my mother called me over, and we got into our car. Just as my mother started the engine, Mel came over and gave us a bag of peanut brittle and told us that justice was a damn hard thing to get, but that we shouldn't give up.

I would have preferred lemon drops, but it was nice of Mel anyway.

"Where are we going now?"

"Going to visit Laetitia."

The guard who came out to our car was all smiles. The television lights were so bright they hurt my eyes, and, if you tried to look through the windshield in certain directions, you couldn't see a thing.

"Morning, ma'am."

"Good morning."

"Where you heading?"

"Salt Lake City."

"Purpose of your visit?"

"Visit my daughter."

"Any tobacco, liquor, or firearms?"

"Don't smoke."

"Any plants or fruit?"

"Not any more."

"Citizenship?"

"Blackfoot."

The guard rocked back on his heels and jammed his thumbs into his gun belt. "Thank you," he said, his fingers patting the butt of the revolver. "Have a pleasant trip."

My mother rolled the car forward, and the television people had to scramble out of the way. They ran alongside the car as we pulled away from the border, and, when they couldn't run any farther, they stood in the middle of the highway and waved and waved and waved.

We got to Salt Lake City the next day. Laetitia was happy to see us, and, that first night, she took us out to a restaurant that made really good soups. The list of pies took up a whole page. I had cherry. Mom had chocolate. Laetitia said that she saw us on television the night before and, during the meal, she had us tell her the story over and over again.

Laetitia took us everywhere. We went to a fancy ski resort. We went to the temple. We got to go shopping in a couple of large malls, but they weren't as large as the one in Edmonton, and Mom said so.

After a week or so, I got bored and wasn't at all sad when my mother said we should be heading back home. Laetitia wanted us to stay longer, but Mom said no, that she had things to do back home and that, next time, Laetitia should come up and visit. Laetitia said she was thinking about moving back, and Mom told her to do as she pleased, and Laetitia said that she would.

On the way home, we stopped at the duty-free shop, and my mother gave Mel a green hat that said "Salt Lake" across the front. Mel was a funny guy. He took the hat and blew his nose and told my mother that she was an inspiration to us all. He gave us some more peanut brittle and came out into the parking lot and waved at us all the way to the Canadian border.

It was almost evening when we left Coutts. I watched the border through the rear window until all you could see were the tops of the flagpoles and the blue water tower, and then they rolled over a hill and disappeared.

CHAPTER TWENTY-TWO

Canada in a Globalizing World

Introduction

This chapter asks what it means to live in a globalized world, in a world of open borders and free trade agreements, of export processing zones and trans-national corporations. Brian Mulroney was prime minister from 1984 to 1993. His most important policy initiative was the Canada-U.S. Free Trade Agreement (FTA) which came into effect on 1 January 1989. On the one hand, the FTA was what Mulroney said it was: a trade agreement between two countries. On the other hand, it raised age-old fears about Canada's sovereignty, its independence and its identity. The free trade debate of 1988 was a divisive one. Supporters of the agreement called its opponents cowards; wrapping themselves in the flag, opponents of the agreement called its supporters un-Canadian. Robertson Davies (1913–1995) entered the fray. An incredibly accomplished novelist and playwright with an international reputation, Davies was Canada's leading man of letters. Why did he object to the Free Trade Agreement?

Thinking about post-1988 Canada, have Davies' fears about the Canadian identity been realized? Thinking about yourself, about the television you watch and the clothes you wear and the stores you shop at and the movies you go to and the magazines you read, can we talk about a Canadian identity while living on Planet America?

Free Trade, 1988†

Brian Mulroney

RIGHT HON. BRIAN MULRONEY (Prime Minister): . . . Mr. Speaker, it is with pride that I rise to support this bill which will give Canada a new, more certain and more beneficial trade relationship with the United States of America.

I believe it is a good agreement for Canada. It is an idea older than Confederation itself whose time has finally come. It will stand the test of honest scrutiny. It is I believe genuinely in the national interest. The free trade agreement is necessary to secure access to our most vital market and is consistent with policies which are already strengthening our economy and improving the well-being of Canadians.

We on this side of the House support the free trade agreement because we believe it will bring prosperity and economic benefits to Canadians from coast to coast.

Some Hon. Members: Hear, hear!

Mr. Mulroney: Free trade will mean lower prices for Canadian consumers, better jobs, and greater individual opportunities. Free trade will help the regions of this country. It will do so by creating a broader and deeper pool of national wealth, not just by redistributing existing resources.

[*Translation*]

Mr. Speaker, free trade will help us to sustain our social security programs. Nothing endangers them more than economic decline. Nothing guarantees them better than an expanding economy. The values we have as Canadians and the distinctive quality of life we bring to North America will be enriched by free trade. By strengthening our economy, free trade will help us support cultural programs that enhance the capability of our artists, writers, and performers to express themselves to Canadians and to the world. Free trade will also improve our capacity to strengthen our national programs ranging from the environment to regional development to child care.

Free trade will strengthen our foreign policy. It will be welcomed globally as a beacon of hope for the forces of more open trade, particularly, Mr. Speaker, among developing nations and as a bulwark against protectionism.

My purpose today is to outline the rationale for this initiative, measure the results against our objectives, separate myth from fact, and assert the reasons why I believe this agreement deserves the support of all Canadians.

---

† Canada, House of Commons, *Debates*, 30 August 1988.

Signing Away Canada's Soul
Culture, Identity, and the Free Trade Agreement

Robertson Davies

IS CANADA A country without a mythology? The phrase is a provocative one, but it talks of an impossibility. Canada has a mythology, but it is only now, after about 400 years of history, being forced to decide what it is going to do about it. Somehow, by sheer weight of geography and the passage of time and a slow accumulation of national wealth, we have forced ourselves upon the attention of the world, and we are now in the uncomfortable position of having to discover, and in some measure to define, our national soul.

It cannot be emphasized too strongly, right at the outset, that the attitude born of this situation is not anti-American; it is simply pro-Canadian. We do not want to lose our identity, and we feel it suddenly threatened. We are different peoples, divided by geography and, most important of all, psychology. As a Canadian artist has said: "The U.S. frontier is in the West and its hero is an outlaw; the Canadian frontier is in the North and its hero is a policeman." Your aspiration toward life, liberty, and the pursuit of happiness is one that we admire, but our own is for public order and good government, which encourages the indigenous culture—the national soul—of which I now write.

Are we late in the day? Not really. I suppose if we were to assign sizes to national souls, as we do to hats, we might agree that the largest, most powerfully defined national soul in all of history—the unquestioned number nine—would be Russia, but it was not until the nineteenth century that anybody began to talk about the Russian soul. We are a little bit slow in getting off the mark, but we have begun; and the talk of the Canadian soul has begun for us, as it began for Russia, with our writers.

Telling Canada that she has a soul used to be rather like telling a stupid and unsophisticated girl that she was beautiful; she laughed coarsely and kicked you on the shins. A great deal of persuasion was needed before she would pay attention to what you were saying and stop calling you a fool. But during the past year or so something has happened which has made the stupid girl listen a little more seriously.

I will not bore you with detail: simply, it is the desire of Canada's Progressive Conservative government, and particularly of the Progressive Conservative's leader and our Prime Minister, Brian Mulroney, to enter into the Canada–United States Free Trade Agreement. As drafted by the Progressive Conservatives and the Reagan administration, the agreement is one of the most sweeping economic accords ever negotiated between two nations. It would eliminate (over a ten-year period) all remaining tariffs on $131 billion a year in merchandise trade between the two countries, the world's biggest trading partners. Barriers to U.S. investment in Canada and to the growth of U.S. service industries in Canada would also be lowered or eliminated. The opposition Liberals forced an election this past November by refusing to approve the pact in our Senate. The Progressive Conservatives won that election—after one of the most bitter campaigns in our history—with a parliamentary majority that appears to insure ratification of the agreement, which is due to take effect January 1. But it is my sense that the agreement will remain the crucial issue in Canadian politics, defining and dividing us. There is a proviso: either country has the right to cancel the agreement with six months' notice. Debate will not cease.

The government insists that such an agreement would enormously enlarge Canada's national wealth, create a great many new jobs, and open up the country to the sort of development that would bring in American capital. The business community is, in the main, delighted by this idea and supports it as big business usually does—by laughing at its opponents as people who do not understand how the world wags, and who should be content to trust their betters in such supremely important matters as money and trade. But there is substantial opposition to the free-trade proposal in Canada, stemming from a strong misgiving that it would threaten and eventually wipe out any indigenous Canadian culture. Loud and clear, a lot of Canadians are saying that there are things in our national life that are more important than money and trade, and the word "culture" is being used on the street, so to speak, in a new sense.

This new sense confuses many people in the United States. They seem to be astonished that Canada is not wholeheartedly in favor of the free-trade agreement between our two countries. That such an opposition even exists seems to them to be something new and inexplicable. In fact it is as old as the history of the two countries. Twice Canada made the decision not to throw in its lot with the United States: first, in 1776, when it did not join the revolution against British rule and became a haven for Loyalists who were forced to flee from what had been their homeland; then again, in 1812, when the United States invaded Canada to free it and was astonished to find that Canadians regarded themselves as free already. Is the free-trade question an occasion for a third such choice?

The immediate American response has been that the United States has no intention of taking over its northern neighbor. But—and here I must write with the uttermost tact—the gap between profession and practice is no less in U.S. foreign policy than it has been in that of any other great power when dealing with a smaller one. While expressing respect for our national sovereignty, U.S. submarines, uninvited, are in our Arctic waters and won't go away. American banks have sought to establish themselves in Canada without regard for our own banking system. We watch with dismay the cavalier treatment the United States gives to international agreements when these agreements do not suit American policy. With our strong Scottish strain, we murmur the words of Robert Burns:

O wad some Pow'r the giftie gie us
To see oursels as others see us!
It wad frae mony a blunder free us,
    And foolish notion.

The new sense in which "culture" is being used confuses our own tycoons, too, because they think they know what culture is. For them it is art galleries and ballet companies and opera companies and theater companies, to which some of them contribute quite generously. But they still live in a world where pictures and ballet and opera and theater are heavily dependent on imported goods, and they do not really believe that the fostering of such things within Canada could mean anything very much or employ any significant number of people. They are determined that the worth of an activity is related to the number of jobs it creates.

The Canadians who resist them know better. These cultural activities now have a local habitation in Canada, and the people they employ are important to the country in a way that the tycoons have not yet comprehended. When we send a symphony orchestra or a ballet company abroad, they make Canada known in an international world; they show we are part of the *internationale* of cultivated people, and that, insofar as international cultural exchange favors a climate of world peace, we are doing not at all badly. Furthermore, we are submitting ourselves to the judgment of the world on a level that asks for no favors and is not directly hitched to the world of business.

It is a matter of history, of an inherited governmental system, and of a national psychology. The question of the governmental system may be dealt with most easily. What virtually all Americans, and too many Canadians who deal in the international world of money, fail utterly to understand is that Canada is that political oddity—*a socialist monarchy*. We have created an elaborate and very successful welfare state under a monarchical setup, which is itself a declaration that there are things of national importance that are above politics and above simple matters of finance.

As to the matter of history: Canadian history is supposed to be dull. I would rather say that until the present century it had been such a sad story that we remembered it, but chose not to dwell on it. Our first European settlers, the French, came to Canada more than 400 years ago because life at home was hard and without hope. My mother's father was descended from a Scottish group for whom I have a special sympathy. Their origin was the uttermost northern part of Scotland, and so the gentlemen who arranged for their transport to Canada assumed that they would be best suited to a latitude comparable to the homes they left behind. So these wretches were deposited on the shore of James Bay, and if you do not happen to know where that is, I can assure you that it is a brutal place even for people from the Highlands.

After the American Revolution, Canada also received many thousands of political refugees from the new republic. When I say "refugees," I use the word in its fullest sense, for they had been deprived of civil rights, of land and money, their children were driven from the schools, and they were subject to all the harassment of the losers in any war. Many of these Loyalists had been prosperous in the American colonies before the revolution, and in Canada they were tireless in their labors to reestablish the economy and the educational and religious institutions that they had been forced to leave behind in the land of the free and the home of the brave.

Does it seem to you that I am talking about a nation of losers, of exiles and refugees? Modern Canada is a prosperous country, but the miseries of its earliest white inhabitants are bred in the bone, and cannot, even now, be rooted out of the flesh.

In psychological terms, Canada is very much an introverted country, and it lives cheek by jowl with the most extroverted country in the world—indeed, the most extroverted country known to history. Let me explain the terms. In personal psychology, the extrovert is one who derives his energy from his contacts with the external world; for him, everything lies outside and he moves outward toward it, often without much sensitivity to the response of that toward which he moves. The introvert, on the other hand, finds his energy within himself, and his concern with the outside world is a matter of what approach the outside world makes to him. It is absurd to say that one psychological orientation is superior to the other. Both have their value, but difficulties arise when they fail to understand one another.

The extroversion of the United States is easy to see. The United States assumes that it must dominate, that its political and moral views are superior to all others, and that it is justified in interference with countries it thinks undemocratic, meaning unlike itself. It has also the happy extrovert characteristic of seeing all evil as exterior to itself, and resistance to that evil as a primary national duty.

Canada, the introverted country, feels no impulse to spread its domination beyond its own boundaries and has shown itself generous and sometimes absurdly permissive in its acceptance of the behavior and customs of the numberless refugees that seek its shores. Now, suddenly, because of a desire on the part of our government and our powerful and vocal business community, we are faced with the likelihood of what many of us see as, eventually, a takeover not immediately political but cultural and, indeed, spiritual. We have built up our arts by means not approved of in the States; a lot of public money, for instance, goes into the support of our national broadcasting company, which is one of the things that knits together a vast land still sparsely populated. We have a flourishing National Film Board. Music, opera, ballet, and theater receive public support in a measure which is not adequate—when have artistic people ever considered any degree of support adequate?—but which recognizes their significance in our national life. Although the performing arts are important and are easily seen to be important, it is by our literature that we have made our deepest impression; the state, of course, cannot beget a literature and can do very little to support it, except for grants to writers thought to be promising. But grants cannot ensure public acceptance, and the acceptance Canadian literature now enjoys all over the world rests simply on the quality of the work—quality and individuality.

How gratifying this is to Canadian writers I cannot begin to express. I have traveled a good deal in Europe during the past five years, and everywhere I've gone I've been astonished and somewhat breathless to find how much we mean to friends abroad of whom we know nothing. Canada, through its writers, has suddenly come under international literary scrutiny.

You may ask why I suppose that the free-trade agreement with the United States, and all that it implies, would alter or endanger this situation. But I can remember— and many other Canadian authors can remember—being offered publication in the United States on the condition that I make a few alterations that would transfer the scene of my novel to the United States. To this day that is virtually a condition of having a motion picture made of a Canadian novel. We have a Canadian film industry, and our films are much respected at international festivals. But we cannot get distribution for them in the United States because they are seen as a form of competition with Hollywood, and Hollywood is not the most generous or culturally conscious part of the great Republic—it doesn't like any sort of competition. Film distribution throughout the North American continent is in U.S. hands, and the free-trade agreement will not change that.

Nor is the free-trade agreement going to be friendly toward our publishing industry, which is substantial and has had to maintain its position through adroit maneuvering and government assistance of an indirect kind. Such governmental assistance will undoubtedly be opposed by American publishers as a restraint on their freedom of trade and as unfair competition.

Will it matter? Yes, it will. Canada is waking up. Canada, where biblical references are still understood by quite a few people, sees itself suddenly as Naboth's vineyard. You remember that the great King of Samaria coveted Naboth's vineyard and made him an offer for it. Naboth replied, "The Lord forbid it me that I should give the inheritance of my fathers unto thee." Poor Naboth lost the fight and was traduced and stoned to death. But those of us who have Canada's newly found nationalism and national culture near to our hearts have hopes of reversing that nasty story and keeping our vineyard for ourselves and our children.

This dispute is particularly difficult because one of the parties to the difference does not see that there is any dispute at all. An American tycoon, commenting on the free-trade proposal, said, as if he were disposing of a trivial objection, "It's all business, isn't it?" But that is precisely what it is not, and why it is not so is extraordinarily hard to make clear to what may be called the extroverted Front Office mentality. A few months ago a friend of mine, an important Canadian publisher, spoke on this theme before an influential group of businesspeople in New York City. My friend was trying to explain why a distinctively Canadian culture was important and why we were determined to preserve it. After she had done her best she was astonished to be asked by the wife of an American publisher, "I don't get it. You keep talking about *Canadians*. Aren't you all Americans too?"

Americans are precisely what we are not and what we don't want to be. And Americans, charming, extroverted, certain of their acceptance everywhere, simply cannot understand this. And, of course, it is a problem. A Canadian historian, Arthur Lower, once said that we Canadians love England but don't like Englishmen, and that we love Americans but can't stand the United States. I have been trying to explain why this is so.

Why am I so obstinate in this matter of the trade agreement? What am I defending? In part it is our land. I believe strongly that the land upon which one lives influences one's character, and our land has given us qualities that are more akin to the Scandinavian countries than to any part of the United States except New England. I have spoken of our national introversion, and I see sympathies in our national feeling that attach us more strongly to the lands of Ibsen and Strindberg than to anything to the south of us. And as our land makes us what we are, it of course gives its quality to the best of our literature. Douglas Le Pan speaks in one of his poems of the Canadian as a "wild Hamlet, with the features of Horatio." That is a striking figure and one I have pursued in my own work.

A country's literature is a crystal ball into which its people may look to understand their past and their present, and to find some foretaste of their future. The pictures are never simple, never wholly clear, and certainly never didactic. They need interpretation; not the interpretation of the literary critic, unless the critic is a person of gifts comparable to the writer, but the interpretation of the heart, the sympathy and understanding that are the partners of insight. Canada has, over the years, produced such a literature, and during the past quarter of a century, that literature has grown to an extraordinary maturity. It has done so with the encouragement of a growing body of readers who want to hear what their writers have to say and make it part of their national consciousness. I avoid the term "national culture" because it has been abused by people who think of culture as a commodity, separable from the rest of the national life. Culture is an ambience, a part of the air we breathe.

That special ozone is now to be breathed in Canada, because it arises from the land itself—not a few acres of snow but a country of immensely varied beauty of landscape and of season, including our lovely and dangerous winters. It arises from our history, not dull but simply not dwelled upon, somber in palette but with wonderful flashes of brilliance. It arises from our psychology, which takes its color from the land and the history. Political unity with a more aggressive and powerful country may not mean the death of the essence of one's own country. But such a link could be dangerous and in some respects depleting, and I wish the majority of Canadians had had the good sense to declare against it. A strong link already exists, and it is sufficient without turning the link into a shackle.

CHAPTER TWENTY-THREE

Destinies

Introduction

This reader ends where it began: with Arthur Lower and Margaret Conrad and Alvin Finkel. Lower's conclusion to his classic 1946 survey of Canadian history, *Colony to Nation,* is very different in both content and style from Conrad's and Finkel's conclusion to their 2002 survey of Canadian history. How are these two conclusions different? Perhaps more importantly, how are they similar? And finally, what does that similarity tell you about Canada itself?

Reflections

Arthur Lower

WHEN THE FALL of France made the possibility of the fall of England very real, strange currents began to course through English Canada: it was not merely the loss of naval control over the Atlantic which loomed up, but personal tragedy. The occupation of Great Britain would have been painful to contemplate, but more painful still was the apprehension of there being disrupted something that was infinitely deep: ways of thought, views of life, traditions, familiar associations, the whole framework of existence that proceeded from the unbroken continuity of English history. The children saw the death of a dear parent approaching and for the first time looked at life through their own eyes.

The moment passed; the parent recovered; English Canadians slid easily back into the attitudes of children. French Canadians, orphaned generations before, had long since learned self-reliance, and for them, however touched they might be by the fall of France, the psychological shock had not occurred.

When Japan attacked the United States, another high emotional moment presented itself. On the west coast everything was confusion, for once again the prospect of direct attack was opened. Canada's two mainstays, the two great world powers which overshadowed every aspect of her life, were wounded and bleeding. Half the American fleet lay on the bottom of the sea, and the British navy seemed to be rapidly following it. Colonies went over like nine pins: armies of white men surrendered to the Japanese. In the midst of it all came the dagger in Canada's own ribs: the news of the fall of Hong Kong, with the loss of two Canadian regiments.

Here were deep experiences shared by English Canadians in common, and partly shared by French Canadians too. Of such are communities made. Compared with the trials of many other people, they were slight enough and far from sufficient to impress on the inhabitants of Canada a common character. They did not do that for the English, and their influence was far weaker on the French. Yet through one medium or another, during the Second World War, a common character was emerging in English Canada. Whether there was any prospect of a general Canadian community or not, as the end of the war drew in sight it was plain that an English Canadian community with traits of its own, neither English nor American, was taking shape.[1]

From *Colony to Nation: A History of Canada* by Arthur Lower. Copyright © 1946 by Estate of Arthur Lower. Reprinted by permission.

[1] This community has since been more or less upset by the huge immigration of the 1950's, and as has happened more than once before, several generations will be required for building another one of close-knit character.

Unfortunately the government of the day, with all its good points, was singularly lacking in the creative imagination which might have given form, balance, and purpose to the English-Canadian people and encouraged both them and the French to understand their common destiny. No group of men could frame a better set of exchange regulations, but they could not rise to the height of a national occasion. No Churchillian speeches came out of Ottawa. No national symbols were born from that source, no national pageantry set going. The Prime Minister of a country of two languages would not even make a speech in French. When the Canadian navy received its first cruiser, instead of this being the occasion for a flourish which would have made her an object of pride to all Canadians, she was brought in with a trifling announcement on the back pages of the daily newspapers. An imaginative touch would have named her after one of the great provinces; instead of that she was accepted with her original English name and called H.M.C.S. *Uganda* "after the protectorate", as it was lamely explained. The real explanation no doubt lay in the higher personnel of the Navy, which could hardly distinguish itself from the British Navy[2] or possibly in departmental leadership of a colonial rather than a national turn of mind. Whatever the reason, the action was all of a piece with the general conduct of the government in such matters of national symbolism.

An outstanding opportunity for creative statesmanship was missed in the forces themselves. Nearly a million men were embodied in the land, sea, and air services. They constituted a magnificent expression of the country's will and as fighting men, like their fathers before them, were unsurpassed. The ability with which they were organized was splendid. Canadians were intensely proud of them. They were intensely proud of Canada. They could have been made the basis for a national feeling that would have stamped character and unity upon the country. As it was, it seemed as if the fighting services became Canadian almost in spite of the spirit of their organization and direction, which would have made them little more than subordinate branches of the British. If the spirit of colonialism could have been completely dissipated (the circumstances of war did make great inroads upon it), such men might have become the vehicle to integrate the Canadian community, French and English, curing it of those schizophrenic ills, that suicidal diffusion of loyalties, from which it chronically suffers. A nation might have been forged from the fighting men but the government of the day would not have dreamed of initiating the project.[3]

---

[2] This is borne out by the Royal Commission report on the navy, tabled in Parliament, October, 1949.

[3] This statement no doubt assumes that the government, that is, Mr. King, had clearly formulated ideas upon the direction in which it would like to see Canada go. A close observer has remarked that this was not the case, and that Mr. King merely reflected the ordinary views of the moment upon such matters.

Little criticism, however, was made of it on that score. Government was condemned in Quebec for contributing too much to the allied cause and it was condemned in Ontario for not contributing enough, but it was condemned nowhere for not being imaginatively and creatively Canadian. At the end of this long survey, that fact alone provokes the question whether, in the course of the century and three quarters since the Conquest of 1760, anything vital had been created.

French Canadians would have summed up by contending that they were a people in themselves, but that they were willing to keep the spirit of Confederation and agree to a frankly bilingual, bicultural state. They would have pointed to the numerous occasions on which the English had broken their faith and would have claimed that only by insistence on every jot and tittle of their rights could they hope to survive as a group. They would have rejected with horror the idea of assimilation. Clearly the first of Canadian problems was the last, and the primary antithesis of Canadian history remained largely unresolved.

Honest effort at a judgement forces the conviction that the heavier share of responsibility has lain with the English Canadians. They have been more numerous, but as a group, and with many honourable exceptions, they have not been magnanimous. They have been the stronger, but they have not hesitated to use their strength. They have been greedy and intolerant, and then have turned naïvely round and wondered why the French (under their command) would not enter their wars. They might have made at least a Switzerland out of Canada and they have created an Austria-Hungary.

Admittedly, the French, considered also as a group and with as many individual exceptions as among the English, have been a difficult people. Parochial, oversensitive, and self-centred, they have been so conscious of their rights within Canada that they have had no adequate sense of their duties towards Canada. In face of the defence mechanisms set up for the protection of race and creed, the very real efforts of many of the English to be fair, friendly, and just have gone unheeded and unappreciated. They have had before them innumerable examples of the fate of small peoples: if they had wished, they could have seen Ireland, Poland, or others of the miserable subject minorities of Europe; instead, they have seen mainly those legal privileges that they have not succeeded in attaining. Their conception of *race* has become an obsession and it has been carried to un-Christian and almost Hitlerian intensities.

But the English Canadians have been little fitted to deal with a sensitive minority: they are a dour and unimaginative folk. Having failed to find a centre in themselves, they borrow the heroes, the history, the songs, and the slang of others. With no vividly realized *res publica* of their own to talk about, they take refuge in silence, unable to formulate their loyalties, confused over their deepest aspirations. Yet they are surcharged with a sense of duty, and when the great occasion of war comes, their efforts seem to know no limit. They must surely have an intuitive faith in the unexpressed essence of their traditions, for few of them have a formulated creed.

Canada with its divisions of race presents no common denominator in those profundities which normally unite—in race, language, religion, history, and culture. If a common focus is to be found, it must come out of the common homeland itself. If the Canadian people are to find their soul, they must seek for it, not in the English language or the French, but in the little ports of the Atlantic provinces, in the flaming autumn maples of the St. Lawrence valley, in the portages and lakes of the Canadian Shield, in the sunsets and relentless cold of the prairies, in the foothill, mountain, and sea of the west, and in the unconquerable vastnesses of the north. From the land, Canada, must come the soul of Canada. That it may so come is not as fanciful as some might think. When in 1763 the experiment was begun in the northern wildernesses, no one foresaw the strong state that was to be. Canada has been built in defiance of geography. Its two coasts were bridged by a transcontinental railway almost in defiance of common sense. Canadian statesmen reconciled the irreconcilable when in the 1840's they joined dependence to independence. They accomplished one of the greatest acts of state-building in history when in 1867 they brought together scattered provinces and two peoples into one country. Though the extremists would more than once have wrecked it, the structure so built has never failed in crisis to rally to it the support of moderate men from both races. It has stood through the storms of two world wars. In every generation Canadians have had to rework the miracle of their political existence. Canada has been created because there has existed within the hearts of its people a determination to build for themselves an enduring home. Canada is a supreme act of faith.

Never was there greater need of faith than in the days when the second great world war reached its closing stages: it seemed as if the dream dreamed in 1867 would either be realized or the country would disintegrate. Perhaps victory would be accompanied by a renewal of the faith, something of that tolerance and magnanimity without which Canada could not continue. Perhaps the cleansing torrent of war would bring the self-knowledge and the self-reverence that would mean new strength for the country's institutions, for the freedom which alone could keep them sweet and clean, and for the faith upon which that freedom rested. Perhaps for the one great thing its two peoples have in common, this strange and difficult land itself, this maddening land, there might be at hand a destiny not less enduring for the slow and bitter travail of its birth.

> My roots are in this soil,
> Whatever good or bad, what vain hope or mighty triumph lies in you
> That good or bad, that destiny is in me.
> Where you have failed, the fault is on my head.
> Where you are ignorant or blind or cruel, I made you so.
> In all your folly and your strength I share
> And all your beauty is my heritage.[4]

---

[4] From the unpublished poem, "Oh Canada, My Country" by Gwen Pharis Ringwood.

Conclusion from *History of the Canadian Peoples*

Margaret Conrad and Alvin Finkel

WHERE THEN HAD the national journey taken Canadians in the years since Confederation? In many respects the issues confronting Canadians in the early 2000s were much the same as those defined in the 1860s: relations between French and English, regional disparities, the status of Native peoples, the roles and rights of women and men, the relations between workers and capitalists. Although none of these were new, much had changed in nearly a century and a half. Canada had been transformed from a largely rural nation closely allied with Great Britain to a largely urban nation dominated by the United States with which it shared what amounted to a common market. Its governments had gone from being primarily the financiers of railways and promoters of trade to being the organizers of vast social welfare programs, the desirable size of which was, however, in some dispute. The churches, which once had been able in large measure to direct the lives of most, played a far more modest role in a secular society.

In the context of such changes, the form in which class, gender, regional, and ethnic issues played out changed dramatically as well. Canadians in 1867 might have been largely content to accept traditional social relationships, but their struggles over the years had created very different Canadians by the 2000s, with far more demands for democratization of social institutions and for inclusion in decision-making within society. Although no one could predict how long the nation-state known as Canada would exist and particularly whether Quebec would remain part of it for the long haul, it was clear that Canadians had achieved a great deal collectively since 1867. Many Canadians hoped that the new millennium would become the occasion for new achievements that would make Canada a more just and civil society, and strengthen its sense of purpose to remain an independent nation despite the pressures for integration with the United States, a global superpower with a determination to recreate the world in its own image.

Sources

Arthur Lower, *Colony to Nation: A History of Canada*, Don Mills, Ontario: Longmans Canada, 1946

Margaret Conrad and Alvin Finkel, *History of the Canadian Peoples, vol. 1: Beginnings to 1867*, 3rd edition, Toronto: Addison, Wesley, Longman, 2002

Samuel de Champlain, *Voyages to New France, 1615–1618*, Ottawa: Oberon Press, 1970

D. Peter MacLeod, "The Amerindian Discovery of Europe: Accounts of First Contact in Anishinabeg Oral Tradition," *Arch Notes* (July/August 1992): 11–15

Grey Owl, *Tales of an Empty Cabin*, London: Lovat Dickson, 1936

M.T. Kelly, *Breath Dances Between Them*, Toronto: Stoddart, 1991

Armand Garnet Ruffo, *Grey Owl: The Mystery of Archie Belaney*, Regina: Coteau Books, 1996

Donald Creighton, *The Empire of the St. Lawrence: A Study in Commerce and Politics*, Toronto: University of Toronto Press, 2002. First published as *The Commercial Empire of the St. Lawrence, 1760–1850*, Toronto: Ryerson Press and New Haven: Yale University Press, 1937

Michel Brunet, "The British Conquest: Canadian Social Scientists and the Fate of the *Canadiens*," *Canadian Historical Review* 40, 1 (1959): 93–107

Mark Starowicz, "Plains of Abraham: The abandoned battlefield," www.cbc.ca/history

Cecilia Morgan, "Creating a Heroine for English Canada: The Commemoration of Laura Secord," *Canadian Issues/Thèmes Canadiens*, October 2003

Agnes Maule Machar, *Lays of the True North*, Toronto: Copp Clark, 1899

Katharine Livingstone Macpherson, *Pictures from Canadian History for Boys and Girls*, Montreal: Renouf Publishing, 1899

J.G. Bourinot, *The Story of Canada*, Toronto: Copp Clark, 1896

David Duncan, *The Story of the Canadian People*, Toronto: Morang, 1904

Louis Fréchette, "Le dernier des martyrs," no publisher, 1885

Pierre Trudeau, "[Dialogue] . . . with Riel," in Pierre Trudeau, *PM/Dialogue*, Hull: High Hill Publishing House, 1972

J.M. Bumsted, *A History of the Canadian Peoples*, Toronto: Oxford, 1998

Marilyn Dumont, *A Really Good Brown Girl*, London: Brick, 1996

Alexander Muir, "The Maple Leaf Forever" 1867

Adolphe-Basile Routhier, "O Canada" 1880

R. Stanley Weir, "O Canada" 1908

E. Pauline Johnson, *The White Wampum*, Toronto: Copp Clark, 1895

National Anthem Act, Statutes of Canada, 29 Elizabeth II, Chap. 5, Assented to 27 June 1980

Vivienne Poy, Second Reading of Bill S-39 An Act to Amend the National Anthem Act to Include all Canadians, Debates of the Senate (Hansard), February 21, 2002

W.D. Lighthall, *Old Measures: Collected Verse*, Montreal: A.T. Chapman, 1922

E.J. Pratt, "In Memoriam," in Albert Watson and Lorne Pierce, eds., *Our Canadian Literature*, Toronto: Ryerson Press, 1923

David Macfarlane, *The Danger Tree: Memory, War, and the Search for a Family's Past*, Toronto: Vintage Canada, 2000. First published by Macfarlane, Walter & Ross, 1991.

J.M. MacCallum, "Tom Thomson: Painter of the North," *Canadian Magazine*, 50, 5 (March 1918)

Arthur Bourinot, *Tom Thomson and Other Poems*, Toronto: Ryerson Press, 1954

George Whipple, *Life Cycles: selected poems of George Whipple*, Toronto: Hounslow Press, 1984

Margaret Atwood, *Wilderness Tips*, Toronto: McClelland and Stewart, 1991

David Frank, *J.B. McLachlan: A Biography*, Toronto: James Lorimer, 1999

Sheldon Currie, *The Glace Bay Miner's Museum*, Ste. Anne de Bellevue, Quebec: Deluge Press, 1979

Harold Innis, *The Fur Trade in Canada*, Toronto: University of Toronto Press, 1999; first published by Yale University Press, 1930.

Harold Innis, "A Plea For Time," in *The Bias of Communication,* Toronto: University of Toronto Press, 1951

R. Douglas Francis, "The Anatomy of Power: A Theme in the Writings of Harold Innis," in Michael Behiels and Marcel Martel, eds., *Nation, Ideas, Identity: Essays in Honour of Ramsay Cook,* Toronto: Oxford University Press, 2000

Goldwin Smith, *Canada and the Canadian Question,* Toronto: Hunter, Rose, 1892

David Taras, "Swimming Against the Current: American Mass Entertainment and Canadian Identity," in David Thomas, *Canada and the United States: Differences that Count,* Peterborough: Broadview Press, 2000

Evelyn Lau, "America," in *Descant 95,* vol. 27, no. 4, Winter 1996

René Lévesque, *Memoirs,* Toronto: McClelland and Stewart, 1986

Solange Chaput Rolland, *My Country, Canada or Quebec,* Toronto: Macmillan, 1966

Michèle Lalonde, "Speak White," in David Taras and Beverly Rasporich, eds., *A passion for identity: an introduction to Canadian studies,* Toronto: ITP Nelson, 1997. This poem was first published in French in 1970.

Pierre Trudeau, "New Treason of the Intellectuals," in Gerard Pelletier, ed., *Against the Current,* Toronto: McClelland and Stewart, 1996. This essay was first published in French in the journal *Cité Libre* in 1962.

Pierre Trudeau, "Speech at the Paul Sauvé Arena, Montreal, Quebec, May 14, 1980," *Transcript of a speech given by the Right Honourable Pierre Elliott Trudeau at the Paul Sauvé Arena in Montreal on May 14, 1980,* Ottawa: Office of the Prime Minister, 1980

Catherine Annau, "The Sphinx 1984–2000," in *The Trudeau Albums,* Toronto: Penguin, 2000

Tara Nogler, "Snapshot: My Life as Anne in Japan" in Irene Gammel, *Making Avonlea: L.M. Montgomery and Popular Culture* (Toronto: University of Toronto Press, 2002)

"Did Our Anne of Green Gables nurture gay fantasies?" *Edmonton Journal,* 26 May 2000

Laura Robinson, "'Big Gay Anne': Queering Anne of Green Gables and Canadian Culture," 2004. Dr. Robinson, Nipissing University, wrote this article for this reader.

Doug Owram, *The Promise of Eden: The Canadian Expansionist Movement and the Idea of the West 1856–1900,* Toronto: University of Toronto Press, 1980

Di Brandt, "This land that I love, this wide wide prairie," in Pamela Banting, ed., *Fresh Tracks: Writing the Western Landscape,* Victoria: Polestar, 1998

Carl Berger, "The True North Strong and Free," in Peter Russell, ed., *Nationalism in Canada*, Toronto: McGraw-Hill Ryerson, 1966

F.R. Scott, *The Collected Poems of F.R. Scott*, Toronto: McClelland and Stewart, 1981

Karen Connelly, *This Brighter Prison: A Book of Journeys*, London, Ontario: Brick Books, 1993

matt robinson, *A Ruckus of Awkward Stacking*, Toronto: Insomniac Press, 2001

Neil Earle, "Hockey as Canadian Popular Culture: Team Canada 1972, Television and the Canadian Identity," *Journal of Canadian Studies*, 30, 2, Summer 1995

David Adams Richards, *Hockey Dreams: memories of a man who couldn't play*, Toronto: Anchor, 2001. First published in 1996.

"Canadian Multiculturalism Act," Statutes of Canada, 35–36–37 Elizabeth II, Chap. 31, Assented to 21 July 1988

J.M.S. Careless, *Careless at Work: Selected Canadian Historical Studies*, Toronto: Dundurn, 1990

Irving Abella, "Jews, Human Rights, and the Making of a New Canada," *Journal of the Canadian Historical Association*, vol. 11, 2000

Lawrence Hill, *Black Berry, Sweet Juice: on being black and white in Canada*, Toronto: Harper Flamingo, 2001

Shani Mootoo, "A Garden of Her Own" in Shani Mootoo, *Out on Main Street*, Vancouver: Press Gang Publishers, 1993

Tamara Vukov, "Performing the Immigrant Nation at Pier 21: Politics and Counterpolitics in the Memorialization of Canadian Immigration," *International Journal of Canadian Studies*, 26, Fall 2002

George Sioui, "Canada: Its Cradle, Its Name, Its Spirit: The Stadaconan Contribution to Canadian Culture and Identity," *Canadian Issues/Thèmes Canadiens* October 2003

Thomas King, "Borders," in *One Good Story That One*, Toronto: Harper Collins, 1993

Brian Mulroney, "Free Trade 1988," Canada, House of Commons, *Debates*, 30 August 1988

Robertson Davies, "Signing Away Canada's Soul: Culture, Identity and the Free Trade Agreement," *Harper's Magazine*, January 1989

Margaret Conrad and Alvin Finkel, *History of the Canadian Peoples, vol. 2: 1867 to the present*, 3rd edition, Toronto: Addison, Wesley, Longman, 2002